MW00861002

FOSS
Ninety Years of Towboating

Tugs HENRY (stb. fwd.), *MATHILDA (stb. aft), and ARTHUR (port fwd.) assisting tanker TULLAHOMA into Vancouver, B.C. The tanker was holed by the freighter P & T ADVENTURER in a collision off the Washington coast on August 4, 1951. (Courtesy of Foss Tug Co)*

FOSS

Ninety Years of Towboating

By

Michael Skalley

*"**The End of One Era and the Beginning of a New One.**" Photographed at the Foss dock in Port Angeles in 1966 is the veteran THEODORE (ex-ARTHUR) 77 years old with the new MYRTLE, less than 7 weeks old. The two tugs worked together towing logs for the next two years and prior to THEODORE'S well earned retirement. (Photo courtesy of the author's collection)*

Copyright 1981 by Michael R. Skalley

Seattle, Washington

Library of Congress Cataloging in Publication Data

Skalley, Michael R., 1951–
  Foss: ninety years of towboating.
  Bibliography: p.
  Includes index.
  1. Tugboats. 2. Towboats. 3. Foss
Company—History. I. Title.
VM464.S56   338.7'6238232'0979   81–16684
ISBN 0-87564-224-1   AACR2

FIRST EDITION

Original pen & ink drawings copyright 1981 by James A. Cole
Original cover concept by Joe Salisbury
Cover design by Bonath & Associates

Photographic reproduction by Artcraft Colorgraphics—Seattle, WA.
Layout and book design by Phyllis Berg

TABLE OF CONTENTS

DRAWINGS BY JAMES A. COLE

ACKNOWLEDGEMENTS

I wish to extend my grateful thanks to the members of the Foss family who so generously provided background information on the company's Founders and to the Foss personnel—active and retired—for their keen interest in this book and for relating their experiences on the green-and-white tugs. Special thanks is extended to Jay Peterson, former operations manager, for his patient reading of the manuscript for accuracy and sequence and for his constant encouragement. Particular mention is also due the *Marine Digest* for making back files available and to marine photographer Joe Williamson for his courtesy in supplying many fine pictures. *H. W. McCurdy's Marine History of the Pacific Northwest (volumes I & II)* and the government publication *Merchant Vessels of the United States*, have been invaluable for reference information.

My associates in the Foss office have my lasting appreciation for their interest and enthusiasm in following the daily progress of the book—may gales and rough seas be only in the story.

The Foss Piers in Ballard photographed at years end, *1961 with several of the ocean going tugs and barges tied up for the winter months. (Courtesy of Foss Tug Co)*

COMMENTARY

From the standpoint of a past chairman of the Foss Launch & Tug Co. Board of Directors and a 62-year member of the Foss family, I found "Foss—Ninety Years of Towboating" an absorbing account. It is a fine portrayal of my grandparents, Thea and Andrew, my father Henry Foss, and his brothers Arthur and Wedell, whose visions and zeal made possible a Foss enterprise that started with rowboats and led to a fleet of one of the largest in the U.S.

The book recalls the trials, disappointments, and problems that faced our family in establishing their livelihood. Faith and perseverance carried them through many uncertain and trying times. Overcoming adversities along the way further strengthened the family's chances of success. Step by step, year by year, dollar by dollar, a thriving company developed and was brought to maturity by steadying principles and hard work. The "introduction" has this theme and depicts the successful progression of both family and company.

In "Foss—Ninety Years of Towboating" the tugs come alive and present individual personalities that make for engaging reading. Being associated with the tugs for many, many years, it was a pleasant experience to re-live the many adventures of the ocean towboats and relax with the local exploits of Foss tugs in and around Puget Sound.

> Drew Foss
> Past Chairman of the Board of Directors
> Foss Launch & Tug Co.

All's quiet at the Foss Seattle docks on Christmas Eve with many of the Foss tugs tied up for a 24 hour break in the action. (Photo courtesy of the author's collection)

FOREWORD

Material for this book came largely from personal contact with active and retired Foss personnel and from existing log books. Considering that there are 144 tugs involved, some with records dating back seventy-five years and more, it is possible that there were errors and omissions in the material available and in interpretation of events. Nevertheless, a determined effort has been made to accurately report all significant details of each tug in the Foss ocean and inside fleets.

For nearly a century, the maritime services of the Foss boats have been closely involved in the growth and prosperity of greater Puget Sound. The productive work of Foss crews and tugs is evident throughout this book in both the regional and worldwide assignments that make up the interesting and varied life of the tugs.

So stand by fore and aft. We're ready to get under way with the unique Foss organization for a lifetime of voyages on 144 tugboats.

INTRODUCTION

THE FOSS COMPANY FOUNDERS

America's greatness came from people like Andrew and Thea Foss, people with a drive for success, but not at the expense of others. They didn't wait for opportunity to come—they searched it out. Imbued with a strong pioneering spirit, they persevered and overcame the trials and tribulations of establishing a new life in a foreign land. With keen foresight they recognized and used the flood tides to counteract the ebbs—the runouts that leave undertakings high and dry.

Having the courage to act on his conviction that this welcoming country, the United States, had the elements of the type of life and success he was looking for, Andrew Foss left Norway and arrived in America in 1878 making a ten-year stopover in St. Paul, Minnesota. He left there a 33-year old family man, to move westward and settle down in a region of vast and largely untouched resources, the Pacific Northwest. Probably because of his Norse ancestry, he ended up on the waterfront at Tacoma, Washington—a city with Mt. Rainier pointing heavenward as a backdrop reminder and the blue waters of the Pacific connecting it with half the world. He had found his home. Andrew, more in his natural element beside the sea, had suffered from inland Minnesota's climate and he hadn't made any real headway in house-building while in St. Paul—just breaking even—his heart was not in it. It was in boat building.

Fourth in a family of eight, he was born Andrew Olesen (son of Ole-Ole Thorvaddsen) in 1855 at Skirfoss, Norway. Unschooled, able only to write his name, but not untalented, he learned the shipwrighting trade by going to sea. When seventeen years old, he walked sixty miles to Christiana (now Oslo) to his brother Theodore's home and then first shipped out as a cook on the Norwegian brig *Urania*, carrying ice frm Christiana to Liverpool, England. Andrew stayed with seafaring for six years, ending up as a ship's carpenter, a skilled craftsman and a seasoned seaman. During his time at sea, he sailed on the frigid run to Murmansk and went as far away as Australia. He also sailed to South America and the Gold Coast of Africa in the bark *Lubra*. His goal, however, was to cross the Atlantic.

But he first met an exceptional girl. Whenever his ship was in Christiana, Andrew stayed with his brother Theodore, who was ten years older and had married Julia Christiansen. There, Andrew met Julia's sister Thea when she visited them at the same time as Andrew. They were immediately drawn to each other and when sure of their feelings, agreed to make their home in America, where from all reports, it was like the promised land.

Thea, born in 1858 at Eidsberg had long flaxen hair done up in coils, a dignified carriage and a well-proportioned figure, appealing to the eyes of a born craftsman like Andrew. Time proved she had a well-balanced character to match. In turn, Thea liked what she saw. Andrew's air of competency and his strong features gave an impression of confidence and understanding. He always seemed to be thinking, bringing ideas to fruition. Thea saw these qualities, ones that would stand the test of time. As their life together revealed, they were well matched, a complement to each other. In later years, Andrew was always ready to assert that his wife was his greatest asset and fortune.

Fired with the desire to establish himself and marry Thea, Andrew left his homeland and crossed the Atlantic to Quebec as a forecastle hand on a sailing ship. Upon paying off from the vessel he received a generous cash gift from the captain, who was impressed with Andrew's diligence and industry. Andrew, now feeling truly blessed, had funds enough to pay his way to St. Paul, Minnesota, with its large Norwegian community. At 23 he left his family in Norway to improve his lot in life in the land of opportunity—not necessarily to seek a fortune, but to find fulfillment in the freedom of the new world with a diligent wife working and sharing beside him. His brother Theodore had similar convictions and he emigrated to St. Paul after Andrew, but he didn't live to reach his goals, he died before Andrew left Minnesota.

Settling among his own Scandinavian people, Andrew went right to work building houses instead of boats, saving every nickel. When he had earned enough for Thea's passage he sent for her, but to his surprise his brother Iver, two years older, came in her place. Andrew didn't give up and when he had earned more passage money, he again sent for Thea. This time his sister Kristina came over. By now Andrew was ready to go back for her himself, but Thea arrived in time to save the expense. She had turned over the money Andrew sent her to his family as she was determined to pay her own way, hiring out as a housekeeper to earn money for the trip. Though the wait had been very trying, Andrew now knew he had a competent, independent and self-reliant girl to marry and they happily made their vows at a Lutheran church in Saint Paul in 1881. A case of all's well that ends well.

With so many Olesens in Saint Paul, Andrew changed his name to Andrew Olesen Fossen—the last name meaning waterfall. It seemed appropriate: his home in Norway was near cascading water flowing from a nearby lake. Later on, to simplify the name, he shortened it to Andrew Foss—a fortunate decision as it would be a stronger-sounding name when Foss became synonymous with worldwide towing and identified with a large fleet of tugboats.

Andrew and Thea lived in Minnesota for almost eight years and during this time Thea added three children to the family—Arthur, born in 1885, Wedell in 1887, and two years later, in 1889, Lillian—a particular joy to Thea. Andrew supported his family by continuing to build houses, but it was not a profitable undertaking although they managed by dint of sacrifice to send for Andrew's brother Peter and sister Mina—resulting in another increase to the number of relatives in St. Paul. But not for long, Andrew's brothers and sisters ended up in Tacoma, with Andrew the first with a family to head west. Minnesota's cold weather didn't agree with Andrew and a natural yearning for the sea prompted a move to the Puget Sound country in Washington State.

To find the right place, Andrew left his family in 1888 and worked his way to the Coast, earning money as a carpenter for the Northern Pacific Railroad in order to leave what funds they had saved for the family's needs. After two months enroute, he arrived in Tacoma, terminus of the N.P. and then naturally, he headed to the waterfront and found work as a deckhand with the Tacoma Tugboat Company. Here he could again breathe salt air! In his free time he beachcombed cedar logs for a float to build a house on and he hauled mill slabs and salvaged lumber to the location for a one-room structure. By using secondhand hardware and scrounging a stove, beds, table, benches, and simple shelving, the float house became habitable.

Fresh water, however, was a quarter-mile away and every bucket had to be hauled from a small creek. Living wouldn't be easy, but it was a start. Andrew could now begin counting days not months until his family would leave Minnesota and at long last, after a painful separation of eight months, he could send for them.

They arrived in the late spring of 1889 coming out on an immigrant train—one with stoves to cook on at each end of the cars and sleep almost impossible with all the confusion—the journey taking seven weary cinder-filled days. A trying experience for Thea, looking after the needs and safety of three lively children, all under five.

Happily, but with some trepidation, Andrew took them right to the float house from the N.P. station. Fortunately, the foot of Twelfth and Dock Streets was set in a spring-green world of budding trees and blue water with anchored sailing ships among diving seagulls, so the slab-sided, tarpaper roof float-house with its meagre furnishing and no water or conveniences, didn't completely dismay Thea. Seeing Andrew's zest for life, she put her worries aside. After all, it wasn't permanent! There was a growing city back of them and Andrew would want to better himself, and none too soon for her! Before the day was over, Wedell fell in the water and later on Arthur—both requiring rescuing by Andrew. Even this didn't turn Thea back to Minnesota, though she never conquered her fear of the water.

After the thankful reunion, Andrew and Thea took time to re-assess their state. The family's material assets consisted of a few dollars and Andrew's woodworking tools. But their greatest assets were themselves—stout hearts to face adversity and sound minds to exercise good judgment combined with common sense in making decisions. And having a sincere dependence on Divine Providence, they both had a deep spiritual sense of right and wrong, and a feeling of responsibility to their Creator and their fellowmen to an unusual degree. These characteristics and concepts never failed to guide Andrew and Thea and they ultimately gave life and form to their dream of security and success.

True, the float-house was not much—but it was their own and rent free. In time, Andrew would batten the cracks, add more comforts and refinements on his after-work hours and when he could, haul water and wood to relieve Thea. Though washing, cooking and three children underfoot was a job in itself, and she was soon an expectant mother, the float-house nevertheless was well organized and home-like—she would accept whatever came. Though Thea did not realize it then, they were to remain on the waterfront—and with far-reaching effects, fortunately for the towing industry.

But the start was at quite a cost to the family. Three weeks after their arrival in Tacoma, and with some of the shipping boxes still unpacked, Thea became deathly sick and lay helpless for three months. It was a daily struggle against typhoid-pneumonia and a question of survival. Answering Andrew's plea, a kind and friendly doctor did what he could and without remuneration. Andrew was nurse not only to his wife, but also to his three small children. Fortunately, Thea did get well and had reasonably good health for the rest of her life. Andrew, however, never quite got over his exposure to Minnesota's below zero effects and was not robust throughout his long life. (The doctor's kindness to Thea was not forgotten, as in better times Andrew made substantial donations to the Pierce County Hospital in thanksgiving.)

When Thea was back on her feet and the house in order, Andrew went back to his first job as a deckhand for Tacoma Tugboat Company. Then to earn more money, he secured work in a shipyard where he could put his skills to work more profitably. With Thea expecting another child, this was imperative.

Before the new arrival and within a year of their coming to Twelfth and Dock streets, they faced the stress of another upheaval. The family was forced to move due to the City's diversion of the Puyallup River to allow a dredge landfill to be made for industrial development. Andrew's float-house ended up at Hallelujah Harbor, so named

The Foss's early home on the Tacoma waterfront.

because of the many "Salvation Army" shacks in the neighborhood. The area was later known as the Wheeler-Osgood Channel. Water carrying was a problem there too, and living still wasn't easy.

As Andrew's cash income was sporadic and to provide better for his family, he had to leave home and take a contract to build a house at Henderson Bay, a day's sail away. While on the two-month job, Providence really took a hand in their affairs. A nearby-beach resident, leaving town, let Thea have a $10 rowboat for $5 when he saw that was all she could scrape up in small coins. It was an inspired buy. Sprucing up the boat with green and white paint—the eventual Foss colors—she was able to sell it at a profit and with the gain, she bought more rowboats. This trading in boats went on until she could afford to keep the rowboats and rent them out. Recreational boating was at its height. The Foss float became the center of boats for hire at all times, day and night, and originated the Foss slogan "Always Ready" which Thea advertised from the housetop and brought in customers with its appeal. When Andrew returned, amazed that Thea had made more money in a few weeks than he had in two month's hard labor, he set right to work building more boats. By the end of the year, rowboat rentals were producing a substantial income.

The early beginnings....circa 1918.

The bread-and-butter anxiety settled—a third move was in order. Henry, the third boy, made his appearance in 1891 and the Hallelujah float-house now had to house a family of six. A larger home had to be provided and a more suitable place found to carry on the boat business. Andrew found another tide-water location at the foot of the Union Pacific Railroad Bridge, but as a home, they would have to endure the roar of trains going by and it proved to be a hazardous site for the children. Andrew set to work, and Arthur and Wedell, as young as they were, helped on the project by carrying salvaged lumber and going to the hardware store for materials to keep Andrew supplied. After eighteen months, the building was ready—with three family rooms above and a storage room below for the rowboats. Fresh water now was no longer a problem. There was a faucet right outside the door! Pleased wtih all this home-making space, Thea could now expand her natural gift of hospitality and invite more Norwegian friends, so that Sunday potluck dinners, many times with twenty to thirty people, were a regular event and the new home became a social and business center.

Thea realized great satisfaction from the rowboat business, but Andrew's creative hands had to have an outlet, so he joined his two brothers, who were working in a local sawmill, in building a fifty-foot steamer for re-sale. The float-house had, of course, been moved up to the boat-house location and it became a workshop. With Iver and Peter's mechanical ability and Andrew's skill with wordworking tools, they made a good team. however, not having money enough for new boat equipment to fit into the planned hull, they bought the parts, rusty engines and boiler, from the wrecked steamer ST. PATRICK, lying in Tacoma harbor.

THE BLUE STAR, first Foss-owned boat on Puget Sound, was powered with the engine and boiler of the wrecked steamboat St. Patrick.

Although the three brothers worked only in their spare time, building the vessel on the beach near Andrew's boathouse, by 1892 she was ready—a freight and passenger steamer 55' × 13.6' × 5.3' and named BLUE STAR. It should have been called RED STAR. The Fosses sold the boat, but it was a losing venture. The BLUE STAR was eventually converted to a tugboat, but not by the Foss yard, and while in the hands of Captain E. Weston, she was destroyed by a fire in Olympia in 1902.

As was to be expected, the young Foss boys found the beach life engrossing. Thea was hard put to get them up town to school. In 1894 Arthur was nine years old, Wedell seven, Lillian, five years old, and Henry born at their Hallelujah Harbor location, was just three, not quite old enough to join his brothers in beachcombing. But the two older boys were taking to the water like ducks. Thea at first spent considerable time pulling the boys away from the water, but eventually she gave up, trusting in the special Providence that looks after fledgling sailors. She knew experience was the best teacher and after all, they had to learn the ways of tides and examine what the waves brought in. By the time Henry was old enough to safely get his feet wet, the older boys were doing their water adventuring in boats, so Thea's worries were slightly lessened.

Henry was the last hand signed on the family ship. But prior to Henry, a daughter named Lela had arrived stillborn a year after their coming to 12th and Dock streets—no doubt Thea's three-month illness, the privations, and the somewhat primitive living conditions had taken their toll. However, Lillian lived long enough to share in the early

The Foss Family around 1900. *(From left to right) Back Row: Arthur, Lillian, Wedell Front Row: Andrew, Henry & Thea.*

struggles and early success of her parents, but not in the heyday of the business. Only the boys were a part of the ceaseless work of their parents that would eventually turn a harbor operation into a seven-ocean company.

But it started slowly, on a pay-as-you-go basis. After Andrew's unprofitable experience with the BLUE STAR, his next step was to search for a cheap boat to rebuild and make a profit, he found the LIZZIE A—a small stern-wheeler. Built for freighting on the Duwamish River out of Seattle, she proved difficult to handle by trying to plane like a speedboat, raising her bow when under way. Andrew bought the LIZZIE for $50, floated her off the beach and brought her home. He practically rebuilt the boat, but failed to cure her bad habit, and she was not successful on a freight run Andrew started to Vashon Island. Since the LIZZIE was not Thea's idea of a good business investment, and with Andrew's blessing, she found a buyer who agreed to pay $500 and a team of horses for the wet-ender. Between them, Andrew and Thea, much to their relief had made a profit on the LIZZIE A. However, she was the Foss' only sternwheeler, although this same type of tugboat was later used for towing logs down the Skagit and Snohomish Rivers.

Andrew's shipyard at the time of rowboat construction and just before the LIZZIE A, consisted of nothing more than saw-horses, beachcombed and salvaged lumber and the tool chest. But, under Andrew's skilled hands and with an eye for proportion the work was exceptional. The yard produced its own rowboats and oars. Uniquely, the oars were fashioned from rived spruce flitches. Andrew split out his oar blanks so the rower would be pulling against vertical grain and not flat grain—he had few broken oars. To test the wood, he used a pricker to lift up the grain and if the raised sliver broke he discarded the piece as unfit for the strain put on an oar. The same test was used by spruce mills in determining the tensile strength and safety of spruce flitches during W.W. II when sawed for export to Britain for spars in trainer aircraft.

The boys took part in every undertaking, as they did in building the boat-house, except in fashioning oars or building rowboats. In the rowboat days they were charged with bailing out the boats and keeping them clean and ready to go. One compensation, they collected all the herring bait left in the boats and resold it the next day to the new crop of fishermen. Some of the skiffs were equipped with a sail and the boys gave instruction on how to use it. There was a slight charge for this, of course. But not all their jobs brought in cash. They had to collect spilled wheat from the grain cars that rumbled by on the Northern Pacific roadbed above the boat-house. Some of the wheat went to the chicken yard, and the better portion, sifted out, went to the kitchen. Thea soaked the wheat for twenty-four hours then boiled it for another four—the end result with thick cream, was a nourishing and tasty gruel, with a few cinders included for roughage. Among other chores the boys also prepared kindling for the morning fire by shaving cedar splints into a cluster of curls—a trick they learned watching Andrew's skilled hand. With the many jobs at home and going to school, the boys had little idle time. In fact, they never lost the habit of being constantly at work.

With Arthur and Wedell now able to handle small boats, Thea had a chance to buy a two-horsepower naphtha-powered launch called HOPE. She didn't have pleasure-cruising in mind for the boat, but business. She reasoned that the boys could run a faster delivery service than the competition with rowboats for the merchants who were supplying the anchored sailing ships in the harbor. Andrew readily agreed to the idea of the launch and with the necessary cash in hand from the sale of the LIZZIE A, the deal was made and the Foss family had their first power boat and "Foss Launch Company" became a reality.

The venture was an immediate success. Like many of Thea's undertakings her perception was accurate. The boys had an eye for the main chance too, and they soon had a corner on the delivery business. To keep up with the demand for service, more and better equipment was necessary, so Andrew, together with Iver and Peter, now spent full time building launches in addition to rowboats. And before long, "Foss Launch Company" had ten launches in their fleet. Launch construction started Andrew out in a more complete shipyard. He enlarged the site and bought second-hand woodworking machinery, the expansion eventually led to the building of his own heavy-duty tugs. But it was the little HOPE that gave the boys the zest and the drive that carried them beyond the delivery service—to have a Foss tug serving every incoming ship.

Before long, the enterprising boys developed a lucrative sideline. They started a rescue service in the harbor using their small launch. With a telescope, they could spot tired rowers or windless sailboats in need of help. They were especially solicitous of young couples, becalmed and in danger of incurring the ire of parents by not returning before dark and ending up in a compromising situation! If the boat in distress had been rented from the Foss float, the boys did not charge for towing, otherwise the rate for rescue was twenty-five cents. They did very well financially, taking in $5 some evenings with their first fling at moonlighting and of course, they didn't have to file a tariff or keep books for a silent partner because of having an income!

At the time the launch service was initiated, Thea's nephews, Fred and Charles Berg, came out from Chicago and joined Andrew and Thea. Her three brothers and one sister that came to America changed their name to Berg. Fred assisted in formally organizing the "Foss Launch Company". With the launch LILLIAN D., Andrew's work of art, performing so well, the future use of launches seemed assured, so more equipment was added to the growing business. Fred Berg, knowledgeable about engines recommended buying a heavy-duty gas engine for their launch COLUMBIA, then under construction. Fred had to revamp the engine before it was efficient. Two more launches were quickly built, the COLUMBIA II and the UNCLE SAM. Then the Foss Company bought out the Alger fleet of launches giving Foss a better opportunity to take on most of the harbor service business in and around Tacoma, ultimately including ship-docking.

ANDREW FOSS and THEA FOSS during their life in Tacoma.

In keeping with their high standards, the Fosses continued to provide excellent service for the sailing ships anchored in the harbor. At times they were serving twenty-five vessels, not only delivering supplies, mostly fresh meat and produce, but providing water-taxi transportation for the crews if the ship's own shore-boats were not used. Andrew had six launches to be kept busy in ship service and due to the stiff competition, Arthur and Wedell were delegated to convince the captains that Foss gave the best service. In the early going, school interfered with their boat activities. However, Arthur was able to work full time after the eighth grade as it became necessary to leave school and help his parents in the family business. Wedell continued with his schooling, but even so he was still a working member of the family.

The boys arranged to receive a wire from Port Townsend—the clearing and entering port for all ships—whenever a vessel headed for Tacoma and at the proper time, they headed out in one of the launches for Point Robinson to wait there for the ship to show up, usually towed by a tug. The young Foss salesmen always carried a box of Washington apples or fresh produce to pass up to the captain and the crew. Not only did it delight the sailors after a long voyage, but it helped Arthur and Wedell's pitch for the ship service job. Sometimes to beat competition, they would go all the way to Port Townsend, seventy-five miles, to meet a ship and if the weather was cold, windy, and rainy, traveling in an open launch all night was an ordeal. But business was business.

Arthur, when only 13 years old, started delivering the U.S. mail from Tacoma to Seattle by launch, under a government contract. The railroad at the time bypassed Seattle and ended up in Tacoma. Arthur on his daily run always admired a beautiful, recently logged area called Hidden Valley, near Des Moines and in 1938 he purchased the property for development and as a place for his retirement. He didn't live to realize his plans, but his daughter Patricia does live at Hidden Valley. It is still owned by the family.

By 1902, after Andrew put more power in the launches, they were able to help dock the big ships and this added revenue, combined with the delivery service, usually totalled about $1,500 for each vessel—that is if the ship waited the usual time in port before loading. At last they no longer had to deal in coins.

With the increased business, more working space became a necessity. A third move had to be made to provide tie-ups for the launches, storage for the rowboats, and housing for store, office, shop and living quarters. Salmon Bay, a half-mile away was chosen as there was ample room and a pile bulkhead to build against already there that retained a sand fill alongside the railroad tracks. The boat-house (later on a dormitory and store) ended up on piling next to the bulkhead and the floating work-shop was moved and joined to the end of a new floating pier built for launch tie-ups. All facilities were grouped together and a more unified operation was now possible. By 1906 the Foss Company address was 400 Dock Street.

With the ship-assist business flourishing and rowboats in good demand, the Fosses continued to buy and build more boats, so the picnickers, fishermen, duck hunters, merchants, and ships were well-provided for and there was always a boat ready. Everyone in the family was busy, but there just weren't enough of them to cover the work. Help had to be hired. They naturally drew on the steady influx of Scandinavian immigrants flocking to the Pacific Northwest, a region similar in beauty and climate to their own native shores. And logically the newly arrived were drawn to the language, food, and social attitudes of their own kind. The Foss family was never short of help—and good help at that.

Thea provided for the men in her own practical way. In order to provide satisfying meals, and a spirit of unity for the growing number of Foss crews and workers, she had Andrew build a simple two-story building adjoining their quarters. The addition consisted of a dormitory above for the men and an adjoining dining room served from her own kitchen, and below a general store on the float level, which she ran herself. Twenty-five to thirty men were housed in the dormitory. The family ate with the crews and they helped with the housekeeping. She listened to them and gave them good counsel on money matters. She ran a "happy ship" and they in turn repaid Thea and Andrew with loyalty and good work. Andrew, however, insisted that all his countrymen become citizens. And moreover, he instructed them from his own citizenship texts and saw to it they appeared before the judge when they were qualified. To Andrew, U.S. citizenship was an honor and a must.

The Foss store furnished all supplies for launches and later on the tugs—from food to towing gear. And the crews on the boats and in the yard were furnished all their needs from the store. It was a popular place. With most necessities available, there were few regular paydays, but money was on hand when asked for. Otherwise, payment for work came at termination and it was always generous. Indeed, "Mother Foss" and "Father Foss" as they were called by the crews, looked after their men as if they were family—with solicitude, but without overdoing it. The habit of concern was so ingrained in Thea and Andrew, which Arthur, Wedell and Henry carried on, that those who worked for Foss soon considered themselves part of the family and the end result was a solidarity of purpose.

How Thea managed to do as much as she did remains a mystery. And without fuss. Her hands and mind were never idle. And Lillian, though she helped, didn't inherit Thea's stamina for taxing work. The tasks were endless. To keep the boarding house supplied with her own products, Thea kept about forty chickens, two pigs, and a cow named Annie. Fortunately a nearby field had room for Thea's animal farm, however, the pigs were under Andrew's care. He had a special feeling for animals and they responded to him, especially the pigs. Understandably, the turnover in chickens was heavy, but Annie kept her position without fear of ending up in an oven. She was a good milk provider and in exchange for her bounty, she demanded and received direct from the kitchen window a generous helping of hot cakes every morning. She considered herself a member of the family too. According to the boarders, Annie's milk turned into griddle-cake batter by just beating it.

Annie performed another important function, so the story goes, she provided an answering service for the boat captains. When the weather was foggy and an incoming Foss boat needed a bearing on the launch dock to come in on, the captain would keep his whistle blowing every sixty seconds until Annie had time to amble out on the dock and give an answering blast, cow-style. Apparently the captains fed Annie on the wharf whenever they tied up after announcing their arrival with the whistle. They kept her in practice so she would be on hand whenever the weather was thick. Annie's dual role certainly conformed to the Foss idea that any worker should be able to do more than one job—the specialist of today was unheard of in that era.

With a notable friendliness that brought people to her, Thea continued to run the boarding house, store, and office not only in the interests of the Company, but as a base to carry on charitable works, with the help of her sister Mathilda, who had married Andrew's brother Iver. Every day they made someone happier in helping the needy, attending the sick, comforting the afflicted. And for fifteen years they sheltered and aided green girls from the Old Country.

Thea's life was one of dedication, perseverance and enthusiasm for all her undertakings and without sparing herself. She was honest but shrewd, never exuberant, seldom laughed, a serious-minded, mentally-active woman whose business acumen and success was only the means to an end—service to others, on land or water.

Occasionally Thea expressed her feelings in a diary and the entry on January 19, 1907 is indicative of her philosophy.

"The law imprinted in all men's hearts is to love one another. I will look at the whole world as my Country and all men as my brothers. We are made for cooperation and to act against one another is to act contrary to nature. Say not, I will love the wise and hate the unwise, you should love all mankind. Let us not love in word and in tongue, but in deed and in truth. "The only word missing is "Amen."

With Thea's beliefs and Andrew's standards safely imbued in the boys through example and practice, Andrew and Thea felt the time had come for Wedell and Henry to acquire a degree in law and business, so necessary now with the expected growth of the Company. After a family conference, the decision was for Wedell to obtain a law degree from the University of Washington and for Henry to take a business course at Stanford. Arthur with his natural ability, discernment and foresight was to assist in the management as Andrew, by this time, required rest periods during the day, and he had a couch in the boathouse where he could lie down and recuperate.

With the Company deciding to embark in the purchase, construction and operation of regular tugboats, Arthur's young outlook and ideas were necessary as the simpler life style of centuries was ending and modern mechanization was taking over. The stately windships gradually disappeared in the changeover to steamships—self-propelled vessels that didn't need Foss help. And at the time, in the early 1900's the bicycle craze was sweeping the country, dropping pleasure boating to a low level. Then with the advent of the automobile a short time later, the use of rowboats and sailboats was further curtailed. Most of the rowboats and launches were idle.

All effort now had to be concentrated on further developing the towing business—principally log towing. Old growth timber still covered the hills and Puget Sound was dotted with lumber mills, humming night and day, cutting up large quantities of logs. The consumption was so great, logs had to be towed in. The need for more tugs was certain. In short order Foss Launches, readied with a towing bitt installed just aft of the exhaust stack, were able to tow logs, but proved underpowered—using up the revenue for gasoline in trying to buck the two-a-day tides.

The Foss Company heads—Andrew, Thea and Arthur, along with Fred Berg, decided on a remedy. Clearly, the launch-tugboats as they were, would not do—but the family was not disheartened. Instead, local mills were contacted up and down the Sound to make sure of an abundance of towing jobs and then the Company invested in new and more powerful engines to make the launches practical. Time was money in contract towing—there simply had to be enough power to keep a log raft moving even in an adverse tide. Foss' long history and expertise in log towing had started.

Though economics at this point was forcing a change in engines, there would be more and varied advances to come, bringing an end to an uncomplicated era. However, the Company being flexible and having cash on hand, was able to meet the challenges. This ready reserve was due to Andrew and Thea's firm policy of saving as much money as possible during prosperous years so that when depressed times came along and bargains were available or upgrading was in order, they could buy what equipment they were able to pay cash for. In building up their business they acted on the theory that prosperity and depression came in cycles and so they were always prepared to act accordingly.

The future in towing looked very bright with mills in every harbor, consuming millions of feet of logs and they would for many years to come. To take full advantage of the towing potential, though the launches were improved, Foss planned to go all out to better their position by converting to boats designed and built especially for log towing. The decision led to Andrew's revolutionary tug design.

Inspired to build an efficient tugboat, Andrew spent his evenings at home carving out a flowing type model hull. He had streamlining and minimum water resistance in mind as he whittled. After many trials, the model ended up with a teardrop shaped underbody and a rounded stern on the above-water after-section. Andrew knew little about hydrodynamics, but his teardrop design ultimately became an industry standard—even today the bulbous-bow ocean liners have the same concept. His sharp practical eye had seen and had fashioned a vastly improved boat hull. Andrew went one step farther in planning an efficient tug. He designed a balanced rudder, plating ahead as well as in back of the rudder post, giving better control and tighter turning. He didn't patent any of his inventions. He said they were for the common good. Satisfied, the Company, with Andrew's tug design to bank on would be able to out-perform the present towing competition. The long range plan was to improve the shipyard and turn out tugs on a continuous basis.

But Andrew's prototype tug, the FOSS-6, fashioned after his whittled model, did not become a reality until 1916. She was in fact, the third Foss tug launched. The first two, the FOSS 9 (a purchased tug, rebuilt) and FOSS-12, were turned out at Gig Harbor for Foss-Tacoma in 1912 and 1914, but were not of the teardrop type. Andrew's home shipyard was not equipped at the time to handle the FOSS 6 job, so to prevent any delay, the Company had her built by Robert Crawford at Gig Harbor, but under Andrew's supervision. It was good insurance as FOSS 6, from the moment she left the ways, performed as Andrew had visualized—with minimum water disturbance and maximum stability. He hadn't really worried about the outcome, nevertheless, the favorable comments, especially from his sons and the complimentary marine articles, did please him. A rare case of the knife being mightier than the pen—Andrew could hardly write.

Two years after the towing program was functioning successfully and the business outlook still bright, the family in spite of all they could do, suffered a heavy personal loss. No longer would there be a golden-haired girl to share in the family success. Lillian Deborah, who had been in failing health, passed away in 1914 from T.B. To Thea, the loss of her beautiful Lillie was a heavy blow from which she never completely recovered and losing her brought back the sorrow of the death of her first daughter Lilly Marie at age four in Minnesota. However, in her depth of understanding, she accepted the sorrow. Now she would immerse herself more than ever in the productive, burgeoning business and in the family good works.

By 1914 Andrew's health was such that he was forced to curtail his physical activities and even with Arthur and the Bergs actively engaged in the business, more management help was imperative. Andrew's brothers who had been the mainstay in the shipyard had passed away, Peter in 1909 and Iver in 1906, so Andrew had assumed the responsibilities of the yard and this added to the demands on his strength. Thea had her hands full with the store, boarding house, office, and personal projects—she couldn't do more. Henry was the answer to their need. Without hesitation, he left Stanford after only a year at school. It was now necessary to reorganize the Company. A new name resulted: Foss Launch & Tug Company. And incorporated by Andrew, Arthur, Henry and Fred Berg.

The Company's next move, in order to take care of the immediate log towing jobs that had been developed, was to charter the three Tacoma Towboat Company's steam tugs to augment their own three gas tugs. And they still had six launches operating on harbor jobs. Then the newly organized company expanded into another area—contract work. Early on, they accepted and successfully completed a chancy contract, calling for providing and delivering 100,000 cubic yards of brush matting for a fill to be put in at the site of a new Todd Shipyard in Tacoma. Ever since, Foss has never hesitated to undertake, and to successfully perform unusual or difficult maritime jobs.

Foss Launch and Tug was able to take care of their towing commitments with six tugs and six converted launches until World War I, then to make sure they could meet the surge in wartime cargo movement, the Company bought outright, the three chartered tugs. Arthur also purchased a 55% interest in the Chesley Tug & Barge Company of Seattle and under his direction this connection helped meet the increased demand on Foss, however, later on Arthur sold the interest back to Chesley.

With the war over, Arthur, Henry and Wedell, in August 1919 put on a water sports carnival at the boathouse to specially honor Thea's great contribution to the Company's success and to commemorate her starting in the rowboat business. It was a festival long remembered by the hundreds in attendance at 400 Dock Street, especially by Wedell, just out of the Navy and happy to be back with the family.

Wedell, before the war, was not directly connected with the Company affairs, but he did take care of what legal matters arose. As planned, he graduated from Law School and was practicing in Tacoma, when in 1917, the Navy called him for duty in the Militia. He joined the battleship SOUTH DAKOTA as a Junior Lieutenant. The SOUTH DAKOTA spent several months in South American waters chasing the commerce-raider, SEEADLER, commanded by Count von Luckner. Then convoy duty in the Atlantic was the SOUTH DAKOTA's next and final assignment during the war. She was eventually scrapped in Seattle. After the war, Wedell spent several months at the Naval Academy before being discharged in June 1919. While practicing law, Wedell had married Edith Eaton of Yakima and Tacoma. They had two daughters, Barbara who married Sidney Campbell, and he in time became chairman of Foss Launch & Tug Company. Justine, the other daughter, married William Wood, who became a vice-president of Foss.

Arthur and Henry had also married. Arthur in 1904 to Ellen Eggers of Tacoma. They had two daughters, Christine and Patricia, but their husbands did not become part of the Foss organization. However, Patricia became active in the Foss Company and during 30 years of participation she held various executive positions, including serving on the board of directors. Henry married his boyhood sweetheart, Agnes Hanson in 1914, and they had one son, Drew, now retired—a former board chairman—and a daughter, Henrietta.

It so happened that the third generation of Fosses ran to daughters, five to one, so there are few present members with a Foss last name. But of course, there are many members with a middle name of Foss. However, all the names of the present line of tugs end with Foss.

The growth of Company operations in the 1920's spread to Seattle, when Wedell preferring boat towing to law, re-entered the towing business by buying a half-interest in the Rouse Towing Company of Seattle. To establish a position, he took over the inventorying and towing of boomsticks from Seattle north to Blaine. One job led to another, and before long with Arthur's help, he was in the log towing and barge business. Arthur felt that their Seattle venture should not be separated from Foss-Tacoma, so in due time, Wedell bought Fred Berg's stock in the Foss Launch & Tug Company and the Company, through Arthur, bought the balance of Rouse stock from the widowed Mrs. Rouse. Now there was one Company—entirely Foss. Arthur had moved to Seattle to assist Wedell in expanding the area operations on all fronts and in the merger Arthur became president, Wedell vice-president, with Henry secretary-treasurer of the combined operations.

The Foss division in Port Angeles showing the HENRY, MARTHA, IVER, FOSS #21, NANCY and FOSS #9 *on a July day in 1945 between assignments.*

Wedell first located his Seattle base on the north side of the Lake Washington Ship canal at the Bolcom Dock, under the Ballard Bridge. Later on the base was moved to the south side of the canal, a half mile east of the bridge. An office, shop, and a short finger pier comprised the plant. However, year by year, the area, facilities, buildings, and piers were enlarged to accommodate the growing fleet until the 1970's the plant covered several acres. The greatest expansion came in 1973 when the Foss-Tacoma shipyard and related units were shifted to Seattle in the move for consolidation of activities, leaving only a small supervisory force for local work. However, up to World War II, Tacoma continued to be headquarters for Foss. Henry, in charge of Tacoma operations, and Arthur and Wedell in Seattle, proceeded to put a Foss tug on every local towing job of consequence. But they ran out of tugs. During the 1920's more tugs were added and still there weren't enough. All tugs were running and the Company prospered.

Though the business was progressing and healthy, the heart of the Company—Thea Christiansen Foss—was slowing down, bringing on a mother's lament, "there are so many things yet to do". And no doubt she missed being at the center of the Company's activity on the waterfront. The family had built a new home at North 25th and Cheyenne St., but it was uptown and out of sight of tugs and launches. However, Thea's interest in company affairs never waned and she continued on with her "helping hand" work as her strength allowed. But at sixty-nine, Thea's physical side was no longer able to respond as she wished—her time was drawing to a close.

Anxiously, Andrew and many times, the boys, put aside their immediate business concerns to come and spend time in her company, keeping her informed of their activities and recounting the many past successes she had a hand in. Then in May of 1927 Andrew's beloved Thea, the boys' attentive mother, the founding mother of the Company, the friend and benefactor of uncounted people—passed away. It is no wonder hers was the largest funeral to occur in Tacoma up to that time. The green and white tugs flew their flags at half mast. Time has continued to show how remarkable she was in a man's world of business, a woman not at all like the amusing caricature protrayed in "Tugboat Annie" but a unique and unforgettable personage whose innate dignity, extraordinary perception and charity left its permanent mark.

Shortly afterward, Andrew, to ease the shock of losing Thea, went back to Norway, to visit his birthplace and their relatives. Then to re-live his family's train trip West, he came back to Tacoma across the country on a Canadian Pacific immigrant train, still operating, and typically gave helpful information and encouragement to the eager new arrivals.

As Thea would have wanted, her sons went right back to work, more determined than ever to achieve the long planned goals. The Seattle division fully occupied Arthur and Wedell, and under their guidance, foresight, and initiative, they had Foss into all phases of tugboating—assisting ships in docking and undocking, engaging in all types of barging, salvage and rescue work, and most important at the time—log towing. In three years the log towing range increased widely and the Foss coverage included all of Puget Sound, British Columbia waters, Alaska and Coastwise to California. Arthur's next move was to purchase the Wagner Towing Company, their four tugs and established runs. Counting the Wagner acquisition, thirteen more tugs were joined to the fleet in the 1930's including three new boats turned out from the Foss-Tacoma shipyard, by this time able to build most any size tug, and at the same time keep the operating tugs "Always Ready".

All Foss divisions successfully weathered the long business depression of the 30's and in the general up-swing, Henry in Tacoma, took on more and bigger jobs. In 1939 he contracted to place the pier anchors and deliver the pier concrete for the Tacoma Narrows Bridge. It was quite a feat and the Foss brothers all had a part in it. They were able to take justifiable pride that their company successfully laid the anchors, though working under unfavorable conditions. The builders, Pacific Bridge Company, faced with an extraordinary problem, laid a drawing of the pier locations on Henry's desk. To anchor the pier caissons in the nine-mile-an-hour current, the plan called for submerging forty-eight huge concrete blocks. The blocks, twelve feet square by fifty-one feet long, each weighed 550 tons. Could Foss rig barges to carry such loads and slide them into the water at mapped locations, accurately fixed by triangulation? The job would tie up six barges as the concrete was to be poured right into a form on each barge and then six days of stand-by would be required waiting for the concrete to set.

The Foss Company, with their shipyard, marine railway, and two machine shops, with fifty men working on Foss equipment exclusively, agreed to undertake the job. They would put all their resources to work. It was certain the barges would be subjected to a terrible impact when the 550-ton loads suddenly slid off into the water and the barges pitched sideways. Heavy wood barges were selected and watertight compartments fitted in and braced with large timbers and stay irons. Fresh oakum was driven into the bottom seams and layered over with galvanized sheathing.

Ted Kuss, the Narrows Bridge engineer who designed the block-anchoring system, poured the huge concrete monoliths, at the Scofield Plant at Tacoma, into plywood forms that rested on skids secured to the barge. Foss plan-

Photographed in 1944, the MARTHA *passing under Deception Pass Bridge with a log tow bound for Everett.* (*Courtesy of Foss Tug Co*)

ned to tip the barges by flooding sea water into the compartments on one side. Because of the danger in using hand-operated sea valves, they used eight-inch wooden plugs placed below the water line. The plugs were rigged by rope lanyards, leading to a bridle, so they could be pulled by a stand-by tug.

Everyone concerned was tense with anxiety when the first barge, showing only 12″ of freeboard, with its great concrete block, was towed into Tacoma Narrows at slack water. No one knew just what might happen; the method was untried. Arthur, Wedell and Henry aboard an accompanying tug checked every move. Maybe their barge would be shattered. If each of the forty-eight concrete blocks destroyed a barge—Foss would have to go back to square one, Thea's rowboats!

From various triangulation stations, the bridge engineers directed the four tugs jockeying the barge into position. At their signal, the plugs were pulled. Water poured into the barge. It listed sharply, heeled deeper, began to sink sideways. The three Foss men at the rail of the lead tug stood tense and alert. If the barge and block planed to the bottom together, the whole unit would drift yards out of position.

Then suddenly the canted block shifted, moved, gathered momentum, and plunged off the half-sunken barge. Geysers of water sprayed up in the air and a six-foot wall of water started to fan out. The barge shot from the water like a projectile, leaped high, and then smacked back on the water with a clap of thunder.

Tugs rushed in—suction hoses ready, but were not needed. When the congratulations were over, the barge was taken to the Foss shipyard and hauled up on the marine railway for examination. Except for two large bracing stringers sheared off the bottom, it was practically undamaged. Success! The Fosses breathed easier—and the engineers had their block in place 120′ below the surface. The work went ahead. Five similar barges dumped the other forty-seven concrete anchor blocks. Each time it was a breath-holding event. But only one anchor was lost overboard five miles from its destination when a rip tide jerked the barge out of control. An ever-present danger faced by the crews was the chance that a strong, swirling tide-rip would slam the tug between one of the 550-ton barge loads and a bridge pier, which could have meant the end of the tug and crew.

With the anchor work successfully underway, Foss took on the second contract with the bridge builders in which luck had to be on their side, or more probably inexhaustible attention to every facet of the job. They agreed to deliver 20,000 tons of mixed concrete from the shore mixing plant to the Narrows Bridge piers. According to specifications, the concrete was to be poured in the pier forms within thirty minutes after it was mixed. And once again, barging through the Narrows began. The entire pouring operation, often extending over thirty hours, had to be completed without a hitch. Day and night, two tugs towing barges of mixed concrete fought their way through tidal currents, delivering the perishable cargo on schedule, regardless of rain, wind or fog. The responsibility was nerve-racking, so the tug skippers worked very short shifts. Some of the experienced captains entrusted with the tugs on the bridge jobs were Henry Schoen, Roy Hall, Tom McInnis, Milton Ness, Henry Harder and Vern Wright.

As a result of good planning and execution, Foss did not end up with any loads of hardened concrete to dispose of. More congratulations were received on the success of both jobs, but Arthur, Wedell and Henry did not attribute the successful outcome all to their own ingenuity, they well knew that every contract was more or less an out-and-out gamble, and success, in addition to the human role, was influenced by the natural elements. Weather, tides, and winds determined the ease or difficulty of carrying out a towing contract. Henry Foss said many times, "Even with the best crews and far-sighted planning, the unexpected is the expected in the towing business."

The 1930's in spite of the Depression, brought them continued fame and fortune, as well as sorrow and near-tragedy. In 1932 during the time Henry was state senator, the Foss-Tacoma headquarters building burned down, endangering the lives of twenty men. Fortunately, they escaped, though the material loss was great. But Arthur located and purchased an unused seaplane hangar in Seattle and towed the building to Tacoma for conversion to an office and shop. They were back in business and within a year, all damaged appertaining buildings had been replaced. However, by 1944 more group space was needed, necessitating the Company's relocation. As a result, all the old worn out buildings at 400 Dock Street were burned down after they established a new base at 220 "F" Street. Modern structures, more efficient, housed all departments necessary to a major tugboat operation and the complex remained intact and functioning until the consolidation with Foss-Seattle in 1973.

All of the improvements were too far in the future for Andrew. Though he experienced the 1932 rebuilding after the fire and many pioneering towing jobs, he was not destined to share in the great development of the ocean-going fleet. On March 13, 1937 Andrew, aged 82, passed on after a two-month illness. He had been more or less retired for several years, though he did spend time almost every day in Henry's office, resting on the couch—still thinking and planning, his inventive mind still active. His judgment when asked for, as sound as ever. He was blessed with great patience and through perseverance, had accomplished the difficult. His example inculcated this attitude in his sons. One of Henry's guidelines was inspired by his father: "Be impatient for success, but be patient in acquiring it." And the

AGNES and JUSTINE towing the ex-passenger ship LELANI from California to a Seattle shipyard, in 1960, for conversion to the American President Lines passenger vessel PRESIDENT ROOSEVELT. (Photo courtesy of Roger Dudley)

Many years prior to the Ocean tow pictured above the Foss tugs, FOSS 16, WINONA (later HAZEL) and ROUSE (later WALLACE) were engaged in moving log rafts through the Government Locks to Ballard sawmills, pictured about 1920. (Photo courtesy of the Hiram M. Chittenden Locks)

boys never forgot Andrew's prime axiom: "Keep out of debt!" Andrew remained true to his belief to always stay on a cash basis and not add the worry of owing money to the unavoidable trials of living. Just before he died he asked his sons, "Do I owe any money? Is there anything that anyone needs with whom I am acquainted? Are there any obligations that I have to anyone that you may know of? Is there anything you boys need? I do not want to leave this life with any unpaid bills or anything that I should have done and after you have taken care of any you may find, I want it said that I did not leave this life in debt to anyone but my Maker. And to pay my way after all my obligations are paid, the balance goes to the County Hospital." Andrew had never forgotten the good doctor's care of Thea in their hour of need and his continued gifts to the hospital for the needy continued to the very end.

To quote Henry's final tribute: "And so passed this immigrant boy, who made his way under all circumstances, asked no favor of any man, was loyal to the United States of America, and whose final services were performed by his three sons."

Andrew, who was a born inventor, had witnessed a world changing from rowboats, horses, buggies, and windships to bicycles, motor cars, self-propelled ships and airplanes. He had seen his Company develop from rowboats to launches to tugs and to the universal acceptance of his own style of tugboat. And it would have been satisfying for Andrew and most fitting, had he been able to witness the advances in tug operation and the extraordinary growth of the Company from 1940 to 1950. Twenty-two more tugs of every variety were added, bringing the total acquired to sixty-one with the end not in sight. The tugs were ranging from Alaska to the Central Pacific, largely moving supplies and equipment for the Army and Navy in the Second World War. As a result, many of the Foss crews were working in the war zones and some lost their lives in the cause.

The Company was now actively engaged in the government's supply line and in order to centralize control and allocate more tugs and barges to the war effort, the Foss stockholders purchased Pacific Towboat Company of Everett, Washington. And ever since the change in ownership, Pacific Tow has remained united to Foss; and their six tugs handle most of Foss' towing and harbor work in the Everett area. However, Pacific's Anacortes office closed down in 1965; and the tanker-assist tugs all work out of the Bellingham base.

Early in the war, with able supervision in the Tacoma office under Orville Sund and George Maddock, Henry felt free to join the Navy to lend his talents in piloting ships—he had held a pilot's license since World War I. But the Navy preferred to use him as a salvage officer. He joined as a lieutenant commander and at the war's end he held the rank of captain, although he retired as a rear-admiral. Henry received many citations and commendations for his rescue of ships and men in the South Pacific. Later on at home, he was honored for his civic services—the new Tacoma High School built in 1975 bears his name.

Wedell, with his prior naval service tried to get back in, but due to physical disabilities, the Navy couldn't take him, so he remained with Arthur keeping their tugs and barges working in connection with the Seattle Port of Embarkation all during the war.

HENRY FOSS and drydock AFDM #6 *departing Puget Sound for Guam, 4,000 miles away. (Courtesy of Dudley, Hardin & Yang and Foss Tug Co)*

Four Foss tugs, CAROL, SHANNON, PATRICIA and AGNES towing the battleship COLORADO from Puget
Sound Naval Shipyard at Bremerton to Todd Shipyard in Seattle for Scrapping in July, 1959.
(Courtesy of Roger Dudley and Foss Tug Co)

Drew Foss, Henry's son, while serving the Navy on Wake Island, was captured by the Japanese and spent four years in a prison camp. The story of the JUSTINE FOSS (1) notes Drew's ordeal. Henry, quite unexpectedly, by good fortune met Drew on board the U.S.S. TRYON at Pearl Harbor in 1945 when Drew, along with 300 other P.O.W.'s, arrived in Honolulu on their way home. The two, war-weary father and son, arrived in Seattle on the U.S.S. TAKANIS BAY in November 1945.

However, Henry and Drew were back in the tugboat business in short order. Having witnessed the practicality of ocean towing during the war, Henry, Drew, Arthur and Wedell started purchasing at government sales the capable MIKI tugs that performed so well for the Army and Navy in offshore towing. Four MIKI-class tugs were bid in and put to work coastwise and on long hauls to Alaska.

Then to have a base in northern Puget Sound, Arthur and Wedell purchased in October 1949 the Bellingham Tug & Barge Company from Mrs. F. E. LaFehr, the daughter of Barney Jones, the company founder. Foss acquired four outside tugs and three harbor boats in the sale. Bill Wood, husband of Justine Foss, moved to Bellingham to take over the management.

About the same time, Henry arranged for Foss to buy a sixty percent stock interest in Turner & Judd's harbor taxi operation in Long Beach, California. T. & J. wanted to get started in the tugboat business and with Foss. The venture, named Pacific Tow & Salvage Company, was a success and through the affiliation, Foss obtained representation in Southern California.

Foss now had bases in all their operating areas except Alaska. However, the northern runs all originated from Seattle. But in the mid-50's Foss did establish a base in Anchorage. In 1969 Drew Foss took over the management and remained in charge until he retired in 1974.

With the great increase in customers served by Foss and doing business in so many different places, Henry in 1950 felt they should again bring groups of their customers together for contact with each other and with the Foss people as they had done sometime before when they operated a small yacht, named THEA. The purpose was to gain better understanding and furtherance of mutual interests and goals. Of course, combining pleasure with business. And what better way to accomplish this than aboard a large, comfortable cruising yacht?

Henry heard that the ex-Barrymore yacht was for sale and after a favorable survey, he made the purchase. Given the name THEA FOSS, the 120″ yacht has more than fulfilled its purpose. The THEA has a reputation for friendliness and hospitality so the yacht is aptly named.

The next great advance for Foss after the stress and strain of the post-war adjustment was to the Far North. And the Tacoma and Seattle divisions, planning together for Foss' part-to-be in the great oil development in Alaska, were able to add twenty-one more tugs to the fleet. But again, the Company had a price to pay for its success.

Wedell in January 1955 passed away at 67 from natural causes. The loss simply could not be measured. His reputation for integrity and success in business life was a by-word, but publicly he was best known for fostering the Tugboat Annie stories. Wedell was largely responsible for developing Norman Reilly Raine's interest in writing Northwest tugboat episodes. Wedell furnished the material for the first story plot in 1931. A succession of stories in the "Saturday Evening Post" provided amusement to a wide readership, among them the Foss family who enjoyed the tugboat antics never before seen on land or sea. But after many Tugboat Annie stories, Raine switched to writing largely for the movies, much to Wedell's disappointment, as he had hoped for more publicity on the Northwest, resulting from the stories. Interest was rekindled however, when a Tugboat Annie film was made in Seattle and a Foss tug, the WALLOWA, later the ARTHUR FOSS, was disguised to represent a fictional counterpart. The owner of the storied Deep-Sea Towing & Salvage Company, Alec Severn, was undoubtedly fashioned from Raine's knowledge and association with Wedell. Both Wedell and Alec were prudent, knowing, thrifty, and enterprising. However, the character of Tugboat Annie had no resemblance to Wedell's mother, Thea, either in appearance, manner, attitude, action, position or philosophy—Annie was completely fictitious.

As Foss vice-president and lawyer, Wedell had looked after the legal side of the business, but he also was ready and willing to resolve any emotional or family problems that his employees, both ashore and afloat, became involved in. Being a strong family man he would make every effort to restore harmony—with financial help if necessary. Thea's characteristics of discernment and concern were very much in evidence in Wedell.

The LORNA shown assiting the MARTHA in towing a mill refuse burner from Hoodsport to the Standard Export Lumber Mill on Seattle's Duwamish River in 1942. (Courtesy of Joe Williamson)

Captain Ray Quinn, left, of the AGNES FOSS, receiving departing wishes from Foss management, Sid Campbell, left and Paul Pearson, prior to departure of the AGNES and DONNA for Panama with the liner REPUBLIC. (Courtesy of Joe Williamson)

The CATHERINE underway from Seattle for *North Vancouver, B.C. with two Foss Railcar barges on a regular run first established by Foss in 1957. (Photo courtesy of Foss Tug Co)*

The close family bond between the three brothers was altered by Wedell's death. It left a tremendous personal loss. In the business, a realignment of the Company officers was now necessary and Arthur became board chairman; Henry, president; Drew, vice-president; Orville Sund remained manager in Tacoma with George Maddock as assistant. Paul Pearson, a Foss employee since 1920 continued as Seattle Manager with Sidney Campbell as Assistant.

The Company, with its aggressive management continuing, added to the 1960's an almost unbelievable number of tugs to the fleet. Forty-three more units, including the acquisition in 1961 of the five small Delta Smyth tugs in Olympia. There were few idle tugs, yet few jobs were turned down. But the greatest growth period in Foss history and the most profitable was tempered by the death of Arthur in October 1964 at 79 years.

Arthur's entire business life was devoted to the well-being of the Foss Company and its members—over seventy continuous years of dedication. However, he did lead a varied life, evidenced by his interest in public projects. Consequently, though somewhat reserved, he enjoyed membership in several prominent clubs in Seattle and three Scandinavian groups. But it was always business first and free time was at a premium. In addition to his Foss Launch & Tug chairmanship, he was chairman of the board of other Foss companies and interests—Milwaukee Log Boom Company in Tacoma; Pacific Towboat Company of Everett; Bellingham Tug & Barge Company of Bellingham; and the Star Towing Company, Ltd. of Vancouver, B.C., a company later absorbed in the forming of Island Tug & Barge Company of Victoria and Vancouver.

Like Thea, his life was one of activity, yet he found time to collect and preserve memorabilia—pictures and souvenirs of all types of ships, principally sailing ships. However, his marine license was for "engineer, steam and diesel"—one of his prized possessions. He even bought the windjammer ST. PAUL and turned it over to the Puget Sound Academy of Science for the public to view. Unfortunately, he did not live to see the largest of Foss tugs—named in his honor—in operation. The ARTHUR wasn't completed until February 1966 after four years in the Foss shipyard.

Two words express Arthur's code of conduct: Trustworthy—Dependable. He often said that he and Wedell and Henry were raised on the application of those words and they became a Foss tradition. One of his most ardent wishes has yet to be fulfilled, "We found our niches and I hope our future generations will continue to find their own place in the world of towing and transportation." In time it could be realized.

Henry now had the full load on his shoulders. He carried it well, but two years after Arthur's death, Henry reached his seventy-fifth year and he elected to retire from active work in favor of younger talent. Henry's many contributions to the Company's success are attributed to his tact, diplomacy, initiative and salesmanship—he left his mark.

Sidney Campbell, in the Seattle Division, became president. He took over when the Company was at its peak with 800 employees, 75 tugs, and as many barges in operation from the Gulf of Mexico to Alaska. It was a high-pressure situation. However, the management personnel came up through the hawse pipe; they knew where the rocks and reefs were—so there was little costly trial and error and the Company carried on in the Foss tradition of dependable service.

At Henry's retirement in 1966—and he is still living on Day Island—Drew, Henry's son, and Arthur's daughter Patricia were the only remaining third generation members active in the business. Of the fourth generation only one member, Peter Foss Campbell, remained in a Foss executive position. On Andrew's side, his brother Peter married Anna Reid and they had three children, but they were not directly connected with the Company. Andrew's brother,

Two Foss Miki class tugs departing San Francisco with drill jacket for an oil exploration site in Cook Inlet, Alaska, 1964. (Photo credit unknown)

27

Five Foss tugs, LESLIE, EDITH (3), WEDELL, ANDREW and CAROL (just visible) positioning one of the center spans of the Hood Canal Bridge in 1960. (Courtesy of Foss Tug Co)

Iver, married to Thea's sister Mathilda had one son, but he only worked for the Company a short time. However, their names were "Foss." Thea's brothers Anton and Lewis worked in the yard and the store, but they were not involved in administration.

Therefore, by the 1960's it was obvious the Foss family would in the near future face a serious problem of family personnel to perpetuate the business. The Company had experienced and competent hands at the management level, but very little succession at the active stockholder level. In 1969 the stockholders, Henry, and the family heirs of Arthur and Wedell, decided to insure the Company's position by joining in a stock exchange with an established, reputable, and successful company with maritime interests. The Dillingham Corporation of Honolulu was selected as the ideal corporation to associate with, the one to continue the success Foss enjoyed throughout the years.

Foss became a part of Dillingham's maritime group on July of 1969 and three years later Sidney Campbell changed from president of Foss Launch & Tug Company to chairman of the board of the directors of the Foss Division of Dillingham. The Company continued to grow by building more new and powerful tugs and developing additional markets for tug service. And now, ten years after the amalgamation, the advance continues in a sophisticated manner, but in Andrew's simple rule of improving as you go.

In Andrew's time and in his early tugs he installed fifty-horsepower gas engines, then as more towing developed he increased the tug power to insure prompt and safe log delivery. This policy has been followed by Foss Company throughout the years and the single-tug horsepower went up to 6,000 in the HENRY and ARTHUR FOSS. Their high horsepower tugs are used in barge and ship movement where power and speed are important.

Foss' one-time mainstay, log towing, has decreased through the years in volume and importance with the heavy shift to barge towing replacing it as the Company's main source of revenue. Fortunately, the high income from the barge runs offsets the capital expenditure for today's heavy investment in equipment and compensates for the inflated cost of operation. In the pioneering era the rate of hiring a Foss rowboat for a day was twenty-five cents—the cost of hiring an ocean-going tug for a day at present is $6,000. The building cost of a rowboat was $10, a launch $150, a primitive tug $500, a modern ocean tug $3,000,000. Tugboats have not been exempt from inflation.

From Andrew and Thea's time the Company has advanced to heavy ocean-going tugs towing to the Orient, South Pacific, South America, and East and West Indies, Africa, Central America, Inter-Coastal and Coastal United States, Hawaiian Islands, and most importantly, Alaska. These days the "Always Ready" tugs tow on the seven seas, making voyages of 12,000 miles or more and of many months' duration, delivering items impossible to transport except by tug or tug and barge.

The Foss slogan—ever since Thea originated it by making it known that she was "Always Ready" day or night to rent a boat or take on a job—has been justified through the years by close attention to service and responsibility to customers. That same spirit still applies to the Foss offices in Seattle, Tacoma, Port Angeles, Anchorage, Alaska, and the subsidiary bases in Everett, Bellingham, and Long Beach, California. From these many stations, approximately seventy tugs and seventy barges are in operation day and night, efficiently moving all types of commodities around the world.

However, Foss does not limit their operations to towing. Rescue and salvage has always been a part of their service and with a ready response. They raised a ditched Northwest Airlines plane sunk in 600 feet of water off Maury Island and Foss launches, first to arrive, assisted in saving the 200 passengers from the rammed and sunk steamer City of Kingston at Brown's Point. From the tragic to the comic, they towed and safely landed a cow adrift in the flooding Puyallup River—diversified service!

Though Foss Launch & Tug Company has been successful in its service by making the right move at the right time, it hasn't always been easy what with the inherent hazards of tugboating—adverse weather, machinery failure, human error, and the wear and tear of participation in two wars. Surmounting the obstacles made the Foss Company what it is today—one of the largest and most competent tugboat organizations in the world.

The AGNES towing the ELMER and a general cargo barge in Icy Bay, Alaska during oil exploration activities in the early sixties. (Courtesy of Foss Tug Co)

The Barge FOSS 243 with 3,000,000 fbm. of lumber departing Port Gamble, WA. for Willmington, CA. in 1970 under tow of the JUSTINE. (Photo courtesy of Foss Tug Co)

Tugs SHANNON, CAROL and WEDELL assisting P & O Lines cruise ship ARCADIA on a rare visit to Seattle. (Photo credit Joe Williamson)

James A. Cole

SECTION I – TOWING BECOMES A BUSINESS FOR FOSS

Tugs Acquired 1910 – 1919

FOSS 9, FOSS 12, FOSS 6, FOSS 15, FOSS 16

ECHO – FOSS 18

Prior to 1910 the Foss Boathouse Company was engaged solely in renting rowboats and operating launches for hire. Thea purchased the first rowboat in 1890 and Andrew built the first gas launch, the COLUMBIA, in 1901. Their first marine revenue came from fishermen, pleasure boaters, and later on from carrying supplies to sailing ships at anchor in Tacoma Harbor.

Then in 1912 Andrew, with boat use curtailed, realized that log towing would take up the slack and would increase in volume through the years. Wisely deciding to take advantage of the potential, he purchased and outfitted his first tugboat—the FOSS 9. With the 40-horsepower boat performing well and profitably, Andrew knew what to do. He had a second tug built—the FOSS 12. Then two years later he launched the FOSS 6, a tug of his own design.

Andrew expanded the tug side of the business as rapidly as his resources would allow. He would not contract for a boat until he had the money, then he knew the Company was prospering and he could go ahead safely. Neither Andrew nor Thea believed in operating mortgaged tugs, disliking the idea of being responsible to a second party in case of loss.

However, in another two years, with sufficient earnings, they were able to add three more ready-built tugs—much larger than the pioneering boats. Andrew and Thea were now committed. They were in the tugboat business to stay—come winds, waves, or woes.

FOSS 9

Built:	1907	Propulsion:	General Motors
	Astoria, Oregon		165-Horsepower
Length:	37-feet	Primary Service:	Tacoma Harbor day-boat
Beam:	12-feet	Final Foss Operating Day:	September 11, 1968
		Status:	Sold - Domestic

FOSS 9, originally the VIOLET, was built as a harbor tug for use at Astoria, Oregon, however she worked only five years on the River before Andrew purchased the tug and brought her to Gig Harbor, Washington for renovation.

He didn't change the 40-horsepower gas engine, but he changed her name to FOSS 9. She held the distinction of being one of the first two of Foss' regular-type tugs, along with FOSS 12, to serve Tacoma Harbor.

But when the 9 started work, there were twelve Foss launches on Harbor duty as the Foss reputation for service was first established by launches. They carried passengers and freight to and from anchored sailing ships and took excursion parties and work gangs around the Tacoma area. This type of service accounted for the origin of the first part of the name "Foss *Launch* & Tug Company." However, during the rowboat-launch days and prior to 1914 Andrew and Thea did business under the name "Foss Boathouse Company." They built their first gas-propelled launch, the COLUMBIA, in 1901, followed by over fifteen more launches in a period of twenty-six years. Largest of the launches, the FOSSBERG—of 15 tons, 100-horsepower (gas) and 64-feet in length—was built at Gig Harbor in 1912 as a combination passenger and freight boat. But she could be used as a tug and many times turned around Black Ball Lines' Seattle-Tacoma passenger steamers in Tacoma's narrow waterway. Among the better known of the launches was the LILLIAN D, the first Foss boat to be repowered with an oil engine. The LILLIAN D was named for Andrew and Thea's daughter, and surprisingly, the cruiser-launch is still afloat, tied up at the Foss-Seattle terminal and presently owned by Sidney Campbell.

The FOSS 9, outliving the launches in usefulness and after twenty years of towing and ship service, left Tacoma for Port Angeles to carry on as a harbor work-boat. Foss had established an operating base in 1926 at Port Angeles. Foss reconditioned the 9 for a long stay, building a new deckhouse and installing a 100-horsepower Hall-Scott gas engine.

A disastrous fire in September 1944 nearly destroyed the 37-year old boat, but upon inspection, Foss found her worth repairing. They towed her to Tacoma, completely rebuilt and repowered her with a safer 110-horsepower General Motors diesel. She returned to Port Angeles to operate with the FOSS 8 and NANCY FOSS. Then in 1947, the new OMER FOSS joined the Port Angeles' fleet and for several months a record four tugs worked the area. But by December 1948 Port Angeles could no longer support four harbor tugs so the FOSS 9 returned to Tacoma and remained in and around the harbor for the balance of her towing life. Due to her light draft, the tug proved most useful to Foss-Tacoma for working in shallow-water log storages.

After fourteen years of wear and tear on the G.M.-110, Foss repowered her with a 165-horsepower G.M., and the new engine lasted the rest of her working life. By 1968 even though she had a sound engine, the 61-year-old hull had many leaks, requiring constant attention. She lost so much working time it was impossible to compete with the new high-powered and efficient steel tugs in service.

"Old Number Nine" bucked her final tide when Captain Quentin Henderson delivered the last of many log rafts to the St. Paul & Tacoma Mill. After tying off the six sections, he headed for the dock to turn in the FOSS 9's Logbook for the last time. On September 11, 1968 she completed fifty-four years of steady work for Foss, establishing a record length of service. The FOSS 9 stands as the senior vessel in terms of years spent on the active list, an honor for a 37-foot tugboat. Only four other tugs—the 12, 15, 18 and WALLACE—reached a Golden Anniversary Year as Foss operating units.

After being pier-bound in Tacoma for nine months, the FOSS 9 was purchased for a fireboat by the City of Renton as she was equipped with a high-capacity fire monitor. For some reason they renamed her SNOOPY!

After several years' service in Lake Washington, Renton declared the SNOOPY surplus and sent her to Tacoma for storage. The tug was lifted out of the water and set on dry land beside the Hylebos Waterway. In 1978 and still out of salt water, the FOSS 9 timbers show many areas of decay—she is slowly losing the qualities that kept her staunch and serviceable for over sixty years.

FOSS 12

Built:	1914	Propulsion:	Cummins
	Gig Harbor, Washington		140-horsepower
Length:	43-feet	Primary Service:	Tacoma Harbor
Beam:	14-feet	Final Operating Day:	December 2, 1966
		Status:	Dismantled and burned

The FOSS 12, built in Gig Harbor especially for Foss Boathouse Company, was the first Foss vessel planned and ordered exclusively for towing. Robert Crawford designed her so that one man—the captain—could run the

FOSS #12 In Tacoma Harbor about 1940. (Courtesy of Joe Williamson)

75-horsepower gas engine, pilot the boat, and tend lines. The 12 handled well, so in addition to harbor towing, she was one of the boats that assisted the Seattle-Tacoma passenger steamers to turn around in the limited area of Tacoma's West Waterway. Eventually the steamship captains wanted faster turning, so in September 1933 a 175-horsepower Hall-Scott gas engine was installed. With a hundred more horsepower the captains were happy and the 12 was able to run at an amazing thirteen knots!

But the FOSS 12, even with her speed, on one occasion wasn't able to stay above water. The Log Book says she left the Foss dock for log-storage work on the night shift with Captain Hank Schoen and his deckhand Quentin Henderson. Unknown to the two men, a timber had been dislodged from a section around the counter, apparently happening when the tug was backing and filling in getting away from the pier float.

By the time they reached the harbor, the FOSS 12 began taking in water, though the crew was not aware of the problem until the engine began missing, due to water reaching above the deck boards and splashing over the motor. Upon shining a light into the engine room, they could see water pouring in so rapidly that sinking was inevitable. Hank Schoen radioed the office and other tugs in the area that they were heading for the log storage to abandon ship. But in the excitement he forgot to mention which storage and right after signing off their radio went dead! However, the active Foss harbor tugs now alerted started a systematic search of the storages and in time the LELA found the two crewmen safe on a log raft—the tug had sunk right alongside the storage. Luckily, they didn't have to take off in the 12's skiff as it had not been in the water for a long time and leaked so badly when launched that Captain Schoen made no attempt to row for shore, but hauled the boat upon the logs and waited for rescue.

The next day Foss' A-frame derrick raised the 12. The Foss shipwrights repaired the damage and while at the dock yard, they outfitted her with a monitor on the forward trunk cabin for washing down barges and doubling as a fire-boat. Water for the monitor was supplied by a six-inch pump, directly connected to the main engine providing 125-pounds nozzle pressure.

In 1942 a 140-horsepower Cummins replaced the Hall-Scott and the diesel, with overhauls, outlasted the hull. The FOSS 12 and her Cummins remained a steady workhorse in the Tacoma Harbor until 1966 completing nearly fifty-two years of service. With her "over-fifty" status, she became a member of the very select group reaching a Golden Anniversary Year.

Having served her time and well, Foss laid her up and removed all the machinery. Then on July 4, 1967 the hull was towed out into Commencement Bay and set afire as part of the Tacoma Fourth-of-July celebration.

The FOSS 12 ended literally in a blaze of glory—commemorating the Nation's 191st year of independence.

FOSS 6

Built:	1916	Propulsion:	Gasoline
	Gig Harbor, Washington		40-horsepower
Length:	45-feet	Primary Service:	Tacoma Harbor
Beam:	11-feet	Final Foss Operating Day:	October 1933
		Status:	Sold - Domestic

The FOSS 6, also built at the Gig Harbor boatyard, was the Company's third pioneer harbor tug, but the first formed from Andrew's whittled model. Every timber that went into the 6 was approved by Andrew and when the hull was planked, he was pleased with the smooth-flowing run aft from the teardrop bow. The 6's performance on her trial runs justified his confidence in the design.

Though Andrew still engaged in running launches, his tugboat business gained in importance; and he realized that launches would become passe, but tugboats would not. Nor did they. FOSS 6 and her sister-tugs performed the same type of work in 1916 as harbor tugs do today—rafting and towing logs, shifting and towing barges, and assisting ships in docking and undocking. The work concept of the tug is still the same regardless of the year—only the sophistication and horsepower changed.

The FOSS 6 with her 40-horsepower gas engine continued on regular harbor service until 1932. Then with the world-wide economic depression, Foss was forced to reduce the number of Tacoma tugs in service. The 6 operated only intermittently in 1933 and then with no foreseeable use she was permanently retired during the winter and her machinery removed the following year.

In March 1936 Foss sold the 6 to Mr. C. F. Nelson of Seattle. The sale price an amazing $35! During the next few years the tug (renamed JERRY) changed ownership twice. And in 1940 she was sold again, this time to Mr. C. A. Heston of Seattle. He installed a 180-horsepower diesel engine and did odd towing jobs for a short period, then he sold the JERRY to Upper Columbia Towing Company. Her home port was Seattle, but she operated on the upper Columbia River.

The tug had experienced a variety of owners, but the changes ended when after three years of service, Upper Columbia Towing junked the boat. It could be said the FOSS 6 spent her thirty-two working years to get from upper Puget Sound to upper Columbia River—but by then so work-worn she couldn't carry on any longer.

ELF Later to be the FOSS #15, on the Tacoma Waterfront in 1909. (Courtesy of Joe Williamson)

FOSS 15

Built:	1902 Tacoma, Washington	Propulsion:	Washington 240-horsepower
Length:	63-feet	Primary Service:	Puget Sound
Beam:	16-feet	Final Foss Operating Day:	August 12, 1970
		Status:	Sold - Domestic

The FOSS 15, built for Olson Tugboat Company of Tacoma, started out as the ELF—a rather fanciful name for a tugboat. Olson powered her with a 125-horsepower steam engine and a coal-fired boiler, the usual power plant at the time. The ELF and her running mates, the ECHO and OLYMPIAN, towed on Puget Sound under Olson management for sixteen years handling logs, barges, scows, and salvage work.

During the summer of 1915 she towed scow-loads of fish from fish traps near Cherry Point to the Pacific American Fisheries Cannery at Bellingham. When the run of fish ended, she returned to her regular line of work—without free fish dinners for the crew.

The men responsible for the safe running of the ELF during Olson's time were Captain H. J. Gillespie and Captain Thomas Torgesen, the latter in charge for eleven years. Captains William Anderson and A. J. Bale also had command of the tug at various times. After so many years, it was most fortunate to find the names of the Foss 15's early skippers and associate them with a tug still in operation after 77 years. She had to have T.L.C. all along the way to last out.

And she did, falling into good hands in January 1916 when Captain Olson sold the ELF, ECHO, and OLYMPIAN to the Foss family. They were the first full size tugs acquired by Foss. Then in 1919 Andrew changed the Company's name more appropriately to Foss Launch & Tug Company, and so it has remained. The next year, in keeping with the numbering sequence of boat names, the ELF became FOSS 15, the name she carried for fifty years.

By 1922 coal-fired tugs were proving uneconomical so the FOSS 15's boiler was converted to oil, but her oil bunker capacity of 2,940 gallons provided a cruising radius of only 280 miles, a major drawback, though typical of the early steam tugs. Regardless, the 15 continued to operate with her steam engine until January 1926 when she went into temporary lay-up due to a poor towing market. She returned to work in July 1928 but by 1930 with her steam plant causing many problems she was withdrawn from service and laid up in Tacoma. Five years later Foss transferred her to the Seattle yard as a back-up boat, but in June 1936 she returned to Tacoma for repowering and rebuilding.

The yard work lasted several months as the tug was practically stripped to the water line and all machinery removed. The only distinguishable mark left was the curved stem. An entirely new and up-to-date three-tiered deckhouse graced the main deck. But the galley and crew's quarters were put forward and below. However, they were modern (for 1936) and well appointed. With the new engine, a 210-horsepower Western Enterprise, and the cruising range increased to 2,000 miles, she now had a chance at the longer and more profitable tows. The engine was fresh-water cooled by circulating the coolant through pipes on the outside and low on the hull. This arrangement allowed the tug to work in shallow and muddy water and prevented salt water corrosion in the engine. Last but not least a new heavy-duty towing winch, carrying 1,250 feet of 1-inch wire, was installed.

The Foss family was proud of their remodeled tug, for during the summer months in the late thirties they often withdrew her from regular towing jobs and with family and friends aboard made excursion trips on Puget Sound and occasionally to the west coast of Vancouver Island. On the yachting trip of the week of August 1938 she was piloted by the Company president, Henry Foss, as the FOSS 15's regular Captain, Vern Wright, had a week's vacation. However, in the 30's the tug crews generally worked right through with very little shore time except for a few days a month when the tug tied up for maintenance and general repairs that couldn't be performed while working.

One of the 15's frequent jobs was towing lumber scows between the Simpson Mill at Shelton and the deepwater port of Olympia. In the days before tugs had radio communication the 15 would leave Tacoma on a Sunday night for the Olympia-Shelton run and, except for a land phone call, if the opportunity arose, the crew would go about their routine job day after day with no reason for contact with the Tacoma office. Those were the days of free enterprise.

Late in 1938 the 15 engaged in a new and demanding service, towing bargeloads of slush pulp from the Shaffer Pulp Mill in Tacoma to Rayonier, Inc., in Shelton. Four 130-foot barges were used to keep the pulp moving, and the covered house-type barges with convex roofs and rollback roof hatches could be loaded right up to the roof joists with the "dissolving" pulp. Upon arrival in Shelton, high pressure hoses sluiced the pulp into a sump on the barge bottom

FOSS #15 *On the Lake Washington Ship Canal, 1966. Note the striking change from the ELF. (From the author's collection)*

for the heavy delivery pumps to pick up and feed into the Rayonier Pulp Mill. With four barges in use, Captain Vern Wright and his crew were constantly on the move shuttling loaded and empty barges back and forth. After five years the service was discontinued and the barges were converted for carrying bulk cement. But the FOSS 15 wasn't out of a job for long—she was called on to join the Army.

With the outbreak of World War II, additional tugs were needed by the Army Transport Service for work around the Seattle Port of Embarkation, and Foss was asked to supply two tugs—the FOSS 15 and 18. On December 19, 1942 the 15's documents were cancelled and she became ATS 15, a Government vessel. However, by September 1943 the Army no longer required her services, and they returned the tug to Foss—she became FOSS 15 again on September 9. Her former skipper, Vern Wright, took over and started shifting log rafts delivered by Canadian tugs to Port Ludlow. The 15 towed the logs through Hadlock Cut to the pulp mill at Port Townsend, their every move watched by Army boats patrolling the waters near the entrance to Puget Sound. The patrol boats worked out of Fort Worden on a day and night vigil checking on all marine traffic.

After the war, the FOSS 15 earned a living towing chip scows, lumber barges, and log rafts in the Puget Sound area and with very little down-time. However, all engines wear out and after twenty-three years the Western Enterprise was the worse for wear. A major breakdown occurred on October 14, 1959 while towing logs in Lake Washington.

Inspection of the engine indicated replacement, so the 15 took 120 days off and came out of the Yard with a new 240-horsepower Washington diesel. The repowering was completed March 1, 1960 and with alternate captains, Bill Shaffer and Chet Sweeney, she was assigned to the Port Townsend chip run.

The 15 continued in steady service on the Sound for the next eight years, but in 1963 her skippers changed—Ed Stork and Walter (Yobbie) Torgesen took over. Both captains stated that the 15 was one of Foss' best seaboats, though she had one major disadvantage—it was necessary to go out on deck to get to the head, the pilot-house or the captain's quarters from the engine room, galley or crew's forecastle. When towing in stormy weather, it was often impossible to enter or leave the pilothouse and it resulted in some long "between times" and lonely watches for whoever happened to be on duty.

Captain Stork related that on a stormy night while he was on watch in the Straits, the tug was taking green water over the bow at each pitch. The rest of the crew were below deck in their quarters when the emergency escape hatch on the fore deck lifted up and cold sea water gushed into the forecastle like a waterfall. The crew tried holding the cover down from the inside—an impossible task—each breaking wave dumped a deluge down the hatch, soaking the crew and the forecastle. But like all heavy weather, it ended eventually and the forecastle returned to normal and the sloshing water was returned to the sea—mostly by bucket.

By 1968 the FOSS 15, though still in good condition for her sixty-six years, was costly to maintain and sadly underpowered for current towing requirements, so in late July she was tied up and put on standby reserve, operating only seven days the remainder of the year. All of 1969 except for thirty days she spent rubbing the dock and for 1970 her last with Foss she had only eleven operating days. For her final job with a full crew aboard she towed twenty-one sections of logs from South Bay to Tacoma.

On her last running day, August 12, 1970 the tug completed fifty-two years of service for Foss Company. Only three other tugs had longer or equal service records: The FOSS 9 (54 years), the WALLACE FOSS (53 years) and FOSS 12 (52 years). However, the FOSS 18 had achieved the Golden Anniversary Year with 51 years of Foss service.

Foss signed away their ownership to the 15 on April 29, 1971. Olson Brothers of Tacoma were the purchasers and they renamed her KARLYN. But they kept the boat only until September 1971 and then sold her to Stephen Tate of Suquamish, Washington. Tate gave her the name SKOOKUM CACHE and used the boat as a family yacht as well as a commercial tugboat. He towed with her in southeastern Alaska during part of 1973—working out of Sitka. Recently she hauled materials into Bangor for construction of the Trident Nuclear Submarine Base.

In 1978 the Tates gave their antique tug a special honor by restoring her original name, ELF. And, appreciating the sound condition of the tug, but realizing the age of the ELF's heavy-duty engine, the lack of spare parts, and the heavy upkeep expense, they decided to repower their 76-year-old pride and joy.

In the fall of 1978 the ELF entered Dave Updyke's shipyard on Lake Union for installation of a new 350-horsepower Caterpillar diesel and by mid-November 1978 the new Caterpillar was ready to roar.

Captain Tate is pleased with the performance of the ELF and he credits the builders of the boat for her staunch construction and the Foss Company for her excellent condition after so many years of exposure to the elements.

Will the ELF be around for her "Centennial Anniversary"? The way she looks, it is a good bet she will.

FOSS 16

Built:	1908	Propulsion:	Enterprise
	Tacoma, Washington		200-horsepower
Length:	63-feet	Primary Service:	Puget Sound
Beam:	16-feet	Final Foss Operating Day:	November 22, 1963
		Status:	Sold - Domestic

The FOSS 16, with over 55 years of successful towing to her credit, was built by James Reid as the coal-burning steam tug OLYMPIAN for Olympic Tug and Barge, A. J. Weston, president. Her first skipper, V. C. Young, later became the well-known captain of the popular little Sound steam MIZPAH. In November, 1909, after only a year's ownership, Mr. Weston sold the OLYMPIAN to O. G. Olson of Tacoma. The OLYMPIAN remained in good hands and during her nine-year stint with Olson, under competent Captains John Peterson, Tom Toregeson, and T. W. Phillips, all well thought of skippers around the Sound, she never missed a day's work.

The OLYMPIAN, along with the ECHO, ELF, and the OHIO—a later launch-type addition—were purchased by Foss to further the towing side of their business. Acquisition of the Olson fleet gave Foss a total of sixteen tugs and launches and the means for taking on longer towing assignments to the upper Sound ports of Everett, Anacortes, and Bellingham. In order to promote the Foss name, the OLYMPIAN became the FOSS 16, so named in keeping with Andrew and Thea's policy then of giving numbers to their boats.

Another major change took place to the 16 in late 1919. Foss removed the old steam plant and repowered her with a modern 200-horsepower Fairbanks-Morse heavy duty engine. She became the first of the Tacoma-based tugs to be equipped with a heavy oil semi-diesel, otherwise known as a surface ignition engine. A tremendous improvement.

OLYMPIAN *On a quiet day in Tacoma in 1909, later to be the FOSS #16. (Courtesy of Joe Williamson)*

The 1922 edition of "Pacific Motorboat" explains the operation of a surface ignition engine: "Combustion is produced by injection of fuel oil into a combustion chamber and against a heated surface. Initial heating of surface is attained by torches. Then the heat of combustion maintains the surface at a proper temperature. The engine will burn any available type of fuel oil that is free-flowing."

Installation of the new engine was completed in the spring of 1920 and the tug went right to work on log towing with Oscar Rolstad in charge. The new power-plant proved a success as Captain Rolstad reported completing an eight-section log tow from Anacortes to the Buffelin Lumber Company in Tacoma in a record thirty-six hours.

Statistics recorded by Foss show the 16 was a real money-maker. During four consecutive years after being repowered—1921 through 1924—she earned more revenue per year than any of the other tugs. Even when larger tugs were purchased in the early and mid-Twenties, the 16 continued to be one of the two top producers. However, the excellent bottom line results were at a time when inflation was not a factor and costs could be controlled.

The cost of operating the FOSS 16 in 1926 averaged an amazing $6.41 per hour and the expense of feeding the five-man crew came to $3.50 per day. Proportionately, the fuel was the least expensive item. She burned about 320 gallons per twenty-four hour operating day at a rate of about three cents a gallon, with a total daily cost of under $10.00. By comparison, fuel for a comparable tug in 1979 would be $148.00 per day—a ratio of fifteen to one!

The FOSS 16 operated well with her heavy oil semi-diesel Fairbanks, but in 1939 to make the 16 still more efficient, a more modern 200-horsepower Enterprise full diesel was installed. Cabin improvements were made at the same time though apparently nothing was done to improve the odd towing gear lash-up.

The unusual arrangement consisted of a combination towing winch and anchor windlass, both located on the foredeck. The tow wire leg from the winch drum down through the deck and following along the length of the tug, passed alongside the engine and then up to the main deck through the crew's quarters and out through the end of the house to a set of tow bitts on the after deck. A "Rube Goldberg" contrivance—but it worked. The tow winch was operated by a chain drive from a gasoline engine located in the engine room and right next to the Model "A" engine was an open Arcola furnace for heating the boat. At times the leaky carburetor dripped gasoline to within inches of the old-fashioned heater—but luck was with the FOSS 16, she didn't catch fire or suffer an explosion.

The 16 with her Enterprise engine and with Captain Chet Elmquist in charge worked successfully on the lower Sound towing lumber barges between Shelton and Olympia, fuel scows from Olympia to Tacoma, gravel scows from pits to both Tacoma and Bremerton, log rafts between Tacoma, Shelton, Olympia, and the Nisqually log storage. She also made occasional trips to Everett with a chemical barge or a chip scow.

By the 1960's she was sadly underpowered and she had a further handicap, the hull, not rebuilt during either time of repowering was showing defects and the slack joints of age. On several occasions, so the report goes, with the tug running in a following sea, the crew by standing on one end and lining up the opposite end fore and aft, could see the deck twisting in opposite directions at the same time!

The true condition of her seams was evident by an occurrence in June 1963. The 16 had delivered a log tow to Quendall on Lake Washington and on the way back, going down the Canal, stopped for diesel at a dock near the Foss office. As soon as the fuel was on board the tug, now lower in the water, she developed a starboard list from water pouring in at an alarming rate. The crew hurriedly shifted the 16 to the Foss pier and put a portable pump aboard. At the same time they transferred the fuel to another tug. Close investigation revealed an open seam on the starboard side below the guard. The repair crew, headed by Wally Barber, caulked and cemented the seam, stopping the leak. However, with other weak spots showing in the fifty-five year old hull and no chance of making a seaworthy boat by just patching, Foss tied up the tug in Tacoma and placed her on a standby basis to be used only if absolutely necessary.

The necessity came about five months later in November when Captain Ed Nelson and a four-man crew fired up the 16 for six days to tow logs and chip-barges, to help work off a backlog of short haul jobs.

A week later she operated as a two-man day-boat and on November 21, after the day's work, the captain reported the tow winch brake was shot. Then during the day of November 22, when attempting to reverse the heavy-duty diesel, the engine exhausted through the air intakes rather than the exhaust outlets—a hazard in direct reversible engines. The engine continued firing and the 16 kept driving ahead without reversing and she rammed a waterfront pier and damaged the tug's stem. In the meantime the engine room continued to fill with exhaust smoke until the engine was stopped and the camshaft shifted to the reverse position.

This last incident clinched the decision to retire the 16 in favor of tugs with newer and clutch engines—so she went into permanent lay up. Several months later the machinery was lifted out, the stern tube sealed, the rudder

FOSS #16 Basically unchanged in appearance from her earlier days as the *OLYMPIAN*, pictured on lower Puget Sound, September 2, 1944. (Courtesy of Joe Williamson)

removed, and on November 27, 1964 the FOSS 16's official documents were surrendered to the Coast Guard giving as a reason: "Vessel dismantled and abandoned."

Two years later the stripped-down FOSS 16 was sold to a party in Seattle and they towed her to a pier on Lake Union. The purchaser did very little to the boat, although some attempt was made to update the cabins. However, the hull was the problem and she apparently opened up and sank—remaining underwater for a year and a half until the City of Seattle Engineering Department found someone to raise and remove the hulk. Fortunately, Diver's Institute of Technology, as a public service and to provide experience for their apprentice divers, volunteered to do the job. In a week they had the boat raised and towed to their school in Ballard where they removed the pilot house but left the lower cabin intact. The galley, refrigerator, and range were still in position, but hardly recognizable.

The Diver's Institute continues to use the FOSS 16 as a diving platform for their students, so after seventy-one years the 16 still performs a service of a kind, but it is far removed from the heyday of the "Twenties" when she was a breadwinner of the Foss fleet.

ECHO

Built:	1900	Propulsion:	Steam
	Crawford & Reid Shipyard		175-horsepower
Length:	67-feet	Primary Service:	Puget Sound
Beam:	18-feet	Final Operating Day:	September 1930
		Status:	Intentionally destroyed

The ECHO, a coal burning steam tug of 175-horsepower, was built by F. M. Crawford for Captain O. G. Olson's Tugboat Company in Tacoma.

Olson put his red and white tug to work in June 1900 towing log rafts from up-Sound points to Tacoma sawmills and a great portion of the resulting sawn lumber ended up aboard Olson's barges for transfer by tug to sailing ships anchored in Commencement Bay. The ECHO had it coming and going. She brought in the raw material and moved the finished product out to waiting ocean carriers for transport to world-wide markets.

The tug worked steadily delivering logs and lumber for Olson until the January, 1916 sale to Foss of all the Olson tugs. Little change occurred in the tugs' life as Foss used them in the same manner—towing logs and barging lumber.

The ECHO towed out of Tacoma until late 1923 when she was loaned to the Seattle base, opened by Wedell Foss in 1920 and known at the time as the "Foss Company of Seattle." Then in 1925 the Seattle branch having become part of the Foss Launch & Tug Company of Tacoma, assumed title of the ECHO and immediately converted her boilers from coal to oil and installed new fuel tanks with a capacity of 3,360 gallons, giving her a cruising range of 800 miles. The power plant ended up first class, but the hull had numerous weak spots.

Foss-Seattle, under the direction of Arthur and Wedell continued to use the ECHO for the same type of work as before the boiler conversion and they happily noticed a difference in efficiency. The boiler pressure held up with oil-firing and the surpassing results with oil burners brought on high-power tug era.

The well-known skippers who ran the ECHO were Captains Harold Butcher, Lee Rice, and Walt House, but they only enjoyed five years of ECHO's oil-fired performance. According to official documents dated September 10, 1930 Captain House was the last skipper to run the vessel, for by mid-summer the wood hull had deteriorated to such an extent repair appeared impossible—the question was where to start and stop, with one soft spot leading to another. The fact that she had been coal-fired for many years, with no insulation around the bunkers, speeded dry-rot deterioration. Foss naturally was disappointed that her hull did not stand up like the ELF and OLYMPIAN.

Pending a decision on her future, the ECHO was laid up at the Foss-Seattle yard and she apparently remained tied up between 1930 and 1938 as her official papers were surrendered January 3, 1938. The listed cause was abandonment—unfit for further service. Final disposition of the ECHO was reported to have been by burning near Shilshole Bay.

Her two companion tugs, the ELF and OLYMPIAN, both similar in size, lasted much longer—the FOSS 15 until 1970 and the FOSS 16 to 1963. With the sale of the 15, the last reminder of the Olson Tug Company acquisition of 1918 ended—a span of fifty-two years.

The Olson tugs led very commonplace lives, they belonged to the class of small tugs that accomplished the lesser assignments without fanfare or recognition and little adventure, but it was the small jobs that created big jobs for the larger and far ranging tugs.

ALICE As a coal burning tug around the turn of the century later to become the FOSS #18. (Courtesy of Joe Williamson)

FOSS 18

Built:	1892	Propulsion:	Enterprise
	Alameda, California		450-horsepower
Length:	69-feet	Primary Service:	Puget Sound
Beam:	19-feet	Final Foss Operating Day:	September 11, 1970
		Status:	Sold - Domestic

The FOSS 18, designed and built as the steam cannery-tender ALICE for Pacific Packing & Navigation Company was enroute to southeastern Alaska within a month after launching to service canneries on the west coast of Prince of Wales Island. Then after eight years, the P.P.& N. ceased operation and the ALICE became a unit of the Pacific American Fisheries of Bellingham, Washington. For the next five years she hauled fish in the San Juan Islands during the canning season and in the off-seasons she wintered at Eliza Island, near Bellingham.

Her time as a cannery tender ended in 1905 when Crosby Towboat Company of Seattle purchased her. Crosby sent her to the shipyard to be remodeled for towing on Puget Sound. She came out two months later from her conversion and became an active unit of the Crosby fleet—remaining under their ownership for the next seven years. Then in 1912 Crosby merged with the Chesley Towboat Company and so for the next seven years the ALICE operated under Chesley's control.

In 1919 Chesley retired the tug from active work and Foss purchased her for service out of Tacoma, renaming her FOSS 18.

They used her only occasionally the first year and she towed but a few months in 1920. The 18 was idle in 1921 and in 1922 she operated only four months as her outdated steam plant required extensive maintenance and her operating cost was excessive.

Foss decided to remedy the deficiency, and in October 1922 the 18 was withdrawn from service for rebuilding and repowering. In February 1923 Foss ordered a new 250-horsepower Sumner semi-diesel from Todd Shipyard in Tacoma. An unusual feature of the engine, patented by Mr. H. Sumner, was the open face or side allowing the engineer to see the working parts and hand lubricate them. The purpose was similar to the open-side steam engine. Ignition of the fuel was accomplished immediately by the use of a hot electric bulb in the cylinder head, but the engine had to be first turned over by air at 150-pounds pressure. The tug's nineteen tanks held enough air for 135 starts. With the installation of the new heavy-oil engine, the 18 was able to run for thirty days without re-fueling compared to twice-a-week with steam power. A great asset on long slow log tows.

The rejuvenated FOSS 18 when she started out again in October 4, 1923 was as modern as Foss could make her and able to tackle the heaviest log tows required on Puget Sound. A published report in April 1924 on the success of the FOSS 18, stated in part that on a log tow from Utsalady to Tacoma and leaving at the same time as a steam tug of comparable horsepower and both towing the same number of sections, the FOSS 18 arrived with her tow seventeen hours ahead of the steam tug! She also did well on her tows from Shelton to Tacoma by making the run on one less tide than other tugs. Her largest tow during the report period consisted of forty-five sections of logs and 160 boomsticks from Tacoma to Anacortes—a heavy drag of over 4,000 tons. When running light she had an average speed of 11½ knots at 265-RPM's and her fuel consumption a low 13 gallons per hour. The fuel and lube oil cost combined, averaged out at 46¢ per hour—the figures were impressive even for 1923.

During the next eleven years, the FOSS 18 was concerned primarily with towing logs between Shelton, Olympia, Seattle, Tacoma, Everett, and Anacortes. Howeever, for a brief time in the late Twenties she tried towing logs to Grays Harbor from the Ozette River on the northwest coast of Washington.

Towing slacked off seriously for Foss Company in the Depression years and with insufficient work to keep the fleet going, some of the tugs were laid up. In October 1934 the 42-year-old FOSS 18 was placed in reserve status to wait out the economic low.

Then in 1940, with the general economy surging ahead due to war preparation, there were jobs for all boats, so Foss decided to reactivate the 18—but first she had to be rebuilt. The Tacoma yard stripped the boat down to the bare framing and then started the rebuilding. The refit was a complete job from keel to truck. To suit the upgrading, Foss also installed a modern 450-horsepower Enterprise diesel, making her one of the more powerful units of the fleet at the time. When viewed on her trial runs in September 1941 there wasn't a sign of an elderly tug, launched nearly half a century before.

With Captain Milt Ness in charge, the FOSS 18 returned primarily to log towing out of Tacoma. Then during early 1942 she started towing rafts on a regular basis from the Pysht River and Sekiu to Port Angeles. But World War II changed the 18's routine completely as the U.S. army requisitioned her services along with other Foss tugs. On March 8, 1942 the 18 changed her colors from green and white to wartime drab grey. Captain Milt Ness and his crew joined the Army Transport Service along with the 18, and they remained for the duration of the war. The army used the tug, renamed ATS-18, in harbor service in Seattle and Tacoma, principally assisting government and commercial ships in docking and undocking.

Shortly after the war ended, the FOSS 18, along with other requisitioned tugs, were returned to their former owners. The 18 changed back to Foss colors, but she remained in Seattle harbor as a ship-assist tug. Ed Saling and Wally Keezer were her captains during the early post-war period of barge and ship shifting.

In early 1951 the tug with Captain Jim Henshaw in charge, took time out from her harbor duties to join the SANDRA and HENRY to help lay the world's largest submarine cable (up to that time) from Fidalgo Island to Lopez Island in the San Juan Islands. The job required very tricky maneuvering due to tidal ranges and the strong and variable currents encountered. However, placing the cable was accurately carried out by the three tugs. The assignment consisted of laying two underwater lines—the first a 24,800-foot cable from Fidalgo Island to Decatur Island and the second, an 11,000-foot segment from Decatur to Lopez Island. The taxing job required precise readings every two minutes for cable tensions, drum revolutions, angle of cable, and speed of the cable entering the water. The cable barge, PUGET POWER, had 2,000 feet of cable left over indicating the accuracy of the work. It was a challenging job well done, especially so as the cable brought much needed low-cost Bonneville power to the Islands.

The FOSS 18 returned to her former occupation and she continued on as an active member of the Seattle harbor division, doing ship-assists until 1958 when the new "twins" CAROL and SHANNON FOSS took over all ship-

FOSS #18 On the Duwamish River, Seattle, a far cry from the ALICE of 1910. (Photograph from the author's collection)

assist work. The displaced harbor tugs SANDRA and ERIK were assigned to other ports, but the 60-year old 18 remained in the harbor for barge and scow shifting.

Attrition caught up with her in the mid-Sixties, caused by a hull weakened from years of hard work, so Foss relieved the 18 of harbor duties and put her on less demanding jobs—the sand and gravel run from Steilacoom to Seattle and on general towing around the protected waters of the Sound, but no farther north than Everett. Bill Archer nursed the 18 through the final years of operation, and she completed all her assignments without help.

During the summer of 1970 Foss decided that by the end of September, the 18 would be laid up, as her age did not warrant the expense of a major hull rebuilding, and her 30-year old main engine was about worn out. The final day of operation came on September 10. Foss informed the crew that upon completing the gravel run, they were to dock at the lay-up farm. By October all operating gear was removed, and in November the main engine and towing winch were taken out—making her a bare boat.

During the first month of retirement Foss captain, Roy Durgan, purchased her "as is" for re-sale, and he didn't have to wait long before a party in LaConner, Washington, made a deal with him. For several years the tug was berthed in LaConner while undergoing a slow rebuild, but with very little accomplished she was sold to another party in Anacortes for further renovation; and from all appearances, it will be some time before she will be off and running again.

Though the 18 no longer has a piece of the Foss action, she is not forgotten but remembered as a top producer of the fleet with a successful record of 51 years—one of the five veterans to reach a Golden Anniversary Year.

James A. Cole

SECTION II
FOSS SERVICE PERMANENTLY ESTABLISHED

Tugs Acquired 1920 – 1929

FOSS 19 - HAZEL - HIOMA - MARY FRANCES - ANDREW (1)

PEGGY (1) - FOSS 21 - RUSTLER - FOSS 17 - IVER (1)

MARTHA (1) - FOSS 11 - GRACE (1) - LORNA (1) - ARTHUR (1)

BARBARA (1) - DREW (1) - WALLACE - ROLAND (1)

The second decade, a time of major expansion in equipment and services, completed the coverage for Foss in all areas of tugboating. With the addition of nineteen tugs to the fleet, including twelve large boats, all types of linehauls (direct point-to-point runs) were now possible. The scheduled hauls were on inside waters—towing log rafts, oil barges, and gravel scows; but the tugs did make intermittent barge runs to Alaska and along the coast.

Earnings were high in this period enabling Foss to install nine new oil engines and build, rebuild, or remodel ten tugs. The Foss-Tacoma facilities expanded to accommodate all types of shipyard work and the workmanship was thorough and expertly done—one of the reasons for Foss' reputation of being "ALWAYS READY."

FOSS 19

Built:	1895	Propulsion:	Enterprise
	San Francisco, California		200-horsepower
Length:	72-feet	Primary Service:	Puget Sound
Beam:	17-feet	Final Foss Operating Day:	May 14, 1965
		Status:	Sold - Domestic

The FOSS 19 started her active service as the Government steamer WIGWAM, patrolling the fishing industry in Alaska, with special attention to the salmon fisheries. In 1895 there were many canneries from Ketchikan to Bristol Bay and many fish traps in operation during the time of the fish runs, so the WIGWAM was as much on the go as the salmon she looked after.

However, after only two years of Alaska duty she was transferred to Semiahmoo Bay, near Blaine, Washington and to more agreeable weather. However, the WIGWAM returned to Alaska in 1900 when the Alaska Fish Commissioner requested her to provide transportation for inspection trips.

She was a good choice. The boat was handsomely finished inside and out and her accommodations for eighteen people were first class. Painted all white and with fine lines she had a yacht-like appearance. She was given a new name, the OSPREY—a fish hawk.

After several years roaming the inlets of Alaska, the OSPREY was superseded by the Fisheries' new boats and they sold her to Alaska Packers Association as an inspection and utility vessel for their salmon canning operations around Blaine, Washington. To update the boat they rebuilt the deck houses and installed a 100-horsepower Fairbanks-Morse surface ignition diesel.

The OSPREY's new job lasted until the early 1920's when APA built several dispatch-inspection boats that were better suited for the job than the yacht-like OSPREY, so APA sold her to Foss.

After a two month's conversion in the Foss yard—her identity changed and ready to tow—she became a tug, the FOSS 19. She started out doing linehaul towing out of Tacoma, and showing she could handle Puget Sound to towing, Foss increased her range and sent her to Alaska—the first Foss tug to go North.

With Andrew Foss aboard, she left Tacoma on August 11, 1922 towing a new Foss lumber barge bound for the sawmill at Wragell, Alaska. She made the 750-mile trip in a week. Upon arrival 350,000 feet of spruce lumber was loaded aboard the barge. Almost two weeks were required for the 100-horsepower tug to make the return trip, but she never stopped and arrived safe and sound with her tow.

OSPREY *Operated by the United States Fisheries for many years, pictured in Southeast Alaska. Later to become the FOSS #19. (Courtesy of Joe Williamson)*

The 19 went back on linehaul work and she operated steadily for the Tacoma office until engine problems forced her into temporary lay up in February 1925. A new engine was ordered, but didn't arrive until June. So in the meantime the galley and cabins were renovated to make the tug more livable for the crew on long hauls. The new engine, a 180-horsepower Fairbanks-Morse was installed and all shipwrighting completed by October. She went right to work as the machinery tested O.K., remaining with the Tacoma Division for the next five years. Then starting in October 1930 she worked out of the Seattle office as more tugs were required to satisfy the ever-increasing number of customers.

FOSS #19 *Shown in the form she maintained from the early forties to her retirement in 1965. (Courtesy of Joe Williamson)*

During the period 1934 through 1938 the cost-accounting on the FOSS 19 showed figures that are a revelation compared to today's costs. The Captain earned $170 per month, Deckhands received $80 per month. The average 24-hour day, hourly labor cost for four crew members was 80 cents. Galley supplies averaged $4.08 per day and deck supplies averaged 96 cents per day. The average fuel consumption was eight gallons per hour with an hourly cost of 42 cents. The cost of diesel in the five-year period came to 5.4 cents per gallon. Using these costs and today's revenue, the tugboat business would be better than an oil well!

In the late 1930's the FOSS 19 was assigned to the Union Oil Southeastern Alaska oil-barge run with Captain Henry Butcher in charge. The tug worked six months a year delivering oil to southeastern Alaska communities, then when the season was over she came south to spend the winter months towing on the Sound.

However, during the winter and spring months of 1940, she remained in the Foss-Seattle yard for rebuilding and repowering. In place of the old Fairbanks, a 200-horsepower Enterprise full-diesel was installed. The deck house was again rebuilt to give her a more up-to-date appearance and to improve the cabins for better living. Coming out of the yard in May, she looked like a new boat and after outfitting she headed North to resume her oil deliveries.

By 1945 the demand for oil had continued throughout the year, so the 19 remained in Southeastern•to provide year-around service. She was based in Juneau, where the supply tanks were located, and her route covered over 1,500 miles, calling at some twenty-five locations. The 19 remained on the run until September 1950 when the larger and newly acquired MARGARET took over. A stronger tug was desirable due to the stormy weather encountered on the winter runs.

The FOSS 19's performance record was good all during her Alaska service. Walt Davis, the tug's skipper, related that only one serious mechanical problem occurred during his years in charge. In October 1949 they were south-bound to Seattle for annual drydocking when one of the main engine crank bearings broke in several pieces. They anchored up at Namu Harbor and instead of waiting for assistance and parts which could have taken three days, the 19's ingenious engineer coated the pieces of the bearing with Permatex, fitted them back together and reinstalled the bearing. Strange as it may seem, the bearing held together all the way to Seattle!

The tug now back on the Sound, worked out of the Seattle office towing gravel scows and oil barges, with the oil-barge runs taking most of her time. Her principal job was towing the small (94-foot) refined-oil barge FOSS-94 to various Union Oil distribution points on Puget Sound. However, weekends were generally free and she tied up at the Foss pier in Seattle until the Sunday night start on the oil run.

The 19's orders usually read: "Crew to report Sunday noon, pick up groceries in commissary. Pick up the FOSS 94 at the Ballard dolphins and tow to Union Oil, Edmonds. On arrival, load 12,000 gallons of regular gas, 36,000 gallons of super gas, 23,000 gallons of stove oil, and 32,000 gallons of diesel. Deliver to Coupeville, Anacortes, Orcas Island, and Friday Harbor—topping each plant as you go. Return the barge to Edmonds and load for Gig Harbor, Bremerton, and Poulsbo. Return to Edmonds and load for Hoodsport, Port Townsend, and Port Angeles."

She continued in the oil delivery business until age, wear and tear caused serious delays and repair expense. Foss was undecided as to what action to take on the tug's future. Then in May 1965 on the routine run to Bremerton with the FOSS 94, the engine developed knocks and loss of power forcing her to return to the Foss yard for repair. After inspection of the engine and considering the cost of repowering or rebuilding the engine, Foss decided with little delay, that any further outlay on the seventy-year old tug would not be practical.

She went into lay-up in Seattle, but only for a short time as Pat Stoppleman of Seattle asked to purchase her. Foss agreed and in June 1965 she changed hands. Stoppleman repowered her with a D-343 Caterpillar diesel and renamed the tug KIOWA.

Mr. Stoppleman used the KIOWA for two years doing general towing around the Sound; then he traded her to Samson Tug & Barge Company of Sitka, Alaska for their tug the INVERNESS.

For eleven years the KIOWA was successful in log towing around southeastern for Samson T & B. For an 82-year old tug (in 1977) to stand up under the pounding of the many yearly storms was quite remarkable.

But in October 1978 her good fortune came to a sudden end. In a typical Alaska blow, generating high and break-ing seas, the KIOWA with a log tow was caught out in open water near Point Gardner in Frederick Sound. The Cap-tain headed for the protection of Herring Bay and began shortening the towline. But the heavy seas tumbled logs out of the raft and driven by wind and seas, the loose logs bore down on the tug. Like battering rams they slammed into the tug's stern, opening up the planking. Water poured into the boat so fast there was no chance to pump or make the beach. Providentially, another Samson tug was able to reach the KIOWA in time to safely take off the crew. Shortly after, the tug plunged to the bottom—ending a long, varied, and productive career. The WIGWAM-OSPREY-FOSS 19-KIOWA in eighty-three years accomplished her "reason for being" many times over for her five owners.

HAZEL FOSS

Built:	1907	Propulsion:	Buda
	Bolcom Boat Company		165-horsepower
	Seattle, Washington	Primary Service:	Puget Sound
Length:	60-feet	Final Operating Day:	December 1956
Beam:	12-feet	Status:	Sold - Domestic

The HAZEL came out of the Bolcom yard as the WINONA, built for Captain Walter Griffin of Tacoma. He equipped her with only a 50-horsepower gasoline engine. Regardless, he sold her to a Captain Green for several years towing in the lower Sound. Then he sold her, after installing an 80-horsepower gas engine, to Crosby Towboat Company of Seattle, later to become Chesley Tug & Barge Company, based at the Grand Trunk Dock.

HAZEL FOSS *Formerly the WINONA, photographed in the early fifties. This particular deckhouse design was the third and last for the vessel. (Courtesy of Joe Williamson)*

Once again, in December 1918 the tug changed hands—going to Rouse Towing Company of Ballard for towing logs and boomsticks. Then in the 1919-1920 sale of Rouse to Foss, the WINONA and Rouse's three other tugs came under Foss ownership. Wedell and Arthur operated the tugs from the Foss office on the canal, but under the name of Rouse Towing Company. However, all the tugs eventually carried Foss family names—the ROUSE became the WALLACE FOSS, WINONA changed to HAZEL, the RIVAL became ROLAND FOSS, and PEGGY had FOSS added to her name.

Foss Company in 1923 with the coming age of diesel power re-engined the WINONA with a 120-horsepower Western Enterprise diesel, a slow-turning heavy duty engine. Ballard Marine Ways made the installation. Repowered, Foss used the WINONA to tow logs, boomsticks, and lumber scows around the Sound until the Depression hit the country, immobilizing the economy. With the serious decline of business in 1931 Foss laid up the WINONA at Ballard to wait out the world-wide debacle. Not until June 1933 was it possible to have a go at log towing again.

With Captain Jess Delong in command, the WINONA first headed north to assist the BARBARA FOSS with a log tow from Canada; but when rounding Partridge Point off Whidbey Island about three in the morning, the WINONA's hull began working in a heavy ground swell, and she started leaking under the heavy strain. Apparently in the long lay-up, the planking shrank more than anticipated and did not have time to take up. The bilge pump could not keep up with the flooding, so the crew launched the life boat, stood off, and unable to help, watched their boat sink.

Fortunately Foss was able to salvage her. Several days later divers put slings around the WINONA and raised her to water level with a floating derrick. Then lashing her to an accompanying barge, the salvage crew pumped her free of water. Now safe for towing, but still lashed to the barge, the Foss tug WALLOWA towed the entire unit to Lake Union to clean up the mess. The WINONA's engine was removed and being relatively new, was installed in the ROUSE (later WALLACE FOSS). Then the WINONA again moved into lay-up on the canal to await more prosperous times to justify the expense of an extensive rebuilt.

At last in mid-1935 the towing work in sight warranted a renovation. The WINONA's entire deck house was removed and the former engine of the ROUSE, held in storage, a 110-horsepower Western Enterprise diesel, was put in the WINONA. The ROUSE was operating with the 120-horsepower diesel that had been removed from the WINONA after the salvage. A modern deck house was then built on the WINONA consisting of a pilot house with Captain's Quarters adjoining and a low trunk cabin extending over the engine room. The galley and adjoining forecastle for three men was arranged below decks. With renovation completed in November 1935 she went right to work—dispatched out of Seattle.

Strange with all the extensive remodeling a towing winch was somehow omitted. The tug had only a set of tow-bits, the tow line was 300-feet of heavy manila, commonly referred to as "wooden line." Pulling in and coiling the wet unwieldy rope was an exhausting job. The WINONA did tow alongside when possible and that helped. When the crew could get away with it, they put out a short tow line, but on the Captain's watch they couldn't get away with a short line. Fortunately that was only half the time. Unfortunately for the crew, the tug finished out her Foss life with the same old tow-bits.

In the late 1930's the WINONA went to Bellingham to tend booming grounds, replacing the RIVAL which was due for a major rebuilding at Foss-Tacoma, but her stay in Bellingham was short. Foss ordered her back to Seattle and on the way down she was to tow fourteen sections of logs from Bellingham to the McMasters Shingle Mill at Marysville, near Everett. The distance, though only about sixty-five miles turned out to be a time-consuming job—fighting weather, tides and mechanical problems. In fact she lacked power to pull the fourteen sections past Northwest Point through Deception Pass during the short period of slack water. To make any headway the crew had to go with two separate tows of seven sections each to get the logs through the Pass, then reassemble the raft near Hope Island, east of the Pass.

Due to the tug's poor showing in towing logs she was used principally on barge work for the next several years. Then in 1944 the WINONA went back to the yard for further modifications and improvements. The galley was moved to the main deck making more living space below and most important, a high speed 165-horsepower diesel was installed. During the yard work in July 1944 and after 24 years, she was given a Foss name, HAZEL, in honor of the wife of Elmer Foss, a grandson of Theodore.

The HAZEL worked primarily out of Seattle for the next ten years, mainly on log and boomstick tows in Lake Washington and Lake Union. But she did have another lake job to look after—towing the 96-foot concrete petroleum barge FOSS-102 from the Seattle Gas Works on Lake Union to the tar plant at Quendal on Lake Washington. The tar was a by-product from coking coal, a process to obtain coal gas for home and industrial use.

On one of her frequent ventures away from home base, the HAZEL made a run to Anacortes towing boomsticks. With the sticks safely delivered she headed for Seattle, and when coming out of Burrows Pass and exposed to a heavy westerly swell, the narrow HAZEL took several extreme rolls. Captain Langstaff wasn't worried, but the near-sighted cook complained that it must have been a real bad sudden storm they went through, as he had just completed preparing dinner—including mashed potatoes—when during the successive rolls the entire meal ended up out on the deck—for dinner they had "rolls," but nothing much else!

By late 1953 the HAZEL was succumbing to age and to keep up with the leaks, the bilge pump ran constantly, so she worked only as a day-boat in Ballard. In February 1954 she went up-Sound to tend the Bellingham boom, but due to her poor condition she did very little work. To prevent any mishap, the HAZEL was brought back and put in lay-up at Foss-Seattle in December 1956—her working days for Foss at an end.

She remained in lay-up until sold in September 1960 to Mr. Stanley Hill in Alaska. After a considerable amount of time and work restoring the boat to a safe and seaworthy condition, he ran her to Alaska for use in the fishing industry. Her new home port, Juneau, and her new name, GYPSY TOO.

Some time prior to 1971 the GYPSY TOO changed hands, however, she retained her name and home port. But strangely she ended up in Seattle and for a period in 1968 the GYPSY TOO sat on blocks just off Westlake Avenue undergoing hull work to remedy the constant leakage which nearly sank her in past years.

Then in early 1974 the GYPSY TOO was sold to Eric Carlson of Seattle and he tied her up at the Ewing Street moorage—right next door to the Foss docks! During the next several months, Mr. Carlson installed new fuel tanks, renewed most of the decking, overhauled the old Buda engine, and remodeled the galley. And he renamed her WINONA—to take fifty years off her age.

Mr. Carlson lived on the boat while doing miscellaneous towing on the Sound, including a number of jobs for Anchor Towing Company, a firm engaged in house-moving by barge. The upkeep on the 68-year old tug was a burden to Mr. Carlson, so he sold her in the fall of 1975 to Mr. Ed Squibb of Petersburg, Alaska. Mr. Squibb uses the WINONA to tow logs and tend logging camps in southeastern Alaska. Mrs. Squibb acts as Mate, Cook, and Deckhand, but in his very responsive letter, Ed Squibb failed to mention whether she was a paid hand or not. The Squibbs converted the house just aft of the pilothouse into a stateroom. They have replaced considerable wood in the hull and expect to do more as they intend to do barge towing in the near future and they want the boat in good shape.

The WINONA started out handling logs in 1918 and regardless of a little barge towing it looks like she will be a lumberjack to the end of her days.

HIOMA

Built:	1907	Primary Service:	Dayboat—Duwamish River
	Seattle, Washington		and Lake Union
Length:	49-feet	Final Foss Operating	
Beam:	12-feet	Year:	1957
Propulsion:	Superior	Status:	Sold - Domestic
	200-horsepower		

The HIOMA's early activities have faded out of the records up to the time Webster Towing Company became the owner. Webster owned the tug in 1923 as they removed the HIOMA's gas engine at that time and installed a 38-horsepower 600-RPM Dodge diesel. The small, but strong engine proved very economical with a total fuel and "lube" cost of only 20¢ per hour!

After operating several years for Webster, Gilkey Bros. of Anacortes purchased her for log towing and harbor duties in the Anacortes—Bellingham area, but first-off they repowered her with a 120-horsepower gas engine to handle heavier tows and to increase her speed. She remained in Gilkey's service until their harbor boats were purchased by Pacific Towboat Company of Everett.

As a unit of Pacific's fleet, the HIOMA performed the same type of work she did for Gilkey Bros. After a short stay with Pacific, by that time controlled by Foss, the tug came down to Seattle to handle log rafts around the Duwamish River area, tending sawmills on the East and West Waterway. At times Foss also used her as a day-boat on Lake Union and Salmon Bay, towing and shifting rafts for the Stimson Mill, Seattle Cedar, U. S. Plywood, Phoenix Shingle Mill, Motor Mill, and the Whalen Shingle Mill.

After almost fifty years of steady work, the limitations and deficiencies of old age caught up with her and she towed her last raft for Foss in 1956 ending up at the lay-up farm on the Canal. Her time chaffing tie-up lines was short, for in February 1957 she was sold and found a new home at Shaw Island, San Juan Islands. There she went right back to her same old trade juggling logs and boomsticks.

In 1978 she was still operating in the Bellingham and San Juan Island area but as a licensed log-patrol boat. Strange as it may seem, her name is still HIOMA—very rare for a small commercial vessel to carry the same name for over seventy years.

MARY FRANCES

Built:	1905	Primary Service:	Seattle-Tacoma Harbors
	Olympia, Washington	Final Foss Operating	
Length:	44-feet	Year:	Early 1930's
Beam:	12-feet	Status:	Sold - Domestic
Propulsion:	Frisco-Standard Gas Engine		
	50-horsepower		

The MARY FRANCES' known history is very sketchy. Built in Olympia in 1905 and designed for Olympia harbor work and upper Sound towing, she was equipped with a 130-horsepower Pierce-Arrow gas engine.

Rouse Towing Company of Seattle eventually bought the tug and moved her to their area of operation around Seattle to tow logs for the sawmills and shingle mills in Lake Union and Salmon Bay.

In 1920 when the Rouse Towing Company became part of Foss, the MARY FRANCES was included. The tug continued as a log-handling dayboat in Lake Union for a number of years. Then in the early 1930's Foss sold her to an independent tugboat operator in Tacoma who installed a fifty-horsepower Frisco-Standard gas engine, but her life in Tacoma was short. She was sold again, this time to Captain Bud McCarty for harbor work in Seattle, but her time there was also limited, for in 1949 Walton Mill Company of Anacortes purchased her for use as a log-boom boat. The move to Anacortes was the last recorded change. Apparently the MARY FRANCES went out of business at the same time the Walton Mill Company closed their plant in the early 1950's. However, she spent the last years of her life rotting along the bank of the Snohomish River.

ANDREW FOSS As she looked as a powerful diesel tug in the 1940's operating on both Puget Sound and Alaska. (Courtesy of Joe Williamson)

ANDREW FOSS (1)

Built:	1905	Propulsion:	Western Enterprise
	Puget Sound Engineering Works		450-horsepower
	Seattle, Washington	Primary Service:	Puget Sound and Alaska
Length:	97-feet	Final Foss Operating Day:	August 4, 1951
Beam:	23-feet	Status:	Sunk by Collision

The ANDREW started out in Government service, a regular member of the U. S. Army and at the time of her commissioning she was given the name of LT. GEORGE M. HARRIS. The steamer was to act as a tender for the then-active coastal defense forts, so she was ordered to San Diego for duty at Fort Rosecrans. The soldiers of the coast

Artillery Corps manning the Fort, plus their families, numbered over two hundred and they depended on Government vessels for transportation between San Diego and the Fort. Passengers and supplies, including guns and ammunition, were handled by the tender GENERAL DeRUSSY, but she had proved too small to adequately supply the Fort, so the HARRIS took over the run.

The HARRIS' cargo hold and crew's quarters were in the forward part of the hull and the dining room, galley, and a spacious passenger cabin were part of the long deckhouse.

The HARRIS operated on the Fort run until shortly after the end of World War I and at that time land access to the Fort had improved to the point where steamer service was no longer practical. However, the ship remained in San Diego until sold to Foss in March 1923. With the HARRIS still in good condition, Foss ran her to Tacoma, where she arrived in early April 1923.

During the next four months, the yard of A. M. Hunt & Son transformed the HARRIS into a proper tug. The after-house was cut off eliminating the dining room and passenger cabin, and in its place a large steam towing winch was installed. The new power plant consisted of an oil-fired Almy boiler feeding a 600-horsepower triple-expansion engine. She carried enough fuel for thirty day's steaming. By way of amenities, Foss equipped her with a complete bathroom for the comfort of the crew—the first tugboat crew to be so fortunate!

Before undergoing seatrials in late August 1923 the HARRIS was renamed ANDREW FOSS to honor the co-founder of the family Company. The ANDREW was the first of nearly 120 tugs to be named for members of the Foss family and their names were carried to hundreds of ports.

In September with all the machinery running smoothly, she entered regular towing service on Puget Sound, towing logs, and barges. During her first full work year, the ANDREW earned $30,000—an exceptional revenue in 1924 when true values were the standard of reckoning.

Then in December 1924 the ANDREW entered the Ballard Marine Ways yard for extensive hull work which had previously been by-passed at Tacoma in order to get the tug water-borne as soon as possible. By March 15, 1925 the ANDREW was again ready to assume her position as flagship of the Foss fleet. She continued towing without problems for the next five years, until ravaged by a fire that nearly destroyed her.

The fire started on July 28, 1928 when the ANDREW, with Captain Archie Cameron in charge, pulled out of Port Angeles with a log tow for up-Sound. An oil burner in the steam boiler backfired into the engine room causing a flame up on the oily surfaces of machinery and timbers. The crew was able to smother the fire for a time, but it flared up again in the structure several minutes later. Quickly spreading out of control, the fire did considerable damage to the machinery and destroyed nearly all of the upper works before burning out. The crew "abandoned ship" and escaped without injury to a boat standing by. Foss towed the ANDREW to Tacoma for inspection and survey, sorely disappointed at the damage to their fine tug. After examination on August 7th, Foss decided to rebuild the ANDREW and install a diesel engine in place of steam power. They engaged a naval architect, H. C. Hanson, to draw up plans and specifications so the tug could be built to the highest standard of efficiency.

The ANDREW's reconditioning in the Foss shipyard lasted nine months, but when she came out in May 1929 she looked like a new boat inside and out. A shining new 450-horsepower Western Enterprise diesel now filled the engine room. Then, from the day she again returned to service and for the next twenty years, the ANDREW's steady performance was a Company by-word—no doubt doing honor to her namesake.

In her long Foss life the ANDREW ranged from Seattle, her home base since 1933 to British Columbia, Alaska, Oregon, and California—an accomplishment in her day. Included in her Alaska runs was carrying out the Foss contract for towing the oil barge FOSS-100 from Edmonds to southeastern Alaska for Union Oil Company. The ANDREW owned the run except for an occasional relief trip by the MARTHA. During the spring and summer months, with Captain Bill Stark, the ANDREW and her barge supplied the major oil distribution ports of Ketchikan and Juneau with up to six thousand barrels of oil a trip. Foss used a smaller tug and barge, based in Ketchikan, to distribute the oil to outlying towns, villages, and canneries. But during the fall and winter months, the ANDREW being a much larger and better sea boat, performed the final delivery service as well as the mainline tow from Edmonds. The ANDREW alone was able to maintain the slower winter schedule as the canneries were closed for the season and all the various village tanks were topped off in early fall.

Captain Ingval "Northern Exposure" Wick—nicknamed due to preferring the Alaska runs, who handled the ANDREW during the winter months reported that they could tow the loaded barge at a speed of six knots and the empty barge at 7.8. The average round-robin trip covered 2,700 miles and required between seventeen and twenty days. Usually fifteen trips a year were necessary to deliver sufficient oil to keep Union's southeastern Alaska customers satisfied.

At times the ANDREW engaged in another of the Foss Company's more important functions—log towing. She towed part time out of Port Angeles and the Straits' log dumps and then more frequently during World War II while the ARTHUR FOSS was in Government service. The ANDREW's longest and hardest tows were the occasional large log cribs, not in the Straits, but towed all the way from Alaska to Puget Sound. The heavy cribs containing up to a million feet had to be worked with the tide and the advance was about thirty miles a day—an average trip even in good weather lasted over three weeks!

After WWII and as Foss had purchased ocean-going MIKI-class tugs from the Government, the ANDREW was used primarily on runs in Puget Sound and the Straits—towing both rafts and barges. However, during the summer months with MIKI-class tugs fully occupied on a new Anchorage barge service, the ANDREW was frequently called upon to handle barge tows to-and-from southeastern Alaska and it was a barge tow on this run that proved to be her last.

On July 27, 1951 with veteran Captain Bill Erickson in command and a ten-man crew, she left Seattle with the empty cargo barge FOSS-138 bound for the Polaris-Taku Mine at Taku, Alaska, south of Juneau. They pulled into the mine wharf late on July 31st and loaded the barge with ore concentrates. On August 1, with 719 tons of ore aboard, valued at $70,000, they left Taku for the smelter at Tacoma.

In the early morning hours of August 3rd, the ANDREW made an unscheduled stop at Ketchikan to set the ailing First Mate ashore, then at 0300 hours they resumed their southbound course at a speed of slightly over 5½ knots. During the evening when the ANDREW entered the north end of Grenville Channel, Captain Erickson made radio contact with the Captain of the MIKI-class tug MACLOUFAY of Alaska Ship Lines, who was nearing the south entrance of the 42-mile Grenville Channel with a barge load of ammunition and dynamite; northbound for Valdez, Alaska.

Grenville Channel leads northwest from Wright Sound to Arthur Passage and Chatham Sound in the northern reaches of British Columbia. It is part of the usual route taken by vessels using the famed "Inside Passage" to and from Alaska.

Volume II of the British Columbia Pilot (1969) describes Grenville Channel as "a channel deep throughout its entire length, and the land on both sides very high and densely wooded. The mountains rise almost perpendicularly, and cause the southeastern portion of the narrow channel to appear even narrower than it is. The general effect of so many mountains rising one behind the other renders Grenville Channel one of the most beautiful landscapes on this coast." The seven-mile stretch between Ormiston Point and Morning Point in Grenville Channel is about 2,000 feet wide and in the middle of this seven-mile stretch are two spectacular waterfalls—Serpent Waterfall and Waterfall No. 2, both on the mountainous port hand, in travelling north.

At 0015 on August 4th, with an overcast sky and a light wind, the ANDREW and barge FOSS-138 approached Morning Point at a speed of 5.5 knots. The MACLOUFAY and her barge were between Ormiston Point and Serpent Waterfall, heading north just to the left of mid-channel. The tugs were about eight miles apart and would meet each other in about thirty minutes.

Shortly after midnight the tugs spotted each other's running lights. The MACLOUFAY was still near mid-channel, while the ANDREW, southbound, was close to the east shore. Both tugs were clear for a starboard to starboard passing. At about 0020, the MACLOUFAY passed Serpent Waterfall while the ANDREW was just past Morning Point. They were now five miles apart, both vessels holding parallel courses.

At about 0038, the MACLOUFAY passed Waterfall No. 2 and the ANDREW was one mile north of Waterfall No. 2. At their present course and speed the two vessels would have passed clear of each other in slightly less than four minutes—free of the danger of collision.

Then at about 0040 when the two tugs were about one-half mile apart, the ANDREW began swinging slowly to the right—the crew on the MACLOUFAY assumed the ANDREW was giving the east shore a wider berth. Continuing to swing to the right, she blew one whistle. The MACLOUFAY interpreted this to indicate that now ANDREW wanted a port-to-port passing, so they answered the whistle and started turning right. By this time the two vessels were less than 500 yards apart with a combined approach speed of 15½ knots, thus allowing little time for successful major course changes. But it did appear that both vessels would pass clear of each other, port-to-port.

However, in the developing tragedy, when about 400 yards apart, the MACLOUFAY blew two blasts of the whistle, indicating she was now altering course to port, in the direction of the ANDREW. This action was taken, according to the crew of the MACLOUFAY, minutes earlier, when both vessels were on the new courses to pass port-to-port. But the green running light on the barge FOSS-138 was observed to be right ahead, which meant to the MACLOUFAY that the ANDREW's barge was not following or responding to the ANDREW's pull on the towline, but that the barge was still heading parallel to the shore, contrary to the ANDREW's heading which was across the Channel. The MACLOUFAY reasoned that continuing on her course, they could not clear the loaded ore barge, hence the MACLOUFAY blew two blasts and altered course left to avoid the oncoming barge.

The ANDREW recognizing the MACLOUFAY's sudden maneuver started a major evasive turn to the right, in less than a minute the MACLOUFAY realized she would not clear the ANDREW who was still turning right and slowing in speed due to the unresponsive barge. The MACLOUFAY immediately backed full astern, but there wasn't time to get the way off, and she plowed into ANDREW's port side just forward of amidships, nearly cutting the ANDREW in half. The forward motion of the MACLOUFAY pushed the ANDREW around, and the crew climbed from the bow of the ANDREW to the deck of the MACLOUFAY.

Eight men got off safely—however the Cook, tragically, did not. He was still attempting to put on his wooden leg in his cabin when the ANDREW suddenly rolled over toward the MACLOUFAY and sank stern first in about 380 feet of water. Total time from collision to sinking was between three to five terrifying minutes.

When the tugs collided, the two barges continued past, then the bow of the barge loaded with explosives struck the ore barge, holed it below the waterline, and in minutes the FOSS-138 sank with her load of ore, but fortunately the dynamite barge did not explode or the collision would have been a major calamity.

As soon as possible, the MACLOUFAY got underway with her barge for an inlet a few miles away to inspect tug and barge and make repairs. However, the MACLOUFAY suffered very little damage and she continued on her way north, but before arriving at the inlet, the rescued Foss crew were put aboard another Foss tug which happened to be in the Channel southbound for Seattle.

The crew of the ANDREW, in spite of the accident, stayed with tugboating and Captain Bill Erickson continued with Foss as Master until his retirement in the early sixties.

The facts of the collision were obtained from the court case resulting from the accident. Two versions were presented to the court; one by the Foss Company who sought damages against Alaska Ship Lines; and a second interpretation in a counter libel suit by Alaska Ship Lines against the Foss Company. Both cases claimed negligence and lack of communication. No conclusions were drawn and only actions and circumstances were related to the court.

Any attempt to fix responsibility for collision and the ''why's'' and ''why nots'' concerning the crews involved were put to rest as the case was closed with an out of court settlement. Regardless of the terms of the settlement, Foss did end up one tug short, but with the coming of the big MIKI tugs, Foss' towing commitments were well-covered and there would be another tug to carry on the name of ANDREW.

PEGGY FOSS Classed as a "Bayboat," one of the smallest units of the Foss fleet. Powered by a small gas engine, retired in the forties. (Courtesy of Joe Williamson)

PEGGY FOSS (1)

Built:	1912	Primary Service:	Lake Union and Lake Washington
	At Seattle	Final Foss Operating	
Length:	32-feet	Year:	1944
Beam:	8-feet	Status:	Sold - Domestic
Propulsion:	Hall-Scott (Gas)		
	75-horsepower		

Foss ownership of the PEGGY dates from March 28, 1923 when Ballard Hardware, Inc., sold the undocumented boat for $550. Foss was not added to her name until early 1940 and then she had the dubious distinction of being the first tug with a girl's name not honoring a member of the family line—maybe it was done as a hint for one of the Foss families to come up with a daughter nicknamed "Peggy."

Prior to Foss ownership, the PEGGY was a salmon troller and in good condition except that her engine was ready for replacement. Foss altered her to a tugboat and installed the 16-horsepower N & S gasoline engine removed from the launch FOSS 5.

The PEGGY spent most of her twenty-year Foss life as a bay-boat towing logs and boomsticks around Salmon Bay and Lake Union, but not for the entire twenty-years with the 16-horsepower engine. By 1934, the old N & S had served its time and to give the PEGGY more oomph, a 75-horsepower Hall-Scott gas engine was set in. With the added power she no longer was limited to towing only one log raft at a time.

The PEGGY continued towing on the Ship Canal until 1944 when the newer GRACE FOSS replaced her. The outdated PEGGY was consigned to permanent lay-up and with no further use planned—the PEGGY's future was grim, but her retirement was short-lived. Foss sold her to the U.S. Plywood Corporation at Mapleton, Oregon, for handling logs on the Siuslaw River. But old age finally got the best of her by 1969 and she had to be junked. U. S. Ply replaced her with a dozer-boat to service the mill's log pond on the river.

According to the latest check, there still is no PEGGY FOSS—that is in the flesh.

FOSS #21 In Port Angeles, shortly after being rebuilt and repowered. (Courtesy of Joe Williamson)

FOSS 21

Built:	1900	Propulsion:	Superior
	Tacoma, Washington		400-horsepower
Length:	80-feet	Primary Service:	Puget Sound
Beam:	19-feet	Final Foss Operating Day:	April 30, 1966
		Status:	Sold - Domestic

Tacoma Tug & Barge Company built the Foss 21, but she carried the name of FEARLESS for twenty-five years and she lived up to her name. T. T. & B. powered her with a 400-horsepower steam engine, making her one of the strongest tugs at the turn of the Century. The owners wanted a tug powerful enough to handle heavy log tows, lumber barges, and most importantly, able to assist large sailing ships down the Straits, through the Sound and into port.

In 1908 the FEARLESS made towboat history when the Company installed a Massie wireless telegraph set—the first tug on the West Coast to be equipped with wireless communication. T. T. & B. bought the Massie to maintain contact with the FEARLESS on her long tows in order to direct her from job to job without loss of time. The reasoning was correct then and seventy-one years later it still is.

Tacoma Tug & Barge retained the FEARLESS in regular towing service until they sold her to Foss in February 1925. The tug was renamed FOSS 21, and sent right off to the Foss-Tacoma shipyard for eight months of overhaul and rebuilding.

Foss reconditioned the hull from stem to stern, modernized the cabins, recaulked and rewooded the decks. Then, and in conformity with Foss policy of converting all linehaul tugs from steam to diesel, a 240-horsepower 256-RPM Ingersoll-Rand full diesel was installed.

The new engine, and the one installed in the MARTHA FOSS in 1927 had an unusual history. They were originally shipped to China by the French Government during World War I, but were not removed from the packing crates. The crates apparently were used as revetments of a sort from the marks on the outside. Several years after the war, Foss bought the two engines on speculation, but after delivery and inspection the engines were found to be in the same condition as the day they left the factory!

Fortunately, in view of the engine size, the FOSS 21 had very heavy timbering, in fact the engine-bed timbers were eighteen inches square, twenty-five feet long, through-bolted to minimize vibration and to prevent any give in the engine frame. Even her fuel tanks were over-size, they held 13,000 gallons, allowing thirty days of continuous operation.

Foss included in the rebuilding program an air steering system and a modern tow winch. The towing machine and anchor windlass were powered by compressed air, furnished by a compressor connected to the main engine. For ship's lighting, a 14-horsepower Frisco-Standard gas engine directly connected to a generator was installed in the engine room wing.

For cost comparison, a similar renovation in 1980 would be over $200,000—the total cost of the 1925 refit came to $20,000. In November she started paying it back.

The FOSS 21 was assigned to towing barges of pulpwood from the Quillayute River on the Washington coast to Port Angeles. Under command of Captain Orville Sund, later to become General Manager of Foss, she relieved the ANDREW, the original tug on a run that started in early 1925. The pulpwood barging contract was the first Coast towing job Foss engaged in, heretofore they had confined their services to Inside waters. The FOSS 21 continued on the run until the pulp mill closed down the pulpwood camps in 1930.

The cost of operation in the 21's early days is shown in the report for the first full year on the pulpwood run. During 1926 she consumed 48,000 gallons of diesel in 4,000 operating hours—this figured an economical 12 gallons per hour. Her total operating cost was $9.04 per hour! And by the end of the run in 1930 the total operating cost per hour decreased to $7.60 per hour or $182.00 per day! In mid-1979 the fuel alone for a 240-horsepower tug would cost $175.00 per day! To compensate for present-day costs, a tug would have to earn ten times the 1926 amount.

At the conclusion of the Quillayute run, the 21 towed logs on the Straits of Juan de Fuca but with an occasional trip to southeastern Alaska. With the exception of the Alaska runs and two one-year lay ups, she made Port Angeles her base and the Straits' log towing her business for the next thirty years.

But there were occasional breaks from the usual routine. In the early morning hours of August 13, 1947 the 21 was lying at the Foss dock in Port Angeles waiting to start another log towing job later in the day. The harbor was enveloped in fog obscuring all lights and objects ashore and afloat. Caught in the heavy gray shroud, the DIAMOND KNOT, a 5,525-ton freighter owned by the U. S. Maritime Commission and under bareboat charter to Alaska Steamship Company, was inbound fully loaded and nearing Ediz Hook. Her cargo contained 7,407,168 cans of Red, Chum, King, and Coho salmon from canneries in Bristol Bay, Alaska and valued at $3,500,000. Herring oil and miscellaneous equipment was also on the manifest.

Another freighter, the FENN VICTORY (10,000 tons) outbound from Seattle, was also nearing Ediz Hook. She was light, carrying only 200 tons of general cargo. At 0115 August 13, the two ships collided. The bow of the FENN VICTORY rammed fourteen feet into the DIAMOND KNOT's starboard side. With the side opened up, the river of inrushing water submerged the smaller ship to the main deck in a matter of minutes. The ships remained locked together and drifted west down the Straits in the strong ebb current.

With the first radioed "MAYDAY" FOSS 21's Captain Joe Tisdale, who had just taken command less than two hours before, answered the call. The tug left the dock at 0200 and groped through the fog blanket until by whistle they found the two ships at 0310—five miles northwest of Ediz Hook. Another tug, the MATHILDA FOSS, in the area and hearing the talk between ships headed for the scene to render assistance.

At 0330, with the two tugs on hand it appeared safe to separate the rammed vessels and after the big freighter's forecastle was freed from the crosstrees on the mainmast of the DIAMOND KNOT the ships were allowed to drift apart. The entry in the FOSS 21 logbook states: "0400 hooked on to Motorship DIAMOND KNOT, pulling dead slow toward South Beach." Joe Tisdale towed her stern first toward Crescent Bay where they were hoping to beach the foundering freighter and salvage the valuable cargo. With only bow damage, the FENN VICTORY was able to reach Seattle under her own power for repairs. However, water continued to pour into the DIAMOND KNOT through the deep gash, flooding Number Two and Three holds, so the ship's crew was taken off as a precaution as she was steadily losing buoyancy.

The tugs struggled with their waterlogged tow, making slow progress for the next 4½ hours. Finally at 0830, Captain Tisdale reported in his Logbook, "Start heaving in towline—DIAMOND KNOT sinking fast!" At 0857 she rolled over on her side, then plunged to the bottom in 135 feet of water. The 21 didn't have time to release or cut the towline—they were still hooked to the ship. At 0900 the tug's Log read: "DIAMOND KNOT on bottom, heave in wire short and lay over wreck with towline still fast." They remained on stand-by over the ship until the following day, August 14, until 1500 then they were instructed to cut the towline and return to Port Angeles for a new towline and orders.

The sinking of the DIAMOND KNOT entailed one of the largest cargo collision losses on the West Coast, but the insurance companies, principally the Fireman's Fund, made prompt payment of the nearly 3.5 million dollars, including compensation to the crew for loss of possessions.

On August 17th, a plan was devised by Walter Martignoni, salvage master from San Francisco, to recover the fish oil and canned salmon. Foss furnished barges, miscellaneous equipment and with the FOSS 21 kept the salvage operation in supplies. Walter MacCray of MacCray Divers was in charge of the undersea work. Heavy duty hoses were rigged in the DIAMOND KNOT's fish-oil tanks and connected for discharge aboard the standby barges. The time and material was well worth it as the recovered oil was valued at $22,000.

The salmon was next on the recovery plan. First, a salvage equipment barge was anchored over the wreck by twelve heavy anchors. Then, great volumes of air were circulated in pipes to the ship's hold to create a suction—acting like an underwater vacuum cleaner—to pick up the salmon cans that were released from the cases by using a directed nozzle at 300-pounds water pressure, breaking open the cases and freeing the cans. The siphons sucked up 1,000 gallons per minute and with the water came the cans of salmon! Water and cans were deposited on the deck of the barges where the cans were retrieved and the water drained over the side. The work continued twenty-four hours a day for nearly two months. Out of a total of 7,407,168 cans aboard the DIAMOND KNOT, 5,774,496 were recovered, but ten thousand cases remained in an inaccessible area of the ship. Seventy-five percent of the cans recovered were undamaged and went to market. The operation was unique in underwater salvage and brought a return of over two million dollars.

For the next sixteen months after the salvage feat, the 21 with alternate skippers Joe Tisdale and Ellis Bundy, continued log towing on the Straits with an occasional tow to Everett and Tacoma. then the tug's 25-year-old engine developed too many aches and pains to run steadily and efficiently, but she was still sound of body and limb, so Foss decided to repower her. Their survey showed a new engine was amply justified as was a refit of the galley, living quarters, and pilot house. On January 28, 1949 after delivery of 36 sections of fir and cedar logs in Tacoma, Captain Tisdale and his crew turned the FOSS 21 over to the Foss yard for the scheduled improvements.

During the nineteen months' yard work, the hull was reconditioned from the keel up and the decks resurfaced and recaulked—no areas were overlooked to bring the boat to A-1 classification. For added power a 400-horsepower Superior diesel was installed and the new engine was figured to burn 20 gallons per hour, an eight-gallon increase over the old Ingersoll, but also an increase of 160-horsepower.

At last on September 6, 1950 the FOSS 21, with the blessing of the Tacoma yard crew, was ready to start proving her worth. Captain Joe Tisdale returned to his old berth and at 1730 the rejuvenated 21 left Tacoma for Seattle to take on fuel, run up to Everett, pick up a tow of boomsticks and head for Port Angeles.

She went right to work on the straits, and during the remainder of the year showed her ability by safely delivering twenty-two separate log tows to Port Angeles from Pysht and Sekiu River. The same months she also towed 184 sections in five separate tows from Port Angeles to Puget Sound ports.

Captain Joe Tisdale remained with the FOSS 21 as her senior skipper through October 1952 and for his relief skipper he had his younger brother Captain Don Tisdale, two of four brothers and all four employed by Foss in Port Angeles.

The FOSS 21 for the most part of her life was free of mishaps, but a strange one occurred on June 23, 1951 when enroute from Port Angeles to Neah Bay with a set of log-crib sticks, Captain Don explained the odd happening in his Logbook entry: "At 0300 on June 23 started to get foggy and at 0350 with the Mate and Deckhand on watch in wheelhouse, tug went off course until we swung around and ran full speed into our own crib sticks! Iron bark sheathing is loose on each side of stem and engineers report boat is leaking quite badly and needs pumping every four hours." The men on watch must have had a hard time explaining that one! However, the tug delivered the sticks to Neah Bay and returned a crib to Port Angeles and then went on to Tacoma for drydocking and stem repairs. The round-turn Mate and Deckhand no doubt were transferred to a tug with automatic steering.

In November, 1951 the 21 became a family tug as Jim Tisdale joined the crew as Deckhand and Don was still Mate and Joe, Captain. The fourth Tisdale, Ron, was skipper on another Foss tug in Port Angeles. Maybe the FOSS 21 should have been renamed Tisdale-FOSS. In October 1952 Don took over as senior skipper and remained so for the next 5½ years.

With the arrival of the MATHILDA FOSS in Port Angeles in 1946 the ARTHUR FOSS in 1948 and the HENRY FOSS along with the FOSS 21 already in service in Port Angeles, made four tugs on log towing. The tows were between Neah Bay, Sekiu, and Pysht to Port Angeles and from Canada to mills in Tacoma and Everett. But by the mid-Fifties there was not sufficient business to keep all four tugs running full time on logs, so the HENRY was transferred during the summer months to supplement Foss-Seattle's ocean division boats on Alaska and California runs.

By 1957 the MATHILDA had left Port Angeles for temporary lay up in Tacoma and the ARTHUR, FOSS 21, and HENRY part-time, were easily handling all the log work. Then in February 1958 with fewer and fewer logs being rafted, the FOSS 21, now 56 years old, was laid up in Tacoma, her towing future in Port Angeles uncertain as the ARTHUR, with the HENRY's help, was able to keep up with the log input.

However, the tragic sinking of the HENRY FOSS on her way to Ladysmith, Canada in February 1959 brought the 21 out of retirement. In March 1959 work was started to reactivate her and after several weeks of repair and outfitting she returned to the same job in Port Angeles she was doing previously—log towing, with Ron and Don Tisdale again alternate captains.

The FOSS 21 operated steadily until engine breakdowns started slowing her down indicating the need for a major engine overhaul. On January 24, 1961 while towing a crib from Neah Bay to Port Angeles, the engine hammered to a stop. This hang-up was one too many for the Company and Foss ordered the tug to Tacoma and sent over the EDITH as a replacement boat. Within a month of her breakdown, the FOSS 21 was placed in the lay-up fleet—but she was not down for the count yet. In early 1964 the Seattle Division, realizing they would be short of tugs for local work due to the heavy oil activity in Cook Inlet requiring all the major tugs, decided to reactivate the 21 in Seattle and use her for linehaul work. In late April she was towed over to the Canal and for two months repair crews worked over the tug—a tough job after three years of inactivity. The real problem was the engine and all that could be done in the time allowed was to put it in running condition. On June 26, 1964 she started to work, but not towing logs—she was assigned to the chemical and cement barge tows between Seattle and Bellingham.

Because the engine did not receive a major overhaul she spent considerable time at the dock for repair, but even so she operated 113 days the last half of 1964 and 235 days in 1965. But on April 30, 1966 when underway for Texada Island, B. C. she developed tail shaft problems and returned to the yard for repair. They were made—for the last time. The FOSS 21 would no longer be calling in for orders—her name was deleted from the vessel position report.

She was placed on the "for sale" list and on June 13, 1966 Bob Shrewsbury of Western Tugboat Company, Seattle, bought her. He changed the name back to FEARLESS and operated the tug for two years, then sold her to Schnabel Lumber of Haines, Alaska for towing barges and logs in southeastern Alaska. The 68-year-old tug was to become a sourdough and permanent resident of Alaska.

Ownership changed again in the fall of 1969 when Schnable sold the FEARLESS to Don Starkweather of Ketchikan. In late 1970 he removed the old Superior and installed a Waukasha diesel providing more power and most of all, dependable service.

Don Starkweather reported that while docked in Juneau a fire broke out in the galley destroying the whole area and portions of the cabins on the boat deck. The FEARLESS was given a new modern galley and the damaged rooms were restored and paneled.

The FEARLESS spent her time through 1977 in general towing and charter jobs, but starting in 1978 she had more interesting work—ship-assist tug at Skagway, Haines, and Juneau. Don Starkweather says she will continue "juggling" ships and she was still at it on her 80th birthday, in 1980!

RUSTLER

Built:	1887	Propulsion:	Cummins
	Hoquiam, Washington		200-horsepower
Length:	53-feet	Primary Service:	Duwamish River and Ballard
Beam:	14-feet	Final Foss Operating Day:	April 4, 1968
		Status:	Sold - Domestic

Early records of the RUSTLER list her as a steam-screw tug built in Hoquiam, Washington for use in towing logs from up-river booming grounds to mills located on the Chehalis River at Aberdeen, Hoquiam, and Cosmopolis.

In the pioneer days of lumbering on Grays Harbor, 1885-1910 there were over twenty lumber and shingle mills in operation and in 1900 these mills were cutting 250-million feet of virgin timber a year and a fleet of tugboats was necessary to keep them supplied in logs. The tugs were used also to tow ocean lumber-carriers from the Chehalis River bar to mill-loading wharfs and then back down the river to sea.

The first official papers of the RUSTLER in 1908 showed her as being owned by the Northwestern Lumber Company who had operated a sawmill in Hoquiam since 1882. Then in 1909 they sold the tug to Wishkah Boom Company of Hoquiam and two years later she acquired another owner—this time Soule Tug & Barge Company who operated her on the Chehalis River for eight years before selling her to R. J. Ultican, owner of the Ultican Tugboat Company. He used the boat for only a year and then sold her to four working partners who operated the tug for the next five years towing in Grays Harbor and Willipa Harbor, farther down the coast. Her last job around the Twin Harbors was in February 1925 for the Nemah Lumber Company.

An accident changed her area of operation and gave her a seventh owner. The RUSTLER when pulling a tow of logs out of Willipa Harbor grounded on a sand bar and before the tide could float her off, the wind and seas drove her across the shoal and up on the beach. From all appearances she would end up a complete wreck. But two far-sighted men from Tacoma thought otherwise. After a close inspection, Andrew Foss and Henry had the courage, discernment, and perseverence to rescue the tug for a better fate. For nearly two months after buying the boat from the Benson Tugboat Company a Foss crew worked with the beached tug to get her waterborne. Using three horses, twelve men, and heavy rollers, they dragged her 8,500 feet to calm waters where she could be safely launched.

When the RUSTLER was ready to go in the water April 19, 1925 the ANDREW FOSS, flagship of the fleet, came down to make the final pull. Her 2,000-foot towline was run ashore and made fast to the RUSTLER. The tug easily slid into deep water and the ANDREW suddenly had a towing job from Willipa Bay to Tacoma.

Two days later the RUSTLER arrived at the Foss repair yard and during the six weeks of reconditioning, the hull and cabins were fully renewed and most importantly, she came out with a new 100-horsepower Fairbanks-Morse semi-diesel engine. The cost of putting her into first class condition came to $4,600—in 1925.

The RUSTLER was put to work as a linehaul tug out of Tacoma, towing barges and logs on a regular basis until January 1936. Then to modernize the tug and bring her up in appearance and capability to the new tugs recently built by Foss, they put the RUSTLER in the yard for upgrading.

Her old deck house, 19th century style and her semi-diesel were removed and during the next two months a new 110-horsepower Washington diesel was installed, a modern deck house and roomy pilot house built with all around visibility and the galley and living quarters were redone.

When the RUSTLER returned to service in the spring of 1936, she was equal to any boat of her size in the fleet. All she had to do now was act out her name. Foss-Tacoma used her for harbor work and linehaul runs barging lumber, hogged-fuel, gravel, and occasionally as with all Foss tugs, towing logs.

The RUSTLER through the years had a good performance record on linehauls, considering she only had 110-horsepower. One of her regular jobs, with Captain Bert Hill, was towing hogged-fuel scows from the Dickman Lumber Mill in Tacoma to the Wycoff Creosote Plant at Eagle Harbor on Bainbridge Island. On another of her frequent runs she towed loaded lumber scows from the Reed Mill at Shelton to Tacoma. In March 1942 the RUSTLER proved her worth on this job by successfully towing six empty lumber scows from Tacoma to Shelton in a total elapsed towing time of sixteen hours. Quite a run! All her jobs were not so close to home base as she made many tows with loaded limerock scows from Westsound, San Juan Islands to the Soundview Pulp Company Mill at Everett, making the run in twenty-one hours.

The RUSTLER in May 1942 went to Port Angeles for harbor duty while the HENRIETTA worked the Waada Island breakwater job at Neah Bay for the Austin Company. The RUSTLER remained in Port Angeles through the summer of 1942 then returned to Tacoma. Four years later she went to Everett to tow logs for Pacific Towboat Company and she remained in Everett until 1951 then Foss assigned her to Seattle as the day-boat on the Duwamish River relieving the GRACE FOSS. She worked on raft and barge shifting for the Duwamish mills until 1954 when her Washington diesel was worn out and Foss put her in the yard for installation of a 200-horsepower Cummins diesel. She then did shifting work at Ballard, Lake Union, and Lake Washington until 1957 when she went back to river work, replacing the HIOMA. The RUSTLER was the last Foss tug based on the Duwamish River as most of the lumber mills closed down and the regular Seattle harbor tugs could handle the curtailed shifting.

At the end of the working day on December 1, 1965 the RUSTLER left her long-time berth at Seattle Export Lumber Company (SELCO) for the final time, moving to her new base at Foss-Seattle on the Canal. She became a day-boat serving the shipyard and doing local towing on the lakes for the next 2½ years.

Increasing mechanical problems combined with a hull age of 80 years brought an end to her service for Foss in April 1968. When the HENRIETTA FOSS came over from Tacoma to take over her job, Foss then offered the RUSTLER for sale.

Her lay-up ended in November of the same year when Robert Boren of Seattle bought her, then sold her to Bob Richards and the RUSTLER became the ESTHER J—her first name change in 83 years. In June of 1972 she changed hands again, going to the Bay Tug & Barge Company of Tacoma. They operated the ESTHER J for two years in the lower Sound area, then anchored her in Gig Harbor where the tug remained for three years, unattended. Eventually she broke loose from the anchor buoy and ran aground. The beached tug was refloated and then sold for the ninth time to Steve Tate of Suquamish who needed a second tug. Captain Tate purchased the ESTHER J in May 1977 and four months later renamed her RUSTLER. He repowered the tug with a Murphy diesel, replacing the old worn-out Cummins.

Captain Tate used the RUSTLER as a backup boat to his primary tug, the ELF—ex-FOSS 15—seventy-seven years old. He made several tows with his second tug to the new Trident Submarine Base at Bangor, Washington and by so doing she became the oldest active tug on the West Coast. At 92 years of age she could also be the oldest working tug in the United States. Her longevity is a compliment to those men, ashore and afloat, who gave her such thorough care all during her most productive years and prolonged her life—perhaps even to the 100 mark!

FOSS 17

Built:	1903	Propulsion:	Cummins
	Ballard, Washington		140-horsepower
Length:	48-feet	Primary Service:	Tacoma Harbor
Beam:	14-feet	Final Foss Operating Day:	December 21, 1964
		Status:	Sold - Domestic

The FOSS 17 started her towing career as a 75-horsepower coal-burning tug named HAROLD C. She operated as a unit of Crosby Towboat Company of Seattle for nearly twenty years before being sold to Delta Smyth of Olympia for towing on the lower Sound. She changed hands again in January 1926 this time to the Foss Company and the HAROLD C then became the FOSS 17. Shortly after, Foss rebuilt and repowered her with a 120-horsepower heavy oil Fairbanks-Morse engine. They also installed a fire monitor on top of the pilothouse and the 17, with her high pressure pump poured tons of water on many waterfront fires during her life in the harbor. The fireboat-tug paid off her cost in November 1942. She was alongside the dock when the PETER FOSS caught fire and it was the 17's monitor that helped save the number one harbor tug PETER from becoming a total loss.

After twelve years in steady towing around Tacoma and the lower Sound, the 17 was ready for a new engine, so in late 1940 she was repowered—this time with a 140-horsepower Cummins diesel. The change made her the first diesel-powered tug in Tacoma.

Always on the go, the FOSS 17 spent 38 years of her Foss life in Tacoma harbor work until the Company decided to retire her at the end of 1964—and her engine, still useable, was removed and stored. Her retirement only lasted until November 1965 when a real estate agent on Orcas Island purchased her for $750.00. Later on he bought and reinstalled the 17's Cummins engine and by 1966 the ex-tug was running in the San Juans as a private yacht named EDNA.

About 1969 the EDNA was sold to R. W. Hughs of Vashon Island and he changed the name to BILLY RAY and then at some time in the early 70's he gave her another name, SEA ROAMER. But again, in 1974 the veteran tug-turned-yacht was sold for the fifth time—the new owners the Dyson family who renamed her FREDERIC J and berthed the boat just one block from the Foss offices in Seattle! Ownership changed for the seventh time in 1981 and the tug became the TORTUGA, still homeported in Seattle.

With new bulwarks, new bright work, and a remodeled interior, the TORTUGA doesn't look her age—78 at the last count.

IVER FOSS Ex-ANGELES, in Seattle Harbor on July 28, 1965 delivering the Killer Whale NAMU and his sea-going pen. Note sign by smokestack designating the IVER as part of the "NAMU NAVY." (Courtesy of the author's collection)

IVER FOSS (1)

Built:	1925	Propulsion:	Enterprise
	Angeles Gravel & Supply Yard		400-horsepower
	Port Angeles, Washington	Primary Service:	Puget Sound
Length:	65-feet	Final Foss Operating Day:	August 21, 1972
Beam:	16-feet	Status:	Sold - Domestic

The IVER, originally named ANGELES, was designed by L. H. Coolidge of Seattle and built by Angeles Gravel & Supply for towing gravel scows to the Company's dockside bunkers. All the shipwrighting was done in Port Angeles and upon completion in May 1925 the boat was towed to Commercial Boiler Works in Seattle to install a 200-horsepower Sumner semi-diesel. The deck machinery, towing winch, and windlass—built by Markey Machinery Company of Seattle—were all mounted and approved while the engine was being made ready. By July 24, 1925 the ANGELES was complete.

She started right in barging sand and gravel and towed steadily for the next ten months. Then her ownership changed, but not her area of operation. On May 22, 1926 Foss purchased the assets of Angeles Gravel & Supply Company which included the tug ANGELES, plus a number of gravel scows. To honor Andrew's next to youngest brother, the ANGELES was renamed IVER.

As a result of the acquisition, H. F. Berg, a Foss executive in Tacoma, was appointed to establish a Foss division in Port Angeles with responsibility for generating business along the Straits, supervising the IVER's gravel run, and the barging of Quillayute River pulpwood to Port Angeles, now in its third year of operation. To take care of the work load, Henry Berg had the IVER and the FOSS 21, then at times the ANDREW if the press of business warranted it.

The IVER struggled along with her original underpowered engine until 1930, then relief came with the installation of a new 275-horsepower Atlas. IVER's production went up 40 percent and so did the confidence of crew and management.

Then in the winter of 1935 Foss-Seattle dispatched the IVER to the Nehalem River in Oregon to tow spruce log rafts up the coast to Astoria. With Captain Ralph Oliver in command, the IVER successfully delivered the first log tow to Astoria. For wintertime, the ocean weather held remarkably good with light wind and sea. However, on the second trip the IVER ran into trouble at the Nehalem River bar. Gale force winds and rough seas made the bar a seething cauldron of breaking waves. The IVER had no warning of the treacherous conditions, so she had no alternative but to plunge into the steep heavy seas—retreat was impossible. In minutes the seas heaved out the logs and broke up the raft, scattering logs along the beaches.

The break-up decided the Astoria mill against further towing in the winter season, so the IVER was reassigned to Port Angeles for log towing on the Straits where there were no bars to cross.

The IVER continued towing logs out of Neah Bay and Port Angeles under Captain Mel Gobrillson and Captain Arnold Tweter until September 1946. Then with the assignment of the larger and more powerful HENRY and MATHILDA to Port Angeles for towing heavy log cribs, the IVER was transferred to Foss-Tacoma for towing rafted logs on the lower Puget Sound.

In November 1954 while on a routine job, the crankshaft broke on the Atlas diesel and the IVER came home on the end of a towline. Foss-Tacoma remedied the problem by installing a new 400-horsepower Enterprise. After repowering she went back to towing logs, chip scows, and chemical barges. The same routine went on for the next ten years—then novelty came her way. In July 1965 she took part in one of the most unusual tows ever attempted and completed by Foss.

On June 30, 1965 Ted Griffen, Director of the Seattle Marine Aquarium, on the lookout for a killer whale to add to his waterfront aquarium, heard that two fishermen near Namu, British Columbia had a 4-ton killer whale in their net. Ted Griffen flew up to Namu to view the whale. Satisfied, he made a deal with the fishermen, paying $8,000.00 for his prize. Griffen named the whale "Namu", after the small fishing village nearby.

In order to tow Namu to Seattle he built a large log and wire pen for the whale to frolic in while underway. He hired the purse seiner, CHAMASS BAY, to tow Namu to Port Hardy on the southern side of Queen Charlotte Sound. The slow towing speed of 2 knots and the constant worry made the Captain of the Chamass Bay reluctant to continue past Port Hardy. After all, he did have to get back to his livelihood—fishing not towing.

At this point in the drama, Foss Launch & Tug Company volunteered the services of the IVER. Acceptance was immediate, so the IVER with veteran skipper George Losey in charge, left Seattle on July 10th for Port Hardy. Arriving on July 12th, Captain George sized up his strange tow and decided to give it a go—he hooked on to Namu's cage and started on the 350-mile trip to the Seattle Aquarium. The official escort boat, ROBERT E. LEE, followed along with the Seattle newsmen, a film crew, and radio broadcaster Robert Hardwick aboard to cover the unique event in the daily papers and over the air for an eager public.

IVER and Namu cooperated well on the run down the Inside Passage and the weather was friendly until July 15th when the "Namu Flotilla" had to take shelter in St. Vincent Bight, a small cove on Vancouver Island, as small-craft warnings were raised. Ted Griffen and Captain Losey spent the anchor time conferring on procedure for the most dangerous part of the journey still ahead—passing through Seymour Narrows where the currents ran up to 12 knots except at the few minutes of slack water occurring at each tidal change. The particular problem was the slow speed of the tow now averaging only 1½ knots. However, with good weather and perfect timing, Namu and his escort went through the Narrows safely at 0400 on July 17th. Captain Losey stated that the passage went just the way it was planned out after studying tide and current tables, charts and weather reports for the precise time to start through—taking into account the slow speed and the mile to travel through the Narrows.

A week later Namu became an American whale as he crossed the International boundary. A Bureau of Customs official from Friday Harbor flew over to Namu's pen and cleared the flotilla for Seattle. Captain Losey and Dave Rosenboom, the tug's oiler, had run up the colors on the tug several hours earlier to denote the nationality of their charge for the Customs and Immigration inspection.

Just before sunset on July 25, the IVER and the strange tow passed under Deception Pass Bridge. Sightseers were everywhere, packed along the bridge rails, clinging to the girders, perched on surrounding cliffs and hillsides—all striving for a first look at the lively antics of Namu. A convoy of countless boats of all sizes and descriptions surrounded the IVER and Namu. Expedition members later said they were speechless—some were shivering from the tremendous ovation. Captain Losey said, "This display really made it soak in."

At last, on the morning of July 28th, the IVER pulled into Seattle's Pier 36 about 0900 with Namu, followed by the ROBERT E. LEE photographing the arrival celebration to complete a full-length film.

The crew of the IVER reached down for lines from Seattle's official greeting barge and tied Namu's pen to the pilings. It was the final act in the long touch-and-go trip.

The IVER was through. The four tons of live cargo now disporting before an awed and enthusiastic audience was safely delivered and for the first time in two weeks Captain Losey of the "Namu Convoy" had a full night's sleep. He stated that worry for Namu's safety kept him awake—Namu had become a real person.

Namu remained a star attraction at the Seattle Aquarium for nearly a year, but on July 9, 1966 in a desperate attempt to get free, Namu drowned. He had been moping for several days, surfacing frequently and anxiously. Then at 2200 on the 9th he made a shallow dive and rammed the netting full force. Namu couldn't surface. He became tangled in the cables just as he was about to break free—only one fin was caught. Ted Griffen felt that there was no question—it was a break for freedom. Perhaps Namu had heard a soundless call from passing whales . . .

With the strangest of tows in the Logbook, the IVER went back to bread-and-butter towing and for the next seven years continued in steady service on pulp-chip and sawdust runs with an occasional log and oil barge tow.

With the IVER and similar tugs of the IVER's vintage and type of equipment, repairs became more and more frequent and the maintenance expense less and less justified. This situation combined with the new tugs arriving on the scene brought on the IVER's retirement.

The time came in August 1972. Her 46-year service with Foss ended when she developed engine problems while towing chip scows on the Port Townsend run for Crown Zellerbach. The IVER came to Seattle for repairs but instead she was laid up "as is" at the Foss yard on the Canal and listed as surplus.

She remained in lay-up until sold in March 1974 to Mr. L. H. Clark of Tenakee, Alaska. He towed her to a nearby yard where all the necessary repairs were made and the IVER outfitted for towing in Southeastern Alaska.

Before leaving for Alaska, Mr. Clark renamed the tug BONNEY-GAL. She remained with him for three years and then returned to the more familiar waters of Puget Sound when she was sold to Mr. Bob Waterman. He had a contract for towing the Lone Star Industries gravel scows from their pit at Steilacoom to the Lone Star concrete mixing plant in Lake Union. Bob Waterman had one tug, the 76-year-old TILLICUM, but needed a second tug to fulfill

James A. Cole

the Lone Star contract, so he bought the BONNY GAL, renamed her MARILYN and at the same time gave her the somewhat prosaic color scheme of black and white.

The IVER, now MARILYN, with the change in sex, lives on.

MARTHA FOSS Departing Port Angeles on a foggy day in 1944. Two years later fog caused her demise. (Photo courtesy of Foss Tug Co)

MARTHA FOSS (1)

Built:	1886	Propulsion:	Ingersoll-Rand
	Astoria, Oregon		240-horsepower
Length:	88-feet	Primary Service:	Puget Sound
Beam:	22-feet	Final Foss Operating Day:	May 21, 1946
		Status:	Sank

The MARTHA FOSS commenced service as a steam-powered fish packer named DOLPHIN, built for the Alaska Fish Salting & By-Products Company. They used her in Alaska until 1916 then sold her to the W. S. DePierris Company who employed her as a cannery tender. Her home port was Juneau, Alaska, but she frequently tied up for the winter in Lake Union, Washington—being a cannery boat she operated only during the fishing season.

When the DOLPHIN was put up for sale in 1925, while laid up at the owner's dock on Lake Union, Foss, always on the lookout for usable boats to expand their fleet, bought her, closing the deal on January 6, 1926.

Built as a single ender, the DOLPHIN's cabins with accommodations for eighteen persons and the 150-horsepower engine were all located aft—the large fish hold was forward. Foss realized the general condition of the house and machinery were below average, but the 40-year-old hull was still sound and good for many years.

So on February 1st the DOLPHIN was towed to the yard of Ballard Marine Ways where for the next several months she went through a major transformation. The deck house and all the old steam-powered machinery were removed and the hull recaulked and planking renewed where necessary. Before decking-over the new midship house, a 240-horsepower Ingersoll-Rand diesel was installed. The engine was identical to the one recently put in the FOSS 21. Some of the machinery removed from the old crude-oil barge CAPTAIN BARKER, owned by Foss, was rebuilt and installed in the DOLPHIN—fittings, hardware, and even hand rails were reused. She could have been reclassed as a composite vessel.

By mid-summer, after shifting to the Foss yard, and with outfitting nearly complete, the "new" tug was renamed MARTHA FOSS in honor of Andrew's mother. At this time only one other Foss tug carried the name of a Foss family member, the Tacoma-based tug ANDREW FOSS, known as the flagship of the Tacoma-Foss fleet—the MARTHA now became the flagship of the Seattle division. In 1926 in addition to the premier ANDREW and MARTHA, there were twenty-three other boats owned by Foss—nineteen tugs and four launches and all working.

Ready for a trial run in August 1926 the MARTHA with Captain House in charge left for the gravel pit at Steilacoom taking along two barges to load. Entering Shilshole Bay on the return trip, the crew attempted to shorten up the towline before going into Ballard Locks, but the winch lacked sufficient power—the air compressor in the engine room could not deliver enough pressure to bring in the towline and the barges at the same time. Captain House had to chance the line fouling the propeller by backing under power toward the barges. The trial run had served its purpose and in short order the MARTHA had a large air compressor running directly from the main engine, solving the problem.

During the next 17 years the MARTHA performed steadily and well for Foss-Seattle hauling gravel and oil barges on the established Sound runs. Then during the summer months of the 1930's, she towed the oil barge FOSS-100 carrying diesel, gasoline, and stove oil between Edmonds, Ketchikan and Juneau for Union Oil Company.

But she lost the oil run in April 1943 when the Seattle and Port Angeles divisions made an exchange of tugs. The MARTHA with Captain Roy Hall went to the west end for towing heavy log cribs and the CATHERINE, a lighter tug, relieved of the log towing, came to Seattle. The MARTHA joined the veteran tugs FOSS 21 and IVER FOSS to help keep the mills in logs, even bringing in rafts from Canada.

The MARTHA's tows out of British Columbia were her heaviest and longest, especially those from Crofton to St. Regis Paper Company at Tacoma—the rafts of 40 sections, 2 wide, stretched out 1,600 feet end-to-end. The total time expended on a tow was usually 14 days. However, only half were actual towing days, the rest were usually spent at anchor along the way waiting out foul weather and adverse tides.

As it turned out, the MARTHA worked out of Port Angeles all through the World War II years towing logs except for intermittent runs with limerock scows from a quarry at Smallpox Bay on San Juan Island to the Rayonier Mill at Port Angeles. From limerock back to logs was quick and easy as Port Angeles was the home base for both services.

In towing log rafts the MARTHA was supreme as shown by her operating report for the period of May 1945 through May 1946 during the time Warren Waterman was skipper:

Total number of log tows delivered—30

Total number of sections moved—775

Total number of log cribs towed—4

The board-foot volume approaching 25 million—enough to build 1,000 houses! A remarkable achievement for a 240-horsepower tug in her 60th year.

MARTHA FOSS Only the pilot house remained afloat after being rammed and sunk by the freighter IROQUOIS in May of 1946. (Courtesy of Foss Tug Co)

But unfortunately, her remaining time afloat was measured in hours. On May 21, 1946 early in the morning, the MARTHA with Captain Waterman still in charge, left Port Angeles for Washington Harbor 18 miles away to pick up a log tow and due to zero visibility she ran at reduced speed. Then at about 0530, when off Green Point and unknown to the MARTHA, the Steamer IROQUOIS approached the Point on a scheduled run to Port Angeles. In the dense fog neither vessel could see the other and whistle signals were muffled. Suddenly and without warning, the bow of the IROQUOIS broke out of the fog on the MARTHA's starboard bow revealing the vessels to be on collision courses. Before evasive action could be taken the fast-steaming IROQUOIS plowed into the starboard side of the MARTHA just aft of amidships, nearly cutting the tug in half. The MARTHA's crew had just time enough to jump into the water and swim away before the tug rolled over and sank.

The IROQUOIS' crew pulled six wet and gasping survivors aboard, but tragically the seventh man, First Assistant Engineer Nelson Gillette, on watch in the engine room went down with the tug. The MARTHA's long and profitable life ended abruptly and with it, to the shock and dismay of the crew, a valued shipmate.

FOSS 11

Built:	1927	Propulsion:	Caterpillar (Single)
	Foss Shipyard		230-horsepower
	Tacoma, Washington	Primary Service:	Tacoma Harbor
Length:	52-feet	Final Foss Operating Day:	August 18, 1973
Beam:	16-feet	Status:	Sold - Domestic

FOSS 11, built entirely in Foss' own shipyard, was planned for harbor work or linehaul towing and so to give her adequate power they installed a high-torque heavy-duty Fairbanks-Morse C. O. engine. For her first two years, starting in July 1927 the FOSS 11 engaged in Tacoma harbor work and linehaul towing, port-to-port. Then in 1929 she went outside with an assignment to tow small general-cargo barges between Seattle, Tacoma, and the Hoh River on the northwestern Washington coast. Her cargo was material for construction of the coast-side stretch of Highway 101 between Gray's Harbor and Port Angeles. Equipment and supplies could only be delivered by tug and barge, as no road connection existed from either end of the project.

On July 13, 1929 the FOSS 11 had a close call while towing her barge to the Hoh River unloading site—she ran aground on the river entrance bar. The situation was precarious should the wind make up or the swell become heavy, but fortunately, the sea remained calm—and the crew, too. At high tide she backed off and no serious leaks showed up. Inspection in Seattle revealed only minor damage.

Still on the same job and faced with the same hazards, the FOSS 11 in March 1930 with Captain Eckberg in charge and in company with another Foss tug, the RUSTLER, towed the barge FOSS-44 from Tacoma to the Hoh loaded with 200 tons of lumber, cement, pipe, steel, and a number of dump trucks. With the variety and quantity of cargo aboard, the discharge was prolonged and worrisome—the vagaries of Pacific Ocean weather a constant threat to the safety of the crew, tug, and cargo. The same dangers faced them on each of twelve trips required to complete the job for the road contractors, Strom & McDonald Company, but the weather cooperated which was unusual for the Washington coast. By summer the Hoh River job was successfully completed and the FOSS 11 returned to her regular duties—towing lumber scows and chip barges between ports and mills on the Sound.

Because of natural engine wear and to prolong the usefulness of the otherwise sound tug, Foss repowered the FOSS 11 in January 1941 with a new six-cylinder Waukesha-Helleman spark-ignition oil engine, developing 170-horsepower at 900 RPM. Her fuel capacity was increased to 1,700 gallons to give her greater range and the upgrading proved timely in view of her sudden change of occupation and environment.

In late February 1941 she was chartered bareboat by Pacific Airbase Contractors building airbases in the mid-Pacific and to save time and reduce the risk of an ocean crossing, they shipped the FOSS 11 to Hawaii on the deck of a cargo ship. Arriving safely as planned, she went to work in the contractor's barging service for the ''duration''.

After World War II she worked for the Naval Air Arm in Honolulu about two years. Then her tour of duty in the land of luaus and leis ended in July 1947 and she was returned to Foss, FOB Tacoma, and as in her first ocean crossing she came home on the deck of a freighter.

Back with Foss and after a thorough inspection, the tug was found to be in good condition generally, except for a worn-down engine, but even so it was not until 1949 that the FOSS 11 was repowered, this time with a Buda diesel. After the strain of hectic war service, she settled down to a quiet routine by operating as a day-boat in Tacoma Harbor and for many years.

As a proof of constant hard work she wore out four engines during her active towing life—the fourth was installed in October 1961 a 230-horsepower Caterpillar. Each change gave her more power and the final one lasted the rest of her days. For thirteen years the Caterpillar operated without a major overhaul, but the day finally came. Faced with the expense on the "Cat", plus the over-age wooden hull, Foss decided to lay up the tug as soon as possible. The time came in August 1973 when she was towed over to Foss-Seattle for permanent lay up in the Canal.

Five months after retirement in January 1974 the FOSS 11 was sold to Larry Finneson of Bellingham. He renamed her PAMELA J and turned her into a fishing boat. Then a few years later the PAMELA J passed to another fisherman, Dean Croft of Blaine, Washington who reported he moved the engine ahead eight feet, added a mast, boom, and winches so he could drag for bottom fish.

The ex-FOSS 11 works out of Blaine and is still in a sense towing—but the drags now pull easier.

GRACE FOSS Ex-ROSEDALE, on a barge tow in Lake Union while operating as a dayboat for Foss-Seattle. (Courtesy of Joe Williamson)

GRACE FOSS (1)

Built:	1911	Propulsion:	General Motors
	Astoria, Oregon		165-horsepower
Length:	55-feet	Primary Service:	Seattle area
Beam:	13-feet	Final Foss Operating Day:	December 17, 1954
		Status:	Sold - Domestic

The GRACE FOSS, originally documented as a passenger vessel under the name of OLLIE S was built with a long, closed-in deck house and powered with a 75-horsepower Eastern Standard gasoline engine. Her home base was Portland and she operated on short runs up and down the Columbia River and later in Willapa Harbor until Drummond Lighterage of Seattle bought her in 1918. They renamed her ROSEDALE and rebuilt her into a linehaul tug for use on Puget Sound.

Drummond Lighterage, with a plant located along the West Waterway in Seattle, operated a shipping terminal and a number of first class barges, both open and covered. The barges were used for carrying general cargo and they had a riding crew aboard, usually two men housed in a small cabin on the stern. Drummond's principal business was lightering cargo onto beaches and to locations where no piers were available, which was the case at most logging camps along Hood Canal. The tug would tow a barge into shallow water at the cargo-discharge site and lines then run ashore from capstans and made fast so the barge crew could heave away on the drums and pull up on the beach. When the cargo was discharged, the tug at high water with a towline to the barge pulled the barge into deep water and tug and tow moved on to the next unloading point.

The ROSEDALE, captained by Clarence Lampman, worked with a smaller tug, the GLENDALE, in the lighterage service. Both the Drummond tugs were named for communities on Puget Sound. The ROSEDALE's original gas engine, after 15 years steady work, was breaking down and it was completely outclassed by the new semi-diesels now on the market, so a change was in order.

The ROSEDALE entered the Ballard Marine Ways in September 1926 for repowering and rebuilding a portion of the deck house, including construction of a new pilot house. She ended up with a roomy galley, two bunks below decks forward and a bunk for the Captain in the after-part of the pilot house. Her new engine, popular at the time, was a 100-horsepower Fairbanks-Morse heavy oil semi-diesel. The refit was completed on October 9.

But the rejuvenated ROSEDALE still had a serious defect due to her heavy sheer and now aggravated by the heavy diesel engine. When the tug had a full load of fuel aboard, the main deck was awash amidships, her lowest point—a nuisance, worry, and a hazard. This was one tug the crew preferred not to keep the fuel tanks topped off.

The ROSEDALE's service with Drummond Ligherage ended in November, 1927 when she was sold to Foss. They worked her on linehaul towing with a three-man crew on runs from Shelton to Tacoma and from South Bay to the Defiance Mill at Tacoma, also from booming grounds at Bremerton to the Nettleton Mill at Seattle.

In November 1936 Henry Harder assumed charge of the ROSEDALE, taking over from Captain Art Wickstrom and the tug continued on linehauls until April 1937 when Foss assigned her to harbor work and the crew reduced to two men. The change in crew and service was due to a new union requirement calling for a four-man crew on linehauls and the ROSEDALE could not provide accommodation for a fourth hand.

Foss-Seattle in 1939 asked for the ROSEDALE to shift logs on the Duwamish River and to tend the various sawmills including West Waterway Mill, Seaboard, Seattle Export Lumber and the Standard Mill Company. The ROSEDALE's low freeboard, for once, when shifting log rafts for the mills proved advantageous to the crew in jumping onto logs and back aboard.

In early 1942 the semi-diesel installed in 1926 was replaced by a high speed full diesel, a 165-horsepower General Motors. While in the repair year the ROSEDALE was renamed GRACE FOSS in honor of the wife of Oswell, a son of Peter Foss. The renaming came about due to the changed Foss policy of naming all tugs after family members.

The GRACE with her new engine and with Sam Stout as Captain, worked as a day-boat on Lake Union, Lake Washington, and Salmon Bay, but only for an engine break-in period. Then with all parts running dependably, the GRACE was again assigned to the Duwamish River mills and due to the increased work load, she operated day and night to keep the plants supplied with logs and lumber barges.

However, the month after month steady grind put too much strain on the weak hull, so after several years on the Duwamish Foss sent her to Ballard as a day-boat tending the mills on Lake Union and Salmon Bay as well as vessel shifting at Foss' own terminal. But even with an easy schedule, the hull became a steady leaker and the bilge pump kept her afloat. When idle at a pier, a portable pump was always aboard and the crew in the Dispatching Office had standing orders to check on the water level.

Captain Russ Gross related an incident showing just how delicate the hull was. The GRACE had orders to run to Shilshole Bay and assist in picking up logs spilled from a raft. She made it only as far as mid-channel at Shilshole Bay before slight waves began nudging the tug. She immediately started taking in water so fast the bilge pump couldn't keep up, so they headed back to the calm surface of Salmon Bay. After that experience and until her retirement, the GRACE remained in the protected waters of Lake Union and the Ship Canal.

By late 1954 the GRACE's hull was oozing water at the seams and she had to be pumped continuously. On one occasion the dockside pump wasn't equal to the task—she filled up and sank. The yard crew raised her to carry on a few more years, but for other owners.

The GRACE could no longer hold her own in any type of work, so after completing her day's orders on December 17, 1954 Foss laid her up permanently, removed the engine, and surrendered her official documents to the Coast Guard listing the reason simply as "out of service".

The reason for the incessant leaking was attributed to the composition of the hull—red cedar planking on oak frames. The hull fastenings in time would not hold in the soft cedar and they worked out allowing the seams to give.

After lying idle for a considerable time at Ballard and later at Kennydale, the GRACE was finally sold, minus the engine, for fishing and yachting. She was not documented, but she again became the ROSEDALE. Her owner installed an 80-horsepower six-cylinder Lathrup diesel.

A few years later the ROSEDALE changed hands again, this time to a minister who used the vessel for recreation and to take young people from his church on excursions. The leaking was never corrected and by the early Sixties her hull leaked at the rate of 300 gallons per day! The minister had his fill of troubles with the old tug and he sold her to a computer technologist. The owner put up with the leaks until 1967 then sold her to Dan Grinstead of Seattle and Dan kept her afloat until 1971 when he bought a more seaworthy tug, the 68-year-old LORNA FOSS. He sold the ROSEDALE to a Tacoma newspaperman and he moved the tug to Gig Harbor and began the long battle of refastening the hull below the water line. The work progressed until the winter of 1974 when his automatic pump stopped and the tug sank at the dock. For three weeks attempts were made to raise the boat, but all efforts failed. Later on a seine boat ran over the sunken craft damaging the cabins. The remains were dragged into deep water to remove any possible danger to navigation.

In June 1978 Jon Paterson of Gig Harbor made a dive on the ROSEDALE to see what changes had taken place. He reported the pilot house and forward trunk cabin missing, but the deck rails were still fastened to the bulwarks and the hull was in one piece. Patterson salvaged the propeller and shaft, but left the rest of the boat to the marine life.

The ex-GRACE finally made it to the bottom as a permanent resident after 25 years of trying—she apparently preferred to be wet inside and out!

LORNA FOSS *Outbound in the large locks. (Courtesy of Phil Henry)*

LORNA FOSS (I)

Built:	1903	Propulsion:	Superior
	Hoquiam, Washington		200-horsepower
Length:	63-feet	Primary Service:	Puget Sound
Beam:	13-feet	Final Foss Operating Day:	August 6, 1957
		Status:	Sold - Domestic

The LORNA FOSS was originally the steam tug PILOT built for the Polson Logging Company of Grays Harbor, Washington. Polson powered her with a 200-horsepower reciprocating engine and used her to tow logs down the Hoquiam River from their railroad log dump to Grays Harbor mills where the logs were sawn into lumber for shipment world-wide. However, not all the PILOT's logs were sawed for export lumber. Some of the select logs ended up in structural timbers in the fine sailing ships and steam schooners built by local yards.

The PILOT towed hundreds of millions of board feet of logs to the Grays Harbor plants during her life, as at times Polson produced a million feet of logs a day!

After 23 years of towing service by the 1903 tug, Polson built a new PILOT of the same size and installed the old PILOT's boiler and engine. The new boat was ready for work in 1927.

The first PILOT was laid up alongside the Polson headquarters' wharf in Hoquiam to prepare her for the boneyard, but Foss rescued the old tug from a scrapping fate. In August 1927 they purchased and towed the hull to the Foss-Seattle yard where she remained in an "as is" condition until March 1928 when reconstruction plans began. On March 5th Foss moved the PILOT to the yard of Ballard Marine Ways for major renovation. New engine timbers and foundation for a diesel were placed, the hull was recaulked and refastened and new main deck cabins built. A new main engine, a 150-horsepower Eastern Standard diesel, bought from McLaughlan Engine Company of Seattle, was installed.

Ready to go in July 1928 as the LORNA FOSS, named in honor of the wife of a son of Peter Foss, she began her towing career on Puget Sound.

Then, beginning in the early 30's, the LORNA under Captain Emil Wick, was assigned to Ketchikan, Alaska along with the small oil barge FOSS-11 to distribute oil from the Union Oil Company's Ketchikan base during the months April through September to the many canneries, reduction plants, and Indian villages in southeastern Alaska. During the off-season in Alaska, the LORNA worked out of the Seattle office on local tows. She continued in the dual service until the FOSS 19 took over on the Union oil run at the start of the 1942 season.

But by 1954 the LORNA, now over fifty years old, was showing signs of age, loss of power, hull leaks, and timber deterioration—all necessitating heavy maintenance. In view of the defects, Foss decided, beginning 1955 that she should be assigned to the Seattle office as a day-boat on Lake Union and Lake Washington, replacing the GRACE FOSS, recently laid up.

The LORNA continued as a day-boat until the morning of August 6, 1957. At that time Captain Sam Stout and his Deckhand were making up a set of boomsticks at Northwest Steel, near the Foss office and when ready to pull the sticks out, Captain Sam realized he didn't have rudder control. He was able to work the tug back to the Foss dock, a quarter of a mile away and discovered the trouble—the rudder had dropped off! This event, plus the continued hull-leaking of the past months decided Foss to lay up the LORNA immediately. The OMER FOSS came over from Port Angeles to take over her duties.

The veteran tug became available for sale and on October 24, 1958 Foss sold her to one of her former Captains, Bob Allison, for use as a pleasure boat. He retained the name LORNA FOSS even though the Company tried for several years to force a change, but he kept the name and the tug until his death in 1964. His widow sold the tug to Phil Edwards, a local fisherman, and he held ownership for seven years, using the boat as a yacht and fishing vessel and still carrying the name LORNA FOSS.

Another sale took place in 1971—this time to Dan Grinstead of Seattle. He also wanted the boat for a yacht. In 1973 Dan bought two 130-horsepower 1946-model Atlas diesels from New England Fish Company and he installed one engine in the LORNA and held the other for spare parts.

Dan has an affection for the boat and keeps the engine and the boat in top condition. He uses the LORNA for cruising, a floating repair shop, and occasionally as a tugboat. Each year at the Antique Tugboat Race or Parade, the LORNA always makes a creditable showing under Dan's care and guidance—just as she did when she was hard at work for Foss.

WALLOWA *Prior to purchase by Foss Company in 1929 and later rebuilt and renamed ARTHUR FOSS. (Courtesy of Joe Williamson)*

ARTHUR FOSS (I)

Built:	1889	Propulsion:	Washington
	Portland, Oregon		700-horsepower
Length:	110-feet	Primary Service:	Puget Sound
Beam:	24-feet	Final Foss Operating Day:	July 26, 1968
		Status:	Donated to "Save our Ships"

The 80-year history of the ARTHUR was one of adventure and action ranging from Alaska to the South Pacific, although she wasn't planned to be a roving tug. She was designed and built by David Stephenson of Portland for the Oregon Railway & Navigation Company—they named her WALLOWA, with no change for 40 years. Though no expense was spared to insure the best of tugboat construction, for some strange reason the first engines installed in the brand new hull were a pair of used and obsolete twin steam "bilge" engines, so called because they were set diagonally in each bilge.

For the first nine years of her life the WALLOWA worked on the Columbia River assisting sailing vessels over the dangerous shallow bar at the mouth of the river and then towing them on upstream to Astoria. However, in 1898 Captain E. Caine of Seattle bought her for barge towing between Seattle and Skagway during the Alaska gold rush. The Captain had arrived in the Pacific Northwest from the mid-west in 1895 and to get in on the big push, he purchased several barges, three sailing ships, and three tugs for Alaska service, operating them under the name of Pacific Clipper Line.

The WALLOWA, now a part of the action, began 1898 with a tough break while southbound from Skagway to Seattle towing the sailing vessel COLUMBIA. Heavy weather drove the barque ashore near Mary Island, but fortunately suffered no damage. She was refloated on the next high tide. However, three days later, the COLUMBIA, still under tow, swung wide under gale-force winds and grounded on the rocks near the entrance to Portland Canal. Impaled, flooded, and battered, she became a total loss.

Then in 1900 the WALLOWA's life and work simplified when her ownership passed to Mike Earles of Puget Sound Sawmills. With Frank Harrington as Captain, Earles used the tug for towing logs between his booming grounds at Port Crescent in the Straits and sawmills at Bellingham. In 1901 to give her more power in keeping with her well-found condition, Earles installed a modern steam engine with a new boiler and so ended the WALLOWA's expensive breakdowns with her ridiculous "bilge" engines.

After many years of log towing for Puget Sound Sawmills, Earles sold her to Merrill & Ring Logging Company who used her in the same type of work as Earles—towing log rafts, but out of their own Pysht River log storage on the Straits to Port Angeles.

Then in 1929 Merrill & Ring sold the 42-year-old tug to Foss for towing logs. She continued towing rafts for several years and then by an unexpected chance, she was suddenly in the public eye—and by way of the movies!

In the early 1930's a new instructor and lecturer came to Seattle to teach writing at the University of Washington—the soon to be world-famous Norman Reilly Raine, at the time a short-story writer for the Saturday Evening Post, the quality weekly founded by Benjamin Franklin, no less. Raine, as was natural, after observing waterfront activities around Puget Sound found a wealth of story material. He conceived the idea of developing and using a middle-aged vociferous woman tugboat captain and central character for a series of short stories depicting her shrewd maneuvering in towing episodes. The Saturday Evening Post published the stories under the title of "Tugboat Annie" and their appearance made tugboat history. The Post stories ultimately led to the filming of Annie Brennan's antics in keeping her tug NARCISSUS out-maneuvering arch-enemy Bulwinkle.

Drawing on the resources of Foss, in 1933 the WALLOWA temporarily became the NARCISSUS for the filming of the first "Tugboat Annie" movie in the proper locale. Raines' material for the movie as well as for the Post stories was largely provided by personal contact with Wedell Foss and other tugboat men on both the Seattle and Tacoma waterfronts—sixty years of tugboating had produced many authentic incidents to draw from. So much so, that "Tugboat Annie" became an industry by-word typifying the steam tugboat era in heart-warming terms.

After her glamorous "career", the WALLOWA lost her movie guise in a 1934 major conversion in Tacoma. She was torn down nearly to the water line and all machinery removed. In July 1934 renamed ARTHUR FOSS to honor the Company President, the rebuilt ARTHUR came out with a new 700-horsepower diesel and new auxiliary machinery as well as new modern deck cabins and pilot house. "Tugboat Annie" would have had a hard time recognizing her for the hard-used NARCISSUS!

Relating to the ARTHUR's new engine, an advertisement by the Washington Iron Works appeared and stated: "This 700-horsepower engine makes the ARTHUR FOSS the most powerful diesel tug on the West Coast. The selection of this powerful motor by one of the largest and most conservative tugboat companies on the Coast is another added instance of universal approval of Washington diesel power for difficult marine service." A new high-power, high-speed era was getting under way!

In November 1935 the ARTHUR continued meeting the unexpected. A fire broke out in the engine room and crew's quarters. To save the boat, Captain Bowers beached the burning tug near Discovery Bay. The Coast Guard responded and were able to get close enough to extinguish the fire. Then Foss pumped out the ARTHUR, refloated and towed her to Tacoma for repairs.

Rejoining the fleet several months later, after again undergoing extensive restoration, the ARTHUR engaged in the recently developed Foss Alaska and Coastwise towing service by making a lumber run to California. In 1936 the ARTHUR was welcomed with public fanfare to Los Angeles when she arrived towing the famous four-masted schooner COMMODORE loaded with 1,500,000 board feet of lumber from mills on Puget Sound. The ARTHUR's Captain Sporman reported that the voyage was far from smooth, with rough seas most of the way, however, as the COMMODORE's rigging was still in good shape, the sails were set for two days to take advantage of favorable northerly winds, making the unusual 7-day voyage possible.

The ARTHUR made another record lumber tow in 1940 with Captain Vince Miller when she towed a barge of 1,800,000 feet of lumber to Los Angeles without loss of time or cargo. The special tow just preceded the end of the ARTHUR's pre-war towing—she was about to enter a long period of military duty.

On February 8, 1941 the ARTHUR, with Captain Vince Miller still in command, left Tacoma for Honolulu via Oakland to take in tow a closing-gate for one of the Navy graving docks at Pearl Harbor. The ARTHUR started out from Oakland with the cumbersome load on February 15 and arrived in Honolulu with no misadventures two weeks later.

She went on charter to the Pacific Naval Airbase Contractors right after delivering the dock gate and in her first assignment towed barge loads of gravel from Kanehoe to Honolulu for construction of airport runways. After completing the gravel haul in June, the ARTHUR began towing barge loads of material from Honolulu to Wake Island for construction of an airbase. She continued on a regular run between Honolulu and Wake Island until December 1941—a momentous date. The ARTHUR with Captain Oscar Rolstad now in charge had left Wake Island after delivering two barges from Honolulu just 12 hours before the Island was captured by the Japanese! But another Foss tug, the JUSTINE, was not so fortunate. The Japanese sank her in the lagoon at Wake Island and the crew, after a period of forced labor, lost their lives at the hands of the Japanese long before the enemy's evacuation.

With airbase work increasing in tempo, the ARTHUR had a part in the construction of the French Frigate Shoals Landing Strip, starting the job by towing a clamshell-bucket dredge from Oahu to the Shoals, a crescent-shaped reef 18 miles long and 3 miles wide, located 500 miles northeast of Oahu. Fern Island, one of the eleven small coral sand islands making up the Shoals was to be made into an emergency landing strip by the Pacific Naval Airbase Contractors for refueling fighter planes on runs between Oahu and Midway. The ARTHUR delivered the bucket dredge to the Shoals on August 8, 1942 and remained as a tender to the dredge scooping up coral from the lagoon and depositing it on the 4-foot high Fern Island to build up and form the runway. The French Frigate Shoals job occupied the ARTHUR for three months, then she went back to towing around the Hawaiian Islands for the Airbase Contractors and the Navy.

At the end of the ARTHUR's service, lasting several years, she was laid up in Honolulu awaiting disposition, but still under charter to the Contractors. Finally in the fall of 1947 the ARTHUR was released and made ready for her return to Foss Company in Tacoma. The Contractors placed her in a sea-going drydock and towed dock and tug across the Pacific, but due to rough weather, she dropped off the keel blocks and suffered hull damage. Upon final delivery to Tacoma, the tug went through a period of extensive repairs, much needed after six non-stop years of hard service and the damage suffered aboard the drydock.

By August 1948 the ARTHUR was ready to begin peacetime work, at a slower tempo. With Captain Arnold Tweter in charge, she started towing logs out of Neah Bay, Sekiu, and Pysht, to mills in Port Angeles and up-Sound

THEODORE FOSS *Better known as the ARTHUR FOSS from 1933 until becoming THEODORE in 1964. Shown here between log towing jobs in Port Angeles, August 28, 1967 – her final summer of operation. (From the author's collection)*

ports. Now a veteran of 57 years, the ARTHUR was not used for coastwise and Alaska towing as the recently purchased MIKI-class tugs with their greater horsepower and size could more effectively handle the long tows. Ably suited for log towing, the ARTHUR remained on the Straits for the next 22 years, taking time off only for annual drydocking and repairs at the Foss yard in Tacoma.

While undergoing annual repairs in December 1964 she was renamed THEODORE FOSS to honor Andrew's oldest brother. ARTHUR's name was to go on one of the new super ocean-class tugs about finished at the Foss-Seattle yard.

Now, at 75 years of age, the THEODORE was still going strong towing heavy bundled rafts from Neah Bay to Port Angeles for Crown Zellerbach. But new Foss tugs were being turned out at various West Coast yards in the replacement program and their superiority eliminated any chance for continued use of the veteran tug.

The reconditioned wartime tug PACIFIC towed out of Neah Bay along with the THEODORE and they were joined by the new MYRTLE FOSS in 1966, then in 1968 another new tug, the MARTHA FOSS, arrived in Port Angeles for log towing. With the presence of the three newer vessels, the THEODORE, now close to 80 years old, was forced out of the running and slated for retirement. Her final tow was a log crib on July 26, 1968 from the Rayonier dump at Sekiu to Port Angeles, and after completing the job, Captain Tweter rang the engine room telegraph to "Finished with the Engines," ending the tug's productive and outstanding towing career, much to the regret of Arnold Tweter and Lynn Davis, her regular skippers for so many years. They liked the old "ARTHUR," always so comfortable and quiet.

After lying idle at Port Angeles for the remainder of the 1968 summer, the THEODORE was towed to Tacoma and put in permanent lay-up. She remained dock-bound until May 1970 then the Foss Company decided to donate the tug to the non-profit historical society "Save-Our-Ships". On June 24, 1970 Foss officially presented her to the S.O.S. Society in appropriate ceremonies on the Seattle waterfront. The Society renamed her ARTHUR and gave her a new coat of green and white paint—colors that for nearly a hundred years indicated a Foss tug ready to render service in a Foss manner.

Being truly representative of the shipwright's art, the ARTHUR became a unit of Antique Ships of the Northwest, joining the sailing schooner WAWONA and lightship RELIEF. The ships were moved to a permanent home at Kirkland, Washington, where they are open for tours to the general public year round. The ARTHUR, inside and out, looks as she did when still actively towing, and by visiting the tug, many decades of service and adventure can be re-lived aboard perhaps one of the finest tugs of her time built on the West Coast—and one of the pioneer tugs contributing heavily to the Foss reputation. With proper care the ARTHUR will be around for her 100th birthday in just ten years, and it will be a fitting compliment to the man who built her, David Stephenson, who stated at the beginning of construction that the tug was to be his finest work ever—and so it proved. Most of it under the Foss banner.

BARBARA FOSS (1)

Built:	1925	Propulsion:	Washington (Single)
	Nelson Shipyard		110-horsepower
	Seattle, Washington	Primary Service:	Puget Sound
Length:	53-feet	Final Foss Operating Day:	May 31, 1942
Beam:	14-feet	Status:	Sunk

The first BARBARA FOSS, built as the tug WEGO at John Nelson's shipyard next to Fisherman's Terminal in Seattle, was from a design by Lee & Brinton, Seattle naval architects. The WEGO was named for Webb and Gould who owned Pleasant Harbor Towing Company on Hood Canal and owned part of Snow Creek Logging Company. Their new tug, costing $30,000, was launched on September 25, 1925. She had the distinction of being the heaviest boat of her size ever to be built in a Northwest shipyard and a special feature of construction was a steel engine foundation to provide for a heavy-duty diesel. The original and only engine used in the tug was a 110-horsepower Washington-Estep diesel.

Mr. A. C. Estep, Chief Engineer at the Washington Iron Works where the Washington-Estep diesel engines were built, had determined that he could improve on the earlier "hot bulb" type diesels. Changes were made in the

BARBARA FOSS *As an operating unit of the Seattle division during the thirties and early forties until destroyed by fire. (Courtesy of Joe Williamson)*

cylinders, heads, and pistons. A new fuel system was used as well as high pressure injection-nozzles. The new type engine started on compressed air, the air being used to rotate the crankshaft. Once the engine began firing, the compressed air was shut off and the air intake-valves opened to outside air; then the engine continued to run on diesel fuel. The first Washington-Estep was installed in the tug ELMORE of American Tugboat Company of Everett in 1923. This was the first of nearly 400 Washington diesels to be installed in vessels on the East and West Coasts and the Mississippi River. The engines were slow turning with a full-speed RPM of between 225 and 300, depending on the size of the engine.

Through the years nine Foss tugs were powered by Washington diesels, ranging from 110-horsepower in the RUSTLER and BARBARA to 700 in the ARTHUR. Foss found the heavy-duty Washingtons quiet running, dependable, and in general living up to the excellence expected of them.

The WEGO, powered with the favored Washington, started her career in November 1925 towing logs and boomsticks on Hood Canal. Then after about four years of working for Snow Creek, the WEGO in 1929 was sold to the Foss Company and renamed BARBARA FOSS in honor of the eldest daughter of Wedell and Edith Foss.

Foss put her right to work towing oil barges around Puget Sound, but unfortunately on February 15, 1931 during a winter storm the BARBARA stranded on a reef off Puffen Island, Rosario Straits. For three days units of Bellingham Tug & Barge attempted to pull the grounded tug free of the reef, however, the unrelenting wind and sea held her fast. Then while waiting for more favorable conditions, the BARBARA unaccountably slipped off the reef and sank.

The next day a Foss tug and scow with salvage equipment arrived on the scene with salvage-master Glen Petterson aboard. Divers found the BARBARA lying in 60 feet of water at the edge of a rocky ledge which formed the top of a 300-foot submarine cliff. Lines from the scow were fastened around the sunken tug and on February 23rd, winches raised her to the level of the scow and then the crew lashed her alongside. Scow and tug were towed to Echo Bay where the BARBARA was beached and a temporary patch put in place. At high tide they started for Seattle to make permanent hull repairs and overhaul the engine due to the submersion in salt water.

The BARBARA, fit again, re-entered service in the spring and continued moving barges successfully for the next ten years and it appeared her 1931 stranding would be her only accident, but unfortunately that was not the case.

Foss lost the BARBARA on March 31, 1942 by fire while on a tow with the empty gasoline barge UNION OIL COMPANY #3 from Port Angeles and Port Townsend to Seattle. The crew believed that sparks from the generator ignited oil around the motor base and the rising flames set fire to the overhead paint. Captain Hank Hall, noticing the swirling smoke, stopped the boat, then rushed down and with hand extinguishers smothered the flames. However, shortly after getting underway, the fire started again, but to the crew's dismay all the extinguishers were empty and the fire spread out of control. With the boat dead in the water, the towline snagged on the bottom and the gas barge came surging up to the tug's stern—a possible catastrophe in the making! By this time the deck of the BARBARA was too hot to walk on and the Deckhand climbing up on the cooler bulwarks gained a higher place to jump from just before the auxiliary gas tank blew up. The quick-thinking Deckhand had jumped far enough out into the water so the shooting flames did not reach him. Fortunately, Captain Hall and the rest of the crew were on the opposite side from the explosion and unharmed. They went after a 40-gallon foam extinguisher on the barge, disregarding the danger of another explosion. Grabbing the extinguisher, they sprayed the stern of the tug and at the same time attempted to shove the burning tug away from the dangerous gas barge. At this point, and luckily, an Army tug arrived on the scene, took off the crew and pushed the BARBARA into a kelp bed about a mile southeast of Marrowstone Island. The Army tug stood by with the barge until the burning tug sank.

Two weeks later a search was made for the BARBARA, using a wire drag from an A-frame scow. But after two days of searching, she could not be located and so the insurance company declared the tug a total loss. The disappearance of the BARBARA without a trace is still a mystery. Perhaps the undercurrents were responsible for radically changing the BARBARA's position. The boat is gone, but the name lives on in a fine new modern ocean-going tug.

DREW FOSS (I)

Built:	1929	Propulsion:	Caterpillar
	Foss Company		325-horsepower
	Tacoma, Washington	Primary Service:	Puget Sound
Length:	53-feet	Final Operating Day:	December 11, 1975
Beam:	16-feet	Status:	Sold - Foreign

The DREW, named for the son of Henry and Agnes Foss, was built by Foss Company at their Tacoma yard following the plans of FOSS 11 constructed two years before. Both tugs were designed for harbor work, also light towing on Puget Sound, so they were fitted with a galley and crew's quarters. The DREW began service on April 1, 1929 in Tacoma Harbor as a utility tug. Her 120-horsepower heavy oil Fairbanks-Morse diesel was adequate for barge and log raft shifting, but on linehaul towing, which she did occasionally, she was the slow boat to Port Townsend. Even so, the DREW's earnings were remarkable. In 1929 during nine months' operation, she made a profit of over $12,000—regardless of the stock market crash. The FM engine proved very economical and that helped her profit account. For the first year her average fuel consumption figured only 7.8 gallons per hour.

The DREW built up a record of reliability and prompt service for seventeen straight years working in Tacoma and around the Sound. She performed so well, Foss decided the tug was well worth spending money for betterment, so in early 1946 she entered the Foss shipyard in Tacoma for rebuilding and repowering. The old style heavy-oil engine was removed and new engine beds for twin high-speed 150-horsepower Cummins diesels were installed. The two engines were connected to a common shaft driving a single propeller. The DREW was the only Foss tug to have this type of installation until the SEA KING, purchased in the late 1950's, came similarly equipped. During the repowering, the deck house was rebuilt, providing a Captain's stateroom aft of the pilot house and a W. C. and shower on the main deck. The galley and crew's quarters were refurbished, but remained below decks.

In July 1946 the DREW, appearing fresh as a new boat from the builder's yard, re-entered service. She towed logs and lumber or chip scows, ranging from Shelton to Port Angeles.

She had a special assignment acting as a tender in dredging operations: the FOSS-301, a clam shell bucket-dredge, when in operation, dropped the spoils on flat-deck scows tied up alongside, and when loaded, the barges were towed by the DREW to a deep-water dump site and the dredgings washed overboard by the tug's high volume monitor. The DREW's dredge tending included work at Chambers Creek, Nisqually, Milwaukee Boom in Tacoma, Shelton and log dumping sites on the Straits of Juan de Fuca. She also towed the FOSS-301 and two waste-material barges to Bellingham for a dredging operation at the Bellingham log-booming grounds.

The longest and most important dredging operation the DREW tended occurred in Seattle harbor, dredging out the area of Pier 46 in preparation for the construction of the new container-terminal and deep-sea ship berth. She worked with the FOSS-301 and the much larger FOSS-300 from December 20, 1961 through February 28, 1962.

Then three weeks later she returned to the Pier 46 site to tow loaded gravel barges from Sound Sand & Gravel on Maury Island to pier 46 for the major landfill forming the terminal base. On May 21, 1962 the DREW towed the first load to Pier 46 and within a week three tugs and five barges were engaged in delivering sand and gravel on an around-the-clock basis. The DREW spent just two months on the gravel haul then left to resume dredge tending.

She continued to work until developing gear-box trouble in March 1964. The 18-year-old Cummins engines were worn out so Foss decided to repower her with a single 325-horsepower Caterpillar diesel. The repowering was done in 2½ months and then with only a few hours testing, the DREW was sent to Sekiu on the Straits to resume dredge-tending.

DREW FOSS *Shown with a log tow bound for Lake Washington, February 5, 1967. (From the author's collection)*

For the next five years she continued her assist work, rarely laid up and never missing a job, but by mid-1969 with the newer and larger tugs available and the 49-year-old DREW showing her age, the demand for her services was waning. Customer requirements were for high power, fast tugs, and the DREW couldn't compete, but she did work steadily into early 1970. In February she worked her final dredging job—at Shelton. After washing the waste off the last two scowloads on February 28, she returned to Tacoma and the following week she was re-classed as a two-man dayboat for operating in and around Tacoma Harbor doing light towing.

Her linehaul towing days were supposed to be finished, especially with the more powerful tugs taking over all the long haul and heavy towing, but the West Coast longshore strike in July 1971 required the services of every Foss tug that could tighten a towline.

With all the larger tugs towing Japanese export logs to Canada for loading aboard the diverted log ships, there was a lack of tugs for local work on Puget Sound. The DREW was outfitted once again for a live-aboard crew and on August 11, with a full crew aboard she went on the chip run between Shelton, Port Townsend, and Port Gamble. She took several hours more to complete the run than her newer counterparts, but she always brought in her tow. After a month and a half of fill-in service, and as the tugs towing to Canada returned to local work, the DREW returned to her two-man operation in Tacoma Harbor. She continued in harbor support activity until additional new equipment arrived to handle all assignments. So in September 1975 she was placed in ready-reserve.

In November Foss shifted her to company moorings in Seattle to be in fresh-water storage, and they kept her in ready-reserve status—it was just as well.

On December 4, due to major flooding along the Snohomish River in the Everett area, all the major log storages broke loose, spilling hundreds of sections of logs all over Everett's outer harbor. The DREW was immediately sent to Everett and worked around the clock, along with the Everett harbor tugs rounding up logs into bag booms and rafts. After five days, and with the emergency work done, the DREW returned to Seattle towing an empty chip scow. The next day, after finishing shifting log rafts at the Renton log storage and tying up at the Foss pier, her active career with the Foss Company came to an end.

The DREW was declared surplus on December 19, 1975 and her engine removed. After remaining in lay-up for 18 months, Foss sold her in 1977 to Mr. Gary Bolderson of Campbell River, B. C. He towed the DREW north and had her repowered with a 200-horsepower Buda diesel. Mr. Bolderson used the tug in log-salvage work in Quatsino Sound on the west coast of Vancouver Island. Then after about a year he sold the boat to Mike Lloyd of Squamish, B. C. who converted her for cruising and renamed her BEVERLY ANN II.

Now a second and new DREW FOSS is ably carrying on the reputation of the name.

WALLACE FOSS

Built:	1897	Propulsion:	Caterpillar
	Tacoma, Washington		230-horsepower
Length:	58-feet	Primary Service:	Puget Sound
Beam:	15-feet	Final Foss Operating Day:	March 10, 1972
		Status:	Sold - Domestic

The WALLACE FOSS, built in the "Old Town" district of Tacoma, was originally designed as a steam passenger vessel, but when only half completed her owners, Blekum Towboat Company of Seattle, changed the plans and she ended up as a tugboat named OSCAR B.

With her 100-horsepower fore-and-aft steam compound engine she did well in towing logs, boomsticks, and barges between all ports in Puget Sound—becoming the flagship of Blekum's fleet. The OSCAR B worked for Blekum until 1911 then they sold her to Captain Pearson of Thompson & Pearson Company in Everett, Washington. She operated only a few months under Pearson's ownership; apparently she didn't work out well as they beached her near a hay field close to Lowell on the Snohomish River. Forgotten and rapidly falling into a deplorable state, she was given a new lease on life by the Rouse Towing Company of Seattle who bought her in 1913. After making the rescued tug seaworthy enough for the short trip to Seattle, Rouse towed her to the Ballard Marine Ways for renovation.

During the next few months, the Ballard yard rebuilt most of the hull and installed a two-cycle two-cylinder 100-horsepower surface ignition engine that was originally used as a stationary engine in Sweden.

When the tug was ready for service, Captain Rouse gave her his family name and the ROUSE towed for her salvors until Wedell and Arthur Foss acquired Rouse Towing Company for their Seattle program. The new addition to the fleet was a milestone in Foss engine history being the first Seattle tug owned and operated by Foss to have an oil engine.

The ROUSE continued in regular Foss service until 1925 then she went to the shipyard for deckhouse modernization and engine replacement. Her semi-diesel was removed and a new 110-horsepower 4-cylinder Western Enterprise full diesel installed, also new fuel tanks with a capacity of 1,700 gallons were set in. Three cabins aft of the pilothouse were added, all on the main deck, making for comfortable accommodations.

ROUSE *Formerly the small steamer OSCAR B, owned by Rouse Towing of Seattle, later the WALLACE FOSS.*
(Courtesy of Joe Williamson)

The rebuilt ROUSE began service in September 1925 and went immediately on short charter to Nooksack Pack-ing Company of Lummi Island. She lived up to expectations, performing well with her new engine, so well, in fact, that in 1935 Foss gave her a stronger engine, another Western Enterprise, salvaged from the recently sunk WINONA. The ROUSE towed steadily for Foss-Seattle except for a short period in the early 40's for Foss-Tacoma under the command of Gene Allen.

In 1945 following the latest Foss policy, the ROUSE officially became a member of the Foss family by being given the name WALLACE FOSS, a son of Theodore's son Joe.

The 48-year-old WALLACE, having a sound hull decided Foss in 1949 to further improve the boat. Her house was entirely rebuilt, including a brand new pilothouse above the main deck cabin to increase visibility. Her new accommodations and galley greatly added to the comfort of the crew. Foss increased her power output with a new high speed 225-horsepower Buda diesel, replacing the slow-turning Enterprise.

She re-entered service in the fall of 1949 with Captain Haaken Berg, formerly of the HILDUR, in charge. Cap-tain Berg had lost his home afloat when Foss retired the HILDUR because of incurable afflictions—leaks and shakes. The WALLACE served Foss-Seattle for the remainder of her long career towing oil barges and gravel scows month after month—a going concern.

The WALLACE must have had a charmed life because in 1959 after sixty years of work she was again favored with repowering and a hull refit. Deciding to go all out, Foss sent her to the Pacific Shipyard in Anacortes in April 1959 where she remained for ten months to undergo revision.

When in February 1960 the WALLACE emerged with an upgraded hull and a new 230-horsepower Caterpillar high speed diesel—the first "cat" to be installed in a Foss tug—she made Foss engine history the second time. Twenty years later fifty Caterpillar diesels were providing main propulsion power for Foss tugs along with many Caterpillar auxilliary engines furnishing power for tug utilities.

In 1969 the WALLACE logged her Golden Anniversary becoming one of only five to operate fifty years or longer with the Foss Company. Even with new tugs on the line, the WALLACE was still used on the Steilacoom-Seattle gravel haul. But by the fall of 1970, 230-horsepower was not sufficient to keep up with an advanced schedule on the gravel run, so the veteran tug went to Tacoma and operated as a two-man harbor boat on an as-needed basis.

The Tacoma assignment lasted through March 1971, but with better utilization of the regular harbor boats, the WALLACE was no longer needed and she returned to Seattle as part of the ready-reserve fleet. Then in August, due to the longshore strike, every available tug was put to work, so for the next three months, in order to release the regular tugs for log towing to Canada, the WALLACE towed a railcar barge from Tacoma to the Simpson Mill at Shelton and gravel scows on the usual local runs.

With the strike-fostered activity ended, she returned to lay up in Seattle, but she did operate several days a month during the winter tending log storages and making up log tows in Lake Washington. Her last operating day was March 10, 1972 and she was officially laid up on April 6th, having completed 52 years of service for Foss.

Six months later, on October 26th, Foss sold her to Mr. Dennis Strong of LaConner. The yard crew had removed the engine and the towing winch, so Mr. Strong set in a D-13000 Caterpillar—her seventh engine! He painted the tug black and white covering the Foss green and white colors and suddenly the WALLACE FOSS became the yacht LAURA E. She now berths in LaConner and her smart look belies her eighty-two years.

WALLACE FOSS *In the locks outbound June 15, 1968. There are no similarities from her early days as the Rouse. (From the author's collection)*

ROLAND FOSS (1)

Built:	1910	Propulsion:	Waukesha
	Seattle, Washington		170-horsepower
Length:	43-feet	Primary Service:	Puget Sound
Beam:	12-feet	Final Foss Operating Day:	February, 1944
		Status:	Sold - Domestic

The ROLAND FOSS, first known as the RIVAL, was built for Captain N. L. Johnson's Seattle-based towing company. Following the habit of the early tugs on Puget Sound, she changed owners several times and in her fourth year was sold to Rouse Towing Company of Seattle to augment their fleet of small harbor and Sound tugs. Edwin Hedman and William Stark, two of their regular captains, were in charge of the RIVAL. However, the RIVAL and her two skippers came into the Foss organization in the 1919-1920 change-over.

The RIVAL operated out of Foss' new Seattle base for the next twenty-five years as a bay-boat, the class name used at the time for a small harbor boat. Her efficiency improved in 1925 by replacing the gas engine with a 65-horsepower diesel. Shifting log rafts and boomsticks in Ballard and on the Duwamish River was now easier and she could even make an occasional long tow, as far as Bellingham.

Later on the RIVAL had difficulty in holding on to her captains—or so it seems. During a span of twenty years she had a record twenty-six different skippers, including Clarence Bale, Dave Pearson, Bill House, Ralph Murrow, and Amos Hilton—all well-remembered Captains that piloted Foss tugs for many years.

In June of 1929 Foss sent the RIVAL to Bellingham, with Captain Noel Ferras in command, to tend the rafting grounds of Bellingham Boom Company. The RIVAL, first of the green and white fleet to work out of Bellingham, shifted rafts and sticks at the log dump until early 1941 then she returned to Seattle, as a bay-boat. With the increase taking place in harbor shipping due to hostilities in Europe, the RIVAL had to have more power to keep up, so in the spring of 1941 Foss installed a new 170-horsepower Waukesha diesel and rebuilt the hull and cabin.

The job was completed in July and before leaving the pier the RIVAL became the ROLAND FOSS to honor another son of Theodore's son Joe. The ROLAND spent some break-in time in Tacoma Harbor and then returned to her old stand in Seattle.

However in 1942 the ROLAND had a change of environment for three months, when working in Port Angeles as a harbor tug, filling in for the HENRIETTA during the Neah Bay breakwater job.

After completing the Port Angeles stint, the ROLAND took over the log and barge shifting work on the Duwamish River in Seattle and she held the station for her remaining two years with Foss.

In March 1944 the U. S. Navy purchased the ROLAND for use out of Portland, Oregon on the Willamette and Columbia Rivers. The tug remained in active service until shortly before declared surplus in 1949. Her next owner, Mr. D. L. White of Oregon, purchased the boat in July and converted her to a fish boat and installed a 140-horsepower gasoline engine. He had the boat registered as the ROLAND FOSS, apparently to give the boat some importance. Then in 1957 Mr. White sold the ROLAND to Sidney Keyes who continued to use the boat for Columbia River fishing.

Mr. Keyes retired the boat in the early Sixties as she was no longer seaworthy due to age and deterioration. She finally sank at her berth in Skamokawa on the Columbia River in 1965 at the age of 55, having spent twenty-five years under Foss aegis.

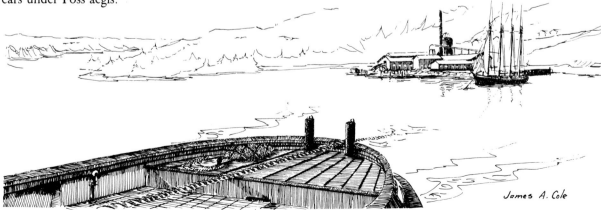

James A. Cole

SECTION III – OCEAN AND COASTWISE TOWING INCREASES IN IMPORTANCE

Tugs Acquired 1930 – 1939
JUSTINE (1), PETER (1), HENRIETTA, ANNA (1)

MATHILDA (1), PATRICIA (1), WANDERER

AGNES (1), CATHERINE (1), MYRTLE (1), FOSS 8

HILDUR, NANCY, CHRIS (1)

With five additional tugs capable of long open-water tows, Foss, even during the Depression, handled more and more towing jobs to California, Oregon, and Alaska. In 1933 the first of many future regular runs to southeastern Alaska started with the MARTHA towing the FOSS 100 for Union Oil Company.

As the tows became longer and heavier in the 1930s the engine horsepower continued to increase up to 1,500 in the AGNES. All the new engine installations were slow speed heavy-duty diesels.

Foss purchased Wagner Towboat Company of Seattle in 1937, adding another four tugs to the Puget Sound fleet and adding the established Wagner runs to the Foss schedules.

In 1939 a new type of venture came about for Foss when the U.S. Navy Airbase Contractors chartered the MATHILDA to tend defense projects at islands in the Central Pacific. The MATHILDA was the first of many Foss tugs to take part in the military programs of World War II.

1930 to 1940 was the last decade of "business as usual" for the Foss Company. Due to the war, post-war prosperity, oil discoveries, and world-wide industrial expansion, business growth and Company growth became greatly accelerated and continuous.

JUSTINE FOSS Photographed by Mr. Drew Foss at Taku Glacier during the summer of 1938 while operating in S.E. Alaska for Union Oil Co. (Courtesy of Drew Foss)

JUSTINE FOSS (1)

Built:	1930	Propulsion:	Atlas
	Foss Launch & Tug Company		200-horsepower
	Tacoma, Washington	Primary Service:	Pacific Area
Length:	57-feet	Final Foss Operating Day:	December 23, 1941
Beam:	16-feet	Status:	Sunk by Enemy action W.W.II

The JUSTINE, named for the youngest daughter of Wedell and Edith Foss, was the third of five similar tugs built by the Foss Company in their own yard. Each of the five tugs varied slightly in length and were powered by four different makes of engines, but all tugs had the same general design of pilot house forward and a long trunk cabin aft with crew's quarters below decks.

At the time the JUSTINE started towing on January 31, 1930 she was the largest of the look-alike tugs and with her 200-horsepower she outclassed the DREW and FOSS 11 with their 120.

Within the first eleven months of operation the JUSTINE reached a new high for the Company in potential profit: In 4,345 hours, she earned $30,000 and her 1930 operating cost was an amazing $5.42 per hour. She made money whether working on Puget Sound, towing Coastwise, or in Alaska. For her first six years of service she produced average yearly earnings of over $23,000 and this in the Depression 30's.

The JUSTINE's Puget Sound work consisted in towing log rafts or barges of sawmill waste, like the run, with Captain Ralph Oliver, towing chips and hogged fuel from the Canyon Mill in Everett to the Port Townsend Pulp Mill.

In 1932 the JUSTINE helped in the construction of Oregon's scenic Coast Highway (101) by barging rock and gravel between the Umpqua and Siuslaw Rivers where the JUSTINE's loads were transferred to trucks for final delivery to the new highway.

Besides the scenery, fishing on this particular job was excellent. With an Oregon State fishing license to stay legal, the crew became part-time fishermen. On one trip they caught ninety salmon and by the end of the month the "fishing vessel" JUSTINE FOSS had caught 3½ tons of "silvers" which the crew sold at 2½¢ per pound, netting $175.00—at today's prices $10,500! Then after three months on the job, the JUSTINE was relieved by the PETER FOSS. The fishing was over anyway.

During the years 1933–1935 the JUSTINE engaged in some tough jobs on the Straits and the Washington Coast. She towed heavy log cribs from the Sail River to Port Angeles and in a more risky assignment she moved bundled log rafts from the Hoh River on the seacoast to various ports on Puget Sound. The tows were worrisome with the chance of the weather turning bad on the long open-water haul and breaking up the brailed rafts. The great danger on the trip up the coast and rounding Cape Flattery came from the long ocean swells, at times heavy enough to make the raft undulate and part the gear. Logs in bundles were made up on the Hoh River and floated down to just inside the breaker line where they were formed into a raft—logs in bundles and rafted together proved to be the most practical method of towing logs in the ocean. The JUSTINE, anchored outside the breaker line would ferry a line across the Hoh River Bar to the raft, then pull the raft to the tug and get underway. Five miles out she turned north and the more challenging part of the trip began.

The JUSTINE carried out another chancy assignment when she towed a loaded Union Oil Company barge from Edmonds to Mora village located five miles up the snag and bar-prone Quillayute River and with another ocean estuary to cross at the entrance. They arrived safely and discharged the oil, but a mass of fishboats blocked the main channel on the down-river run. While waiting for the boats to disperse, the tide ebbed and the JUSTINE grounded, but by holding her upright she lifted off at high water with no apparent damage.

She spent most of 1936 away from home base—performing tasks a much larger boat would have trouble doing. In early February, with Captain Tom McInnis and a 3-Man crew, the JUSTINE had orders to pick up a dump scow at Oakland and deliver it to southern California. Upon arrival in Wilmington she picked up a second dump scow and proceeded to El Sugundo and began towing the scows, loaded with sludge from a sewer excavation project, to a dump-site 25 miles out to sea. The crew only worked five days a week so the operation lasted four long months.

With no lost time or rest, the JUSTINE started on another assignment in California tending a derrick barge used in lifting ground tackle, anchor gear, and large mooring buoys out of the water on to a barge for inspection and repair. The buoys were used for harbor mooring by Navy vessels and oil tankers. She worked with the derrick at San Pedro, Long Beach, Ventura, Gaviota, and other southern California ports. The job went on for five months and to the "away from home" crew it seemed like fifteen!

The JUSTINE made one more run before tying up at the Foss pier—she towed the U.S.A. GORDON from Los Angeles to Tacoma where the GORDON, purchased by Foss, was to be rebuilt, emerging as the big heavy-duty tug MATHILDA FOSS. The JUSTINE and her crew—Captain Tom McInnis, Leonard Sund, and George Maddock, later to become a Foss Vice-President, arrived in Tacoma with the GORDON on November 25, 1936 after almost ten months of continuous action.

After completing voyage repairs, Foss returned the JUSTINE to routine towing on Puget Sound. However, by the spring of 1937 she left for a new area. To start the new job she towed the oil barge FOSS-11 to Ketchikan and began oil delivery shuttle service, replacing the LORNA FOSS for the 1937 and 1938 seasons. She distributed oil to the fish canneries and processing plants during the six month season, then with the onset of winter, she returned to Puget Sound and towed chip scows.

In the spring of 1940 the JUSTINE worked in yet another region. This time she crossed the Gulf of Alaska to Woman's Bay, Kodiak Island where she towed for Puget Sound Bridge & Dredge, tending the dredging operating at the U.S. Military Base. By winter the job was finished and the JUSTINE headed for home, again crossing the Gulf—a rugged trip for a small boat. Though the seas stove in the pilot house windows and the tug labored and rolled and pitched in the heavy southerly weather, she came through by careful handling of the throttle and wheel. They were fast alongside the Foss pier in Tacoma on January 4, 1941.

The tug went into the shipyard for voyage repairs and then towed on the Sound until early 1941 when the Pacific Naval Airbase Contractors, a joint venture of Morrison-Knudsen, Hawaiian Dredging, and other firms, required towing service at proposed airbase sites in the Central Pacific. The MATHILDA FOSS was already on the job and the JUSTINE, FOSS 11, and ARTHUR were to follow in the spring of 1941.

The JUSTINE first went to San Francisco to be towed to Honolulu by a cargo vessel, but on the way over the towline parted and the tug finished the trip on her own. The same situation prevailed on the run from Honolulu via Midway to Wake Island, her ultimate destination, 4,500 miles from Seattle. The JUSTINE ran the last thousand miles under her own power arriving at Wake no worse for the experience.

Her Captain on the long ocean voyage was Tom McInnis, the JUSTINE's regular skipper. Had he known what he was headed for, maybe he would have remained on the Sound, but it isn't likely—he would have gone anyway, he was that kind of a captain.

The JUSTINE went right to work lightering equipment, supplies and material ashore by barge from deep-draft vessels lying outside the shallow, coral, v-shaped lagoon. Tug and barge had access through dug channels to the shoreside construction sites around the three islands forming the sides of the lagoon.

The Foss-Tacoma crew soon returned home except for Captain McInnis and Mate Ralph Van Valkenberg. But Drew Foss, son of Henry, came over to assist in the JUSTINE's project and worked aboard until a foot injury forced him ashore. The barging continued rapidly right through most of December, and after Pearl Harbor the pace increased.

On December 23, 1941 the Japanese after many air attacks, captured Wake Island and took possession of all the facilities that the construction crews had so laboriously built as part of the Navy's Pacific defense program. A relief task-force under Rear Admiral Frank Fletcher, built around the Carrier SARATOGA, had been sent to Wake Island before the Japanese attack, but Cincpac (Commander in Chief Pacific) recalled the force as the risk of loss to the ships was too great in view of major setbacks and the desperate need of combat vessels.

Wake Island was the most important outpost between Honolulu and Guam, but there were only five hundred officers and men, mostly Marines, stationed on the Island. Their defense consisted of a squadron of fighter planes and some 5-inch coastal defense guns. Not a formidable repelling force, but the time was in the first month of a unprepared-for war.

The Japanese invaders sent the American combatant prisoners to Shanghai and the civilian workers, around eight hundred, were shipped to various prisoner-of-war camps. Drew Foss ended up in a prison camp in Japan, there to remain for almost four years of suffering and toil, eking out a bare existence—the fate of all the prisoners sentenced and abused for defending liberty and justice.

About 100 civilian employees were detained on Wake to work for the enemy. Included in this group was the crew of the JUSTINE, composed of Foss men Tom McInnis and Ralph Van Valkenberg together with four residents of the Island. They remained aboard the tug and were compelled to lighter cargo from Japanese ships to the lagoon.

The JUSTINE's captive crew was forced to slave away for the Japanese until lightering was no longer required. At that time, the JUSTINE, much worse for wear was intentionally sunk by the Japanese in the lagoon. The tug was expendable and the crew must have been considered in the same category as they were taken ashore, lined up and executed—why? Victims of the complete disregard for human life in the lust for power.

The first indication to the Foss Company that all was not well with the JUSTINE came in January 1942 when both the ARTHUR and MATHILDA in the South Pacific during the Japanese takeovers, reported in safe. But no word was received from the JUSTINE. Constant inquiries were made but to no avail. Then in December 1943 information came from the Red Cross that Drew Foss was a prisoner of war. So by inference the Foss Company knew the JUSTINE, Captain McInnis and Ralph Van Valkenberg were in the hands of the Japanese; but at that time they didn't know the men had lost their lives. After U.S. re-capture of the Islands, the navy sent the bodies to Honolulu for proper internment.

Late in 1945 Drew Foss arrived home in Tacoma with the sad sordid JUSTINE FOSS story. Drew, after four years in prison camps undergoing toil, humiliation, and living on a diet of rice and grasshoppers had survived man's inhumanity to man. This is well-illustrated by a reprint of the orders given U.S. prisoners when taken aboard the Japanese prison ship at Wake Island in December 1941:

Commander of the Prison Escort
Navy of the Great Japanese Empire

REGULATIONS FOR PRISONERS

1. The prisoners disobeying the following orders will be punished with immediate death.
   a. Those disobeying orders and instructions.
   b. Those showing a motion of antagonism and raising a sign of opposition.

c. Those disobeying the regulations by individualism, egotism, thinking only about yourself, rushing for your own good.
d. Those talking without permission and raising loud voices.
e. Those walking and moving without orders.
f. Those carrying unnecessary baggage on embarking.
g. Those resisting mutually.
h. Those touching the boat's materials, wires, electric lights, tools, switches, etc.
i. Those climbing ladder without orders.
j. Those showing action of running away from the room or boat.
k. Those trying to take more meal than given to them.
l. Those using more than two blankets.

2. Since the boat is not well equipped and inside being narrow, food being scarce and poor you'll feel uncomfortable during the short time on boat. Those losing patience and disobeying the regulations will be heavily punished for the reason of not being able escort.
3. Be sure to finish your "nature's call" evacuate the bowels and urine, before embarking.
4. Meal will be given twice a day. One plate only to one prisoner. The prisoners called by the guard will give out the meal quick as possible and honestly. The remaining prisoners will stay in their places quietly and wait for your plate. Those moving from their places reaching for your plate without orders will be heavily punished. Same orders will be applied in handling plates after meal.
5. Toilet will be fixed at the four corners of the room. The buckets and cans will be placed. When filled up a guard will appoint a prisoner. The prisoner called will take the buckets to the center of the room. The buckets will be pulled up by the derrick and be thrown away. Toilet papers will be given. Everyone must cooperate to make the room sanitary. Those being careless will be punished.
6. Navy of the Great Japanese Empire will not try to punish you all with death. Those obeying all the rules and regulations, and believing the action and purpose of the Japanese Navy, cooperating with Japan in constructing the "New order of the Great Asia" which lead to the world's peace will be well treated.

These orders to Wake Island prisoners from their captors are typical of the pernicious effect on human behavior in a war of aggression.

PETER FOSS (1)

Built:	1930	Propulsion:	Enterprise
	Foss Company		600-horsepower
	Tacoma, Washington	Primary Service:	Tacoma, Washington
Length:	62-feet	Final Foss Operating Day:	March 5, 1973
Beam:	19-feet	Status:	Sold – Domestic

PETER was the fourth tug in the series of the five similar tugs built by Foss-Tacoma during a ten-year program. The tug was named for Andrew's brother Peter who worked in the family shipyard in the early days. Knowing the tug would be used extensively around log rafts and boomsticks, Foss built her with a high deck rise forward to hold up her head in a sea, but a low freeboard aft to enable the crew to step from the after deck to log rafts and jump back aboard without doing a high hurdle over the bulwarks.

The early tugs built by Foss were planned and the construction supervised by Andrew, who before shipwrighting started, whittled a pine model of the proposed tug for everyone's guidance—and the tug always ended up having the shape of the model. The symetrical lines of the PETER and others of the class were the result of Andrew's attention to detail, a quality instilled in his sons and his shipwrights.

Foss installed a 375-horsepower Western Enterprise diesel which made the PETER one of the most powerful harbor tugs on Puget Sound. With the big engine she burned more fuel than most harbor tugs, using nearly eleven gallons per hour. Figuring other tug expenses in with the fuel, her hourly cost in 1932 was an exorbitant $8.80, nearly double the operating cost of the other harbor tugs—but the PETER produced more work in a shorter time, so her revenue more than offset the higher hourly cost.

The PETER was equipped with a galley and sleeping quarters for a day and night crew should she go on long-term work. And she did in 1932 on a towing job up the Umpqua River on the Oregon Coast. She relieved the JUSTINE FOSS towing gravel barges on the Highway 101 construction project. The PETER remained until the barging was completed later in the year and then returned to Tacoma harbor duty.

The PETER maintained a record of steady service until a calamity in November 1942 put a stop to her activities. Captain Glen Case and his crew had tied up the PETER and shifted to one of the smaller harbor tugs to do raft work in the shallow water log storages and while away on the early evening job, fire broke out on the PETER. Fortunately, the Foss dispatcher, Lucien Landry, spotted the flames at the first flare-up and called the Fire Department. About the same time the CARL FOSS with Captain Faye Hopkins pulled in to the Foss pier and the CARL's crew jumped on the FOSS 17, lying idle at the float, started the engine and trained the 17's fire monitor on the PETER. The Fire Department arrived in minutes and with heavy streams from hoses and monitor, the fire was smothered and out before enveloping the entire boat. Later when the smoke cleared, a quick inspection revealed Foss' pride of the harbor fleet to be a charred fire-scarred hulk. The detailed inspection confirmed that the pilot house, trunk cabin, and galley space below were destroyed. All furnishings in the pilot house, galley, and crew's quarters were ruined. The engine room, auxilliaries, and windless engine were now submerged in salt water, but they had been subjected to intense heat and all electrical wiring had melted. The evidence indicated the fire could have been caused by the galley range leaking diesel, igniting and catching the wood deck and bulkhead—although the galley range fire had been extinguished by the PETER's crew before leaving.

The damage report was not encouraging, but regardless, the Foss shipwrights went right to work and in a matter of months the superstructure was entirely rebuilt. The deck house was fashioned into a modern, three-tiered structure with the Captain's quarters just aft of the pilot house.

The PETER looking as good as new resumed towing, but in a dual role—as both harbor and linehaul tug. The combination continued during World War II years, as many of the regular linehaul tugs were assigned to the Army Transport Service. The PETER helped to make up for their absence. With the return of the war-duty tugs, the PETER was able to remain in the harbor and reclaim her title as Tacoma's chief harbor tug. She held the position until 1952 when the new BRYNN FOSS with her 800-horsepower assumed the Number One spot. However, due to the continued port growth the PETER remained a necessary part of the harbor action.

In early 1956 the PETER's 1930 Enterprise became unreliable, so she entered the Foss shipyard on March 16, 1956 for repowering. With improvements to cabins and hull and a new 600-horsepower Enterprise, the PETER didn't leave the yard until 1957 a 12 month's revamp. However, she again came out almost a new tug, which insured her position in the harbor, especially so with the 600-horsepower to widen her use.

For the next 16 years the PETER held her own with BRYNN, and the two tugs kept the harbor work right on schedule. But by 1973 and after 43 years the PETER was the worse for wear. The hull had lost its resiliency and considerable new wood was necessary to bring her up to acceptable standards and to add to her plight the engine needed a major overhaul.

She completed her last harbor assignment on March 2, 1973 and on March 5th the day crew delivered the PETER to the Foss shipyard in Seattle for a drydock survey. The result was negative, stating the wooden hull to be badly deteriorated, especially in and around the stern. To rebuild the hull and engine was not practical in view of the new, powerful steel tugs now available for harbor work, so Foss consigned her to the lay-up yard.

Shortly after retirement an offer to purchase the PETER came in and Foss accepted, so on April 1, 1974.Lutak Trading & Stevedoring Company of Haines, Alaska, purchased her. The new owners towed her to Duwamish Shipyard in Seattle for a complete overhaul. The hull repair was extensive and turned out to be very costly, but also successful. Engine rebuild and other mechanical repairs were made to bring the tug up to her former class. After many weeks of yard work she was accepted and ready for sea, but before starting for Haines, the PETER became the LUTAK PRIDE.

For several years she operated in the northern waters of southeastern Alaska, towing barges and logs for Lutak, then ownership passed to Samson Tug & Barge Company of Sitka for further towing in Alaska. The timing of the purchase was excellent as Samson shortly after lost one of their tugs, the KIOWA (ex-FOSS 19) in a surprise fall storm.

Samson Tug, to keep the LUTAK PRIDE efficient, repowered her with a new Caterpillar diesel and they made other refinements. The LUTAK PRIDE went back to work in the spring of 1979—towing logs in southeastern Alaska, keeping the Alaska Pulp & Paper Mill near Sitka supplied with rafts.

With all her various transplants, facelifts, and restorative operations, the LUTAK PRIDE will no doubt be pulling hard long past her fiftieth birthday—July 1980.

HENRIETTA FOSS

Built:	1931	Propulsion:	General Motors
	Tacoma, Washington		165-horsepower
Length:	49-feet	Primary Service:	Foss Yard – Seattle
Beam:	15-feet	Status:	In Service – 1979

The HENRIETTA from the time of the keel laying has always been a member of the Foss fleet, retaining the name of Henry Foss' daughter all through her long towing life. Due to her similarity to the PETER FOSS, she was called the "LITTLE PETER" by the designers of both boats, Henry Foss and Louis Berg. The HENRIETTA, built in Foss' own yard, was fashioned by expert workmanship, using the best of materials and proving it by still going strong after nearly fifty years of hard work.

The new tug had two special features—a fire monitor atop the wheelhouse with a pumping unit delivering 700-gallons per minute at 100-pounds pressure. The unit was used primarily for washing scows, but available and effective for fire fighting. The "LITTLE PETER" was the first Foss tug to have a bumper encircling the stern for protection from chaffing and bumping against barges. The fender, built of rubber tire sections, each about four inches wide and seven inches long, was held together by a steel cable passing through each piece and made fast to the bulwarks with tightening turnbuckles. After the HENRIETTA's prototype, the horse-shoe fender, with variations became a common installation on all tugs doing shifting work.

Foss powered her with a 160-horsepower Washington diesel—at that time considered powerful for a 50-foot boat.

HENRIETTA FOSS Shown here in 1971 towing a loaded cedar chip barge from Ballard to Shilshole Bay. (Photo from the author's collection)

After outfitting and working off the stiffness of the original heavy-duty engine, she started out towing on a schedule of 24 hours a day, 5 days a week and with no lay-ups. The original crew stayed with her for several years—in the 1930's a job was a job—they were hard to come by. The crew consisted of Captain, Mate, a combination Deckhand-Cook, and they all had a hand in oiling and maintaining the engine.

Her early years while based in Tacoma were spent towing hogged-fuel barges between Shelton and Everett; chip scows from Shelton and Tacoma to Port Townsend; and towing log rafts and lumber scows between Shelton and Olympia. Then about 1940 the HENRIETTA was sent over to Port Angeles as a harbor day-boat, but on occasion she had tows like the 30-hour run with boomsticks from Morrison Mill at Anacortes to Port Angeles.

The HENRIETTA's service in Port Angeles was interrupted for a few months when on January 11, 1942 she left for Neah Bay to work for the Austin Company, constructing the large breakwater from the Neah Bay shore to Waada Island. Her job was to run crews and supplies between the village of Neah Bay and Waada Island, also she shifted rock barges at the construction site. The HENRIETTA kept the job well serviced—and the skippers responsible were Captains Ed Reid and Don Price.

The job at Neah Bay ended in the spring and the HENRIETTA returned to Port Angeles, but only for a short stay. The time had come to replace the original engine as the cylinders of the 12-year old Washington were getting soft and the upkeep was too much for the crew to handle and do the harbor work at the same time. So on July 21, 1943 the rebuilt NANCY FOSS just out of the Foss-Tacoma shipyard went to Port Angeles and the HENRIETTA returned to Tacoma for repowering with a 140-horsepower high-speed Cummins diesel, which unlike the worn-out Washington required very little attention from the crew.

The HENRIETTA stayed on in Tacoma for harbor work with an occasional tow to Olympia and Shelton. Then after 22 years of steady service in her port of origin, she again went to Port Angeles to tend rafts for log ships. But after only 14-month's work the LELA FOSS with 325 horsepower replaced her. The LELA is a new steel harbor-class tug built by Foss to provide greater power.

The HENRIETTA then returned to Tacoma in April 1967 but not for long. In late 1968 she made another change, this time to Seattle for work in the Foss yard. Her chief duty was to provide service for the maintenance and repair division, shifting tugs and barges in and out of drydock and the repair piers. She also was delegated to maintain the Foss log storages in Lake Washington.

A special job the HENRIETTA performs in her new environment takes place in August at the hydroplane races during Seattle's Seafair. She tends the small-boat tie-up log boom on the eastside of the race course—much to the pleasure of her crew enjoying course-side seats.

The Seattle office kept her on the go until January 1978 when on a routine assignment towing logs in Salmon Bay, the main engine seized up. Foss decided the tug was still worth the cost of a new engine so the Yard repowered her with a 6-71 General Motors diesel and had her ready to go again in late February 1978.

The HENRIETTA has become the senior member of the Foss fleet and along with the CHRISTINE are the only wood hull tugs still operating under Foss ownership. From all appearances the industrious HENRIETTA will still be a working member of the Foss fleet on her 50th anniversary.

ANNA FOSS (1)

Built:	1907	Propulsion:	Enterprise
	Tacoma, Washington		300-horsepower
Length:	69-feet	Primary Service:	Puget Sound
Beam:	18-feet	Final Foss Operating Day:	August 2, 1968
		Status:	Sold – Later Sank

The ANNA FOSS, originally the VIGILANT, a wood two-deck boat with a 75-horsepower steam engine, was built by Ed Heath for the Wallace Towboat Company of Tacoma. After 13-years service for Wallace, they sold her in 1920 to Captain O. G. Olson for use by the newly formed Cascade Tugboat Company. Her stay with Cascade was short as in 1922 Gilky Bros. of Anacortes bought her for log towing in northern Puget Sound and British Columbia. Some three years later Captain C. C. Croft of Seattle traded his tug COLUMBIA for the VIGILANT. Then Captain Croft and partner W. A. Baker formed the Vigilant Towing Company of Seattle.

The VIGILANT operated 5 years for her new owners, but just one year with her old steam plant. On her last job as a steam tug she towed a scow loaded with three donkey engines, a steam shovel and miscellaneous logging equipment from Kirkland to the Campbell logging operation at the Hoko River on the Straits of Juan de Fuca.

In May 1926 a 200-horsepower 2-cycle Worthington diesel was installed and with the greater power of the new engine, she could tow heavy gravel scows. On one particular trip she completed a tow of 650-tons of gravel from the Friday Harbor pit in the San Juans to Ballard Locks in eleven hours—a new towing record at the time for a vessel her size and with only 200-horsepower. Her average speed for the trip was a surprising 5.7 knots!

In mid-1927 the VIGILANT shifted to another gravel run between Producers Rock & Gravel Company at Royal Bay, B.C. and Lake Union. Arriving at Royal Bay with two empty scows after a rough trip, the Captain, to be

ANNA FOSS Ex-VIGILANT shown entering Seattle Harbor. (Courtesy of Joe Williamson)

safe, made the tug and scows fast to the mooring buoy before going ashore to clear Customs at Victoria. But during the two hours he was away, the wind increased to a southeast gale and one scow broke loose from its tie and ground to pieces on the rocks. In the meantime, the buoy cable parted, and the VIGILANT with her second scow was driven ashore. Fortunately, the wind moderated and with a rising tide, the VIGILANT with her scow pulled free. Tug and scow were able to make Seattle for repairs.

The tug worked three additional years for Vigilant Towing Company, then they sold her in February 1930 to Anchor Tugboat Company of Portland, Oregon. The Anchor Company used her on the Columbia River, but only until 1933 when the firm ran into difficulties due to the Depression and as a result the VIGILANT went under the hammer at a U.S. Marshall's sale on August 1, 1933. Foss bid $5,300 and went home with the title.

They brought the VIGILANT back to Puget Sound and within a week after her return she was ready to tow, with Captain Lefty Howden in charge. For the tug's first Foss job she towed 32 sections of logs from Ladysmith, B.C. to Seattle. Since that first tow the VIGILANT brought down millions of feet of Canadian logs for the many mills operating in Salmon Bay and Elliot Bay.

When Captain Howden stepped aboard the tug for the first time in October 1933 he little realized that his home away from home for the next thirty years would be the VIGILANT—better known since 1938 as the ANNA FOSS, her name honoring the wife of Andrew's brother, Peter.

In 1938 the Worthington diesel started having breakdowns, causing delays, a result of the piston rings sticking. Her resourceful Chief Engineer Bert Thompson provided a remedy—he poured kerosene in the heads and that freed up the rings. However, Foss had a permanent cure in mind and to better fit the ANNA for heavy barge work, they repowered her with a 300-Enterprise diesel. The bigger engine was a boon to ANNA, she was able to chug along for years with few interruptions towing gravel scows, oil and rail barges and Monsanto Chemical waste-liquor barges.

On one of the ANNA's log towing jobs Captain Howden became involved in a game of lost-and-found. He had a 16-section log tow from Puget Sound to Victoria, B.C. and after going through Deception Pass it was necessary to make a run to Anacortes to clear at the U.S. Customs. The Captain tied the rafts to a rock pinnacle on the lee side of Burrows Island while he was away with the ANNA on the run to Anacortes. At daybreak he was back at Burrows Island and much to his chagrin the logs had vanished—the rock pinnacle had broken off!

The Captain figured, since the tide was flooding, the log tow must have drifted into Guemes Channel or continued up Rosario Straits. His first choice was Guemes Channel so he headed towards Anacortes and just past Shannon Point and still drifting east was the runaway tow. The ANNA, her 16 sections intact, was only a few hours late in arriving in Victoria even with the log-hunt diversion.

For many years the Foss-Seattle tugs had white painted hulls in contrast to the green hulls of the Tacoma-based tugs. But in 1940 there was an unexpected color alteration to one of the Seattle boats—the crew of the ANNA while southbound with a log tow for Seattle, decided white hulls required too much maintenance and green hulls would be less work, besides being better looking. So without further ado, the Mate Sam Stout, lowered a skiff over the side and in one afternoon painted the entire hull dark green. The ANNA became the first, though unauthorized, Seattle-based tug to display a green hull. When the ANNA arrived at the Seattle dock a few days later, the Seattle office staff voiced their disapproval and called the entire crew traitors! However, the green remained and as time went on other tugs, still without permission, were given green paint jobs. Eventually the Seattle and Tacoma divisions were no longer distinguished by color—the green prevailed.

By 1960 the ANNA completed more than 50 years of towing and the wood hull showed the strain. Even when idle alongside the Foss pier, it was necessary to keep a shoreside bilge pump going. Sometimes when running, abnormal leaks developed and the ANNA would be forced to give up her tow and head for home. This happened to her on October 11, 1961 when towing a Navy gasoline barge from Seattle to Whidbey Island. The water started coming in around the stem at the waterline, flooding into the chain locker and with the bilge pump running continuously the water still gained, so the ANNA gave up her barge to a relief tug and headed full bore for the Foss yard and drydocking. The ANNA's water problem was cured by recaulking around the stem and hood ends of the planking.

But more trouble was in store for the tug. What could have been a major disaster occurred on January 16, 1962 while she was shifting gravel scows in the Duwamish River. A mechanical failure prevented her from reversing at a critical moment, and she plowed into a moored barge inflicting serious damage to the tug's entire bow section. The stem, apron, planking, and bulwarks were sprung out of place, even the deck planking was buckled ten feet back from the stem. After three month's of shipwrighting, she was back on the oil and gravel runs.

Captain Howden continued with the ANNA until well past his sixty-fifth birthday and with forty-three years of towboating to his credit, he decided it was time to go ashore. So at the conclusion of a trip to the San Juan Islands on November 23, 1963 he turned in his accounts for the last time. The ANNA was able to continue on for only another six years, but Captain Howden is still going strong.

The ANNA continued with her Sound runs until the fall of 1967. Then as with all the veteran tugs, she was laid up when the fleet of new "J" and "D" class boats returned from the season's work in Alaska and were available for towing on the Sound.

The ANNA had a poor operating year in 1968 as there were sufficient new vessels to take care of the work, so the 60-year old tug was away from the pier for only 19 days between January and mid-July. However, she remained in ready-reserve, but the end was in sight.

Her final work for Foss began on July 30, 1968 at the time when the DEBORAH FOSS with her crew aboard was under repair at the Foss yard. In the morning a call came for a boat to do an immediate shifting job in Lake Washington. The ANNA was handy so the DEBORAH's crew commandeered the tug and two hours later they were under way. When they returned from the lake, the DEBORAH was still under repair, so the ANNA filled in and left for her much-visited gravel pit with two scows to load and return to Lake Union. She stayed on for three round trips and on the last one when nearing Ballard late in the evening of August 2nd, Captain Arlie Grimes and his crew were advised that when they delivered the loaded scows to the Seattle Ready-Mix Plant in north Lake Union, they were to return to the Foss dock and tie up the boat in an out-of-the-way berth as the ANNA was being permanently retired—at midnight the ANNA ended her hardworking career.

Foss sold her to the ANNA's former Chief Engineer, Everett Atkinson, in May 1969. Prior to the sale, Foss changed the name back to VIGILANT and painted the Foss green hull a nondescript black. Mr. Atkinson anchored the VIGILANT in Colvos Passage in front of his Vashion Island home. He kept a bilge pump going to take care of leaks, but on September 16, 1969 the pump apparently failed and the boat, with no one aboard, filled and sank in 40 feet of water, 20 miles from her birthplace.

No attempt was ever made to raise the VIGILANT and the hull soon became a home for all types of marine life. In a 1978 inspection only portions of the hull and the encrusted machinery were found.

MATHILDA FOSS *Hardly recognizable in 1937 when photographed in Tacoma prior to conversion. (Courtesy of Burton Thurber)*

MATHILDA FOSS (1)

Built:	1909	Propulsion:	Western Enterprise
	Willamette Iron & Steel		500-horsepower
	Portland, Oregon	Primary Service:	Puget Sound
Length:	91-feet	Final Foss Operating Day:	October 31, 1957
Beam:	22-feet	Status:	Sold – Domestic

The MATHILDA FOSS, ex-CAPTAIN GREGORY BARRETT, was originally a U.S. Army Quartermaster Corps passenger and freight vessel powered by a 375-horsepower compound steam engine. Her manning scale while based at the Presidio in San Francisco consisted of two officers and six crew men. The CAPTAIN BARRETT remained in active service as an Army supply boat until 1931 when the government declared her surplus and available for sale.

In September 1932 two brothers from Wilmington, California, George and Alfred Machris, purchased the boat and documented her as a private steam yacht, renaming her GORDON. The Machris' used the yacht for four years and then in the fall of 1936 removed all the machinery, equipment, and furnishings.

Foss saved the GORDON from a scrapping fate when they bought the dismantled vessel in November 1936. The steel hull was still in good condition and Foss figured that with new deck cabins and a powerful diesel engine they would have a superior tug capable of long range ocean or coastwise towing.

The JUSTINE FOSS towed the GORDON to Foss-Tacoma for rebuilding. After seven month's yard work, the boat came out with a new pilot house, new officer's quarters on the boat deck, and a remodeled galley, staterooms, and W.C.'s on the main deck. New on-deck equipment included an anchor windlass and a towing winch. In the engine room new auxilliaries were set in and a 500-horsepower Western Enterprise diesel installed for propulsion. The new engine enabled the tug to cruise 4,000 miles at 10 knots on a fuel capacity of 10,000 gallons. During the conversion, completed in late July 1937 she was given the name MATHILDA FOSS, honoring the wife of Iver Foss.

The MATHILDA began her career in August on local tows, then in December she started running to Alaska due to the ANDREW FOSS needing engine repair. The MATHILDA relieved her on the oil-delivery run from Edmonds to Southeastern ports for Union Oil Company.

After the ANDREW returned to the run, MATHILDA continued towing to Alaska, but with cargo barges to Southwestern. On the second voyage in 1939 she delivered a load of 140-foot fish-trap piling to Kodiak Island, arriving a little later than scheduled because of having to beach the tug to replace a broken propeller. With the piling delivered and when just starting the return trip, Roy Hall, the MATHILDA's skipper, picked up an SOS from the 4-masted codfish schooner SOPHIA CHRISTIANSON aground on a sand bar in the Aleutian Islands.

Captain Hall headed right out to the stranded ship, arriving a few days later. He found the schooner high and dry at low tide and imbedded in the sand, but Roy Hall was not dismayed. At high tide he made a hawser fast to the ship and opened up the MATHILDA's engine to full power. After pulling all out and even changing the angle, he had to give up—the sand friction held her fast. Then the resourceful Captain had another plan. He would wheel-wash with the propeller, a channel from the ship to deep water and also wash away the sand packed tight along the side. The next day he started the dredging and after two day's churning he had the channel dug and the sides free of sand. At the next high tide the Captain again put a line on the schooner and this time she broke loose, slid into the channel and followed the MATHILDA to deep water. An hour later the SOPHIA CHRISTIANSON with all sails drawing was underway. The MATHILDA headed for home—mission accomplished, a feat for the Foss record book.

The MATHILDA on arrival at Foss-Tacoma October 22, 1939 found a new venture in the offing. The U.S. Engineers required a strong sea-going tug to assist in the construction of airbases at Midway and Wake Islands—part of the planned Pacific Defense Program. Henry Foss arranged a charter for the MATHILDA on the Midway project—4,200 miles out in the Pacific, 1,300 miles west of Honolulu. Sand Island, one of the two circular atolls forming Midway, with an encircling reef, was picked for the airbase. It remained in U.S. hands in spite of the wartime Japanese attack.

The charter-party for the MATHILDA was dated October 18, 1939 only four days prior to the MATHILDA's return from Alaska. For the next six weeks the Foss yard crew conditioned and outfitted her for distant long-term work and ocean crossings. The charter was bareboat, however Foss did provide the crew with charters paying all expenses.

On December 3, 1939 the MATHILDA with Captain Hall again in command left Tacoma running light to San Francisco, arriving four days later. Instead of heading out for Honolulu under their own power, they were towed by the navy ship, SIRIUS, along with a dredge—a rather humiliating experience for an able-bodied tug. The reason was economy and safety—and they did arrive safely.

After loading stores at Honolulu, the MATHILDA was ordered to tow the bucket dredge on to Wake Island to scoop up coral sand from the lagoon and deposit it shoreside to build up the runways. The MATHILDA delivered the buck-dredge, made a fast turn-around and headed for Honolulu where a new skipper, Captain Gertulla, relieved Roy Hall and ran the MATHILDA on to Midway.

Then in September 1940 while still barging material for the U.S. Engineers and the Airbase Contractors, the navy took over the charter. The bareboat rate to Foss was $3,000 per month plus expenses with the same specified operating area, including the Hawaiian Islands, Midway, Wake, Palmyra Islands and the intermediate areas. The MATHILDA remained in navy service through 1945 towing supply and material barges and equipment to navy bases; and through all the years of exposure, she wasn't touched by enemy action—a charmed life indeed.

Right after W.W. II ended, the MATHILDA was placed in lay-up in Honolulu, her naval service over, and shortly after she returned home to resume the ordinary life of a commercial tug. She arrived in Tacoma on January 17, 1946 after an absence of seven years—entitled to Bronze Stars and Campaign Ribbons—if awards were made to tugs.

After the years of arduous work, the MATHILDA was in need of a complete reconditioning, as evidenced by the off-hire inspection reports. The survey stated that in general the vessel showed signs of hard usage, limited upkeep, and that the war-time alterations made in the hull and deck houses should be rebuilt and rearranged to suit Foss' requirements. Also the report warned that sections of the hull-plating forward and under the lower guard were wasted and when scale and rust were chipped off, a number of holes developed. Ten days in drydock were required to complete the hull repair, but several months for house repairs and alterations. Over fifty items were replaced or repaired throughout the boat and all machinery reconditioned. However, before starting any work the tug had to be fumigated to kill a dangerous breed of rats infesting the boat.

The "refit" required six months to accomplish and when she came out of the Foss yard in July 1946 decked out in shining green and white, there was no sign of the dull-grey, battered, and worn-down tug that had gone through the entire war. Under command of Captain Warren Waterman and Chief Engineer Ed Hansen, the MATHILDA re-entered Foss service out of Port Angeles, towing log rafts on the Straits and to Puget Sound ports. She joined the FOSS 21 and HENRY FOSS in regular service until the summer of 1951 when Foss-Seattle needed a tug for service

MATHILDA FOSS *Shown in tow of U.S.S. SIRIUS, December 1939 departing San Francisco for Government service in the Pacific at Midway Island. (Courtesy of Foss Tug Co)*

to southeastern Alaska, and the MATHILDA was their choice. Her principal run turned out to be towing loaded ore barges from the Taku Mine at Juneau to the smelter in Tacoma.

The MATHILDA went back to log towing in the fall and then in the summer of 1952 she towed on the southeastern barge runs. Except for the two summer seasons in Alaska service, she worked steadily for the Port Angeles division for several years and most of the time under the command of Captain Ron Tisdale.

The career of the MATHILDA came to an end due to engine wear and the deterioration of the hull plating between wind and water. During her later log towing days, extra care had to be exercised when working alongside a raft so not to heavily rub or bang the hull. Her Foss log-towing life ended in the evening of November 29, 1956 when the engine broke down off Clallam Bay. The crew tied up the log tow at Clallam and the NANCY FOSS towed the MATHILDA on to Port Angeles.

The engine repair was too extensive for the Port Angeles crew, so Foss towed her to Tacoma. However, with the usual winter curtailment in towing, Foss decided not to repair the engine at the time, so the MATHILDA went into lay-up until spring.

MATHILDA FOSS *Photographed in Seattle Harbor, September 1957. (Courtesy of Joe Williamson)*

In May 1957 the Seattle division required an additional tug for intermittant linehaul towing and MATHILDA came over for the job. The yard repaired the engine, but no work was done on the hull as the assignment was temporary and not too rigorous. She went to work in mid-May with Captain Roy Hough in charge and her former long time skipper, Ron Tisdale, as alternate.

For 5½ months she towed the Seattle-Port Townsend car-barge and at times she towed on various oil barge runs. Though the MATHILDA was an awkward boat to handle, she docked and undocked ships in the intervals between tows, generally in the Anacortes area helping tankers in and out of the oil refineries and in company with the PROS-PER and PALOMAR.

With the arrival for the winter of the newer and higher horsepower Seattle-based tugs from the seasonal Alaska runs, the need for the veteran MATHILDA was over, so on October 31, 1957 Captain Hough ran the tug to Foss-Tacoma where she went into permanent lay-up.

The outcome of a survey in drydock early in 1958 ended any possibility of the MATHILDA ever towing again for Foss. Most of the hull plates were badly wasted, some paper thin. The cost of replating, around $2,500 per plate, was prohibitive especially for a 50 year old tug with a 20 year old heavy-duty engine—Foss had no alternative, but to close her expense account.

The MATHILDA remained idle in Tacoma for the next 5½ years and then in August 1963 she had a buyer, Jensen Hardware & Marine of Ketchikan, Alaska, wanted her for use as a floating bunkhouse. Foss removed all machinery and readied her for the trip North as a towed vessel. On September 13, 1963 the WEDELL FOSS took her in tow for Ketchikan strung out behind the rail barge FOSS-250.

In Ketchikan, Jensen used her to house men in connection with a logging operation. This lasted for several years, then she was remodeled for use as a cafe. This wasn't successful so she ended up abandoned on the far side of Pennock Island. She had the name ROXANNE painted on her bows and her last-known owner, in 1975 was Jim Church.

The once-able MATHILDA continued to deteriorate, neglected and unwanted. Then a severe windstorm broke her loose from the tie-up and she drifted down the main channel past Ketchikan, becoming a menace to navigation. She was corralled and tied up—but not for long. An eyesore and a potential danger if she sank, certain people decided to remove the hulk, so on a dark night sometime in 1978 the ROXANNE was towed to deep water outside the greater Ketchikan area. Explosives were fastened to her sea cocks and detonated. The explosions tore out the sea cocks and she filled and sank, several hours before dawn—so passed the MATHILDA, but her eventful history remains.

ARCATA Shown as U.S. Revenue Cutter operating on Puget Sound during the First World War. Later to be rebuilt as the PATRICIA FOSS. (Courtesy of Joe Williamson)

PATRICIA FOSS (1)

Built:	1903	Propulsion:	Atlas
	W.A. Boole & Son Company		350-horsepower
	Oakland, California	Operating area:	Puget Sound
Length:	80-feet	Last Foss Operating Day:	November 3, 1957
Beam:	18-feet	Status:	Scrapped

The PATRICIA FOSS, originally known as the ARCATA, was built for the U.S. Revenue Service to carry compliance officers around the San Francisco Bay area in the course of enforcing Revenue-Customs laws. However, the ARCATA's operating time around the Golden Gate was very short.

PATRICIA FOSS *Running lite to Seattle Harbor in the mid-fifties. (Courtesy of Joe Williamson)*

The Revenue Service was inadequately represented on Puget Sound around the turn of the century, as the government had only two small underpowered boats to patrol many miles of shoreline. This situation brought on the golden years of smuggling goods and aliens into the country. For whenever the weather was stormy, the small Revenue cutters were harbor-bound, unable to face the rough going. Confining weather was the time of greatest illegal activity as the gales provided safe smuggling conditions—the most common and lucrative game was running in Chinese.

However, in 1904 after only one year of service in San Francisco Bay, the ARCATA with her crew of fifteen transferred to Puget Sound to make smuggling a costly business. The Revenue Service stationed her at Port Townsend, relieving the two small vessels for duty in the more sheltered waters of the Sound. For the next 14 years, she continued with Revenue law enforcement, search, seizure, and general harassment of smugglers until war changed her long-established use.

During the World War I years, the ARCATA operated as a naval vessel doing patrol duty on the west coast. Then when the war ended in 1918 the navy turned her over to the Coast Guard, as the U.S.C.G. had assumed the marine side of the Revenue Service—now known as the Customs Service.

With the passage of the Volstad Act in 1919 prohibiting the possession of intoxicating liquor, "rum running" became a flourishing business on all coasts and inland waters, including Puget Sound. The ARCATA became part of the Coast Guard enforcement fleet; and with her speed and firepower, she gave the rum-runners "a run for their liquor" and made many captures.

In 1926 the ARCATA changed stations; she transferred to the Seattle Port of Embarkation and operated out of the Port until 1936. At that time the need for the ARCATA-type cutter had ended and so the government declared the 33 year old boat surplus. Shortly after, Foss bought the vessel, but not for law enforcement.

Foss put the ARCATA in their own shipyard for conversion. They cut away the after-end of the wardroom and made space for a towing winch. Next the bulwarks were cut down to the lines of a tug, particularly around the fantail. Her 13 × 26 × 20 steam compound-engine and the boiler were removed and replaced with a 250-horsepower, open-base Sumner diesel, a rather primitive engine for 1936 but probably greatly reduced in price.

The ARCATA started her towing life under Captain Mike Hilton in late 1936, but as the tug PATRICIA FOSS, named for the eldest daughter of Arthur and Ellen Foss. She operated reasonably well with the Sumner diesel doing general towing on Puget Sound with occasional trips to Alaska. Although after five years, the engine had to be changed. Fortunately Foss had just the right one on-hand at the time for a replacement. Having a 350-horsepower Atlas engine readily available came about as a result of an event that occurred several years earlier involving a vessel-sinking in Alaska.

In February 1937 the Alaska Transportation Company's freight and passenger vessel ZAPORA left Seattle on a regularly scheduled run to southeastern Alaska. While northbound from Ketchikan to Hoonah, the 155-foot vessel struck a rock on the western shore of Admiralty Island near Angoon. The 31-year old ship sank rapidly with no loss of life, but taking with her 10,000 pounds of frozen salmon and 53,000 pounds of sable fish. In March of 1937 being in shallow waters, the ZAPORA was sold on an "as-is-where-is" basis. The ZAPORA's engine, a 350-horsepower Atlas diesel, was recovered by divers and subsequently sold to Foss. They barged it down to Seattle and completely rebuilt the engine for future use, and the time came just prior to World War II when the PATRICIA's Sumner diesel was ready to give up.

The PATRICIA entered the Foss shipyard in 1941 and in three months she had her new engine ready to take on heavier tows. She operated for the Seattle office on Puget Sound and adjacent waters for the remainder of her career—towing all types of barges and gravel scows. She worked steadily without major breakdowns, except in July 1942 when she lost her propeller towing a log raft up the Duwamish Waterway. Hard to believe today, but true, the total cost of the new wheel, renewing a plank, repairing the rudder and stock, drydocking and shipyard work, came to only $1,243!—just 37 years ago.

During the early 1950's the PATRICIA made countless barge trips to Nanaimo, British Columbia, to pick up lumber barges for delivery to Seattle and Tacoma. During this time she was in charge of Captains Walt Davis and Walt Stark, with Captains Bill Erickson and Sam Stout finishing out the last years of the PATRICIA's service.

By 1957 the tug had seen her best days and the Maintenance and Repair Department worked on her engine almost every trip. Before a decision was made as to the proper long-range corrective action, the answer came on November 3, 1957 when relief Captain Sam Stout brought the PATRICIA to the Foss dock and advised the M & R Department that the engine exhaust blow-by was so bad that the gasses were causing a definite health hazard.

After several hours of engine inspection, the results clearly indicated the need of a complete overhaul and rebuild. With the report in hand and in a matter of days, Foss decided the PATRICIA had reached the end of her useful life. The yard shifted her from the operations pier to the lay-up float at the Foss farm where she stayed for the next year. Then Foss towed her to more permanent moorings at Kennydale on Lake Washington. The next move in 1963 was to the Tacoma yard to remove the engine and all other machinery. Stripped to the hull, she then joined several other Foss tugs in the Tacoma lay-up fleet for final disposal.

That time came on the evening of July 4, 1967 when the PATRICIA, looking like an active tug in the concealing dusk, was towed out to Commencement Bay and set afire along with the FOSS 12, no doubt to represent the Torch of Liberty as part of Tacoma's Independence Day celebration—a patriotic finish for the PATRICIA.

Even tugboats have embarrassing moments as shown when the old PATRICIA missed the channel at Shilshole Bay and ended up out of the water. (Photo courtesy of Foss Tug Co)

WANDERER *Photographed during a 4th of July celebration in 1903. (Courtesy of Joe Williamson)*

WANDERER

Built:	1890	Propulsion:	Steam
	Port Blakely, Washington		800-horsepower
Length:	128-feet	Primary Service:	Puget Sound
Beam:	24-feet	Final Foss Operating Day:	February 16, 1947
		Status:	Dismantled

Tugboating started on Puget Sound as a means of transporting logs produced from local forests to sawmills built in deep-water ports around the Sound. The logs were dumped in the water and made up into towable rafts for the wood and coal-burning tugs to hook their towline on and deliver to the waiting mills.

As the output of lumber increased, so did the number of ocean sailing ships increase to keep the lumber moving to world markets. The sailing ships gave the Sound tugs a second line of work—towing the windjammers from Cape Flattery to the mill loading-docks.

The WANDERER, one of the better early tugs was built for the Port Blakely Mill Company to handle logs and tow ships, through any type of weather. She carried her name all through her towing career, even though she was later owned by Foss.

With the increase in number and size of ships calling on Puget Sound for forest products, it was necessary for each of the four major mill companies to have a tug standing by off the Cape at all times to pick up and tow, without delay, vessels scheduled to load at their respective mills. However, the mills found they could not afford this individual expensive service. Their log towing was handicapped and stand-by tug time on the boats assigned to the Cape Flattery station proved far too costly.

To rectify the situation cooperation between the mills was essential, so in 1891 four of the largest mills formed a tugboat pool, with each company supplying one tugboat from its fleet for the purpose of escorting and towing sailing ships. Port Blakely Mill Company supplied the WANDERER; Tacoma Mill Company the TACOMA; Washington Mill Company the 14-year old RICHARD HOLYOKE; and Pope & Talbot Puget Mill supplied the TYEE, which had been built in Port Ludlow in 1884 and was the most powerful tug at the time in the Unied States.

These four large steam tugs burned coal and had powerful reciprocating engines turning a screw propeller, a big improvement over the big sidewheels which were still in evidence even in the late Nineties. The four tugs made up the first organized towing company on Puget Sound and it was appropriately called Puget Sound Tugboat Company with the first headquarters at Port Townsend. Captain Libby of the Puget Mill Company was appointed manager of the company. By 1900 nine additional tugs had been added to the fleet, including a new 128-foot steel tug named TATOOSH, built in Seattle at a cost of $80,000 and Seattle became the new company base in 1900.

Wages on these big tugs were high for the time and Puget Sound Tugboat Company paid the highest of any outfit in the business—Captains received $200 a month; Chief Engineers $150; Mates $75; Cooks $50; and others $40. Fringe benefits were unheard of in 1900. In 1979 wages for tugs of comparable size and service without overtime would average $1,800 for Captains; $1,700 for Engineers; $1,600 for Mates; $1,200 for Cooks, and $1,000 for others—plus all the welfare extras.

With thirteen tugs in the fleet, four could be spared to cruise between Cape Flattery and up to fifteen miles off shore to meet incoming vessels. Ships rarely had to wait for a tug to take them in tow. On the outbound runs, the tugs towed loaded ships well clear of the Cape—about 130 miles from Seattle. The tug fleet was successful and fully occupied until late 1907.

That winter a business slump occurred affecting the whole country. Shipping and lumber demand on the West Coast slowed so much that sailing ships and steamers arriving on the Coast and Sound ports were unable to obtain charters and they were forced to stand by until conditions improved. The owners of the lumber carrying ships could not obtain full cargoes and the rates offered for the small amount of lumber to transport was too low to continue operating. With freight rates way below the break-even point, it was more economical to lay up the vessels than attempt to send them to sea only partially loaded and at a heavy loss.

By the summer of 1908 some twenty lumber carriers were in lay-up at Port Townsend and Eagle Harbor. With shipping on the Sound tied up for lack of cargo, tugboats were hard pressed to find work. Four of the P.S.T.C. boats were idle, including the WANDERER, and unfortunately during the next several years she rarely left the dock.

As an economy move, P.S.T.C. in 1914 started to dispose of their floating equipment. They realized that with the opening of the Panama Canal and the increasing dissolution of the merchant sailing ship fleet, the need for ocean-going assist tugs was practically over.

In 1916 the WANDERER was sold to Merrill & Ring Lumber Company for towing logs produced by their logging operations on the Straits of Juan de Fuca. Puget Sound Tugboat Company continued selling the rest of the fleet and so after 1920 only the veteran tug PIONEER remained and six years later they sold her. With the liquidation of all the company equipment, the corporation finally dissolved in 1931 after forty years of operating a fleet of the most eye-appealing tugs ever to travel the waters of Puget Sound and the Straits.

The WANDERER operated with Hudson Morrison as Skipper for the next twenty years, towing logs for Merrill & Ring primarily out of the Pysht River on the Straits to Port Angeles and Sound ports. Then in 1936 they sold the tug to Foss.

The WANDERER with Foss crew and colors continued to tow M. & R.'s logs from their Pysht River dump to Port Angeles. However, she was not an exclusive log-tower as she towed barges for the Seattle office, especially during the World War II years. As the WANDERER approached 50 years in age, her timbers were becoming slack in the joints and the crew related that when running in the Straits with a westerly swell, the bilge pump ran continuously to take care of the leaks. She was so loose that hull, deck, and house did a *double* twist as she rolled and pitched!

Nevertheless, the WANDERER carried out an unusual towing job in 1939. She moved the massive concrete pontoons from the builders' yard in Seattle to the construction site for the first Lake Washington Floating Bridge built by the State Highway Department.

Also in May of the same year, the WANDERER took part in the Maritime Day tugboat race—Puget Sound Tug & Barge's diesel flagship NEPTUNE won the race at an average of 13.3 knots and American Tugboat Company's diesel tug PETER came in second. The sentimental favorite, WANDERER, with Captain Lloyd Davis ended up third, but with her tall stack belching steam and her long smooth lines, she presented the most thrilling sight of all the tugs—and most of the cheering was for her.

The WANDERER spent her final towing years on barge runs as the linehauls were easier on the veteran tug and they no doubt extended her useful life. In the middle 40's for her principal job, she towed Milwaukee Railroad car barges between Seattle, Port Townsend, and Bellingham, and while on this run she ended her career.

WANDERER *Aground at Doublebluff on Puget Sound February 16, 1947. Fog caused the grounding. (Courtesy of Joe Williamson)*

On the foggy morning of February 16, 1947 the WANDERER under Captain Walt Stark, her skipper for four years, was running on compass courses between check points due to the fog blanket. Then due to a strong current-set, the WANDERER ran past her next course change and she grounded near Double Bluff. The 57 year old hull was further strained, although not holed or severely damaged. However, it was a case of the "last straw." Her unseaworthy condition, plus the disadvantages of steam power and the presence of many World War II diesel tugs available for commercial service meant the WANDERER's time was over—she could only be run on sentiment, a very expensive item.

Two days later Foss pulled her off at high tide, towed her to the Foss pier, and the yard crew removed all usable items. She ended up sunk at the mouth of the Nisqually River as part of a breakwater. However, her remains were visible for many years. Finally the ravages of time, wind, and sea reduced her to only a memory, but she had her day—the pride of Puget Sound's first towing fleet.

AGNES FOSS (I)

Built:	1904	Propulsion:	Enterprise (Twin)
	Philadelphia, Pa.		1,500-horsepower
Length:	142-feet	Primary Service:	Ocean and Coastwise
Beam:	30-feet	Final Foss Operating Day:	December 4, 1969
		Status:	Sold—Foreign

The AGNES FOSS, long before becoming a tug boat, served the U.S. Army as a mine planter, one of eight built from 1904 to 1909 on the East Coast. The second ship in the series;, the Col. GEORGE ARMISTEAD, later became the AGNES FOSS. The ARMISTEAD, carrying a crew of five officers and thirteen enlisted men remained in active Army service for 32 years.

She began her career on the Atlantic Seaboard, but eventually transferred to the West Coast with Fort Winfield Scott, California, her home port. After a number of years the Army again relocated her, this time to Portland, Oregon—the ARMISTEAD's working base for the next nine years. 1934 was her last active year for the Army. After that she remained in lay-up at San Francisco, until the Foss Company purchased her in 1937. Prior to the sale, the Army removed the upper deck, lifted out the engines and all equipment, leaving a bare boat.

Foss towed the dismantled ARMISTEAD to Seattle in mid-1937 and placed her in dead storage at the Foss moorings until early 1941 when she entered the Lake Washington shipyard for rebuilding to an ocean-going tug. The survey report made before conversion stated that the remaining wood deck and wood pilot house were badly deteriorated; however, the condition of the hull and steel superstructure was good and had been well-maintained. The survey gave and as-is value of the bare boat at $80,000.

For the next six months she received a thorough refit and repowering, including a new pilot house and a rebuilt main deck house. All the quarters above and below decks were renewed. Twin Enterprise diesel engines were in-stalled as well as new auxilliary machinery. The cost of the refit came to $300,000 and the completed tug survey in early 1942 gave a fair replacement value of $480,000. Foss' largest tug was given the name of AGNES in honor of the wife of Henry Foss.

On her trial run in February, the Agnes averaged an 11-knot speed under adverse conditions and her crash-stop test took only forty seconds. The trim-appearing AGNES had very little opportunity to demonstrate her worth on the usual Foss runs as the navy drafted her soon after completion to assist in the World War II Western Pacific defence program.

COL. GEO. ARMISTEAD At the Foss moorings in Ballard shortly after being towed up from California by the AR-THUR FOSS in 1938. Three years later she emerged as the AGNES FOSS. (Courtesy of Joe Williamson)

The navy had contracted with a joint-venture group of Hawaiian Dredging Company, Raymond Concrete Pile Company, Turner Construction Company, Morrison-Knudsen, and the J. H. Pomeroy Company, to construct airbases around the Western Pacific. In late 1941 the Naval Airbase Contractors began chartering ocean-going tugs to service dredging and construction sites. Foss Company turned over a number of their vessels to the contractors, both ocean and harbor tugs. The agreement included the AGNES FOSS, which at the time, December 1941 was still in the shipyard. When ready, the AGNES would be used by the contractors at Pearl Harbor, around the Hawaiian Islands and at Midway, Wake, Johnston, and Palymyra Islands.

After completing her test runs in February 1942 Foss delivered the AGNES to the U.S. Navy at Seattle as the navy acted as agent for the joint-venture group. Later in the month the AGNES, now covered with navy-gray paint, left for Honolulu in charge of Captain Vince Miller.

The AGNES remained in the Contractor's hands all during the war covering approximately 200,000 miles towing supply barges, scows, and equipment, servicing navy military bases in the Pacific. In all her traveling and many times exposed to enemy action, she escaped without damage and earned a reputation for "well-done" assignments. She was most deserving of a Citation Award after so many years of armed services duty and taking a vital part in two wars.

After 5 years she was returned to Foss in April 1947 at Seattle, and the necessary refitting and repair work at Todd Shipyard and the Foss yard took only until mid-May.

Foss put the AGNES right to work towing to Alaska, delivering heavy tandem tows, with no problems—summer or winter. In 22 years of post-war towing for Foss she completed hundreds of trips to Alaska, Hawaii, the South Pacific, Central America, the Orient, and Southeast Asia. In her time she was a top revenue producer.

One of the AGNES' noteworthy voyages to Alaska occurred on June 16, 1950 when she delivered the first barge load of bulk cement from Puget Sound to Anchorage. The recently converted LST, FOSS-205, carried 3,016 tons of cement on the pioneer run and shortly after there were four Foss tugs and barges on a regular schedule towing bulk cement to Anchorage. The 30-year old cement service is still in operation, an important run to the Foss Company and for the Foss tugs, lasting eight months a year during the ice-free season.

In December 1951 the AGNES made an interesting voyage from Honolulu to Long Beach towing half of the W.W. II-built tanker, FORT DEARBORN. In March 1947 the tanker, enroute to Shanghai from San Francisco with a full load of fuel oil, broke in two sections 800 miles northwest of Honolulu. Some of the crew lost their lives in the accident and the surviving members were rescued from the floating sections. The forepart, a menace to navigation, was sunk by gunfire and the after section still intact and containing the machinery was towed to Honolulu and sold to the Hilo Electric Light Company for use as a municipal power plant. Then in December 1951 the machinery-end of the FORT DEARBORN was sold to National Iron Company of Long Beach, California for scrap and the AGNES with Captain Ray Quinn went to Honolulu to pick up the strange tow. Captain Quinn reported the eastbound voyage required 33 days of hard towing at a speed of about 6½ knots. The ship carried 2,000 tons of scrap metal for ballast and that gave her a deep draft and more resistance. Upon arrival the Captain was ribbed for arriving with only half a ship.

The AGNES spent the next two years towing cargo barges to Alaska. Then Captain Miller and his 14-man crew worked for Phillips Petroleum Company in exploration work at Icy Bay, Alaska. Until the winter storms started to buffet the coast of western Alaska. Vince Miller headed the AGNES home and they arrived on November 12, 1954 looking forward to time off—but it was not to be. Thirty-six hours after arrival, the AGNES with her regular crew headed out to sea again.

A Panamanian freighter, the MARGO, broke her propeller-shaft and was drifting helplessly in the North Pacific. Foss won the competitive bid for the tow and the AGNES was picked for the job—she was stored and fueled in a matter of hours. In six days the AGNES reached the disabled ship, wallowing in heavy seas 875 miles off the Washington Coast. During the entire westbound trip the AGNES' crew battled hurricane-force winds and fifty foot seas. The storm was one of the season's worst and from November 20 through November 23 the wild tempestuous weather continued unabated. The AGNES and a Coast Guard cutter could only stand by the helpless ship and hope she held together. The storm moderated sufficiently on the 24th to hook up towing gear and get under way for the Columbia River. However, the weather remained stormy all during the return trip, so it wasn't until November 29 that the AGNES safely delivered the battered MARGO, with the crew still aboard her at Tongue Point on the Columbia River. The AGNES arrived in Seattle the next day, and this time the crew did have an uninterrupted shore leave.

After another two years on the established runs North, the AGNES in June 1957 left Seattle on another pioneering trip towing the barge FOSS-207 to St. Lawrence Island in the Bering Sea. This voyage and another similar trip by the JUSTINE FOSS in the same month marked the first time that private operators handled the so-called "Mona

AGNES *Shown in typical rough seas of the Pacific Ocean, an area often traversed by the AGNES between 1942 and 1969. (Courtesy of Harry McDonald)*

Lisa'' project, supplying the far North military installations that the Navy had taken care of since their establishment. The AGNES' trip was the start of countless DEW Line voyages for the government.

For a number of years the AGNES took part in the annual resupply program to the Bering Sea and the Arctic Ocean, at times running as far east as Barter Island and as far north as Point Barrow. Included in the supply missions were mid-winter fuel re-supply runs to the Air Force Base at Shemya Island in the outer reaches of the Aleutian Islands and the AGNES was always assigned to the job. The weather at Shemya was generally stormy and many times too violent to discharge cargo. It was not unusual to lay off the dock for days on end waiting for a slight moderation in weather to enable the tug and barge to dock and unload. Two winters in a row, the 5,800 mile round-trip voyage took nearly two months to complete for Captain Erskine Nicol and his crew—the wind on one trip held above 50 knots for two straight weeks!

A welcome change of climate for the AGNES occurred in February 1964 when Foss assigned her to tow the large suction dredge McCURDY from Seattle via Honolulu to Kwajalein Atoll in the Marshall Islands. Tug and tow left Seattle on February 21, 1964 and after stopping in Honolulu on March 10, to add a barge to the tow, they continued on to the South Pacific. Fortunately, one of the crew members aboard the AGNES was a ham radio operator and through another "ham" in Seattle, was able to maintain daily contact with the Seattle office—this was three years before the advent of long-range single side-band communication radios on ocean-going tugs. After a good-weather voyage, the AGNES arrived at Kwajalein on March 29, the same atoll the U.S. Marines battled to regain in W.W. II. With the dredge anchored and the cargo discharged, the AGNES headed for home towing the empty barge, arriving on April 25 completing a 64-day voyage of 9,400 miles.

After a short period in the yard for voyage repairs, the AGNES returned to Alaska runs, including a trip to the Arctic late in the summer, handling the re-supply to the Bering Sea stations.

Then in 1965 with oil drilling exploration going full swing in Cook Inlet and drilling platform construction under way, the AGNES barged supplies to the Inlet until mid-1966.

In August she was given a long-term and long-distance assignment. Her orders called for picking up a floating machine shop at Panama and delivering it to Vietnam—the War was very active at the time. With her regular skipper, Captain Nicol, aboard, the AGNES left Seattle August 14th on her way to assist in her third war. She arrived in Panama on August 30th and departed the next day for Vietnam via Kwajalein for fuel. After an uneventful voyage across the Pacific at an average speed of 7.8 miles, the AGNES and her sea-weary crew arrived at Qui Nhon, South Vietnam on October 28th after a 49-day crossing. With less than a day at Qui Nhon, the AGNES headed for home by way of Guam. But upon arrival at Guam the crew learned that the AGNES was to go on charter to Alaska Barge & Transport, the private tug and barge operator in South Vietnam, working on a long term contract for the Military Sea Transportation Service. A.B.&T. tugs were in need of drydocking and repairs and to maintain the vital tug and barge service without interruption they chartered outside tugs for interim duty.

The AGNES first went to Hong Kong for voyage repairs, then back to Vietnam and started on charter to A.B.&T. December 2, 1966. (Story of MARTHA FOSS 2 details the tug and barge operations in Vietnam.) The AGNES, with Captain Nicol and later Captain Salo, along with MARGARET FOSS continued barging war material around Vietnam until mid-May of 1967 when the regular fleet of A.B.&T. returned to work.

Then the two Foss tugs proceeded to Hong Kong for voyage repairs, drydocking and off-charter inspection. After acceptance by Foss, the AGNES, being in better condition was ordered to tow the MARGARET to Seattle. Captain Jay Jacobson who had been on the MARGARET for the past eight months assumed command of the AGNES and left Hong Kong on June 7th for the non-stop voyage. The A.B.&T. crewmen on the two tugs remained for further Vietnam service and the unneeded Foss men went home by plane.

After an uneventful crossing of 32 days, the tugs arrived home in Seattle on July 10th. The AGNES served without failure and returned home in good condition after 330 days of continuous operation under hazardous conditions.

She remained at the dock for the next six weeks undergoing voyage repairs and re-outfitting. Then in mid-September she returned to the Alaska run hauling bulk cement until freezing weather closed the season in Cook Inlet. But the AGNES' season wasn't over, she had yet to buck the North Pacific winter weather by towing a 32,000 barrel loaded oil barge from Seattle to Amchitka Island in December 1967, this time under the guiding hand of Captain Tom King. After a storm-tossed 54-day round trip voyage, the AGNES and her barge arrived at the Foss pier, with fresh rust streaks decorating the hull.

While the tug crew prepared for the next trip, with several weeks leave, the AGNES during the time was being prepared by the yard crew for a long voyage to Japan and Cook Inlet, Alaska.

On March 19, 1968—again with Captain Tom King in command, the AGNES left Seattle with a tandem barge tow for Hiroshima, Japan. The tow turned out to be a slow drag what with bucking a heavy westerly swell and so taking 51 days to make the crossing.

After a three week lay-over in Hiroshima, the AGNES headed out with her same two barges loaded with pipe for the Cook Inlet Alaska oil fields. After a much better eastward run with following wind and sea, the AGNES arrived in the inlet after a 31-day voyage, on July 4th. With only a few hours lay-over and not taking time to join the Day's celebration, the AGNES returned to Seattle, arriving home on July 11th, completing a 10,000 mile trip lasting 114 days.

The AGNES made only one additional voyage in 1968 but it was another long one of 68 days covering three separate assignments in western Alaska. She left Seattle on July 16 with a fully loaded general cargo barge for the Kuskokwim River port of Bethel in Alaska's Bering Sea. Arriving two weeks later, and after a week discharging cargo, she headed with the empty barge for Cook Inlet and her second assignment, to tow a general cargo deck-barge to the Arctic Ocean port of Kotzebue. The PATRICIA brought the Kotzebue barge to Cook Inlet and exchanged tows with the AGNES as she was better suited to make the run to the Arctic.

By September 26th she had arrived at Kotzebue, discharged the cargo and was on her way to Dutch Harbor in the Aleutians. Upon arrival, the AGNES tied up the empty barge and then ran light to Cold Bay on the south side of the Alaska Peninsula to relieve the ELLEN FOSS of a loaded diesel barge for delivery to a land-based oil exploration site near Port Moller of the north side of the Alaska Peninsula. The AGNES stood by at Port Moller for several days until the barge was moved to the beaching site and discharging commenced. Four days later, the ELLEN returned for the barge and the AGNES headed for Dutch Harbor to retrieve her own barge. With all assignments now complete, the AGNES with Captain Howard Kuehny, pulled out for home, arriving October 22nd, disappointed to find out the AGNES wasn't listed on the Foss board for a winter job.

During the early months of 1969 prospects for a spring job appeared remote. However, in late April ocean and coastwise work increased to the point where the use of the AGNES was necessary to take care of the up-surge. And so four days after the order came to ready the AGNES, she was under way for Eureka, California on a 10-day run towing the chemical barge FOSS-260 to the Louisiana-Pacific Pulp Mill. Her second assignment in her last year with Foss was towing a loaded bulk-cement barge to Anchorage. A fitting run for her last voyage to Alaska as the AGNES had initiated the haul nineteen years before.

Her final long-distance tow for Foss began on July 4, when the AGNES, under Captain Tim Lyness, left Seattle with equipment and explosives for a construction job in the Hawaiian Islands—the crew losing out on the national holiday. Arriving Honolulu after a fair-weather trip and with the cargo discharged, the AGNES and the empty barges started for Seattle, but two days out they were diverted to Alameda, California under new orders to tie up the barges and make up a tandem ship tow. Arriving on September 7th, the AGNES proceeded at once to line out the special tow—two Navy destroyer escort vessels for delivery to Portland, Oregon. The D-E's were safely delivered a week later and on September 17th, the AGNES was back in Seattle, her last long ocean voyage for Foss Company in the Log Book.

After a three week lay-up, the AGNES completed three trips from Bellingham to Eureka with the chemical barge FOSS-260. Her last trip in late November was also her last run under Foss colors. She had then completed 28 years of proficient service for Foss and 30 years for the government.

The economics of operating an underpowered and super-annuated tug indicated permanent retirement, especially so in a competitive towing market demanding high horsepower, efficient and sophisticated tugs. Foss' replacement program was constantly bringing into action modern competitive boats able to out-produce the one-time highliners of the fleet.

The AGNES had to give way to progress, so she joined the lay-up fleet in Ballard rubbing the piling until November 1970. Then a second chance came her way—Luzon Stevedoring Company of Manila, Philippine Islands purchased the AGNES, along with the retired MIKI tug ANNA FOSS (ex DONNA FOSS), for towing in the Philippines and the South China Sea. After transfer of title Luzon renamed both tugs—AGNES became CELTIC and ANNA changed to BRUIN.

Then on November 14th, after voyage preparation and outfitting, the tugs with Filipino crews left the Foss pier for the last time and headed for Manila. They arrived in the Philippines safe and sound, less ocean wear-and-tear after a month's voyage.

The latest word from Luzon, in mid-October 1978 advised that the CELTIC was still towing barges around the Philippines and going strong in spite of her 58 hard-working years and twenty-seven of those spent under Foss care and guidance, a contributing factor to her long life.

CATHERINE (1)

Built:	1899	Propulsion:	Union
	Hanson Shipyard		350-horsepower
	Seattle, Washington	Primary Service:	Puget Sound
Length:	67-feet	Final Foss Operating Day:	November 5, 1964
Beam:	17-feet	Status:	Sold - Domestic

The coal-burning steam cannery tug KATHADIN, long before she became CATHERINE FOSS, was owned by the Anacortes Packing Company and used in northern Puget Sound towing fish-scows and floating fish-traps. Her service for Anacortes Packing turned out to be very brief for they sold her in July 1901 to Alaska Packers Association of San Francisco. However, A.P.A. made Blaine, Washington, the KATHADIN's home port and she spent the next thirteen years working on Puget Sound. Her skippers during the A.P.A. ownership were Captains Krull and Humphreys, old hands in the fish packing business.

In April 1917 the KATHADIN's life as a cannery tender ended when Cary-Davis Towing Company of Seattle bought her for use as a tugboat. Captain J.R. Thurston was first in charge, followed by Elmer Olsen and Roy Small. Cary-Davis, within a year, had three other tugs in operation, the EQUATOR, CHEHALIS, and OREGON, giving the new Company good coverage for all of Puget Sound.

The KATHADIN continued in service until the mid-'20s when Cary-Davis laid her up in favor of newer oil-fired steam tugs and economical diesel tugs. Her firebox remained cold for several years and from all appearances, the KATHADIN would never tow another raft of logs. But the Wagner Tugboat Company of Seattle could see a use for the tug and they bought her in June 1930.

Wagner updated the KATHADIN; they removed the engine, boilers, and deckhouses, then installed a 6-cylinder, 350-horsepower Union diesel. New fuel tanks with a capacity of nearly 5,000 gallons, giving a cruising

CATHERINE *Photographed abeam of Seattle, January 24, 1961 three weeks prior to a thirteen month lay-up at Seattle headquarters. (Courtesy of Foss Tug Co)*

range of 1,800 miles, were fitted down below. With the addition of a new modern deckhouse, she appeared as a late-model and powerful linehaul tug.

The KATHADIN started her Wagner service in September 1930 and on one of her early tows, with Captain William Spurgeon, she towed 24 sections of logs from Anacortes to Shilshole Bay in 25 hours, a distance of 65 miles. Good time with a drag of almost 4,000 tons. However, the KATHADIN was planned for international towing and shortly after her trial runs, she started on long hauls from Union Bay and Chemainus, B.C. to Seattle with log rafts — a 115-mile tow.

In the following years she earned a record of superior performance even though her operating cost was high, caused by having the engine controlled only from the engine room and not from the pilot house. The arrangement required an engineer on watch at all times when running, but it had one advantage, the engineers were able to maintain the big diesel in excellent condition and the Union never let them down. The general appearance of the tug always drew compliments, she had the reputation of being one of the best cared-for tugs on the Sound and with this in mind another owner was ready to acquire the KATHADIN's excellence and reputation.

In the Wagner Towboat Company purchase, Foss obtained the showy tug and Captain Frank Reardon, her skipper at the time of the transfer, continued to run her on the Wagner routes until late 1939 when she was transferred to Port Angeles for log towing on the Straits and to up-Sound ports.

The tug retained her original name until July 1940 when in keeping with Foss' current policy of using family names, the KATHADIN became the CATHERINE FOSS in honor of a daughter of Chris and Hildur Foss.

The CATHERINE continued her long-time log-towing career by towing Merrill & Ring Logging Company rafts from the Pysht River to Port Angeles. She did this on a regular schedule, weather permitting, often bringing 18 log sections to Port Angeles making the 40-mile tow in 17 hours. For variation, she occasionally delivered one of her tows to the Crown Zellerbach Mill at Port Townsend. During her four-year stint in Port Angeles, the CATHERINE was involved in two serious incidents, one of which ended in tragedy.

The first occurred in the early morning fog in Admiralty Inlet on November 26, 1941. Captain Russ Benthein's Log Book entries state that the CATHERINE was running light from Seattle to Discovery Bay to pick up a log tow. At 0100, Point-no-Point was passed and at the time the sky was overcast, but within twenty minutes, the Mate had to slow the tug to half speed due to a fog bank. Echoes from whistle blasts were used to determine their position and at 0115 the Mate rang the engine room for slow as an echo came back from the land. The next entry reads: "At 0125 the CATHERINE went aground in thick fog. Established position as between Lip Lip Point and Oak Bay. After making a survey of the tug, called Tacoma office for assistance to aid vessel to right herself when the tide rises as at present she is listing 45 degrees to starboard. Caulked doors on low side and after-hatch to keep water out as tide rose. At 0700 vessel on nearly even keel." But the problems were not over. Shortly after 0700, the CATHERINE heeled over, but to port, letting water in all the side doors. The doors were then secured and the crew began pumping with a portable pump furnished by the FOSS 18, arriving in the meantime to render assistance. The CATHERINE's pump was inoperative due to the list, but the FOSS 18 pump was gaining on the inflow of water until it overheated and stopped. The crew then decided to leave the flooded boat, take their gear and row ashore to await new pumps and the evening tide.

At high water, and with help from the FOSS 18 and DREW FOSS, the water was pumped out and the CATHERINE floated free. The FOSS 18 took the crew to Tacoma and the DREW towed the water-soaked tug to the Foss yard.

After several days of clean-up and repair, she left for Port Angeles to resume herding logs. Captain Benthein remained with the tug until mid-1942 when three other Port Angeles skippers followed—Captains Bundy, Read, and Oliver — all experienced in log-towing.

The CATHERINE's second misfortune occurred in late 1942. She had left Port Ludlow at noon on November 21st with 32 sections of Grays Harbor hemlock logs for Port Angeles. But she only ran as far as Washington Harbor before worsening weather forced the crew to anchor in the sheltered bay to wait for flatter water. From the 24th on and for the next 15 days, the 6-man crew waited in vain for safe log-towing weather. Hoping for a break, on December 9th, they left the logs in the Harbor and headed out to check the sea condition. Unfortunately, on the way they ran afoul of Middle Ground Shoal and the boat took a sudden heavy roll to port. At the time she hit, the Cook, Carl Feyh, was in the W.C. washing up before turning-to in the galley. The W.C. door was open and when the CATHERINE took the quick deep roll, the Cook was thrown through the doorway and right over the side into the cold dark water — a strange accident to happen to a cook! Hearing the Cook's yells the Mate and Deckhand launched the skiff, towed over to the Cook and pulled him aboard. Rowing at double-time for the dock, they set the shivering Cook ashore at Bugges' Cannery for transportation to the hospital. But the exposure was too much for him and he passed away the following day — greatly to the grief and surprise of his shipmates.

Fortunately, they were able to back the CATHERINE off the shoal and 12 hours later, in moderate weather with a flood tide, they were under way for Port Angeles with the long tow, arriving on December 11 after a 20-day trip of 33 miles! She continued towing for the Port Angeles division until she exchanged places with the Seattle tug, MARTHA FOSS. So the CATHERINE went on barge work and the MARTHA took over log towing.

On one of the CATHERINE's routine barge tows and during a black night, she became involved in a costly accident, but through no fault of the tug or crew. She was towing the loaded 6,000-barrel oil barge FOSS-99 from Edmonds to Seattle. Having a maximum load aboard, the barge's deck was awash making it difficult to see the vessel even with the sidelight and the pumphouse at the stern. As frequently happens, a ship approached the barge on a collision course and unaware of the danger. A Navy tug, with a crash and rending of metal, heard up ahead on the CATHERINE, plowed into the side of the barge at full speed. In a matter of minutes the oil barge broke in two and sank, just off Meadow Point near Shilshole Bay, but the tug escaped with only a bashed-in bow. Today such a spill would be an environmental disaster, though in 1945 it was just considered a tough break — losing a barge and an oil cargo. The CATHERINE's luck changed for the better after the barge loss and she was free of accidents for the rest of her Foss life.

An interesting job came up for her in June and July 1959. She had a part in the construction of the Hood Canal floating bridge by towing gravel scows from Steilacoom pit to the bridge construction site where the gravel was used for anchor ballast. The sand and gravel was poured by chute into the anchors after they were sunk into position. Two tugs, primarily the CATHERINE, and five scows delivered 45 loads, 25,000 tons, of sand and gravel to hold the anchors and the bridge in place. The anchors are still undisturbed, but not so the bridge — the western half broke loose from the anchors and sank in a freak storm in February 1979 — causing a circuitous re-routing of traffic.

The CATHERINE continued on routine towing until mid-February 1961 then tied up due to a drop in the work load and the extra-expense handicap of engine room control, requiring two engineers. She remained at the Foss dock on standby reserve throughout the year. Then in mid-January 1962 the ANNA FOSS suffered serious bow damage due to her engine failing to reverse, so the CATHERINE was re-activated as substitute tug. She left the pier with Captain Pat O'Malley aboard, but four hours later a breakdown occurred forcing a return to the yard for electrical repairs. Much of the tug's wiring shorted out due to dampness from the long idle period.

During the spring of 1962 towing orders increased and even with the ANNA returning to service in April, the CATHERINE continued to operate on a regular basis until November 1963 when, due to usual winter curtailment, she again went into lay-up to await the spring activity.

But she didn't get away until May, with alternate Captains George Walker and Skip Lampman. The 65-year-old tug ran steadily and trouble-free through the summer and fall barging oil and gravel. Then in October, with the return of two new tugs from Cook Inlet, Alaska, the CATHERINE's usefulness was over. So after delivering two gravel scows to Lake Union on Friday, November 5, 1964 Captain Walker was informed that the "CAT" was being retired and all gear, supplies, and stores were to be taken ashore.

In early 1965 Foss towed her to Tacoma where the engine and other machinery was removed and the CATHERINE placed in dead storage alongside the FOSS 16, MARGARET, and MYRTLE FOSS — all waiting for some final disposition.

The CATHERINE and the MYRTLE were sold in June 1969 to Foss Captain Roy Durgan, who bought and sold boats as a sideline. Roy Durgan held the CATHERINE until 1974 then sold her to Alex Vaughn of Seattle. Vaughn towed her to Lake Union and began a major rebuilding program. However, in less than a year, he sold the tug to the present owner, Joseph Kenna of Anacortes. Kenna installed a used Atlas diesel and other machinery to make the CATHERINE operational and he had the hull repaired and much of the deck replaced. In April 1977 Mr. Kenna renamed the tug KATHADIN and shortly after, with the shipyard work completed, he towed the tug to LaConner where the rehabilitation of the 80-year-old tug is continuing.

The KATHADIN should now be ready to make her debut on the Sound and join the unique and select club of octogenarian tugboats, many of them like herself graduates from Foss.

MYRTLE FOSS (1)

Built:	1909	Propulsion:	Atlas
	Seattle, Washington		200-horsepower
Length:	57-feet	Primary Service:	Puget Sound
Beam:	15-feet	Final Foss Operating Day:	December 8, 1962
		Status:	Sold - Domestic

Ainsworth & Dunn Fishing Company in 1909 had James Chilberg of Seattle build a small Puget Sound cannery tender, to be equipped with a 75-horsepower gas engine. At her launching, the Company named her KINGFISHER and she retained the name until joining the Foss fleet 28 years later.

The KINGFISHER worked on Puget Sound for many years as a fish packer, generally in the Blaine and Lummi Island area of the northern Sound. During the time, she was in charge of Captains Nels Nelson, her first master, then Roger Cook, R. R. Ginnett, and W. Haraleroad.

In the mid-Twenties, with the coming of semi-diesel engines, Ainsworth & Dunn replaced the KINGFISHER's old gasoline engine with a 180-horsepower Fairbanks-Morse and they increased the fuel-tank capacity to 2,000 gallons, giving her a cruising range of 1,600 miles.

Ainsworth & Dunn then sent her to Southeastern Alaska to tow fish scows, traps, and to barge general cargo now that she had the capacity to work in Alaska. But the KINGFISHER, as with other tug cannery tenders, had the deckhouse aft, which called for the towing winch to be located forward by the anchor windlass, with the tow wire leading aft and out between the towbitts on the afterdeck — an awkward arrangement.

The KINGFISHER spent a number of seasons in Alaska towing for and tending canneries, but after the winter of 1928-1929, her owners sold the boat to Wagner Towing Company of Seattle. Captain H. Nelson and a 3-man crew stayed with the tug at Wagner's request. After some modification, she started towing logs from British Columbia to Puget Sound.

MYRTLE FOSS *Formerly the KINGFISHER of Wagner Towing. Shown nearing Ballard Locks on December 26, 1954. (Courtesy of Joe Williamson)*

She became involved in a rather strange predicament when she and another Wagner tug, the CREST (later CHRIS FOSS) were southbound at night near Vancouver, B.C. towing 1,000,000 feet of logs for Seattle delivery. The two tugs, lashed side-by-side, were progressing slowly and favorably through the dark water until they stranded on rocky Atkin's Reef. The KINGFISHER partially passed over the reef before hanging up on the deep-water side, but the CREST rammed high and dry on the backbone of the reef. The tugs listed away from each other so the crews relashed them to prevent falling over on their beam ends. Fortunately the tugs were not holed or opened up, so at the next high tide they floated free and continued on with the tow. Inspection in Seattle revealed only minor damage from the stop-over at Atkin's Reef.

In late 1937 when Foss purchased Wagner Tugboat, the assets included the KINGFISHER. She continued to operate for some time under the Wagner corporate name. Then, in June 1940 KINGFISHER became the MYR-TLE FOSS, named for one of two daughters of Chris and Hildur Foss. With the name change, a new Captain took over, veteran skipper Clarence Bale.

By 1941 the MYRTLE's old Fairbanks-Morse showed signs of age with holes developing in the piston heads. More and more of the yard's time was used for repairs, so Foss decided to change engines. At the same time, the entire deckhouse and foredeck was rebuilt. Ole Brekke, a Foss shipwright, designed and built the new deckhouse. The main deck cabin was conveniently arranged so that the pilot house, galley, and W.C. were all located in the same 9 x 14 house with access to all compartments from the inside — a decided advantage in bad weather. The forecastle or living quarters were located just below the pilot house. The MYRTLE was repowered with a 200-horsepower Atlas which had recently been removed from the tug CHICKAMAUGA, but the engine was still in top condition.

By mid-1941 the tug was ready and Foss assigned her to tow logs and oil barges for the Seattle office, with an occasional gravel barge run between Steilacoom and the cement plants in Lake Union.

CREST & KINGFISHER *Later to become CHRIS and MYRTLE FOSS, caught in an embarrassing position on Atkins Reef near Vancouver, B.C. (Courtesy of Joe Williamson)*

Three years later, in early 1944 the MYRTLE was taken over by the Foss-Tacoma office to tow chip-scows and logs with Henry Hall her skipper. In late 1944 Jack Harropp relieved Captain Henry Hall and he stayed with the MYRTLE until she returned to Foss-Seattle in March 1946.

For the next fourteen years she worked on all the regular Foss-Seattle linehaul runs, another of the hard-working Sound tugs, doing the commonplace port-to-port jobs, moving products and material for local industry. Outside of two minor groundings, the MYRTLE carried on her day-to-day routine with little trouble for the yard crew until the problems of age finally slowed her down at the 50-year mark.

The MYRTLE continued in service for the Seattle office through August 1960 with George Walker, the Captain of long-standing, in charge. However, during her last year of service, Foss used her only 15 to 20 days per month and she didn't run after August 31st, because the old diesel was causing problems and her 200-horsepower was less than the other linehaul tugs. Nevertheless, Foss maintained her in a semi-ready state.

A contributing factor to her lay-up was her troublesome air-driven towing winch. Before bringing in the tow wire, a full head of air was pumped into the tanks; the tug stopped; and as much towline as possible spooled in on the winch drum until only enough air remained in the tanks to start the engine twice. The tug had to run ahead while building up additional air because the service air-compressor was driven by the main engine and the engine had no clutch, so the propeller drove ahead whenever the engine turned over. This run-and-reel-in was usually necessary two times before the line was all aboard. There was little margin for error when the air supply was critically low and, with only one or two starts of the engine possible, the MYRTLE was a difficult tug to handle if extensive juggling or shifting was required.

The MYRTLE remained idle for 19 months, then in early April 1962 she returned to the active list.

Captain George Walker again took her out and they were busy throughout most of the year towing the rail-car barge FOSS-116 between Seattle and the Simpson Mill at Shelton. However, it was on this run that she ended her active career with Foss.

On December 6, shortly after leaving Shelton with the FOSS-116, a loud detonation occurred and continued in the cylinders. The crew changed injectors, but with no improvement, so they realized there was a serious problem so they anchored off Squaxin Island to await a tow to Seattle by the LORNA FOSS.

Inspection at the Foss yard indicated that the heads be overhauled, but instead the company decided the MYRTLE should be retired. She remained in lay-up at the Seattle yard for the next three years, then Foss towed her to Tacoma, removed the engine, and placed her in dead storage.

The MYRTLE remained in this state until 1969 and then Foss sold her to Roy Durgan, a Foss employee, who in turn sold the tug to George Erskine of Seattle. Erskine installed a Hendy diesel and made modifications to the deckhouse so he could use her as a yacht. He changed the name to RUTH B, but the gender remained the same. She is berthed along Seattle's Duwamish River and easily recognized as the former MYRTLE FOSS.

FOSS #8 Photographed in Port Angeles Harbor, August 1966, her base for most of her active career with Foss. (Courtesy of the author's collection)

FOSS 8

Built:	1935	Propulsion:	Cummins
	Wrang Shipyard		140-horsepower
	Bellingham, Washington	Primary Service:	Port Angeles Harbor
Length:	32-feet	Final FossOperating Day:	August 24, 1972
Beam:	11-feet	Status:	Sold - Domestic

FOSS 8, built as the YAMOTO by Wrang Shipyard for the yard's own use, was'a small, harbor-type tug powered with a 50-horsepower gas engine. Besides the YAMOTO, the Wrang yard, with three marine ways, repair, and boat storage facilities, built fifty boats of various types during the first ten years of operation. One of the later boats was identical to the YAMOTO and took over most of the yard work so George Wrang decided to sell the YAMOTO while she would still bring a good price. Foss, knowing the tug was like a new boat, bought her on July 25, 1938. Renamed FOSS 8, they assigned her to Tacoma and she went right to work though underpowered. Then after operating for three years, Foss repowered her with a 140-horsepower Cummins diesel.

In September 1944 the Tacoma office sent her to the Port Angeles division to replace the fire-damaged FOSS 9 and she stayed on tending log rafts for most of her working life.

When the new 300-horsepower harbor tugs became a reality in 1966 older tugs were put on light work and so in 1967 with two new harbor tugs in Port Angeles, the FOSS 8 returned to Tacoma where she worked until 1970; then she went to Everett as a spare harbor tug.

By 1972 with the new fleet of steel harbor tugs in all the ports, the usefulness of the FOSS 8 ended and she came over to Foss-Seattle for lay-up and sale. After less than two months in retirement, Mr. Maynard Daum of Tacoma bought her and under the name of LOU ANN used the boat for general dock work at the Zidell ship-dismantling operation in Tacoma. Then in the fall of 1973 Mr. Daum and the LOU ANN left Tacoma for Wrangell, Alaska to work around the harbor — beachcombing and salvaging stray logs.

By the fall of 1977 the local log market had dropped off drastically, so Mr. Daum moved the LOU ANN to the small community of Point Baker, Alaska where he planned to make the boat into a shrimp dragger. He recently reported that the sturdy old tug, newly painted and worked over, looks like new and ready for anything, just as she did when Foss bought her from the Wrang yard in 1938.

VENTURE *Shown in the thirties while under ownership of Wagner Towing. Foss made no changes to the interior or exterior. She became the HILDUR FOSS. (Courtesy of Joe Williamson)*

HILDUR FOSS

Built:	1907	Propulsion:	Eastern Standard
	Jensen Brothers Yard		150-horsepower
	Friday Harbor, Washington	Primary Service:	Puget Sound
Length:	63-feet	Final Operating Day:	April 1, 1949
Beam:	15-feet	Status:	Intentionally sunk

The HILDUR, like many Foss tugs, was originally a Puget Sound cannery tender named the VENTURE and powered with a 175-horsepower steam engine. After ten years in the fishing industry, ownership passed to Mr. B.L. Jones of Bellingham. With minor modifications, he turned the VENTURE into a tugboat and used her for log towing on the northern Sound.

Then in 1925 Wagner Towboat Company of Seattle became the owner. They operated her for several years with the original steam engine, but in 1926 Wagner repowered her with an Eastern Standard diesel. The VENTURE was primarily a log tower, but occasionally she towed an oil barge for General Petroleum Company.

The tug was handy with logs, but not all her skippers were. In one instance bringing a tow out of Shelton, tricky piloting even for an experienced Captain, and under the command of an ex-freight boat Captain who knew little of tugs and towing, the VENTURE tried going overland. The Chief Engineer, an old hand at towboating, related that at the particular time he had been down in the forecastle installing a steam heater and decided to come up on deck for a breather. Arriving topside he was amazed to see the VENTURE heading for the beach at the narrowest portion of Hammersley Inlet. Before the Chief could get to the pilot house, the tug was aground — but the log tow kept on coming, rammed the stern, pushing the tug farther up the beach. Fortunately no serious damage resulted and the VEN-TURE floated off on the next high tide — the Captain wasn't consigned to limbo, but to less-exacting tows.

The VENTURE became a Foss tug at the time of the Wagner acquisition in 1937. Foss operated all four of the acquired tugs using the Wagner names until 1940 then following the policy of using family names, the VENTURE became the HILDUR FOSS, named for the wife of Chris Foss, a son of Iver.

The HILDUR was dispatched from the Seattle office, working frequently on the gravel run from Steilacoom to the Salmon Bay Sand & Gravel plant, just inside the Government Locks at Ballard. The gravel haul was inherited by Foss in the Wagner purchase and they continued with the job for many years. However, the HILDUR quite often towed refined-oil barges for Union Oil Company.

The HILDUR had inherent structural weakness — Foss discovered that her condition was not equal to the other three Wagner tugs. The crews reported that the HILDUR's main deckhouse in rough weather, or when shaking from pulling hard on a heavy tow, would sway off-center to port and starboard—a threat that must have kept the crew outside.

Even with her peculiarity, the HILDUR was one of the few boats to have only one Captain. He was Haaken ''Peanuts'' Berg and, although he had a wife and home, he seemed to think the HILDUR had priority over both. The HILDUR usually worked Monday through Friday and then tied up at Ballard for the weekend. Captain Berg would stay aboard and have his wife bring down his week's supply of clothes and join him for dinner on the home-away-from-home. Apparently he was a dexterous skipper as few men could operate, as he did, the primitive pilot house engine controls, consisting of three buttons — one for AHEAD, one for NEUTRAL, and one for ASTERN. The trick was in the timing so as not to confuse the proper sequence — the right button at the right time or the engine did strange things. On the rare occasions when Captain Berg took a vacation, the HILDUR stayed dockside, awaiting the return of the Skipper's foolproof button routine.

An important operation, from a timing of delivery standpoint, that Captain Berg and the HILDUR participated in, was the part they had in the construction of the Seattle-Tacoma airport. The tug was assigned the job of towing two scows, on a time schedule, with sand and gravel aggregate between Steilacoom pits and Des Moines, the truck relay point. The runways were paved with HILDUR's sand and gravel, with the help of a little cement. However, the HILDUR's Captain didn't favor hauling gravel scows and evidence of his aversion occurred during a boomstick tow from Seattle to Tacoma. While underway the Captain had calculated the HILDUR would arrive in Tacoma about the time the Salmon Bay gravel scow would be loaded and ready to tow to Ballard. Returning to Seattle hooked to a slow-moving gravel scow didn't fit in with the Captain's plans, so he pulled into Tramp Harbor and began turning in circles with the HILDUR and the boom sticks. When his Mate, Bob Quinn, came on watch the Captain told him to continue turning in circles, marking time. About two hours later Captain Berg returned to the pilot house and told Quinn to continue on for Tacoma as the Salmon Bay scow would most certainly have been dispatched with another tug by now — he was right — and nobody told him he was wrong in making all those round-abouts.

By 1948 even with Captain Berg's fine hand at the wheel, the HILDUR's age was slowing her down and the open-seam hull leaked non-stop. To further aggravate her condition, the cabins by now were shaking about six on the Richter scale, and the old engine was breathing her last. Also, the air-ports on the engine controls had to be continuously cleared of rust and water or the engine could not be controlled. The valves were shot and the engine threw grease like a spray gun — the crew had to be bilge rats to work in the engine room. Her case appeared to be hopeless, and so the Company thought, for they operated her only as a back-up boat.

But to make sure her failings were fatal she went to Tacoma on April 1, 1949 for drydocking and inspection. The result turned out as expected. The hull was soft, perforated, and not worth repairing. It would be difficult to make a sieve water-tight, especially a real big one. During the next several months at slack time, the yard crew removed the machinery and articles of value. Her official documents were surrendered to the Coast Guard, but the bare boat remained at the Foss yard in Tacoma and the crews of the PETER and BRYNN FOSS were obliged to pump her out regularly.

Finally, orders were issued not to spend any more time on the HILDUR and soon after Captain Vern Wright of the BRYNN had the job of sinking her in Commencement Bay. He towed the HILDUR and a partially loaded gravel barge to the middle of the harbor and, using the BRYNN's monitor, washed nearly five tons of gravel into the hapless HILDUR. Due to the buoyancy of the empty fuel tanks, she held up longer than expected, but inch-by-inch she gave way and then suddenly the house lifted off and the hull broke up, plunging to the bottom of the bay.

Captain Berg's long-time home, fittingly filled with gravel, was no more — but "Peanuts" didn't complain, he now had the WALLACE FOSS to live on.

CALCITE Shortly after purchase by Foss, operating as a four man linehaul tug. (Courtesy of Joe Williamson)

NANCY FOSS

Built:	1907	Propulsion:	Cummins
	Lopez, Washington		140-horsepower
Length:	45-feet	Primary Service:	Port Angeles Harbor
Beam:	12-feet	Final Foss Operating Day:	March 21, 1975
		Status:	Sold - Domestic

The NANCY FOSS started out life as the yacht CALCITE, owned by Mr. John McMillin of the Roche Harbor Lime Company. The CALCITE, Mr. McMillin, and the Lime Company are all closely related to the development and island life of the San Juans, for during the entire history of the Islands the most important source of income to its residents came from mining limestone. The Lime Company's mining operations terminated in the late '50s and, though fishing and tourism have taken over and prospered during the last two decades, they will probably never surpass the contribution of the limestone industry, which goes back to before the turn of the century.

In 1886 Mr. John McMillin, associated with the Tacoma Lime Works, arrived on San Juan Island and purchased property rich in limestone deposits. Shortly after acquiring the property, Tacoma & Roche Harbor Lime Company was formed to handle the venture and many quarries were opened up on high ground. The mined stone was loaded into dump cars and railed downhill to thirteen lower-level kilns. Then the burnt lime was chuted to even lower-level rooms for barreling, weighing, and then trucking to waterfront warehouses at Roche Harbor.

By 1890 Roche Harbor had a population of 247 and every building and house was built and maintained by the Lime Company. The Company also owned the brig WM. G. IRWIN, the steam tug ROCHE HARBOR, and five barges for transporting limestone to Puget Sound markets. The only method of transportation around the Island was by boat so vessels of all types were necessary to support the lime works and the Roche Harbor community. Even the Yacht CALCITE had a function to perform. She had good accommodations and so provided interesting quarters for overnight guests and comfort in extensive cruising.

The CALCITE, named after the calcium carbonate substance in limestone, was powered by a 50-horsepower Frisco-Standard gasoline engine giving her a speed of 9 knots. She had a 4-KW generator set, electric lights, a gas galley stove, pilot house engine control, and McMillin equipped her for off-shore navigation so she could cruise the inland and open waters of British Columbia. A typical CALCITE trip took place shortly after the yacht was completed.

Mr. McMillin ran the CALCITE on a 17-day cruise through the Canadian Gulf Islands and into the British Columbia inlet-fjord region. Joining him on the cruise was Canadian lime baron, R.P. Butchart whose wife developed the popular public Butchart Gardens in Victoria, B.C. R.J. McCormick, Seattle photographer, was also a CALCITE guest. McMillin's son acted as Captain and for crew they carried a Chief Engineer and Cook. McMillin and his party cruised, fished, and hunted from the yacht, with the entire voyage recorded on photographs by Mr. McCormick, showing they visited areas from Chemanus and Vancouver to Campbell River and Princess Louisa Inlet.

The CALCITE continued as McMillin's yacht until 1915 when the vessel was redocumented for hauling freight, but that did not deter her use as a part-time yacht. The CALCITE continued in freight service until early 1934 then went to the shipyard for rebuilding to a tugboat, radically changing her function. When the conversion was completed in late 1934 she still retained the 60-horsepower diesel engine that had been installed in 1930. As a tugboat she operated with a 4-man crew towing limerock barges between Roche Harbor and mills at Everett, Lowell, Bellingham, and Tacoma. Her skipper on the new service was Pete Larson with Gene Allen as Mate.

The 60-horsepower engine proved inadequate for towing heavy limerock barges, so in 1936 McMillin repowered her with a 110-horsepower Atlas diesel—the big, heavy-duty engine cut the towing time by 20 percent. The CALCITE continued barging limerock until early 1939 when the Lime Company sold her to Foss.

The Company put the tug to work out of Tacoma, towing logs and lumber scows in the Seattle-Tacoma-Olympia-Shelton area. With a Captain, Mate, Deckhand, and Cook, she operated as a 24-hour, on-call boat for the next four years.

In January 1943 the CALCITE was ordered to Port Townsend to relieve Crown Zellerbach's tug DIAMOND Z scheduled for overhaul. The Captain of the CALCITE at the time, Jack Harropp, worked the tug on a 12-hour day shift, usually with the help of a deckhand. However, at times he was a one-man crew which, as his notes in the Log Book show, was not to his liking. On January 30th he recorded, "No Deckhand again today—I don't like this . . . ." Next day, after putting in 13½ hours of steady work, his log entry ended at 2115 stating, "All done—thank God!"

On February 5, the CALCITE returned to Tacoma and operated infrequently until April 1943; she then entered the Foss shipyard for a major rebuild. Three months later she came out of the yard and went to work as a 2-man day-boat instead of a 4-man linehaul tug. While in the yard, she was renamed NANCY FOSS in honor of a great grand-daughter of Theodore.

On July 28 Foss sent her to Port Angeles, to relieve the HENRIETTA. Ed Reid of Port Angeles, familiar with Port Angeles routine, took over the NANCY. She worked in the harbor until November 1946 then the necessity of a change of engines sent her to the shipyard. The NANCY, as with the HENRIETTA and all tugs with heavy-duty engines requires regular attention, and the necessary time was hard to find on a 2-man day-boat running 12 hours a day and, quite often, non-stop. So the Tacoma yard installed a compact, easily maintained, 140-horsepower, high-speed Cummins diesel. On February 10, 1947 the NANCY returned to Port Angeles, to take over from the JOE FOSS, substitute boat for the past three months.

For 20 years the NANCY worked day-after-day, adhering to the Foss motto and experiencing few mechanical woes. However, in the summer of 1966 the new LELA FOSS with her 325-horsepower showed up in Port Angeles to replace the NANCY—the NANCY had tenure, but the LELA had the power. The NANCY remained in Port Angeles until October; then she shifted to Tacoma for harbor duties and she operated steadily until 1971. An extra

The CALCITE *after a major rebuild. Named NANCY FOSS and shown here in Port Angeles in August 1966. (From the author's collection)*

boat was needed in Everett harbor, so the NANCY headed north, stayed a year in Everett, then returned to Tacoma for part-time work until early 1973. Foss finally retired her on March 21, 1975 and later in the year they towed her to Foss-Seattle for storage in fresh water.

Then on December 17, 1975 Foss sold the NANCY to the Olson Bros. of Tacoma for private use and they named her NANCY BEAR. The Olsons sold the boat soon after and the purchaser at LaConner resold the boat to Will Park who berths the tug at Kingston and uses her for fishing. Present information indicates she is once again for sale, and judging from her steady operating record of 72 years, she may outlive another owner or two. The hull is still sound and the Cummins diesel has a good healthy roar.

CHRIS FOSS (1)

Built:	1925	Propulsion:	Eastern Standard
	Sieverson Shipyard		150-horsepower
	Seattle, Washington	Primary Service:	Puget Sound
Length:	51-feet	Final Foss Operating Day:	December, 1946
Beam:	14-feet	Status:	Sold Domestic

The Wagner Towboat Company of Seattle engaged naval architect, L.E. Coolidge to design a small tug for use on inland waters and then contracted with the Sieverson Shipyard on Seattle's West Waterway to build the boat. The tug was completed in May 1925 and given the name, CREST.

After completing trial runs in early June, she left for Ketchikan, Alaska on a sixty-day charter to Alaska Consolidated Canneries. The CREST made the run to Ketchikan in seventy-three hours, averaging 8.9 knots, a good speed for 1925. At the end of the salmon season she returned to Seattle and remained towing on Puget Sound until Foss purchased Wagner's Company in 1937. When Wagner Towing was dissolved and the tugs operated directly by Foss, the CREST became the CHRIS FOSS in honor of a nephew of Andrew.

The CHRIS had two major disadvantages—she drew nearly nine feet of water, a serious handicap in shallow water areas, and she had only semi-pilothouse control. The engine speed could be controlled from the pilothouse, but the engine could not be stopped, started, or reversed, except from the engine room. The arrangement required an engineer to be available for all maneuvering.

The CHRIS had accommodations for only four men: Captain, Mate, Engineer, and Cook. There were no deckhands and when arriving or leaving port with a barge, the Mate and Cook were required to assist on deck. With this crew set-up, the CHRIS was usually given the longer barge-towing jobs on the Sound, so her principal job was towing refined oil and gasoline barges to some twenty different Union Oil stations located from the San Juans to Gig Harbor.

However, Foss did vary her work and on one occasion she had orders to proceed to Ladysmith, British Columbia and assist the PATRICIA FOSS with a log tow to Puget Sound. Before leaving Seattle, the crew pilfered six gallons of white paint and during the slow five day return tow, the CHRIS' crew repainted the entire hull. The fresh paint gave the CHRIS a yacht-like appearance and upon arrival at the Foss pier, the "Front Office" was somewhat taken-back as they were about to repaint the hulls of the Seattle tugs a dark green to correspond with the hull color of the Foss-Tacoma tugs. However, to get some benefit out of the six gallons of paint, the CHRIS retained her lily-whiteness for a

CHRIS FOSS *In the early forties. (Courtesy of Joe Williamson)*

few months. when the crew of the CHRIS saw some of the tugs now with green hulls, they said the boats had turned green with envy.

During the construction of the Bremerton Airport, a great quantity of gravel was needed for the runway bases, so the CHRIS, with Captain Ken Norton, towed gravel scows between the pit at Steilacoom and the Port Orchard delivery site. The gravel haul had the CHRIS busy for several months—then she went back to general towing around the Sound.

On one of the CHRIS' runs in 1945 she narrowly avoided disaster when inbound to Seattle Harbor towing the empty concrete-hulled FOSS-102. At the same time the CHRIS was coming in, a Government 350-foot Knot-Class freighter was making a wide swing out of the harbor. The freighter's officers seeing the large deckhouse of the FOSS-102 assumed that the barge was a self-propelled vessel of some type and completely independent of the tug, so the freighter continued in her wide turn going between tug and barge, severing the towline. As the freighter neared the tug and barge, the Captain of the CHRIS stopped the engine, but, with the towline severed, the barge veered to the left and into the ship's starboard bow, punching a hole in the freighter and cracking the bow of the FOSS-102. Both vessels entered the shipyard for necessary hull repairs, but the CHRIS was undamaged and ended up as only a spectator and witness, free of any damage claim.

The accident with the freighter had no direct connection with the sudden installation of full pilothouse engine control, but nevertheless the controls were put in right after the event. With full pilothouse control the need for an engineer was eliminated and a deckhand was added to the crew.

The year after the encounter with the freighter, and on a wintry December day while inbound from Port Angeles with an empty oil barge in tow, the CHRIS ran aground on Dungeness Spit, at the east end of the Straits of Juan de Fuca. A few days later during high tide, but because of strong winds still buffeting the Straits, the CHRIS had to be pulled off the inshore side of Dungeness Spit. The salvage operation was successful and the CHRIS floated into the sheltered waters of Dungeness Bay. When the weather moderated, Foss towed the CHRIS to Seattle for survey and repair and the yard crew found the hull to be strained in several places and the engine in doubtful condition. The adverse report decided Foss to lay up the CHRIS indefinitely, so the engine was removed and the tug tied up at the Foss out-of-service moorings.

The CHRIS remained on the roster of Foss tugs for several years, even without an engine. Then by 1956 after eight years in lay-up and no possible use in sight, Foss sold her to Mr. R. Wertz of Seattle in October 1956 for conversion to a fishboat. However, his plans did not work out and he sold the boat to Mr. Charlie Jacobs of Winslow, Washington. Mr. Jacobs installed a 200-horsepower Fairbanks-Morse diesel and made the necessary repairs to the hull. By summer 1957 the CREST was again towing on Puget Sound, showing up occasionally with a log tow in Hood Canal or the Government Locks.

After eleven years of towing, Charlie Jacobs retired from the business and sold the CREST to George Perreault of Portland. Prior to his retirement he had installed an air-controlled 200-horsepower D17000-Caterpillar engine.

Mr. Perreault and family use the vessel for cruising, going as far as Canada, but more often up the Columbia and Snake Rivers. Eventually, they intend to cruise Alaskan waters. the hull has been completely refastened and recaulked and modern electronics and an auxiliary generator installed. The ex-CHRIS has had a long and varied life, with no end in sight—according to Mr. Perreault.

James A. Cole

James A. Cole

SECTION IV – THE WAR AND POST-WAR PERIOD

Tugs Acquired 1940 – 1949

CARL, EDITH (1), OSWELL, SANDRA (1), ADELINE (1),

SIMON, EDITH (2), HENRY (1), JOE (1), LELA (1), ELAINE (1), BARBARA (2),

CHRISTINE, JUSTINE (2), KENAI, PHILLIPS (1), WEDELL, DONNA (1),

OMER (1), GARY (1), JERRY

The need for tugs in the war years to handle government barges and ships was intense and vital. Foss responded by selling, chartering, and working their boats as the Military Forces required. The Army and Navy used the tugs locally, in Alaska, and the Central Pacific. Shortly after the war ended, the requisitioned tugs were turned back to Foss. However, two were sunk during the war, one by enemy action.

The adjustment to peace-time and commercial operation for Foss was rapid and with a greater than ever expansion in all phases of the towing business. At the end of 1949 Foss' established barge runs consisted of lumber hauls between Shelton and Olympia—car barges, Seattle to Bellingham and Seattle to Bremerton and Eagle Harbor to Tacoma or Seattle, also Shelton to Tacoma—log rafts from Straits' log dumps to Port Angeles and Port Townsend—gravel barges, Steilacoom to Lake Union—Limerock from the San Juan Islands to Port Angeles—seasonal oil runs to Bristol Bay and southeastern Alaska—year-round oil runs in Puget Sound—pulp-chip and hogged-fuel barges from and to Sound mills. In addition to the scheduled runs, the tugs made countless contract tows around the Sound, the Coast, and Alaska—there were few idle tugs or days.

BACKGROUND ON THE MIKI TUGS

The Foss Company owned and operated nine World War II MIKI-class tugs—purchased as they had proven dependable, seaworthy, and heavy "pullers." In their over 30 years of Foss ownership, the tugs, with minimum expense, operated profitably and well. However, the type was a confirmed success long before they were built in quantity for use during World War II.

The prototype was designed by naval architect L.H. Coolidge of Seattle in 1929 and built by Ballard Marine Company for Young Brothers Towing Company of Honolulu. The tug was given a Hawaiian name, MIKIMIKI—this accounts for the origin of the name "MIKI." She more than proved herself, towing successfully in the Hawaiian Islands for many years.

Early in W.W.II there was a decided lack of ocean-coastwise tugs to assist in the movement of supplies and equipment for the Army Transport Service from West Coast ports to Alaska and also, along the Atlantic and Gulf coasts. Mr. Coolidge, at that time a member of the Army Transport Service design staff, recommended that the 1929 plan of the MIKIMIKI, with modifications, be adopted for the Army's needs. So late in 1942 the A.T.S. authorized construction of the Hawaiian type, affectionately to be known as the "MIKI's."

The tugs were constructed at eight shipyards on the West Coast and by two in New England—out of 61 built, 51 came from West Coast yards. The first 25 tugs were powered by twin Fairbanks-Morse diesels, and the last 36 were powered by single Enterprise or Superior diesels—the 10 East Coast MIKI's all had Superior diesels. Other than the main engine, the major difference in the East and West Coast MIKI's was the type of construction-wood used. East Coast tugs were built of oak and pine and the West Coast tugs of fir and Alaska cedar.

While running for the A.T.S., the tugs operated with engine-room controls and the manning scale called for three oilers and three engineers with a total crew of eighteen. But the crew size was first reduced to fourteen after the tugs were sold to private interests. Then by the late 1950s and early 1960s engine room control was changed to pilot house control, eliminating two oilers and later on the third oiler was dropped. With the installation of an automatic dishwasher, the messman was no longer necessary and the crew size cut to ten.

By the mid-1960's the MIKI's, with their ten-man crew and only 1,500 horsepower, were operating at an economic disadvantage compared to the new breed of sophisticated tugs requiring only eight men. They could not compete with the new technology in the high-powered steel tugs built after 1966, so the aging MIKI's were slowly phased out.

Then, with the escalation of the Vietnam War in 1966 tugs were needed to assist in towing and lightering operations off the coast and in rivers and ports of South Vietnam. Alaska Barge & Transport of Vancouver, Washington purchased nine MIKI's some of which had been laid up for a number of years. they reactivated and outfitted them for the long voyage and duty in Vietnam.

Eventually, ten MIKI's were working in Vietnam and those same ten tugs began their towing service for the Government in World War II and they returned to Government service twenty-one years later in Vietnam. One Foss MIKI, the MARTHA, served the cause in Vietnam, leaving for the War Zone on January 2, 1966 (See story on MARTHA FOSS).

The nine MIKI's owned by Foss are listed, showing year purchased and year removed form service:

1. BARBARA FOSS (2)   1946 - 1973
2. JUSTINE FOSS (2)   1946 - 1971
3. CHRISTINE FOSS   1946 - In service
4. DONNA FOSS (1)   1947 - 1970
5. MARTHA FOSS (2)   1951 - 1965
6. LESLIE FOSS (1)   1951 - 1968
7. MARY FOSS (1)   1957 - 1976
8. PATRICIA FOSS (2)   1958 - 1976
9. ADELINE FOSS (2)   1958 - 1976

As of December 1979 the CHRISTINE FOSS is the only MIKI still operating on a regular commercial basis on Puget Sound.

CARL FOSS

Built:	1912	Propulsion:	Enterprise
	Anacortes, Washington		200-horsepower
Length:	57-feet	Primary Service:	Puget Sound
Beam:	16-feet	Final Foss Operating Day:	October 6, 1969
		Status:	Sold Domestic

The CARL FOSS, originally named SOUND, was a steam-powered cannery tender built for the Coast Fish Company of Seattle to tend Puget Sound fish packing plants during the salmon season. She operated eight years for Coast Fish Company, then Gilkey Bros. Towing Company of Anacortes acquired ownership. The company was run

SOUND *As a steam powered tug owned by Gilkey Brothers of Anacortes prior to her 1926 conversion to diesel. (Courtesy of Joe Williamson)*

by six Gilkey's, all Skagit County residents and all the six owners were directly involved in towing on Puget Sound and in British Columbia through a subsidiary company doing business as International Towing Company. The Gilkeys started business in 1918 by buying Captain Charles Norton's Anacortes harbor tug and a second harbor tug, then in 1919 they started acquiring larger boats for general towing.

The Gilkeys operated the SOUND for six years with her costly steam plant before sending her to Seattle for installation of a new heavy-duty diesel. The SOUND's thirty-year-old steam engine had a history—it was originally installed in the Puget Sound steamer ALBION, the first steamer on the Seattle-Everett-Whidbey Island route. Then in 1907 the ALBION was sold to Angeles Brewing & Malting Company for hauling beer from Port Angeles to Seattle and a few years later she was sold to W.A. Lowman and repowered. The ALBION's steam engine then ended up in the new cannery tender, SOUND.

The SOUND towed logs for Gilkey Bros. until 1940 then they laid her up in Anacortes and offered her for sale. Foss purchased the tug on December 18, 1940 and towed her to their Tacoma yard for complete rebuilding and repowering. All the cabins were removed and the heavy engine replaced. The Washington Diesel only thirteen years old, was later installed in a larger tug, the BAER (later the SEA OTTER), owned by Pacific Towboat Company of Everett.

During the early months of 1941 Foss erected a three-level deckhouse on the SOUND and built accommodations for a five-man crew with the Captain's room just aft of the pilothouse. The forecastle and galley were located below decks, forward of the engine room. A smaller diesel engine was installed, better suited to the hull size. The 200-horsepower Enterprise, was one of the last of the Enterprise engines with exposed valve push-rods. They were later enclosed—the up-and-down motion gave the engineer something to watch!

CARL FOSS *Many years later towing logs on the Lake Washington Ship Canal.*
(Courtesy of Joe Williamson)

When ready for service in the fall of 1941 the SOUND was renamed CARL FOSS for a son of Theodore. After trial runs in Tacoma Harbor, the CARL, with Faye Hopkins aboard as Captain, towed a small drill barge from Tacoma to Sitka, Alaska. The equipment was used for drilling shot-holes in the rocky sea bed near Japonski Island, a U.S. Engineer's project to improve the bottom. The CARL made the return voyage running light to Anacortes in four days and arrived ready for the next job.

With Norm Carlson as skipper, Foss-Tacoma dispatched her to the vicinity of Tatoosh Island to meet the sailing Schooner WAWONA and tow her to Anacortes. Arriving off the Cape early in the morning they ran into a thick fog that enveloped the entire area. Fortunately they were able to make radio contact with the schooner, and the Master advised he wasn't sure of his exact position, though he knew he was off lower Vancouver Island, heading for the entrance of the Straits. The CARL searched all day, checking foghorns in the pea-souper, but to no avail. Late in the day the fog lifted about seven feet off the water, but it wasn't much help to Norm Carlson in the wheelhouse. Then by sheer happenstance, one of the crew members, Walt Olsen, sitting on the low after bulwarks and looking out over the water, spotted the dark hull of a ship. He called out the bearing to the pilothouse and Captain Carlson headed for the vessel. In minutes a hail across the water identified the elusive WAWONA—she was just off Neah Bay. The CARL hooked on and began the tow to Anacortes, arriving with the cod-fisher twenty hours later.

For the next twenty-six years the CARL towed on Puget Sound and adjacent inland waters with Tacoma her base. Her routes and assignments were similar to the other Tacoma-based tugs towing on the regular Foss runs with chip-scows, caustic-barges, lumber-barges, and log-rafts. The routes ranged from southern British Columbia to Olympia and Port Angeles. On the CARL's one major international assignment, she towed lime-rock barges from Texada Island, B.C. to Tacoma.

With the advent of larger, more powerful tugs in the mid-sixties, use of the low-powered CARL became limited. On May 1, 1967 she tied up at Tacoma, waiting for a possible surge in business to put her back to work, but five months went by before she came out of lay-up to make a one-day gravel run from Steilacoom to the Kenyon Materials plant near Bremerton. Then on October 9, 1967 Foss gave her another chance in Olympia, working as a two-man day-boat to assist ships in and out of berth and towing Foss gravel scows between the Steilacoom gravel pit and Graystone's plant in Olympia. The CARL's presence eliminated the need for a fully-crewed Tacoma tug to make on-demand runs to Olympia. Two smaller harbor tugs, the PARTHIA and RUFUS, were stationed in Olympia, but were too low-powered to do more than handle light shifting work.

For two years the CARL remained in Olympia providing ready service, but the combination of old-age, costly maintenance, and the Foss replacement program for over-age tugs, forced the CARL to the sidelines. The new PEGGY FOSS arrived in Olympia to take over the CARL's duties, and so on October 6, 1969 with Captain Don Jennings, she made her final run towing a loaded gravel scow from Steilacoom to Graystone.

Late in the fall, the CARL came back to Tacoma and permanent retirement. But in June 1970 Captain Dick Wright, a Foss Company employee, purchased her and changed the tug's name to JENNY W. He used the boat as both a tug and family yacht. Then in 1976 he sold the JENNY W. to Mr. Jon Paterson of Gig Harbor, President of the Retired Tugboat Association, an organization of sixty members and forty boats. He changed the boat's name back to SOUND—after being the CARL for twenty-five years. In making the boat into a regular yacht, Mr. Paterson added a main-deck lounge with view windows and he is working at remodeling the interior. He hopes to have the conversion complete and to his satisfaction in a few years, so another Foss tug lives on, earning the title "venerable."

EDITH FOSS (1)

Built:	1901	Propulsion:	Atlas
	San Francisco, California		500-horsepower
Length:	115-feet	Area of Operation:	Alaska
Beam:	24-feet	Final Operating Day:	December 4, 1943
		Status:	Sunk by collision

Alaska Packers Association of San Francisco built the steam cannery tender CHILKAT for use in Alaska during the Bristol Bay Salmon canning season. APA owned and operated canneries in the Bristol Bay area and a heavy tug-tender was necessary at the time to assist APA's sailing vessels in and out of port. The ships carried supplies and men north to fish and operate the canneries, then at the end of the salmon run the ships headed south with the season's pack. After many years using a 250-horsepower steam engine, APA in the 1930's gave the CHILKAT more power, they powered her with a 500-horsepower Atlas diesel.

Six years afterward, APA decided to sell the boat and Foss was right on hand to purchase her, so on January 21, 1942 the CHILKAT became the property of Foss Launch & Tug. A Foss crew brought her up from San Francisco to her new base in Seattle and the Atlas diesel never faltered on the four-day run.

Before fitting-out started, Foss renamed the CHILKAT, EDITH FOSS, to honor Wedell's wife. Actually, the boat was the second EDITH FOSS, the first EDITH was sold after only a year of Foss ownership. However, with the sinking of the CHILKAT-EDITH and re-purchase of the original EDITH, the CHILKAT-EDITH was then designated as EDITH number one.

After minor changes and outfitting, the tug under command of Captin Emil Wick, left on April 28, 1941 with the oil barge FOSS-100 in tow, for Alaska's Bering Sea region to begin an annual delivery run for Standard Oil Company supplying petroleum products to the towns of Naknek, Dillingham, and Bethel in Western Alaska. Unfortunately, the EDITH's first season on the oil re-supply run was marred by several incidents. On June 5th she grounded on a bar at Goodnews Bay during a falling tide and at change of tide the strong current caused her to drag over the gravel bottom giving the crew a good shaking up but no apparent damage to the tug.

A month later while docking her barge at a Port Moller cannery, the tow-winch brake failed causing the towline to pay out, making it impossible to control the barge. Caught in a strong current, the barge sheared and grounded on a mud bar, damaging the skegs so badly they were removed to prevent further damage to the bottom.

Then on September 7th, two cylinder heads cracked while towing the same unruly barge. With the engine stopped the barge, still on the towline, surged alongside, damaging the hull planking.

To climax her run of hard luck, the next day tug and barge grounded on the Kuskokwim River Flats due to peculiar mirage conditions which distorted the land position and led the tug into shoal water. The tug's sudden stop brought the towed barge hard against the EDITH's stern, damaging the after-bulwarks. The tug floated free soon after, but the barge was fast aground for two weeks. However, inspection revealed only denting to the bottom plating of two tanks. Fortunately there were no more delaying mishaps and the EDITH with FOSS-100 was able to finish her work and return to Seattle, arriving November 2, 1941.

After spending the winter on Puget Sound, the EDITH returned to the Western Alaska oil run in April, 1942. The season turned out as normal as the last one was frustrating so the EDITH was able to complete the deliveries weeks earlier than the previous year.

With the EDITH available for use and with military supplies urgently needed in Alaska due to World War II, the Army Transport Service requisitioned the tug and designated her LT-239. Captain Bill Stark, the Foss Skipper of the EDITH went along at the start of her Army service to assist the ATS captain.

The LT-239 was assigned duty at Amchitka in the Aleutians and while there she worked at pulling cargo barges off the beach. On one of the hard pulls the rudder palm broke loose and being unable to steer, the crew dropped the anchor to hold position, but the tug ended up dangerously close to jagged rocks. Unfortunately they let go of the towline to the barge and the LT-239, free of strain, swung right over on the rocks, gouging a hole in the hull below the waterline. The tug filled and sank, but luckily in shallow water so she could be patched, pumped, and raised. Four days later and again seaworthy, she left Amchitka to begin towing in Southeastern Alaska—but not for long, her Army service was about to end.

On December 4, 1943 while bound for Seattle with a tow, the Alaska Steamship Company vessel VICTORIA rammed and sank the LT-239 in Dixon entrance near Prince Rupert. The fifteen crewmen on the tug were rescued and returned to Seattle as distressed seamen—entitled to compensation for loss of possessions. In this her second and fatal sinking, unlike at Amchitka, she went down in water too deep for salvage and so her name was added to the long list of wartime marine casualties cradled in Alaskan water.

OSWELL FOSS

Built:	1940	Propulsion:	Enterprise
	Foss Company		450-horsepower
	Tacoma, Washington	Primary Service:	Puget Sound
Length:	74-feet	Final Foss Operating Day:	August 28, 1974
Beam:	19-feet	Status:	Sold Domestic

The OSWELL, named for a son of Andrew's brother Peter, was the largest and the most seaworthy of the six tugs built by the Foss Company after 1927 in their Tacoma yard. For longevity they planked the hull with Alaska cedar and for strength the timbering was clear Douglas fir. The four to one ratio of beam to length gave her good stability.

She started work in late April 1940 but Foss used her for only five months. With a Pacific war threatening and few late-model tugs available, the Navy requested the OSWELL and Foss, most willing to help the cause, sold the tug on October 15, 1940.

The Navy named her U.S.S. METEA and assigned the tug to Los Angeles for harbor work and eventually for tending anti-submarine nets. The METEA served the Navy for six years and then in March 1947 the Navy offered her back to Foss as the government policy was to return requisitioned vessels, if possible, to their former owners. Foss acquired the tug on March 21, 1947 and they were pleased to have their hand-built tug back in the fold. After a thorough check-out, painting, and renaming, Foss started her out doing general towing on Puget Sound and occasionally' helping the regular tugs in towing log-cribs from Neah Bay and Sekiu to Port Angeles.

During her career with Foss, the OSWELL carried out a number of special assignments, some out of her usual operating area. An unusual away-from-home job was carried out for San Francisco Bridge and Dredge Company at Coos Bay, Oregon. With Captain Oscar Rolstad in command, the OSWELL left Tacoma in late May 1948 for the two-day run down the coast. Her job was to tend the dredge ALABAMA employed in dredging at Coos Bay, using a 27-ton clamshell bucket. In addition to tending the dredge, shifting anchors, and crown buoys, the OSWELL towed

OSWELL FOSS *Eastbound in the Locks with a raft of logs for Lake Washington on September 25, 1966. (From the author's collection)*

the loaded dump scows out to sea, dumped them and returned the empties to the dredge. To keep up with the work, the OSWELL operated two twelve-hour shifts every day.

Much of the Coos Bay bottom was hard limestone so dynamite was often used to break up the bed and the blasting was usually done at low water. On one occasion, the OSWELL was ordered to shift an anchor and a mooring buoy into the clear before preparing another blast and unknown to the OSWELL the anchor had been placed dangerously close to a sub-surface rock. The OSWELL headed for the anchor buoy and unfortunately, in a heavy groundswell, she hooked the anchor and came down hard on the rock, severely damaging the propeller. The rising tide lifted her off the rocky perch and the crew worked the tug into Empire a mile away, where the OSWELL could be beached to change the wheel and repair any damage.

Within minutes of arriving at Empire, the crew heard over the marine radio that the ALABAMA had just suffered a major explosion. Regardless of the tug's condition, the crew immediately headed for the dredge to render assistance. Arriving alongside they were informed that fortunately no one was killed, but the ALABAMA's sponson compartments were blown out and the galley area practically destroyed.

Inspection revealed that an old W.W. II Japanese mine had floated in and exploded upon contact with the dredge. Providentially the OSWELL was not alongside the dredge in the usual place she occupied during blasting times. The mine exploded right at the OSWELL's tie-up spot—it was a case of a minor accident preventing a major catastrophe! The ALABAMA and the OSWELL were repaired at Empire and finished the job, without help, in November 1948.

With the project successfully completed, the OSWELL returned to Tacoma and resumed her former work—towing chip-scows, log rafts, and cribs. Towing logs and scows became a regular routine for the OSWELL and her five-man crew, continuing without interruption until a break came in 1960.

The change in scenery came about when the OSWELL was used by the Foss Ocean Division for service to the U. S. Government on the re-supply program for the Mona Lisa radar stations. On May 4th, with Captain Don Williams in charge, the OSWELL left Seattle with Foss Barge-167, a barge with bow doors and ramp for beaching operations. Her first stop was the station at Middleton Island in the Gulf of Alaska, then across to Naknek on the Bering Sea side of the Aleutians, arriving there May 24th. The OSWELL assisted in lightering cargo from the AGNES FOSS' large cargo barges to the beach unloading sites. During the next two and one-half months, the OSWELL worked several more beach operations, then she headed for home via Anchorage arriving in Seattle August 29th. After voyage repairs she returned to her regular duties out of Tacoma—the extended trips away from home over with until July 1961.

Then the OSWELL, with Captain Bud Thweatt in charge, left Seattle with two small flat-deck barges in tow for Yaquina Bay, Oregon. The barges were to be used in connection with sample core-drilling in the entrance channel and the harbor.

Once the OSWELL delivered the barges, she began a regular work routine with the three-man crew of Captain Thweatt, Budd Turner (later Captain of the MARTHA FOSS) and Gene Otis—they worked the OSWELL five days a week. The job consisted in tending several small three-legged drill towers, setting and pulling anchors and tending two equipment-barges, one with a large air-compressor aboard furnishing air for drills penetrating the sea floor.

The crew naturally was curious to know the purpose of the three-month program of drilling, but the answer was not revealed; apparently the work was secret. But they did know it was a Government-sponsored job and the Army Corp of Engineers were overseers on the entire operation. Rumors of all sorts came from the workers, the most common story had the Government testing for an eventual deepening of the channel for a submarine base. Time has proved there must have been another reason.

The OSWELL, her work finished, returned to Seattle on October 10, 1961 and after two days of voyage repairs, she began her usual routine towing.

For the next fourteen years the OSWELL built up a continuous operating record, except for annual drydocking and repairs. She lived up to the Foss reputation, delivering the tows as scheduled. But by early 1974 with complete utilization of the new and powerful steel tugs, the OSWELL was relegated to back-up service—used only when an extra tug was needed. She did sporadic duty the first eight months and completed her last job on August 27, 1974. After delivering a log tow to Quendal on Lake Washington she returned to the Foss dock and went on the "on call" list. She remained available throughout the fall, but by November her reprieve time had run out and she was shifted to the Foss lay-up fleet, the final step before being sold.

The OSWELL remained dormant until September 2, 1975 then Foss sold her to Captain Dick Wright of Tacoma for use as a yacht and a tug. Captain Wright changed the name from OSWELL to JENNY W and he worked the boat on small towing jobs in the Sound. He also did house-moving by barge, landing homes on beach sites.

In 1977 the JENNY W began regular towing, hauling gravel scows between the Steilacoom gravel pit and Schofield Materials Co. in Tacoma. As of late 1979 she was still in the gravel business and pulling hard.

SANDRA FOSS (1)

Built:	1925	Propulsion:	Enterprise
	Chilman Shipyards		750-horsepower
	Hoquiam, Washington	Primary Service:	Puget Sound
Length:	77-feet	Final Foss Operating Day:	March 1, 1973
Beam:	21-feet	Status:	Sold Domestic

The Allman-Hubble Tugboat Company of Grays Harbor built the Sandra, but under the Indian name of TYEE. They used the tug for local work in Grays Harbor and towing log rafts to and from ports on the Oregon and Washington coasts.

She was built in the transition period between steam and diesel, as most of the new tugboats constructed after the early 20's were diesel powered. However the TYEE was an oil burning steam tug of 340-horsepower, but by 1930 her owners joined the trend to diesel and repowered the tug even though she was only five years old.

The TYEE ran light to Seattle and arrived at the Ballard Marine Ways on June 7, 1930. The shipyard removed the steam plant, laid down new foundation timbers and installed a 500-horsepower Atlas diesel together with the usual auxiliary equipment. The shipyard accomplished the conversion in a record time of two months including fit-

TYEE *Shown as a steam powered tug, operating in Grays Harbour. Later to become the Sandra Foss. (Courtesy of Joe Williamson)*

ting new fuel tanks and a hot-water system. After trial runs on Puget Sound, the TYEE returned to Grays Harbor and Coast log towing—a hazardous occupation.

Her first brush with disaster came in March 1933 when sounding for the channel off the mouth of the Nehalem River near Brighton, Oregon. She ran aground by the entrance and the swells drove her up on a sandspit near the Brighton jetty. Due to her position it was impossible to work equipment for refloating the tug on the outer side of the sandspit, so the services of a Salvage Master and the Ballard Marine Railway were enlisted to move the stranded tug back to deep water. The salvage crew cut down trees and hewed them into rough timbers for building a cradle under the entire length of the tug. Then they brought in two logging yarders (self-powered winches) mounted on heavy sleds and pulled the cradle and tug across the sandspit, a distance of 1,000 feet, to the inner side and into water deep enough to float the TYEE over to the channel.

Surprisingly, she made the run up to the Ballard Yard under her own power, but with an escort. During several weeks work, the shipyard fitted a new keel, recaulked the hull, and replaced the iron bark sheathing. By July she was able to resume towing and again on the unsheltered coasts.

Another expensive incident happened to the TYEE in March 1938. While towing the 1,251-ton steel barge NISQUALLY, loaded with 600,000 feet of peeler logs, the barge broke away off the mouth of the Columbia River and stranded on Clatsop Spit. Most of the high-grade logs were lost and the barge severely damaged. However, after several weeks of salvage effort, the barge was refloated, repaired, and returned to service.

The TYEE's next accident was tragic and almost finished her off. On December 6, 1940 she delivered a tow in Tillamook Bay and on her way out she encountered high, steep seas, particularly when crossing the bar. Before she cleared the rough, shallow entrance, the steering gear failed allowing the tug to swing broadside at the mercy of the wind and the battering waves. In a matter of minutes she was swept into the pounding surf on the shoal side of the channel, overwhelmed and eventually driven ashore. Sad to relate, two crewmen, John Henderson, Deckhand, and Julius Long, Cook, were washed overboard and drowned. The rest of the crew, headed by Captain Hillary Hubble, successfully launched the tug's lifeboat before the TYEE foundered and they battled gale-force winds and high seas for six hours, to keep away from the breakers, before they were rescued by the Coast Guard Cutter ONANDAGA.

After a survey of the wreck, Allman-Hubble sold the TYEE, as-is-where-is, to Columbia River Salvage and during the ensuing months they stripped the tug while high and dry on the beach. Then Foss Company was asked to take a look at the TYEE, so they made a thorough inspection with the idea of purchasing.

Foss found the tug to be structurally sound so they bought her direct from the Salvage Company and began at once on a long and tedious salvage operation. The same method was used as proved successful eight years before at Nehalem. A cradle was again built under the boat and the unit skidded to Barview where they launched her into Tillamook Bay, nearly a year after her stranding. Then Foss towed her to their Tacoma shipyard where she spent the next several months under repair. The deckhouses were rebuilt and much of the hull renewed and new machinery installed. The tug's crews claimed that the Yard never did get all the sand and gravel out that accumulated during her stay on the Tillamook Beach. Pockets of sand remained between the inner and outer planking of the hull in the spaces alongside the fames—the same type of void spaces were packed with salt to inhibit dry rot in the days of sailing ship construction.

In June, 1942 completely rebuilt and repowered with a 750-horsepower Enterprise diesel, and when fully outfitted, Foss gave her the name SANDRA, in honor of the daughter of Sidney and Barbara Foss Campbell. After only a few short weeks of towing for Foss-Tacoma, the Army Transport Service requisitioned her along with several other Puget Sound Foss tugs.

The SANDRA worked out of the Seattle Port of Embarkation on local towing and occasionally on barge tows for the Army between Seattle and Excursion Inlet, Alaska, the staging area for barges waiting to be towed across the Gulf of Alaska by the ocean-going Miki-class tugs. At times, there wasn't a southbound Army tow and the SANDRA then would go to Edna Bay in Southeastern Alaska and pick up a crib of spruce logs and deliver them to Puget Sound for sawing into clear flitches to be used in England for the manufacture of training-aircraft.

The tug remained in use by the Army until August 1946 then they returned her to Foss for commercial towing, and Foss immediately placed her as primary harbor assist-tug in Seattle, helped as necessary by the FOSS 18. Now and then the SANDRA had time to make the rail-car barge run between Seattle and Port Townsend for the Milwaukee Railroad, but even on the simple car-barge run, Murphy's Law again applied to her.

This time the Milwaukee Rail-barge-6, while under tow of the SANDRA, sank as a result of a collision with the 6,000-ton FAIRLAND while entering Seattle Harbor. The riding crew aboard the barge was rescued by the tug in a matter of minutes, but six of the railcars loaded with lumber later washed ashore. Normality was not a part of the SANDRA's life!

She continued as the primary ship-assist tug for Seattle and in 1953 to give her more help, the ERIK FOSS came up from the Long Beach operation of Pacific Tow and Salvage. But by 1957 ship tonnage in and out of the Port of Seattle increased so rapidly that new and more powerful ship-assist tugs were needed. So in 1958 to meet the demand, two new sister-tugs of 1,200-horsepower, the SHANNON and CAROL FOSS, assumed all Port ship-assist work.

At the same period of general Port expansion, Anacortes and Ferndale started handling more and larger ships, principally tankers. The tugs BELLINGHAM BAY, 400-horsepower, and the sixty-year-old PROSPER, 350-horsepower, were not adequate to handle the heavy and many tankers arriving at the refineries, so in the summer of 1958 after arrival of the SHANNON and CAROL in Seattle, the SANDRA was transferred to Anacortes as a ship-assist tug. Her coming was a great help to the Captains and Pilots of the large ships by making the docking and undocking safer. Then to further improve ship assistance, late in 1958 the ERIK was assigned to Anacortes. This allowed the SANDRA to shift her base of operation to Bellingham, to take better care of the shipping in and out of Bellingham and Ferndale.

The SANDRA remained in Bellingham until late May 1959 then relieved of her job, she returned to Seattle to help out on the ever-increasing harbor activities, but again she made occasional rail-car runs to Port Townsend for the Milwaukee Railroad. In September 1960 she traded ports and jobs with the ERIK, and this time the SANDRA remained in Bellingham only until October 1961 when the recently purchased 1,200-horsepower tug LUMMI BAY arrived to take over the ship-assist work. The LUMMI BAY's sister-tug SEA KING, stationed in Anacortes at the time, handled the heavy ship jobs in that area.

SANDRA FOSS *Navigating the Lake Washington Ship Canal with an LST-Class barge alongside, October, 1966. (From the author's collection)*

Another switch took place in October 1962 when more power was needed to supplement the SHANNON and CAROL's work. The LUMMI BAY was sent to Seattle and the SANDRA once more ended up in Bellingham. She remained there until a fire almost destroyed her, but the ex-TYEE once again refused to be written-off.

The SANDRA, as most tugs of her time, had an Arcola stove for ship's heating and the SANDRA's was located in the upper engine room, an unfortunate location. In October 1963 while lying alongside a tanker at Anacortes after finishing the ship-assist, the Chief started up the Arcola and really turned the heat on. Captain Dick Lamont had backed the tug away from the tanker and headed for Bellingham, but half-an-hour later, shortly after the SANDRA passed the SEA KING, flames erupted from the upper engine room and within minutes the entire engine room and officers' quarters on the boat deck, which had a direct stairway-access from the engine room, were engulfed in fire and smoke. Captain Lamont put out a "MAYDAY" on the radio which the SEA KING, an ex-Navy fireboat, picked up and immediately reversed course to the SANDRA, readying her fire-fighting equipment on the way, including a large fire monitor.

In the meantime the crew, to escape the scorching heat, retreated to the bow of the SANDRA to await rescue by the SEA KING since the fire had melted their plastic lifeboat within minutes; it was swim or chance the SEA KING arriving in time. The fire quickly burned through the pilot house engine and rudder-control cables, so the SANDRA continued on her course running all out in the general direction of Bellingham. But after going a mile, the fuel lines burned off and the tug rapidly lost way, allowing the SEA KING to approach the blazing inferno.

After taking off SANDRA's crew, Captain Dick Blake and his crew immediately began pouring water into the SANDRA from a stand-off position and with the tremendous volume the SEA KING threw aboard, the fire was extinguished in ten minutes. Of major concern now, with the fire out, was the seaworthiness of the water-logged tug. However, under careful towing by the SEA KING, she arrived at Anacortes and was immediately pumped out. The next day Foss towed the SANDRA to the Foss shipyard in Tacoma for survey and repairs.

Foss decided the tug was worth repairing and immediately began the job of rebuilding the upper deck-quarters, galley, and engine room. After several months of repair work, the SANDRA re-entered service in late March 1964. She was rebuilt to her former configuration and arrangement, the Tacoma yard doing a top job—her appearance a compliment to their skill.

The SANDRA was assigned to Seattle again as a harbor and ship-assist tug. However, since the Foss tug replacement and building program was underway and new tugs were taking over more and more of the jobs, the SANDRA's work load became much lighter, easing the wear and tear on her forty-year-old hull. The Seattle office gave her less harbor work and more routine linehaul towing between the principal Sound ports. In the late 60's Foss had her on the cement run to Bellingham and the chemical or oil run to Anacortes and Bellingham.

On one of the oil delivery runs in July 1969 the tug again was afflicted with the "TYEE-SANDRA" syndrome and a most unfortunate and very strange accident occurred. Most people would only recall July 20, 1969 as the day the American astronauts walked on the moon, but for the dispatchers on duty at Foss-Seattle and all the operations personnel the day will also be remembered as the day the fully loaded oil barge FOSS-114 sank while under tow of the SANDRA.

At about 0600, July 21st while nearing Pt. Wilson, the SANDRA's Captain reported the barge had developed a list. Tug and barge were southbound with 14,000 barrels of diesel from Anacortes to Ballard, a routine job and good weather prevailing. According to the report of the dispatcher on duty in Seattle, the barge suddenly flipped over at 0720 hours and the towing bridle legs dropped off, allowing the barge to drift free. Shortly after, the JOSIE FOSS and a Coast Guard vessel arrived to render assistance, but there was no way of making a line fast to the 114 in the overturned condition and with the available gear. The boats stayed close-by and at 1245 the SANDRA reported the barge sank.

Both tugs and the Coast Guard remained over the site, as the barge held its position 150 feet off the bottom. Then at 1825 a strange situation arose, literally. While the Coast Guard vessel was circling over the sunken barge, the 114 mysteriously rose to within six feet of the surface, struck and damaged the propeller of the Coast Guard vessel and then the 114 sank seventy feet below the surface and started to drift away with the tide—the depth sounder indicated 250-feet of water. The barge remained buoyant, drifted with the tides for two days, impossible to corral. Then by the twenty-fourth, the 114 apparently lost all buoyancy and sank to the sea floor, its exact location could not be determined until three days later.

As the 114 remained in the same position for the next month, a salvage plan was discussed, but with the barge lying in 240-feet of water any attempt to raise her even with hard-hat divers and sophisticated equipment was considered too risky. However, divers did make a quick inspection and found the barge sitting level, but capsized, slightly bedded and intact. After more technical conferences, Foss decided to write off the barge and cargo as a total constructive loss.

There is considerable difference in attitudes between authoritative comments on the oil barge loss in 1969 and oil spill reaction in today's pollution-conscious society under influence of the Environmental Protection Agency. A leading water pollution expert at the University of Washington commented at the time: "The greater loss was to the owner of the barge—the oil spill appears bad, but from a biological standpoint, the barge-load (14,000 barrels) is not measureable from any practical standpoint." A fisheries expert agreed by advising: "The damage to sealife will be minimal." Unfortunately no distinction is made in today's assessment between the light oils (diesel) and the heavy black oils—yet there is a great difference in degree of damage. The Foss-114 was loaded with diesel—no known deleterious effects developed.

The consensus of opinion was that by the time the barge finally came to rest on the bottom, most of the 588,000-gallons aboard had drained out. The spill was and would be broken up by biological action. Yet ten years later an accidental spill of a quart of diesel is considered a punishable offense. The diesel hasn't changed but attitudes have. Fines and reprimands on minimal spills, by the Coast Guard and EPA are supposedly assessed to develop an awareness, but the punitive action under accidental circumstances could be considered harassment by the spiller. The case of the SANDRA's barge causing but little identifiable pollution would indicate that in today's spills the "punishment should fit the crime."

The SANDRA operated on linehaul tows only until mid-July 1970 then there were enough new high-powered efficient tugs to take over most of the runs. The SANDRA couldn't compete, so Foss laid her up pending a final decision on her future.

After lying idle at the Ballard yard for two months, she had a short reprieve—Pacific Towboat at Everett needed another tug for ship-assists and the SANDRA got the call. She handled about twenty ships a month, using a crew from one of the smaller harbor tugs. The SANDRA's expense was minimal and the saving in costs by not having to run tugs up from Seattle or other ports with full crews aboard was considerable.

While still based in Everett the SANDRA had a sudden change of scenery in August and September 1971 during the West Coast Longshore strike. With the strike in effect there were no ships arriving in port, but there were several hundred rafts of logs to be towed to Canada where they could be loaded for Japan with no Longshore problems. A full crew was put aboard the SANDRA and she returned to log towing for the first time since her Grays Harbor days, more than thirty years previously. She proved equal to the task and during her month-and-a-half towing logs to Canada, she delivered eight tows amounting to about six million feet.

At the settlement of the strike, the SANDRA remained in Everett harbor assisting log ships in and out of port. Then with more and more mechanical problems to contend with, Foss ordered the tug into permanent lay-up early in 1973. But the SANDRA's career wasn't over yet, regardless of her age and condition.

In May 1974 Don House of Wrangell, Alaska, realizing the need for a tug of the SANDRA's power and weight for ship-service in southeastern Alaska, purchased the tug and renamed her TYEE. After drydocking and engine repair she left for Alaska in late June.

The TYEE is fully occupied serving the ports of Wrangell, Juneau, Haines, and Skagway—working at her old trade—assisting ocean carriers. After forty-five years and three near-terminal disasters, the TYEE is still responsive and seems to have shaken off the "TYEE-SANDRA" syndrome.

ADELINE (1)

Built:	1898	Propulsion:	Steam
	Tacoma, Washington		175-horsepower
Length:	72-feet	Primary Service:	Puget Sound
Beam:	18-feet	Final Operating Day:	April 1949
		Status:	Disposed of by burning

Foss company's first ADELINE started out as a steam powered tug named FLOSIE and apparently built for resale by LaConner Trading & Transportation Company of Seattle, Joshua Green, President. In May 1899 after just one year under LaConner's ownership they sold her to the Juneau Ferry & Navigation company for towing service in connection with gold mining operations in Southeastern Alaska.

While based in Juneau, the FLOSIE on August 15, 1901 unexpectedly played an important part in the rescue of passengers and crew from the ill-fated steamer ISLANDER. The ship had left Skagway for Juneau shortly before midnight on August 14th with 112 passengers and 71 crew members. Shortly after leaving port, the ISLANDER encountered dense fog in Lynn Canal and it is assumed the current set her inside the course and eighty miles from Skagway she ran on the rocks near Pt. Hilda. Her steel hull was holed in many places and she sank rapidly. The lifeboats were launched, but due to the short time available to abandon ship, many people were unable to reach the boats and they perished in the cold water. The Chief Engineer and a few other survivors were able to swim ashore and then hike along the beach 14 miles to the Treadwell Mine. Fortunately, they found the FLOSIE and another tug, the LUCY, lying alongside the mine wharf just south of Juneau. The tug crews were informed of the tragedy and having steam up, they raced to the scene of the wreck and found the lifeboats milling around still looking for survivors. The tugs took aboard everyone alive and brought them back to Juneau. Out of the 183 persons aboard, forty-two perished. More would have been lost due to exposure except for the heroic struggle of the Chief Engineer's hardy group and the timely action of the FLOSIE and LUCY—true sisters of providence to the survivors.

After five years of plowing up the water in and around Juneau, the FLOSIE joined the Army, her commercial career suspended. The War Department in November 1903 purchased her for use as a supply boat in southeastern Alaska and based in Skagway. She remained in government service for twenty years and then in March 1923 the government sold her to the Wilson & Sylvester Mill Company at Wrangell, Alaska. But before starting service for Wrangell Mill, the Company gave her an extensive rebuild and they eliminated a portion of the cabin to give her a longer open after deck so the towline would have a longer lead.

The Wrangell Mill used the FLOSIE for log towing until March 1929 when they sold her to Carl Isakson of Seattle for general towing on Puget Sound. She remained in the area until April 1933 then Mr. Isakson sent the tug to Southern California for a year-and-a-half, then with the California work completed, she returned to Seattle for another change of ownership.

ADELINE FOSS *Running light inbound to Seattle Harbor off Magnolia Bluff in the mid-forties. (Courtesy of Joe Williamson)*

Delta V. Smyth purchased her for towing out of Olympia, using the tug for seven years. FLOSIE lost her 59 year old name in July 1939 when Smyth renamed her OLYMPIAN, to give the tug local identity.

The ex-FLOSIE acquired a seventh owner in April 1941 when Smyth sold her and another tug, the ALICE, to Foss. The ALICE became the SIMON FOSS based in Tacoma, and the OLYMPIAN became the Seattle-based tug ADELINE FOSS, named for a daughter of Andrew's brother Peter—how melodious if only the tug could have been named FLOSIE FOSS.

The ADELINE had an active but short career with Foss, she didn't fit the Company's long range plans and she had two serious operating handicaps. For a steam tug to have a fuel capacity of only eighty-eight barrels, providing just two or three days steaming time, was a decided disadvantage, especially with a slow long-distance log tow. Her range was further limited as she carried only enough boiler feed water for fifty to sixty hours steaming.

By 1941 with the heavy operating expense of steam tugs, only eight remained in active service on Puget Sound, including the ADELINE. However, their life-span was extended due to the shortage of tugs in the early years of World War II.

During the War, the ADELINE was primarily used in towing ammunition barges between Tacoma and Indian Island near Port Townsend or to Ostrich Bay near Bremerton. On every trip a Coast Guard vessel was required to escort the ADELINE and her barge. All the ammunition-barge runs were uneventful except one. On this particular voyage, the ADELINE and her barge had left Ostrich Bay and they were heading for the bridge at Port Washington Narrows and bucking a strong current. Her skipper, Sam Stout, only had 150-feet of towline out, but even so the barge suddenly caught an eddy and took a sheer for the bridge. Captain Stout, seeing the possible danger of explosion, blew the danger whistle to warn the riding crew of the barge and the accompanying Coast Guard boat. The deckhand, standing by the brake on the tug immediately, on orders, slacked off the towline and the explosives-laden barge swung just enough to miss ramming the bridge, by one foot!

When collision appeared inevitable the Coast Guard escort-vessel turned around and headed full bore back towards Ostrich Bay and as the ADELINE was not allowed to continue her trip without a Coast Guard escort, she had to stall and wait for the "escort" to return. Apparently the ship didn't know the danger was over in minutes for she stayed completely away from the area. Eventually, Coast Guard Headquarters sent another vessel over from Seattle to continue the run.

Captain Stout stated that in towing "ammo" barges, the ADELINE was at a disadvantage and a bit risky because she did not have sufficient steam-capacity. After bringing in the towline with her winch there was very little steam left for backing and filling when making a landing and the docking could easily get out of control. There was little margin for error in handling the ADELINE, both in the wheelhouse and engine room.

On another occasion, in August 1943 the ADELINE was towing a rail-barge into Bremerton and as she neared Pt. Glover, the fast streamlined ferry KALAKALA suddenly showed up outbound from Bremerton. The barge sheered while rounding the point and the KALAKALA, unable to take evasive action, collided with the barge, holing the side and toppling two railcars into Rich Passage. The barge was beached, a temporary patch put on, then towed to Tacoma for repairs.

The ADELINE had a second railcar barge-run and this particular haul required a steam tug. She towed the barge between Seattle and the Baxter-Wycoff Creosoting Plant at Eagle Harbor. The barge had a small steam engine and winch aboard for pulling the rail cars on and off at the Plant. The ADELINE, lying alongside, furnished steam for the winch, using a flexible-joint pipe. Tug and barge were self-sufficient, a complete towing, loading, and unloading unit.

Occasionally, the ADELINE did ship-assist work and on one assignment, in company with a second Foss tug, she was dispatched to Lake Union Drydock to shift a cargo vessel. In coming alongside, the ADELINE's skipper bounced her hard against the ship, just below the big vessel's bridge. No damage was done to either the tug or the ship, but by the heavy jolt, all the accumulated soot in the tug's stack broke loose and shot up like a black sand storm, covering the bridge of the ship and the Pilot standing in the wing. The shower of soot blackened him from head to foot and his descriptive language more than matched the color of the soot!

The ADELINE, in spite of her failings, served Foss for eight years and the Captains handling her were Ralph Paschal, Norm Driggs, Clyde Smith, Clarence Geddes, and Noel Ferris.

By late 1948 the era of steam tugs was about over and as Foss had acquired several war-surplus diesel tugs, with their proven economy, the ADELINE was only used a few days each month. By early February 1949 on her fiftieth birthday, she tied up at Foss-Seattle with no hope of running again. At this time, only two steam tugs, the MARY D. HUME of American Towboat Company and the MILWAUKEE owned by Milwaukee Railroad, remained in operation on the Sound. The other steam tugs operated by Foss, the WANDERER and KENAI were retired in 1947 and 1948.

The ADELINE remained at the Foss-Seattle moorings for several months before being shifted to the boneyard moorings at Kennydale on Lake Washington. She became a forgotten boat as she remained in the Kennydale farm for nearly twelve years. Then on June 16, 1961 the ANNA FOSS went to Kennydale, picked up the ADELINE and towed her to the Foss-Seattle yard for removal of the steam engine—for posterity. On June 27th, with the engine out, Foss towed her to Tacoma and on July 4th as part of the Independence Day celebration, she was set afire in the harbor as a symbol of the torch of Liberty.

Sixty-four years earlier she existed only in a set of plans and in 1961 she ended up as only a set of plans—the ADELINE should have been named Sockeye, Coho, Silver or Chum as like them she returned to her place of birth to expire.

ALICE On lower Puget Sound in the early thirties as a steam tug owned by Delta Smyth of Olympia. (Courtesy of Joe Williamson)

SIMON FOSS

Built:	1897	Propulsion:	Superior
	Crawford & Haskell Yard		175-horsepower
	Tacoma, Washington	Primary Service:	Puget Sound
Length:	65-feet	Final Foss Operating Day:	April 13, 1962
Beam:	16-feet	Status:	Sold Domestic

The SIMON's first owner, Captain William Bradford of Tacoma, since he intended to use the boat in his own business, built her with the best Douglas fir lumber and the best workmanship. To honor his wife, Captain Bradford named his new passenger steamer ALICE. He operated the boat on the Tacoma-North Bay passenger run, replacing the smaller steamer SUSIE, built in 1879 and sold to Franco-American Canning Company of Bellingham.

The ALICE stayed with the North Bay route until February 1901 then Bradford sold her to the Pacific Coast & Norway Packing Company, with Wrangell, Alaska the home port. She worked as a passenger-freight vessel and cannery-tender for two years, then in late 1902 PC&NPC rebuilt her at Juneau into a combination tender and tug. However, in August 1918 they sold her to Todd Packing Company for use at their own canneries. Todd kept the name ALICE and ran her with only a four-man crew even though she had steam power. The ALICE hauled fish scows during the Alaska season then she generally tied up for the winter in Seattle.

In December 1925 her work for Todd, after seven years, was completed and they sold her to the Delta V. Smyth Towing Company of Olympia. The ALICE continued in Smyth service for five years, basically unaltered in form from her Alaska days. During this period, Captains Art Mix, Andrew Lunde, and Henry Butcher had charge of the ALICE.

By 1930 with modern diesels proving efficient and economical, Delta Smyth decided the time had come to give the thirty-three-year-old tug a new start in life, so he installed a 135-horsepower Washington diesel. In addition to the new engine, Smyth increased the fuel capacity to 3,000 gallons, giving her a cruising range of 1,000 miles. He removed the old cabins and built a one-level deckhouse, eliminating the raised pilothouse. The streamlining gave her a modern appearance and distiction for a vessel of her size. She was ready to go again in December 1930 with Lorene Jacobson as Captain.

Smyth continued to use her in his up-Sound towing operations until February 1941 when he sold her, along with the OLYMPIAN, to Foss. The OLYMPIAN became a member of the Seattle division and the ALICE, renamed SIMON FOSS, to honor a son of Theodore, became a unit of the Tacoma fleet. Shortly after taking possession of the tug, Foss removed the Washington diesel and installed a 175-horsepower Superior diesel. Foss hired the Smyth crew to man the tug so there was no lost motion in putting the SIMON to work. Captain Carl Woge ran her for several years, then Captain Jack Harropp took over, followed by Ed Stork.

During her career with Foss, the SIMON spent most of her time towing logs and barges between Tacoma, Olympia, and Shelton. Even though comparable in size with most Puget Sound tugs of her time, she had disadvantages compared to other linehaul tugs. The SIMON, very simply equipped, was without a freezer or reefer unit. She did have an icebox which kept perishables cool for up to three days, then more ice had to be found. Another inconvenience, her fresh-water capacity was a mere 150-gallons and it had to be pumped by hand. Hot water for washing was obtained by heating on the galley stove, a nuisance to the cook. And the crew was always careful not to work up a sweat or get too dirty as the SIMON had no shower. The W.C. also was primitive, flushing was accomplished with a bucketful of saltwater borrowed from Puget Sound.

The Captain and Mate slept aft of the pilothouse and the Cook with the Deckhands slept below in the foc's'le with the only source of heat an open-flame Arcola. If the heater was off the crew shivered, if left on the crew roasted—either on or off it was a penance.

With the SIMON's living deficiencies, Foss usually assigned her short jobs, primarily towing hogged-fuel scows five days a week from the Buchanan Mill in Olympia to the St. Regis Mill in Tacoma, where the waste chips were used for boiler fuel. For another short range job the SIMON towed barge loads of export lumber from the Simpson Mill at Shelton to Olympia for loading aboard deep-water ships. Captain Ed. Stork, the SIMON's regular skipper for many years, related that one of his exciting trips out of Shelton occurred when towing five loaded lumber barges from Shelton through the Narrows in Hammersley Inlet to Olympia. Three barge loads were considered maximum to safely bring through the narrow passage and at this time, in 1961, there were no docks or buoys to tie off extra loads—once a start was made there was no turning back. Captain Stork said he had "butterflies" watching the currents swing the barges shorewise and stretch his towline to the limit. But he came through with his charges—it was quite a feat and he only had 175-horsepower.

Captain Ed related another incident in the early 1950's with Captain Jack Harropp, another Foss skipper, aboard. They were lying in Oakland Bay at Shelton waiting to pull a log tow out of storage, but meanwhile the tide ebbed and dropped the SIMON on a deadhead. Then when the tide flooded, water flowed right through the hole in the planking made by the sunken log and nothing could be done to stop the heavy inrush of water. They had to abandon ship as the SIMON was fast filling to deck level. At high water only her two masts showed.

During the next low tide the hole was patched and the remaining water pumped out. Foss then towed her to Tacoma for drying out and refurbishing. The Captain figured there was a lesson in the accident—don't assume the bottom is just mud, even if the chart says so.

By the early 60's, after more than thirty years turning the propeller, the SIMON's old Superior finally balked at the heavy and constant use. The crew said the tug ran her last two years with the engine held in place with bailing wire, the machinists at Tacoma winced every time the SIMON came to the pier as it always meant a taxing repair job. However, after April 13, 1962 they had no further cause to fret.

The remedy came about at the time relief skipper Captain Ron Crabtree was aboard. The SIMON had just delivered a tow of peeler logs from Tacoma to Quendal in Lake Washington and they were running light to the Foss-Seattle office for orders, when a crash with a loud cracking of metal came from the engine room and the SIMON went dead in the water. After a tow to the Foss yard, an inspection revealed a sad situation: one of the rod-bearing cap studs failed and went right through the engine base causing bad breaks. Extensive repair would be required and considering other weaknesses, Foss decided the overall costs would be prohibitive for a sixty-five-year-old tug, so no time was wasted in laying her up at Tacoma.

Then in October 1963 Foss sold her to Gordon Newell of Olympia for use as a beach house and office. Mr. Newell, author of many fine seafaring books and articles, was editor of the "H. W. McCurdy Marine History of the Northwest" and the SIMON provided an inspiring retreat for the maritime oriented writer. Foss removed the old Superior engine and other equipment, then at Gordon Newell's request, the DREW FOSS, on one of the high tides, towed the SIMON, once again renamed ALICE, to a sandy beach area near Olympia and pushed her up to the

SIMON FOSS *A completely rebuilt version of the former Alice. (Courtesy of Joe Williamson)*

bulkhead facing Mr. Newell's property. She was firmly entrenched in the sand and made fast to prevent her from floating away on later high tides. In short order the Newell family had a beach cabin and one with a sixty-six-year history. The pilothouse, captain's quarters and foc's'le were left as they were when she functioned as a tugboat.

For ten years the ALICE remained on her sandy perch, her old hull growing more brittle with each year out of water. No one passing the old relic ever considered the ex-tug would float again—but she did!

Apparently Captain Miles Hargitt of Anacortes had the courage to undertake a rebirth of the ALICE for in July 1974 he purchased the 77-year-old tug from Mr. Newell as is, where is. Then he set about the task of excavating, caulking and patching after bulldozing the gravel away, exposing the hull so it could be made reasonably watertight. On a high tide later on, the ALICE floated free after ten years ashore. Miles Hargitt, satisfied with what he bought, towed the resurrected ALICE to Bellingham with his other tug, the LIL' LOUIE. The ALICE went on drydock for hull rebuild and installation of new machinery. Thirty-three hull planks had to be replaced in order to make her seaworthy and the frames had hardened so much that the heavy boat spikes bent when driven in. Finally the bonehard frames were drilled to receive the planking spikes and that solved the problem.

A 500-horsepower supercharged Enterprise diesel was installed at Anacortes in 1976 and the new engine gave her three times more power than any of the ALICE's former engines—her speed increased to thirteen knots. Finally in mid-1976 rebuilding was complete, however, the main deck house, dating back to 1930 was left intact so as to preserve her long low flowing lines.

The ALICE, seventy-nine years old, disregarded the restraints of old age, prudent towboat practice, and with minimum fuel and less water, took on the job of towing the former Canadian crusie ship GLACIER QUEEN from Seattle to Anchorage, Alaska. She had to cross the very unpredictable and often stormy open water of the Gulf of Alaska, but Captain Hargitt felt his pride and joy would deliver the goods. His confidence wasn't misplaced. The ALICE successfully made the run to Anchorage, averaging 6.9 knots. Limitations and age were not deterrents in favorable weather.

Captain Hargitt and the ALICE worked on several assignments for General Construction and on the first job they towed tandem rock barges to Port Angeles, and each barge carried 1,500 tons. The haul lasted only three weeks, but Captain and tug had little idle time. The Foss motto must have remained with the tug—she is always ready to go. ready to go.

In May 1977 the ALICE made a fine showing in the Seattle Antique tugboat races, placing second and beating out four other ex-Foss tugs in the race.

In 1981 the ALICE was sold by Capt. Hargitt. The new owners converted her to a shrimper for work in the San Juan Islands and later S.E. Alaska. The ALICE lives on—a tribute to Capt William Bradford's foresight.

EDITH FOSS *Departing Foss dock January 26, 1968 bound for the S.E. Alaska oil run, her final operating season under Foss ownership. (From the author's collection)*

EDITH FOSS (2)

Built:	1919	Propulsion:	Union
	New Orleans, Louisiana		560-horsepower
Length:	81-feet	Primary Service:	Puget Sound
Beam:	21-feet	Final Foss Operating Day:	October 11, 1968
		Status:	Sold Foreign

Government shipbuilding programs through the years provided tugboat companies with the opportunity to purchase ready-made tugs to build up their fleet and this was the case with the second EDITH FOSS. She was built as a combination steam tug and passenger vessel at a cost of $137,000, and put on the Navy roster with the number A-49. The navy assigned her for service on the West Coast, but she eventually ended up in Honolulu where the navy decommissioned her in the mid-1920's.

Shortly after her loss of status, R.J. Ultican of Ultican Tugboat Company, Grays Harbor, Washington, purchased the A-49 and had the vessel towed across the Pacific to Aberdeen, Washington. Ultican removed all the old machinery and then temporarily berthed the hull along the banks of the Wishkah River while he planned the conversion.

By mid-1928 major rebuilding was underway, including new deck houses. For power, Ultican ordered a 425-horsepower diesel from Washington Iron Works in Seattle. The engine arrived in early February and was promptly set into the machinery space and bolted to the engine bed. After a years' work of renewing, the tug was complete and ready to tow. Renamed RUSTLER, her trial run on July 5, 1929 was a great success for those days—she attained a speed of 11½ knots. Ultican put her to work towing logs from the Oregon Coast to Grays Harbor and towing logs around the Grays Harbor area.

Then after eleven years with Ultican the RUSTLER, in January of 1940 was purchased by Foss and as the tug was in fine condition, they started her right out for San Francisco, with Oscar Rolstad in command, to pick up three barges for Honolulu. Returning from the Pacific crossing, she went North and worked at Kodiak Island, towing for the local canneries, not as the RUSTLER, but as the EDITH FOSS.

After little more than a year's towing, Foss sold the EDITH in April of 1941 to Hubble Towing Company of Hoquiam and they changed her name to DAUNTLESS. Once again she went to work in the fresh water ports of Grays Harbor.

When Foss sold the EDITH, another vessel recently purchased by Foss (the CHILKAT) was given the name of EDITH FOSS, and the CHILKAT, for the official records, became the first EDITH FOSS due to the DAUNTLESS eventually coming back to the Foss fleet.

At the outbreak of World War II, the DAUNTLESS was transferred to the U.S. Army for coastal service and remained under Army control until the conclusion of the war. Shortly after, tugs requisitioned for support duty were returned to their pre-war owners. However, during the war, Hubble Towing was temporarily disbanded, but the Hubble family remained in Grays Harbor, so they were able to take possession of the DAUNTLESS. But not having any immediate use for the tug, they sold her back to Foss two days later. The DAUNTLESS returned to Tacoma in mid-1946 and became the EDITH FOSS on September 26, 1946. EDITH could be given to her again as the earlier EDITH, ex-CHILKAT, was rammed and sunk in 1943 while under allocation to the Army Transport Service.

During the post-war years the EDITH, operating out of Tacoma, was used primarily for the wood products customers of Foss, towing logs between Puget Sound ports and chip and sawdust scows to pulp mills on the Sound. In July 1956 Foss withdrew the EDITH from service as her 1929 vintage engine was worn out and the tug generally in need of modernization, so for the next fifteen months the EDITH was in the hands of the shipwrights. Both her upper and lower deck houses were completely rebuilt and a new 560-horsepower Union diesel installed. The EDITH, with her new look, re-entered service on December 2, 1957. However, less than a month later, she came back to the yard in Tacoma with rudder stock and quadrant problems. The troubles remedied, she went back to work with Captain Faye Hopkins in charge.

The EDITH, though based in Tacoma, operated a good portion of the time towing logs on the Straits of Juan de Fuca and from ports in British Columbia to Port Angeles. During the winter months log towing became very trying and time-consuming in seeking shelter and waiting out one storm after another. A tow in January of 1959 from Ladysmith, British Columbia to Port Angeles, a distance of 100 miles, required nineteen days for the EDITH to complete due to adverse weather. She continued log towing until May 1960 then the Seattle office requested her for use in Alaska.

With Captain Jerry Clark in command, the EDITH towed the oil barge FOSS-100 to Dutch Harbor, Alaska, the base for extended oil service to Bristol Bay ports. For six months she delivered petroleum products from Dutch Harbor to Naknek and Dillingham for Standard Oil. (This was supplementary service to the CHRISTINE and FOSS-95.)

With the open-water season over in Bristol Bay, the EDITH returned home in November 1960 to resume log towing in the North Sound. Then in February 1961 on assignment to the Port Angeles division, she replaced the veteran tug FOSS 21 for towing log cribs from Sekiu to Port Angeles. She continued towing in the Straits for the next several years and until Foss rebuilt an ex-Army T.P. tug into the 1200-horsepower PACIFIC to take over the Port Angeles job. The EDITH now engaged in lighter work, general barge towing round the Sound.

In 1968 she went to Ketchikan as a replacement tug to relieve the ROGER FOSS on the Southeastern Alaska oil barge run for Union Oil Company. From April into October the EDITH, with the oil barge FOSS-109, supplied liquid and packaged petroleum products to towns, logging camps, and canneries. Then in October a new "D" class boat took over the run and the EDITH returned to the Sound, arriving Tacoma October 11.

Shortly after her return, a fire starting in the main switchboard spread and caused considerable damage in the engine room. The cost of repair, combined with her age, low horsepower, and the new efficient boats in operation, eliminated any foreseeable use for the EDITH, so Foss laid her up in Tacoma to await final disposition.

In October 1969 Navieras Consolidadas, a firm based in Ensenada, Mexico bought the tug even with her deficiences. Electrical repairs and outfitting were carried out at the Foss-Seattle yard before she headed into the Pacific. She left for Mexico in late October, towing two ex-Foss deck barges and appropriately the name RUSTLER was again on her bows.

*The **HENRY** with steam tug **WANDERER*** (alongside) assisting the army freighter, CAPE PERPETUA into Lake Washington in 1945. (Courtesy of Joe Williamson)

HENRY FOSS (1)

Built:	1900	Propulsion:	Enterprise
	Seattle, Washington		1,000-horsepower
Length:	90-feet	Primary Service:	Puget Sound
Beam:	21-feet	Final Operating Day:	February 13, 1959
		Status:	Sunk

The HENRY FOSS, originally a cannery tender built for Pacific American Fisheries of Bellingham, was designed by L.H. Coolidge and built by E.H. McAllister in the record time of six months. She was powered with a 450-horsepower Vulcan steam engine. PAF named her JOHN CUDAHY, a name more appropriate to Chicago than Seattle, although she did belong to a packing business, even though it was salmon.

The CUDAHY had a change of occupation in 1905 when PAF sold her to Grays Harbor Stevedoring Company of Aberdeen, Washington for use as an assist-tug to vessels entering Grays Harbor over the Chehalis River bar. She also acted as a pilot vessel and a coastwise tug. After fourteen years with the Stevedoring Company, they sold her to the Merrill & Ring Logging Company for towing log rafts from the Pysht River log dump on the Straits of Juan de Fuca to Port Angeles. Then after only three years with M & R, in 1922 Allman Hubble Tug Company of Hoquiam, Washington purchased the CUDAHY and returned her to Grays Harbor.

During her river-bar service, she made many daring rescues of ships and their crews, all occasioned by the wild winter storms prevalent along the Northwest Coast. In one incident occurring in February 1925 the steam-schooner CAOBA, southbound from Willapa Harbor to San Francisco, loaded with lumber, was just north of Ocean Park, Washington when struck by a sudden strong gale. Wallowing and pitching in the heavy seas, the CAOBA's caulked hull seams opened up allowing a great inrush of water. The engine room flooded, stopping all machinery and forcing the engine room crew to the main deck.

With no power and no chance of saving the ship, the crew took to the lifeboats and fortunately launching the boats in the rough sea was successful. The CUDAHY responded to the SOS call, located and rescued the men in one lifeboat and a freighter picked up the rest of the crew in a second lifeboat. The men suffered from exposure, but otherwise they were able to carry on. Their decision to leave the CAOBA was wise as the ship ended up a wreck in the breakers just north of Ocean Park.

For the fourth time, in the mid-thirties, the CUDAHY was sold; this time going to Knappton Towboat Company for general towing on the Columbia River and Oregon coast. She worked for only five years under Knappton's ownership before being laid up due to hull deterioration and poor engine performance.

The CUDAHY was offered for sale "as is" and the Foss Company examined the tug and decided she could be rebuilt, so they purchased the boat on June 19, 1941 and towed her to the Foss Shipyard in Tacoma.

The CUDAHY spent the next twelve months under repair, going through a complete renovation. The hull framing and planking was renewed wherever necessary, with new guards, deck beams, and weather deck installed. Then a deckhouse and pilothouse were constructed on the rebuilt hull. Below decks all new machinery was set in, including a 1,000-horsepower Enterprise diesel. Only one other Foss tug at the time had more horsepower, the AGNES FOSS with 1,500—she had entered service just four months ahead of the CUDAHY.

On May 26, 1942 with the conversion completed, the pride of the Foss yard was christened HENRY FOSS, shortly before Henry Foss joined the navy.

With Captain Walt Stark in charge, the HENRY in early June commenced her break-in trips. But after only two week's running, she was requisitioned for military duty in World War II and assigned to the U.S. Army Engineers.

The HENRY served the Engineers for eighteen months on regular barge runs to Alaska, including a special voyage, safely made, to the War Zone in the Aleutian Islands. By mid-November 1943 the HENRY was no longer required by the Government as many new Army tugs were then in operation. The tug was returned to Foss and in good condition, so only a few days of outfitting and painting were necessary before she rejoined the Foss fleet.

Again a green and white tug, her first job on November 23rd with Captain Norm Carlsen in command, was towing the dead ship S.S. KAIMENEZ POPALSK from the Shaffer dock in Tacoma to the Olympia Port dock. The HENRY then started what was to be her specialty for her entire career with Foss—towing log rafts. The first of her countless tows consisted of thirty-two sections of Simpson hemlock from Tacoma to the Rayonier mill at Port Angeles, her new base of operation.

Captain Carlsen continued as senior skipper on the HENRY with Arnold Tweter as alternate. They towed logs month after month on the Straits and to mills on Puget Sound. Then a tragic accident occurred on September 15, 1944 ending the career of Captain Carlsen.

The HENRY had left Tacoma on September 12th with thirty-seven sections of logs for Port Angeles, but due to impending bad weather, anchored in Port Townsend Harbor late on September 14th to wait for favorable towing conditions. During the afternoon of September 15th, Captain Carlsen informed the Chief Engineer Jack Gilden that he had to go ashore and call the Port Angeles office. The Mate, Mr. Talbert and one Deckhand by the name of Fish accompanied the Captain. According to entries in the Logbook, the three men failed to return during the evening and at 2200, Chief Gilden had to start the engine and shift tug and tow back to a safe anchorage as a sudden strong wind caused the HENRY to drag anchor. He kept the engine going to maintain position until 0300 on the 16th when the wind eased and he was able to cut the engine and hold her with the anchor. The Chief stated he was not overly concerned about the missing men as due to the severe weather he assumed they had remained ashore for the night not wanting to risk going back to the HENRY in a small rowboat. But by 0730 the Chief was definitely worried so he had the Assistant Engineer, second Deckhand, and the Cook launch the lifeboat to begin a search for the missing men. They were unable to find a trace of them or the boat so they returned to the tug. Then at 0900 the Coast Guard patrol boat came alongside with the missing Deckhand aboard.

He reported that returning to the tug in the dark and in very rough seas, the work-boat capsized throwing all three men into the water. The Captain and the Mate disappeared immediately and the Deckhand struck out for shore, reaching the beach after a half-hour's swimming and struggle to keep afloat. Upon recovering enough to walk, he went for help and was taken to the Coast Guard Station for care and later returned to the HENRY to relate the circumstances. Shocked by the tragedy, Chief Engineer Gilden had difficulty recording the loss in the Logbook, but he did, and then went ashore to notify the Port Angeles office.

Three relief crewmen were sent to Port Townsend, headed by Captain Oscar Rolstad, to take over the tug and they completed the tow to Port Angeles on September 20, 1944.

The HENRY continued for the next several years in her prime service out of Port Angeles. However, during slack logging periods especially in the 1950's, she assisted the Seattle office whenever they came up short of equipment, particularly during the summer and fall months. At times she also helped out on the Milwaukee rail-car barge run between Seattle, Bellingham, and Port Townsend.

Her regular skipper, Captain Warren Waterman, remained with the HENRY except for the several voyages she made to Southeastern and Southwestern Alaska to supplement the Seattle ocean-division tugs in 1956, 1957, and 1958. When the HENRY went North, Captain Waterman transferred to the MATHILDA for linehaul towing out of Seattle.

After October 1958 the HENRY towed steadily for the Port Angeles office with Warren Waterman again the Captain. But as of October she had just three-and-a-half months to go before becoming only a claim number in the files of the insurance companies.

In the early evening of February 12th, the HENRY, with relief Captain Vince Miller aboard, had just delivered a log crib from Rayonier's log dump at Sekiu to Port Angeles—the last tow in her fifty-eight years of life. After tying up the tow the HENRY quickly shifted over to the Foss Pier as it was crew-change time and the men were anxious to go home for their two weeks off. The new crew, headed by Captain Warren Waterman consisted of Lawrence Berg, Mate; Oswald Sorenson, Deckhand; Richard Lothian, Deckhand; Erick Danielson, Cook; Ed Hansen, Chief Engineer; and Martin Gullstein, Assistant Engineer. They came aboard and took over at midnight, leaving shortly after under orders to run light to Ladysmith, British Columbia and pick up a log tow for Port Angeles.

The night turned wet and stormy with poor visibility as the HENRY angled across the Straits to the Canadian side. The weather remained foul going up Haro Strait and on the run between Pender and Saltspring Islands. A fifty-knot gale buffeted them accompanied by rough seas and driving rain.

Suddenly, without warning, at about 0400, the HENRY came to a grinding and abrupt stop near Beaver Point on Saltspring Island. Apparently she had not been making her course good, running way inside the proper track. With impaired visibility and the land mass obscured, she came up standing so quickly there wasn't time to haul away from the rocks. The Mate on watch rang the engine room for full-astern and the HENRY slowly backed off the rocks into deep water and to disaster. In his report, Chief Engineer Ed Hansen stated that although he hurried to the engine room, the water was already over the floor plates and the bilge pumps were unable to keep up with the flood coming in from the ruptured bottom.

The HENRY sank so rapidly the crew had to abandon ship without delay. The seven-man crew hurriedly launched the lifeboat and then the work-boat, but as the crew started to climb into the lifeboat, the water-logged tug took a sudden and heavy list causing all the deck gear and mast to come crashing down alongside the two boats, swamping them. A minute after, the HENRY rolled completely over and sank throwing all seven men into the cold and rough water of Swanson Channel. All the men reached the overturned lifeboat and hung on, but not for long—numbness from the exposure overcame the crew and one by one they slipped below the surface, except the Chief and Deckhand Richard Lothian. The two men were able to hold out until rescue came.

Unfortunately, with the tragedy taking only a matter of minutes, no radio MAYDAY had been sent, so it was not until the ferry CY PECK made her first run of the day out of Ganges Harbor on Saltspring Island that help arrived. While nearing Beaver Point, the ferry Captain spotted the overturned lifeboat and the two clinging survivors. He ran alongside and the crew pulled the helpless men aboard. The ferry went all-out for Ganges Harbor and the two men were rushed to the hospital. Chief Hansen survived the ordeal, but Richard Lothian, sorry to relate, died of exposure after arrival at Ganges. The loss of the HENRY's six men was the most painful calamity in the Foss' long history of tug boating.

Ed Hansen, after a period of recuperation returned to work and resumed his position as Chief Engineer for Foss. Fortunately Ed did not experience another HENRY-type tragedy and he retired in October 1979 after forty years of service with Foss.

The HENRY was not salvaged although she sank in only 150 feet of water. There were reports at the time that an attempt might be made to raise the tug, but nothing happened. No doubt the cost involved compared to the value of a 58-year-old wood tug was out of proportion, so Beaver Point became the HENRY's final destination.

JOE FOSS (1)

Built:	1942	Propulsion:	General Motors
	Foss Launch & Tug Company		165-horsepower
	Tacoma, Washington	Primary Service:	Tacoma Harbor
Length:	43-feet	Last Foss Operating Day:	August 18, 1972
Beam:	14-feet	Status:	Sold Domestic

The first JOE FOSS, named for a son of Theodore, was designed and built by the Foss Company for use in Tacoma Harbor. Completed and ready for service in October 1942 she was considered in her day, the flagship of the Tacoma Harbor fleet.

A special feature of the JOE was a high-capacity fire pump and monitor, capable of pumping a large volume of water at great pressure. The monitor was used primarily for washing barge decks. However, she was called upon for all waterfront fires, assisting the city fire department from the water side. The JOE pumped over a million gallons of water on two of the most recent, largest, and most spectacular waterfront fires—the Milwaukee dock fire in the early sixties and later the extensive fire at Pier Seven. Not only the JOE and her monitor, but the entire Foss-Tacoma harbor fleet turned out to help extinguish the two huge fires.

The JOE spent nearly her whole thirty-year towing life, except for a short spell in Port Angeles, operating in and around Tacoma Harbor towing barges, shifting log rafts, and tending log ships. The exception happened on November 16, 1964 when the JOE went to Port Angeles to help while the NANCY FOSS came to Tacoma for engine replacement. The NANCY returned to Port Angeles on February 10, 1972 and the JOE then left for her own back yard.

In May 1971 with the new steel replacement tugs in Tacoma, Foss sent the JOE to the Scott-Pacific log dump at Renton on Lake Washington to make up and shift log rafts on an "as needed" basis. The arrangement continued until early December 1971 when she came to the Foss-Seattle yard for a two-month overhaul.

Ready for service again in February 1972 the JOE returned to Tacoma and familiar surroundings. In May, with no further work in sight for the JOE, she went into lay-up alongside the other tugs with doubtful futures—caused by the new high-power steel tugs taking over around the Sound. By mid-August the time came to officially declare surplus the one-time pride of the Tacoma Harbor fleet.

However, the JOE remained dormant only until November 13th, when George Peterson, owner of Peterson's Boatworks next door to Foss on Tacoma's middle waterway, purchased the tug. There she began life anew as a yard tug, serving Peterson's repair docks and marine ways. Too bad she didn't have a steam whistle to go with her affectionate new name: LITTLE TOOT!

LELA FOSS (1)

Built:	1942	Propulsion:	General Motors
	Foss Launch and Tug Com-		110-horsepower
	pany	Primary Service:	Tacoma Harbor
	Tacoma, Washington	Final Foss Operating	
Length:	32-feet	Day:	October, 1953
Beam:	11-feet	Status:	Sold Domestic

The first LELA, named for a daughter of Andrew and Thea, was designed and built by Foss-Tacoma as a light draft tunnel-stern type tug for use in the shallow water log storages of Tacoma Harbor.

Her original engine, a 140-horsepower Cummins diesel, proved to have too much power for the small tug and caused the stern to sink several inches when running full out. She had very little freeboard under normal conditions and at full speed the freeboard aft was zero. When slowing down from full-ahead, her considerable stern swell would pour over the low bulwarks and cascade against the back of the pilothouse. If the door was open the rush of water flooded into the pilothouse, sloshing around until time could be spared to bail out.

The problem continued until 1950 when the LELA was repowered with a 110 horsepower General Motors diesel, recently removed from the tug FOSS 9 during her repowering. With the 9's smaller engine, the LELA performed in a normal manner and sea boots were no longer necessary in the pilothouse.

However, for general towing she didn't perform effectively due to the hull design. With this handicap, combined with the FOSS 9 performing well in the log storages and in general harbor towing since returning from Port Angeles, the LELA had to give way. So in October 1953 she was lifted out of the water at the Foss dock in Tacoma and placed on the beach near the shipyard.

The LELA remained on dry land until 1959 when Foss sold her to work as a boom-boat at log dumps in Southeastern Alaska. After reconditioning and repainting at Foss-Tacoma and changing her name to MOLLY HOGAN (a logger's grommet), the ex-LELA headed for Alaska.

For the next several years Wrangell was the center of the MOLLY HOGAN's activity in Southeastern. Then information came from DuPont's manager in Southeastern, the all-knowing Bob Jacobson, that she sank in 1965 while berthed at a dock in Wrangell Narrows, south of Petersburg. She was never raised although she sank in relatively shallow water. The G.M. diesel was salvaged some time later, but the hull of the MOLLY was sprung so much that salvage was out of the question, so the final whereabouts of the ex-LELA FOSS can never be in doubt.

ELAINE FOSS After completing an oil barge assignment in Seattle, shown here heading to the Ballard yard for time off, July 1965. (From the author's collection)

ELAINE FOSS (1)

Built:	1925	Propulsion:	Enterprise
	St. Helens, Oregon		250-horsepower
Length:	60-feet	Primary Service:	Puget Sound
Beam:	16-feet	Final Foss Operating Day:	June 21, 1967
		Status:	Sold Domestic

The ELAINE, first known as the LARCH, was built for the United States Lighthouse Service as a buoy tender on the Columbia River. She was a single-ender with a well-deck forward for carrying navigation aids and a swinging boom mounted over the well for lifting buoys on and off. For power she had a 160-horsepower Washington diesel, giving her a 9-knot speed.

In 1935 she came to Seattle following purchase by Puget Sound Bridge & Dredge company. They renamed her LOYAL and after installation of a towing winch, she began specialized towing for P.S.B. & D. Co.

The LOYAL towed barges between the rock quarry at Mats-Mats and Port Townsend for the construction of a boat-basin breakwater. She also engaged in several dredging and construction jobs on Puget Sound just prior to doing similar work in Wrangell Narrows, Alaska during the early 1940's.

By 1945 P.S.B. & D. had occasion to sell the LOYAL and Foss purchased her. With little work coming in for the Foss-Seattle shipwrights, the time was favorable to undertake an extensive rebuilding job so they put the LOYAL in the repair yard for a major refit. The forward well-deck was altered to the more familiar lines of a tugboat and her deckhouse altered to make room for a galley, and the Captain's cabin enlarged. Major rebuilding was necessary to the horseshoe around the stern as considerable dry rot had developed. For power Foss set in a 250-horsepower Enterprise diesel. After several months of heavy expense, the LOYAL was finally ready to start paying her way. But before leaving the outfitting pier, Foss joined her to the family group by naming her ELAINE, in honor of a daughter of Hazel and Elmer Foss.

The ELAINE worked out of Seattle for the next twenty years, towing oil barges, rail-car barges, and gravel scows. The scows, loaded at Steilacoom and Maury Island pits, were delivered to Glacier Sand and Gravel Company's two plants on the Duwamish River and to Washington Asphalt Company in Lake Union, also to the Graystone plant in Ballard. A round trip between gravel pits and mixing plants averaged only twenty-four hours, which made a routine and unvaried run, week after week, for the alternating five-man crews. In the 1950's and early 1960's Foss had twenty gravel scows in use, keeping two and sometimes three tugs busy.

The ELAINE at times towed the wood railcar barge FOSS-116 from Seattle to the Simpson Mill at Shelton and her oil-barge work consisted of shifting around Seattle Harbor and frequently towing the oil barges to the lower Sound ports of Shelton and Olympia.

By 1965 the ELAINE began to show signs of her forty years hard work. Mechanical troubles constantly plagued her, with repairs becoming frequent and costly. Leaks in the wood hull became a constant annoyance. So after 1965, she was only used as a fill-in tug, working for only seventy-two days in 1966—largely due to the use of the new, efficient, high-power tugs.

After lying idle for nearly seven months, the ELAINE had a chance to go back towing. The sudden need for her on the Sound came about when the new boats were sent to Alaska for assist-work in the construction of offshore oil platforms. The ELAINE was crewed up on June 13th, 1967 to go on her old gravel run and for eight days she plugged along, the crew keeping her running by ingenuity and luck. But on June 21st, mechanical failure crippled her permanently. However, the old tug made it home and right into lay-up. Foss decided that to continue what no doubt would be a never-ending round of repairs would not be practical, so the ELAINE ended up on the "For Sale" list.

Her retirement at the Foss-Seattle moorings lasted for a year. Then she was sold to Annette Timber Corporation of Ketchikan who purchased her along with the JERRY FOSS, another retired tug. The ELAINE, renamed TRINITY 1, left Seattle for Ketchikan after completing the owner-ordered repairs at the Foss yard.

For the next three-and-a-half years the TRINITY towed logs in the area of Prince of Wales Island and in the harbor of Klawock. Then on February 6, 1972 while running light from Prince of Wales Island to Ketchikan, she encountered driving rain, snow, and strong winds. In poor visibility, late in the afternoon, she ran on the rocks near Lincoln Rock Light in Clarence Straits. As the tide rose, the engine room flooded and the main deck was soon completely awash. The TRINITY was in Clarence Straits—but she was also in dire straits. After dark, the tug, MOGUL, spotted distress signals from the stranded boat and stood by during the stormy night until the Coast Guard buoy-tender BITTERSWEET arrived and rescued the two-man crew, leaving the TRINITY to her fate. She slipped off the rocks during the next high tide and sank into deep water—forty-seven fathoms down in her forty-seventh year.

BARBARA FOSS (2)

Built:	1944	Propulsion:	Enterprise (Single)
	Barbee Marine Yard		1,500-horsepower
	Kennydale, Washington	Primary Service:	Alaska-Coastwise-Ocean
Length:	117-feet	Final Foss Operating Day:	June 8, 1973
Beam:	28-feet	Status:	Transferred to Hawaiian Tug & Barge, Honolulu

Foss Company, after World War II, purchased three of the ten Miki-class tugs built by Barbee for the Army Transport service and the BARBARA, ex-LT-376, was the first of the three.

ATS used the 376 on the Pacific Coast and in Alaska, towing barges of military cargo until shortly after the War's end, when the LT-376 and many other Miki-class tugs were declared surplus and sold by the government to commer-

BARBARA FOSS *August 1969, towing the C-2 freighter CAPE TRYON from Bangor to a site off the Washington Coast for disposal. (Courtesy of Foss Tug Co)*

cial interests. Due to the Miki's record of dependable service during the War, the demand for the LT's was strong at every sale and Foss was an active bidder, purchasing nine Mikis over a twelve-year period. The acquisitions gave the Company greater capabilities and added the necessary horsepower to enable Foss to take advantage of the foreseen potential for tugs in ocean transportation.

At the government sale in Seattle on April 12, 1946 Foss succeeded in buying the LT-376 along with a sister-tug. The two LT's were towed to the Foss-Seattle yard for outfitting to company standards and during the refit the 376 became the second BARBARA FOSS.

The new member of the fleet was out of the yard and running in mid-May 1946 with Walt Davis, one of Foss' able Captains in command. She started her career towing Milwaukee rail-car barges between Seattle and Bellingham, the usual break-in run for new tugs. Graduating from the car-barge run the BARBARA went on to Alaska towing and general towing in Puget sound, but on the Sound only during the off-season when cargo movements to Alaska were at a minimum. Working the two areas kept the BARBARA humping—grass didn't have much chance to grow and foul the bottom.

One of the BARBARA's bread-and-butter runs was the newly developed cement-barge tow from Bellingham to Anchorage. To provide the equipment, Foss, in 1949 and 1950 acquired three surplus LST's from the government and converted them to combination barges carrying bulk cement below and general cargo on deck. With three barges, three tugs were required, so the BARBARA had two running mates, the DONNA and JUSTINE.

An additional LST was purchased in 1952 for conversion to a cement carrier and by April 1952 four barges were in regular service to Anchorage. An average of eighteen voyages per season were made, with all three tugs participating during the first five years on the route. The first trip of the year left Bellingham in early April and the last in late September.

The BARBARA's Alaska-Puget Sound schedule remained the same for several years until the advent of the Honolulu lumber trade, giving her a chance to go on the pineapple run—so termed by the tug crews. Foss had been barging lumber down the coast for many years, so they were prepared in 1961 to include the Islands when Honolulu became the main barged-lumber market. for many years the JUSTINE FOSS, another Miki with Barge #207 and #200, served the Pacific Coast lumber ports, but with Honolulu scheduled, a second tug was needed, so the BARBARA was favored to make a monthly sailing to Hilo and Honolulu.

On August 23, 1961 the BARBARA left Seattle with Barge #201 on the pioneer voyage to load lumber at Coast ports for the new destination. She made a good first run and kept doing it continuously for four years except to return home occasionally for voyage repairs or to wait a day or two for the barge to be loaded.

The year 1966 was the last for the BARBARA on the lumber run and for good reason as only four round trips were logged in the twelve months. The high-horsepower tugs with their new high-capacity barges were taking over, so the BARBARA had to give up and look to the North Country for steady towing. Intermixed with the last four Hawaii trips were runs to Cook Inlet, Alaska, barging vital supplies and equipment for the oil and marine construction companies engaged in the new oil field development—the BARBARA now had a new line of work to keep her busy.

Weather allowing, a steady stream of tows entered Cook Inlet and the BARBARA this time held her position on the rapid delivery program. From 1967 through June 1970 she towed equipment to the oil rig constructors, but she also made trips hauling bulk cement and mobile homes from Seattle to Anchorage.

Between trips to Anchorage, in August 1969 the BARBARA carried out an interesting job for the navy. She towed the USS CAPE TRYON from the navy ammunition dump at Bangor, Washington to a disposal site well off the northern Washington Coast.

The CAPE TRYON was a freighter built in 1944 for service in World War II, but she also served in the Korean and Vietnam wars. By 1969 she had outlived her usefulness as an operating unit, so the Navy brought her to Bangor and loaded her with 6,000 tons of out-dated bombs, mines, and ammunition. Navy personnel cut many holes in the old hull and covered them with soft plugs that could be knocked out to scuttle the ship at the disposal site.

The BARBARA left Bangor on August 11th and arrived at the predetermined location in the Pacific at 0700 on the 13th. Upon arrival demolition teams boarded the ship, knocked out the plugs, and opened the main sea valves. The CAPE TRYON slowly sank. At 0912 the ship performed her last duty for the navy as she settled below the surface with her cargo and vanished from radar. Sixty seconds later a tremendous explosion gently rocked the BARBARA and the two escort vessels waiting at a safe distance. The tons of assorted bombs and ammunition exploded at a depth of one mile and became fragments on the sea floor. This was the first job that the BARBARA irretrieveably lost her tow. Captain Fred Strang with a farewell whistle salute headed the BARBARA for the Columbia River to pick up the dredge McCurdy for delivery to Ventura, California.

A slowdown in towing activity, as well as the new modern ocean tugs taking over, forced the BARBARA in July 1970 after returning from Alaska, to go on inactive status. She remained so for the next thirteen months, not leaving the dock, but the longshoremen inadvertently were about to put her in motion. The major West Coast dock strike beginning in the summer of 1971 stopped all shipping by freighters and intensified the use of tugs and barges, so the BARBARA was re-activated and during the next three months she had all the work a Miki could possibly handle. Then when the strike ended in December, the BARBARA went to Bellingham as extra ship-assist tug for the winter of 1971-1972 and then back to the same job in late 1972 and through April 1973.

By May the BARBARA's services were no longer needed on Puget Sound or in Alaska, but Dillingham Tug & Barge in Honolulu required a large tug, so on May 21, 1973 the BARBARA, towing two dump scows, left Seattle for the Islands with Captain Ken Payne in charge. After an easy trip across, she arrived on June 8th and Dillingham had the tug they needed. With only a day's R&R in Honolulu, Captain Ken Payne and his crew returned home by air in four hours as compared to four hundred on the outbound run.

The BARBARA operated on the inter-island routes until the early summer of 1975, then she permanently retired from towing after almost thirty years work. In October 1976 Dillingham donated her to the Navy's Third Fleet to be used for target practice and in this cause the BARBARA ended her days. She started out serving the Army and she finished up serving the Navy.

CHRISTINE FOSS *April 1974, enroute to Points Wells for loaded oil barge FOSS 111, to tow to S.W. Alaska. (From the author's collection)*

CHRISTINE FOSS

Built:	1943 Sagstad Shipyard Seattle, Washington	Propulsion:	Caterpillar (Twin) 1,530-horsepower
		Primary Service:	Puget Sound and Alaska
Length:	117-feet	Status:	In Service,
Beam:	28-feet		

The CHRISTINE FOSS, a Miki-type Army tug, LT-187, was one of a class of sixty, built for the Army Transport Service during World War II. The 187 was powered by two Fairbanks-Morse diesels, delivering 1,380 horsepower to twin propellers. The later Miki tugs, due to a shortage of engine, were powered by single large engines driving a single propeller.

The LT-187 was used by the ATS to barge supplies to Aleutian Island bases from a supply depot at Excursion Inlet in southeastern Alaska. Army plans called for early development of an extensive tug and barge line to and in Alaska because of the scarcity and vulnerability of cargo ships. But as the active war concentrated in other areas and left Alaska comparatively untouched, the need for a barge line lost some of its importance and many Mikis ended up as harbor tugs.

Soon after World War II, the ATS had no further use for a number of the Miki's, so they were sold at Government sales. The LT-187 was included with two other Miki-class tugs in the Government's April 1946 sale and Foss was the successful bidder. LT-187 became the CHRISTINE FOSS, named for the youngest daughter of Arthur and Ellen.

After minor repair work at the Foss yard the CHRISTINE was ready to tow, the first Foss Miki-class tug to receive towing orders. For her initiation into commercial service she towed the former United States mine-planter AROOSTOOK from Puget Sound to California with Captain Oscar Rolstad in command.

Prior to the War, Foss had acquired a contract from Standard Oil Company to barge petroleum products between their Dutch Harbor distribution base at the tip of the Alaska Peninsula and various ports in Bristol Bay and the Bering Sea. The run was handled by the EDITH FOSS and FOSS BARGE-100 with Captain Emil Wick in charge of the pioneer operation. But after the War, heavy demand required bigger and better equipment, so in January 1947 the CHRISTINE, under Captain Bill Stark, left Seattle for New Orleans, Louisiana, to pick up a larger barge which Foss had purchased at a government sale. After a layover in New Orleans, during Mardi Gras—a break for the crew—the CHRISTINE headed for home with a 14,000-barrel oil barge, designated FOSS-95.

After voyage repairs and modifications to both vessels at Foss-Tacoma, in May of 1947 the CHRISTINE, still under command of Bill Stark, left Seattle with the FOSS-95 for the first of many six-month seasons in Alaska delivering petroleum products to isolated villages located all the way from Kotzebue and Nome, south to the Aleutian chain.

There was always a great rush and a feeling of immediacy with the tug's crew during the early-season deliveries as the oil was urgently needed to replenish near-empty shore tanks after the long ice-bound winter. So the added speed and efficiency of the CHRISTINE and the capacity of her new barge was a great boon to the anxious villagers. By mid-summer the crew raced the weather calendar in an attempt to have all shore tanks topped off before the Bering Sea bays and tributaries froze over, usually in late October or early November, for another long winter. By the middle of October, with the last deliveries made and ice already forming, the CHRISTINE and her barge headed south to Seattle, arriving in early November at the Foss dock and there she waited for the spring thaw and another six-month's season in the Bering Sea. This six-on-and-six-off schedule for the CHRISTINE continued for the next twenty-eight years!

During the many seasons the CHRISTINE served on the oil run, she travelled nearly 700,000 miles in making calls at Port Moller, Naknek, Dillingham, Bethel, and Platinum. The CHRISTINE's longest-term Captain, Robert Burns, has put in thirteen years on the run, and he still goes back to do the job, but now on one of the new high-power tugs.

Regardless of the routine and the lack of relaxation there were extra compensations for Captain Burns and his crew during the annual, long six-month spell. Next to letters from home, the excellent and varied meals served were a wonderful morale builder for the crew leading a simple and uniform life. The cook kept his men well fed and contented—many of them returning year after year. The cook of the CHRISTINE had the variety of a floating supermarket to choose from, and what the tug couldn't carry, the oil barge stored. The entire six-month food supply was put aboard in Seattle with the exception of fresh fruits and vegetables, which could be purchased at Bethel and fresh fish when the runs were on. The Steward's voyage list included, along with many other items: 360 pounds of ground beef, 150 cube steaks, 50 pounds of Polish sausage, 200 pounds of bacon, 72 bottles of catsup, 540 rolls of paper towels and even a case of ice cream cones! On the oil barge alone, nearly two tons of food and galley supplies were carried—and all for ten men.

In the off-seasons of 1957 and 1958 the CHRISTINE took part in two historic tows. On January 18, 1957 she arrived at the Milwaukee Railroad slip in Seattle with a rail-car barge loaded with lumber from central British Columbia. The cars were unloaded at the Pier slip and then shipped on to the Midwest and East. This was the first car-barge of lumber ever shipped from British Columbia through Seattle to Eastern destinations. The new Foss service made it possible for the Milwaukee Road to engage in railroading lumber from British Columbia to the Midwest and East. The rail-barge delivery system functioned so well that in twenty years of continuous service, Foss tugs and barges were able to make three hundred trips per year, hauling over nine thousand railcars between Vancouver and Seattle, adding considerable tonnage to the Milwaukee's long-haul freight volume.

The CHRISTINE's second pioneering run came about in January 1958 when she towed two barges loaded with dynamite to supply the Hawaiian Islands for six months of tunneling, construction, and mining projects. New safety regulations enacted in Hawaii in 1958 discouraged the import of explosives to the Islands by ship. Foss was called upon to solve the transportation problem and they did by the use of tug and barge. There were no detonations or repercussions as the CHRISTINE was back in the Foss-Seattle yard in February, safe and sound.

In the winter of 1963-64 the CHRISTINE was given new life by repowering with two 765-horsepower Caterpillar diesels, installed by Foss-Tacoma. The new engines came at the right time as she needed more power for the new and larger oil barge replacing the FOSS-95. The Bering Sea villages had grown into towns and more oil was needed at each stop, so the new barge named FOSS-111 was built to carry an additional nine thousand barrels. The CHRISTINE had to hump with the bigger barge as the calls were just as many, but the big "Cats" gave her the needed extra push.

For the next twelve years the CHRISTINE went North each spring to deliver oil to the Bering Sea ports. But, though progress was about to displace her after so many years on the run, she would never lose the honor of being the *first* FOSS tug to be able to fly the flag of the mythical "Alaska Sourdough Fleet"—a flag with blue background and seven silver stars forming the "Big Dipper," similar to Alaska's state flag with blue background and eight gold stars. Each season North gave the CHRISTINE one star—seven seasons, and she became a "Sourdough."

Prior to the 1976 Bering Sea sailing, Foss decided that a new tug with more horsepower and efficiency should take over the oil route in conformity with the policy of continued upgrading of the Company's ocean and coastwise fleet. A deep feeling of nostalgia prevailed in the dispatch office when in late April of 1976 the voice of Captain Burns was heard talking to the Foss dispatcher and reporting that the newer WENDY FOSS, not the customary CHRISTINE, was underway with the oil barge, FOSS-111, for the Bering Sea. But the CHRISTINE wasn't champing at her moorings, she had sailed two days earlier with an LST barge for Shemya Island in the westernmost of the Aleutian Islands—so far west that the longitude was "East"!

The CHRISTINE holding her own continued to operate coastwise through August 1976 but with the Prudhoe pipeline construction completed and the cargo movements to Alaska dropping off, the newer boats were favored for the rest of the year. The CHRISTINE remained idle during the next four months—her first September in port for many years.

Then in January 1977 her number again came up. A tug was needed by the Port Angeles office to relieve the MARTHA FOSS for towing log rafts from Neah Bay to Port Angeles. The CHRISTINE was activated and outfitted with log-towing gear for the first time in her towing life. Captain Arne Nielson, an experienced log-towing Skipper, took over the tug and began moving rafts down the Straits for Crown Zellerbach.

With the return of the MARTHA in June, the CHRISTINE returned to coastwise work, towing loaded chip-barges between Port Gamble, Washington and the pulp mill at Wauna, Oregon on the Columbia River. The job was short-lived and in July she went into lay-up.

Progress in tug sophistication and efficiency was over-shadowing the thirty-five-year-old wood tug. Her chances of working lessened further by the new boats with 3,000 horsepower compared to the CHRISTINE's 1,500.

In August 1977 the CHRISTINE was put on the inactive list and placed in the Foss reserve fleet in Seattle, but, unlike the other Miki's, Foss kept her in a state of semi-readiness. This was fortunate for in the spring of 1978 the towing business in Puget Sound suddenly boomed and a busy year was indicated in Alaska. With the increased demand for tugs the CHRISTINE was called out to help take care of the unexpected surge.

After two weeks of outfitting, she started towing on the car-barge runs. Then in May she transferred to the ocean division, making successive round trips between Seattle and Anchorage. Late in the season, with the new steel tugs again available to make the run to Anchorage, the CHRISTINE returned to Puget Sound for towing the Milwaukee railcar barges between Seattle and Port Townsend, on the contract that Foss had with the railroad since 1955.

She continued on the run until October 1978 then came into the yard for stem repairs and while tied-up and with the need for tugs still strong, Foss decided to "major" both the CHRISTINE's engines. With her engines rejuvenated she returned to the car-barge run for three days a week and did general Puget Sound towing on the off days. Since the CHRISTINE performs best with a towline out, she gets the longer hauls, and with her machinery running smoothly again, she will be well able to celebrate her thirty-sixth birthday—with a tight towline.

JUSTINE FOSS (2)

Built:	1944	Propulsion:	Enterprise (Single)
	Barbee Marine Yard		1,500-horsepower
	Kennydale, Washington	Primary Service:	Coastwise-Alaska-Hawaii
Length:	117-feet	Final Foss Operating Day:	June 14, 1971
Beam:	28-feet	Status:	Sold - Domestic

The second JUSTINE FOSS, Army class number LT-378, a MIKI-type tug built for coastwise and Alaska use in the tug and barge program instituted by the Army Transport Service early in World War II, was the last of ten MIKIs turned out at the Lake Washington yard.

After serving the Army less than two years, LT-378 in 1946 was declared surplus and offered for sale. Foss purchased the tug along with the LT-376 in a competitive bidding Government sale. Both vessels were in good operating condition when sold, so within a month the tugs were taking part in Puget Sound and coastwise towing—but under Foss names. The 378 became the JUSTINE FOSS and the 376, the BARBARA.

Each year the JUSTINE towed to Alaska during the summer and fall and in the winter and spring she towed on Puget Sound. The same schedule was followed more or less through 1958 but during the elapsed twelve years there were several unusual episodes recorded in her logbook.

One of the JUSTINE's special events occurred in July 1953 with Captain Bob Redd in command—they were principals in a pioneering towing project starting with the JUSTINE leaving Tacoma towing the barge FOSS-250 bound for the Ketchikan Pulp Mill at Ward Cove, Alaska. The tow was historic as it marked the first time a barge left Puget Sound carrying empty railroad cars switched on to the barge at a slip in the United States for delivery to a manufacturing plant in the Territory of Alaska and the loaded cars returned to the States. For the next twenty years Foss continued to tow rail-car barges between Puget Sound and the Ward Cove mill on a regular schedule.

The JUSTINE added a page to Foss history in 1957 when she sailed in June with a tandem tow to the Bering Sea for the Government's MONA LISA radar warning project. This was the first year private operators handled the annual re-supply to the MONA LISA military installations—in past years the Navy was charged with the responsibility. The first year of commercial operation, 8,000-tons of cargo had to be delivered in the short open season. Foss was awarded a contract to handle half of the tonnage. So on June 15th, the JUSTINE left Seattle with a tandem tow and the AGNES followed a few days later with a similar tow. The two tugs in one trip delivered the required 4,000 tons.

Then in September 1957 the JUSTINE went to Kendrick Bay on Prince of Wales Island with the barge FOSS-208 to load 3,000 tons of uranium ore from the Bokan Mountain Mine for delivery to Seattle. The JUSTINE's barge carried the first shipment of uranium ore from Alaska and upon arrival in Seattle, the ore was trans-shipped to the Climax Molybdenum Company of Spokane, Washington. Later on, Foss barged out an additional 12,000 tons of ore.

On November 11, 1958 the JUSTINE left Seattle with ocean cargo-barge FOSS-204 bound for Crescent City, California to load two million feet of lumber for San Pedro. The JUSTINE's trip came about as a result of the new Foss lumber run to California, initiated by the LESLIE FOSS in April 1958. In the new service, lumber was loaded at Longview, Newport, Bandon, Coos Bay, Port Orford, Crescent City, and Eureka with discharge at San Pedro and San Diego—usually three ports provided a full load.

The Operations Department personnel little realized when the JUSTINE left Seattle with her lumber barge on November 11th, that the day would start nearly eight years for the JUSTINE on the Coast and Honolulu lumber runs—except for an occasional run to Alaska when a special need arose. And the need did come after six straight months towing lumber barges on the Coast when the JUSTINE was diverted to Seattle for towing a cargo-barge to Anchorage. Completing the trip she returned to the Coast lumber haul. Then, once again at the height of the seasonal movement to Alaska, the JUSTINE was called back for six weeks to assist in towing general-cargo barges on the Northern run, but by mid-September she had returned to barging lumber.

In May 1960 after a thirty-day overhaul in Seattle, she left for Oregon with the first of three newly rebuilt LST-type barges specially designed for lumber service. She towed this same barge, FOSS-200, trip after trip, year after year, on the lumber runs. But of all the years, 1961 deserves special recognition. The JUSTINE's 1961 operating record was extraordinary—one for the book. She ran 362 out of 365 days, trouble free—in fair weather and foul. Then in August she began what turned out to be another memorable record. She left Crescent City August 30th on the inaugural voyage of the Honolulu lumber run and kept at it for forty round trips accumulating a total towing distance of over 200,000 miles and all accomplished in five consecutive years. During this time there was a period between April 1963 and November 1964 when she ran without failure for 584 consecutive days—a remarkable performance for a tug nearing her twentieth year of towing and also considering the lack of adequate fuel capacity for making long trips—a handicap common to all MIKI tugs. The remarkable performance record owes a good deal to the JUSTINE's Captains and crews who kept the tug in top condition and on schedule.

The MIKI's were at a disadvantage in ocean crossings—a one-way trip to Honolulu was the cruising-range limit of the tugs. With a fuel capacity of 28,000 gallons and daily consumption of 1,600 gallons and towing a loaded barge, there was little margin for safety. Towing an extra heavy load or in adverse weather, the consumption rose to 1,750 gallons per day making the safety margin even less. On the average trip, however, the JUSTINE arrived in Honolulu with 6,000 gallons remaining in the tanks if the weather was kind. But on many voyages, bucking bad weather, she arrived in port with only one day's fuel left in the tanks. Not a comfortable margin when on ocean voyages a twenty-percent reserve is considered necessary.

After a two-week overhaul in late 1964 the JUSTINE returned to the lumber trade and continued on the Pacific run until mid-October 1966 when she was ordered to Seattle due to a change in lumber barges. The new super lumber barge DIAMOND HEAD had just arrrived on the Coast from Houston under tow of the HENRY FOSS and with the new barge's large capacity the use of two smaller LST-type barges, each with its own tug, would be eliminated. The new barge required a high-horsepower tug, so the JUSTINE's days on the lumber haul were over except for special assists, as the larger and more powerful tugs like the HENRY were able to move the 10,000-ton drag at 10 knots.

JUSTINE FOSS *Photographed passing under the Ballard Bridge after returning from Aleutian Islands, September 4, 1967. (From the author's collection)*

Back in Seattle the JUSTINE loaded fuel and stores then left with two cargo barges for Anchorage, Alaska—a decided change of climate for Captain Tauno Salo and his crew. Returning from Anchorage in December 1966 the JUSTINE tied up at Foss-Seattle for complete overhaul, the first in ten years.

With the awarding of the Holmes & Narver Amchitka contract to Foss in early 1967 the JUSTINE shifted from mid-Pacific to the North Pacific, leaving Seattle in March with Captain Stan Thurston in charge, on the first of eight voyages to the Aleutians—hauling construction equipment and drilling material for the Atomic Energy Commission's project. Captain Thurston had the tug on all the early Amchitka voyages and during the May trip he ran the JUSTINE to Adak and picked up the burned-out tug PACIFIC TITAN (see DONNA FOSS #1) and towed it to Seattle for the owner, Pacific Tow & Salvage.

The JUSTINE continued on the Amchitka run through 1967 except for two Anchorage voyages worked into the Amchitka Fall schedule. A serious accident befell the tug on the November voyage to Amchitka—at the time Captain Jay Jacobson was in command. They left Seattle with loaded barge FOSS-202 and dodged in and out of storms all the way across the Gulf, finally arriving at Dutch Harbor for refueling on November 24th—a week behind schedule. After taking on fuel, the JUSTINE continued on her way west, with the weather along the Aleutian chain deteriorating by the hour. During the early hours of November 26th, the barometer dropped rapidly with the wind howling from the southeast at 40-50 knots. By 0800 the wind increased to over seventy knots and the glass continued to fall; by noon the barometer read 28.75 inches! The JUSTINE labored and wallowed in fifteen-foot seas driven by steady hurricane-force winds. The air filled with foam and driving spray caused zero visibility. The tug, still holding on to her barge, tried to reach shelter in the lee of Yunaska Island, but at 1635 on the 26th the towline parted and the barge drifted rapidly to leeward.

Captain Jay ordered the towing winch started to wind in the two-inch wire to determine what had parted. The cause proved to be a broken shackle between the tow wire and the heavy surge chain used as a shock absorber or catenary. In the violent weather it was impossible to retrieve the barge, all that could be done was to track the barge on radar and wait for the weather to moderate.

Help from the weather did not come, in fact by 1830 the seas had increased to "mountainous" with the wind gusting to over 80 knots. A particularly vicious sea struck the JUSTINE along the port side and cascaded aboard, breaking pilothouse windows and springing the hull planking, allowing water to pour into the engine room. Sea water shorted out the refrigeration unit, the heating plant, electric steering motor, and the fresh water pump. Fortunately, the bilge pumps continued to operate and the engineers were able to keep ahead of the incoming water, otherwise the storm would have claimed a victim.

Captain Jay had changed course immediately to protect the damaged port side and again he headed for Yunaska Island. By 1400, November 27th, they were able to gain some shelter close to the island and for the next eighteen hours in a cold ship they circled in the lee waiting for the savage winter storm to abate.

As soon as the wind and sea dropped to just "gale conditions," the JUSTINE headed for the quiet safety of Chernofski Harbor on the west end of Unalaska Island to effect repairs, arriving safely at 1930 on November 27th. During the day of the twenty-eighth, the deck crew re-caulked the damaged areas under the port guard and on the fore-deck while the engine room crew repaired the shorted-out motors and electrical system. In the afternoon the ANDREW FOSS with barge FOSS-183 returning from Amchitka, pulled into Chernofski Bay to exchange tows. Due to the questionable conditions aboard the JUSTINE, the ANDREW had orders to take over for the JUSTINE. The ANDREW borrowed fuel and supplies from the JUSTINE and leaving the FOSS-183, headed out into the somewhat moderated weather to retrieve the JUSTINE's FOSS-202. They found the barge intact, re-rigged the tow gear and headed for Amchitka, taking a full three weeks to arrive—in spite of the distance to travel only 550 miles! For eighteen of the twenty-one days, the ANDREW bucked heavy weather making it impossible to make time without breaking the towline.

In the meantime, with temporary repairs complete, the JUSTINE hooked on to the FOSS-183 and headed for Seattle, but cautiously! They did arrive safely on December 17th, with sighs of relief and with no lost motion the crew hurried home, thankful to have brought the JUSTINE through her trials and yet be back in time for Christmas.

The experience with the JUSTINE apparently didn't faze Captain Jacobson because two weeks later he headed for the Aleutians with the MARGARET FOSS on a trip that had enough challenges for a skipper to wish for a life with "Old MacDonald"!

The JUSTINE, to become seaworthy again, went to the Foss Shipyard where she spent the long winter undergoing hull and machinery repairs. By mid-March 1968 again ready to tow, she left on March 26 for her old nemesis, Amchitka. But 1968 turned out to be trouble-free for the JUSTINE as she made three uneventful round trips to Amchitka and several routine trips to Anchorage.

In March 1969 after a relatively quiet winter in the Hawaiian lumber market, a sudden surge in demand brought the JUSTINE and Captain Jacobson back on the run to assist the regular tugs CRAIG and HENRY. The JUSTINE, for her part, made two round trips to Honolulu, feeling right at home, and no wonder with so many years previously spent on the run. With the help of the JUSTINE's two trips and one assist trip by the ARTHUR, the CRAIG and the HENRY then with their big barges DIAMOND HEAD and KOKO HEAD were able to handle the volume without further help.

The JUSTINE went back to Seattle and spent the summer towing to Alaska and in the fall she towed lumber barges again, this time between Crescent City and Wilmington, California, remaining on the coast through November.

Returning to Seattle in late November and with Captain Jay still aboard, the JUSTINE left for Cook Inlet to make the last general cargo delivery of the ice-free season. On the 1600-mile return trip to Seattle they ran into violent storms in the Gulf of Alaska and all down the coast. Hampered by wind and seas, a normal nine-day run stretched into three weeks!

After the winter lay-up the JUSTINE was crewed-up for a supplementary lumber run from Coos Bay and Crescent City to Honolulu. A second trip was required and so on May 10th with Captain Arnold Reynolds in charge, the JUSTINE and the FOSS-202 left Longview for Honolulu on what was to be her last voyage to Honolulu and the final round-trip lumber voyage to the Islands by any Foss Miki-class tug.

For the remainder of the 1970 season, the JUSTINE towed general cargo barges between Seattle and Alaska. Then in October she went into winter lay-up, not to emerge until spring, which was usual procedure. With the new high-power ocean tugs in use, the aging and under-powered Mikis's were laid up during the Alaska off-season. But the JUSTINE had orders early in March to go on the coast lumber run. So after four and one-half months of inactivity and with Captain Fred Strang in command, she headed for Coos Bay, Oregon to pick up a barge-load of lumber, the first of five round trips between Coos Bay, Crescent City, and Wilmington, California.

The weather during the JUSTINE's three months on the lumber run was most unfavorable; time and again she took a battering from the strong winds and heavy seas. On her fourth trip she was slammed especially hard against her barge while lying alongside at Crescent City, the result of a sudden squall striking the open part of the harbor. The JUSTINE, in spite of her protective fenders, suffered planking and structural damage to the port quarter and fantail. The condition required inspection and correction so Captain Strang took her down to Long Beach where temporary repairs were made to stop some of the leaking. However, inspection revealed the timbering in the damaged area of the twenty-seven-year-old wood tug to be deteriorated, so the JUSTINE was ordered to return to Seattle.

She arrived at the Foss pier at midnight June 14th, and in the morning a general survey was made of the hull, especially the area around the stern section. The report came in as expected advising that considerable rebuilding of the members around the stern and port quarter would be necessary to put the vessel in seaworthy condition. The estimated expense involved proved to be prohibitive, especially for an under-powered World War II vintage tug. Considering the superior qualities and the availability of the new steel tugs there was no practical reason to repair the JUSTINE, so Foss ordered her into lay-up.

All deck gear, supplies, and navigation equipment was stored ashore and the machinery winterized. In three days the yard crew turned the JUSTINE from the most active Miki in Foss history to a stripped, forlorn vessel, now suited only for salvage.

The next weekend Foss towed her to their moorings in Tacoma, there to remain for the next five years. However, the JUSTINE still continued to serve the Company in a very vital way; she became the spare-parts provider for the three remaining Miki's in active service. Up until 1976 when the last of the three Enterprise-powered Miki's were laid up, parts from the JUSTINE kept the ADELINE, MARY, and PATRICIA running.

Contrary to appearances the JUSTINE was not junk, she was again to feel the flow of water past her stem. In October 1976 Foss sold her "as is" to Mr. Al Walover of Seattle for conversion to a fishing vessel. He shifted the JUSTINE to his berth near Fisherman's Wharf for installation of a high-speed modern engine and to fit large fish tanks in the after-end. The JUSTINE is now the ODIN—to be used for towing drags under the water instead of on the water, but still a towboat of sorts!

KENAI

Built:	1904	Propulsion:	Steam
	San Francisco		750-horsepower
Length:	123-feet	Primary Service:	Puget Sound
Beam:	27-feet	Final Foss Operating	
		Year:	1948
		Status:	Dismantled

The KENAI was built as the U. S. Army Fort-tender GENERAL MIFLAN, for duty at Fort Warden, near Port Townsend, Washington. A second, smaller vessel, the MAJOR EVAN THOMAS, was also assigned to the Fort at the same time. The THOMAS later became the Pacific Towboat Company's tug, SEA RANGER, and she remained in Pacific's fleet, but the MIFLAN had a succession of owners.

With a crew of four officers and ten enlisted men, the GENERAL MIFLAN served Fort Warden and other Army installations in the Puget Sound area for over a quarter of a century. Then in August 1932 the government declared her surplus and Cary-Davis Tug & Barge Company purchased her. They berthed the MIFLIN in Lake Union, and she remained idle for over a year until the Alaska Steamship Company bought her. In the winter of 1933-1934 Alaska Steam rebuilt the vessel into a mail, freight, and passenger steamer for Alaska service. The conversion, costing $35,000, was done at Alaska Steam's yard in west Seattle, and when completed, they named her KENAI after the town in Alaska on the east side of Cook Inlet.

Alaska Steam had received a government contract for supplying the ports of Juneau, Sitka, Hoonah, and a number of out-ports with mail. So on July 4, 1934 the KENAI, carrying thirty passengers and 200-tons of cargo and mail, commenced eight years of Alaska Service that ended in early 1942 when Alaska Steam sold the KENAI to Harbor Plywood Corporation of Aberdeen, Washington.

They retained the name and converted her to a tugboat for coastwise towing; principally for bringing peeler log rafts to Gray's Harbor. With a bunker capacity of 27,000 gallons, she had a cruising range of 2,000 miles, so fuel consumption even in time-consuming log towing was not a problem, but rough weather encountered in ocean towing was a problem.

With a change in wartime Log allocation, the KENAI was released in July 1944 to new owners, Pacific Towboat Company of Everett, Washington.

During the next year-and-a-half under Pacific's ownership, the KENAI made several trips between southeastern Alaska and Puget Sound, towing huge log cribs, providing millions of feet of timber for sawmills to turn into lumber—fir and spruce needed in supporting the Government programs of the Second World War.

Another change of ownership was in the offing for the KENAI. In 1944 when she became the property of Pacific Towboat, the Company was not considered a part of Foss even though Pacific was owned by the Foss family. However, in 1946 Pacific was recognized as part of Foss and the KENAI then became a member of the overall Foss fleet, operating out of the Seattle office.

Foss retained her name and with Captain Clyde Smith in charge, she started towing on the Seattle-Bellingham rail-car run. Because of her weight she also was the principal tug involved in moving government ships and other types of floating equipment around the Sound between Army docks, bases, storages, and the reserve-fleet moorings in Olympia, Everett, and Port Townsend. However, Captain Smith maintained that the KENAI was not a practical tug for maneuvering ships. When ringing astern on the engine, extreme care had to be exercised because he never knew for certain which direction the tug would swing. Usually she backed in the direction of movement before going astern, no matter how slight or undetectable the movement was at the time. It was a question of behavioral patterns. But regardless of the KENAI's peculiarities, the tug was liked by her crews, she had so much inside space which made for comfortable living.

In 1948, due to the economics and advantages of their diesel powered tugs, Foss layed up the forty-four-year-old steam tug. With the extra men in her engine and boiler room, she was not competitive. Nevertheless, in event of converting to diesel, she had the advantage of good condition—her steel hull was still sound, as deteriorated plates had been replaced. But until a final decision could be made on the KENAI's future, Foss sent her to their moorings on Lake Washington to join the other "idlers."

In May 1950 while still in storage, the KENAI was legally transferred from Pacific Towboat Company to Foss Launch & Tug Company. Five days after the transfer of ownership, her Coast Guard documents were surrendered with the option for the right to apply for new papers should she ever be reactivated.

During the next year, 1951 the machinery and all usable parts of the KENAI were removed. However, the idea of modernizing the vessel by installing a modern diesel was being considered and in 1955 a Seattle naval architect was asked for recommendations on repowering the KENAI with an 1,800-horsepower Fairbanks-Morse diesel. A study was made and a report submitted to Foss that turned out more negative than positive. The findings indicated the vessel was too narrow for the length compared to modern design and due to the fact she was built as a supply ship for carrying freight, her lines and displacement were excessive for a tug. The report also stated that 120-tons of concrete ballast would be necessary to trim her properly. Further, with gross tonnage way over two hundred, she would require extra crewmen. Structurally, considerable stiffening would be necessary in the stern and regular maintenance would be necessary due to the riveted construction of the hull. However, the report did state she was in reasonably sound condition and with a new engine, along with extensive modification, the result would be a "usable vessel;" but not a practical vessel by modern standards. The efficiency of a rebuilt KENAI as compared to a new and modern steel tug of smaller size and comparable horsepower would show a difference of twenty-five percent in favor of a new boat.

With the preponderance of factors on the negative side, Foss easily decided to leave the KENAI "as is" and save any further expense. She remained at Kennydale in the Foss boneyard until late 1962 then they towed her to the Foss yard to be cut up for scrap.

Regretfully, from a nostalgic point of view, another veteran steam tug, the MILWAUKEE, the last steam tug to operate in Puget Sound, was also in the yard for scrapping, after forty-two years of Milwaukee Railroad service. By 1963 the cutting torch had reduced the two tugs, MILWAUKEE and KENAI, to only names.

PHILLIPS FOSS In the Lake Washington Ship Canal in August 1966 during her final six months of operation. (From the author's collection)

PHILLIPS FOSS (1)

Built:	1916	Propulsion:	Atlas
	Oakland, California		300-horsepower
Length:	75-feet	Primary Service:	Puget Sound
Beam:	20-feet	Final Foss Operating Day:	February 13, 1967
		Status:	Sold Domestic

The PHILLIPS FOSS, originally a cannery tender-freight vessel, powered with a 150-horsepower Union gas engine, was built under the direction of W. F. Stone for the Red Salmon Canning Company of San Francisco, with canneries located on the Ugashik River, Bristol Bay, Alaska. The boat carried the name FRANK B, in honor of Company President-Manager, Frank B. Peterson. The FRANK B hauled fish in her hold and towed loaded fish scows to the canneries during the canning season. Then in the winter she idled at dockside either by a Company cannery or her home base in San Francisco.

The same routine continued until the spring of 1939 then Mr. Peterson sold the boat to T.J. Badaraco of San Francisco—she remained documented as a cannery-tender and freight vessel for use in California.

Shortly after the outbreak of World War II the FRANK B was laid up in San Francisco Bay and offered for sale. Puget Sound Tug & Barge Company was the successful purchaser. They had been combing the market for a tug to buy as the Government had requisitioned many of the Puget Sound area tugs and the commercial companies were hard-pressed for boats to meet their committments.

PST&B purchased the FRANK B in August 1942 and towed her to Seattle for repowering and outfitting suitable for Puget Sound towing. The Company had in the meantime located and purchased two 300-horsepower Atlas diesels for installation in the FRANK B and another tug, the RETRIEVER. The engines were originally sold to a dredging firm in Asia, but at the outbreak of the War, the engines were held in San Francisco and could not be shipped foreign. .

The FRANK B, renamed LIVELY, was ready in early 1943 to put the new Atlas to work. For the next three-and-a-half years she towed barges, assisted in docking and undocking all types of ships, and seldom left the Sound, what with all the local waterfront activity. Claud McCain and Clair Kellogg, the LIVELY's Skippers, kept her on the move, especially during the War years.

In August 1946 the LIVELY changed hands along with the NEPTUNE in a settlement of Foss claims against PST&B Company. After the transfer to Foss-Seattle, the LIVELY became the PHILLIPS FOSS, named after a son of Justine Foss Wood. The PHILLIPS started out on Puget Sound tows in September 1946 with Captain Lyle Green in charge. She operated only a few months then entered the Foss shipyard for remedial alterations asked for by Captain Green and Chief Engineer Morris Pixley.

According to Chief Pixley, the PHILLIPS had hand steering combined with an oversized rudder and to move it required "four men and a boy at the wheel." Further, the Atlas diesel was salt-water cooled which promoted corrosion and trouble. Also, her only auxiliary power was a one-horsepower Briggs-Stratton gas engine, driving an air-compressor to provide air for starting the big Atlas. The utility generator was only a one-kilowatt 32-volt unit and totally insufficient for lighting a tug of the PHILLIPS' size.

The yard crew corrected all the troublesome deficiencies by installing an air-steering system, changing the engine-cooling method from salt water to fresh, and putting in a larger auxiliary engine along with a higher yield generator. To improve the crew's accommodations the galley was modernized, a new stove set in, and steam heat, hot water, and a shower provided. In addition, a special installation for the Skipper consisted of a bell and jingle system between the pilothouse and the engine room, to be used as a back-up in case the pilothouse engine controls should fail. Some of the relief Captains who were used to the bell and jingle insisted they be used, disregarding the pilothouse engine controls. They maintained it was the engineer's job to run the engine. Today their reasoning wouldn't apply—with computerized and unmanned engine rooms!

When the PHILLIPS was ready, a month later, she began towing gravel scows to the local concrete mixing plants and oil barges port-to-port. She stayed on the same routes for many years with no changes except for the crew.

Though the PHILLIPS' skippers changed, Chief Engineer Morris Pixley remained on the tug for many years, until Foss transferred him to the THEA FOSS, the Company's hospitality boat, where he monkey-wrenched for the next twenty seasons, keeping the twin Atlas engines running.

From 1948 through 1964 the PHILLIPS had several skippers with long terms aboard; Gene Langstaff, Jim Henshaw, and Dave Davis. Gene is now operating a farm, Jim is a Puget Sound pilot, and Dave is just plain retired.

After her 1946 refit, the PHILLIPS towed in linehaul service through 1964 working an average of 300 days per year. Then in 1965 and 1966 she operated only 200 days a year, still a good record for a fifty-year-old tug. The PHILLIPS' usefulness, as with all the old wood tugs, declined due to the superior qualities of the new steel tugs.

Foss planned to retire the PHILLIPS at the end of 1967. However, her career was shortened several months by an accident in February 1967. She had delivered the loaded oil barge FOSS-97 to a Bremerton oil dock and stood by until the oil was discharged. Then on approaching the Port Washington Narrows Bridge, returning to Seattle, a strong cross current caught the PHILLIPS, quickly setting the tug hard against the bridge pier. She hit the pier nearly head on, severely damaging the entire bow section. Leaks developed around the sprung planking, but she made the Foss-Seattle yard under her own power. The inspection revealed extensive damage and the cost of repair was out of proportion to the value of the boat, so Foss put the PHILLIPS in lay-up to await final disposition.

During the summer the yard crew removed the towing winch, main engine, and other machinery, and on August 25, 1967 her official papers were surrendered to the Coast Guard, with the reason stated as "dismantled."

On August 21, 1968 the PHILLIPS was patched and towed over to Port Orchard, Washington to serve as a floating breakwater for the small-craft floats. She remained as a breakwater for many years, until through lack of upkeep and care leaks developed in the deteriorated hull. The PHILLIPS finally sank in place and the cabins later broke away from the deck and floated to the head of the inlet where they washed ashore and were eventually broken up. The hull probably remains in the same position, unless displaced by bottom currents.

With the sinking of the PHILLIPS, fourteen Foss tugs, in a seventy-year span, have bottomed-out. They are not forgotten; in most cases their names live on in their modern counterparts, and this is true of the PHILLIPS.

WEDELL FOSS

Built:	1904	Propulsion:	General Motors
	Baltimore, Maryland		1,600-horsepower
Length:	109-feet	Primary Service:	Puget Sound and Southeastern
Beam:	23-feet		Alaska
		Final Foss Operating Day:	June 9, 1977
		Status:	Sold – Domestic

The WEDELL FOSS began her working life as the R. M. WOODWARD, a 500-horsepower steam vessel owned by the Public Health Service, U. S. Treasury Department, and costing a mere $60,000 to build—1904 prices. She was classed as a boarding steamer operating out of the Quarantine Station on San Francisco Bay. The WOODWARD met incoming ships and put Public Health doctors aboard to make examinations and issue a clearance or order quarantine detention, as all vessels arriving from a foreign port were subject to inspection for contagious diseases and contamination from rats and other carriers.

The WOODWARD functioned in the bay area until the mid-1930's when the government de-activated and laid her up at San Francisco. Then in May 1937 she was sold to Puget Sound Tug & Barge Company of Seattle. They towed her to Seattle for conversion to a modern diesel sea-going tug.

Todd Shipyard spent six months on the refit, including fitting a heavy steel engine bed and installing a 1,050-horsepower Fairbanks-Morse diesel. The big FM made her the most powerful tug on the Pacific coast at the time. To provide sufficient engine fuel, Todd increased the tank capacity to 40,000 gallons, giving her a cruising range of 8,000 miles. The shipyard also installed an anchor windlass and towing winch. With the machinery set, new decking was laid and three staterooms on the main deck rebuilt to accommodate six seamen. A new galley, messroom, and lounge were also constructed on the main deck.

With a raked, red smokestack, well-proportioned houses with eased corners and good hull sheer, she made an imposing sight on her trial run. The seventy-five guests on the test run, made on April 9, 1938 were very impressed with her 13.3 knot speed and remarkable absence of vibration—the designers on the revamping and repowering knew their business.

The updated tug, now carrying the appropriate name of NEPTUNE, was assigned to tow the Milwaukee car-barge from Seattle to Bellingham and return. She made the northbound run in nine hours, nineteen minutes and the return trip, covering 85 miles, in nine hours, twenty-five minutes—her reputation for fast service had started.

The NEPTUNE continued handling car-barges, but on an intermittent basis as she spent considerable time on Coastwise assignments during the next several years. Her first outside job came in May 1938. She ran light to San Francisco and picked up the former Southern Pacific Railroad ferry GOLDEN SHORE for delivery to Seattle. The ferry was scheduled to join the Blackball fleet in Puget Sound service, under the name of ELWHA.

The NEPTUNE made another interesting coastwise tow in October 1939 when under Captain Ray Quinn she successfully towed a Benson log raft from Astoria to San Diego on a risky seventeen-day voyage. The raft was 960 feet long, 55 feet wide, drew 27 feet of water and contained 5,000,000 board feet. However, ocean log towing, in general, proved impractical due to stormy weather generating heavy seas and swells, breaking up the rafts and scattering logs for miles along the beaches. Today, the monetary loss of a 5,000,000-foot raft would come to over $1,250,000. Due to the hazards, the NEPTUNE's log towing was short-lived and she returned to the more commonplace runs on Puget Sound until 1940.

Then in April she made a fast run to the Unimak Pass area in Southwestern Alaska where the States Steamship Company freighter WASHINGTON, enroute from Vladivostok to Portland, was disabled and drifting. The ship's boilers could not be fired and hold steam due to contaminated fuel purchased at the last bunkering port. The ship had used up all the good oil taken aboard in the "States" at the outset of the voyage. The NEPTUNE averaged 13 knots on the run North, located the ship, hooked on and headed for the Columbia River, 1,700 miles away. Tug and tow arrived safely, experiencing moderate weather during the fourteen-day trip.

The NEPTUNE, as did many local tugs, joined the Army Transport Service for the duration of World War II. She worked out of the Seattle Port of Embarkation towing barges of equipment and supplies to the Army bases in Alaska. Her Army duty lasted until shortly after the war when she was returned to her former operators and put back on commercial towing in Puget Sound and the West Coast.

Then in August 1946 the NEPTUNE was allocated to Foss through a court settlement satisfying certain obligations owed by Puget Sound Tug & Barge Company to Foss Launch and Tug.

Shortly after acquiring the tug, Foss renamed her WEDELL, the one and only tug to carry the name. For the next fifteen years the tug was used exclusively on Puget Sound and adjacent waters, spending much of her time for the Milwaukee Railroad, assisting their tug MILWAUKEE on rail-car runs between Seattle, Port Townsend, and Bellingham. The railroad retired their own tug in 1954 so the WEDELL had the Port Townsend run all to herself. This single haul lasted until 1957 when the Seattle-Squamish, B. C. rail-car barge run was established by the Milwaukee Road and the WEDELL then worked on both routes for the next eighteen months.

The WEDELL temporarily ended her service, and rather abruptly, on the evening of September 15, 1959. While southbound from Squamish to Seattle, with one loaded rail-barge, the tail shaft broke and the propeller dropped off, effectively changing her from a tugboat to a boat towed.

Foss dispatched the MARY to Strawberry Island, where she retrieved the WEDELL and her barge, and towed them to Seattle and on to Tacoma next day for survey. Foss decided to repower the tug with a 1,600-horsepower General Motors diesel, as inspection revealed the hull in good shape and the 20-year-old engine in poor condition. During the lay-up the cabins were remodeled and the boat generally brought up to current standards. The job worked under a slow bell, so the WEDELL remained at the Tacoma yard for twenty months.

On June 19, 1961 the transformed tug was ready, so the WEDELL went right to work—where she left off—towing on the Seattle-Squamish rail-barge run.

The WEDELL continued towing rail-barges on the local runs until 1962. Then she became an "outside" boat, towing the rail-barge FOSS-250 from Tacoma, and later Bellingham, to the Ketchikan Pulp Mill at Ward Cove, Alaska for loading and return with carloads of pulp. The WEDELL worked under a long-term contract and she made a round trip in eight days, usually completing three trips per month, depending on the mill's shipping schedule. For the next ten years the tug, with Captain Ed Paine in charge, remained on the run. The WEDELL travelled close to 400,000 miles during her time on the haul, establishing a Foss record for miles covered on one job by one tug on successive trips. The WEDELL could have earned a pilot's license many times over.

Foss' towing contract with the pulp mill expired in November 1972 and the WEDELL joined the ranks of the unemployed, but not for long. She transferred from the Ocean Division to the Sound Division and they assigned her to Seaspan International in January 1973 for towing their rail-barges between Seattle and North Vancouver. Apparently the WEDELL's destiny was towing rail-car barges. The Seaspan job lasted fourteen months, ending in March 1974.

For the next three years the WEDELL had a partial respite from car-barges by towing oil, chemical, chip and cargo-barges on the usual Foss Puget Sound linehauls. Though to keep in practice, she occasionally towed on the Port Townsend-Seattle Milwaukee rail-barge run. During the three-year period, and in the peak movement of cargo to Valdez, Alaska in 1975 for the Alaska Pipeline, she again towed for the Ocean Division. Her job was to bring barges from Seattle to a point south of Cape Spencer on the inside passage where one of the new, high-powered Ocean Division tugs, better suited for crossing the Gulf, would meet her and exchange barges. The WEDELL then returned with the empty barge to Seattle for another load. In March 1976 she went North again, towing the black-oil barge FOSS-99, loaded with 14,000 barrels of fuel, from Seattle to Sitka for the Bureau of Indian Affairs School Building. This was the final revenue voyage to Alaska that the WEDELL made for Foss, and after completing the ten-day run she returned to railroading.

The WEDELL ran full time on the Townsend-Seattle route after the ERIK FOSS was retired in June, 1976, but the WEDELL only held the run for a year. She became a retiree due to the Foss tug-modernization program. With a seventy-two-year-old hull and an ailing engine, she had to give way to the newer "D"-Class boats. In early June she tied up at the Foss pier for de-activation and all operating gear and supplies were sent ashore. Until 1980 the WEDELL's address was Foss West-Tie-Ups, Lake Washington Ship Canal. She no longer is standing by waiting for somebody to come along and put her back to work. She is owned in and is working out of San Francisco.

In her time she moved approximately seven-and-a-half million tons of rail-car freight by barge, almost 190,000 carloads and end-to-end they would make a train 1,900 miles long! Quite an accomplishment for a tug without the benefit of a train crew. The WEDELL was in the railroad business from 1946 to 1956 on the Townsend and Bellingham routes and to 1959 on the Squamish to Seattle run, then ten years on the Ketchikan haul and over a year for Seaspan, with most of her final two years on the Townsend run. Thirty years elapsed time, largely spent towing a floating railroad. The Milwaukee Road operated the car-barge system, but a more apt name for the Company would have been: The Milwaukee and Wedell Road.

DONNA FOSS *Passing under the Ballard Bridge outbound for another routine tow to Alaska on February 19, 1969.*
(Courtesy of Foss Tug Co)

DONNA FOSS (1)

Built:	1944	Propulsion:	Enterprise (Single)
	Barbee Marine Yard		1,500-horsepower
	Kennydale, Washington	Primary Service:	Alaska and Coastwise
Length:	117-feet	Final Foss Operating Day:	September 25, 1970
Beam:	28-feet	Status:	Sold - Foreign

Foss Company's DONNA was one of the ten Miki-class tugs built for the Army Transport Service in Kennydale on Seattle's Lake Washington. The hull, LT-377, was a regional product in every sense. All of her structure came from Washington forests and her timbers were processed in local sawmills.

During the last year of World War II, LT-377 towed for the ATS on the West Coast and Alaska. When her brief service for the Army was over in 1946 she went into the lay-up fleet in Antioch, California to await final disposition. That came in 1947 when she was put up for sale and purchased by Foss. The LT-377 went on the Company roster as the DONNA FOSS to honor the wife of Drew Foss. After receiving title to the tug, Foss shifted the DONNA from Antioch to the Fulton shipyard for two weeks of conversion to commercial use. Then a Foss crew, under Captain Oscar Rolstad, ran the DONNA to Seattle—ready to start twenty-three years of towing for Foss.

During the first decade of her new life, beginning in June 1947 the DONNA towed on Puget sound with occasional trips coastwise and to Alaska. A noteworthy coastal run occurred in early 1952 when she towed, with the help of the AGNES, the forty-five-year-old Army Transport Service liner, REPUBLIC, from Puget Sound to Panama. The AGNES and DONNA delivered the 20,000-ton vessel on the 4,000 mile voyage in forty days. It was an awkward, light draft, slab-sided tow, and no pleasure cruise for Captain Ray Quinn and Captain Mike Hilton. They had to contend with the REPUBLIC's bad case of the "yaws," sluing from side to side. At Panama the big transport was turned over to Moran Tugs to complete the tow to an East Coast yard for scrapping.

The REPUBLIC had an interesting history. Launched at Belfast, Ireland in 1907 as a German passenger ship, she ended up for the Germans as a troop transport in World War I, until captured by the Allies. After the War she became a unit of the United States Lines and during the 1920's and 1930's sailed in trans-Atlantic passenger service. Just before and in World War II she served the Army as a troop transport and later as a hospital ship. The long and demanding service finally aged her right into the scrap-yard.

In August, 1959 the DONNA and PATRICIA, another Miki-type tug, delivered the battleship, MARYLAND, from Bremerton to Oakland, California, a slow, heavy drag, but with fine weather the tow followed along on course. From California the DONNA towed the Seattle dredge, MANSON #7, to Panama. Then with no northbound tow available, she returned home to take on whatever the Seattle Operations Department had to offer.

During the next several years only routine Alaska towing assignments came her way—long ocean tows were scarce. Her primary runs consisted of towing Foss LST barges loaded with bulk cement from Puget Sound or Portland to Anchorage and towing the rail-car barge, FOSS-250 between Tacoma and the Ketchikan pulp mill. Interspersed with these regular tows were occasional runs to ports in Southeastern and Southwestern Alaska not regularly served by scheduled barge service. Having served a long stint on Alaska runs, the DONNA was entitled to a change of scenery and climate.

It came about in 1962 when the increased demand for lumber in Hawaii and southern California required the services of a third tug-and-barge unit to supplement the regular sailings of the BARBARA and JUSTINE FOSS. During the first five months freighting lumber, the DONNA and her LST barge made two trips to Honolulu and several trips from Oregon and northern California lumber ports to Los Angeles and San Diego. With the DONNA's help, enough lumber poured in to keep up with the demand, but even so, the DONNA's services were necessary for almost two years.

A change of assignment came about for the DONNA in 1964 when she took on the job of towing the container barge, COLUMBIA, for Sea-Land, Inc. between Portland and Oakland from January through November. The DONNA's coastwise haul occurred at the time when containerization was in the early stage of development and container movement by tug and barge on a trial basis. However, the run continued, but not with the DONNA, the PACIFIC MARINER of Pacific Tow & Salvage took over so the DONNA could return to the Alaska runs.

The first half of 1965 the DONNA, with Captain Ed Saling, kept on the move towing supplies to the oil fields in Cook Inlet. Then in July a pressing call came for a tug to go on the Honolulu lumber run to relieve the BARBARA FOSS, in need of an overhaul after serving non-stop for nearly four years. So the DONNA returned to hauling lumber, leaving Seattle in July to begin the first of seven round-trip voyages. Each round trip lasted between thirty-five and fifty days including the discharge time, keeping the DONNA literally "on the run" for ten months. The Captains responsible for the DONNA's performance were Ed Saling, Jay Jacobson and, for the last two months, Joe Uskevich. Captain Joe remained with the DONNA, except for an occasional trip off, for the next four years, and until he assumed command of the new JEFFREY FOSS, the tug that more or less replaced the DONNA and brought on her lay-up.

When the BARBARA returned to the Honolulu run in mid-1966 the DONNA returned to the cooler Alaska climate, hauling barge loads of oil-company material and equipment to Cook Inlet for construction of sea floor pipelines. At the end of the open season, she tied up in Seattle to wait for the spring push to put her back to work. But while waiting for the Alaska season to open, the DONNA, in March 1969 played a major role in a ship rescue.

She was dispatched to a location about 1,000 miles southwest of Cape Flattery, Washington, on a mission to find and take in tow the disabled and helpless Liberian freighter, BELO HORIZONTE. The ship was in darkness and the crew struggling through several days without heat, electricity, or warm food. The HORIZONTE was out of control, drifting and wallowing at the mercy of the Pacific. Captain Uskevich figured the probable position of the HORIZONTE, steered accordingly and in time the ship showed up on the radar. The tug's crew went right to work and with a messenger-line, put the tow wire aboard with the eager help of the HORIZONTE's crew. The tow to Seattle was safely accomplished in seven days, and the dead ship delivered to the shipyard right at the estimated time.

An earlier rescue operation for the DONNA occurred in May 1967 in the Aleutian Islands. The PACIFIC TITAN, owned and operated by Pacific Tow & Salvage Company at Long Beach, had been towing a small cargo barge around the Aleutian Islands, discharging cargo at Adak, Shemya and Attu, one of the westernmost islands of the Aleutians. On May 18 with discharging finished at Attu, the TITAN was returning to the Navy facility at Adak, but when less than five miles from Attu, a broken oil line in the engine room started a fire which engulfed the tug in minutes. But the Captain was able to get out a "MAYDAY" call. Then he had the lifeboat launched and the eight-man crew jumped aboard, rowed away and from a safe distance, waited for the fire to burn out. The barge was undamaged and still on the TITAN's towline. A search plane spotted the lifeboat next morning and later in the day the Coast Guard cutter, CONFIDENCE, arrived on the scene and assisted the eight cold and cramped crewmen aboard. To save the tug and barge, and to prevent night collisions, the cutter hooked on and headed for Adak.

Fortunately, on May 17 the DONNA, with Captain Uskevich aboard as usual, had departed Amchitka Island for Seattle, towing an empty cargo barge. As soon as word of the fire reached the Foss-Seattle office new orders were sent to the DONNA, via high-seas radio, to drop her barge at Adak and head for the Attu Island area to relieve the CONFIDENCE. By the night of May 18 the DONNA had left Adak and was underway for the TITAN. She met the CONFIDENCE on May 20th and took charge of the burned tug and barge and headed back to Adak, arriving on May 22nd. The TITAN's crew had already landed at Adak from the cutter and were on their way to California by air.

The DONNA's next orders were to load return cargo at Adak before returning home. In two days time the navy cargo was aboard the barge and the DONNA underway for Seattle, towing the TITAN's barge and her own.

The PACIFIC TITAN was held at Adak to await the arrival of the JUSTINE FOSS on her way from Amchitka and the following month the JUSTINE towed the TITAN to Seattle.

After inspection at Foss, the TITAN was declared a total loss. However, it was not until the following year that Foss sold her for salvage to Marine Power and Equipment Company. Then after lying at their Seattle yard in her burned-out condition for ten years, they sold her for rebuilding into an ocean fishing vessel to operate in the Alaska crab industry.

A possible serious accident befell the DONNA in heavy weather crossing the Gulf of Alaska in late November 1967 while southbound with two barges from Cook Inlet to San Francisco. At 0115 on November 23, with winds southwesterly 40-45 knots and rough seas, a freak wave hit the starboard quarter of the tug, caving in the door, frame and house planking of the cook's cabin. Fortunately, the sleeping cook was not injured, but he was flooded out. Captain Joe immediately headed the DONNA into the seas and hove-to until necessary repairs could be made. The crew patched the area with stiffeners, heavy plywood and canvas over all. The tug remained hove-to and waited out the storm to ensure no more damage would happen to the weakened starboard side of the deckhouse, which could allow a flood of water to swamp the engine room. After the storm eased up, the DONNA and her tow headed for Port Angeles via the Inside Passage and arrived safely on December 5th. The MARY FOSS took over the tow at Port Angeles and the DONNA went to Tacoma to repair the deckhouse.

In September 1968 after several trips to Alaska during the spring and summer season, the DONNA completed a barge tow from Seattle to the Kona Coast of Hawaii. The barge carried construction equipment and several tons of explosives to be used in the construction of a small boat harbor near the town of Kona, Hawaii. Upon returning from the Islands she headed right out for Amchitka—from fair weather to foul—the run to the Aleutians was the DONNA's last trip of 1968. Routine assignments to Anchorage, Amchitka, and Valdez kept her on the move through 1969.

In June 1969 on arrival home from a voyage to Anchorage, the DONNA FOSS became the ANNA FOSS. The name DONNA was to be used for a new "D"-Class boat which was soon to be completed in Portland. The original ANNA FOSS had been retired and sold in 1968, so the switch caused no complications.

The ANNA, after nearly four months lying idle, in 1970 began her final months for the Foss Company hauling barges between Seattle and Anchorage. Her retirement was largely due to the arrival of the new ocean-class tugs earlier in the summer, combined with a seasonal slowdown in cargo to Alaska. But another influencing factor was the twenty-six-year-old tug's engine needing a major overhaul. After arrival from Anchorage on September 25th, she went into indefinite lay-up with little prospect of ever running again.

Then in late October 1970 a representative from Luzon Stevedoring Company of Manila, Philippine Islands, flew over to negotiate with the Foss Company for the purchase of surplus tugs. A few days later a sale was consummated for the AGNES and ANNA FOSS. As recorded in the AGNES' story, on November 4th, twenty Philippine seamen employed by Luzon arrived in Seattle and established quarters on the two tugs. The vessels were re-activated, necessary repairs and outfitting accomplished, and successful sea trials carried out in preparation for the thirty-five to forty day voyage to Manila. The tugs were repainted to a color scheme of black hull, white house, and blue trim. They were transferred to Philippine Registry and renamed. The ANNA became the BRUIN, the AGNES the CELTIC.

The tugs left the Foss dock on November 17th and arrived in Manila on December 22nd, in time to celebrate Christmas at home after an uneventful and favorable crossing of the Pacific.

The Luzon Stevedoring Company has informed Foss that the BRUIN continued in service in the Philippines for seven years doing ship-assist work, barge towing, and salvage work. However, due to constant engine troubles which were uneconomical to repair, the BRUIN was decommissioned in mid-1978 at Manila. The CELTIC, as of 1979 is still in operation.

OMER FOSS (1)

Built:	1943	Propulsion:	Buda
	Wilson Boat Company		150-horsepower
	Wilmington, California	Primary Service:	Port Angeles Harbor
Length:	46-feet	Final Foss Operating Day:	May 2, 1958
Beam:	11-feet	Status:	Sold - Domestic

The OMER FOSS, built during World War II as the Army tug MTL-1218, was one of a group of small, diesel-powered, wood tugs designed by the Army Transport Service for river and light harbor towing. By using tunnel stern construction, the tugs could float and work in only four feet of water, a decided advantage in shallow bays.

The MTLS had Buda diesels and the auxiliaries, if needed while operating, were driven from the main engine, but for standby service, a 1,500-watt, automatic, gasoline-engine-driven light-plant was available. Accommodations for the crew were forward of the engine room and separated by a bulkhead. The small fo'c'sle contained two berths and a small galley equipped with a portable stove.

When the MTL-1218 was declared surplus, after the Army service in Seattle was completed in late 1946 Foss purchased her at a government sale by sealed bid in June, 1947.

After a complete overhaul at the Foss-Tacoma yard, the MTL, renamed the OMER, Wedell's middle name, started her commercial life in Port Angeles harbor October 17 1947 joining the regulars already there—FOSS 8, FOSS 9, and NANCY FOSS. In addition to harbor work the OMER towed boomsticks across the Straits to Victoria and Esquimalt and on occasion filled in on the chip-scow run to Port Townsend when the larger tugs were not on hand.

The OMER continued in harbor service for the Port Angeles division on a steady basis until August 22, 1957. About this time the original LORNA FOSS, used as the day-boat at the Foss-Seattle yard, was retired, and the OMER came over as a replacement. The move did not affect Port Angeles as the declining log towing business in and out of Port Angeles required only two harbor tugs.

The OMER operated less than a year in Seattle as most of the sawmills had closed, so very little log towing was required in and around the Lake Washington Ship Canal. However, there was still a need for a tug on the occasional job offered, so a serviceable boat was to be on hand. The OMER might have stayed longer as the "on-call" boat, except her old, original engine was causing much trouble and was no longer reliable, so in May 1958 the steel-hulled harbor tug JERRY FOSS was transferred from Tacoma to Seattle as the standby tug. The OMER was withdrawn from service and laid up to wait a decision on future use. After a year in lay-up, Foss towed her to Tacoma and removed the old engine just in case the OMER would ever be repowered.

She remained idle in Tacoma until July 1962 then Pacific Towboat Company in Everett needed an additional harbor tug, so the OMER was given the job and repowered with a 165-horsepower General Motors diesel. After a general outfitting, she started service in Everett, but only for a month. In April 1962 she transferred to the Anacortes division of Pacific Towboat Company where a boat was required to tend log storages. While on the Anacortes job, on May 8th, the title to the OMER was transferred to PTC and the next month she became the SEA PRINCE to conform to PACIFIC's way of naming tugs, all names starting with the prefix "SEA."

In the late sixties, with a decline in log input at Anacortes, the SEA PRINCE was sent to the Scott Pacific log dump on Lake Washington where she did similar work, tending log storages.

By late 1970 the tug was badly in need of recaulking—the hull required continuous pumping to keep afloat. However, the poor condition of the planking did not warrant the expense of recaulking, so the PRINCE became a leaky problem. Then one weekend, when no one was in attendance, the water level increased to more than the normal height and by Monday morning she had sunk in the shallow water alongside her tie-up float. She was raised, pumped out, and towed to the Foss yard where all machinery and equipment were lifted out. Then to solve the leakage, Foss put her in a cradle at the storage yard.

On December 30, 1970 the remains of the SEA PRINCE were sold to Mr. Roy Durgan, who had purchased other retired Foss tugs. Shortly after, he sold her to Art Lang of Tacoma for conversion to a fishboat.

GARY FOSS (1)

Built:	1943	Propulsion:	Atlas
	Reliable Welding Works		400-horsepower
	Olympia, Washington	Primary Service:	Puget Sound
Length:	69-feet	Final Foss Operating Day:	October 10, 1949
Beam:	20-feet	Status:	Sold to Pacific Tow & Salvage Company

The GARY FOSS started out as the ST-166 for the U. S. Army, ninth in a series of sixteen identical tugs turned out by Reliable Welding Works for use in Army out-ports. Unfortunately, in heavy weather, the ST-tugs, with their extensive deckhouses, large smokestacks, extra topside equipment and round bottoms, were heavy rollers. Moreover, in rough weather with no baffle-plates in the fuel tanks, there was a constant threat of capsize due to "free surface" oil sloshing side to side. To further complicate the ST's tender condition, there were only two watertight transverse bulkheads in the hull, and if a major flooding occurred there would not be sufficient buoyancy to remain afloat.

But regardless of the hazards, the ST-166 operated in Southeastern Alaska during World War II and until the fall of 1948 when the government offered her for sale. On November 12, 1948 Foss purchased the ST-166 and on arrival in Tacoma gave her the name of GARY FOSS, in honor of a son of Justine Foss Wood. As the tug was needed to keep up with towing orders, very little work or change was attempted at the time. She went on linehaul work and remained on port-to-port runs during her stay with Foss on Puget Sound.

The GARY's term in Seattle ended suddenly when Pacific Tow & Salvage at Long Beach decided to enter the harbor ship-assist market, and they asked Foss to release a tug for the new work. So less than a year after her purchase, Foss sold the GARY to PT&S and upon arrival in Long Beach they renamed her PACIFIC ROCKET.

The tug was used on the new work for a year, but Pacific had very little success in the ship-assist part of tug boating, so they shifted her to full-time towing on local barge runs.

The ROCKET's primary job during most of her career in Long Beach was towing Barge-166 for the U. S. Navy on a logistics run between Port Hueneme and the Navy base at San Nicholas Island. The barge carried a variety of cargo, from sand and gravel, to trucks, beer, PX merchandise, miscellaneous Navy equipment and supplies.

She performed well for customers and owners until one weekend in the summer of 1972. Some time prior to her sudden and unexpected immersion, a bolt under the thrust-bearing on the engine let go and was driven straight down into the thin steel bottom. A blister formed which gradually eroded as time went on. Sometime during the night on an idle weekend, with no crew aboard, the steel blister finally broke open, allowing a geyser of water to flood the engine room and eventually the entire hull amidships. Transverse bulkheads would have limited the inflow, but being without this structural protection, the tug filled up and sank at the dock.

Pacific Tow decided to raise the tug and they brought the derrick-barge PACIFIC EAGLE to the scene. After several days of preparation, the ROCKET was raised and shifted to a shipyard at Terminal Island for survey and patching. The insurance company settled the damage claim by taking over the tug and paying off PT&S, then they immediately sold the ROCKET on an "as-is" basis to a San Pedro party, but other than renaming the tug BRONCO, the San Pedro purchaser made no attempt at reconditioning.

In August, 1973 Captain Dave Updyke, owner of Diesel Repair Company in Seattle, had purchased a tuna clipper in San Pedro and needed a tug to tow the vessel to Seattle, so he purchased the BRONCO to do the job, knowing well a major overhaul would be necessary after her submersion in salt water. As he anticipated, the repairs required four men full time for a month to complete. The major work consisted in renewing the electrical system, right down to the generator, and overhauling the Atlas engine, including installation of new rod bearings.

Dave Updyke and his crew left San Pedro in late September with the tuna clipper in tow, but they returned to San Pedro within a day after departure for radar repair. At the next attempt everything went smoothly and they made a fine run to San Francisco to take on fuel.

When they were ready to leave for Seattle a weather report came in that was not encouraging. There was a good possibility of a Pacific storm moving in, and on a tug which had proved a problem in heavy weather, Dave decided to leave the tuna clipper in San Francisco and go on with just the BRONCO. Running light, the tug was able to out-distance the weather, and she arrived in Seattle none the worse for the trip. The tuna clipper was towed up a year later by a private party that Dave said owed him a favor.

In early 1974 Dunlap Towing Company of LaConner, Washington, purchased the BRONCO from Updyke and they stripped the tug down to bare hull and gave her a complete rebuild and refit. When she finally reappeared on the Sound in 1975 as the tug SWINOMISH, she couldn't be recognized as the former WWII ST-166 "beer barrel" tug—so called because the bottom was built like a barrel and rolled like one. But Dunlap, by complying with all the requirements of new tugs built during the mid-70s, had turned the veteran into a trim, modern-looking boat.

The SWINOMISH is now an important part of Dunlap's log towing fleet and she isn't wearing out the clinometer by rolling like she used to do before her transformation and change of locale.

JERRY FOSS

Built:	1943	Propulsion:	International
	Gibbs Gas Engine Company		170-horsepower
	Jacksonville, Florida	Primary Service:	Foss Yard,
Length:	45-feet		Ballard, Washington
Beam:	14-feet	Final Foss Operating Day:	April 20, 1968
		Status:	Sold - Domestic

The JERRY FOSS, built for the War Shipping Administration, was one of twelve identical steel harbor and general service tugs turned out by the Gibbs Engine Company of Florida. Ready for service in 1943 the small tug was shipped to Honolulu where she served the Navy at Pearl Harbor all during and for a time after WWII. Then about 1947 she was sold at a surplus sale to Mr. Ernest Wright of Honolulu. He named the boat JERRY, and the name stuck, even during the time of Foss ownership—which came about as a result of the Foss Company's Bill Wood taking a vacation trip to Honolulu.

Peculiar circumstances developed in connection with the purchase and documentation of the JERRY by the Foss Company. The strange case of the JERRY began in November 1948 when Bill Wood, manager of Foss' Bellingham Tug & Barge Company negotiated for the purchase of the tug through a Mr. Lee of Irish Cabs, Inc. of Honolulu who claimed an interest in the boat. Mr. Wood was informed by Mr. Lee that the vessel was actually owned by a Mr. Ernest Wright and in evidence Mr. Lee produced a bill of sale in favor of Foss and signed by Mr. Wright. The boat was registered by Wright with the Coast Guard as being less than five tons, so transfer of ownership to Foss could be made at Honolulu Coast Guard and no "Marine Bill of Sale" was required under the circumstances. The purchase price to Foss was $2,200!

In early 1949 the JERRY was shipped to Seattle aboard the YC-470, a small cargo barge that became the FOSS-125. The JERRY ended up at Foss-Tacoma for a rebuild that took until October, 1950, as the boat was only worked on at slack repair periods. For power, Foss gave her a new 160-horsepower Gray Marine Diesel. With the tug nearing completion, the next step was documentation with the U. S. Customs. The process turned out to be more than a step—it was a whole staircase!

But in order to allow the boat to run, the Customs Service issued a temporary permit until the proper papers could be provided. With the temporary permit in hand, the JERRY started regular Tacoma harbor work in November, 1950. In the meantime, the U.S. Customs advised that Foss must produce a formal marine bill of sale, a builder's certificate, and a record of the chain of ownership from construction to the present time. This meant a formal bill of sale from Mr. Wright, and a record of his purchasing the vessel from a previous owner, which was probably a U.S. government agency.

So on November 2, 1950 Foss wrote to Mr. Wright in Honolulu requesting information and documents. No reply was received and a second letter was dispatched in late November. Both letters were returned stating Wright had moved and left no forwarding address. The Coast Guard replied to a letter of inquiry that they in Honolulu had no information as to where the boat was built or the name of the shipyard. They also stated that no identifying hull number could be found on the boat. Fortunately Foss found in the engine room a small plate showing the vessel was built by Gibbs Gas Engine Company of Jacksonville, Florida. Foss wrote to Gibbs Company asking for a Builder's Certificate or a statement to the effect that it would be impossible to produce the document. Included in the letter were exact dimensions of the tug as well as the model number of her previous engine, a 170-horsepower Buda diesel—the only clues to the origin of the vessel.

Gibbs Company replied that during 1942 and 1943 they built twelve boats of the dimensions stated. The boats were numbered G.Y.T. 1 to 12 inclusive and all had Buda engines. All twelve were taken over by the War Shipping Administration as soon as constructed. They also stated that the records of the Yard Superintendent had been lost and they were unable to identify the exact hull from the information furnished. The model number or serial number of the engine was of no help to them. So much for Gibbs—Foss had one of twelve, but which one?

Next, a letter was written to the Maritime Administration in Washington, D.C., asking for records showing any Bills of Sale by the War Surplus Division covering G.Y.T. class of tugs issued in Honolulu after the War. The answer came back negative—another dead end.

As a last resort in the title quest, a letter was written to Mr. Lee, the taxicab man, asking for his help in tracking down Mr. Wright. Mr. Lee had given the impression that he had an interest in the boat through some salvage deal with Mr. Wright, so possibly Mr. Lee just might know of Mr. Wright's whereabouts. No reply came back to the last hope for a lead.

By January 30, 1951 Foss concluded that in view of the complete lack of information it would be fruitless to continue the search for title papers, so the facts were presented to the U. S. Customs asking for a waiver of the requirements and on February 12, 1951 a letter came from the Customs Service stating that a waiver was unconditionally granted. The quest was over after three frustrating months.

The JERRY continued in her Tacoma harbor work for the next 7½ years with little change to the tug, except in July 1953 she received a new 170-horsepower International diesel, the only tug in the fleet to have an International. Then in May 1958 she transferred to the Seattle division to take over from the OMER FOSS on log, barge, and boat shifting in Ballard and Lake Washington. The JERRY continued on the job through 1959, then the curtailed activity on Lake Washington Ship Canal and Lake Union did not warrant a full-time tug based at Foss-Seattle, so the JERRY moved back to Tacoma, but only for a short time before being transferred to Bellingham Tug and Barge.

The JERRY kept active in Bellingham for a year and a half on various harbor jobs, including an occasional boomstick tow to Anacortes. Then when the work slowed down, she returned to Seattle. At least the JERRY's life was not monotonous, up until 1962.

During the years 1962-1965 she only operated a total of ninety-three days, but she did make unlogged emergency runs with the Foss night or weekend dispatchers to pump out a sinking scow in the yard or to corral a drifting boomstick in the Canal.

In late December 1965 the Foss tug, RUSTLER, to be closer to the office, came over to the Canal from her berth at the Seattle Export Lumber Company dock (Selco) on the Duwamish River. With the coming of the RUSTLER, the JERRY became the junior tug as the RUSTLER was better suited as a yard tug and she carried a regular two-man, eight-hour crew. The only work for the JERRY occurred when mechanical difficulties tied up the RUSTLER. The JERRY had little chance to earn her keep; from 1966 through June 1968 she operated only 123 days.

By mid-1968 with both the RUSTLER and JERRY suffering from mechanical problems and age, the "old reliable" HENRIETTA FOSS came over to work the Ballard area. The JERRY now could be permanently dispensed with, and on July 17, 1968 she and the surplus tug, ELAINE FOSS, were sold to Annette Timber Company of Ketchikan. The JERRY was renamed TRINITY II and left in late July for southeastern Alaska under tow of the TRINITY I (ELAINE FOSS).

The TRINITY II operated primarily around Klawock in southeastern Alaska, towing logs and tending the sawmill until the mid-Seventies when she sank near Klawock. The tug was raised and towed to nearby Craig, where she remained afloat, but badly deteriorated. In early 1979 she was sold, and the present owner started the long and tedious job of restoration, intending to install a G.M. diesel, and when all is accomplished, he will use the tug for log salvage in southeastern Alaska.

James A. Cole

SECTION V – OCEAN TUGS EXTEND FOSS'S RANGE OF OPERATIONS

Tugs Acquired 1950 – 1959

MARGARET (1), PEGGY (2), DUNCAN (1), EARL, LESLIE (1)

MARTHA (2), BRYNN, ERIK, PROSPER, CRAIG (1), GARY (2)

ANDREW (2), CAROL, ELMER, ELSIE, MARY (1), SHANNON

ADELINE (2), PATRICIA (2), IVER (2), ALASKA CONSTRUCTOR

Of the twenty-one tugs purchased, fifteen came from competitive-bidding government sales. Being able to buy the right tug at the right time was a decided advantage to Foss, enabling them to satisfy the growing demand for their services and with little delay. Foss also added the ex-Barrymore yacht to their fleet as a hospitality ship.

In this decade of Foss activity, ocean barge towing was developed to a high state of efficiency and importance. With nine more high horsepower tugs on the roster, additional regular Alaska and Coastwise runs were established. Barging lumber to California became a steady business. The Bellingham-Anchorage cement run was started. Foss began the first of the annual re-supply trips to the DEW Line Stations.

On Puget Sound, with the number of tankers calling at the refinery ports increasing, additional tugs were assigned to assist in docking and undocking. In Seattle, two special ship-assist tugs of 1,200-horsepower were built to handle the high number of vessels calling at the Port.

Year in and year out there was very little slack in any of the company lines—they were pulling hard and well.

THEA FOSS—YACHT

Built:	1930	Propulsion:	Atlas (Twin)
	Craig Shipbuilding Company		550-horsepower
	Long Beach, California	Primary Foss Service:	Company Yacht
Length:	120-feet	Status:	In Use
Beam:	21-feet, 6-inches		

Foss purchased the THEA in 1950 from a group of geological scientists who had bought the boat from the government after World War II and used the vessel for private surveys off the coast of lower California. The group did not change the boat's name, AMBER, nor did they alter the boat's appearance or fixtures from when the navy used her as a patrol boat during the war. So it was up to Foss to convert the boat to a yacht. The Foss-Tacoma shipyard made the transformation and brought the boat back to her former quality.

The yacht, launched in March 1930 was built for the renowned actor John Barrymore as a present to his wife, actress Delores Costello. At her suggestion he named the boat INFANTA to honor his first daughter, Delores Ethel May—soon to be born. But regrettably, the Barrymores gained but little pleasure from their yacht. John much preferred his former sailboat, as he felt a part of her by working the sails and battling heavy weather—he had no challenge on the well-crewed INFANTA. And, unfortunately, his insatiable need for cocktails resulted in many unpleasant moments between John and the more conventional Delores, even aboard the yacht. With the ever-present problem, they used the boat rather sparingly, although they did make trips as far south as Cape San Lucas in lower California and as far north as Alaska.

The INFANTA carried a full-time crew of ten with Otto Mattheis the captain all during Barrymore's ownership. With such a large crew, the yearly cost of maintaining the yacht came to $35,000 and that was in the 30's. Eventually Barrymore ran into financial difficulties and mortgaged the INFANTA for $40,000. In about 1938 he gave up the boat to his creditors—which is ironic, considering he earned $3,000,000 during his first ten years in Hollywood. However, the INFANTA served no useful purpose for the Barrymores, so she was not missed when they lost her by default.

After the Barrymore era, the boat was named POLARIS by her new owners, the Lowe family. Then when the navy took possession in 1942 they named her AMBER, but she didn't stay forever AMBER as Foss bought her and she became the THEA FOSS—in honor of the mother of the Foss family line. Naming the yacht THEA was wise and discerning as THEA's name and her reputation would become known by hundreds of people as guests on the boat, whereas, her name lettered on a tugboat would receive only limited recognition unless some feat brought her before the public.

Foss has now owned the THEA for thirty years, and each summer season she goes on cruises in and around Puget Sound and British Columbia, hosting Foss customers, giving them a pleasant change from the fast pace of business. Unlike the INFANTA, Foss' THEA serves a useful purpose and her many guests look forward to the pleasant annual trips.

Her guest list has the names of Kings, Ambassadors, and Congressmen, including King Olaf of Norway, who was aboard in 1975 for a trip around Seattle's waterways and harbor. It seems most appropriate that the King and his party chose the THEA in view of the Foss Norwegian background.

Like the trip with King Olaf, most of the cruises are for thirty to forty people on short runs in the close Seattle and Puget Sound area, as the THEA has accommodations for only ten guests on overnight trips.

Occasionally the THEA is free to take special parties on longer cruises like to Princess Louise Inlet in British Columbia to view the many waterfalls cascading over high rock bluffs. And she has also made trips to Rivers Inlet and other salmon fishing areas in B.C. carrying avid fishermen. In Thea's day, the fishing was done around Tacoma, and she furnished only rowboats and launches.

But regardless of time or place, Thea's solicitude, knowingly or unknowingly, started the Foss Company out in their concern for satisfied customers and they in turn considered Thea a very special person. So it is fitting that a very special ship has her name and carries on the hospitality of her namesake—from the ever-ready coffeepot to the spread on the bountiful table.

MARGARET FOSS (1)

Built:	1943	Propulsion:	Fairbanks-Morse
	Clyde Wood, Inc.		450-horsepower
	Stockton, California	Primary Service:	Southeastern Alaska
Length:	89-feet	Final Foss Operating Day:	October 2, 1962
Beam:	25-feet	Status:	Sold

The MARGARET FOSS, an ex-Army tug named SGT. JAMES A. BURZO during her military service, was one of a series of Army tug-passenger vessels with the class number TP99. The BURZO was a sister-tug to the PACIFIC, which later became the third EDITH FOSS.

The BURZO operated solely on the West Coast during and after World War II, including a number of years in Southeastern Alaska while based in Kodiak. She was declared surplus in June 1950 and at a Government sale in August at Fort Richardson, Alaska, Foss turned in the high bid of $7,678.

They purchased the BURZO to replace the 200-horsepower FOSS 19 working on the Union Oil delivery contract out of Ketchikan. By 1950 a more powerful and more seaworthy tug was needed to serve Union Oil Company customers in Southeastern Alaska on a year-around-basis.

The BURZO was a decided improvement for the crew, as the living quarters were larger and more modern. All cabins and the galley were located on the boat deck or the main deck, with ample room for living inside when the Alaska weather turned stormy or frigid.

In September 1950 the BURZO was drydocked and made ready for her new job by the Foss shipyard in Tacoma. She left the yard bearing the middle name of the oldest daughter of Drew and Donna Foss. As the MARGARET FOSS, she started deliveries out of Ketchikan in November, towing an oil barge with 300,000 gallons of petroleum products. Her first and regular skipper until the late Fifties was Captain Walt Davis, a proficient Alaska pilot who has commanded many Foss tugs.

Because of improved docking facilities at Ketchikan, the headquarters of the Union Oil Company's Southeasthern Alaska operation was transferred there from Juneau in 1956. The MARGARET followed along and tied up at the Union Oil float when stopping in Ketchikan.

During spring, summer, and early fall, the MARGARET and her barge were always on the go, delivering oil to the many canneries, salteries, and towns of Southeastern Alaska. Then when logging became extensive after the Ketchikan pulp mill started, floating logging camps sprang up in many bays and inlets with each camp requring oil—adding new stops for the MARGARET.

In late September of each year, with the customers' storage tanks topped off, and the canneries down until the following season, the MARGARET with her barge would head south for annual reconditioning. After a usual four-to-five-week lay-up in Seattle for repair and then drydocking in Tacoma, she would return to Ketchikan in late October.

Winter deliveries were infrequent so the MARGARET and her crew were idle in Juneau or Ketchikan for two or three weeks between trips. However, they were always ready in case oil was suddenly needed along the route.

A great advantage of the MARGARET, according to Walt Davis, over the earlier tugs on the oil run was her ability to withstand the winter weather, especially when crossing Taku Inlet. Winds gusting to 100 knots were not uncommon and they seemed to spring up from nowhere.

In unwinding a few strands of past times on the MARGARET, Captain Davis remembered one incident very clearly. He said it points out the difficulties to be surmounted in operating away from major repair facilities, and it shows the all-out effort made by the Foss crew to be "always ready". According to the Captain, the vessel was laid up in Seattle one fall for annual repairs, including a major engine overhaul. Part of the engine rebuild included installation of a set of pistons that had been taken out of a removed engine from the CHRISTINE FOSS. The engines were similar in size, bore and stroke, and the pistons, in good condition, were supposedly identical. Only time would tell.

On arrival back at the Ketchikan base in November, the Engineer reported the pistons were sticking and leaving metal shavings on the cylinder walls. This caused excessive wear on the rings and necessitated replacement. The crew set to work and changed rings, figuring the problem was now solved since the engine had just had a major overhaul. Alas, the poor crew—the pistons continued sticking and the rings needed replacing after every voyage! Each change of rings took about 20 hours of patient work and the ring change went on all winter, spring, and summer until the MARGARET returned to Seattle in the fall. Upon inspection at Foss-Seattle, the machinists found the pistons were definitely too large, so they were removed, turned down to size and re-installed. This solved the vexing problem—no more 20-hour ordeals.

However, starting in 1961 the MARGARET had progressive engine trouble and since Foss had recently acquired another government surplus tug, more maneuverable and in good mechanical condition, they decided to give the MARGARET a rest. There were other factors influencing the decision. The bays and inlets where logging camps located were usually too restrictive for a vessel of MARGARET's dimensions and then with fall and winter storms to contend with, an engine failure could be dangerous. So the MARGARET returned to Seattle in September 1961—after topping off the last customer's fuel tank.

Five weeks later the recently acquired ROLAND FOSS left the Foss pier for Ketchikan to take over the oil service for the winter, and the MARGARET remained idle in Seattle, awaiting a decision on repowering.

In early May 1962 the ROLAND came back to Puget Sound for special assignment and the MARGARET returned to Ketchikan for one more summer season. The MARGARET relieved the ROLAND on May 15th and continued on the oil run until the regular fall shutdown period. She came back to Seattle in October and the ROLAND once again went north to take over the route.

The MARGARET tied up at Foss-Seattle—but only for a month, then on November 25th the DREW FOSS towed her to the Foss yard in Tacoma and placed her in dead storage, awaiting a decision on her future use. As late as December 1962 plans were still in the making to give her a new engine, but by 1963 repowering was ruled out, so Foss placed her on the retired list. The determining factor for the MARGARET's retirement was the Company's decision to build new high power steel tugs, eliminating the need to spend large sums of money to repower the old wood boats—so the MARGARET could now be offered for sale.

In January 1966 she gained a new owner and a chance to go back to sea. She was bought by Seattle fisherman, Olaf Angell, for conversion to a king-crab fisher and reefer vessel. Mr. Angell removed the worn out engine and installed a new 500-horsepower Caterpillar diesel. He also modified the deckhouse in order to install a fish hold. She started her new career late in 1966 as the fishing vessel BARON, one of ten ex-Foss tugs converted to the less-demanding role of a fish boat. In 1977 she was elevated higher in the fish boat nobility by an important-appearing addition to her name—she is now the ROYAL BARON and, no doubt, gets a salute from passing fish boats.

PEGGY FOSS (2)

Built:	1944	Propulsion:	General Motors (Twin)
	Warren City Tank & Boiler Company		330-horsepower
	Warren, Ohio	Primary Service:	Alaska
Length:	53-feet	Final Foss Operating Day:	November 24, 1961
Beam:	14-feet	Status:	Sunk

The PEGGY was built for the U.S. Navy and named LCM-51776 (Landing Craft Medium), but six months after completion the government sold her to Marine Industrial Supply Company of Long Beach, California who had already purchased a number of LCM's.

In early 1950 Foss bought eight LCM's from Marine Industrial Supply and barged the boats to Seattle in care of the AGNES FOSS. Seven of the LCM's were resold to various buyers in the Northwest and the eighth boat was retained and became the PEGGY FOSS.

For most of her career the PEGGY worked in southwestern Alaska and Cook Inlet doing shallow-draft lightering and landing cargo in beaching operations by use of her bow ramp. She had no crew accommodations and only a small pilot house on the after end for steering and engine controls. Her 2-man crew was supplied by the ocean-going linehaul tug requiring her special ''barge-to-beach'' unloading services.

The PEGGY worked in Alaska until November 24, 1961 when she met with misfortune and sank off Anchor Point while under tow of the AGNES FOSS. The loss occurred traveling southbound in Cook Inlet bucking into rough seas and floating ice. Apparently she struck an ice pan, gouging a hole in the hull. The crew on the AGNES noticed the PEGGY was low in the water, but before they could investigate, the cargo barge also under tow of the AGNES and coming along astern of the PEGGY ran her down and she disappeared from sight.

An air search was made, but to no avail. The PEGGY was on the bottom in only 20 fathoms, but there was no chance of locating her due to the silt. After a short inquiry, the underwriters declared her a total constructive loss.

Her name is a persistent one as there is now a third PEGGY FOSS carrying on, an advanced type of harbor tug.

DUCAN FOSS AT Port Gamble shifting chip scows for Pope & Talbot in April, 1967. (From the author's collection)

DUNCAN FOSS (1)

Built:	1944	Propulsion:	Nordberg
	Victory Shipbuilding Corporation		400-horsepower
	Newport Beach, California	Primary Service:	Puget Sound
Length:	63-feet	Final Foss Operating Day:	December 29, 1971
Beam:	18-feet	Status:	Sold - Foreign

The DUNCAN FOSS, originally a World War II Navy harbor tug, carried the class designation YTL-309. The YTL's were powered by two Buda diesels driving a single propeller and as the tugs had ample power, they were used for harbor shifts and inter-island barging in southern California waters, the Hawaiian Islands, and other established navy bases.

At the conclusion of the war, many of the YTL's were sold to private and commercial interests, but others, including the 309, continued with harbor work during peacetime. The 309 assisted navy vessels around Pearl Harbor for several postwar years before being declared surplus and eventually decommissioned.

In December 1950 the 309 was sold to A. G. Metal Products and without ever using the tug they removed the machinery and sold the bare boat on February 9, 1951 to Foss. The AGNES FOSS, in Honolulu at the time to pick up a barge of equipment for Seattle, made a tandem-tow and brought the 309 to the Foss-Tacoma yard for rebuilding.

The vessel was reduced to just the bare hull before commencing eighteen months of reconstruction. Two staterooms, a W.C. and shower were constructed on the main deck. Below decks a modern galley was fitted out and quarters for the crew built forward of the galley area. A 400-horsepower Nordberg diesel, installed in November 1952 provided the power and new auxiliary equipment was set in place to give the tug a whole new up-to-date engine room. After outfitting, the rebuilt tug in June 1953 with Walt Olsen as Captain, was ready for work, carrying the name DUNCAN in honor of a son of Sidney and Barbara Foss Campbell.

As with all new installations, defects show up on the early runs and the DUNCAN was no exception. On one of her first assignments, she towed 32 sections of logs from Everett to Port Townsend and when nearing her destination, the main engine water pump failed. The big diesel had to be shut down, so the DUNCAN with the force of the tide drifted toward the beach. There were no tugs nearby to offer assistance and something had to be done immediately to provide power. After some quick thinking, Captain Walt Olsen hooked up the 2½ inch firehose between the fire pump, run by an auxiliary motor, and the cooling-water inlet on the main engine. It was a patch job, but the connection held and they were able to deliver the tow intact to Port Townsend. The makeshift cooling system even held together all the way back to Tacoma for permanent repairs. The hook-up was later known as an Olsen coupling.

For the next 18 years the DUNCAN operated for the Tacoma division, handling logs and all types of barges—chips, hogged fuel, caustic, chemical, ammonia—towing them between Puget Sound chemical plants and pulp mills. In October 1969 the last of the new D-class boats were nearing completion, and Foss reassigned the name DUNCAN to the new boat, so the first DUNCAN was renamed ELAINE FOSS.

During the Longshore Strike of 1971 the ELAINE, along with many Foss tugs, was pressed into service to tow log rafts from Tacoma and Everett to the open ports of Ladysmith and Cowichan Bay, B.C. for loading aboard log ships engaged in the export trade to Japan. The B.C. log push worked the ELAINE hard until the strike was resolved in late fall, then she returned to routine Puget Sound towing.

The many years of running with little time for engine overhaul began to show by telltale signs of noise, exhaust smoke, loss of power—all indicating the necessity of a major rebuild. Foss scheduled the ELAINE for the repair yard on January 2, 1972 so after delivering a loaded gravel scow from Steilacoom to Tacoma, Captain Bud Hopkins and his crew removed all loose gear for storage ashore.

The Nordberg engine was completely disassembled and during the time Foss re-assessed the expense and age factors. They decided that rebuilding a heavy-duty engine 20 years old for a tug nearly 30 years old would not serve the best interests of the Company, so all work on the ELAINE ceased.

The tug was placed in dead storage at the Foss yard and after lying idle for 18 months she was sold to John Menzies for use as a log patrol boat based in Ganges Harbor, B. C. During the Menzies ownership she was known as the CUMSHEWA CHIEF.

Title to the tug changed again in the fall of 1974 when Frank Chidley of Kyuquot, B. C., on the west coast of Vancouver Island, purchased her for use in his hand-logging operation. Mr. Chidley with his family moved aboard and ran her to Kyuquot Sound, then he renamed the tug TANIA TOO.

The Chidleys did some renovating to make the boat more suitable for family living. The bulkhead between the two on-deck staterooms was removed to make one large stateroom and Mrs. Chidley, with a skill in leather crafting, converted the forecastle into a workshop—but she did leave one bunk intact for a guest.

The Nordberg engine was rebuilt by Mr. Menzies during his ownership, and he advises that it is still in good operating condition.

In addition to handling logs in Kyuquot Sound, the TANIA TOO, with the Chidleys, has engaged in log salvaging work in the area around Bella Bella, B. C. (on the inside passage to Alaska). The TANIA TOO, according to her owner, continues to perform well and as long as the Chidleys are satisfied, the ex-ELAINE FOSS will no doubt remain a Canadian citizen.

EARL FOSS

Built:	1944	Propulsion:	General Motors (Twin)
	Walsh Construction Company		330-horsepower
	Jersey City, New Jersey	Primary Service:	Tacoma Area
Length:	46-feet	Final Foss Operating Day:	February 10, 1968
Beam:	14-feet	Status:	Scrapped

During World War II hundreds of various types of landing craft were built to debark and land troops, equipment, and supplies at beachheads, including the LCMs (Landing Craft Mechanized). They were carried aboard attack-personnel carriers and supply ships. During the War when the big ships were in action off the beaches, the LCMs were lifted into the water with ship's gear for the runs ashore. With their bow ramps they were the best solution to transferring men and material ashore where no piers or landing facilities existed.

When the war ended, a great number of all types of landing craft were offered for sale and Marine Industrial Supply Company of Long Beach bought several LCMs for resale. In January 1951 Foss, in Tacoma, needed an LCM for shallow water log-storage work at Chambers Creek, Nisqually, and Kamilche. On January 8 Foss purchased the LCM-3 and shipped it to Tacoma aboard a barge. They put a foredeck on the vessel, made other minor modifications, painted it green and white and named it EARL FOSS, the middle name of Roland Foss, a grandson of Andrew's oldest brother Theodore who died in 1888 at St. Paul.

The EARL's working base was Chambers Creek, a mile north of Steilacoom and handy to the West Tacoma Newsprint Company log storage. One of the EARL's primary jobs was relieving linehaul tugs of log tows and shifting the rafts into the WTNC mill storage. She also worked the shallow water Nisqually log storage for the St. Regis Pulp & Paper Company.

As the Steilacoom gravel pits were within a mile of Chambers Creek, the EARL was often called upon to shift gravel scows and assist the linehaul tugs during the loading process. When no shifting was required, which was rare, the EARL often helped a linehaul tug to pull a log tow when trying to make a tide at Shelton or Balch Pass.

Being available around the lower Sound, the EARL also assisted tugs from competing companies needing help with log rafts. She also relieved other tugs of log tows when they were destined for the mill inside Chambers Creek. Foss, of course, received a fee for the EARL's obliging services.

By the late Sixties, the regular water log-storages were used less and less and the logs were stored more and more on dry land in Tacoma proper, however, the EARL continued to be used at Chambers Creek with her long-time skipper, Captain Don Jennings at the wheel. By 1968 the EARL was showing signs of hard use—her steel hull was much thinner, badly dented, and the engine was beginning to complain.

On February 10, 1968 while towing a 6-section bundled raft from Nisqually storage to Chambers Creek, the starboard engine lost all oil pressure. So after delivering the tow, the EARL limped into Tacoma on the port engine.

With curtailed business at the storages and facing heavy repair expense to the engine, Foss decided to lay up the EARL. The retirement created no problems as the FOSS 9, working out of Tacoma, could take care of whatever tending and shifting came up at Nisqually or Chambers Creek.

With no future need or use for the EARL, the machinery was removed in the fall of 1968 and her document surrendered to the Coast Guard, listing the reason as "abandoned". Shortly after, the EARL was scrapped, her steel parts recycled to come out in some other useful form.

LESLIE FOSS (1)

Built:	1944	Propulsion:	Superior
	Minneford Yacht Yard		1,200-horsepower
	City Island, New York	Primary Service:	Alaska and Coastwise
Length:	117-feet	Final Foss Operating Day:	April 19, 1968
Beam:	28-feet	Status:	Sold - Domestic

The LESLIE FOSS, designated LT-495 by the U.S. Army during World War II was one of a series of five MIKI-Class tugs built at the Minneford Shipyard in New York. She operated on the East Coast for the Army Transportation Corps from 1944 until shortly after the War.

When the 495 was declared surplus and offered for sale, the Baltimore Towing Company of Baltimore, Maryland, in July 1946 purchased the tug and renamed her the JOHN MICHAEL. They used the MICHAEL in East Coast service until April 1950 then sold her to Kotzebue Oil Company, Kotzebue, Alaska for $150,000.

Kotzebue Oil owned a number of smaller tugs and several cargo barges and a large oil barge, the ARCTIC CHIEF—all their equipment was used in the Bering Sea and Arctic regions. But with the acquisition of the JOHN MICHAEL, Kotzebue Oil intended to compete in more general towing in other areas of Alaska on a year-around basis rather than be restricted to the short ice-free season in the Bering Sea. The JOHN MICHAEL started work for Kotzebue Oil in 1951 doing general barge towing between Puget Sound and Alaska and it must have been profitable as the Company was able to make payments during the summer to the Sea-First Bank on a marine mortgage against the tug.

But in early November, Kotzebue's fortunes took a turn for the worse. The JOHN MICHAEL left Seattle with the barge ARCTIC CHIEF bound for the Oceanic Fisheries herring-reduction plant at Port Vita on Alaska's Kodiak Island. This was the second trip to Port Vita and the barge was to load 224,000 gallons of herring oil, 18,000 gallons of salmon oil, and 190,000 gallons of fish soluble. By November 25 all of the $307,000 cargo was aboard and the JOHN MICHAEL, with the ARCTIC CHIEF, pulled out for Seattle.

Shortly after leaving, the weather started to make-up, and by dawn on November 26, the tug and barge were caught in a raging gale with 50 to 60 knot winds and very high seas. The JOHN MICHAEL was taking a vicious pounding, but hanging on and hoping for a let-up. But at the height of the storm, the brake on the tow winch failed, and the tow line flew off the drum, casting the barge adrift. Wind and sea took charge, grounding the barge on the rocky shores of Marmot Island. Heavy breakers pounded the ARCTIC CHIEF, and she started to break up. The incessant seas kept the barge heaving and twisting, and she eventually slipped off the rocks and sank in 500 feet of water.

The JOHN MICHAEL, severely battered by the seas, headed for shelter and waited out the storm before beginning her return to Seattle—light. Shortly after arrival in Lake Union, she was placed under arrest by the United States Marshall as Oceanic Fisheries had opened court proceedings against the tug and owners for loss of cargo. Sea-First Bank also filed a claim for $112,000, the amount still owed on the mortgage and Union Oil Company later filed suit for $15,000 to cover unpaid fuel bills.

Oceanic Fisheries claimed the tug and barge left port in an unseaworthy condition, had inadequte towing equipment, and suffered negligence by the crew. However, investigation revealed that the JOHN MICHAEL's towing gear was approved by a marine surveyor before departure. But a new tow line had been installed prior to leaving Seattle, and the wire was 300 feet shorter than the old line, so it was claimed the shortage of weight and catenary effect would be critical in a storm as severe as the one in which the ARCTIC CHIEF was lost.

During the next three months, claims and counter-claims flooded the court while the JOHN MICHAEL remained under arrest at Lake Union. Then after the legal storm subsided, the Federal Court on March 5, 1951 ordered the tug sold at a public sale by the U.S. Marshall. The major reasons given for this decision were to save the tug's value and prevent accumulation of costs during court proceedings and to reduce deterioration of the vessel during a long drawn-out trial. Kotzebue Oil Company protested the action because a Marshall's sale would not bring enough to enable the firm to resume business. Nevertheless, the sale was held on April 9, 1951 at the Federal Courthouse in Seattle.

Foss Launch & Tug Company bid the highest of the competitors. Besides Foss, Crowley Maritime, and Oceanic Fisheries were bidders. The Foss bid of $76,000 was only $1,000 over Crowley's. Foss' explanation of their bid amount was that a MIKI-Class tug in top condition would be worth $115,000; but they figured to spend $40,000 in upgrading the tug to Foss standards—therefore, the $76,000 bid. With the JOHN MICHAEL, Foss now owned six MIKI-Class tugs to serve the flourishing Alaska and Ocean trade.

A few months later the Court dismissed without costs all causes, actions, and claims against Kotzebue Oil Company except the claims of Union Oil Company and Sea-First Bank.

In the meantime Foss towed the JOHN MICHAEL to their Seattle yard for a major overhaul and outfitting to prepare her for long-distance towing. During the period of reconditioning she was named LESLIE FOSS in honor of the eldest daughter of Drew and Donna Foss.

To start off her active Foss life the LESLIE, in late April, towed Milwaukee rail-car barges between Seattle and Bellingham. But with the start of the Alaska summer season, she shifted to the Anchorage barge run, remaining on the haul all summer.

The LESLIE towed on the various Foss Alaska routes between April and September of each year through 1957. The quiet winter months were spent either waiting for the spring activity at Seattle moorings or towing car-barges between Seattle, Bellingham, and Port Townsend. The LESLIE didn't have exclusive rights to the car-barge run, she had to share the work with her five sister-tugs also wintering in Seattle, each one taking the job for a few weeks to keep limbered up.

Ironically, the LESLIE was again at the Oceanic Fisheries dock at Port Vita with barge FOSS-137 on July 2, 1957 loading herring oil and fertilizer for discharge in Seattle—but under different auspices than the LESLIE's call at Port Vita in 1951.

Next came a shift for the LESLIE to southern waters. After a quiet winter in Seattle, she left for southern California in April 1958 with barge FOSS-207 loaded with lumber from Olympia, Washington. The trip marked the beginning of the long-term Foss Coast Lumber Run, so named until after 1961 when the name was changed to Coast & Honolulu Lumber Run.

The LESLIE maintained the Coast Lumber Run and on a regular basis for fifteen months, barging lumber from Puget Sound, Oregon, and northern California ports to southern California. Then in November 1958 a second tug was added, the JUSTINE FOSS, and the two tugs remained on the run through June 1959 then the LESLIE was ordered to resume barge towing to Alaska. She finished out the Alaska towing season in late fall and joined the winter lay-up fleet—but not for long.

In October the LESLIE had a part in the construction of the Hood Canal Floating Bridge as several high-horsepower heavy tugs were needed to shift and hold in place the floating concrete pontoons so they could be joined and anchored to form the bridge structure. The job required the combined strength of the MIKI-Class tugs ADELINE, DONNA, and LESLIE, with the CAROL and ANDREW FOSS assisting. The job was a short one, but it lessened the winter lay-up time.

The LESLIE continued regular Alaska service with few problems from 1960 through 1963, but in 1964 she made long hard tows which took some of the life out of the 20 year old tug—like the one she made in February 1964. With winter weather battering Alaska, the LESLIE was ordered to tow the large refined-oil barge FOSS-98 from the U.S. Air Force oil dock at Mukilteo to the remote airbase at Shemya Island in the farthest reaches of the Aleutian Islands—a 3,000 mile trip from Seattle via the Inside Passage to Cape Spencer and from there across the rough North Pacific to Shemya. Maintaining a respectable speed of 6 knots, the LESLIE, after being weather-bound for nine days, arrived at Shemya on March 20th. After discharging the 36,000 barrels of oil, she returned to Seattle without suffering weather damage, arriving April 6th.

Another wearing assignment was slated for the LESLIE—she was to take part in the 1964 DEW Line re-supply project for the government. So on May 9, 1964 again with the FOSS-98 in tow, she left Mukilteo for the Army base near Naknek in Bristol bay. Arriving off Naknek River the LESLIE and her barge anchored up, and for the next two weeks oil was lightered ashore in small barges towed by the shallow-draft Foss tugs SEA MULE and ELMER FOSS.

During the next six weeks lightering continued at the Bering sea bases of Newenham, Romanzof, and Unalakleet. Then, with her barge empty, the LESLIE returned to Puget Sound for another load and with only four days in port she headed again for the Bering Sea, departing on August 6th. But after only three days, the north-bound leg of the trip suddenly ended at Bella Bella, British Columbia—the LESLIE's engine developed problems. Via radiophone, the Captain reported that apparently a bad load of diesel was dumped aboard in Seattle and he complained that the engine ran erratically and the valves were burning off. He advised that the engine could not be relied on when maneuvering in close stations. The Seattle office directed the LESLIE to continue northward, meet the MARTHA FOSS and exchange tows. The meeting was accomplished and the LESLIE took the MARTHA's light barge and headed for home arriving August 22nd. With repairs made and new fuel aboard, the LESLIE went back to work, but this time on local routine tows until winter lay-up.

On April 9, 1965 the LESLIE, with Captain Stan Thurston in charge, left Seattle with two combination deck-cargo and petroleum barges for a seldom-heard destination, Amchitka, an island 600 miles out in the Aleutian chain. The LESLIE and her crew knew little of the meaning of operation "Longshot" on Amchitka when they left Seattle, even though activity for the atomic project was under way some time before barge-cargo started to arrive.

On May 9, 1964 the first construction crew meal was served on Amchitka and it was the first meal since the Island was abandoned by the Military in 1945. A small camp for about fifty men was set up for the Atomic Energy Commission job. The coordination of the early stages of the base construction was handled by the Alaska District, U.S. Army Engineers. The first cargo to the Island consisted of sixteen bunkhouses and four portable buildings for kitchens, mess, and recreation rooms. The 20 buildings, each 10 × 24 feet, were shipped via Military Air Transport from Tacoma. Power for the camp was supplied by two generators with a total output of 70 kilowatts. The plants were also air-lifted. During the first year all necessary cargo was air-shipped from Seattle. Very little was known about what was going on at Amchitka except that a highly important government project was in the making.

Captain Thurston's sailing orders on the frst barge trip stated: "You will be carefully watched and checked by the contractors (Norcoast Construction Company), the United States Army Engineers, and other government agencies." Norcoast Construction was only involed with the development work, buildings, roads, and utilities.

The initial cargo carried by Foss consisted of 500 tons of general cargo, 60,000 gallons of diesel, and 225,000 gallons of gasoline. The LESLIE and her two barges arrived at Amchitka on May 1st and spent several extra days discharging, due to the very primitive conditions for unloading. Before returning home, she barged extra supplies from the Navy base at Adak to Amchitka. The diversion lengthened out the trip and she didn't return to Seattle until June 28th, after a three months' absence.

The LESLIE spent the remainder of 1965 on routine tows to Alaska and 1966 turned out very similar with the exception of a 43-day Panamanian trip in the spring. With Captain Dale Gudgel as skipper she ran light to Balboa, picked up a floating machine shop and delivered it to Tacoma.

The LESLIE's 1966-1967 winter days were quiet ones and just as well, for the 22-year old tug had to conserve her aging machinery for the coming season when she was scheduled for more long hard tows to the Aleutians.

A year and a half had passed from the start of the project before the major drilling operation for the Atomic Energy Commission, handled by Holmes & Narver Construction Company, got under way, necessitating a tug and barge sealift.

Foss was awarded the extensive Amchitka towing contract and all their available equipment was utilized to keep cargo moving on all routes.

The LESLIE went back to work in April, and with Captain Gudgel she left for Amchitka on Voyage #3 of the Holmes & Narver contract. With good weather she completed the voyage in 34 days, a fast run for the 5000-mile round trip.

However, the rest of her runs did not turn out as favorably. After 16 years pulling heavy barges for Foss, the LESLIE began to experience mechanical failures, equipment breakdowns, and parts replacement. To complicate repair work, she was the only Foss MIKI powered by a Superior diesel and parts were not as readily obtainable as for the Enterprise engines in the West Coast-built MIKI's. Delays and expensive time loss for the LESLIE were unavoidable as evidenced by her performance record for 1967. On her last run to Shemya in August she started out from Seattle with a general cargo barge with Captain Jay Jacobson in charge—Captain Jay had arrived in Seattle less than four weeks earlier after spending several months in Vietnam aboard the MARGARET FOSS. The voyage to Shemya was routine until the evening of August 12 when halfway across the lower Gulf of Alaska the Superior broke down. The engineers opened up the engine and found Number 4 piston in two pieces. Eighteen hours later a spare piston was in place and they were back on course.

Then on August 14 Captain Jacobson radioed that the direction-finder and radar had both failed during the day and to add to the troubles, they were experiencing rough weather. At 0645 on August 19 when about 30 miles from Dutch Harbor, the main engine broke down again. Fortunately, the fishing vessel VIRGINIA SANTOS was in the vicinity and towed the LESLIE and her barge into safe anchorage at Dutch Harbor, arriving at 1800 that night. The engineers checked out the engine and found a valve had gone through the cylinder head. With repairs made, they were ready for a trial run, but the engine wouldn't turn over. Another check revealed a severely bent "con" rod. The LESLIE was considered deadlined at Dutch Harbor and the engineers started tearing down the engine. The Seattle office arranged to ship a new head, rod, and piston by air freight.

Next day the LESLIE received word by radio that four crates of engine parts, totalling 2,007 pounds would leave Anchorage at 0600 August 22 and arrive Dutch Harbor at noon. But the parts failed to show up. They were sent to Fairbanks by mistake. By August 24, the parts still hadn't arrived—the plane was weather-bound at Cold Bay. The parts finally did arrive August 25 and the installation started. However, prior to this, on August 22, the ADELINE arrived in Dutch Harbor from Amchitka and took over the LESLIE's tow for Shemya and the LESLIE, upon completion of the repairs, was to return the ADELINE's empty barge from Dutch Harbor to Seattle. With repairs completed on August 27, the LESLIE left for home and without further incident arrived in Seattle on September 11. But her future usefulness was considerably in doubt as all towing companies had been constantly upgrading their equipment and powerful high-speed tugs were necessary to compete for jobs. Foss had sufficient new and more able tugs to call on, so the LESLIE was towed to Tacoma for drydocking, mionor repairs, and lay-up.

Then a business upswing began in April 1968 and all the fleet was in motion with the exception of the LESLIE. But on April 12 a rush job came up, and Foss brought her out of lay-up to tow oil barges between Tacoma and a severely damaged tanker lying at Nootka Sound, B.C. The oil was to be pumped out of the tanker, the MANDOIL II, into barges for delivery to Tacoma.

The LESLIE left Tacoma on April 14 with the oil barge FOSS-98 bound for Nootka and after delivering the barge, she returned light to Tacoma to take a second barge to the tanker. On the way up the Straits, abeam of Neah Bay, the electric steering broke down and the ANDREW FOSS was sent to take over. The next morning, still at Neah Bay, the LESLIE was ordered to Tacoma for permanent lay-up and by April 19 she was fast alongside the tie-up float—her career with Foss over.

But with one door closed, another opened for her. On June 6, 1969 Foss sold her to Robert Martin of Gig Harbor who ran Gig Harbor Marine Charters. Martin's purpose in acquiring the LESLIE was to register her as a yacht and modify the tug for charter served to any place in the world. He renamed her ENCHANTER. The new owner modernized the galley and upgraded the quarters for comfortable living, accommodating fifteen persons. She could be used for underwater salvage, extended cruising, or fishing charters.

Robert Martin used the ENCHANTER in this type of service for several years then he sold the boat to the well-known tugboat Captain "Jug" Nolze for a return to the work she was built for.

The ENCHANTER was still equipped for towing and with the necessary document changes, Captain Nolze was ready to crash the Alaska towing business as an independent operator. He entered into a bareboat charter with Northland Marine Lines of Seattle for use of his boat in towing container barges to their delivery ports in southeastern and southwestern Alaska. At this time Nolze renamed the tug POLAR NAVIGATOR so as to have a similar name to Northland Marine Lines' own tugs, POLAR SEA and POLAR STAR. For the next several years the POLAR NAVIGATOR towed on a regular basis and in competition to Foss Alaska Line.

Captain Nolze passed away during the life of the charter, but Northland Marine Lines continued operating the tug until November 1976 when, afflicted by serious financial problems, the company filed for bankruptcy.

The POLAR NAVIGATOR was seized by a local shipyard for non-payment of repair bills and several other firms also filed claims against the tug for unpaid bills. To clear the case, the NAVIGATOR was sold in May 1977 at a U.S. Marshall's sale. Her new owners, Mr. and Mrs. Bob Sinkey of Olympia, Washington, planned to live aboard the vessel and use her for private cruising. They berthed the boat in Olympia and spent the next several months transforming the commercial tug into a comfortable well-appointed home afloat. They left the towing gear intact just in case it was ever needed.

In May 1978 the Sinkey family cruised from Olympia to Juneau, Alaska. At Juneau they anchored in front of the old Alaska Juneau Gold Mine as a base of operations. During the summer of 1978 they chartered the tug for several weeks to a geophysical study outfit in southeastern Alaska and the Sinkeys acted as crew.

In early June they received an unusual request for tug services from Southeast Skyways of Juneau. One of their "Beaver" airplanes crashed at the head of Pinta Bay on the west side of Chicagof Island, but the plane could be salvaged. Fortunately, the pilot escaped uninjured and was rescued the next day. The Sinkeys agreed to provide the services of the NAVIGATOR and the next day they left for Pinta Bay. The tug anchored in a deep water bay close by the downed plane and each salvageable piece of the plane was floated out of Pinta Bay on inner tubes and barrels over to the POLAR NAVIGATOR. Both wings, the pontoons, engine, and fuselage were safely towed to the tug and hoisted aboard. Salvage complete, the tug returned to Juneau, her mission accomplished.

The POLAR NAVIGATOR remained in southeastern Alaska through September 1978 and the final few weeks of the cruise were spent relaxing in Pybus Bay, then the family crew of four and dog headed back to Olympia, arriving in early October.

The Sinkeys decided it was time to sell the 35-year old tug as maintenance was costly and operating expense excessive for a boat with but little offsetting income.

So in early 1979 the tug was sold to a construction company in northern California. They berthed her at the Foss-Seattle yard where the Sinkeys had the tug tied up for repairs. The newcomers intended to do general towing out of the Gulf of Mexico, but apparently nothing developed as last report has the former LESLIE now named WESTERN SEA I tied up in Everett in some legal complications.

MARTHA FOSS *Northbound out of Puget Sound, July, 1961 with triple tow for Pure Oil Co. at Pavlof Bay, Alaska. (Courtesy of Roger Dudley and Foss Tug Co)*

MARTHA FOSS (2)

Built:	1943	Propulsion:	Fairbanks-Morse (Twin)
	Northwestern Shipbuilding Company		1,380-horsepower
	Bellingham, Washington	Primary Service:	Coastwise and Alaska
Length:	117-feet	Final Foss Operating Day:	December 20, 1965
Beam:	28-feet	Status:	Sold

During World War II Northwestern Shipbuilding Company built seven MIKI-Class tugs for the Army Transport Service and fifth in the series was the LT-160, later to become the MARTHA FOSS.

During her war service LT-160 operated temporarily on the Pacific Coast and then transferred to the East Coast to take part, along with ten other MIKIs, in Atlantic convoys and general towing along the Atlantic seaboard.

Convoy-118 was typical of the type of towing performed by the LT-160. The flotilla consisted of eleven MIKIs, including the 160, towing ten ST-Class (Small Tug) tugs and several rail-car floats from New York to Falmouth, England between July 23rd and August 17th, 1944. The LT-160 was assigned two floats and the ST-726. To provide extra fuel for the tugs during the crossing, the tanker SAPELO accompanied the convoy. The voyage turned out well, with reasonable weather and no attacks, but most of the tug-and-tow convoys were not so fortunate.

At the completion of her Army Service in 1946 the LT-160 was declared surplus at Port Arthur, Texas. And in May 1946 Cornelius Kroll & Company of Houston purchased the tug, reconditioned her for commercial towing, and renamed her SEA HORSE.

Cornelius Kroll operated the tug out of Galveston for five years and then put her up for sale in early 1951. Foss was advised of the offering and made the purchase in March. The SEA HORSE then became the fifth Foss MIKI and the second with twin engines. Foss drydocked the tug in Galveston and sent down a Seattle crew to bring her home. She made the run to Puget Sound under the name of SEA HORSE, but upon arrival she became MARTHA FOSS, carrying the name of the first MARTHA sunk in a tragic collision with the Steamer IROQUOIS in May 1946.

The MARTHA entered service in June 1951 on the cement bargehaul to Anchorage and continued on the run for the remainder of the season. Then for the next eight years she engaged in towing to Alaska, principally barging freight to the growing city of Anchorage. When the seasonal work finished in late fall she usually tied up and spent her winters alongside a Foss-Seattle pier.

After the long idle winter, November 1959 to April 1960 the MARTHA was given two warm-up trips towing the rail-barge FOSS-250 between Tacoma and Ketchikan, before commencing the major towing job of assisting in the re-supply program of MONA LISA stations (the government's early-warning system) in the far reaches of northern Alaska.

The MARTHA left Seattle on May 12, 1960 for Dutch Harbor with the 32,000-barrel oil barge FOSS-98 and a smaller 4,000-barrel barge for lightering cargo. During the next four months, the MARTHA made deliveries at all the radar sites in the Bering Sea including Cape Newenham, Tin City, Cape Lisburne, Northeast Cape and Kotzebue. This was the second assist for the MARTHA in the MONA LISA program. The first run was in the spring of 1956 towing two barges of construction equipment from Seattle to Sitkinak Island, south of Kodiak, for J. A. Jones Construction Company engaged in erecting one of the many radar installations for the government.

Upon completion of the 1960 re-supply assignment, the MARTHA returned to Seattle arriving on September 10th. Her towing for 1960 was over and for the first time she laid up in Tacoma during the off-season.

Her 1961 start came in April and the work lasted until November. The MARTHA had an interesting tow in July with Captain Ed Saling in command when she made a triple barge tow from Seattle to Pavlof Bay on the Alaska Peninsula with contractors' equipment for the Pure Oil Company. Pure Oil, an Illinois-based firm, had leased a half-million acres in the Bristol Bay and Alaska Peninsula area for oil exploration and intended to sink a well in Pavlof Bay. The 2,000-mile outbound voyage was completed at an average speed of 5.9 knots, a good showing for a triple tow.

The MARTHA from 1962 through 1964 towed general cargo and cement barges between Seattle and the usual Foss delivery points in southeastern and southwestern Alaska. The trips were run-of-the-mill and comfortable, however, the MARTHA was not a favorite of her crews. Unlike the other MIKIs, the tug had a disconcerting trait, she rattled and shook so much the crews swore they could not write legible letters or pour full cups of coffee when the MARTHA was pulling—apparently she suffered from a bad case of marine palsy!

Her last year with Foss, 1965 started in early April when she towed, in company with the AGNES FOSS, the Western Offshore Drilling Rig #3 from Everett to Cook Inlet. The heavy-weight tow was completed in 14 days.

After delivering the rig, MARTHA headed right back to Seattle. For the remainder of the season, through October, she towed the asphalt carrying barge FOSS-182 between Union Oil Company at Edmonds and Anchorage.

In late November 1965 the MARTHA was dispatched to Portland to pick up Foss' new chlorine and caustic-soda carrying barge, FOSS-260. The barge was built specifically for use between the Georgia Pacific Mill at Bellingham, Washington and the G.P. plant at Samoa, California. The towing contract was for ten years and a total of 192 voyages were made before the contract expired in August 1976. During the last year's run Pittsburg, California and Coos Bay, Oregon were added to the route extending the time of each voyage to 14 days.

The first trip of the contract was made with the MARTHA on December 3rd, under the direction of Captain Stan Thurston. As with all break-in voyages, a few problems developed with the chemical barge, but they were able to leave Samoa after a week and arrived back in Bellingham December 20th. The MARTHA left the barge and headed for Seattle, tying up the same day at the Foss pier—for the last time. The MARTHA's life under Foss control was over, as a charterer was standing by ready to send the tug to war for the second time in her history.

In 1965 the sudden buildup of American armed forces in South Vietnam presented a tremendous problem in logistics. The Republic of South Vietnam had only one developed port—Saigon, 42 miles up the Saigon River from the entrance near Vung Tau at Cap St. Jacques. More than 100 ships were jammed in Saigon and many more downriver, clear to the open sea. The ships carried over a million tons of cargo—ammunition, food, fuel, and construction materials. Loaded ships were held at Guam and as far away as San Francisco due to lack of berthing and discharge facilities in Vietnam.

Additional receiving ports were imperative, but construction materials, equipment, and time were sadly lacking. The solution was to use tugs and barges to land cargo on beaches for quick handling, storage, and favorable location. So in late summer 1965 Alaska Barge & Transport Company of Vancouver, Washington met with the Military Sea Transportation Service and described their experience in over-the-beach discharge at remote areas of Alaska, including the North Slope region. Up north they had provided the equipment, stevedoring, towboatmen, heavy-lift operators, and mechanics—they had been successful in Alaska, so why not in Vietnam? Then after several months of negotiating, a contract was signed, dated December 8, 1965.

A.B.& T. expected to be awarded a contract, so they had attempted to obtain options beforehand on the necessary equipment and be somewhat prepared to act quickly when agreement was reached. They were to supply 17 tugs, 38 barges, 27 off-road fork lifts, 10 shoreside cranes, 30 trucks, and miscellaneous equipment—also all the tug crews, 130 shoreside personnel, and 600 stevedores. In addition, A.B.& T. was obligated to provide dormitory and kitchen furnishings, supplies, and food for a year. Altogether a stupendous undertaking—and 8,000 miles away!

By searching up and down the Coast, A.B.& T. had found four MIKI-Class tugs laid up in dead storage and reactivated them during December 1965. The acquired tugs were to work along with the A.B.& T. tugs taken out of West Coast service for use in Vietnam. Also two tugs were purchased from Foss' California affiliate, Pacific Tow & Salvage and Foss-Seattle made the MARTHA available. A.B.& T. chartered the MARTHA bareboat and Alaska barge was pleased to obtain the MARTHA with her Fairbanks-Morse engines, as all their recently acquired MIKIS were F.M.-powered, which would simplify spare parts problems.

The first flotilla of tugs and barges left San Francisco on January 15, 1966 bound for Nha Trang, South Vietnam via Honolulu and Guam for fuel and supplies. The convoy arrived safely on March 31st, after the 8,000-mile voyage.

The MARTHA, assigned to cross the Pacific in group two, was drydocked in late December 1965 for hull work and survey, then sent on charter as of January 8, 1966. At the same time Foss sold two flat-deck barges, the FOSS-180 and 181 to A.B.& T. and on January 20th, the MARTHA left for Vancouver, Washington, the home base of A.B.& T., towing the two ex-Foss barges.

Ater several days in Vancouver, the tow of four barges, with two riding piggy-back, was ready and the tug provisioned for the long haul to Vietnam. They departed January 25 in the second convoy and while enroute to Honolulu, the first stop, A.B.& T. purchased the MARTHA outright, voiding the charter. In Honolulu the name MARTHA FOSS was painted out and the name MAKAH was stencilled on bow and stern. The name comes from the Indian tribe living at Neah Bay, Washington—all A.B.& T. tugs were named after Indian tribes; Seneca, Seminole, Blackhawk, Mohawk, Apache, and many others.

The MAKAH, her tow and companion tugs, arrived at Nha Trang, South Vietnam in April 1966. Making the approach to the Nha Trang delivery site, the starboard tailshaft snapped and as the MAKAH swung around, the broken shaft slid out and the propeller fouled the rudder, breaking the rudder chains. The tug's crew doubled as divers and rigged cables from the tug's winch to the shaft and forced it back in place, then lashed it securely. With the damage temporarily repaired, the MAKAH headed to Hong Kong on one engine for drydocking and repairs. When she returned thirty days later, the tug and barge program was in full swing.

MAKAH formerly MARTHA FOSS shown operating in S. Vietnam during the war. Note the awnings to keep off the tropical sun. (Courtesy of Bert Dahlstrom)

By May 1966 barges were moving up and down the coasts and cargo was being discharged on the beaches in ever-increasing volume. The backlog of ships lying at anchor was reduced daily by using the barge lightering method. The fleet of ocean and harbor tugs delivering and landing cargo from Saigon north to Nha Trang and even Da Nang, near the demilitarized zone, were getting the job done.

Many of the routes covered daily by the hardworking WWII MIKIS were complicated and dangerous, the "Delta Run" in particular. R. Mansfield and William Warden in their informative book "Towboats in the Orient" state: "The Mekong River Delta is a bewildering maze, with the two principal channels connected, not far from the Cambodian border, by a narrow reach known as the "crossover". Can Tho, on the southern channel can be only reached via a crossover, since the mouth of the channel is not navigable. The way to Can Tho is long, arduous, and often under enemy fire." In the same book the knowledgeable authors make an interesting comment on the MIKIS: "It was probably an advantage that A.B. & T. had been forced to send a total of ten MIKIS to Vietnam, especially for the Mekong Delta run. They were wooden-hulled with massive internal beams and bracing. Their fantails were almost solid timber. The Russian-made rockets were designed against steel; in the MIKI hulls, the aging wood absorbed the shock of explosion and tearing shrapnel. There were countless attacks, several hits and hundreds of near-misses. But the MIKIS always came through the attacks although sometimes a little battle scarred."

In late 1967 six additional tugs were chartered for varying periods of time to relieve the worn-down Vietnam fleet. Due to lack of overhaul on the vanguard MIKIS and other tugs since their arrival in the War Zone many months earlier, they were in serious need of drydocking for repairs and mechanical overhauls. In December 1966 the AGNES and MARGARET FOSS went on charter and the next month the PACIFIC MARINER (later WENDY FOSS) of Pacific Towing & Salvage arrived in Vietnam and was placed on charter—allowing the original fleet to be drydocked in Singapore and Hong Kong as time permitted. The AGNES and MARGARET were returned to Foss Company in late May, but the PACIFIC MARINER was utilized until January 1968.

The tugs accomplished wonders during their Vietnam services—the statistics are amazing. From the beginning of operations in April 1966 through December 1969 an estimated total ton-miles traveled was 432,803,000; total port calls—15,932; and number of tows—19,275. An astounding record for a fleet of tugs serving in their second war with twenty-five years of work between conflicts.

During the MAKAH's years of service in Vietnam, she was usually put on the Mekong River runs as she had excellent steering capabilities. Captain Robert Shaw, skipper of the MAKAH at the time, explained that she was more maneuverable than most of the other tugs in the Zone, so she was able to negotiate the sharp turns and current effects of the Mekong with little difficulty. Unfortunately the MAKAH had become afflicted with dry rot around the stern post and a serious leak developed as a result and some type of temporary repair had to be attempted to curb the ever-increasing leakage until permanent repair could be made in a Singapore drydock. So a cement pudding, or patch, was poured inside the tug around the stern post. As long as the heavy-weight collar held in place, the leak was minimal.

The MAKAH continued on the Delta run for two months, then a drydocking date was set for Singapore. However, shortly before she was due to leave, another MIKI-Class tug, the CHARLES, suffered a serious rocket attack and an unexploded rocket lodged in the hull of the tug and could not be safely dug out. The threat of explosion caused many sleepless days and nights for the crew, but they had the courage to run the boat to Singapore in spite of danger to life and limb. The yard crew in Singapore held the CHARLES in the harbor while they cut out a whole hull section in order to remove the rocket safely.

As the MAKAH had given up her turn for drydocking to the CHARLES, the MAKAH, with the risky concrete patch, was ordered to tow a barge from Vung Tau to Cam Ranh Bay during the northeast monsoon season of 1969. The weather deteriorated on the run and the MAKAH's hull began working in the increasing sea and swell. She lost buoyancy just offshore of the city of Phan Thiet. The concrete patch fell out and with the working motion of the tug, the water poured in like a fountain. Captain Shaw headed the tug for protected waters where he could beach her, but the outlying heavy surf prevented him from approaching the shore. Nothing could be done until the weather and seas eased up, but that was not to be and the MAKAH continued to fill. The SOS proved futile, so knowing there was no chance of saving the tug, the crew launched the lifeboat and abandoned ship. Standing off a hundred yards, the men watched the MAKAH slowly sink with both engines still running, holding her head to the seas right up to the final plunge. She finished out the last years of her career effectively fulfilling the purpose for which she was built—delivering material for the army.

The other MIKI tugs continued in operation well into the 70's, but they were largely run by the Vietnamese. When the last of the Americans left Vietnam in 1975 the tugs were still towing on the Mekong River and Basik River. However, after nearly ten years of continuous service in all types of weather, suffering countless enemy attacks, breakdowns, and near sinkings, the remaining eight MIKIS were experiencing fatigue and engine failure. Many returning tugboatmen figured, with the Vietnamese taking over the tugs and without the technical skill or finances to keep the 30-year tugs in operating condition, they would all be out of service before long.

However, in 1969 the vital job was over for the American crews. Together with the intrepid MIKI tugs like the ex-MARTHA FOSS, they had overcome obstacles, accomplished the mission, and earned a "well-done" from the U.S. Government.

BRYNN FOSS

Built:	1952	Propulsion:	Nordberg
	Reliable Welding Works		800-horsepower
	Olympia, Washington	Primary Service:	Puget Sound
Length:	68-feet	Status:	In Lay-up
Beam:	21-feet		

For many years the veteran tug, PETER FOSS, with 375-horsepower, was considered the top tug for ship-assists, barge handling, and towing log rafts in the Tacoma-Commencement Bay area. But by 1950 with the Port growing rapidly and more ships of larger tonnage using the piers, the need for more tug horsepower became apparent. Foss, after a study of port-service requirements, decided that a powerful ship-assist tug was needed to meet the market demands.

Plans for a super harbor tug were drawn up by H. C. Hanson, Seattle naval architect, and a contract for construction—minus machinery—was awarded to Reliable Welding Works of Olympia. Six months later the steel hull with deck house was ready for towing to Tacoma for finishing and installation of an 800-horsepower Nordberg diesel, and auxiliary equipment. Special features installed by Foss included electric heat throughout the boat and electric cooking units in the galley and coffee bar, hydraulic steering gear, air-powered towing winch, anchor windlass, and a powerful fire-monitor for assisting at waterfront fires and cleaning scows and washing snow off barges and logs.

Since she was to operate with crews working only twelve hours, and living at home during the off-shift, the space normally reserved as a Captain's room was set up as a day-room with comfortable seating. However, the cabin was adaptable to a double-berth room if necessary. Down below, in the forecastle, forward of the galley, provisions were made for a live-aboard crew if the tug towed on longer linehauls. In early 1952 she became the new pride and joy, so Foss named her BRYNN in honor of a daughter of Drew and Donna Foss as both BRYNNS started life about the same time—new daughter—new tug.

Excluding the ocean-class tugs in the fleet, the BRYNN was at the time the most powerful Foss tug operating on Puget Sound, except for the 1000-horsepower HENRY FOSS, towing logs on the Straits.

BRYNN's alternate skippers, reassigned from the PETER FOSS, were Captains Leonard Sund, Vern Wright, Art Wickstrom, and with these three in charge, the BRYNN performed to advantage holding the title "pride of the Tacoma fleet" for 20 years. Ship-assists demanded most of the BRYNN's time, but barge and log raft shifting was still part of her work. Then in the 1960's the number and size of the ships calling at Tacoma increased to the point where ship-assists consumed all the BRYNN's time and the tonnage volume rose to such an extent in late 1970 that more tug horsepower became imperative. The situation was eased in September when the new 2,850-horsepower SHELLEY FOSS took over as prime ship-assist tug in Seattle and the 1,200-horsepower SHANNON FOSS became available to relieve the BRYNN on Tacoma ship-assists.

Since the BRYNN would now be free for outside jobs, Foss decided to use her part-time on linehaul work, but this required accommodations for a full crew. So on December 17th she went into the Foss-Tacoma yard to install four bunks in the forecastle and two in the day-room for use by the Captain and Engineer. Remodeling the galley also was necessary for the live-aboard style of operation.

The first full crew (six men) was called for January 28, 1971; however, the BRYNN didn't start her linehaul work until early spring. She worked around Tacoma with her full crew aboard during the waiting period, then started her linehauling with runs to Bellingham, Anacortes, and Port Angeles with chemical and oil barges.

When the Longshoremen's strike hit the West Coast in July 1971 (detailed in MATHILDA FOSS 2), the BRYNN towed log rafts between Puget Sound and various ports in British Columbia. This went on for three months and then she returned to her former linehaul work with an occasional ship-assist in the various ports she happened to be in with a tow.

By 1977 the 25-year old Nordberg engine showed signs of fatigue. Towing the heavy log rafts for days on end to Canada put more wear and tear on the engine in a short time than many years of intermittent ship-assist work. Down time for repairs became more and more frequent and by late summer the BRYNN was no longer able to pull at full throttle. She spent more time in the shipyard for engine repairs than she did out working—or so it appeared to the operations department.

The final breakdown came in January 1978 while on a log tow from Tacoma to Everett—the main engine conked out near Alki Point and she had to give up her rafts and be towed to the Foss-Seattle yard. After analyzing the past year's repair costs, Foss called a halt to any further expenditure and the BRYNN joined the other idle tugs in the lay-up fleet.

No decision has been made if and when to repower the 26-year old tug. Structurally she is in good shape, but the new tugs of her size that are arriving preclude her use. Only an extended surge of business could bring the BRYNN FOSS back to salt water.

ERIK FOSS

Built:	1908	Propulsion:	General Motors
	Bandon, Oregon		900-horsepower
Length:	97-feet	Primary Service:	Puget Sound
Beam:	23-feet	Final Foss Operating Day:	May 22, 1976
		Status:	Sold - Domestic

The ERIK FOSS, a 400-horsepower steam-powered tug came off the ways bearing the name GLEANER. She was built by J. H. Price at Bandon, Oregon and her first documented owner was Gardiner Mill Company of Gardiner, Oregon. They used the tug in their own business, towing logs and lumber coastwise. Gardiner operated the GLEANER for twelve years and then sold her to Rolph Navigation & Coal Company of San Francisco for towing general cargo and coal barges. She remained in this service in the San Francisco area for eight years and then Rolph sold her in November 1928 to C. E. Baen of San Francisco. The new owner used the GLEANER in general towing until February 1938 when he sold her to the North American Whaling Company who wanted the tug for auxiliary

ST 216 *In Seattle, December 1942 showing wartime colors and wartime name ST 216 rather than GLEANER, later to become the ERIK FOSS. (Courtesy of Joe Williamson)*

towing in connection with their whaling fleet operating along the West Coast. But after a year-and-a-half her ownership changed to San Francisco Sea Products Company and she became a support tug to the fishing industry.

The GLEANER remained based in the Bay area until July 4, 1941 when she again changed hands. Columbia Construction Company of Portland, Oregon bought her for towing and tending their floating equipment.

Her life with Columbia ended in July 1942 when the War Shipping Administration, in their requisitioning of available tugs and barges, took over the GLEANER for use by the Seattle Port of Embarkation. The army completely rebuilt the deck houses and cabins, but the steam engine was not replaced. Adequately powered, however, she worked around Puget Sound all during World War II towing barges and shifting all types of vessels and equipment, including derrick-barges.

The Army held on to the GLEANER until July 1948 then they declared her surplus and sold her to West Coast Steamship of California. She was used on non-scheduled barge-runs along the coast until May 1951 and then sold to Pacific Tow & Salvage Company of Long Beach. PT&S Company was the ninth owner to operate the tug and they used her to tow between southern California ports and San Francisco, also from Long Beach to the Channel Islands. In early 1953 PT&S modernized the 45-year old tug by installing a 900-horsepower General Motors diesel.

By mid-1953 the Port of Seattle was experiencing a rapid increase in ship and barge movements and the SANDRA FOSS with FOSS 18 were hard pressed to cover the waterfront. Another and more powerful tug was needed, so the GLEANER transferred to Seattle in September for ship-assist work. The tug performed so well that Foss decided to keep her in Seattle and they assumed direct ownership, renaming her ERIK FOSS, after the son of Patricia Foss.

For the next five years the ERIK was the mainstay of the Foss harbor fleet, but occasionally she wandered away from home in the summer and fall to make a trip to southeastern Alaska in place of the regular coastwise tugs when they were out on long-distance tows.

In late 1958 the ERIK was given a new base of operation as Bellingham needed another tug to assist oil tankers calling at the North Sound refineries. But in July 1959 she lost her job to the 1,200-horsepower SEA KING, then classed as the primary North Sound ship-assist tug. After being relieved, the ERIK made a number of southeastern Alaska barge tows, then returned to Seattle harbor, joining the CAROL and SHANNON. The ERIK remained on the waterfront work until late 1960, except for five months with the Foss-Tacoma division, substituting for the EDITH on log towing while the EDITH towed an oil delivery barge around the Bristol Bay region of Alaska.

New orders, however, in November 1960 assigned the ERIK to the Milwaukee Railroad car-barge run between Seattle and Port Townsend. She made daily round trips on a regular basis for the next nine years.

Then on December 3, 1969 the 61-year-old tug was replaced on the run by the newer and more powerful LORNA FOSS (ex-LUMMI BAY). The ERIK then transferred to Pacific Towboat Company in Everett for use as a short-crew ship-assist tug in Everett Harbor. But after only three months' work she returned to Seattle and operated with a full crew for one month hauling sand and gravel barges between the pits and the new container terminal under construction at Pier 25. When she completed the job she went into lay-up at Tacoma and remained idle all the next year.

But with the Longshoreman strike underway in July 1971 the ERIK was outfitted for log towing and within a week she started on the first of several tows between Everett and Cowichan Bay, B.C. where log ships could still be loaded for Japan. The log towing ended in mid-August for the ERIK as she had new orders to run light to Ketchikan and pick up two loaded fish barges for delivery to Anacortes. After completing the 8-day run, the ERIK returned to Everett for more log towing and ship-assist work. When the strike ended late in the year, she worked only part time as ship-assist tug with no regular assigned crew.

By May 1974 after 2½ years in Everett, Seattle again needed the ERIK to help out on linehaul towing to take care of a sudden surge in business. Foss assigned her to the Port Townsend car-barge run where her slower speed was not a handicap. Only one round trip per day was required and she could do that in twenty hours.

The ERIK handled the car-barges with no complaints for two years on the five-day-a-week run, but by May 1976 the 68-year-old wood hull had developed leaks and soft spots, especially around the stern. The tug was dry-docked to determine the extent of deterioration and the cost of repair.

Inspection revealed the necessity of replacing much of the stern section and considerable planking, at a high cost. Foss decided against the heavy expenditure and so the ERIK in June 1976 went unto lay-up, her towing days over. Then in March 1977 Foss sold her to Douglas Logan of Seattle. He shifted her to his ship canal yard and for the next 18 months, working off and on, installed a new engine and improved the tug's general condition. Logan apparently liked the name GLEANER as three weeks after taking over, he gave the tug back her original name.

In the summer of 1979 the GLEANER was out and running again, as a pleasure boat, painted in a black, white, and yellow color scheme, effectively disguising her 71 years—24 of them under Foss ownership.

ERIK FOSS *Photographed in Seattle in 1966. (Courtesy of the author's collection)*

PROSPER

Built:	1898	Propulsion:	Atlas
	Port Townsend, Washington		350-horsepower
Length:	88-feet	Primary Service:	Puget Sound
Beam:	19-feet	Final Foss Operating Day:	April 30, 1967
		Status:	Sold - Domestic

The PROSPER, a good-omen name for a commercial boat, started out earning her way as a passenger steamer of 220-horsepower for the Hastings Steamboat Company. Then as with most early Sound vessels Hastings sold her after only limited use to Thompson Steamboat Company and they in turn resold her after using the boat for two years on Puget Sound passenger runs.

Puget Sound Navigation Company, the PROSPER's new owner, in 1902 expanded their passenger service by taking over the six vessels owned by Thompson Steamboat Company. Then in 1903 PSN, fostered by its owner Alaska Steamship Company, bought out LaConner Trading & Transportation for $100,000—with the last acquisition the fleet then totaled nineteen vessels.

The PROSPER started on a run between Seattle and central Puget Sound sawmill ports with calls at Fort Flagler and Port Townsend. She stayed on the route until 1905 then she had a change of occupation. PSN sold her to the Puget Sound Tugboat Company for conversion to a tugboat. This marked the beginning of 73 continuous years spent on the pulling end of a towline.

Puget Sound Tug used the PROSPER to assist sailing vessels down the Straits and on to affiliated lumber mills, then she towed the ships back to sea when they were loaded. But by 1916 due to the declining use of wind-ships, many of Puget Sound's tugs were sold or transferred. The PROSPER, TYEE, and RICHARD HOLYOKE were taken over by Port Blakely Mill Company for use at the Skinner & Eddy shipbuilding yard. The PROSPER remained with Port Blakely until 1923 when they sold her to Bellingham Tug & Barge Company for log towing in northern Puget Sound and British Columbia. She continued as a log tower for the next eleven years and on a regular basis even though her steam plant was ready to expire.

To forestall the inevitable, B T & Barge in 1934 sent her down to Seattle for installation of a 350-horsepower Atlas diesel. The new engine was a great success, developing an eleven knot speed. Captain Haines, her regular skipper, remained in charge.

B T & Barge now classed her as an ocean-going tug ready for unlimited service. Barge towing was soon added to her schedule, so for the next eight years the PROSPER alternated between slow log towing and fast barge towing.

Then in World War II she spent a hitch in the Army along with many other commercial tugs drafted in 1942 for duty with the Army Transport Service. The first two years she operated around Puget Sound towing barges and doing ship-assists in Seattle harbor. The FOSS 18 and SANDRA were also in wartime grey and acting as Harbor boats. In 1944 ATS transferred the PROSPER to Alaska using Ketchikan as a base for towing in Southeastern. She remained up North until late 1945 when she returned to Seattle and shortly after, the ATS turned her back to B T & B—then an associated company of Foss.

The maintenance and repair department of the Seattle Port of Embarkation kept the PROSPER in good condition making it possible to assume her former runs with little delay. For the next eight years she held her own even with the newer W.W. II tugs that Foss had purchased to enhance their competitive position.

In 1953 Bellingham Tug assigned the PROSPER to tow loaded chip-barges between New Westminister, B.C. and Port Townsend, Washington for Island Tug & Barge Company. Then by the summer of 1956 Foss needed an extra tug for towing to Southeastern Alaska during the summer season, so with Dick Blake, one of B T & B's long-time skippers in charge, the PROSPER made runs to Ward Cove near Ketchikan to pick up barge loads of lumber cants for delivery to Bellingham. Summer fog on the inside run was always a navigational worry and without radar, piloting was a strain. Unfortunately the PROSPER had no radar, not unusual for a Puget Sound tug at the time. But after several voyages to Southeastern Alaska, Captain Blake requisitioned a seeing eye as close calls were becoming too frequent. The last trip while southbound in thick fog and in one of the narrow channels on the Inside Passage, he had to turn the PROSPER and the barge in tight circles for three hours waiting for the tide to turn, guessing where the rocky shore was and at the same time staying clear of a large Canadian tug with a log raft negotiating the Channel northbound. At the end of the trip Captain Blake informed the office a radar would have to be installed or an E.S.P. Captain assigned the job. When the PROSPER left on her next Alaska run, a new radar was mounted in the pilot house—no more running blind in foggy channels.

At the end of the summer the PROSPER went back to log towing out of Bellingham and she stayed at it until 1959 when she was transferred by document to Foss for barge towing—taking up where she left off in 1956. For the next ten years she towed linehaul for the Seattle office, primarily on the cement, chemical, and oil runs to Anacortes, Bellingham, and Ferndale, but in the summer of 1959 and 1960 she made several trips to southeastern Alaska.

By late 1966 with 68 years of wear and tear, the PROSPER's hull was becoming porous and unseaworthy. With the deterioration and the mechanical problems of a 34-year-old engine, Foss placed the tug in the limited service class—her days of usefulness numbered. She idled away the winter of 1966 and in 1967 she ran only nine days during the month of April, ending up towing a Navy gasoline barge from the Manchester fuel dock to the Whidbey Island Naval Air Station. Foss held her on the active list for three months, then dropped her a grade to reserve status for the next year.

In August 1968 the PROSPER was available for sale and within six weeks, on September 26, 1968 Foss sold her to a Mr. Fitzgerald who resold the tug in May 1969 to Al Wolover of Seattle. He renamed her ODIN and for the next eight years used her for general towing jobs on Puget Sound and along the Coast.

Mr. Wolover entered the ODIN several times in the yearly antique tugboat races on Puget Sound and frequently the ODIN came in first, including the Olympia race in September 1977.

Then in 1978 Al Wolover purchased the retired MIKI-Class tug JUSTINE FOSS for conversion to a fishing vessel and in October he disposed of the ODIN to the Burke family of Seattle and they renamed the tug PROSPER—for good luck. The tug was converted to a "live-aboard" and the Burkes added additional living quarters on the boat deck. They berth the boat in Lake Union and her appearance belies her over 80 years of hard work—a tribute to the upkeep given her by her former owners, among them the Foss Company and now the Burke family.

CRAIG FOSS (1)

Built:	1943	Propulsion:	Atlas
	Lester Alexander Company		600-horsepower
	New Orleans, Louisiana	Primary Service:	Puget Sound and Alaska
Length:	88-feet	Final Foss Operating Day:	November 7, 1965
Beam:	24-feet	Status:	Sank

The CRAIG was built as the MAJOR HENRY J. CONNERS, in New Orleans, for the United States Army to barge equipment and supplies to Gulf Coast ports, but her area of operation suddenly changed. The Army transferred her to Honolulu and she served there for the duration of World War II and for several years after. When her Army hitch was over, the Government declared the CONNERS surplus and laid her up at Rio Vista, California to await final disposition.

Foss purchased the tug at a Government sale in September 1955 and after a short period of preparation in California, towed her to Seattle, arriving in mid-November. After a second satisfactory inspection, she shifted to the Foss yard in Tacoma and they outfitted her for general towing. During the make-ready period, Foss renamed her CRAIG in honor of a son of Sidney and Barbara Foss Campbell.

The CRAIG began her Foss service in February 1956 and for a trial period worked on local Puget Sound runs before being released for the longer runs to Southeastern and Southwestern Alaska.

She spent several seasons towing the oil barge FOSS-100, delivering oil to Bering Sea ports for Standard Oil, supplementing the service of the CHRISTINE with FOSS-95. Ports of call served from the Dutch Harbor base included Naknek, Dillingham, and Bethel. The CRAIG returned to Seattle in mid-October just before the ice started to form in the Bering Sea. Between seasons in Alaska, she usually towed on the established Puget Sound runs, and for the local work she carried an "inside" crew.

In April 1962 the CRAIG was at the scene of a tragic accident in Seattle's Duwamish Waterway. She had just delivered the bulk-cement barge PERMANENTE #1 alongside the Cement Company's wharf, when the PERMANENTE, without any warning, capsized, and as it rolled over, hurled three employees of the Cement Company into the Duwamish. Two of the men from the barge drowned and one struggled to the surface and safety. No one was injured seriously on the CRAIG even though the pilothouse was crushed. However, the Chief Engineer Karl Syvertsen was thrown against a bulkhead and injured his back. The exact cause of the barge losing stability could not be deter-

CRAIG FOSS *Shown in Seattle Harbor shortly after entering service in 1956. (Courtesy of Joe Williamson)*

mined as the "capsize" completely changed the significant factors. But in this case Murphy's Law can be applied, "If anything can happen, it will." The CRAIG, with a new pilothouse and general refurbishing, resumed her towing program, leading barges around Puget Sound and Alaska. The crew, no doubt, kept in mind the sad lesson of the PERMANENTE—constant vigilance versus Murphy's Law.

In 1964 the CRAIG participated in the annual re-supply mission of the DEW (Distant Early Warning) Line for the Government. The project was named MONA LISA for some reason. Foss had secured the Government contract to provide tugs and barges for supplying the Far North military bases and radar stations in Southwestern Alaska. The CRAIG left Seattle on May 1, 1964 with two oil barges—the FOSS-112 and FOSS-183—for the Bering Sea. During the next four months she played an important part in supplying cargo to the lightering and beaching operations carried out in delivering supplies at the military sites near the towns of Port Heiden, Port Moller, Naknek, and the more remote locations at Cape Newenham and Cape Romanzof.

During the 1964 supply season, other tugs and barges besides the CRAIG made rapid trips to the sites because much tonnage had to be delivered in the short ice-free season. The AGNES FOSS, DOROTHY FOSS, LESLIE FOSS and MARTHA FOSS all helped and made voyages to the Bering Sea, towing general cargo and petroleum barges. The small tugs ELMER FOSS, ELSIE FOSS, and SEA MULE—shallow draft harbor tugs carried aboard the cargo barges—lightered the cargo from the anchored barges to the beach unloading sites.

The CRAIG finished discharging her MONA LISA barges by September and arrived back in Seattle by the end of the month, her 1964 "DEW LINE" service completed.

The year 1965 which proved to be the CRAIG's last, started out with the usual coastwise barge tows; a month's trip to California, a trip to Anchorage, and two trips to southeastern Alaska. When not running "outside" or between Alaska tows, the CRAIG kept busy working up and down Puget Sound, making the most of her remaining short life.

Then in October the CRAIG, with Captain Dale Gudgel in command, left Seattle with a small cargo barge for Anchorage. From Anchorage she went down the Inlet to work for the J. Ray McDermott Company, contractors at the Pan American drilling platform, engaged in laying an underwater oil pipeline. The pipe-laying barge was the CRAIG's undoing—her nemesis.

At the time, 1965 the laying of underwater pipelines for transporting oil from the drill platforms to storage tanks ashore was in full swing in the Middle Ground Shoal area of Alaska's Cook Inlet. Many tugs were needed to tend the crane, pipelaying, and equipment barges in the tremendous construction project undertaken by the McDermott Company. When the Inlet tidal currents were at maximum strength, up to 12 knots, all the horsepower the tugs could provide was required to keep the equipment in the assigned position. Foss had several tugs working in the area during 1965 but more boats were needed to tend the large influx of equipment barges, and several towing companies from the West and Gulf Coasts joined in, sending over twenty additional boats North to help get the oil flowing.

But the CRAIG did not live to see the oil flow. On her final day afloat, along with other tugs including the DOROTHY FOSS, she was tending the derrick barge FOSS-300, cargo barge FOSS-281, and the pipe-laying barge #10. As the tide began to ebb in the Inlet about noon on November 7th, the CRAIG was ordered to put a line on the FOSS-281 and hold the barge head-to-tide to keep it from swinging around against the derrick barge. When the tidal current reached its peak at about three in the afternoon, the holding power of the CRAIG proved insufficient to stem the flow, and she started to fall off, swinging broadside to the current. With the towline leading away at 90 degrees between tug and barge, the CRAIG ended up "in irons". Then the towline fouled in the winch when slack was payed out, and the current took command, heeling the CRAIG over to a 45 degree angle forcing even the high boat deck under water. By stopping the main engine, the tug righted herself to a nearly level position but the current carried the CRAIG down to the stern of the pipe-laying barge. The tug's stern hung up on top of the barge's stinger—the stinger or chute projected off the stern of the barge and angled down to the bottom of the sea where the oil transmission pipe was placed on the sea floor as it came off the barge and down the chute.

The DOROTHY FOSS, alert to the danger, put a line on the CRAIG and attempted to pull her free, but the combination of forces caused the CRAIG to again heel to a dangerous angle as the stern fell off the stinger and the crew, sensing the CRAIG was trapped, jumped from the tug to the safety of barge-10. The tug settled rapidly by the stern and listed heavily to port, at the same time the current forced her around to the port side of the barge with the bow increasing in elevation. The current was now in complete control. Her rescue had become impossible. In twenty more agonizing minutes, the bow of the CRAIG took a jump skyward, then settled back and plunged to the bottom, her final resting place in water too deep for practical salvage. The time was 2000, November 7, 1965.

The "schooner rigged" crew, thankful for their narrow escape, were flown home to Seattle the next day and not many days later were back working on other Foss tugs. The First Mate Ken Hendershot, still with Foss, became a Captain on the Foss Alaska Line run to Southwestern.

The loss of the CRAIG was critical as she had proven most versatile, equally useful in the storm-tossed Bering Sea or the quiet and inside waters of Southeastern Alaska, or simply easing a ship into a congested berth on the Seattle waterfront. However, a second CRAIG was in the offing, one with still greater potential and many times the power of the first CRAIG.

GARY FOSS (2)

Built:	1935	Propulsion:	Caterpillar
	Winslow, Washington		765-horsepower
Length:	68-feet	Primary Service:	Puget Sound
Beam:	18-feet	Final Foss Operating Day:	September 6, 1976
		Status:	Sold - Domestic

The GARY FOSS, first named TROJAN, was designed by H. C. Hanson and built in Winslow for the Alaska Gold Mining Corporation to barge away tailings from their Juneau mine.

In 1935 after years of operation, the Mining Company was faced with finding a new method of waste disposal. Prior to the TROJAN's time, the tailings were transported out and into Gastineau Channel on a conveyor, but eventually the weight of the rock pushed up the bottom of the Channel at other points, creating navigational hazards. Mr. H. L. Metzger, manager of the mine, solved the problem with a tug and barge combination. He built the TROJAN, and three roll-over dump-barges to move the tailings to a safer dumping ground. The tug kept an empty barge under the conveyor at all times and moved out the barge when loaded. Loads of fine tailings were dumped into the Channel close to the mine and the coarser material towed and dumped about a mile south of the mine. The self-dumping barges had high, solid wood bulwarks forming bins on both the top and bottom—the top and bottom appeared identical. At each dumping, the barge made a 180-degree roll, thus the bottom became the top and the barge was again ready for filling. No lost time or motion.

GARY FOSS *On sea trials in Seattle upon completion of major repowering. July, 1966. (Courtesy of Foss Tug Co)*

Two round trips were made every day by the TROJAN and her crew, even in the adverse winter weather of Southeastern Alaska, but weather or no, the tug with her 275-horsepower Atlas compiled a reliable performance record in her 20 years of service at Juneau.

In 1956 the TROJAN's work at the mine was over and Foss bought her for their Puget Sound fleet. While undergoing modifications to Foss standards in Seattle, the TROJAN was renamed GARY FOSS in honor of a son of Justine Foss Wood.

Starting in October and for the next several years the GARY served the Seattle office, working on all the Puget Sound runs, including the gravel run out of Steilacoom and the Sound oil-barge runs.

However, after thirty years of continuous service, the old Atlas diesel started giving trouble and causing delays, so Foss laid up the GARY in early September 1965. Then in mid-October the Company decided there were many good years left in the wood hull and to give her new life she should have a modern engine and some house revamping. During the next eight months at Foss-Tacoma, a new 765-horsepower Caterpillar diesel was installed, a new galley built, some streamlining done to the house, and new navigation equipment placed in the pilothouse.

The GARY's refit was complete in July 1966 and she returned to the Seattle fleet. Her first assignment was the usual break-in run towing the rail-barge FOSS-118 between Seattle and Vancouver, British Columbia. With the repowering proving successful, the GARY was assigned to the Tacoma office for towing log and chip barges—the mainstay of the Tacoma division. She remained working out of Tacoma until 1970 when the Tacoma office relinquished all linehaul towing to Seattle Central Dispatch. From then on, all Foss linehaul tugs on Puget Sound were dispatched from the central office. The change-over didn't affect the GARY's work, she continued as a primary mover of logs and chips scows for her remaining years on Puget Sound.

The only serious complaint heard from the crews of the GARY as she neared her 40th year was brought on by the vibration of her high speed 765-horsepower engine. The shaking gradually opened up the deck and planking seams, causing fresh-water and salt-water leaks—most of them difficult to stop. In the last operating year, even with limited duty, the GARY's crew had a lament, "When it rained on the outside, it rained on the inside." The men kept their rain gear handy and plastic drop-cloths to cover the bunks when necessary.

By late 1976 with a general slowdown in the towing industry and better utilization from new steel tugs, the GARY's retirement was only a matter of days. On September 6th, she towed her last log raft—from Lake Washington to Salmon Bay—ending the day in the Foss lay-up farm.

But later in the fall, the GARY had another chance to go towing. Pacific Tow & Salvage in Long Beach and San Diego, California, needed two medium-class, general-purpose tugs and the GARY FOSS and ROGER FOSS were available. The GARY was assigned to Long Beach and the ROGER to San Diego. After a week's reactivation and repair, the GARY and ROGER on November 16, 1976 left Seattle for the final time. Fortunately, the Pacific was calm during the 5-day delivery trip, but unfortunately, the GARY had engine difficulties south of San Francisco and arrived in Long Beach under tow of the ROGER—not a very impressive showing for the new operators.

In Long Beach, the GARY was repainted and renamed PACIFIC JUPITER, going to work again in January 1977. But even in the milder waters and climate of California, leaks continued to plague the boat and mechanical troubles were increasing, largely due to the lack of a steady crew aboard. With her inherent problems and the new steel boats coming to Long Beach, the JUPITER was laid up—impractical to run. She did her last work for Pacific in July 1978.

While in lay-up, the JUPITER and a small harbor tug, the PACIFIC POLARIS, were declared surplus and available for sale. In early November, both the tugs were sold to a firm in Sacramento, California for towing on the Sacramento River.

One advantage the former GARY now has in her new environment that she didn't have in her Puget Sound days—she will not be bothered by teredos or barnacles.

ANDREW FOSS (2)

Built:	1941	Propulsion:	General Motors (Single)
	Jacobson Shipyard		1,600-horsepower
	Oyster Bay, New York	Primary Service:	Alaska and Coastwise
Length:	107-feet	Final Foss Operating Day:	January 28, 1977
Beam:	25-feet	Status:	Sold - Domestic

The second ANDREW FOSS had a very fitting original name, DAUNTLESS #15 and she lived up to it in the trying conditions the tug later faced for Foss on runs to the storm-prone Aleutian Islands. Built for the Dauntless Towing Company of New York and designed for heavy towing, they powered her with an 8-cylinder, 1,440-horsepower Alco-Sulzer diesel directly connected to an 8-foot propeller. Strangely, the towing winch was located below, in the after-end of the engine room and the tow-wire came through a vertical trunk and over a fairlead sheave out to the after deck. Apparently the lower position of the winch increased the stability. Her deckhouse was arranged to provide inside access to all cabins, a convenience and safety feature for an ocean-going tug.

Within days of her completion in 1941 the army requisitioned the tug for World War II service. However, Dauntless Towing was allowed to use the tug to complete a contract to deliver a tow from New Orleans to Ciudad Bolivar, Venezuela. The DAUNTLESS left New York October 25, 1941 for New Orleans and upon arrival she took in tow a landing stage and a ferryboat hull. Tug and tow left for Venezuela on November 4 and arrived Ciudad Bolivar, some 300 miles up the Orinoco River, on November 24. She returned to New Orleans December 7, completing a 7,200-mile voyage.

The next day the Army Transport Service assumed control over the tug and renamed her LT. COL. ALBERT H. BARKLEY. ATS assigned the tug to the Seattle Port of Embarkation, her home base during the time of army control. She operated for the ATS, doing harbor work, including assisting Army and Navy transports in docking and undocking. The BARKLEY stayed in service until ATS declared her surplus in early 1957.

At a government sale on March 15, 1957 the tug was purchased by Foss and renamed ANDREW. Foss put her right to work on Puget Sound and in Alaska, but after 16 months of towing, the Alco-Sulzer engine started giving trouble, causing many hang-ups, so repowering was in order to make her more reliable, especially as the tug bore the name of the company's founder.

In November 1958 the ANDREW tied up at the Foss yard in Seattle for installation of a new main engine and minor modification. She returned to work in August 1959 with a 1,600-horsepower General Motors diesel—now she could compete, and weather permitting, maintain a schedule.

The ANDREW, no longer a problem tug, was able to operate for many years with the rail-car barge FOSS-250 between Tacoma, later Bellingham, and the Ketchikan pulp mill at Ward Cove, Alaska. Car-loads of pulp running on standard-gauge rails were switched aboard the barge at Ward Cove and towed 600 miles to an unloading ramp at

Tacoma or Bellingham, where the cars were pulled off the barge and joined with trains for shipment to Eastern pulp-processing plants. The barge service gave the American railroads a chance at long-haul freight revenue that otherwise would be lost to the closer Canadian roads.

To prevent the ANDREW from going stale from being on one job too long, the Operations Department sent her to an entirely different area. In 1967 the ANDREW, under command of Captain Frank Reardon, made a "trans-canal" voyage towing the T-2 Tanker MISSION CARMEL from the Olympia Reserve Fleet to Galveston, Texas for conversion to a full container-ship for Sea-Land Service, Inc.

The ANDREW returned light to Seattle from Texas and immediately went on the Amchitka run supplying the Atomic Energy Project. With Captain Frank Reardon still the skipper, she made six trips to the Island, crossing the Gulf of Alaska often in adverse weather. The "tow" on most of her trips was oil barge FOSS-98, carrying 34,000 barrels of fuel to supply the Amchitka rolling stock. The ANDREW's after-deck on this open-water run was usually awash, even with a small sea running the deck disappeared in the ever-swirling, ever cascading water. The ordinary freeboard was low due to the heavy towing winch and the tug's topped-off fuel and water tanks. Regardless of the submerged deck and the North Pacific weather, Captain Reardon always brought the ANDREW through. But there were times when he had to dodge from shelter to shelter to avoid heavy seas and winds—the weather had a hard time intimidating the ANDREW's intrepid skipper.

At the conclusion of the AEC project in 1974 the ANDREW was given a change of scenery. With Captain Tauno Salo aboard and Honolulu the destination, she made the 2,400-mile crossing in 12 days towing two general cargo barges. They had a smooth round trip and returned with two dump scows. The trip was Captain Salo's first with the tug and the ANDREW's only voyage to Honolulu.

After visiting the land of pineapples and palms, the ANDREW went back to coastwise and Alaska towing, spending time on the run to Anchorage and making several trips towing the Foss chemical barge between Bellingham and Eureka, California for Louisiana Pacific Corporation. This offshore towing lasted a year then she went on the Valdez run in 1976 barging construction equipment for the Alyeska oil pipeline. Her last coastwise run was a round trip to Valdez in September 1976 just before she had to give way to the new boats with far more power and much less operating cost.

With the arrival of new, powerful, and efficient tugs for the long tows, use of the high maintenance cost WWII-built boats declined and so in October 1976 the ANDREW was transferred to short hauls on Puget Sound and then only until January 1977. On the way to retirement, Foss placed her on inactive status, but in May a break came her way—she went on bare-boat charter to Puget Sound Freight Lines for their barge service between Seattle and Port Albernie, B.C.

After several months on charter, PSFL was satisfied that the ANDREW was the proper boat for the job, so they bought her outright. After modifications at their Seattle base, and renamed the PACHENA, she resumed towing between Seattle and Port Albernie, barging rolls of newsprint on a regular basis. No longer wearing Foss green and white, she is a brown and white tug now, otherwise she looks the same passing by on her twice-weekly run and her original name still adequately describes her defiance to time, wind, and waves.

CAROL FOSS

Built:	1958	Propulsion:	EMD (Single)
	Todd Shipyard & Foss-Seattle Yard		1,600-horsepower
	Seattle, Washington	Primary Service:	Seattle Harbor
Length:	84-feet	Status:	In Service
Beam:	25-feet		

The plated hull and deckhouse of the CAROL FOSS were built by Todd's Seattle shipyard, with all the inside work and equipment provided by the Foss-Seattle yard. After launching at Todd's in late 1957 the skeleton tug was towed to the Foss yard for their share of the work, including the most important item, installing the main engine, a 1,200-horsepower Nordberg. The new tug had early on been named the CAROL FOSS in honor of the youngest daughter of Drew and Donna Foss.

The CAROL easily passed her sea-trials and she started her career July 5, 1958 joining her just completed sister-tug, the SHANNON FOSS, on the Seattle waterfront. The CAROL and SHANNON, designed for ship-assist

CAROL FOSS In the San Juan Islands September, 1966. (From the author's collection)

work, became the pride of the Seattle harbor fleet. They were used almost exlusively in docking and undocking vessels at the Port piers.

However, during the construction of the Hood Canal Floating Bridge in the early 1960's, the CAROL was frequently engaged in towing and placing anchors and positioning the large concrete floating pontoons. Holding the bridge sections in proper position was an exacting job which at times required the help of six tugs, among them the SHANNON.

After 12 years of top place in the harbor, the "twins" had to step down a notch in 1970. With the arrival in Seattle of a new queen of assist-tugs, the 2,850-horsepower SHELLEY FOSS, the CAROL became the number two assist-tug and the SHANNON was transferred to Tacoma. The CAROL, with the SHANNON gone, became the prime barge shifter in the Seattle harbor, so she gained a new importance because of the transfer of the SHANNON.

The CAROL did her work well for 19 years, juggling ships and barges—so well in fact that she wore out her big Nordberg. The engine after so many years of hard steady running had developed a series of problems. With the CAROL afflicted by excessive down time for repair, Foss decided to repower her with a 1,600-horsepower EMD diesel. They towed her to the Tacoma yard of Marine Industries Northwest in June 1977 spending six months for the engine change and general modernization.

Re-engined and revamped, the CAROL went back to her old stand in January 1978 and she proved to be much more effective for the Seattle harbor work-force with her greater power. Her return was well-timed in view of the need for stronger tugs to take care of the heavier tonnage and movement of both ships and barges passing through the Port. The CAROL and her work were recently documented on television so her reputation and position in the Port appear secure with little serious competition in the offing.

ELMER and ELSIE FOSS

Built:	1953	Final Foss Operating	
	Portland, Oregon	Day—ELMER:	May 1976
Length:	53-feet	Status:	Scrapped
Beam:	14-feet	Final Foss Operating	
Propulsion:	General Motors	Day—ELSIE:	May 20, 1977
	165-horsepower	Status:	Sold - Domestic
		Primary Service:	Alaska

The ELMER and ELSIE FOSS, named for grandchildren of Theodore, were originally army boats built at Portland, Oregon, in 1953. They were identified by numbers LCM 6432 and LCM 6388—the LCM indicating "Landing Craft Medium."

After four years in government service, the twin LCMs in September 1957 were sold to Foss for use in unloading cargo at beach sites in southwestern Alaska, the Bering Sea and Arctic Ocean in connection with supplying the DEW Line stations.

The ELMER and ELSIE always wintered at the Foss-Seattle yard until the DEW Line re-supply mission began in the spring. Then both vessels were transported on the deck of cargo barges to the DEW Line's discharge points for use in shallow water lightering. The two boats were lifted off and cargo loaded aboard them from one of the supply barges for transfer to the beach.

The LCMs did not have crew accommodations, but they did have a small house aft for the engine controls and steering wheel. The operating crews were usually formed from crews of the ocean-going tug bringing up the supply barges. The "twins" worked the DEW Line beaches each season for as long as Foss held the supply contract, and they also performed the same service in other areas of Alaska for the oil industry.

Then in 1962 the ELSIE had a change of occupation, but first she was altered at Foss-Seattle. The end result was a crew-boat for transporting men to drilling platforms engaged in the oil exploration program in Cook Inlet. ELSIE's bow configuration changed with her conversion, a tapered bow was added, increasing the length eight feet and giving her better entry, but it eliminated the head-end ramp and any further use as a beach landing craft. The engines were not replaced, the 165-horsepower General Motors diesels provided adequate power.

The ELSIE worked in the Cook Inlet area for the remainder of her active years with Foss, hauling men and supplies for the oil industry—her special work ending May 20, 1977 when Foss sold her to Dan Clausen of Kenai, Alaska, for private use.

Foss retained the ELMER, with no change in use or structure. She remained in seasonal DEW Line service through 1964. Then beginning with the 1965 ice-free season, the ELMER joined the ELSIE in Cook Inlet assisting at the oil platform construction and exploration sites located over the "Middle Ground" and "Forelands" areas, close to the Arness Supply Terminal at Nikiski.

ELMER remained in Cook Inlet making limited supply runs after the platform construction and pipeline program was over. Then in the early 70's Foss had no further use for the ELMER in Alaska so they loaded her aboard a barge and shipped her to Seattle for disposition. But there was no apparent use or need for a craft of ELMER's design on Puget Sound. Foss put her into lay-up and she remained there until January 1975. Then they sent her to Bellingham to serve as a back-up boat for the harbor tug LELA FOSS and to assist the Bellingham oil spill clean-up barges—on call in case of an oil spill at the four refineries on northern Puget Sound.

The ELMER ran only a matter of days during her 16 months in Bellingham, whenever the LELA was down for repairs. She wasn't a practical boat for working with logs, the principal harbor work. Having high sides, the crew had to be acrobats to jump from the boat to a log raft and back again.

Considering her disadvantages compared to a standard-type tugboat and with a hull worn thin from 15 years of beaching work on rough Alaska shores, the ELMER was relegated to the boneyard. In May 1976 she was cut up and sold for scrap after 23 years of service.

MARY FOSS *Running lite to Shilshole Bay for barge tow to Anchorage, Alaska, April, 1974. (From the author's collection)*

MARY FOSS (1)

Built:	1944 Hodgson-Green-Haldeman Yard Long Beach, California	Propulsion:	Enterprise 1,500-horsepower
		Primary Service:	Coastwise and Alaska
Length:	117-feet	Final Foss Operating Day:	July 1, 1976
Beam:	28-feet	Status:	In Foss Lay-Up

The LT 394, later to become the MARY, was the seventh MIKI-type Army tug purchased by Foss and the last of eleven MIKI-Class tugs built by the California yard for the Army Transport Service. During her short wartime duty she towed on the West Coast and Alaska, primarily barging equipment and supplies to ATS outports.

Assigned to the Seattle Port of Embarkation during World War II, she continued to function for the Port many years after the War, even representing the Port of Embarkation in civic harbor events. Commercial and military tugboat races were held each year on Elliot Bay in the 1950's. The races were based on class and rated by horsepower. Four army tugs were entered in the May 24, 1952 race, and the LT 394 came in first by a comfortable margin. Possibly her prowess convinced the Foss Company to purchase the tug whenever the government put her up for sale.

However, five years passed before the Army declared her surplus and then in 1957 the General Assets Corporation advertised her for sale. At the sale in August, Foss submitted the high bid and acquired a high quality MIKI. She came to the Foss-Seattle yard in good operating condition, so very little work was necessary to bring the boat up to Foss standards. To make her a part of the Foss fleet she was named MARY in honor of a daughter of Theodore.

The MARY started out on rail-car barge runs, first between Seattle and Port Townsend and in early 1958 on the Squamish, British Columbia to Seattle run. During the MARY's first summer season, she towed exclusively on the Squamish haul except for a late fall trip to Anchorage. Then she returned to the Squamish run and from January 1959 for the next eight months she was a steady caller at Squamish. Again late in the season she made two barge trips to Alaska and the two tows were an indication of a coming change in the MARY's routine.

By the spring of 1960 sufficient business was offered on both the Alaska and Coastwise routes to employ the MARY full time, so she lost the so-called "gravy train" job to Squamish and started towing on various Alaska runs, but primarily the cement haul to Anchorage.

During the next four years the MARY spent most of her time on the Alaska runs with a variation in the fall of 1962 by making two trips to Honolulu from West Coast lumber ports assisting the regular tugs, BARBARA and JUSTINE.

After the MARY's initiation in handling lumber barges, Foss assigned her to the West Coast lumber run in January 1965 hauling lumber between Oregon and southern California ports. The job lasted for only three months, then she was recalled to go back on the Anchorage run for the rest of the year.

The last half of 1966 turned out to be interesting for the MARY, but the first six months of the year were routine, with regular runs Coastwise and to Alaska. Then on June 29th Foss received word that the tug, PACIFIC RANGER, belonging to Pacific Tow & Salvage, was disabled several hundred miles west of California on a return voyage from Vietnam and the JUSTINE FOSS had taken the RANGER under tow. The MARY was sent to relieve the JUSTINE so she could proceed to San Francisco, her intended destination. On July 3rd, the MARY took over the tow of the RANGER and brought her in to Long Beach, arriving July 8th.

With Pacific Tow's tug in the repair yard, the MARY was ordered to take over the RANGER's next job, a tough one. She was to tow the heavy drill rig RICON from Long Beach, 4,200 miles to Freeport, Texas, a long, hard tow for a MIKI. The MARY's Captain, Dale Gudgel, had recently returned from a round trip to Panama on another MIKI tug, the LESLIE FOSS, and now he was to go back on the same route.

The MARY and her 11-man crew left Long Beach on July 9th and with no complications and good weather arrived at Freeport, Texas on August 2nd, averaging a surprising 7.3 knots on the trip. Next day the MARY headed light for Panama and Seattle since a return tow was not available. The crew were happy to make a fast run home as the tug did not have air-conditioning and the Gulf of Mexico in summer can be unpleasantly hot.

However, the crew's luck gave out in Cristobal. Orders were waiting for them to proceed to Norfolk, Virginia, pick up a floating machine shop and deliver it to the AGNES FOSS at Panama for towing on to Vietnam.

Following orders, the MARY went to Norfolk and left with the tow August 17th, arriving back at Cristobal August 28th.

The MARY and her crew did another turn around, this time going to the Army base up the Cooper River at Charleston, South Carolina to pick up a tandem tow. They arrived on September 4th and left the next day, towing two barges and an Army tug for the Military Sea Transportation Service. The tow, destined for Vietnam, was to be delivered to Long Beach, California where the MARGARET FOSS would take over and make the final delivery.

Now they would surely head for the more moderate climate of the West Coast and with luck end up in the Pacific Northwest in thirty days. They delivered the tow at Long Beach as planned and on time, making a fast 2,800-mile run from Panama to Long Beach in 17 days at a speed of 7 knots, arriving October 3rd.

The crew had been away from home for over three months, but Seattle was still not their destination—the voyage was not over. On October 4th orders came to pick up a disabled ship south of Manzanillo, Mexico and tow her to Long Beach. They arrived at the crippled S. S. HUNTSMORE October 9th, hooked on and got underway. Shortly after, they tangled with a tropical storm which held them back four days. After the storm passed, they towed the ship at 9 knots and arrived safely in Long Beach, October 20th. The crew went home by air the same night for a much needed leave, having spent 113 days at sea.

Then after nine days of rest and relaxation, the crew returned to Long Beach and more work. They left right away with the MARY for Portland to pick up a Foss barge and take on a load of cement at LaFarge, British Columbia for delivery to Anchorage. The MARY finally made it back to Seattle after unloading the cement, touching the Foss pier on November 26th after 142 days absence. She spent a quiet winter at the Foss moorings, apparently resting for the next season. Well deserved, as Captain Dale Gudgel and the MARY had safely delivered six different tows, covering 22,000 miles, since relieving Captain Stan Thurston in Long Beach back on July 8th. If variety is the spice of life, then Dale was a well-seasoned skipper.

The 1967 schedule also began with variety. The first job for Dale Gudgel and his crew was towing the LST-class barge FOSS-208, loaded with beer vats built by Reliable Welding Works in Olympia and loaded in Olympia for delivery to the Hamm's Brewery near Long Beach, California—a once in a lifetime tow.

The MARY had a change of captains in June, Guy Johnson took over and with barge FOSS-201 towed a rather commonplace cargo, that is for the MARY, 3,000 tons of drummed asphalt and an asphalt-mixing plant with associated heavy equipment to the Aleutian Island of Shemya, some 3,000 miles to the westward. Raber-Kief, Inc. used the cargo on a $1.3 million Army Engineers' contract to re-surface the 10,000-foot airstrip.

To finish the year, the MARY completed two round trips to Amchitka for Holmes & Narver on the Atomic Energy project and then two trips to Anchorage.

The years 1968-1970 were routine years, the MARY making the usual runs to Anchorage and Amchitka and several voyages to Eureka, California with the Foss chemical barge. By September 1970 with the new steel tugs in service and work slowing down for the season, the MARY went into early winter lay-up.

A quiet spring in the towing industry held the MARY idle until the Longshoremen's strike in July brought out all available equipment to move cargo to Alaska. The I.L.W.U. did not handle Foss cargo, so barges could be loaded at will alongside the Foss wharf. The MARY towed steadily to Alaska until December and then again tied up for the winter to await the spring activity.

But the MARY remained idle until April 1972 then she began towing for Peter Pan Seafoods. Foss had contracted with Peter Pan to barge supplies to various canneries in Southwestern Alaska and bring back the season's canned salmon pack.

Her first trip for Peter Pan started on April 18 with stops at the cannery ports of King Cove, False Pass, Port Moller, Naknek, and Dillingham—the last three on the north side of the Alaska Peninsula. After discharging the cargo, the MARY returned to Seattle arriving June 7, completing a 50-day voyage. She made two additional trips for Peter Pan. On Voyage #2 in June and July she made stops at King Cove and False Pass, and on Voyage #3, she called at False Pass, King Cove, and Dillingham, loading 75,000 cases of canned salmon valued at $2 million for delivery to Seattle. The MARY, with a successful year in her Log Book, tied up for the winter after delivering the barge to the salmon terminal on August 31.

However, the year 1973 was a most depressing one for the MARY. She ran only 64 days between June and September and the outlook for 1974 appeared as poor as 1973 until in the spring Foss received a contract for barging supplies to Valdez for the Alyeska Pipeline. The MARY started out on contract in April with Captain Don Hudspeth in charge and she continued in steady service, primarily to Valdez, through November 1974—the busiest season for the MARY since her Peter Pan contract. But in December she was back at the Foss pier and spent the three winter months undergoing engine repairs and upgrading for another active season.

Starting out February 11, 1975 the MARY went on the Valdez run and stayed with it until mid-summer when she switched to towing a bulk cement barge to Anchorage. The MARY left Bellingham with her tow on July 15th, arriving in Anchorage ten days later. While berthed at the city dock, an accident occurred that nearly ended MARY's career. The Logbook recorded the succession of events:

"At 0230 July 27 the Second Engineer notified the Chief and Captain that water was flooding into the engine room and it was then above the deck-boards and rising fast. At 0238 all hands were called to render assistance. By 0245 the water had risen above the bilge pump motor and a call for immediate help was radioed to nearby vessels DIANE FOSS and the research ship RAINIER. At 0250 the water, now 3 feet deep and over the generator, killed the ship's power. The RAINIER came alongside and put two pumps to work, but at 0330 even with the RAINIER's pumps throwing out water, the MARY was still flooding at an alarming rate. The Captain then notified the City of their desperate need and the Utility Department rushed down two large-capacity pumps. Finally at 0500 with six pumps operating, the water level started to recede, but slowly. Then at 0630 the Chief was able to reach all the seacocks and close them. This stopped the inflow and by 0700 the engine room was pumped free of standing water, but the machinery, equipment, and structure were salt covered and dripping water. The cause of the flooding was easily determined—a broken stud allowed the hold-down bar on the cap of the inboard strainer on the sea suction to fly open, permitting a full pipe influx of sea water under pressure."

After the MARY's crew had drawn a breath of relief they went right to work along with Anchorage electricians and for several days they worked long and hard to restore all equipment to operating condition, including a new stud in the strainer bowl. And so on August 5th the Captain was able to report the MARY fit for sea. They left the same day for Seattle, arriving a week later and with a dry engine room. For the remainder of the 1975 season the MARY towed on the Valdez run and after completing a fourth voyage in November, the winter season closed in, so the MARY, as usual, tied up until spring.

Her last operating year, 1976 started out very promising. She returned to the Valdez run on April 24th and made four successive trips but by the end of June the greater part of the Valdez cargo for Fluor Company had been delivered. However, the MARY was given one more job to do before coiling down her lines. On June 28th she started out with a barge for delivery to the tug PACIFIC MARINER at a meeting point some 225 miles north of Seattle. The tugs exchanged tows and the MARY returned to Seattle with the MARINER's barge, arriving on July 1st. Captain Stan Johnson made her fast alongside the pier at eight in the evening and it proved to be the last time the MARY would pull in to the slip returning from a tow. But she did remain on active status until August 13th.

Then, with a general slowdown in the towing industry and with new ocean tugs on hand, the future need for the MIKI tugs was negligible, so all operating gear was removed from the MARY and the HENRIETTA shifted her to the Foss Reserve fleet. In 1977 Foss declared her surplus and she is waiting for someone to come along to put her back to work—she can still take a job if it is not too competitive.

Should the MARY leave the Foss fold, her name will survive, as Foss in March 1979 purchased a Puget Sound-type tug and named her MARY, so at the end of 1979 there was an active MARY and a de-activated MARY.

SHANNON FOSS

Built:	1958	Propulsion:	EMD (Single)
	Todd Shipyard and Foss-Seattle		1,600-horsepower
	Seattle, Washington	Primary Service:	Tacoma Harbor
Length:	84-feet	Status:	In Service - 1979
Beam:	25-feet		

As with the CAROL, Todd Shipyard built the SHANNON's steel hull and deckhouse-shell with the Foss-Seattle yard completing the tug. When ready in mid-1957 Todd lifted the tug into Elliot Bay for shifting to the Foss yard. She was the first new tug of Foss design since the pride of the Tacoma fleet, BRYNN FOSS, was built in 1952.

After outfitting and making her trial runs in early March 1958 with a new 1200 Nordberg she started active service in mid-March doing ship-assist work in Seattle Harbor, a job she was to share with CAROL, her new sister-tug. The tugs were soon known as the Foss twins. The prototype twin, the SHANNON, was named in honor of a daughter of Henrietta Foss Hager, daughter of Henry and Agnes.

During the early 1960's the SHANNON was called on several times to tow bulk cement barges between cement plants in Seattle and Bellingham to Portland, Oregon. However, except for these outside voyages the SHANNON remained on inside waters and with the CAROL was the pride of the Seattle harbor fleet until late 1970.

In September, with the arrival from the builders' yard of the new, more powerful ship-assist tug SHELLEY FOSS, the SHANNON became available for use outside Seattle. So in December 1970 she transferred to Tacoma as primary ship-assist tug to handle the rapidly increasing ship tonnage coming into port. She has remained on the same job with the exception of a limited time spent in linehaul work.

In late May 1971 a broken crankshaft laid up the SHANNON for two months. The unavailability of parts was responsible for much of the delay in repair, but the engine was rebuilt and ready to run in mid-August. By that time towing requirements were altered because of the West Coast Longshoremen's strike that began in July 1971. Smaller tugs were assigned to handle the diminished harbor work at Tacoma so that the SHANNON, after running-in the rebuilt engine, could help out on linehaul towing between Sound ports. Her assistance was needed to fill the shortage of tugs caused by over half of the regular linehaul fleet towing Japanese export logs to British Columbia. Canadian ports were not affected by the I.L.W.U. strike.

When the longshoremen returned to work in December 1971 the SHANNON returned to Tacoma harbor duties and she continued tending ships and barges until mechanical failures in 1977 became too frequent for dependable service. With nearly 20 years of continuous back-and-fill maneuvering in Seattle and Tacoma by both the SHANNON and the CAROL, the engines of the Foss Twins as well as accompanying equipment was due for replacement. Repowering was ordered—the CAROL first and then the SHANNON. However, within two months of the CAROL entering the yard of the Marine Industries in Tacoma, the SHANNON had another serious engine breakdown. The expense of temporary repair for only a few additional months' work was too great, so she was laid up to await her turn for a new engine. Scheduled for fall, the change-over was completed in April 1978 and the SHANNON came out with a new 1,600-horsepower EMD diesel and a fixed Kort nozzle propulsion system. Her performance went up 40 percent, giving her much stronger push-and-pull when docking ships, a big help to the Puget Sound pilots.

At present the SHANNON performs under the guiding hands of alternate Captains Bud Thweatt and Ed Nelson. Her able six-man crews alternate as the Captains do—with one week on and one week off, on a year-around basis. Except for an occasional log tow for Weyerhaeuser from South Bay to Everett, the SHANNON is a Tacoma fixture, adding a touch of glamor to the harbor scene, always running with a bone in her teeth.

ADELINE FOSS (2)

Built:	1943	Propulsion:	Enterprise (Single)
	Northwest Shipbuilding		1,500-horsepower
	Bellingham, Washington	Primary Service:	Alaska and Coastwise
Length:	117-feet	Final Foss Operating Day:	August 6, 1976
Beam:	28-feet	Status:	Sold - Foreign

The second ADELINE FOSS, a World War II ocean-going tug, number LT-452, was built for the Army Transport Service—one of sixty MIKI-Class tugs used for towing barges of supplies and equipment to military command bases. However, as part of her war duty, she did general harbor assist work at Whittier, Alaska. And several years after the War she continued in the same type of service for the ATS, but under the name of SGT. RAYMOND BASER.

Like all the MIKIS after postwar service, she was placed in the reserve fleet, remaining at anchor until Foss put her back in action. They were impressed with the capabilities of the MIKI-type tugs, so they purchased the BASER, in lay-up in California, at a Government surplus sale along with a sister tug the PVT. ROMEO LECLAIR—later to become the PATRICIA FOSS.

In late April 1958 the LECLAIR with Captain Nolze in command, left San Francisco with the BASER in tow and the tugs arrived at Foss-Seattle safe and sound after a week's run up the Coast.

The SGT. BASER remained idle and in her wartime gray coat at the Foss lay-up yard in Kennydale all through the spring and summer. In July she became the ADELINE FOSS and by October overhaul work on the engine was under way at the Foss yard along with conversion of the boat to the Company's requirements. By December, painted green and white and ready to go, she began her Foss career on the Seattle-to-Squamish, British Columbia rail-car barge run, but by the summer of 1959 she was towing regularly to Alaska.

For the next seventeen years and with no misadventures, the ADELINE towed on the Alaska runs with the exception of an occasional trip to Hawaii towing a lumber barge or taking part in the ordinary linehauls between Sound ports. Nevertheless, life was not uninteresting during her years as the ADELINE.

On September 10, 1964 she was dispatched to Portland to pick up a new 320-foot rail-car barge for Washington Tug & Barge Company of Seattle. Washington Tug had a contract with the Canadian National Railroad to tow a rail barge, the 266-foot GRIFSON, between Prince Rupert, British Columbia and Whittier, Alaska, using their MIKI-Class tug CAPTAIN. In 1964 rail traffic warranted a second tug and barge, but not having the necessary equipment on hand, they built a new 320-foot barge named GRIFSON and chartered the ADELINE to do the towing. She remained on the run until relieved by the PATRICIA FOSS in January 1965. Foss continued towing the GRIFSON, but only until Washington Tug & Barge built their own tug for the job. The new boat, the MOGUL, took over the GRIFSON in December 1965.

In early 1966 the ADELINE, her crew members and owners were awarded the Maritime Administration's Gallant Ship plaque for the rescue of 17 seamen from the Alaska Steamship freighter, ODUNA, which grounded on Unimak Island on the Alaska Peninsula November 26, 1965. The ADELINE, under command of Captain Guy Johnson, was homeward bound from the Aleutians when they picked up an SOS from the ODUNA. The ADELINE responded and proceeded immediately to the ship, 50 miles away. Upon arrival at the scene they found that the adverse sea and wind conditions precluded rescue of the crew by lifeboat, so an attempt from shoreside was decided on. After finding a suitable landing, the tug's work boat was launched, in spite of the rough sea, with a 5-man rescue party. The seas threatened to swamp the boat, but by keeping from under the breaking waves, they worked their way to shore. Beaching the work boat, the men hiked two miles over rocks and around cliffs, carrying lines and blocks, to reach the stranded ship. With the equipment from the ADELINE they rigged a breeches buoy and aerial line outfit, and 17 of ODUNA's crew were safely hauled ashore. As the weather improved the Coast Guard was able to take off the remaining crew members by helicopter. There was no loss of life, thanks to the efforts of the ADELINE and the Coast Guard, but the ODUNA became a total loss.

The ADELINE's next adventure was more prolonged. She became involved in the Government's "Big Blast" program, delivering supplies for the atomic bomb test on Amchitka Island. In early 1967 Foss began the massive sealift of supplies and equipment from Seattle to Amchitka for Holmes & Narver, the prime contractor for the

Atomic Energy Commission's undergound explosion project. Holmes & Narver provided technology and equipment to construct two base camps and prepare two major sites suitable for boring deep holes below the island's desolate terrain for two controlled underground atomic detonations. The first task facing Holmes & Narver on the remote island was setting up a 360-man base camp. This included sewer lines, water system, the generating and distribution of electricity, and building a network of roads. The World War II airfields and runways, abandoned for 20 years, were to be used, but they had to be rebuilt. Every individual item, and there were thousands, was funneled through Seattle for transportation to Amchitka by Foss tugs and barges, or if time would not allow, by air express.

The first of the two detonations occurred at Amchitka on October 2, 1969. The Atomic Energy Commission exploded a one-megaton nuclear device, the equivalent of one million tons of T.N.T. Rumors of impending earthquakes, tidal waves, deadly radiation and destruction of sea life were spread throughout the world, forgetting that the detonations were controlled. The actual damage recorded were a few fissures at "Ground Zero", cracks in nearby roads, and some displaced boulders.

Many months before the first blast was detonated, operation "Cannikin", the name of the second scheduled blast, was started at drill site "C". This was to be the deepest, single-lift hole ever drilled by mankind. The hole was 7½ feet in diameter, and it was bored to a depth of 6,150 feet and cased to 6,104 feet. The drill rig was larger than any ever before used, with the enormous weight of rig and equipment on top of the hole totaling 5,500,000 pounds. To support the pressure, it was necessary to build a concrete slab 50 feet square and from 4 to 10 feet thick. The drill derrick lowered 5½ million pounds of tubed steel into the 6,000-foot hole. The superstructure was built to withstand winds up to 150 miles an hour.

The end purpose of all the effort for the Atomic Energy Commission was the opportunity of recording in five one hundred millionths of a second, the result of the largest underground detonation of a nuclear device in the history of the United States.

The headlines in the "Anchorage Daily Times" on November 6, 1971 stated, "Amchitka blast conducted with perfect safety at 1100 hours today." The blast was a practical success—and the largest and most controversial atomic warhead ever exploded by the Atomic Energy Commission.

The records show the Foss "Sealift to Amchitka" was spread out over a period of nearly five years (February 1967 to December 1971) and consisted of 73 separate tows, originating in Seattle and Anacortes. Each round trip of 5,000 miles took an average of 40 days. Weather played the most important part in voyage length on all trips as the logbooks of the tugs proved. The longest single round trip voyage to Amchitka required 74 days due to storms that forced the tug and tow to seek shelter several times in protected bays. The shortest voyage was a summertime trip with fine weather both ways, the round trip taking only 24 days. In accomplishing the protracted Sealift 18 different Foss tugs participated with total towing time of 2,834 days, or 7.76 years.

The ADELINE, under command of Captain John Webb, when not running to Anchorage, made seven round trips between Seattle and Amchitka during the period May 1967 through May 1969—this was at the height of the cargo movement. Captain John and his crew had great influence with the weathermaker, for in the seven voyages, the ADELINE's elapsed time per voyage figured only 38 days, two days under the average.

In the following years the ADELINE returned to a quieter life of hauling barge loads of cement and mobile homes from Seattle to Anchorage during the summer and fall seasons. In the winter months the aging tug remained idle at the canal moorings as the newer, more powerful tugs could better handle the limited off-season and ocean-towing work.

The ADELINE came out of lay-up in the spring of 1974 as Foss had secured the contract for towing cargo from Seattle to Valdez in connection with the Alaska pipeline construction and the push was on. The ADELINE's two remaining sister-tugs, the MARY FOSS and PATRICIA FOSS, were also reactivated to tow between Seattle and Valdez and for the next two years, the ADELINE remained on the Valdez run with an occasional trip to Anchorage.

The Foss fleet modernization program, bringing new and faster tugs into service, resulted in the retirement of the MIKI tugs and the ADELINE, when the bulk of the Valdez cargo was delivered in July 1976 was once more placed in reserve status. Then in the fall of 1976 she dropped to an even lower class. Though still seaworthy, she was superseded by the high-horsepower tugs and retired from the active fleet after 18 years of steady towing under Foss ownership. However, her retirement was of short duration.

For in April 1977 the ADELINE was sold to Belco Petroleum Company of Callao, Peru. Belco employed the Foss yard to reactivate and condition her, then she left for Peru under the name of ANN W. After arrival at Callao in July, she began support services for offshore oil facilities. With her ability to handle ocean weather, she should be as successful for her new owners as she was for Foss.

PATRICIA FOSS Photographed on Puget Sound in July, 1967 enroute to the Washington Coast to shift a drilling rig. *(From the author's collection)*

PATRICIA FOSS (2)

Built:	1943	Propulsion:	Enterprise
	Grays Harbor Shipbuilding Company		1,500-horsepower
	Hoquiam, Washington	Primary Service:	Coastwise and Alaska
Length:	117-feet	Final Foss Operating Day:	June 29, 1976
Beam:	28-feet	Status:	Sold-Domestic

In March 1958 the Foss company was the successful bidder at a sale held by the U. S. Army Property Disposal Branch at Lathrop, California. The sale produced two World War II-built MIKI-Class tugs for Foss—the LT-452 (RAYMOND BASER) and the LT-366 (PVT. ROMEO LECLAIR). Both tugs operated in previous years for the U.S. Army and had recently been laid up in California.

The LT-366 was in operating condition so a Foss crew went down to man the LeCLAIR and tow her sister-tug, the LT-452, to the Foss yard in Seattle. Shortly after arrival home in early April, the LeCLAIR was renamed PATRICIA FOSS, but the 452 retained her number and name until mid-summer, then she became the ADELINE FOSS, starting her towing service the following winter.

The PATRICIA, however, started in mid-May 1958 her predecessor of the same name being permanently retired. She was assigned to the close-to-home Seattle to Squamish rail-car run to give the machinery a good try out before towing on the Alaska and the California cement runs. As all her equipment ran smoothly, she was considered reliable and spent the last months of the year on the scheduled Coastwise and Alaska tows.

During the first six months of 1959 the PATRICIA, between her routine runs to Alaska, made three special log-crib tows from Ketchikan, Alaska to Puget Sound. On January 11th, she left Ward Cove with the first crib bound for Everett and arrived 15 days later, after losing four days waiting for favorable weather. Her actual running time speed for the trip was 2.3 knots. The crib rafts were heavy awkward drags and required careful handling to keep the gear intact and a careful watch on the weather to avoid heavy winds and seas.

The PATRICIA delivered the second crib to Anacortes in April and then on June 8th left Ward Cove for Everett with the last tow. The FOB Everett cost was too high to continue the program even though the third trip was made under ideal conditions, taking 11 days for the 649-mile run.

With log towing over, the PATRICIA went back to routine barge tows between Seattle and Alaska, primarily to Anchorage. She became the number one tug in Alaska service for the next 3½ years.

Then the time came in December 1962 for a change in environment—she took over the Coast and Honolulu lumber run and held it until June 1963. But she returned to the lumber haul in December 1963 to assist the BARBARA, ELLEN, and JUSTINE, remaining on the Island run until September 13, 1964.

Upon coming back to Seattle, the surge in lumber demand over, the PATRICIA headed for Alaska with only a day's dock time. She towed the Liberty ship, HAROLD WINSLOW, from Seattle to Nikishka—Cook Inlet's northernmost ice-free port. The WINSLOW slid along with little resistance, tug and tow arriving on September 27, 1964. The PATRICIA brought up the first of a three-ship "ready-made warehouse" to be used for storing oil-drilling supplies.

When oil exploration in the Inlet intensified in the early 60's, Jim Arness, a long time resident of the Kenai area realized that storage facilities, a supply depot, repair shop, and boat moorage would be needed. The harbor project known as Arness Terminal was to be at Nikishka and made up eventually of two more 420-foot World War II Liberty ships purchased from the Maritime Commission with a stipulation of "non-transportation" use.

Two years later, in June 1966 the PATRICIA with Captain Roy Hough in charge, towed the other two "Liberties"—the EDWARD A. FILENE and the HOWELL COBB—from Everett to Nikishka. The ships were sunk at the site by pouring sand and gravel into the holds to fix the hulls in position on the sea floor and up against the existing foreshore fill. The hulls were then fitted with bow ramps permitting trucks to load and unload in the cargo holds. A complete machine shop for overhaul, maintenance, and fabrication of drilling parts and equipment was installed in one of the ships. An abundant supply of fresh water for supplying the drill rigs was piped from a fast-flowing stream to stand-pipes aboard the "Liberties." Crew and supply boats shuttled between the Arness Terminal and offshore rigs for the next four years. Then at the completion of the major oil development in 1975 the Terminal, having served its purpose, was dismantled. The beached ships were cut up for scrap—the end of three more WWII heroes of the Army's supply line.

In 1964 the PATRICIA happened to be in Cook Inlet when the Union Oil Tanker SANTA MARIA and the Dutch Tanker SIRRAH collided in Anchorage Harbor. Flames shot 500-feet in the air from the SANTA MARIA, but fortunately, the greater part of her 100,000-barrel cargo of aviation gasoline failed to ignite. An estimated 80 percent of the afterhouse, containing the machinery, was destroyed and she suffered a 20-foot gash on her starboard quarter. The Dutch ship was relatively free of damage.

The AGNES FOSS was also in the Inlet at the time so both tugs were dispatched to the collision site to take the SANTA MARIA in tow. They left with the tanker November 5th for Seattle, where the ship was to undergo survey and repair. A steady 6-knot rate was maintained except for the delay caused by bucking into a 70-knot gale in the Gulf of Alaska. The tugs and their disabled tow arrived in Seattle safely on November 17th. (The SANTA MARIA was repaired and resumed service for Union Oil Company).

After two months lay-up in Seattle, the PATRICIA began a 10-month charter with Washington Tug & Barge towing their rail-car barges between Prince Rupert, British Columbia and Whittier, Alaska. The charter ended in November 1965.

During the years 1966 through 1972 the PATRICIA towed on all the regular Alaska runs including seven Amchitka trips for Holmes & Narver, supplying the Atomic Energy Commission Program detailed in the ADELINE story. And for a change of climate, the PATRICIA did manage to get a fairweather trip to Honolulu with a barge of lumber.

In April 1973 the PATRICIA was selected to fulfill the second-year towing contract with Peter Pan Seafoods, so with cargo barge FOSS-202 she left for the P.P.S. Canneries on the first of three voyages to southwestern Alaska under Captain Al Anderson. The first voyage was a 45-day run with stops at Squaw Harbor, King Cove, False Pass, Port Moller, Naknek, and Dillingham.

On the second voyage, the Foss crew, doubling as longshoremen, loaded 61,000 cases of red and pink salmon and 3,000 cases of Snow and King crab at King Cove. Then 71,000 more cases of salmon were put aboard at False Pass. Moving on to Squaw Harbor the last of the cargo was loaded—18,000 cases of small shrimp and a 5-ton crab cooker. The entire cargo was discharged at the Foss terminal in Seattle. By the time the second trip was over in mid-summer, Al Anderson was known to his fellow skippers as "Captain Peter Pan."

After a paying season in the fishing industry and completing a run to Anchorage, the PATRICIA was assigned to Puget Sound towing for the winter months—a better fate than going into lay-up.

During the 1974 season, the big year of the Alaska Pipeline construction, the PATRICIA, like her sister-tugs, engaged in hauling cargo barges to Valdez for Fluor Company, contractors at the Valdez end of the pipeline. Towing

continued non-stop to Valdez even in mid-winter and with the newer tugs unavailable due to other assignments, the PATRICIA was put on a Christmas-time voyage. With Captain Earl Cole she left Seattle December 23rd, headed for what literally turned out to be the frozen North—and no chance for a happy holiday season.

The trip was pleasant on the protected Inside Passage, but on December 28th, they were forced to anchor-up near Hoonah and wait for the heavy weather to moderate before crossing the Gulf of Alaska. The PATRICIA remained at anchor for six days beset with blustery winds, snow, and cold, then a break came on January 4th and they were able to weigh anchor and head out into the Gulf.

Early in the morning of January 6th, nearing the Copper River flats, generally a windy area, the temperature began dropping with the wind and sea making up. By mid-day, ice rapidly formed on the tug's weather (starboard) side. Under these conditions something untoward always happens—the furnace quit! By late afternoon the temperature outside stood at 16 degrees with a 60 to 70 knot wind, producing a chill factor of minus thirty degrees. Inside the tug, ice was forming and the temperature continued to drop. The crew, bundled up in all the clothes they could find, huddled in the galley, the only place with heat.

By the morning of the 7th, the weather side of the PATRICIA was a solid mass of ice, causing a heavy list to starboard, but by transferring fuel to the port tanks, the list was reduced. At noon the weather moderated enough for the crew to go on deck and chop away chunks of thick ice to finish righting the tug. Another day of icing and the PATRICIA would have been in danger of sinking.

Valdez was a welcome sight, and Captain Cole's first order of business was the furnace repair. Conditions on the run south were more favorable than northbound, and they arrived in Seattle January 20th, none the worse for their chilling experience.

During 1975 the PATRICIA made one trip to Adak in the Aleutians, several more trips to Valdez and two trips to Anchorage. However on the last trip for Anchorage in the fall, the PATRICIA failed to make port with her barge.

She left Seattle on September 19th with the FOSS-209 in tow for Pacific Western Lines. The 209 carried bulk cement below decks and a general cargo and mobile homes on deck. Excerpts from Captain Ken Paynes' Logbook indicated a progressive loss of stability on the 209 in crossing the Gulf of Alaska near Prince William Sound: "September 26, 1975, 0045 hours; barge towing sideways; appears to be listing to port; unable to straighten heading and put tug down-sea of tow. Weather rough, seas and winds E'ly force 8."

At 0300 same date he records: "Port list now estimated to be 30 degrees. Notified Coast Guard. Some lumber cargo adrift in water. Crew manning search lights and winch brake and await daylight." At 0830 he states, "One house trailer lost overboard."

By mid-morning they were able to change course and head for shelter in Prince William Sound, 38 miles away. The PATRICIA made it safely, but the barge wasn't so fortunate. The entry in the Log reads: "1530, FOSS-209 rolled over, 14½ miles from Cape Hinchenbrook." However, the barge floating upside-down could still be towed, so they continued on to a safe anchorage in the Sound.

Foss-Seattle sent up surveyors and two of the Company officials by plane to appraise the situation and decide on procedure. With a cargo of hardening cement, little time was spent in deciding to consider the barge a total constructive loss. The barge, now like a floating mound of solid rock, was a definite hazard to navigation and had to be sunk.

Demolition experts were called up and they placed explosives on the barge and cut holes to sink the 209 prior to detonation. The new LESLIE FOSS took over the job of towing the barge to a pre-determined location in the Gulf of Alaska and at the appointed spot and time the barge, with the holes now open to the sea, filled up and sank. At a set depth the explosives detonated, insuring the 209 would never rise to the surface. In the meantime the PATRICIA returned to Seattle and went on the Valdez run for the balance of 1975.

The PATRICIA's service in 1976 with Leonard Vetter in charge, lasted less than three months and all spent on the Valdez run, delivering five separate tows. By late June the greatest part of the Valdez cargo had been delivered, so the PATRICIA's job ran out and upon her return to the Foss pier on June 29th, Foss placed her in ready-reserve status.

She remained on standby until mid-August 1976 then Foss decided to shift her the lay-up moorings as no future use was planned. But the PATRICIA, with her good reputation standing out was sold locally in 1980 to Mr. Stan Langaker for use as a live-aboard pleasure tug. She has recently been seen sporting a blue and white color scheme, and now named DOMINION.

IVER FOSS (2)

Built:	1943	Propulsion:	Enterprise (Twin)
	Everett Marine Ways, Inc.		1,270-horsepower
	Everett, Washington	Primary Service:	Northern Puget Sound
Length:	102-feet	Final Foss Operating Day:	October 8, 1976
Beam:	27-feet	Status:	Sold - Domestic

The IVER, built for the United States Navy as the U.S.S. CANOCAN (Navy-class designation, YTB-290) was planned for station work on the West Coast and Hawaii during World War II, and after the war she continued the same service. Being outfitted with extensive fire-fighting equipment her important function was navy yard and ship fire-protection, so she remained on duty in the Navy until declared surplus in 1958.

Foss bid successfully for the CANOCAN and as she was berthed in the Hawaiian Islands at the time, Foss sent over a crew for the run across the Pacific.

Inspection by the Foss-Tacoma shipyard crew did not indicate the need for major repair work. However, there were modifications to be made to ensure top efficiency as Foss intended her to be the new ship-assist tug for northern Puget Sound. In view of her assignment, the bulwarks were lowered to facilitate line-handling in making up to ships and the yard installed a heavy-duty tow winch and bow-winch—the Navy did not need power winches in their use of the tug. A portion of the complete fire-fighting equipment including monitors was removed; two staterooms were added in the main deckhouse, and the crew's forecastle made more liveable. The galley, that most important source of a sailor's comfort, was updated and the messroom remodeled to do double duty as a day-room for the further convenience of the crew. When redone, Foss had another first class tug.

At the time the CANOCAN was ready for service, tanker traffic was increasing at the three oil refineries on northern Puget Sound and more tug assistance was necessary. Several tankers, some close to 20,000 tons and 600 feet in length, were calling regularly for Shell and Texaco refineries at Anacortes and the Mobil refinery at Ferndale. In addition to tanker traffic, there were many general cargo ships needing assistance at Ancortes and Bellingham. The veteran tugs, SANDRA FOSS and ERIK FOSS, were handling the assist work, but a more powerful tug was desirable to safely serve the heavier ships, and the CANOCAN for the 60's had the right equipment and power.

On April 28, 1959 the tug officially became the SEA KING, and the vessel's documents were transferred to Pacific Towboat Company of Everett, as they were handling Foss' tug activities around Anacortes. Then after final outfitting

SEA KING *Later renamed the IVER FOSS, used in the Anacortes-Bellingham-Ferndale area assisting oil tankers.* *(Courtesy of Foss Tug Co)*

and painting in Tacoma, the SEA KING left on June 24th for Everett, her official home port, to take part in sea trials and equipment performance tests. After making a good showing, she left on July 7th for her working base in Anacortes, but while enroute she assisted another Pacific tug, the SEA ROAMER, with a tow of logs across Rosario Straits. However she arrived at Anacortes in time to dock the 11,000-ton tanker BENNINGTON alongside the Shell Refinery pier—the first of countless ship-assist jobs she performed during her 16 years at Anacortes and Bellingham.

With the SEA KING's arrival at Anacortes, the SANDRA and ERIK were reassigned to Foss-Seattle and the SEA KING ended up with the entire ship-assist program. But as ship traffic increased in the early 60's, the SANDRA re-joined the SEA KING, then the LUMMI BAY, a sister tug to the SEA KING, came up in 1961 to help with the heavier ships.

With two other tugs on the job, the SEA KING could be used occasionally for other work and as additional equipment was needed to deliver supplies and cargo to the oil exploration sites in Alaska's Cook Inlet, the SEA KING was temporarily transferred to the Foss Ocean Division.

She ran light to the Foss pier to outfit, crew-up, and bunker. Then on April 11, 1964 she left Seattle with the der-rick barge FOSS-300 in tow for the middle-ground shoal oil-exploration site in Cook Inlet. Three days earlier the ADELINE FOSS had left Alameda, California, for the same drill site, with FOSS-251 carrying the legs for the drilling rig to be set up on the middle-ground shoal by the FOSS-300.

But early on her way north the SEA KING experienced lubrication-pump and tow-winch problems. Less than a day out of Seattle, Captain Guy Johnson radioed the office that the lube pump on the starboard engine was not func-tioning properly. The chief spent several hours rebuilding the pump. Then the next day the SEA KING again called in to inform they were now having tow winch trouble. When shortening up the wire for Seymour Narrows, only half the tow wire could be reeled in and later on the winch was completely without power. As a result of the failure, they received orders to trade tows with the ADELINE at Ketchikan. The ADELINE was to take over the FOSS-300, and after repairs in Ketchikan, the SEA KING was to tow the FOSS-251. Both tugs, even with the Ketchikan delay, ar-rived in Cook Inlet on the same day, April 24.

The SEA KING was assigned to tend and position the FOSS-300, while erecting the drilling platform at middle ground shoal, and she stayed with derrick-tending until called back to her own work at Anacortes. On the way south, she took along the FOSS-184 and dropped the barge at Kendrick Bay in southeastern Alaska for a load of uranium ore. She then continued on to Seattle, arriving June 3. The SEA KING's first and last Alaska venture for Foss was over.

By the late 60's, with addition tanker traffic at Mobil's refinery at Ferndale and additional ship work at Bellingham, the SEA KING's working base was transferred from Anacortes to Bellingham. The shift provided a more central location, 16 miles north to Ferndale and 16 miles south to Anacortes. A new refinery at Cherry Point, north of Ferndale, was under construction, and large tankers needing docking assistance would be calling, so a central base proved practical for many years.

The SEA KING worked on ship-assists from 1959 to 1976 with Captains Bud Klemp and Larry Hafey handling the tug in all her "juggle" work and they were experts—no accidents were ever reported due to faulty assistance.

In February 1975 all major Foss-controlled tugs, including the SEA KING, were to have the familiar Foss colors of green and white to give uniformity and a significant display of Foss markings. To conform name with colors, the SEA KING became the IVER FOSS.

In 1976 with super-tankers calling at the northern refineries and the State Escort Law for tankers in effect, much higher horsepower was needed than the 1,270 of the IVER and her sister tug, LORNA, the ex-LUMMI BAY. So the RICHARD FOSS with 3,000 horsepower transferred from the Ocean Division to the Puget Sound section for ship-assists and tanker escort. The IVER and RICHARD were fully crewed and ready at all times, but the LORNA was put on a standby basis without an assigned crew.

In 1976 the final year of service for the IVER, she was idled three times by engine breakdowns, the repairs requiring several days to two weeks. The failures indicated what was to come; with engine reliability always in question, ship docking and undocking would be dangerously uncertain. To remove the doubt, Foss sent up the STACEY FOSS, less than two months from the builder's yard, packing 3,000-horsepower and well-equipped for tanker escort and docking service—the IVER could now safely be dispensed with.

For her last Foss job, on October 8, 1976 she assisted the 67,000-ton tanker, TAKATORISAN MARU, out of Atlantic-Richfield's Refinery at Cherry Point and then returned to Bellingham to await the STACEY's arrival later in the day. The STACEY tied up alongside and all necessary gear was transferred and the IVER's crew became the STACEY's crew. That same evening the STACEY left Bellingham for the first job in her new role.

The IVER remained idle at Bellingham until November 2nd, when a day crew ran her down to the Foss yard in Seattle, and the next week all valuable ship's gear was removed and stored ashore. Then the HENRIETTA shifted her to the West Terminal, joining the other retired tugs at the Foss farm.

However, the IVER's retirement was short-lived. In February 1978 Foss sold her to Don House of Wrangell, Alaska. He gave her the Indian name TAGISH and for the next two months, with his own Alaska crew aboard, he outfitted her for ship-service in southeastern Alaska.

On May 6, 1978 the TAGISH left the Foss yard for her new home port of Juneau. Her work, which had become a habit through the Foss years, was to assist ocean-going ships in and out of berths at various southeastern Alaska ports. The ex-Foss tug TYEE (SANDRA FOSS) was doing the ship-assists, but could not keep up with the demand, so the ex-IVER, heavier and more powerful, went north to lend a hand and join her former partner.

ALASKA CONSTRUCTOR

Built:	1944	Propulsion:	Caterpillar (Twin)
	Houston, Texas		1,020-horsepower
Length:	113-feet	Primary Service:	Cook Inlet - Alaska
Beam:	34-feet	Final Foss Operating Day:	December 17, 1969
		Status:	Sold - Domestic

The ALASKA CONSTRUCTOR was originally a "Landing Ship Medium" built for the Navy and assigned the number LSM-111. Designed for beach landing operations, she was a self-propelled ship, 192-feet in length, equipped with ramp and bow doors which provided access for shoreside loading or discharge of personnel and cargo. A feature desirable to Foss for use in areas of Alaska having no pier facilities.

After several years of Navy service, followed by a long lay-up, the LSM-111 was declared surplus and in January 1959 Foss purchased her and towed her to their Seattle yard. However, no work was done until 1962, then major alterations were started to convert the vessel to a specialized cargo carrier. The yard shortened her by about 80 feet, rebuilt the hull and fitted a winch on the after-cargo deck for towing barges. The bow door and ramp were re-worked to operate on the tidal beaches of Cook Inlet. Foss also equipped her to transport both dry and liquid cargo to Alaska's newly discovered oil fields.

In May 1963 she sailed light for Cook Inlet under the name ALASKA CONSTRUCTOR and spent the season doing just what she was rebuilt to do—working the beaches, drill sites, and towing supplies and equipment. After her initial season at various oil exploration sites, the CONSTRUCTOR returned to Seattle for repair and winter lay-up. Then when the spring thaw came to the Inlet, she returned to assist at the 1963 locations.

The CONSTRUCTOR worked every 5-month season in Cook Inlet until 1968 then with the oil platform construction at its height, the oil companies decided to work as long as possible in the season to finish up certain jobs. The CONSTRUCTOR then intended to winter in the Inlet, staying on the job and fighting the elements of wind, wave, cold, and the ever-present and unrelenting ice. But surprisingly, by December most of the construction work was finished on the drilling platforms, and with the new Foss supply-vessel ALASKA HUSKY coming up to serve the major platforms, there was little need for the CONSTRUCTOR to remain in the Inlet, so she started a new job—delivering cargo to the "westward."

The first trip was a supply run out to the Atomic Energy Nuclear drilling site on Amchitka in the Aleutian Islands. Completing the delivery, Captain Clarence Burt received orders to pick up a cargo of drilling equipment at Nikiski and proceed to a new dry-land drilling site at Port Moller on the Bering Sea side of the Alaska Peninsula. While beaching the cargo at Port Moller she was joined by the ELLEN and RICHARD ROSS, each tug bringing up two loaded cargo barges from Seattle for the new operation. When the cargo was all ashore, the CONSTRUCTOR returned to Cook Inlet in time to pick up a load for a second trip to Port Moller, arriving back at the beach in time to spend a very simple Christmas. After unloading the cargo, she returned to Seattle for annual repairs and drydocking and to wait for the spring activities.

In March 1969 she returned to Cook Inlet as a supply ship and again as last season, made cargo runs to Port Moller. Then in September, the CONSTRUCTOR, under Captain Roy Hough, was sent to the David River area of Port Moller to move drilling equipment to a new site 10 miles down the beach. Finishing up in December 1969, the ship returned to Seattle for the usual winter lay-up. But due to lack of jobs requiring the specialized services of the CONSTRUCTOR, she remained in lay-up for two years.

Then in 1972 she was taken over on a bare-boat charter by Alaska Shell, Inc. for the purpose of hauling containers of crab and shrimp between ports in Southwestern Alaska. This proved to be a successful operation for Alaska Shell, so in April 1976 they purchased the vessel outright and renamed her SIX PAK, not after the beer carton, but denoting the deck capacity of six cargo containers.

As of August 1979 the SIX PAK is still an active part of the seafood industry in southwestern Alaska. She is not hitting the beaches any more, and the Captain says, "Not the docks either."

SECTION VI – FOSS OBTAINS PARTICULAR TUGS FOR PARTICULAR JOBS

Tugs Acquired 1960 – 1969

ALASKA ROUGHNECK, EDITH (3), LORNA (2), LORNA (3)

ROLAND (2), PARTHIA, AUDRY, OYSTERMAN, HOONAH

RUFUS, ROGER, ALASKA ROUSTABOUT, ARTHUR (2)

CHRIS (2), ELLEN, HENRY (2), DOROTHY, JULIA

SAM, CRAIG (2), DEBORAH, JENNY, JOSIE

MATHILDA (2), ALASKA HUSKY, CATHERINE (2)

DELORES, DIANE, LELA (2), MARGARET (2), MELIA

MYRTLE (2), OMER (2), DAVID, JOE (2), RICHARD

CLAUDIA, DEAN, GRACE (2), MARTHA (3), DONNA (2)

PEGGY (3), PHILLIPS (2)

Of the 43 tug acquisitions, 23 new boats of seven types were produced—Seven "D" Class (66' 1,200 H.P.) -Three "J" Class (60' 600 H.P.) - Three "M" Class (65' 765 H.P.) - Two "C" Class (80' & 84' 1,700 H.P.) - Six "HARBOR" Class (37' to 45' 325-460 H.P.) - One "PHILLIPS" Class (112' 3,000 H.P.) -HENRY & ARTHUR (149', 5,000 H.P.)

Six far-reaching and important developments in the 1960s greatly affected the company's operating plans: the extensive oil programs in Cook Inlet, Alaska; Foss container-barge service to southeastern Alaska; a long-term contract for barging lumber to Honolulu; the need for tugs in the Vietnam War; contract towing for the Atomic Energy Commission to deliver equipment and supplies, for several years, to Amchitka Island in the Aleutians. And, notably, Foss Launch & Tug Company becomes part of the Dillingham Corporation of Honolulu, through a stock exchange.

This momentous and eventful decade shows Foss' triple expansion—a tremendous fleet increase, more and varied towing programs entered into, and the Dillingham prestige insuring continued growth and prominence.

ALASKA ROUGHNECK *March 23, 1967 leaving Seattle for season's duty tending drilling rigs in Cook Inlet. (Courtesy of author's collection)*

ALASKA ROUGHNECK

Built:	1944	Propulsion:	Caterpillar (Twin)
	Houston, Texas		1,000-horsepower
Length:	113-feet	Primary Service:	Southwestern Alaska
Beam:	34-feet	Final Foss Operating Day:	February 28, 1979
		Status:	Sank

The ALASKA ROUGHNECK, a medium class landing ship, LSM-116, was built for the U. S. Navy during World War II for use on beach-heads as they were equipped with bow doors and ramps. Foss purchased the LSM to facilitate cargo discharging at beach sites in Alaska.

The conversion of the LSM-116 began in 1960 following the plans of W. C. Nickum & Sons, Naval Architects. After stripping the ship a seventy-foot mid-section was cut out of the 192 foot vessel and then the two ends rejoined. The cut-out portion contained the conning tower, original machinery spaces and living area. No change was made in the bow doors or ramp.

The LSM-116 became the first vessel under Coast Guard inspection and with an ABS load-line certificate to be granted the right to make regular landings and discharge cargo on open beaches. The LSM-116 also met all requirements for general towing and transportation of dry and liquid cargo in connection with petroleum exploration and allied construction. Foss equipped her with four tanks to carry 60,000 gallons of oil cargo in addition to her own fuel and she had tankage for 15,000 gallons of potable water. She was fitted with nine ballast tanks with a capacity of 375 tons of salt water used to hold her position in beaching operations.

Being unique—the only vessel in the fleet having the characteristics of freighter, tug, and barge—Foss nicknamed her "FRUGGER," but as she would be working with oil-well personnel, she was officially given a more appropriate name, ALASKA ROUGHNECK.

After preliminary trials on Puget Sound, the ROUGHNECK sailed for Cook Inlet on May 14, 1962 and her Captain, Everett Nolze, reported that the propellers apparently had the wrong pitch as her average speed in ideal sailing conditions was a disappointing nine knots. He also reported the crew's quarters were warm and comfortable, but he was unable to get heat in his stateroom or W.C. Otherwise, the boat operated satisfactorily.

The ROUGHNECK ran well until early December then she developed engine trouble just before returning to Seattle for the winter, so the AGNES FOSS towed her home, arriving two days before Christmas.

The ROUGHNECK returned to Cook Inlet for the next five seasons, working during the ice-free months of April through November in oil exploration and drill platform construction. In the final season she spent most of her time supplying the completed platforms with daily operating supplies.

With the height of the construction work completed by late 1967, and with the new Foss supply vessel ALASKA HUSKY now on the job, there was no further need for the ROUGHNECK type of specialized vessel. She remained in lay-up at Foss-Seattle all winter and spring, then in June 1968 she was chartered by Champion Paper Inc. to transport timber surveyors around southeastern Alaska. Champion was making a study of timber resources for a planned pulp mill at Berners Bay, north of Juneau. The ROUGHNECK spent a month in southeastern Alaska, then returned to Seattle in early July. With no "foreseeable" use, she went into indefinite lay-up.

For five and one-half years she remained dormant. Then in early 1974 Foss received a contract from Fluor Construction Company to transport equipment to Valdez for use at the terminus of the Alaska pipeline. In addition to ocean tugs, the ROUGHNECK was needed to transfer equipment from the port of Valdez to the tank farm construction site across the Bay, so she was moved to the Foss repair yard for three months of repair and reactivation. Five years laying idle entailed an extensive restoration job, but finally in mid-June the yard had her ready for service, looking fit in her new coat of green and white.

With Captain Tom Lewis in command, she sailed for Valdez on June 25, 1974. However, her assignment in Valdez was shorter than expected and by late August she was no longer required in the shuttle service.

From Valdez the ROUGHNECK was dispatched to Cook Inlet where she did limited duty for the next two months. Most of her crew was assigned to other vessels, only a skeleton crew remaining for maintenance and security.

But in late October 1974 she transported several mobile home camp units from Seward to a logging camp at Kazakof Bay on Kodiak Island. Upon completion of the delivery she returned to Seattle, arriving on November 18th. She spent the winter in company with the other seasonal Alaska boats waiting for the spring call to action.

For the ROUGHNECK it came in May as Foss Alaska Line required a vessel of her type to carry containers for delivery to villages on the lower Yukon River. After a month of necessary repairs, again with Tom Lewis in charge, she left for the Bering Sea with a small container barge in tow. By June 25 tug and barge arrived at the village of Hooper Bay, the first discharge point. An excerpt from the United States Coast Pilot, Volume 9, describes Hooper Bay:

ALASKA CONSTRUCTOR and ALASKA ROUGHNECK at a beaching site in Cook Inlet during oil exploration activities in 1963. (Courtesy of Foss Tug Co)

"The village of Hooper Bay (population 460) is the most prominent feature in the area. It is on the highest ground, and the school and tin-roof buildings are visible for about ten miles. Emergency supplies can be obtained from a store. Airmail service is weekly during most of the year." With no docks at any villages in northern Alaska, all cargo delivery operations are classed as tide and beach jobs.

After unloading at Hooper Bay, tug and tow proceeded to the Yukon River villages of Emmonak and Mountain Village. Then after discharging cargo and backloading a cargo of fish, the ROUGHNECK and BARGE-185 headed for Seattle, arriving August 5th. Next day the cargo of fish was discharged and the ship's gear sent ashore for storage. With no work in sight, she went into early lay-up.

In May 1976 an opportunity to put the ROUGHNECK back in motion on a full-time basis came about when Deep Sea, Inc., a Seattle-based crab-processing company, required a ship with capabilities of hauling containers between their processing plants on the Alaska Peninsula and Aleutian Islands to the deep-water port of Kodiak. The loaded containers were to be off-loaded at Kodiak for shipment on Sealand ships to Seattle and the empty containers returned to the processing plants for reloading.

The ROUGHNECK with her open deck was well-suited for the job, so Deep Sea, Inc., chartered her on a bareboat basis. She handled Deep Sea's cargo with no problems for almost three years until the morning of February 28, 1979. Then fate took a hand in the destiny of ship and crew.

On the way from the Aleutians to Kodiak, loaded with containers of sea food, she "came up standing" on Illisk Island near False Pass in stormy weather, accompanied by high seas and poor visibility. But with a rising tide the crew was able to back her off the beach. In only an hour from the time of grounding, they were on their way to King Cove for survey. Then just off Bold Cape within a mile of the Cove, the ROUGHNECK lost stability and with little warning she capsized, taking two crewmen to the bottom with her. To the rest of the crew the tragedy was doubly appalling since they had thought the ROUGHNECK safe with the bilge pumps holding down the water level. The surmise was that the sinking could be attributed to the ingress of water from a rupture in the hull combined with the elevated weight of the containers.

The rest of the crew was rescued and taken to Cold Bay to sail again, but the two unfortunate men and the ROUGHNECK, sad to realize, had made their final landing.

EDITH FOSS (3)

Built:	1944	Propulsion:	General Motors
	Newport Beach, California		1,200-horsepower
Length:	89-feet	Primary Service:	Puget Sound
Beam:	25-feet	Final Foss Operating Day:	August 15, 1978
		Status:	Sold

The EDITH FOSS, originally Army tug T-118, was similar in design to the Army's TP-class (Tug-Passenger), both types were built for service in World War II. Foss was familiar with the TP's having purchased the MARGARET, ex-TP-90, from the Government in 1950.

The T-118 operated on the West Coast for the duration of the War and then shifted to Japan, working for the army until 1957 when they released her from overseas service and she returned to Southern California as a surplus tug, relegated to the lay-up fleet.

Pacific Tow & Salvage at Long Beach purchased the tug in September 1957 and they named her PACIFIC. P.T. & S. used the tug for six months then turned her over to Pacific Towboat at Everett. They tied up the tug at their Everett base until 1959 then sent her to the Foss shipyard in Tacoma for renovation. Her 450 horsepower Fairbanks-Morse diesel was removed and replaced with a 1,200 horsepower G-M. The main deck cabins only required minor changes, but the pilot house and upper deck quarters were completely rebuilt. The Tacoma yard crew had to take care of the repair on operating tugs in addition to working over the PACIFIC, so it was August 1960 before the PACIFIC left the dock, but she came out looking like a new boat.

On August 12th the tug's ownership officially changed from Pacific Towboat to Foss Launch & Tug, as she was to be used directly by Foss. After sea trials, she left for Port Angeles to tow logs on the Straits and to Canada and Puget Sound mills.

On August 15th, 1960 the PACIFIC started out by towing eighteen sections of spruce to the north arm of the Fraser River, B.C. and for the next three-and-a-half years she continued towing logs, working with the two veteran Port Angeles' tugs, ARTHUR and EDITH FOSS.

However, the PACIFIC's full time service at Port Angeles ended in April 1965 as the Foss-Seattle Operations Department required an additional tug for the cement haul between Bellingham and Portland. The PACIFIC remained on the run until October, then the Foss Ocean Division transferred her to towing a cargo barge from Seattle to Cook Inlet, Alaska with equipment and supplies for the oil drilling companies. Upon her return to Puget Sound, she spent the winter and the spring towing logs out of Neah Bay.

She continued with the same schedule for 1966 and 1967 as in 1965—summer seasons on runs to Alaska or down the coast and in the off-season towing logs for the Port Angeles office. The PACIFIC had little lay-up time—an important factor in her profit-and-loss account.

The PACIFIC had a part in the launching of Foss' history-making van service to Alaska, when on September 28, 1967 she pulled out of the Alaska Steamship Company's Pier 46 in Seattle, with Captain Walt Davis in command, towing the van-barge FOSS-291 headed for Ketchikan, Juneau, and Sitka. The cargo-barge FOSS-291 had been converted at the Foss yard to a modern container-barge and equipped with a new ballast system below decks to compensate for a deck cargo of vans. A new six-inch timber deck was laid the full length of the barge to reduce sliding. Also two diesel generators with combined output of 225 kilowatts and having special wiring were installed to service thirty-five refrigerator containers, maintaining temperatures from forty degrees above zero to forty degrees below as required by the particular cargo carried.

The purpose of the Foss and Alaska Steam sponsored trial-run was to compare the relative merits of a tug and van-barge cargo operation against a similar steamship run to Southeastern on a two-week turn around basis. For several years the service was handled by Alaska Steam's knot-class freighters TANANA and TATALINA.

James A. Cole

The PACIFIC left Seattle with the FOSS-291 carrying 111-twenty-four-foot vans nearly triple the capacity of the Knot-class ships. The voyage time was close to the same, but the operating cost much less for the tug and barge—even disregarding the added capacity of the barge. The new system proved out, it was to become big business, but in the beginning one of Alaska Steam's freighters continued to make the run on opposite weeks until a second Foss tug-and-barge unit was ready to take over in 1968. Later on Wrangell, Peterburg, and Metlakatla were added to the original itinerary. The service is now known as "Foss Alaska Line" and the Company is the primary freight mover to Southeastern Alaska, having completed by 1980, 625 voyages covering 1,000,000 miles.

The PACIFIC made only four trips on the van-run, giving way to the WEDELL with more horsepower, so she returned to Port Angeles log towing for the winter. During the summer season of 1968 and 1969, she towed to Alaska and Coastwise to Portland. Then starting in August and until the winter weather set in, she towed on the Anchorage-Kodiak container-run for Sea-Land. When the weather drove her South, she ran light to Tacoma and tied up for several weeks of repair and during the idle period Foss changed her name to EDITH so she would be a member of the Foss family in name as well as fact.

The year 1970 was not productive for the EDITH—she operated only 105 days. For the first four months she was used part-time as a Tacoma ship-assist tug with an occasional linehaul run. Then in the summer season she made three round trips to Southeastern Alaska before being called off the run when the new tugs were again able to handle all the work. The EDITH with only 1,200 horsepower and requiring an extra engineer had little chance against the 3,000 horsepower automated tugs, so she again went into lay-up at Foss-Tacoma. However, she did operate occasionally on ship work in Tacoma with a short crew.

The EDITH remained in ready-reserve until June 1971. Then she went to work on the Sound linehaul runs until the Longshoremen's strike in July brought on a re-allocation of all available tugs. The EDITH was assigned to haul fish barges between Southeastern Alaska canneries and Anacortes, staying with the job until the fishing season ended. She then took on the Milwaukee Railroad rail-barge run between Seattle and Port Townsend, on a daily basis. The EDITH held on to the service until January 8, 1972 when she, along with most of the other wood vessels of the fleet, was placed in reserve status. During the curtailed towing to Alaska in the winter months the new tugs were available for local work, so the older boats had to give way.

The Foss Ocean Division put the EDITH back to work for the 1972 Alaska season towing barges to Southeastern Alaska, including the Foss Alaska Line run, the same route she helped start in 1967. When she finished the Southeastern Alaska assignments in the fall, the EDITH returned to the lay-up fleet, but on standby. This time the dormant period lasted five months, then she returned to Port Angeles after an absence of over seven years to again tow logs from Neah Bay to Port Angeles. She towed on the Straits for several months then returned to Seattle in May 1973 to take over the Port Townsend-Seattle-Milwaukee rail-car run. For the next three years the EDITH worked the rail-car run combined with short stints for the Port Angeles office on log towing, but only during the spring and summer. As usual she rested during the winter and let the new generation tugs take over.

The spring of 1977 was the first time that the EDITH wasn't off and running and for the next twenty months she remained in lay-up waiting for her number to be called.

It came in April 1978 due to a surge of business on Puget Sound and the service of the EDITH was required to cope with the demand. She was reactiviated in a week's time, quick work considering the tug had but little maintenance for over a year-and-a-half.

On May 5, 1978, with Captain Gary Kroll in charge, the EDITH went back on the well-worn groove between Port Townsend and Seattle with the rail-car barge. But by mid-August serious tow winch and main engine problems began plaguing her and she spent more time in the repair yard than towing. A determination-survey was made and the results dictated immediate and permanent retirement. The company intended to class the EDITH as surplus in the fall as sufficient new boats were on hand to handle all the projected towing service for the next several years—the EDITH would not be missed even though she had been useful. After removing all stores and gear, the HENRIETTA shifted the EDITH 600-feet down the Canal to the Foss retirement home. But characteristic of her life with Foss, she again came out of lay-up to resume the "active life", though not for Foss.

She was sold in April 1979 to the Schnabel Lumber Company of Haines, Alaska. The Foss crew made necessary repairs for Schnable to condition the tug for the trip and service up North and the yard painted on a new name MAVIS LYNN. The tug crew gave her a new color-scheme—black hull, white house and blue trim.

She left Seattle in May for the sawmill at the head of Alaska's Lynn Canal. Her area of work would be new, but towing log rafts would not. However, during the long-distance tows required, up to 150 miles, in bringing up logs from the logging areas to the South, she will be encountering Alaska weather with greater risk involved than towing in Puget Sound, but the EDITH has the tools, so she should be a success in her new environment.

LORNA FOSS *Eastbound in Locks, February 26, 1967. (Courtesy of author's collection)*

LORNA FOSS (2)

Built:	1926	Propulsion:	Atlas
	San Diego Marine Construction		320-horsepower
	San Diego, California	Primary Service:	Puget Sound
Length:	79-feet	Final Foss Operating Day:	December 20, 1968
Beam:	19-feet	Status:	Sold - Domestic

The LORNA, built as the PALOMAR, was designed by R. L. Prewett for the Star & Crescent Boat Company, parent Company of the San Diego Marine Construction Company.

Star & Crescent installed a 240-horsepower Fairbanks Morse diesel, giving her an 11-knot speed and with a 6,000 gallon fuel capacity she had a 5,000-mile cruising range. Her area of operation for the first fifteen years encompassed San Diego, the offshore islands and Los Angeles Harbor. She was the first tug to be permanently stationed in San Diego since the steam tug BAHADA left in 1917.

With the advent of World War II, the PALOMAR was taken over by the War Shipping Administration and used in barging material along the southern California coast. Then at the conclusion of her war service in 1946, Pacific Tow & Salvage at Long Beach bought her and installed a 320-horsepower Atlas diesel. Pacific used her for the next four years in general towing to the Channel Islands, harbor work in Long Beach, and oil exploration work in Santa Barbara Channel.

In late 1950 ownership and use was transferred to Bellingham Tug & Barge, the transfer was quick and easy with both companies part of the Foss organization. Upon arrival in Bellingham in December, 1950 she officially became a unit of Bellingham Tug & Barge. Before starting regular towing service improvements were made. She ended up with modern living quarters, new keel condenser, rebuilt guard rails, and additional fuel tanks. The last job was to paint her in Bellingham's colors—black hull, red and white house and big "B" on the stack.

The PALOMAR came to the Northwest fitted with a double-drum towing winch, a type not common at the time to Puget Sound tugs. In order to take advantage of the two drums, B. T. & B. put her on a steady run during 1951 and 1952 towing pulp chip barges in tandem, one on each wire, from Vancouver, British Columbia to Puget Sound Pulp and Timber in Bellingham. On the international run, she was in charge of alternate skippers, Chet Carlson and Dick Lamont.

When the PALOMAR left the chip run, she went on general barge towing and log towing, though still working out of Bellingham. But in April of 1960 Foss-Seattle put her on the cement run from Bellingham to Seattle and the chemical run from Monsanto Chemical in Seattle to Bellingham. She worked so well on special barge towing that Foss officially took over ownership on August 15, 1960 and renamed her LORNA FOSS.

During the next several years she worked for Foss-Seattle, on the long runs to Bellingham and on the shorter gravel haul out of Steilacoom and the various oil barge runs around the Sound.

The LORNA came close to ending her career at the finish of one of her oil delivery trips to Olympia. After returning the empty barge to Seattle the evening of December 2, 1964 she proceeded to the Mobil Oil pier to take on diesel fuel, but the one item the LORNA did not need at the time was more fuel. About 2315 the LORNA, alongside the Mobil Pier, reported to the Foss office that the engine room was on fire, and the fire department called. The FOSS 18, ordered to the scene, arrived to find the Fire Department on the job and pouring foam and water into the engine room and the LORNA's crew on the pier out of danger. The first report to the office inferred that the LORNA would be a total loss, but the reporter forgot the efficiency of the Seattle Fire Department, for at 2340 hours the FOSS 18 called in and reported the fire extinguished and the LORNA in safe condition. Inspection showed the probable cause of the fire to be a generator short-circuit and explosion. The engine room was well scorched and all machinery water damaged, but the rest of the tug was untouched. The same night she was towed to the Foss yard for repair.

With the towing business slack during the winter, the LORNA's repair was not rushed, so the work was not completed until May 6. On May 12, Foss had her back on the gravel run for Washington Asphalt Company, Glacier Sand and Gravel, Seattle Ready Mix, and as in the previous year, part-time delivering oil.

By late 1967 with new efficient steel tugs in service, use for the LORNA was rapidly declining, so in December she was placed on standby status. In the first four months of 1968 she worked only twenty-five days, and between April and early December she didn't leave the dock.

Her last call came on December 17 due to a surge of petroleum business. She towed oil barges for three days, then by December 20th oil deliveries were again normal. After towing the Foss-96 to Seattle from Everett, she was ordered to lay-up at Foss-Seattle and the crew paid off. As the LORNA was no longer competitive, she never again operated with a Foss crew aboard.

On May 7, 1969 Foss sold her to the Sweet family of Seattle for use in exploration work and private cruising. They renamed her SEARCHMASTER and for nearly ten years they berthed her on the Duwamish River, occasionally leaving for a cruise or charter work. From her appearance she was well maintained, her white paint job always clean and shining.

Once again, in February, 1979 she was sold—this time to Keith Sternberg of Tacoma, an independent towboat operator, who previously owned the tugs BEE and INVERNESS. His primary work was log towing. After the sale was finalized, he renamed her PALOMAR, her original name. PALOMAR is Spanish for pigeon house, but no doubt the tug was named after the California mountain. Anyway, the PALOMAR tows again.

LORNA FOSS (3)

Built:	1944	Propulsion:	Enterprise (Twin)
	Everett Marine Ways		1,270-horsepower
	Everett, Washington	Primary Service:	Puget Sound
Length:	103-feet	Final Foss Operating Day:	August 23, 1976
Beam:	27-feet	Status:	Sold-Domestic

The last tug to carry the name LORNA was one of several wood YTB-Class tugs built for the U.S. Navy by Everett Marine Ways. Everett's sawmills furnished the clear douglas fir for her planking and timbering. The navy assigned the tug number YTB-289, the number supposedly representing the number of like naval auxiliaries at the time, however, she did have a paper name, SAKAWESTON.

The YTB-289 operated for the navy on Puget Sound, assisting naval vessels in port and towing supply barges, port to port. She continued in the service for several years even after World War II and until the navy declared her surplus and available for sale by sealed bid. Foss entered an offer and on November 29, 1960 they received word that their bid was accepted and that the 289, with extensive fire-fighting equipment intact, could be removed from the Bremerton Navy yard.

Foss towed the tug to their Tacoma base and put her into temporary lay-up for eleven months, but the yard crew did work on her part time. They overhauled the machinery, installed a towing winch and ship-handling gear, but no structural or house changes were necessary. A change of name was called for, and the 289 became the LUMMI BAY, under the ownership of Bellingham Tug and Barge, at the time running the "show" for Foss in the upper Sound.

In 1961 the SEA KING, a sister-tug of the LUMMI BAY, handled all the heavy work for B. T. & B., but a second tug would soon be required for tanker-assists as traffic was increasing at the northern refineries.

The LUMMI BAY, ready for service in early October 1961 headed for Bellingham, her new home base and two days later she made her trial towing run with an empty chip scow to Vancouver, B.C. and a loaded scow back from New Westminster to Bellingham. She remained at Bellingham on local work, assisting the SEA KING, but working only part time as she was not crewed on a full time basis.

The LUMMI BAY was introduced to log towing in March 1962 and with a full crew aboard, she towed thirty-six sections from Bellingham and Anacortes to Everett and Seattle. She continued off and on with log towing until the fall when harbor assist work in the Seattle area rapidly increased, while log towing and ship-assists in the northern Sound were temporarily curtailed, necessitating a switch of tugs. On October 1 the LUMMI BAY was assigned to Seattle harbor duties and the veteran SANDRA FOSS sent to Bellingham. With business demands dictating, the LUMMI BAY, surprisingly, worked out of Foss-Seattle for the next ten years, and not Bellingham as originally scheduled.

The LUMMI BAY was a welcome addition to the Seattle harbor fleet, joining the CAROL, SHANNON, and FOSS-18. In addition to ship work, Foss used her on the rail-car run to both Squamish, B.C. and Port Townsend, with frequent runs towing the large oil barge FOSS-98 from the refineries at Anacortes to tank farms in Seattle and Tacoma.

However, the LUMMI BAY did a stint at Anacortes as ship-assist tug, relieving the SEA KING for two months in the spring of 1964. Then as the summer of 1964 was an extremely busy one for the Ocean Division, they ran out of tugs to fulfill their commitments, so the LUMMI BAY, being the closest vessel to an ocean-class tug, was recruited for the season. After outfitting for coastwise towing, she left on July 17, 1964 on her first Alaska job, towing the bulk-cement barge FOSS-204 from Seattle to Anchorage and return. She remained on the Alaska run until late September when seasonal towing eased off, then the LUMMI BAY returned to the Port Townsend car-barge run.

In late January 1965 with twenty-one years of operation to her credit, she entered the Foss shipyard in Tacoma for a major overhaul of machinery and routine hull and deck maintenance. The repair progressed at a slow pace and it was May before all the work was completed, but she came out almost as good as new. Between late May 1965 and September she made a number of trips to Anchorage and southeastern Alaska. Then as in 1964, she finished up the year and early spring towing in Puget Sound. The same routine was followed from 1966 through 1968—Alaska in the summer season and Puget Sound in the winter.

Among the LUMMI BAY's regular stops in Southeastern were two herring-reduction plants in Chatham Straits, producing oil and fishmeal. In the mid-1920's many herring-reduction plants were opened in southeastern Alaska to process the Chatham Straits' catches. The plants continued in seasonal operation until World War II when the government put a freeze on the production of herring by-products, fishmeal and fish oil. Herring oil was used in the manufacture of soap and the meal used as a food supplement for poultry and livestock. However, many plants remained closed even after the ban was lifted in 1946 as the demand for herring products had seriously declined.

In the late 1940's when Foss tugs and barges relieved Alaska Steamship Company on the runs to the herring plants, there were only three outfits left in operation, located at Port Armstrong, Big Port Walter, and Washington Bay—all in Chatham Straits. The tugs dropped off empty barges at the plants in early summer while enroute to Anchorage with their loaded cargo barges. During the three to four month herring season, the southbound tugs from Anchorage would stop in at one or two of the plants and pick up loaded barges and bring them to Seattle along with the empty cargo barges from Anchorage. The three plants shared the barges assigned to their service and the barges were held in the staging area at Washington Bay, moored to a buoy until shifted to one of the plants for loading.

The three major plants were similar in style and operation, but with different owners. The Washington Bay plant was owned by the Storfold and Grondahl Packing Company with Bud McCartney, plant manager. The plant usually opened in early June and only shut down after the last barge was loaded, usually in late September after the close of the fishing season. Thirty men were required to run the plant, working twelve-hour shifts around the clock. An average of ten tons of herring were processed each hour with a fifteen percent recovery in meal and fifteen percent recovery in oil. The reduction process was simple but interesting, although the tugs' and ships' crews that travel Chatham Straits today wonder how a herring plant made a go of it—with such small fish.

Bud McCartney related that the herring, traveling on a screw conveyor were first cooked in live steam under ten pounds pressure. Then to recover the fish oil the herring went into a meal press, squeezing the fish against a mesh screen and the released oil dropped into collectors and on into tanks—the Washington Bay tanks had a capacity of 200,000 gallons. After the oil was extracted, the solids were fed into a 7' × 60' dryer and when dried they were dropped into a grinder and the pulverized meal sacked in 100-pound bags for storing in lofts until loaded aboard a barge. The meal was stowed in the barge holds and the oil in bulk tanks. During an average season of three months, 12,000 tons of herring were processed at the Washington Bay Plant.

In the late 1950's the catches began to dwindle and government restrictions were placed on the herring industry. The area open to fishing decreased and by the mid-1960's there was literally no place to fish for herring. The Port Armstrong plant closed after the 1963 season. Washington Bay found it impossible to continue operations after the 1965 season and in 1966 only Big Port Walter, owned by Wilber-Ellis, remained in operation. But the season turned out to be short and unprofitable with only a few barge loads of meal and a few tanks of oil produced. In September 1966 the LUMMI BAY made the final trip for the herring industry barging out the last shipment just before the complete closure, ending a long chapter in southeastern Alaska fishing history. At her departure on September 13 with a cargo of 35,000 gallons of herring oil and 300 tons of fishmeal, the last of twelve processing plants in southeastern Alaska closed. A watchman at Port Walter remained to look after the property and machinery until October 1973. By that time the dock was a shambles and several buildings in ruins; only the watchman's house was kept in a state of repair. In 1975 most of the machinery was removed and the old wooden buildings were burned by the Forest Service. Another era, another industry, ended without recourse.

With or without the herring industry, the LUMMI BAY continued to serve Alaska and during the 1969 season, with Captain Trygve Stangland in command, she made six round trips between Seattle and Cordova, towing a container-barge for Foss Alaska Line. The run, only temporary, lasted between May and September 1969.

During the winter of 1969-1970, the LUMMI BAY became the LORNA FOSS, the third tug to carry the name of the wife of a nephew of Andrew Foss. As the LORNA FOSS, she made one trip to Anchorage in 1970 and 1971 and in 1972 she made one trip to Sitka with an oil barge and two trips to Ketchikan to bring back barges of canned salmon. And she wasn't idle the rest of the year. Foss kept her going in the Sound, but the sand had just about run out of her glass.

In December, 1972 with ample new tugs available for towing and ship work on Puget Sound, the LORNA was placed in ready-reserve. Then in April 1973 she finally made it back to Bellingham as second ship-assist tug, remaining on a full-time basis until 1976. But due to the new escort laws for tankers and the increasing size of ships, she was replaced by the 3,000 horsepower RICHARD FOSS. The LORNA held on as the third tug, but without a steady crew.

During the summer of 1976 she was used only to relieve the IVER while the IVER was being repaired. Then in August she was crewed up for just ten days to assist in linehaul towing between Seattle and Bellingham. But after delivering a chemical barge to Bellingham on August 23, 1976 the crew was released—the LORNA had performed her last towing job for Foss. She remained idle at Bellingham for six weeks in event she could be used, but the necessity did not arise.

On October 8 the new 2,900 horsepower STACEY FOSS was ready to join the RICHARD in the Bellingham operation and on October 8 a four-man crew fired up the LORNA and ran her to the Foss-Seattle yard, then they returned to Bellingham with the STACEY.

In a matter of days, the LORNA was stripped of all operating gear, and shifted to the lay-up moorings. Within a month she was joined by her sister-tug, the IVER, also losing her happy home in Bellingham to the new giants.

For a short time the LORNA came out of lay-up and went back on the Foss payroll earning her way as a training-ship for future crews. However, sufficient crewmen became available from the usual sources so the training program was terminated. Another reason for cancelling could have been that the graduates were nicknamed "LORNA DOONES." In June of 1980 the LORNA was sold to Mr. Frank Huff of Seattle who turned his vessel into a pleasure tug with the new name BLACKFISH showing on the bows.

ROLAND FOSS (2)

Built:	1943	Propulsion:	Washington
	Puget Sound Bridge and Dredge		400-horsepower
	Seattle, Washington	Primary Service:	Puget Sound
Length:	77-feet	Final Foss Operating Day:	May 5, 1974
Beam:	20-feet	Status:	Sold - Domestic

The ROLAND, first of three identical Navy tugs, was built by Puget Sound Bridge & Dredge Company during World War II. The tugs were identified by Navy numbers, the ROLAND YTB-361 and the sister-tugs YTB-362 and YTB-363. The YTBs were used in Alaska and Puget Sound as general service tugs. The 361 served the Navy for seventeen years, then in 1960 she was declared surplus and sold by sealed bid on October 28, 1960 to the Foss Company. On November 25, the ELAINE towed her to the Foss-Seattle yard for outfitting.

After three months of yard work the tug was ready to take on a job, under the name ROLAND FOSS. Not since 1946 had the name ROLAND been carried on the roster of active tugs.

The ROLAND began her Foss career on March 2, 1961 with Captain Gil Behrendt in charge, by towing a loaded oil barge between Seattle and Tacoma, to try out the machinery. As all parts functioned normally, the ROLAND became a regular linehaul tug, taking part in all the established barge runs handled by the Seattle office.

Then in September 1961 when the MARGARET with the FOSS-109 came to Seattle from southeastern Alaska for annual repair, Foss sent the ROLAND north as the replacement tug on the Alaska oil run. With more logging communities added to the route and some having narrow harbor entrances and many located in shallow-water bays and inlets, the ROLAND with her light draft was well-suited for the job.

She provided reliable service so Foss kept her on the run for the next five years, but the time came in 1966 to give way to her sister-tug, the ROGER FOSS. The only difference in the two tugs, but an important factor in making the change, was the ROGER's additional 150 horsepower due to a super-charger on the heavy-duty Washington diesel.

The ROLAND returned to Seattle for a major overhaul and then started full-time duty on the Puget Sound linehauls. She remained for the rest of her active status with Foss working out of the Seattle office, never venturing more than 150 miles from home.

Then in the fall of 1970 the ROLAND gave up general towing and went on charter to Puget Sound Freight Lines for towing cargo-barges on the Sound and from southern British Columbia ports. The charter was "bareboat" and the only Foss crewman was Morris Pixley, the Chief Engineer. The rest were P. S. Freight Lines men.

During the charter the ROLAND came close to sinking. It happened while towing a barge loaded with 800 tons of pulp across the Straits, between Port Angeles and Victoria, B.C. When approaching the Canadian side, the weather rapidly worsened and strong winds with rough seas buffeted the tug. The ROLAND began rolling heavily in the trough of the seas and water poured in the engine room from an undisclosed leak in the hull. The Chief started the bilge pump, but the flood of water was too much for the pump and in minutes the water sloshed over the engine-room floor plates. The Captain called the Coast Guard in Victoria for assistance, but they were unable to respond. The Chief warned the Captain that he couldn't keep her afloat for more than an hour. With the tug hove-to and exposed to the seas in open water, the Captain had no choice but to cut the barge adrift and head for the shelter of Beecher Bay. After dropping the towline and the barge, which came to anchor by the weight of the line, the ROLAND made for the Bay as fast as the seas would allow. The ROLAND won the race, but a few minutes more and the water would have smothered the engine room machinery and the tug would have foundered.

Anchored in quiet water, the leak eased up and the chief was able to pump out the engine room. Then he changed oil in the main engine as the oil was contaminated with salt water.

The next day and in calm seas, the ROLAND proceeded to Seattle. With the flat water and the hull not straining, the leaking was minimal, so they arrived in Seattle unaided. The barge was picked up by a Canadian tug and delivered to Victoria none the worse for riding out the gale.

The inspection at the Foss yard revealed twenty-five feet of caulking out below the guards on the port side. After recaulking, the ROLAND went back to her regular work and stayed on the job without lay-up through 1972. But by this time Foss had several new and powerful tugs to call on, so the 400-horsepower ROLAND with a thirty-year-old heavy-duty engine and requiring an engineer, could no longer hold her own against the modern hotshot tugs.

The ROLAND was idle during the first few months of 1973, then as several of the new tugs were assigned to Alaska during the summer and fall, Foss used her on an intermittent basis, but with the arrival of winter, her operating days were few and far between. In the first few months of 1974 the ROLAND operated two or three days a month—only as a fill-in boat.

On her last assignment for Foss, May 4, 1974 she towed the loaded bulk-cement barge FOSS-157 from Bellingham to Seattle. She remained on the active list the remainder of the season, but the tug was never used. The ROLAND was placed on reserve status in October 1974 and declared surplus in 1975.

The tug remained in the lay-up fleet until December 1976 when Foss sold her to Robert Bainter of Longbranch, Washington. Mr. Bainter changed her name to CHIPPEWA and ran the tug to Juneau, Alaska where he made her available for general towing. On several occasions when time was not of the essence, the ROLAND made barge tows between Seattle and Juneau and apparently she pulled on the towline as well as ever. When not towing in Alaska, the CHIPPEWA is berthed at Longbranch on southern Puget Sound, doubling as a family yacht. Tug or yacht—ROLAND or CHIPPEWA—she is only thirty-six years old—and compared to the SIMON, FOSS 15, WALLACE, and the rest of the ex-Foss venerables, she still has a long life ahead of her.

FOSS ACQUIRES FIVE DELTA SMYTH TUGS

In September, 1961 Foss purchased all the tugboats belonging to the Delta Smyth Towing Company of Olympia, consisting of the linehaul tugs AUDREY and HOONAH, plus the harbor tugs OYSTERMAN, PARTHIA, and RUFUS. Foss repainted the boats to their own identifying colors, green and white, but they retained the Smyth names.

Delta V. Smyth, founder of the Smyth Company, started his tugboat career about 1910 working on the tug OYSTERMAN for the Brenner Oyster Company. Later on he purchased the tug and began a towing business in Olympia that lasted until the sale to Foss. Smyth owned and operated thirty-two tugs during forty years of tugboating, but at the time of the sale, the fleet was composed of only five vessels. The tugs were small and low-powered compared to the average Foss tug in the Sixties and Seventies, so they were given only limited use.

The PARTHIA, oldest of the Smyth boats was built at Winslow, Washington in 1906. She started out with a fifty horsepower gasoline engine, then advanced to a seventy-five horsepower heavy-duty oil engine, next an eighty-five horsepower Cummins and her final engine, a 165 horsepower General Motors diesel—all installed during her ownership with Smyth. The timbering to take ever-increasing engine power indicates the hull strength shipyards built into early tugs.

Foss retained the PARTHIA in Olympia for harbor service until the early seventies then transferred her to the Pacific Shipyard in Anacortes for use as a yard tug. In 1975 Foss sold her to Pacific Shipyard and they used the PARTHIA for several years, then disposed of her to private interests for conversion to a fish boat.

The AUDREY was originally a Puget Sound passenger steamer built in 1909 at Tacoma for the Wollochet Bay freight and passenger service. She next became a shrimp trawler and eventually ended up as a tugboat when purchased by the Delta Smyth Towing Company during World War II. Smyth converted the AUDREY for towing, gave her diesel power and used her for local and short-range towing in Olympia and chip-barge towing. Soon after the purchase Foss placed the AUDREY in the surplus category, laid her up and sold her in 1963.

The OYSTERMAN, another wood boat forty-six-feet long, was built in 1913 by the Brenner Oyster Company for use tending their oyster beds. After many years with Brenner, Smyth chartered and then eventually purchased the boat. The OYSTERMAN worked around the harbor throughout Smyth's ownership, but she was not used after purchase by Foss and the tug remained tied up until 1963—then she was stripped of equipment in Tacoma and the hull donated to the Tacoma Athletic Commission for burning in the 1963 Independence Day celebration.

The largest tug in Smyth's fleet, the HOONAH, sixty-six feet in length was built in Bellingham in 1919, a wood hull cannery tender, for Pan American Fisheries. She remained in their service for three decades before becoming a unit of the Delta Smyth Company. She was powered by a 210 horsepower Hendy diesel, a San Francisco made engine; the HOONAH was one of the few tugs in the Northwest powered by a Hendy. Smyth used the tug on lower Sound towing principally on log rafts, but when Foss took over they used her as a back-up tug on linehaul work out of Tacoma. She was frequently on the Graystone gravel run to Olympia and occasionally, especially during her last year of service, made runs with chip scows from Shelton to Everett and Port Townsend.

The HOONAH by 1964 could no longer compete in time, cost or revenue with the new Foss tugs, so she was laid up in late September and twelve months later sold for use as a private yacht in the San Juan Islands. Then in 1975 she was sold to a private party in San Francisco and while under way to her new home, she attempted to go into Grays Harbor for protection from heavy weather, but ran into the entrance jetty. The fifty-six-year-old tug was quickly broken up by the battering of the breaking seas. Fortunately the crew was able to get off uninjured.

The newest tug of Smyth's fleet, the RUFUS, a 46-foot harbor tug, was built by the Henry Long Boatworks at Olympia in 1957. She was modern in all respects and classed as the flagship. With her 300 horsepower, she performed well for Smyth and for Foss in all her harbor chores.

The RUFUS remained in Olympia until mid-1971 then she was transferred to the Tacoma Harbor division where she worked until April 1972. With newer tugs available, Foss put her on the surplus list along with a number of other older tugs, that had served their time. In October 1972 the RUFUS was sold to Lloyd Harding of Tacoma who renamed the tug DENISE H.

With the shift of the RUFUS from Olympia to Tacoma in 1971 the last of the Delta Smyth tugs passed out of Foss hands. Steel had taken over for wood in the Foss modernization program and the wood tugs became expendable. However, Olympia was not slighted as Foss continued to take care of the ship-assists from the Tacoma office with Tacoma boats, and Roy Willey's Olympia Towing Company handled the general harbor work.

ROGER FOSS *Photographed on Lake Washington Ship Canal in February of 1964. (Courtesy of author's collection)*

ROGER FOSS

Built:	1943	Propulsion:	Caterpillar
	Puget Sound Bridge &		765-horsepower
	Dredge Company	Primary Service:	Puget Sound
	Seattle, Washington	Final Foss Operating Day:	September 11, 1976
Length:	77-feet	Status:	Sold - Domestic
Beam:	20-feet		

The ROGER, along with the ROLAND FOSS were identical tugs built by P.S.B. & D. for the U.S. Navy early in World War II. The ROGER was designated YTL-362.

Though classed as a harbor tug it did not prevent her or a third sister-tug, the YTL-363 from venturing over 2,000 miles to remote navy bases in Alaska's Aleutian Islands. They returned across the stormy Gulf of Alaska after a period of service to their fair weather home-base in Bremerton. A three week voyage in a seventy-seven-foot tug with a minimum of living accommodations, combined with typical adverse southwestern Alaska weather, was a trying experience for the crew, but anything goes in war.

After the 362 returned she remained on the Sound until the late fifties. Then she went into lay-up until August 1961 when she was advertised for sale by sealed bid. Foss was the successful bidder and on September 1 they towed her to their Canal moorings to await reactivation and machinery overhaul, so necessary after years of hard work for the navy.

In early 1963 repair began to bring her up to Foss requirements. The yard crew spent nearly six months on overhaul before they were ready to cover the navy gray with Foss green and white. She started work on September 25, 1963 carrying the name of ROGER FOSS in honor of a great-grandson of Theodore.

For the ROGER's test run, Foss sent her to Ladysmith, B.C. on October 2, 1963 to pick up a tow of logs for delivery to Bellingham. However, the tug did very little log-towing during her thirteen Foss years. Her primary service was towing cement, oil, and chemical barges on runs to Anacortes, Bellingham, and Ferndale. With her Washington diesel supercharged to 550-horsepower, the ROGER was able to make a typical 175-mile round trip to Bellingham in about twenty-six hours running time, much less time than the fifty-year-old tugs making the same runs.

After three years of continuous service on Puget Sound linehauls, the ROGER in September 1966 left the security of the Sound for the rigors of southeastern Alaska. She went North to relieve the ROLAND FOSS and tow the FOSS-109 on the Union Oil delivery run. The ROGER remained in southeastern Alaska working out of Ketchikan from September 1966 until December 1967 when she was replaced by the new steel tug, DELORES FOSS, with twice the horsepower and better able to buck the winter weather.

Back home, the ROGER entered the Foss shipyard for voyage repairs and then in mid-January 1967 she returned to her former linehaul runs on Puget Sound, remaining on the job until an engine breakdown idled her in September 1969.

While towing an empty oil barge from Boundary Bay to Seattle, the main engine crankshaft broke—the most serious accident that could happen to the engine. The ROGER called for a tow to the Foss yard and upon arrival a survey was made indicating the engine would have to be disassembled and a new crank fabricated. The estimated cost proved prohibitive. The answer was to install a new 765-horsepower high-speed Caterpillar diesel. An added incentive to make the change-over would be the elimination of an engineer in the tug's crew.

After six months in the Foss-Seattle yard, the ROGER came out with a shining yellow Caterpillar in the engine room. Her performance was excellent with the added power, but Foss only made use of the advantage for three months, then they chartered her to Puget Sound Freight Lines on a bareboat basis for one year. P.S.F.L. was in the process of expanding their covered-barge freight service on Puget Sound and British Columbia and to provide tugs for the new routes two tugs were being built. For interim towing while the new tugs were under construction, a tug with the ROGER's capabilities was needed, so Foss helped out. After the ROGER's charter started in June, but before the year was up, the contract was extended another twelve months, which meant until the second new tug entered service. The contract concluded on May 31, 1972 and after drydocking and repair, the ROGER returned to her customary duty, towing cement, oil, and chemical barges around the Sound.

After four years of "off and on" linehaul work, the ROBER in August 1976 was idled by a general decline in the towing business. She remained inactive at Foss-Seattle until November 1976 when Pacific Tow & Salvage at Long Beach needed two tugs for use on a run to the Santa Barbara Islands and Foss agreed to supply the boats.

On November 16, 1976 the ROGER and another tug in lay-up, the GARY FOSS, left their base of long-standing for P.T.& S., arriving five days later. After a short period of outfitting in Long Beach, the ROGER headed for San Diego, her new home port. After arrival P.T.& S. repainted the tugs to their own identifying colors—black hull, white cabins, and blue trim. At the same time, they painted on a new name: SAN JACINTO!

When Pacific was satisfied with her appearance they put the tug to work towing a supply barge regularly between San Diego and San Clemente Island, on a logistics run for the navy. When she has free time, the SAN JACINTO works as a harbor tug in San Diego, assisting the three regular tugs—PALOMAR, CORONADO, and PACIFIC GEMINI. From all appearances the ex-ROGER has become a permanent resident of California.

ALASKA ROUSTABOUT

Built:	1944	Propulsion:	General Motors (Triple)
	Mare Island Shipyard		675-horsepower
	Vallejo, California	Primary Service:	Cook Inlet, Alaska
Length:	100-feet	Final Foss Operating Day:	September 28, 1962
Beam:	34-feet	Status:	Sold - Domestic

The ALASKA ROUSTABOUT, originally naval vessel YFU-40, was built as a roll-on, roll-off cargo ship for use in beach landings. After her active navy service she was held in the reserve fleet at Long Beach until 1962, then at a government surplus sale in March, Foss purchased the ship for work in Alaska. The YFU type of vessel was ideal for delivering supplies in connection with Alaska oil exploration where no structures existed for cargo handling. Foss decided to outfit the YFU-40 at Long Beach where the ship was tied up, so she would be ready for work at departure from California. As planned, she sailed direct to Alaska and is the only Foss boat never to enter Puget Sound at any time in her Foss life.

The ROUSTABOUT arrived in Cook Inlet after a two-week trip and spent the summer of 1962 shuttling cargo to beach sites and to drilling rigs for the pioneering oil companies. In September, however, the ROUSTABOUT left the protection of the Inlet and crossed the Gulf of Alaska to Icy Bay to pick up a load of drill pipe for eventual delivery to Seward. She remained in Icy Bay for the next two weeks, on-call for Standard Oil Company, before going to Seward.

Though the seas were threatening, the ROUSTABOUT left Icy Bay on September 27, bound for Seward with the drill pipe and for several days no radio contact could be made with the boat. She was reported overdue at Seward so an air search was started by Foss and the Coast Guard. Finally at dusk on October 1, search planes spotted the overturned hull between Cape St. Elias and Cape Hinchenbrook at the entrance to Prince William sound.

There was no sign of survivors and it was feared that Captain Don Gordon and his crew had been trapped inside when the ship rolled over. However, the next day after continued air and sea search, the ROUSTABOUT's life raft was spotted, with men aboard. A Coast Guard Patrol vessel came alongside and took off the entire crew of the ROUSTABOUT! All the men were in stable condition but suffering from exposure. They were taken to Cordova for a routine check-up before returning to Anchorage and then home to Seattle.

When thawed out, Captain Gordon reported that the ROUSTABOUT had capsized on September 28, probably due to loss of stability from hull leaks. Apparently several fractures had developed in the steel hull and the pumps could not handle the great inrush of water, but the men had about an hour to abandon ship from the first sign that the flooding could not be controlled, so they had time to prepare for the worst and it was just as well because they drifted in the open life raft for nearly four days before being rescued. Fortunately they had water, food, and survival gear in the raft; otherwise the experience might have had a tragic ending. The Gulf of Alaska with its 40-degree water, requiring double bottom rafts, the cold air, and stormy weather was a treacherous part of the North Pacific to be adrift on with only an inflated rubber raft.

The crew recovered and so did the ROUSTABOUT. She was towed upside down to Cordova and sold shortly thereafter to Guy Beedle of Cordova in an "as-is-where-is" condition. She was righted, cleaned up, and entered service in 1964 as the small freight vessel HOLLY C—operating for Gulf Navigation and Towing Company of Anchorage.

From recent reports she has been sailing for the last fifteen years—right side up.

ARTHUR FOSS (2)

Built:	1943	Propulsion:	Nordberg (Twin)
	Marietta Manufacturing Company		5,000-horsepower
	Point Pleasant, West Virginia	Primary Service:	Ocean - Coastwise
Length:	141-feet	Status:	In Lay-up
Beam:	33-feet		

ARTHUR FOSS *Shown entering Shilshole Bay upon return from delivering an oil drilling platform to Cook Inlet in Spring of 1967. (From the author's collection)*

During World War II the Army Transport Service built a number of large steam-uniflow tugs on the East Coast and the ARTHUR FOSS, cx-LT-784, was one of the group. She operated out of the New York Port of Embarkation in general towing service along the Atlantic Seaboard and on trans-Atlantic convoy duty.

The record shows she took part in Atlantic Convoy #119 which left New York on September 19, 1944 under command of a Captain Clarke. The LT-784, with her twenty-one-man ATS crew, was assigned two carfloats and a tug numbered ST-510, to tow on the 3,000 mile run to Falmouth, England. Included in the convoy were nine other LT's, three of the LT-784-class. The tugs were to cross the Atlantic, towing fourteen carfloats, twelve deck-cargo barges and fifteen 85-foot ST's (Small Tugs). Sixteen small, self-propelled YO's (yard oilers) were also a part of the convoy. The flotilla covered an area ten thousand yards wide by two thousand, two hundred yards long—quite a target area for submarine attack. Fortunately, none came. But the convoy, all the way from New York to Falmouth, was beset with storm after storm, turning an otherwise manageable convoy into chaos. Towing gear parted fouling propellers and the ST's, not good seaboats in heavy weather, plunged and rolled dangerously behind the towlines of the larger tugs. The riding crews aboard the ST's took a beating, tossed from bulkhead to bulkhead along the bucking slippery flooded decks, often standing on the side bulkheads instead of the flat decks. The tugs and their tows were heaved about like buoys right up to within a few days from destination, but the battered convoy finally reached Falmouth on October 19, 1944. The toll exacted by the wild, overwhelming seas came to three ST's sunk, including the nineteen men serving aboard, eight carfloats and five barges also lost—Convoy #19 ended up one of the most weather-harassed of the small-vessel convoys.

After a few days rest in port, the LT's returned to New York in company with Navy Task Group 27.5. Shortly after arrival the LT-784 was transferred to the West Coast to carry on her war duties and she continued in towing service for some time after the War. Eventually she was put in the reserve fleet in Richmond, California, to wait out her time until she could be declared surplus and sold to private industry.

The LT-784, after inspection by the Foss Company, was later purchased by them at a January 23, 1962 government sale. The MARY FOSS, an ex-Army Miki-Class tug, went down to Richmond and towed the 784 to Foss-Seattle, arriving February 5.

During the next four years, the 784 was entirely rebuilt into a modern ocean-going diesel tug, capable of the toughest towing assignments. Repowered with twin Nordberg diesels, driving a single eleven-foot variable-pitch propeller, she was capable of running light at speeds in excess of fifteen knots. The fuel capacity was 150,000 gallons. Running light at an economical speed (on one engine), she had a cruising range of 12,000 miles without refueling. During the rebuild, in January 1965 the 784 became the second ARTHUR FOSS. At the time of completion in late 1965, the ARTHUR and her sister-tug, the HENRY FOSS (2) were the most powerful tugs in the United States.

During the week of February 2, 1966 dock and sea trials were successfully completed and the ARTHUR was ready for her first towing assignment as a member of the 70-tug Foss fleet. On February 12, 1966 Captain Ed Saling and his eleven-man crew ran the ARTHUR to Port Albernie, British Columbia and picked up the Canadian barge, HAIDA CARRIER, loaded with rolls of newsprint and delivered the cargo to Long Beach, California. All parts were still ''go'' after the first run, so the ARTHUR was ready to take on longer and heavier tows.

The year 1966 was a big one in the off-shore oil industry in Cook Inlet, Alaska, and the ARTHUR helped to make it so. Between April and December 1966 she towed two derrick barges, two drill platforms, and countless flat-deck cargo barges between California and the oil fields of Middle Cook Inlet. After the ARTHUR's successful first season, the Foss Company was pleased to hear the ARTHUR termed ''Pride of the Pacific.''

In March, with the ice breaking up in the inlet, the ARTHUR again started towing platforms between California and Cook Inlet. During the 1967 season, the ARTHUR safely delivered three, ten-thousand-ton drill platforms to the Inlet for the major oil companies. Then with winter approaching, closing off the Alaska season, the ARTHUR left for warmer climates taking along the 525-foot ex-C4 troop carrier, GENERAL H. B. FREEMAN, from Seattle to Galveston, Texas for conversion to a full container ship. After delivering the FREEMAN, the ARTHUR met the RICHARD FOSS at Panama and took over the tow of another C4 type the GENERAL M. M. PATRICK, for delivery to Galveston.

As a container ship, the FREEMAN was renamed the NEWARK and put on the run between Seattle and Anchorage for Sea-Land. The PATRICK became Sea-Land's container ship, BOSTON.

During the next two years the ARTHUR towed two more World War II troop carriers to Texas for conversion. Starting in August 1968 she towed the MARINE SERPENT from Seattle to Galveston for rebuilding to the Sea-Land ship GALVESTON, for use on the Seattle-Anchorage run. Then in 1969 the ARTHUR took the GENERAL MARK HERSHEY from the Gulf Coast fo Alameda, California to be rebuilt for Sea-Land and renamed ST. LOUIS.

The first ship rescue operation the ARTHUR performed occurred in February 1968 when the tanker, MAN-DOIL II collided with the freighter SUWAHARU MARU, about twenty-five miles off the Columbia River. The ARTHUR was dispatched to tow the damaged SUWAHARU MARU to Victoria, British Columbia, for repairs. The tow was short and easy for the 5,000 horsepower ARTHUR, taking only eight days for the round trip.

Returning from Victoria, the ARTHUR picked up two barges and towed them to Japan. Then after a short lay-over in port, she took in tow a large drill platform for delivery to Cook Inlet. The Pacific crossing was made on the stormy northern route but presented no problems. Total time of the round trip voyage, ending in Seattle in mid-July came to one hundred and thirty-one days.

Another long-haul voyage occurred in 1970 when the ARTHUR, under Captain Tom King, completed a record voyage from Seattle to Houston and back around to Prudhoe Bay, Alaska and return to Seattle. Departing Seattle on April 22, 1970 she ran light to Houston and picked up a Foss barge loaded with oil-field equipment for British Petroleum Alaska. The return trip was comfortable and made on schedule. After a fuel stop in Seattle and picking up a second barge of equipment, brought around from the Gulf by one of the new Foss tugs on her way home from the builder's yard, the ARTHUR headed for the ice-clogged waters of the Arctic Ocean. She made it only as far as Port Clarence, Alaska and for the next five weeks waited for the ice to move out from around Pt. Barrow. The wind finally moved the ice away from the shore far enough to enable the ARTHUR to pass around the northern tip of North America—she made it through to Prudhoe Bay on August 11. After discharging the barges, the ARTHUR headed home to Seattle and with no ice problems arrived on September 14. Eighteen thousand miles of water had slipped past in one hundred and eleven days, not including ice-detention time, a laurel page in the ARTHUR's history.

It wasn't long before the ARTHUR made another interesting entry in her log book. In April 1971 under the guiding hand of Captain Guy Johnson, she towed the 27,800-ton aircraft carrier, PHILIPPINE SEA, from San Diego to the Zidell yard in Tacoma for scrapping. After clearing Santa Barbara Channel, the ARTHUR and her tow headed up the Coast one hundred miles offshore so as to have plenty of sea-room in case of heavy weather or heavy traffic. Top speed with the heavy drag was 4.8 knots. The ARTHUR delivered the 800-foot carrier to the Zidell waterway without assistance, but it required seven more Foss tugs to dock the mammoth carrier. The PHILIPPINE SEA was de-commissioned in 1959 and sold for scrapping after twenty-five years of service. During the Korean War her planes flew 7,243 combat missions. The big ship required a crew of 3,000—the ARTHUR moved her with a crew of eleven.

Another aircraft carrier tow came up in June of the same year for the ARTHUR; she returned to southern California and picked up the PRINCETON for delivery to Zidell in Tacoma. The PRINCETON, with a displacement weight of 30,000 tons, drew more water than the PHILIPPINE SEA, but surprisingly, the ARTHUR this time made better time to Tacoma by twelve hours—possibly the underbody was free of marine growth.

The ARTHUR continued to add to her successful record, trip after trip, and on the next voyage with Captain Tauno Salo she left Los Angeles in late August 1971 with an unusual quadruple tow (four barges) for delivery to Galveston, Texas, and Baltimore, Maryland. The final leg of the tow was completed in Baltimore in early October after a no-problem voyage. The ARTHUR then ran light to New Orleans and picked up another special tow of three barges loaded with drilling equipment for delivery to Port Harcourt, Nigeria, West Africa. After making a safe crossing of the Atlantic, she arrived in Port Harcourt on November 18th—the first Foss tug to appear in Africa! In port for only one day, the ARTHUR headed back to the States with a stop at Freetown, Sierra Leone for fuel. She arrived in New Orleans December 13. Then, after a seven-day lay-over for her sea-weary crew, she headed for Portland, Oregon, towing a new covered barge. Good sailing still accompanied the ARTHUR, and by January 24 she had delivered the barge and was headed out of the Columbia River for home. She arrived in Seattle on January 26 after covering over 26,000 miles, once around the world, in five months. With kindly weather, no storms, the ARTHUR looked well cared for upon her arrival—and ready to go again.

There was no rest for the ARTHUR with more long-haul towing waiting. After two weeks of voyage repairs and a new crew under Captain Cecil Mullins, the tug was underway again for San Francisco to take in tow two World War II freighters for delivery to Taiwan, Republic of China. The two ships were on their way to the scrapyard. The ARTHUR, her good luck still holding, crossed the Pacific to Taiwan with her two "charges" without a hitch. Encountering no port delay, she returned to Seattle with a total voyage time of only eighty-two days, arriving home May 1, 1972.

For the next three summers the ARTHUR was involved in the Sealift to Alaska's North Slope. The Sealift voyages of 1973 and 1974 were more or less routine—the round trips Seattle to Prudhoe Bay consumed only forty-nine days and sixty-four days. However, the Sealift of 1975 was a different story. The ARTHUR left Seattle June 30, 1975 with a tandem tow for Prudhoe and arrived at the southern ice limit in mid-July. For the next fifty-four days the ARTHUR and twenty-two other tugs, with forty-seven barges, waited for the ice around the Point Barrow area to move out. It didn't. For the first time in sealift history, the ice held fast. But several tugs and barges, with the help of the coast guard icebreakers, broke through and with luck made it into Prudhoe Bay in late September. Arctic Marine Freighters, Inc., the Sealift contractor, decided that not all tugs and barges could make it to Prudhoe Bay before the ice closed in, so the cargoes of least importance were to go south to the ice-free port of Seward. With the ARTHUR in line to go, she left on September 3 for Seward with two four-hundred-foot supply barges. After making a second trip from the Arctic to Seward with two more barges, she returned to Seattle, arriving on October 21 after a season of one hundred and fourteen days, but half of the time was used running in circles or anchored at the southern limit of the ice pack.

After minor voyage repairs the ARTHUR was called on for another rescue job. The freighter, LONDON PIONEER, disabled and helpless north of Midway Island in the Pacific, enroute to the Far East, was in dire need of help before the weather made up. The ARTHUR left Seattle in mid-December, located the cripple and getting the two-inch wire aboard, towed the ship to Kobe, Japan, arriving all-secure January 26, 1976.

Later in 1976 the ARTHUR made all-time Foss Company history by successfully delivering the world's largest pre-stressed concrete structure from Tacoma to Indonesia. The "structure," a 40 million dollar concrete-hulled, liquefied petroleum gas barge, was built by Concrete Technology Corporation of Tacoma, Washington. The concrete vessel, named ARDJUNA SAKTI, was the first of its kind to be anchored in a stationary position to liquefy and store gas for later transfer to liquid gas tankers. The structure would make it possible to recover and utilize more than $80,000 worth of natural gas a day that was being burned in the atmosphere.

The voyage of the ARTHUR with the ARDJUNA SAKTI, under Captain Paul Plate, began in Tacoma on April 25, 1976. The 461 by 136-foot vessel with a draft of twenty-three feet, turned out to be a heavy drag. With the exception of a six-hour fueling stop in Honolulu, the ARTHUR towed non-stop to Singapore, covering between ninety and one hundred miles per day in good weather. On August 3, after one hundred days of towing with only the lonely sea and the sky for company, tug and tow arrived in Singapore. Then, after some modifications to the barge which required a week, they were underway again to complete the voyage to the Java Sea oil fields off the Coast of Indonesia. At last, on August 22, after four months and over nine thousand miles, they arrived on location, none the worse for wear.

The ARTHUR was released by the owners of the ARDJUNA SAKTI (Atlantic Richfield-Indonesia) and Captain Plate wasted no time in heading for home. After a fast run with fine weather she arrived in Seattle in good condition all around on October 4, 1976 completing a voyage lasting 162 days, another record for the archives.

With the capabilities and lower operating costs of the new ocean tugs operating for the Foss Ocean division, the use for older and less efficient tugs, such as the ARTHUR and HENRY now became very limited. Due to the high tonnage rating of the two big boats, an eleven-man crew was required as compared to eight on the new vessels. To further inhibit their use, there are other binding coast guard rules regulating the operation and licensing of the ARTHUR and HENRY. With such non-competitive conditions, combined with a general slowdown in the towing industry, the ARTHUR remained idle for twenty-two months—but remained in a state of readiness.

At last, in August 1978 a distress call came informing Foss there had been a major collision of two freighters in mid-Pacific and immediate assistance was required. The ARTHUR was selected to go and she was underway in less than eight hours. By running "all out" she found the M.S. STAR K. in only five days after departure. She hooked up to the ship and towed her stern-first, as the bow was torn away and the forward holds flooded. The ARTHUR towed the STAR K. to Portland, Oregon in eight days without complications. A good showing for a tug laid up for almost two years.

After a short stay in Seattle, the ARTHUR then went south to Long Beach, California and picked up a barge tow for Houston, Texas. She remained in Houston waiting for an oil barge to be ready for towing to Long Beach. In April 1979 she left Houston and on May 8 delivered the barge, loaded with lube oil to Long Beach. The new barge, built for hauling black oil, is now being towed by Pacific Tow & Salvage Company's tug PACIFIC MARINER from Oceanside to San Diego for the San Diego Power & Gas Company.

The ARTHUR ran light from Long Beach to Seattle and tied up at the Foss pier to await the next call to action. However, she spent most of the balance of 1979 just waiting, ready, able and willing—but no heavy-duty job came her way. So at year's end Foss decided to remove the portable gear and consign the tug to the decommissioned fleet, berthed along the Foss side of the Canal.

The heavy, powerful ARTHUR played an important part in establishing Foss' position and expertise in ocean towing—she will be missed. Her 5,000 horsepower has moved over a million tons of cargo. With the ARTHUR now immobilized, it is up to the new, sophisticated, high-performance tugs to carry on the reputation and continue making towboat history.

CHRIS FOSS (2)

Built:	1941	Propulsion:	Caterpillar
	City Island, New York		510-horsepower
Length:	61-feet	Primary Service:	Puget Sound
Beam:	17-feet	Status:	In lay-up
		Final Foss Operating Day:	June 9, 1980

The CHRIS FOSS, a steel harbor-class tug number YTL-159, was built for the navy in City Island, New York, but the tug wandered a long way from home, ending up in Puget Sound. She worked for the navy shifting barges and test equipment around the Sound for twenty years before being declared surplus in 1962 and laid up at Indian Island near Port Townsend.

The 159 was purchased by Foss in mid-1962, towed to the Foss-Tacoma yard for major rebuilding and renamed CHRIS FOSS. The engine room was modernized, including installation of a 510-horsepower "Cat" diesel and new auxiliary equipment. Her deckhouse was extensively rebuilt to include Captain's quarters and a W.C. with shower located aft of the pilothouse on the main deck. The below decks galley and crew's quarters were refurbished. The alterations and improved appearance of the CHRIS gave her a distinction not shared with the five other YTL's in commercial operation on the Sound.

The major rebuilding job was completed in late December 1962 and after the holidays, on January 5 with Captain Arne Nielson in charge, she left on her first run for Foss—a job she was to become very familiar with—towing scows of wood-chips from the Simpson Mill Company at Shelton for pulping at the Crown Zellerbach Mill in Port Townsend.

The CHRIS' machinery functioned without fault on the Townsend trips and after two weeks of running, her alternate crew headed by Captain Arnold Ader was then able to take over for their two-week shift, and so it went year after year. Two weeks on and two weeks off was the customary procedure for day and night tugs on Puget Sound with the crews paid for twelve hours a day during the two weeks on board—even with two weeks off a month, the monthly pay averaged out the same as a full-time job. During the sixteen years since becoming a Foss tug, several hundred crewmen have handled lines aboard the CHRIS. Men come and go, regardless of the opportunity for time-off "moonlighting."

The Captain during the last several years, Yabbie Torgeson, has been with Foss for twenty-five years and when asked what the CHRIS is best known for, he replied that towing logs was now her long suit and she has towed about 500-million feet! A real highball logger.

The CHRIS delivered her share of tows but was handicapped with only 510-horsepower — the least power of all the linehaul tugs. With the present heavy bundled log rafts and larger barges, the CHRIS had to struggle, so she was favored whenever possible with lighter tows.

When towing logs, she did her best work with twelve to twenty-four sections, but she was not restricted in range—her operating area in log service extended from Shelton and Olympia north to Chimicum Creek (near Port Townsend), Everett, Anacortes and occasionally, the San Juan Islands—the scenic run.

When not pulling log rafts, the CHRIS for variation towed petroleum, chemical, and chip barges around the Sound, and she helped out on ship jobs in Olympia when the regular Tacoma assist-tugs were "out-of-town."

With more new and powerful tugs showing up, the forty year old CHRIS went the way of all superannuated tugs—she was relegated to the reserve fleet facing an uncertain future.

ELLEN FOSS

Built:	1943	Propulsion:	EMD (Single)
	Calumet Shipyard		3,600-horsepower
	Chicago, Illinois	Primary Service:	Alaska and Coastwise
Length:	115-feet	Status:	In Service
Beam:	30-feet		

Foss Company's one and only ELLEN was originally the LT-57, built by the Army Transport Service for coastwise and ocean towing, though starting out life on the Great Lakes. She shifted from fresh to salt water shortly after her break-in runs.

The Army powered her with a 1,225-horsepower Fairbanks-Morse diesel and the heavy duty engine kept her going for twenty-five years. By today's standards she was greatly underpowered, but at that time U.S. marine diesels had not been developed to the present day type of small high-speed, high-horsepower engines. Reliability was the criterion and the slow-turning, long-life engines provided just that.

At the conclusion of her Army service, the LT-57 was placed in the reserve fleet at Clatskanie, Oregon and remained there until August 1962 when Foss purchased her at a sealed-bid Government sale. She left soon after under tow to Foss-Seattle for overhaul and outfitting.

After four-and-a-half months of repair work to bring her up to Foss standards, the rejuvenated tug was ready to work—under a new name, ELLEN FOSS, in honor of Arthur's wife. With all the mechanical "bugs" worked out in sea trials by early January 1963 Foss assigned her to the lumber barge run between the West Coast and Honolulu. Except for a voyage to western Alaska in her first summer of service, the ELLEN was continuously employed on the Honolulu lumber run until relieved by the Miki-class ADELINE FOSS in March 1966. The ELLEN was then free to return home for a much-needed engine overhaul and voyage repairs.

Concluding a month of conditioning in the Foss yard the ELLEN, with Captain George Ducich in charge, left to resume her service to "the Islands" and take over the run from the ADELINE. She continued towing the lumber barge through mid-October of 1966—then orders were sent by radio informing Captain Ducich that BARBARA FOSS would take over from the ELLEN upon arrival in Eureka, California. The ELLEN was to return to Seattle for a special assignment requiring a heavy boat to buck the winter weather in the Gulf of Alaska—she was to deliver two barges of oil drilling equipment to Cook Inlet. The ELLEN made the run without loss of cargo or damage in spite of the rough sea that tried time and again to take charge.

Returning from the Inlet the ELLEN had to face more ocean weather during a long major tow across the Pacific. She towed a derrick barge from Eureka to Long Beach. After delivering the barge, the ELLEN ran light to Balboa, Canal Zone, arriving January 24th and waited for the arrival of two ferryboats from the East Coast to take on to Vietnam. That January Foss had been awarded a contract to tow two surplus ferryboats from the Panama Canal to Vietnam and the ELLEN was selected for the job. Upon arrival in Vietnam, the ELLEN was to go on charter to Alaska

Barge & Transport to help out on coastal towing work in the South China Sea while units of Alaska Barge & Transport's fleet were under repair in Hong Kong. The tugs, AGNES FOSS, MARGARET FOSS and PACIFIC MARINER, were already serving Alaska Barge & Transport in Vietnam.

On January 30th, the two ferryboats arrived at Balboa and were turned over to the ELLEN. Wasting no time, Captain Ducich had the tow made up and the ELLEN underway late on the 30th, bound for Vietnam with stops at Manzanillo, Mexico, Honolulu and Guam, for fuel and water. The only unplanned delays on the 14,000-mile run occurred when the ELLEN was forced into Acapulco, Mexico for machinery repairs and a four-day lay-over in Guam to wait out severe tropical storms. On April 17th, tug and tow arrived safely at Vung Tau, South Vietnam and the two ferryboats were turned over to local tugs.

Prior to ELLEN's arrival, Alaska Barge & Transport announced that their fleet of Miki-tugs and other World War II tugs had completed overhaul and were ready to return to service, so the AGNES and MARGARET FOSS were released and the ELLEN was free to return home at leisure. The ELLEN's crew didn't let the engine cool down—they headed right out for Seattle. The trip across was easy and fast with no problems and they pulled into the Foss dock a month later on May 18th. Total time on the complete voyage, 131 days; distance covered, 22,000 miles.

After a two-week lay-over in Seattle, the ELLEN was underway again. Captain Mike Hilton and new crew took her out this time to tow a War II-built tanker the MISSION SOLANO from Seattle to Galveston, Texas. The SOLANO, built in Sausalito, California in 1944 at the Marin Shipyard was a 10,000-horsepower T2 tanker.

The MISSION SOLANO and other similar tankers owned by the Navy Department were laid up at the end of the War, but in 1947 the T2 tankers were withdrawn from lay-up and turned over to commercial operators under contract to the Naval Overseas Transportation Service to carry food and supply cargoes to "occupied areas" in connection with the Government relief program. At the conclusion of the aid plan, the Military Sea Transport Service used the SOLANO for several years as a tanker—then in 1957 she was again laid up in the Olympia, Washington reserve fleet. In 1967 the MISSION SOLANO was purchased by Litton Industries for conversion to a full container ship for Sea-Land Service, Inc.—capable of carrying 332 containers and to be named JACKSONVILLE.

The ELLEN, after delivering the SOLANO in July to Todd shipyard, remained in Galveston to await the next call to action, but her crew returned to Seattle for re-assignment.

In mid-August Pacific Tow & Salvage at Long Beach flew a crew over for the ELLEN to run her to New Orleans to pick up a crane barge for delivery to Vietnam. However, the ELLEN towed the barge only as far as Panama where a sister-tug, the Long Beach based tug, PACIFIC RANGER, completed the tow to Saigon.

From Panama the ELLEN returned light to Galveston where she was again laid up to await further orders. A job came in November and this time Captain Mike Hilton and his crew returned to the ELLEN to take her to Morgan City, Louisiana to pick up two barges. On November 18th she left from the Atchafalaya River port of Morgan City with two heavily-loaded barges containing oil drilling equipment for the West Coast. Towing the heavy drag turned out to be a long and hard struggle for the ELLEN—her 1,225-horsepower was just not enough muscle. On November 28th, Captain Hilton reported to the Foss office that their speed was 4½ knots, and with fuel consumption way up, he was concerned about what might happen on the long trip from Panama to Long Beach, so he asked for an assisting tug. The Seattle office agreed, and fortunately, the ARTHUR and RICHARD FOSS were both on tows near Panama. The RICHARD, with 3,000-horsepower, was ordered to turn over her Texas tow to the ARTHUR at Cristobal, overtake the ELLEN and relieve her of the two heavy barges. On December 4th, the RICHARD took over the tow and the ELLEN was free to run light to Seattle, arriving December 21st. The day after arrival she went into the Foss shipyard—scheduled to receive a new high-speed, high-horsepower diesel. During the next six months, the old Fairbanks-Morse engine was removed and a new 3,600-horsepower General Motors EMD turbocharged diesel was installed. Also, new auxiliary engines and generators were set in and a new anchor winch and a modified tow winch put aboard. Fuel and water capacity were increased and a new fresh-water evaporator hooked up to augment the fresh water tankage. The interior of three staterooms was remodeled and the galley modernized. New alarm and engine automation systems were installed as well as a new radar, loran, depth sounder, and radios. A new work boat was chocked in on the boat deck and a two-ton hydraulic service crane installed for handling towing gear. In just six months the ELLEN came out fitted with all the equipment and the capabilities of a new boat.

She went on trials in June 1968 but as with any major engine replacement, problems developed and the ELLEN had her share—they were all mechanical and annoying, lasting through June and July. She remained on jobs close to home base until the defects worked out; then in September 1968 with everything in good running order, she took off with two loaded barges to Port Moller, Alaska for Pan American Drilling Company. Captain Guy Johnson reported the seven-week trip went smoothly with no mechanical problems of consequence. The ELLEN could now justly carry the Foss plaque, "Always Ready."

Since her conversion, the ELLEN has taken part in a number of interesting tows to go along with the usual run-of-the-mill jobs of towing general cargo barges between Seattle and Anchorage; bulk cement barges between California and Seattle and Anchorage; chemical products between Bellingham and Eureka, California. For variety, in April 1969 the ELLEN was assigned the job of towing another T2 tanker, the MISSION DELORES, from the Olympia reserve fleet to Todd Shipyard in Galveston for conversion to the Sea-Land container ship, TAMPA. The 5500-mile trip was made in twenty-seven days at an average speed of almost 8.5. The new engine cut her old running time thirty percent. With no return tow available, the ELLEN headed right back to Seattle where jobs were plentiful.

Before going on her next long and ambitious tow the ELLEN, in 1969 completed three trips to Amchitka for Holmes & Narver Company in connection with the Atomic Energy Commission Project. Then, in the spring of 1970 with Captain Tauno Salo, she towed the Smith-Rice derrick barge 21 from Seward, Alaska to Inchon, Korea. They left Seward on March 22nd, and after an uneventful crossing on the northern route to Japan, stopped at Hakodate for fuel and then through the Sea of Japan and the Yellow Sea to Inchon, arriving April 24th. From Korea, the ELLEN headed back across the Pacific to Kodiak, Alaska to pick up a container barge for Seattle. The 13,000-mile trip, entirely on exposed ocean waters, ended on May 19th, with both tug and crew still looking fit.

During the next four years, the ELLEN was assigned to the shorter, regular runs to Anchorage and down the coast, as the new twin-screw tugs were now making the long overseas and intercoastal voyages. However, in August of 1974 she did make two runs across to the Islands as a shortage of cement in Hawaii necessitated barging bulk cement from Seattle to Honolulu. The ELLEN, with the cement carrying barge, SEWARD, left Seattle on July 23, 1974 and after a fair-weather trip and completing discharge in Honolulu, returned to Redwood City, California for another load consigned to Honolulu. After the two-month interlude, the ELLEN, with her special barge, returned to Seattle and resumed hauling cement to Anchorage.

During 1975 and 1976, she continued on the cement run to Anchorage, making her last trip in October 1976. It was also her last towing job for the next eighteen months due to a slowdown in business. During the 1977 curtailment it was difficult to keep even the new twin-screw tugs busy, so the ELLEN was low on the call list.

During her extended lay-up she was maintained in a state of readiness, but evidence of rust and flaking paint was noticeable by early 1978. Then with signs of an impending busy summer, day crews began refurbishing the tug to give her the "in service" look once again.

On March 31st, the large Ballard Lock was due to close for ten days for annual repairs so all the ocean tugs had to shift to temporary berths on the Seattle Waterfront or be trapped in the lake. Even though there was no immediate job in sight for the ELLEN, she was ordered to go around to the Harbor for a test of the machinery and equipment that had not been used for the past eighteen months. All work in the Foss operations offices came to a halt at 1100 on the morning of March 30th—all eyes were on the ELLEN as Captain Al Anderson was to back her away from the pier she had lain against since November 1976. There was a question whether the ELLEN in some way had become a permanent part of the pier structure, but all doubts vanished when she eased away from the pier with no splinters attached. Captain Anderson, on his way to the Locks, reported everything running fine and smooth.

The ELLEN went back to work in late April—she had the job of towing the disabled fishing vessel VIRGO from Akutan, Alaska to Tacoma and she had the cripple in Tacoma by May 16th.

Once started, the ELLEN kept going throughout the spring, and fall of 1978 hauling general-cargo barges, primarily to Anchorage. Then with the slack winter season at hand, the ELLEN put out her fenders at the Foss Pier to wait for the usual spring activity.

By May, construction work around Anchorage was in full swing and building materials were needed, so the ELLEN was assigned to the Seattle-Bamberton, B.C. cement run to Anchorage. She towed the Kaiser cement barge until the winter ice closed off barge towing in Cook Inlet.

The ELLEN remained on stand-by in Seattle during the winter, assisting in tanker escort-work when needed. No doubt she will be running North again when the weather permits, as her 3,600-horsepower can move the heavy Alaska barges with dispatch. On the Kaiser run, it is said that the cement is still warm when the ELLEN arrives in Anchorage, even after the 1,600 mile run!

HENRY FOSS On sea trials prior to entering service in April, 1965. (Courtesy of Foss Tug Co)

HENRY FOSS (2)

Built:	1943	Propulsion:	Nordberg (Twin)
	Marietta Shipyard		5,000-horsepower
	Point Pleasant, West Virginia	Primary Service:	Ocean - Coastwise
Length:	149-feet	Status:	In Lay-up
Beam:	33-feet		

The HENRY FOSS, an Army Transport service tug, the LT-815, belonged to a group of the largest class of army tugs designed for heavy ocean towing during World War II. In 1971 fourteen of the class were still in service, but with commercial firms—Foss Company operating two—and several working on the East Coast for the Pennsylvania Railroad.

The LT-815, purchased by Foss at a government sale in November 1962 was released in December from lay-up at Rio Vista, California and turned over to the ANDREW FOSS, standing by to tow the new acquisition home. Tug and tow arrived at Foss-Seattle December 14, after a trouble-free four-day trip.

During the next two-and-one-half years the 815 was under reconstruction at the Foss-Seattle yard. The steam uniflow engine was replaced by two 2,500-horsepower Nordberg diesels. New and modern ancillary machinery was installed, and the latest navigation equipment for long-distance ocean towing fitted in the pilothouse. The increase in fuel capacity to 149,000 gallons gave her nearly unlimited towing range. In early 1965 she emerged from her conversion looking like a model tug and bearing the name of HENRY FOSS.

With sea trials completed on March 19, 1965 the HENRY left on her initial run, towing a cement barge on a five-day round trip to Portland. Choosing Portland for the destination of HENRY's first trip was very auspicious as

Foss had recently secured a contract with Sea-Land Corporation to provide tug and container-barge-service between Oakland, California and Portland, Oregon. On April 14, 1965 the HENRY, with Barge FOSS-207, left for Portland to initiate the new run. During the next eight months she made forty-seven trips between Portland and Oakland, covering 30,294 miles, before the contract terminated December 20, 1965.

The year 1966 was another high-mileage one for the HENRY and it started on February 19th, under command of Captain Dick Parenti when she left for Morgan City, Louisiana to pick up the jack-up drill rig, J. W. NICKLE, and tow the rig to oil-rich Cook Inlet, Alaska. The HENRY, in spite of the deep draft and heavy drag, made the run from Morgan City to Cook Inlet, a distance of 6,200 miles, in seventy days. From Cook Inlet she returned to Seattle for minor voyage repairs, then spent the remainder of the summer towing more drilling equipment between West Coast ports and the Inlet.

The HENRY's second long haul of the year started in September from the Gulf Coast. This time she went to Todd Shipyard in Houston and picked up the first of two new lumber barges, the DIAMOND HEAD, for Pacific Hawaiian Lines. Due to the economic growth of Hawaii, new equipment was necessary as the old LST barges could not provide sufficient capacity to handle the increased lumber demand. The DIAMOND HEAD was double-decked, 328 feet by 68 with a capacity of six-million feet of packaged lumber, enough to build two hundred and forty homes!

Under Captain Parenti, the HENRY made an easy and uneventful trip from Houston with the DIAMOND HEAD, arriving in Seattle November 2nd. Then after some minor work on both tug and barge, the HENRY and her new carrier left to pick up a load of lumber at Longview, Coos Bay, and in California at Crescent City and Eureka. The HENRY departed the West Coast for Honolulu on December 11, 1966 arriving twelve days later, and she continued on a thirty day round trip schedule for the next year, operating under a Pacific Hawaiian Line contract. Captain Parenti remained with the HENRY until March 1967; then Tauno Salo took over the run and stayed with the boat for the next three years. On one of his trips he had an observer-reporter aboard, a high school senior on school assignment for on-the-job experience—thanks to the Foss Operations Manager, Jay Peterson. His consideration made it possible for the student to observe and record a tug in action from Seattle to Honolulu. Later the student's day-by-day report of events, JOURNAL OF A JOURNEY, was rated informative and instructive by Foss and High School alike and used by the school as a model type. The purpose of the on-the-job introduction was to fix the student's interest in what appeared to be his field so that after university graduation, he would not have the problem of vocation indecision and uncertainty—and that is the way it turned out.

In January 1968 the HENRY, relieved by the CRAIG FOSS, left for home to effect much-needed repairs in anticipation of a long-haul ocean-towing contract. Though ready to go again in late January, she had to stand by and await contract developments. Finally on February 1st, word came that the potential job had been won by a rival California-based company.

The California tug, MAUNA LOA, came up for the tow and left Seattle in early February with an 18,000-ton floating drydock for Guam. However, on a Coast Guard inspection at Port Angeles, before the MAUNA LOA left Washington waters, they discovered that the tug was carrying fuel oil in ballast tanks, which are exempt from tonnage admeasurement and this substitution rendered her licensing documents invalid. The MAUNA LOA had needed the additional fuel to make the trip to Guam, but that wasn't a justifiable excuse, so the Coast Guard ordered the tug back to Seattle and imposed a severe penalty on the owners—forfeiture of the vessel. As a result of the strange turn of events, the HENRY, with Captain Salo, was awarded the job after all. So on February 25, 1968 they left Seattle with the AFDM #6 for the Western Pacific.

Despite the size and drag of the tow—the drydock measured 488 feet in length, 124 feet in beam, 76 feet high and drew almost ten feet of water—the HENRY averaged 5.7 knots all the way across—almost. She was due to arrive in Guam on April 13th. However, on April 7th the Foss office in Seattle sent a warning to Captain Salo, on the high-seas single-side band radio, of a severe tropical storm six hundred miles south of the HENRY's position. By the next day the storm, called Typhoon Jean, had advanced to within three hundred seventy miles of the HENRY. Unfortunately, evasive action was impossible due to the unavoidable slow towing speed. On Thursday, April 11th, only two days from Guam, the full force of "JEAN" hit the HENRY. The Foss dispatcher's last radio contact with the HENRY came in at 0930 Guam time and Captain Salo reported mountainous seas breaking over the seventy-six-foot drydock, it was still afloat but adrift—the towline had parted. On the HENRY, her twelve-man crew were fighting for survival, trying to hold the tug's head up in the overwhelming seas.

The Log of the tug shows the following dramatic entries:

April 10, 1968   0915   Wind gusting NE 50-60 knots. Drydock turned tug around. Hove to.

2200   Still hove-to in typhoon. Barometer 29.58. Northeasterly wind 65-75 knots. Very rough seas. Drydock pulling us backward at 2 to 3 knots.

April 11, 1968	0115	Hold-down wire parted, starboard towing pin sheared off.
	0150	Middle towing pin sheared off.
	0245	Towline parted—AFDM #6 adrift. Easterly winds of 85 knots.
	0730	Entered eye of typhoon. Barometer 28.00 Northerly wind 120 knots. Steep breaking confused seas and heavy rain. Visibility zero—vessel's motion wild.
	0915	Out of eye. Barometer 27.60! Winds northerly 120 knots. Mountainous seas.

Then by 1530 the wind had died down to southwesterly forty to fifty knots with light rain and very high seas. They had survived! Captain Salo entered a final report in the tug's Log Book for April 11th: "Got caught by TYPHOON JEAN—not ample warning. Lost tow due to high seas and wind—went through the eye of the typhoon and winds up to 150 knots! Stove in both lifeboats, lost antennas for radio—shorted out radios, radar, running lights, hot water heater and gyro. Cracked windows and broke out one. Things in a heck of a mess. Water all over inside and out. No communication with anyone after coming out of eye of typhoon—attempting to locate the AFDM #6, but like trying to find a needle in a haystack!"

Captain Salo's search for the drydock proved futile, so the HENRY proceeded to Guam for emergency repairs and to obtain help to locate the drydock. While repairs were going on, the Navy began an air search. They discovered the drydock some four hundred and fifty miles north of Guam and apparently undamaged; it had been pushed by the force of the typhoon three hundred miles in forty-eight hours.

After emergency repairs were made, the HENRY headed back to sea and returned to the drifting drydock. Taking it in tow, she steered for Guam and at long last, on April 22nd, delivered the AFDM #6 to its proper destination.

Completing five more days of repair, the HENRY left for Hiroshima, Japan, her long run not over yet. By May 6th she was in Hiroshima where she waited a week before going out to meet the ARTHUR FOSS and relieve her of a Phillips Oil Company drill platform. The HENRY, in settled weather, took the platform across the North Pacific to Cook Inlet, Alaska, arriving July 17th. Then after taking on supplies and fuel, HENRY's wanderings still not over, she returned to Hiroshima, picked up two barges of drilling equipment and again crossed the North Pacific to Cook Inlet; arriving without incident on July 28th.

From there at long last, HENRY and her twelve-man crew were ordered home, but she still had to tow a barge on the final leg of the thither-and-yon voyage. The strenuous five months of roaming the seas was over after covering some 17,000 miles—with the memorable Typhoon Jean included, to keep the trip unforgettable.

After four weeks of voyage repairs the HENRY returned to her old run, towing the lumber barge KOKO HEAD between the West Coast and Honolulu. The skipper, none other than "Typhoon Salo"!

For the next four years the HENRY remained on the Honolulu lumber run, but not with Captain Salo, as Cecil Mullins took over in December 1968 and remained with the HENRY for the balance of the Honolulu lumber service—which ended abruptly in 1972. The HENRY, enroute to the West Coast after leaving Honolulu on August 29, 1972 was ordered to Oakland and not to one of the lumber ports. Upon arrival, the crew was informed the lumber-run contract for Foss Company vessels was concluded, ending eleven years of steady service started by the JUSTINE FOSS and Barge FOSS-200 in 1961.

Released from the Honolulu run, the HENRY operated on various Alaska runs for the next four years, including two voyages to Prudhoe Bay and several between Portland and Kenai, Alaska with the liquid ammonia and urea barge, KENAI.

A round-trip voyage the HENRY made with Captain Paul Plate from Seattle to Prudhoe Bay and return in 1975 took four trying months, as she lay icebound for nearly two months waiting for an opening. With only a few days remaining before abandoning the voyage in late September, the ice receded far enough for the convoy of tugs and barges to make the final push to Prudhoe Bay. But the HENRY still had to get out and quick, as winter had already started to set in and ice was starting to re-form. The HENRY and her companion tugs, so as not to be hampered, left the barges at Prudhoe Bay where they were iced in for the next eleven months. The HENRY made it out before the ice closed in and delivered one of the barges to Seward that had been left behind on the dash to Prudhoe Bay. From Seward, the HENRY returned to Seattle, arriving October 31st. After the long and arduous season, necessary voyage repairs were carried out, then she rested for the balance of the year in winter lay-up.

In January, she was out and running again, making two trips to Valdez with house-modules from Long Beach. She returned in time to safely tow the disabled ship PAC MERCHANT to San Francisco from a precarious position 1,000 miles out in the Pacific. For her next ship job she towed two Victory ships from Suisun Bay, California to Astoria for scrapping. Then she made another tow to Valdez and then back to ship towing, delivering the U.S.S. ARLINGTON from Bremerton to Richmond, California. Next, the big drill-rig GEORGE FERRIS was towed from Homer, Alaska to San Francisco and for her last job in 1976 she towed the exploration ship GLOMAR EXPLORER from Long Beach to San Francisco. After the November tow with the GLOMAR, the HENRY tied-up until 1977.

However, with the HENRY's high operating cost, extensive maintenance and Coast Guard manning requirements, combined with the arrival and use of the new automated tugs, she was forced into limited use, operating only six weeks in 1977 and in 1978 she made only one round trip Seattle to Valdez.

1979 was a little better, she made a series of tows coastwise to California and then completed a tandem tow of two seafood processing ships from Seattle to Dutch Harbor, Alaska in late summer with Captain Paul Plate in command.

It was now quite obvious that with the fuel cost, crew size, upkeep expense and the limited towing market for tugs like the ARTHUR and HENRY, they would have to be retired at the end of 1979.

However, the HENRY had one final assignment before retirement—towing the decommissioned heavy cruiser ST. PAUL from the inactive fleet at the U.S. Naval Shipyard in Bremerton to the Navy base in Long Beach, California. The voyage under command of Captain Jay Jacobson went well except for running into a winter storm that delayed the arrival in Seattle by one day, causing a disappointed crew to spend a cheerless Christmas Day at sea.

The crew of course will return to sea, but the HENRY is slated to retire from the sea after fifteen years of hard towing, enhancing the Foss reputation from the North Pacific to the South Pacific. The HENRY will not be pensioned-off like a veteran Foss employee, but she will receive free moorage and care at the Foss haven for deactivated tugs, alongside the Ship Canal.

DOROTHY FOSS *Shown on Puget Sound during a routine assignment, July 1967. (Courtesy of author's collection)*

DOROTHY FOSS

Built:	1963	Propulsion:	Caterpillar (Twins)
	Albina Shipbuilding Company		1,200-horsepower
	Portland, Oregon	Primary Service:	Puget Sound
Length:	66-feet	Status:	In Service
Beam:	24-feet		

Albina Shipbuilding, a Dillingham subsidiary, built eight "D"-class tugs for Foss in a seven-year period beginning in 1963. The DOROTHY, named for Andrew Foss' sister in Norway, was the first of the class and the first tug constructed for Foss Company from keel up since the Foss Shipyard, in cooperation with the Todd Shipyard in 1958 built the CAROL and the SHANNON.

The DOROTHY started out towing in June 1963 and spent the year on Puget Sound and in Cook Inlet, Alaska. Oil exploration in the Inlet was just getting underway in 1963 and the DOROTHY, being well-suited for tending oil drilling rigs, went right to work for the drilling contractors.

After a successful first season in the Inlet, the DOROTHY returned to Seattle in mid-December of 1963 and resumed general towing on Puget Sound for the winter months. Then with the spring thaw in Cook Inlet, the DOROTHY headed north and delivered two barges to Anchorage, but she didn't tarry in the Inlet—a special job was waiting upon her return.

Ten days later, April 29th, she was back in Seattle taking on stores. The DOROTHY was to be part of the supply fleet for the U.S. Distant Early Warning System as Foss held the contract to re-supply the many radar sites of the DEW Line in the remote areas of northwestern Alaska during the ice-free months. Since the season was short, eight Foss tugs and many barges were involved in the transport and lighterage operation—thousands of barrels of petroleum and hundreds of tons of cargo had to be safely and positively delivered to the sites to keep the stations in operation until the following summer.

With less than twelve hours in port, the DOROTHY headed north for the DEW Line with a Foss oil barge and a flat-deck cargo barge carrying the small landing craft, ELMER FOSS on deck. Enroute to the Bering Sea she picked up another Foss landing craft, the ELSIE FOSS. The job was a tough one for a sixty-six-foot tug not designed for heavy ocean towing, but a shallow-draft boat was required for the northern in-shore work and the DOROTHY was the best compromise.

The DOROTHY and her barges continued on to Naknek, the first discharge point on the annual "Mona Lisa" re-supply project for the DEW Line. After arrival at Naknek on May 24, she waited three days for the LESLIE FOSS with the FOSS-98 to arrive, then using the DOROTHY's small transfer-barge, the lightering service of the 98's oil began. The small oil barge FOSS-100 lightered the oil to the beach from the large 38,000-barrel barge, anchored well off-shore. Then the ELMER and ELSIE pushed the FOSS-100 up on the beach for transfer of the oil by hose to shore tanks. General cargo was handled much easier by off-loading over ramps to the beach.

The long and slow process continued for two weeks at Naknek and then the DOROTHY and a flat-deck barge proceeded north to the remote radar site at Cape Newenham, to lighter cargo ashore from the cargo barge FOSS-207, held on station by the AGNES FOSS. After several days of discharge at Cape Newenham, the Foss fleet re-assembled still farther north at the Cape Romanzof radar site. After supplying Romanzof, the operation shifted to Unalakleet, Nome and south to Dutch Harbor—then to the final beach-discharging site, Cape Sarichef at Unimak Pass.

On July 28th, the DEW Line mission completed, DOROTHY returned to her former work in Cook Inlet, tending floating oil drilling rigs and she stayed with the job until winter ice formed. In December she was forced to give up and return home, arriving December 23rd, completing eight months' service in Alaska. Her voyage repairs after the demanding season went on for sixty days.

In early March with the ice moving out of Cook Inlet, the DOROTHY went north again to tend drill rigs at last year's sites. This lasted until mid-summer when she made a barge run to Puget Sound and back to the Inlet to assist in a pipe-laying operation at the new Shell Oil Company platform. She continued with the pipe-laying work until winter ice halted construction for 1965. Instead of returning to Seattle, the DOROTHY wintered in lower Cook Inlet. During the winter at Kachemak Bay, near Seldovia, she tended floating equipment including drill barges in winter lay-up owned by Western Offshore Drilling and Exploration Company.

During the 1966 season, the DOROTHY again tended oil drilling platform construction and pipelaying work in the Inlet. She continued looking after the platforms, their anchors and barges through November and then returned to Puget Sound for extensive repairs required after a year-and-a-half of strenuous work and subjection to the rigors of an Alaskan winter.

In June 1967 the DOROTHY made a round trip from Seattle to Amchitka, towing a 10,000-barrel oil barge. This was the first time a "D"-class boat ventured west of Dutch Harbor, but with the Aleutian weather cooperating for a change, she made the round trip in twenty-nine days—surprisingly below the average of the regular ocean-going tugs used on the Amchitka run.

In August and September the DOROTHY made two more runs to Southwestern Alaska. The second trip involved towing a floating cannery (ex-Canadian ferryboat SMOKWA) from Seattle to Sandpoint, fishing center in the Shumagin Islands, the area where sea otter, with their luxurious silver tip fur used to abound. In the poaching days (after 1910) the skins brought $1,500 each on the London Fur Exchange.

From Sandpoint the DOROTHY went to Cook Inlet where she took part in the usual rig-tending until late November. She arrived back in Seattle December 5, 1967 and went through a thirty-day overhaul, then started towing on Puget Sound. During the months January through April the DOROTHY, dispatched from the Seattle office, towed on the rail-car runs, oil-barge runs and occasionally she helped on ship-assists.

In late April 1968 the Tacoma Division (which still dispatched and handled several Sound tugs in 1968) needed a high-horsepower tug to help on linehaul work. So on May 1st, the DOROTHY transferred to the Tacoma Division to tow logs, chip-scows, and the chemical barge from Hooker Chemical in Tacoma to Puget Sound Pulp Mills.

Then in August 1968 Foss, with the DOROTHY, began service for Ideal Cement Company of Seattle, towing a Foss barge loaded with 1,400 to 2,400 tons of clay from a quarry at Twin Rivers between Port Angeles and Sekiu for delivery to Ideal's Seattle plant. The DOROTHY made a round trip of thirty-six hours once a week for the next several years and with no failures or mishaps and overcoming all hazards at the loading point.

Timing the arrival at the quarry was critical due to both weather and tide, as docking and loading at the quarry could only be done during high tide. The higher the tide, the more loading time at the dock and the more clay hauled. At extreme low water, the entire berthing area and channel entrance went completely dry! Even at high water, the channel was shallow and only wide enough for the tug with barge alongside to squeeze through. Range markers on the beach aided the captain to stay in the channel, but good judgment was most important. By estimate from 1969 through 1974 the DOROTHY made over 325 trips, transporting over 500,000 tons of clay without mishap. Then after 1974 the "J"-class boats were put on the clay run, freeing the DOROTHY for more diversified service on Puget Sound.

The DOROTHY became the prime tug in towing rail-car barges between Seattle and the Simpson Mill in Shelton, also from the Pope & Talbot Mill in Port Gamble. When not on rail-car service, the DOROTHY tows chip barges and chemical barges to the Sound pulp mills and she still takes part in ship-assists at the major ports. Working days for the oldest "D"-boat on the Foss roster have been full and plenty.

JULIA FOSS

Built:	1964	Propulsion:	Caterpillar (Twin)
	Albina Shipyard		600-horsepower
	Portland, Oregon	Primary Service:	Puget Sound
Length:	60-feet	Status:	In Service
Beam:	21-feet		

The JULIA, named for the wife of Theodore Foss, Thea's sister, was second in the series of new steel tugs built to upgrade Foss' aging Puget Sound fleet and provide new equipment to serve the booming oil industry in Cook Inlet.

She left the shipyard in early May 1964 bound for Foss-Seattle for a week of outfitting. Then on May 12th, she pulled out for Cook Inlet to tend the drill rigs working day and night locating oil well sites.

At the end of an active season the JULIA returned home and started right in towing a rail-car barge between Seattle and the Simpson Mill at Shelton. The JULIA, drawing less water than her turn-of-the-century predecessors and having twice the horsepower, was ideal for a run requiring precision timing on account of tides and currents and twin propellers made her more maneuverable in navigating the shallow and winding Narrows in and out of Shelton. She remained on the Shelton and other Sound runs until mid-summer 1966 then her operating area changed 1,600 miles to the north.

In early August the J. Ray McDermott Company, a prime contractor in the extensive oil-pipeline and offshore well construction program in Cook Inlet, needed another tug, so the JULIA with her performance record returned to the Inlet, regardless of the lateness of the season. She became the seventh Foss tug stationed in Cook Inlet during 1966. After an active four months working near Nikiski and Granite Point, the winter weather finally turned her south and she headed for home in convoy with the DELORES and JENNY FOSS, arriving in Seattle a week before Christmas, much to the crew's delight.

The JULIA did not return to the Inlet and for ten years she was strictly a Puget Sound tug, taking part in all the various types of local towing that Foss is noted for—towing logs, chip scows, oil barges and lowly gravel barges. In late 1977 the JULIA was tranferred to Tacoma, working as a two-man harbor day-boat for several months, but in late

JULIA FOSS Inbound to Foss yard, December 17, 1966 upon returning from tending drill rigs in Cook Inlet. NOTE DELORES FOSS in background returning from the same operation. (Courtesy of author's collection)

1978 she returned to Seattle and to full-crew status for linehaul towing, but by mid 1979 was again a two-man day-boat in Tacoma.

The JULIA and the other "J" boats, or junior boats, are the only Foss tugs adaptable to either five-man-crew linehaul work or two-man, twelve-hour-shift harbor work. This means no idle days in the life of the JULIA or her sisters. Tugs are like crews, inactivity makes them rusty.

SAM FOSS

Built:	1964	Propulsion:	Caterpillar
	Pacific Shipyard		325-horsepower
	Anacortes, Washington	Primary Service:	Tacoma Harbor
Length:	37-feet	Status:	In Service
Beam:	14-feet		

Pacific Shipyard built the SAM, another addition to the modernization and replacement program of the Foss Puget Sound fleet. SAM was the third boat to come out in the series of nine new steel harbor tugs, and to give the boat a wider range of use, a special fire pump and monitor were installed. The fire pump, operating from a power take-off on the main engine, has a ten-inch sea suction and an eight-inch discharge line capable of delivering three thousand gallons per minute. The monitor has a five-inch nozzle and produces enough force to drive the tug rapidly astern if the stream is shot over the bow into the water. The setup made the SAM into a fireboat-tug, handy for washing down scows and barges as well as fire-fighting and towing.

Completed in December 1964 and named for the son of Henrietta Foss Hagar, the SAM headed right to Tacoma, first of the new tugs to work on Commencement Bay. The entire life span of the SAM centers in and around Tacoma Harbor, tending log storages, servicing log ships, and shifting barges. Occasionally, with her two-man crew, she starts barges out of Tacoma for Seattle until met and relieved of the tow by larger tugs. The SAM operates for the most part with a short crew on eight-hour days, five days a week and usually within the Harbor area. Though the SAM's work is not adventurous like the ocean tugs, her daily routine of handling log rafts is vital to the export log industry.

In case of Harbor fires, the SAM's monitor is a valuable asset to the Tacoma Fire Department. The tug might be short in length, but not on service.

CRAIG FOSS (2)

Built:	1943 Tampa Marine Corporation Tampa, Florida	Propulsion:	EMD (Twin) 4,000-horsepower
		Primary Service:	Coastwise and Alaska
Length:	115-feet	Status:	In Service
Beam:	30-feet		

The CRAIG, number LT-648, built for the Water Division of the Army Transportation Corps during World War II, began her Army career towing on the Atlantic Coast and then shifted to the Pacific until laid up about 1950 in the California reserve fleet. She was declared surplus in March 1960 and put up for sale in July 1965. Foss purchased her as they had been on the lookout for a sizable tug to put on the Honolulu lumber run and the LT-648 appeared to be the answer. The only drawback was the 1,225-horsepower diesel engine, adequate in 1943 but decidedly under-powered for 1965.

Foss towed the tug to their Seattle yard, but kept her in mothballs until 1966 when the major repowering and rebuilding job started. To insure close supervision, all the work was done at Foss' own yard where any day-by-day alteration in plans would not cause shipyard problems. The engine room received the most attention in the conversion. All the WWII auxiliary machinery was removed and replaced by modern motors, generators, pumps, and equipment. In place of the F-M single main engine, two new Electro Motive diesels were installed, driving one variable pitch propeller. The engine room was made fireproof and full machinery-automation installed later. Deck house, including the crew's quarters and galley, were modernized and forced-air ventilated. All the latest electronic and navigational aids were installed in the pilot house to provide safe navigation. Outside, the hull and decks were repaired as necessary and then Foss' green and white colors brought the tug up to first-class appearance.

Then in mid-April 1967 the newly christened CRAIG, with Captain Dick Parenti in command, ran light to San Francisco to pick up Pacific Hawaiian Line's new lumber-carrying barge KOKO HEAD, which had recently been delivered to San Francisco from the builder's yard in Houston, Texas. The KOKO HEAD was identical to the earlier built DIAMOND HEAD, with both barges capable of carrying between five and six million board feet of lumber. The CRAIG, running without complaints, took the KOKO HEAD to Everett, Longview, Portland, Crescent City, and Eureka to make up a load for the first voyage to Honolulu. She completed five round trips between the West Coast and Honolulu in 1967 with alternate Captains Dick Parenti and Stan Thurston seeing to the CRAIG's success on the run.

However, good fortune and good sailing did not remain with the CRAIG and KOKO HEAD. On December 17th, when northbound from San Francisco to Eureka, the CRAIG ran into a typical Pacific Coast storm. All during the day the weather continued to deteriorate with seas mounting to very high and steep with a hardening wind making up to storm force. Unfortunately, at the height of the blow, the towline parted and the wind and seas drove the KOKO HEAD ashore. Unable to retrieve the beached barge, the CRAIG proceeded to Eureka to wait out the storm.

The following day a salvage crew succeeded in boarding the KOKO HEAD and they spent the next ten days patching and making the barge watertight before trying to pull her into deep water. The large Astoria salvage tug

SALVAGE CHIEF arrived after the tenth day for an attempt to refloat the KOKO HEAD. They were unsuccessful on two tries and decided to stand by and wait for higher tides later in the week. At the time of the highest tide of the month, the KOKO HEAD was pulled off and towed to Portland by the SALVAGE CHIEF. Hull repair and renewing of parts required nearly six months before she was finally fit for service.

The CRAIG, after two days of standing by in Eureka, and unable on her own to assist the KOKO HEAD, received orders to return to Seattle and much to the joy of the crew, they arrived just in time for Christmas!

In mid-January 1968 the CRAIG returned to the Honolulu lumber run and started out by relieving the HENRY FOSS of the barge DIAMOND HEAD at Eureka. Taking a full barge-load from Eureka, she left January 22nd on the first of twenty-eight consecutive successful voyages during a three-year period between the West Coast and Honolulu. The CRAIG maintained a good trip record, averaging only forty days on each voyage including loading and discharging.

Captain Stan Thurston, her regular skipper during 1968 and through March of 1969, left the CRAIG to take a management position in the Operations Department at Foss-Seattle. The CRAIG needed another skipper like Stan Thurston to maintain the reputation of dependable service and Captain Chuck May did just that from April 1969 on.

After the twenty-eight voyages for Pacific Hawaiian Lines, the CRAIG entered Long Beach for a period of lay-up, arriving January 17, 1971. This was the first time in over a thousand days that the CRAIG was idle and without a crew.

After two months in lay-up, she returned to the lumber run with the DIAMOND HEAD and completed three trips to Hawaii. On arrival in the Columbia River for a fourth barge-load in early July, she ran right into the West Coast Longshore strike. The strike was in full swing and all shipping on the West Coast shut down, including lumber shipments to the Islands. The CRAIG and the DIAMOND HEAD were idled in Portland for nearly three months until called out for a voyage in late September from New Westminster, British Columbia to Honolulu with a barge-load of Canadian lumber. The strike was over by the time she returned to the Coast, so she was able to make two more lumber runs from California and Oregon ports in 1971.

In early 1972 the lumber movement to Hawaii was temporarily curtailed and Pacific Hawaiian Lines laid up the DIAMOND HEAD in Oakland and Foss, in turn, laid up the CRAIG until conditions improved. But in March, Pacific Hawaiian Lines worked out a charter for the DIAMOND HEAD to carry a load of lumber from Coos Bay to the Atlantic seaboard. So on March 6th the CRAIG, with Captain Chuck May, left Oregon with the DIAMOND HEAD for Camden, New Jersey and Portsmouth, New Hampshire.

Tug and barge arrived without incident in Camden on April 15th and Portsmouth the next week. From Portsmouth the CRAIG towed the empty barge to Mobile, Alabama where the DIAMOND HEAD was released to new charterers for service on the East Coast. The CRAIG then returned to Long Beach where she picked up a new ship's mid-body and towed it to Todd's Seattle shipyard, arriving home May 31, 1972.

By May 1972 the U.S. Reserve Fleet in Olympia, which at one time numbered some two hundred moth-balled vessels, had been reduced to ten ships and even the ten were scheduled to leave Olympia's Budd Inlet. On June 1st the CRAIG pulled out three of the remaining vessels, all "knot-class" ships—the ANCHOR HITCH, CLOVE HITCH, and SAILOR'S SPLICE—and delivered them to Seattle in one triple tow. The three ships were to be towed across the Pacific to a Taiwan shipbreaker, but by a Japanese tug.

The following week the CRAIG towed the former aircraft ferry and cargo ship, BAEDONG STRAIT, from the Puget Sound Naval Shipyard at Bremerton to Portland for scrapping. The BAEDONG STRAIT was launched in February 1945 by the Seattle-Tacoma Shipyard in Tacoma and she compiled an interesting record in experimental submarine warfare. Between February 1947 and June 1950 she operated in the Pacific, testing new anti-submarine equipment and training personnel in anti-submarine warfare. During the Korean War she operated off the coast of Korea on anti-submarine duty and as part of the blockade escort force. After three tours of duty off Korea, the ship was modernized and then continued with her experimental work in combination with new naval aircraft and helicopters. After the final tour of duty in the Far East in 1956 the BAEDONG STRAIT returned to Bremerton for decommissioning in May 1957.

Following the BAEDONG STRAIT tow in June, the CRAIG, in July 1972 made her initial trip to Alaska towing barge FOSS-202 to the Navy base at Adak in the Aleutians. With good weather both ways, the round trip was made in three weeks.

There was no let up for the CRAIG during the remainder of 1972 and 1973 towing to Alaska and along the Pacific Coast. Her hardest tow during this period was delivering the decommissioned aircraft carrier, BUNKER HILL, from San Diego to Tacoma for scrapping. The trip north required sixteen days at an average speed of just over three knots! Departure San Diego was July 19th and arrival Tacoma, August 3rd. Towing the BUNKER HILL was the heaviest tow the CRAIG ever attempted. The carrier, 872 feet in length, had a beam of 93 feet and a displacement tonnage of 27,000. She was commissioned in 1943 and served many fronts during World War II, including engagements at the Gilbert Islands, Marshall Islands, Truk, Marianas, Hollandia, and the Battle of the Philippine Sea. The BUNKER HILL received eleven battle stars for her World War II service and the CRAIG's crew felt keen regret at docking such a veteran for scrapping.

In June 1974 the CRAIG and Captain Chuck May began another long-term towing job, but this time to Alaska. Construction of the tank farm and bulk terminal at Valdez, to store and handle North Slope crude oil, required housing, utilities, and related equipment for the many crews working on the installations. Material for the camps was to be delivered by tug and barge, with the CRAIG getting the prime towing job.

In early June she left Long Beach, towing two Foss barges loaded with eighty module housing-units. The modules, 54 feet by 10 feet, were constructed by Atco Structures at Riverside, California and provided living quarters, recreational facilities, offices, dining rooms, and other facilities for the workers. The CRAIG continued in this service for the next eighteen months, hauling tandem tows from Long Beach to Valdez. With the last of the modules delivered, the CRAIG's part was finished and she returned to Seattle with her two barges on November 18, 1975.

During the remainder of 1975 and all of 1976 the CRAIG towed general-cargo barges between Seattle and southwestern Alaska, right up to the end of the season.

Due to the general slowdown in towing to Alaska after completion of the major work on the pipeline, the CRAIG remained idle until May 1977 then she was assigned to the bulk-cement run between Seattle and Anchorage. The CRAIG and Captain May continued in this service throughout the balance of the year and until the summer of 1978 when she had a complete change of environment.

On June 2nd the CRAIG, and as usual with Chuck May in charge, left Tacoma with the barge FOSS-288 loaded with several small Navy waste-oil barges riding piggyback, consigned to Navy bases on the Atlantic Coast. The eastbound voyage lasted thirty-two days and except for having to tighten lashings, the on-deck barges gave no problems. They were off-loaded at Chester, Pennsylvania and then towed separately to bases at Earl, New Jersey; Norfolk, Virginia; and Charleston, South Carolina.

From Charleston the CRAIG went down to Jacksonville, Florida to wait for an upcoming job, and as it turned out, a six-week's wait. So the crew was flown back to Seattle except for the Captain and Chief Engineer remaining aboard on standby.

The lay-up ended the later part of August and the CRAIG, with most of the old crew aboard, headed north to Bay City, Michigan via the St. Lawrence Seaway, marking the second time a Foss tug sailed the waters of the Great Lakes. The DREW had been the first, as in early summer she had towed the dredge NEW YORK to Bay City on a Foss history-making voyage from New Orleans. The CRAIG's orders now called for returning the dredge NEW YORK and a support-barge to Baltimore.

After delivering the dredge and barge to Baltimore, the CRAIG picked up a dump-barge and headed for Miami where she added a second dump-barge and towed both barges to Puerto Cabello, Venezuela. After safely delivering the tow to Puerto Cabello, she made a two-day run to Port of Spain, Trinidad, arriving October 18th. After taking on fuel and stores at Port of Spain, the CRAIG was underway again with two off-shore supply vessels, the LAFAYETTE and the TOUGH TIDE, bound for Seattle. After a comfortable voyage of thirty days, the CRAIG and her tow arrived in Seattle on November 20th, having been away for one hundred and eighty-eight days. There were signs of channel fever as the fragrance of the fir forests drifted aboard the tug plowing down the straits, passing familiar landmarks only eight hours from home.

The TOUGH TIDE was shifted into Foss-Seattle shipyard to go through a $500,000 renovation to fit her for handling refrigerated containers according to plans of her new owners, Clipperton Inc. of Seattle. The LAFAYETTE was moved to another Seattle shipyard for conversion to a crab fishing vessel.

In late December 1978 the CRAIG entered the Foss Shipyard for voyage repairs and annual maintenance to be ready for the spring activity. The 1979 season was slow in starting and the CRAIG rubbed the fender piles until April, then she made a quick trip to Anchorage followed by general towing until June when, with Captain Chuck May, she left for San Francisco to pick up a Navy ship for delivery to Balboa, Canal Zone. Completing the tow, they headed back for Seattle, but on the way orders were received to locate a disabled tuna boat 500 miles north of the Equator and tow the boat to San Diego. The CRAIG made easy work of the assignment and they were heading out of San Diego after bringing in the tuna clipper when word came through that a ship required an escort from Acapulco, Mexico to Long Beach. The CRAIG turned south for Acapulco, joined the vessel and accompanied her to Long Beach, arriving in early August. With no more diversion, the CRAIG made Seattle non-stop and started right out running to Alaska.

The CRAIG must believe variety relieves monotony as she has a penchant for the unusual jobs, but being in the right place at the right time has made it all possible.

DEBORAH FOSS

Built:	1965	Propulsion:	Caterpillar (Twin)
	Albina Shipyard		1,200-horsepower
	Portland, Oregon	Primary Service:	Puget Sound
Length:	66-feet	Status:	In Service
Beam:	24-feet		

After passing acceptance trials on the Columbia River, the DEBORAH, second in the series of eight "D"-class tugs built by Albina, entered service out of Seattle in May 1965. DEBORAH's name came from the middle name of Lillian Foss, Andrew and Thea's daughter.

After stores were put aboard at the Foss pier, the DEBORAH left for Southwestern Alaska to work for the next two seasons in the Gulf of Alaska and Cook Inlet, assisting in the construction of offshore oil platforms. During the winter months when weather conditions prohibited construction work in the Inlet, she returned to Seattle and became a linehaul tug on Puget Sound. The DEBORAH and other tugs returning to Seattle from a season in Alaska enabled Foss, during the off-season months of the year, to make use of the new boats and reduce use of the under-powered older tugs—some of them dating back to the turn of the century.

The DEBORAH returned to the Inlet in 1966 during the height of the offshore platform construction. Foss Company in 1966 had seven tugs, two supply vessels and two launches operating in Cook Inlet. The DEBORAH and most of the tugs worked for the J. Ray McDermott Company of Houston, Texas. Marine activity in "66" was at an all-time high as the oil companies were making up for the time lost due to past winter shut-downs.

So the DEBORAH didn't return home until December and since then, except for special assignments, she has remained on Puget Sound, doing ship-assist work, towing oil, chemical, chip or bulk-cement barges.

However, a special assignment did come up for the DEBORAH during the 1969 May-to-September fish-canning season in Southwestern Alaska. Under command of Captain Karl Hansen she worked for Sea-Land Corporation, hauling containers of canned fish by barge from canneries on Kodiak Island and Prince William Sound to Anchorage for trans-shipment to Seattle via Sea-Land container ships. After five months hauling fish, the DEBORAH returned to Seattle and more routine towing.

Since the Sea-Land job, the DEBORAH has remained close to her home base, working on Puget Sound runs, year-in and year-out. She is classified as a Sound tug along with two other "D" boats. The three "D's" do most of the Foss linehaul work on the Sound, and they do it with little down-time—apparently no improvements are needed in their original specifications. The classification "D" boat could readily mean "dependable."

JENNY FOSS

Built:	1965	Propulsion:	Caterpillar (Twin)
	Martinolich Shipyard		600-horsepower
	Tacoma, Washington	Primary Service:	Puget Sound
Length:	60-feet	Status:	In Service
Beam:	21-feet		

The JENNY, second of three "J"-class tugs built to replace Foss' veteran wood boats, was named for a relative of Andrew by marriage. The all-steel tug was completed, outfitted, and ready for towing by mid-April 1965; and to test the equipment, she towed the rail-barge FOSS-118 on a round trip from Seattle to Vancouver, B.C. During the run all parts held a green light on the display board so she was cleared to take on long-haul jobs.

The JENNY would have been a welcome addition to the Foss-Seattle Puget Sound Division as they were then working with seventeen boats averaging forty-three years in age and four built before the turn of the century; however, assisting in Cook Inlet oil exploration had first call on the JENNY's service. Assigned to Anchorage, she left Seattle on May 3, 1965 with a tandem barge tow, making the 1,600-mile run in nine days. After an active first season in the Inlet tending oil rigs, winter conditions forced her to return to Seattle in mid-December. Her first winter at home was not spent rubbing the fender piles—she worked steadily at general towing on Puget Sound for Foss-Seattle.

With the start of the spring thaw in Cook Inlet, the JENNY returned to take part in the busiest year ever for the company in the Inlet. Foss tugs barged in supplies, delivered equipment, serviced oil-platforms, and the JENNY's part was acting as tender to an oil-drilling rig. She finished her work in time to return home for Christmas 1966 and then repeated last year's program of starting out the New Year towing on the Sound until the Inlet was free of ice.

In March 1967 she left for the inlet on what was her last departure from Puget Sound for four-and-a-half years. At the end of each season's work, when the ice became too thick for tugs to maneuver, the JENNY headed for southern Cook Inlet to spend the winter in the ice-free harbors of Seldovia or Homer. But in September 1971 she left Cook Inlet early and went to "southeastern" for the General Construction Company on a job at Wrangell Narrows. The job finished up in mid-October and at long last she returned to the Foss-Seattle shipyard to repair four years' wear and tear.

After a long reconditioning followed by a spell of towing on Puget Sound, she headed back to Anchorage for the usual round of jobs. Completing an active season at various drill and project sites around Cook Inlet, the JENNY left to spend the winter in the small-boat harbor at Kodiak. Then as usual, when the Inlet opened up in mid-March, she returned to the familiar waters around Anchorage. But by early June 1973 need for the JENNY's particular type of service was over, so she returned to Seattle towing a general cargo barge via Kenai, Juneau, and Sitka, arriving home the end of June. She went right to work for the Puget Sound division doing routine light and intermediate towing for the next three years.

Then, for eight months in 1976 the JENNY operated with a two-man crew working five twelve-hour shifts per week towing chip-barges between the Pope & Talbot Mill at Port Gamble and the Crown Zellerbach Mill at Port Townsend. This was the first time one specific tug was assigned to a steady run hauling forest by-products from one mill to another, although Foss provides general service all over the Sound for barging chips and hogged fuel.

After her eight months with the "chips," the JENNY returned to regular full crew status for line-haul work out of Seattle. Then in January 1977 she was transferred to the Everett division, Pacific Towboat Company, to assist in harbor operations and towing Weyerhaeuser log rafts from Everett harbor to the Snohomish River long storage—again, as in Port Gamble, with two-man day crews. A shortage of line-haul tugs on the Sound in March put JENNY back with a full crew for longer runs.

The JENNY's record has proved the versatility of the "J" boats; they are a decided advantage as they adapt so readily from harbor day-boats to long-haul day and night boats. The "J" must stand for "Jack-of-all-trades"!

JOSIE FOSS

Built:	1965	Propulsion:	Caterpillar (Twin)
	Martinolich Shipyard		600-horsepower
	Tacoma, Washington	Primary Service:	Puget Sound
Length:	60-feet	Status:	In Service
Beam:	21-feet		

The JOSIE, named for the daughter-in-law of Andrew's sister Dorothy, was third in the series of "J" class tugs ordered by Foss for light towing on the Sound and in Alaska. Ready for service on May 19, 1965 she successfully made her trial trip to Vancouver, British Columbia, towing rail car barge FOSS-118. She spent her first year on Puget Sound doing general towing for the Seattle division, waiting out her time before ranging far and wide.

Then JOSIE's range widened considerably due to the construction of offshore oil platforms and laying oil pipelines in Cook Inlet. The program reached a peak in 1966 making the JOSIE's services more important in Alaska than Puget Sound, so on May 18, 1966 she left Seattle for the Inlet with a small supply barge in tow. She worked all season tending oil rigs and supplying them with materials by barge. The open working season ended in December when the Inlet iced up, so the JOSIE returned home to wait out the winter and to prepare for the spring activity.

By March the JOSIE was able to return to the Inlet for an eight-month season, performing the same supply service for the oil rigs as the previous year. At the end of the 1967 season she again returned to home waters for general towing until August of 1970 when she was sent back to Alaska, but not to Cook Inlet. This time Sitka was in need of her services. She spent four months towing a sand, gravel, and rock barge of 1,450-yard capacity from pits and a quarry at Leesoffskaia Bay to Sitka. The material, thirty-eight barge loads, went into the fill to make the approaches of the new high-level bridge spanning the channel between Sitka and Japonski Island.

When the adverse winter weather came in November, the JOSIE was relieved of the operation by the DEBORAH FOSS, as a larger tug was necessary to buck the elements. Captain "Red" Hendershot, and later Bob Washburn and their crews, played an important part by their "on schedule" deliveries in the construction of the very important bridge linking Sitka with all the major government installations on Japonski Island, previously serviced by ferry and launch.

The JOSIE's crew transferred to the DEBORAH so the experienced "local knowledge" men could remain to finish the job and the DEBORAH's delivery crew returned the JOSIE to Seattle.

She remained on Puget Sound towing for the next two-and-one-half years, until mid-1973 when Foss dispatched her with a small cargo barge for Anchorage to move heavy equipment to various drilling sites.

Then in August 1973 the JOSIE became the first "J" class boat and the smallest Foss tug, under its own power, to venture into the open Gulf of Alaska and on to the west end of the Alaska Peninsula. She made two trips to Cold Bay towing barges in connection with improving the airport runway. The asphalt for the runway came up from Seattle, a barge load in drums via the WENDY FOSS. Unfortunately, for the JOSIE's crew, their arrival times didn't coincide so they lost out on a looked-for visit.

After another month in Cook Inlet the JOSIE's Alaska adventures were over, and she returned to more routine towing on Puget Sound. She hasn't left her home waters since the fall of 1973 the "Call of the North" has been answered by the larger and more powerful tugs.

SEA QUEEN (Later MATHILDA FOSS) departing N.C. Marine dock, Lake Union during first week of operation for Pacific Towboat Co., her original owners – October 1965. (Courtesy of the author's collection)

MATHILDA FOSS (2)

Built:	1965	Propulsion:	Caterpillar
	Martinolich Shipyard		765-horsepower
	Tacoma, Washington	Primary Service:	Puget Sound
Length:	65-feet	Status:	In Service
Beam:	21-feet		

The MATHILDA FOSS was completed in October 1965 as the SEA QUEEN, for Pacific Towboat Company in Everett. Pacific built her to replace the veteran tug GEORGE W. in Pacific's log-towing service on Puget Sound.

With alternate Captains, Tom Crowley and Jerry Biddle, she worked out of Everett for several years towing logs around Puget Sound for pulp mills, sawmills, and logging companies.

The SEA QUEEN was also used by Foss-Seattle on barge tows and ship-assists if log towing turned slack. But such was not the case in 1971 during the longshoremen's strike; then the QUEEN had no slack to pick up, not even in her towline.

On July 1, 1971 the longshoremen on the entire West Coast went on strike, resulting in a tie-up of shipping at all ports. Many ships spent weeks at anchor, but cargo vessels scheduled for loading logs on Puget Sound for Japan were diverted to open ports in British Columbia—Vancouver, Nanaimo, Ladysmith, and Cowichan Bay. A big problem in logistics developed by the sudden call to rapidly move millions of feet of logs from Puget Sound storages to British Columbia.

Foss, the principal log tower on Puget Sound, was expected to supply tugs to tow the countless log rafts to Canada, so it became necessary to reactivate boats from lay-up status and also put full overnight crews on the small wooden tugs, relegated to only harbor duty the past few years. The larger reactivated tugs along with the active tugs began towing to Canada. The fully-crewed small tugs were used on Puget Sound, towing barges to relieve the larger tugs to take part in the log exodus.

The LEA MOE, one of the small reactivated tugs, had a special but important part in the log movement—her job was to assist the log tows through narrow, winding Deception Pass. The Pass, connecting Skagit Bay with Rosario Straits, was used by tugs coming up from Everett and lower Sound ports enabling them to tow for as long as possible in sheltered waters.

The SEA QUEEN from July on safely delivered five tows from Everett to Cowichan Bay, four tows from Everett to Ladysmith, one tow each from Everett to Nanaimo and Vancouver and two tows from Port Angeles to Ladysmith and Nanaimo. The tows ranged in size from twenty-four sections to over forty sections, mostly bundled logs, so the volume ran from one to two million feet per tow.

At one period in mid-August, with the strike still on, a record number of tugs with log tows headed for British Columbia. The following report from the crash towing program shows the tugs and tows involved on just one day, August 16th.

BRYNN FOSS	(Regular ship-assist tug)	33 sections, Everett to Cowichan Bay
DOROTHY FOSS	(Regular barge work)	36 sections, Tacoma to Cowichan Bay
ELAINE FOSS	(General towing)	20 sections, Tacoma to Ladysmith
ERIK FOSS	(Out of reserve status)	31 sections, Everett to Cowichan Bay
GARY FOSS	(General towing)	48 sections, Tacoma to Ladysmith
MYRTLE FOSS	(Reg. Neah Bay log service)	25 sections, Port Angeles to Cowichan Bay
OSWELL FOSS	(General towing)	300 boomsticks, Cowichan Bay to Tacoma
SANDRA FOSS	(Out of reserve status)	30 sections, Tacoma to Ladysmith
SEA CHICKEN	(Log towing)	29 sections, Everett to Cowichan Bay
ISLAND VALIANT	(Chartered tug from B.C.)	24 sections, Everett to Vancouver

The day's towing for the ten tugs totaled 276 sections containing approximately 12-million board feet. Eight other Foss tugs, with 100 sections of logs, were also towing on August 16th, but between ports on Puget Sound for domestic use. Three hundred acres of timberland would be required to yield the total volume of logs towed on the record day.

The hectic race to keep up with ship-loading schedules continued for another six weeks beyond the record towing-day of August 16th. Finally, President Nixon invoked the Taft-Hartley Act, giving a forty-five day cooling-off period and returning the longshoremen to the docks. The big push to British Columbia with log rafts was over.

When the Taft-Hartley Act expired, the strike had not been resolved, so the work stoppage resumed, but only for a short while. In the meantime, in early December the SEA QUEEN made two more log tows from Everett to Ladysmith before a new contract was agreed upon by the I.L.W.U. and the Stevedoring Companies. After over five months of strike, tension, and negotiations, the shipping and towing industry returned to normal work. The SEA QUEEN resumed her routine log towing between Puget Sound ports and she continued pulling log rafts for the next several years.

In October 1974 while in Seattle for annual drydocking and repair, the SEA QUEEN was painted in the green and white colors of Foss and renamed MATHILDA FOSS to conform with the current policy of using Foss family names. By using the name MATHILDA, Foss then had three boats similar in type, enough for a new name-class of tugs, the "M" boats. MATHILDA, the 1965 SEA QUEEN, was followed in 1966 by two sister-tugs, the MELIA and MYRTLE. They were built according to plans and design of the SEA QUEEN and they are living proof of the capabilities of the original "M" boat.

The MATHILDA still continued to earn her living towing logs. Once a log tower always a log tower—according to the MATHILDA's record. Though it is a slow, time-consuming and rather monotonous job, occasionally an incident happens to provide a little spice.

Such was the case on a summer evening in August 1978 when the MATHILDA was running light entering Elliott Bay. Captain Gordon Wright spotted a swimmer just ahead, so he slowed and came up alongside what looked like a mermaid with long flowing hair. The crew, all at the rail, asked if they could be of any assistance. The young lady refused until told that she was in the main shipping lane—then she asked to be taken ashore. The Log Book read: "She was stark naked so we gave her a towel and some clothing and set her ashore at Pier 70. She appeared healthy and cheerful and refused further help or money. She offered no explanation for her strange behavior, but she did appear to be spaced-out."

Now, no doubt, whenever even a hair seal pops up on the surface, the MATHILDA will check just to make sure before going on!

ALASKA HUSKY Shown operating in the icy waters of Cook Inlet, servicing offshore drilling platforms. (Courtesy of Foss Tug Co)

ALASKA HUSKY

Built:	1966	Propulsion:	Caterpillar (4)
	Todd Shipyard		3,200-horsepower
	Houston, Texas	Primary Service:	Cook Inlet, Alaska
Length:	182-feet	Status:	In Service
Beam:	36-feet		

The ALASKA HUSKY was designed and built especially for Foss as an advanced type of supply boat for serving the oil-drilling platforms in Alaska's Cook Inlet on a year-around basis, even in heavy ice and below freezing temperatures.

The HUSKY's measurements of 182 feet by 36 by 16, and with a gross tonnage of 447, made her the largest supply boat serving Cook Inlet's oil industry. She was also the most powerful with four "Cat" diesels driving two propellers, providing ample power in ice and in the strong tidal currents of the Inlet. She has a specially formed cutaway bow, made of heavy plating with extra frame strengthening for ice navigation. Her propellers, shafts and rudders all meet the requirements of the American Bureau of Shipping for work in ice. With her generous size, she is able to deliver more cargo and also more driller's mud and bulk cement in her two 830-cubic-foot below-deck tanks, than any vessel of her type in Alaska. She was made to order!

The new boat left Houston on November 14, 1966 with Captain Don Gordon in charge and Chief Engineer Dexter McDaniel looking after the engine room. Captain Don reported a cruising speed of 15 knots and a 16½ knot flank speed. Her home-bound trip was uneventful, arriving in Seattle on December 4th, and after a brief two-day stay for inspection, stores and fuel, she left for Cook Inlet, arriving on December 12.

Immediately upon arrival and disregarding the usual restrictive winter weather, the HUSKY went on charter to Pan American Petroleum Corporation, a major subsidiary of the Standard Oil Company of Indiana and a Foss account since Pan American pioneered offshore oil operations in Cook Inlet several years previously. Pan American markets petroleum products in the Northwest through American Oil Company service stations and dealers.

The HUSKY remains in Cook Inlet servicing the offshore platforms on a year-around basis, but the charter does allow the ALASKA HUSKY three weeks every two years for drydocking and repairs—so every other May she makes the biennial visit to her home port. However, all of the maintenance and much of the repair is accomplished up North by the tug's crew. With four "Cats," there is no down time for engine repairs, as one engine can be repaired while the remaining engines carry the load. For minor hull repairs, she simply runs up on a beach and waits for the tide to go out, exposing the plating for any necessary work. The beach and tide combine to form an inexpensive drydock.

Her present Captains, both from the Puget Sound area, Tom Lewis and Don Hudspeth, work three months on and three months off. The Captains and their crews keep the HUSKY on the move and the platforms well supplied. Phil Henry on shoreside takes care of ship supply, accounts, and coordinates the work with little lost motion.

The HUSKY has belonged to the mythical Alaska Sourdough Fleet for several years, having put in the necessary seven years of Alaska service in 1975. The Big Dipper flag with seven silver stars on a blue background can fly from her yardarm—she's a new breed of Alaska Husky.

CATHERINE FOSS (2)

Built:	1966-67	Propulsion:	Caterpillar (Twin)
	Martinolich Shipyard		1,700-horsepower
	Tacoma, Washington	Primary Service:	Tacoma Harbor
Length:	80-feet	Status:	In Service
Beam:	25-feet		

PACIFIC MASTER was the original name of the CATHERINE as she was built for Pacific Towboat Company. The tug started work in April 1967 on ship-assists for the ports of Anacortes, Bellingham and Ferndale. A good break-in service for a new tug with all the backing and filling that is part of docking and un-docking big ships. The MASTER turned out to be handy in assisting ocean carriers, but she had yet to be tried at heavy towing.

Towing bundled log rafts would be a good test, so Pacific, being a prime mover of logs in Puget Sound, tried the tug at towing log rafts of 500,000 board feet and weighing up to 5,000 tons. Towing the rafts didn't prove too difficult, though care was exercised to prevent breaking up the rafting gear with her 1,700-horsepower. However, Pacific, knowing the MASTER could be used to better purpose than towing logs, sent her north to Cook Inlet to take part in the lucrative oil boom.

By the summer of 1967 the oil exploration and offshore drilling platform construction was at its height in the Inlet, so the PACIFIC MASTER was able to go right to work as an oil-rig tender, working for the contracting companies that were engaged in platform erection and pipeline laying. The very strong tidal currents flowing up and down the Inlet made it necessary to have sufficient tug power to hold equipment and sections in place during construction.

The PACIFIC MASTER had a long, hard season of 24-hour work days, continually bucking tidal currents until freezing winter weather stopped the action. When the icy winds took over, the PACIFIC MASTER headed south to Puget Sound and a milder environment.

Pacific put her back to work towing logs through February 1968 then in March she started a more sophisticated job hauling Foss container-barges between Seattle and southeastern Alaska for Alaska Steamship Company. Six months prior to this time, in September 1967 the Foss Company with their tug PACIFIC had replaced Alaska Steam's ship on their long-established run to southeastern Alaska. But by 1968 the PACIFIC alone could not handle the freight volume so Foss added the PACIFIC MASTER with Barge #275.

With the tug and barge operation a tried and true success, Alaska Steamship Company permanently retired the WWII knot-class freighters that for years had been on the run to Southeastern. The two tugs were able to provide a weekly sailing out of Seattle and the pioneer container-barge service grew into what is now the well-established Foss Alaska Line.

The PACIFIC MASTER appeared to be set on the van-run for some time, so for better identification and in keeping with tradition, the ownership of the MASTER was transferred to the Foss Company and the name changed to CATHERINE FOSS.

The CATHERINE remained on the run for two-and-a-half years, then with the advent of larger van-barges, resulting in heavier tows, and to maintain the tight schedule, tugs with more power and weight like the LESLIE and RICHARD FOSS were necessary. So the CATHERINE was shifted to a new area of action, but not to a new type of towing.

In February 1971 she left Seattle with Foss Barge #290 to work out of Anchorage for Sea-Land, Inc., delivering and returning containers to the out-ports. The CATHERINE remained in this service until released by Sea-Land in the fall of 1972 but she finished up the season doing spot jobs in Cook Inlet and southwestern Alaska. With the slack winter season at hand, she returned to Puget Sound in December to do general towing and Foss-Seattle kept her on the move for the next twelve months.

Then with the increasing size, tonnage, and number of ships arriving and departing from Tacoma every day, a high-horsepower twin-screw tug was needed to help the locally based SHANNON in harbor shifts and ship-assists. The CATHERINE was the likely boat, so Foss outfitted her for ship-assist work and at the end of 1973 transferred her to the Tacoma Division.

Except for an occasional relief job for the linehaul tugs, the CATHERINE stays with harbor work and she has become the prime ship-assist tug for Tacoma Harbor, with Captains Sam Emmerson and Chet Sweeney expertly handling the levers—they haven't dented a plate yet.

DELORES FOSS

Built:	1966	Propulsion:	Caterpillar (Two)
	Albina Shipyard		1,200-horsepower
	Portland, Oregon	Primary Service:	Southeastern Alaska
Length:	66-feet	Status:	In Service
Beam:	24-feet		

Named for a grandniece of Thea Foss, the DELORES began service in August 1966 fourth of the eight "D"-class boats designed for intermediate-range towing on Puget Sound and Alaska. After the usual few days of outfitting at Foss-Seattle, her home base, she started on her way to Cook Inlet, Alaska to work for the McDermott Company in the construction of offshore oil platforms and the accompanying underwater oil pipelines to shoreside terminals.

The DELORES, along with several other Foss tugs, continued rig-tending until the winter weather dictated a return to Seattle. Running in company with the JENNY and JULIA FOSS, dodging winter storms along the way, the three tugs hauling four barges arrived at the Foss pier in mid-December on a cold and rainy Sunday—weatherwise it was from the freezer to the refrigerator.

After voyage repairs were completed in January, the DELORES towed between ports on Puget Sound, but only until early March when the Cook Inlet tugs again headed North. The DELORES arrived at her station in mid-March and remained tending oil rigs until October 15, 1967 when she left for Port Angeles with a Smith-Rice derrick barge in tow. She arrived safely with the derrick in late October and went right to work on the usual Puget Sound runs, but not for long. Foss sent her to Ketchikan to relieve the ROGER on the Southeastern Alaska oil run for Union Oil Company. The DELORES, with her steel construction and having double the ROGER's horsepower, was a safe boat

DELORES FOSS *Shown assisting a container ship into berth in Seattle, January 1980. (Courtesy of Susan Willott)*

for contending with the Southeastern Alaska winters—an ordeal for the staunchest vessels. The DELORES remained through the worst of the winter weather, until Febuary 1968. She was then recalled to Puget Sound and replaced by the veteran tug EDITH FOSS. With milder weather ahead the EDITH could safely take over the run.

The DELORES worked on linehauls around the Sound through April, then she was given a new and significant Alaska job. Foss was awarded a contract by Standard Oil to deliver oil in Southeastern Alaska, similar to the service performed by Foss for Union Oil. After outfitting for her new assignment, the DELORES left Seattle on May 10, 1968 bound for Ketchikan, towing the refined-oil barge FOSS-110, loaded to capacity with 8,000 barrels of fuel.

Then in August 1968 Foss took delivery of a new 12,000-barrel oil barge built specifically for the Standard Oil run and appropriately named CHEVRON TONGASS. The barge was teamed up with the DELORES in mid-August and put to work on the route, and she has towed the CHEVRON TONGASS on the same run year after year. Captain Ernie Johnson of Ketchikan has been her skipper on all her travels since 1972. By good service she has worked steadier and longer in Alaska than any Foss tug with the exception of the CHRISTINE and the ALASKA HUSKY. The only time she leaves Alaska is for drydocking and engine overhaul at Foss-Seattle.

Captain Johnson, when he brings the DELORES down, always has an unusual experience to relate. The stop-and-go run, calling at port after port and small isolated logging camps lacking usual discharging facilities, causes complications, some odd, some serious and occasionally humorous.

An amusing incident occurred while the DELORES was discharging diesel to shore tanks at one of the small communities and the customer's dockman yelled that he wasn't getting any diesel in his tank. The Foss tankerman replied that he had discharged nearly 10,000 gallons. Where was it? After checking, the dockman found his hose hooked to the wrong tank and the product all went into another customer's heating-fuel tank. They changed headers, filled the proper tank, and to rectify the mistake, the customers temporarily exchanged tanks.

On a more serious occasion Captain Johnson and his crew assisted the U. S. Forest Service in removing some 45,000 gallons of oil from storage tanks on the dilapidated dock of the herring reduction-plant at Big Port Walter.

The crew, at some risk, worked on the rotted decking hooking up lines and then pumped the oil into their barge. They also cleaned up oil that had for some time been seeping out of the old tanks. Transferring the oil and cleaning up the dock prevented what could have been a serious oil spill, had the decayed dock given way and allowed the tanks and pooled oil to drop into the bay. The cooperative effort of the tug's crew and the Forest Service—industry and government—got the job done.

Sometimes locations in Alaska can be deceiving as evidenced by an odd situation that developed in 1978 when Captain Johnson had orders to deliver fuel to a new logging camp at Humpback Creek, which to all intent and purpose was located at Port Frederick in Cross Sound. Since most of the Southeastern Alaska logging camps are portable, being on floats, they can be towed from one tract of timber to another. They are able to shift sites with little notice and tug skippers are sometimes hard-pressed to find a new camp location, especially at an uncharted spot. Captain Johnson's Logbook seems to agree.

After leaving Elfin Cove in Cross Sound, the DELORES headed for Humpback Creek, which shows on the chart as being in Port Frederick near Hoonah. They arrived off Humpback Creek in early evening, and Captain Johnson entered in his Log: "No sign of logging camp, piling, or life." So they continued on to Hoonah, discharged fuel, then returned to Humpback Creek. The Pilot House Log Book had this entry. "Made three passes with searchlight, examined entire shoreline. No sign of anything." They tried once more after daylight, but no camp in sight, so Captain Johnson headed for Angoon, the next regular stop. However, while crossing Icy Straits, he received word on the radio that the Humpback Creek he was looking for was not on a chart, but was to be found in Excursion Inlet on the north side of Icy Straits and not in Port Frederick on the south side. Two hours later they located the camp, delivered the oil and packaged petroleum products as ordered—in large red letters the Captain marked Humpback Creek Number Two on the chart.

The DELORES also took part in an unusual type of oil delivery for the Alaska Communications System when they were asked to deliver fuel to the communications station on a mountain top near Mud Bay, a rather strange request for a water-bound craft. Upon arrival at the bay, they were advised to stand by until the fog shrouding the mountain top cleared. Captain Johnson had no idea what he was expected to do. However, in a few hours the fog lifted and a helicopter dropped down to transfer fuel in barrels! A slow but practical method—and easier than back-packing.

Though the crews of the Foss "oilers" operating in Alaska live a routine life, it is interesting because of the unexpected. Even the weather, especially in the winter, prevents monotony. The satisfaction of the job comes from performing a vital service to the communities, at times carried out under trying and adverse conditions, but they get the job done—the oil must get through—and it has for fifty years.

DIANE FOSS

Built:	1966	Propulsion:	Caterpillar (Twin)
	Albina Shipyard		1,200-horsepower
	Portland, Oregon	Primary Service:	Puget Sound
Length:	66-feet	Status:	In Service
Beam:	24-feet		

DIANE, number three in the "D"-class line of eight tugs, was named after a daughter-in-law of Justine Foss Wood. The new boat left Portland for Seattle on May 28, 1966 after acceptance trials on the River. The run to Foss-Seattle indicated that all parts were operating smoothly, so with only a short lay-over at the Foss Pier to take on stores, she left for the Gulf of Alaska on a three months' Mobil Oil charter to tend and service a drill rig.

Returning to Seattle for a brief period during September and early October, the DIANE was introduced to barge towing on Puget Sound, but the initiation didn't last long for better use could be made of the four-month-old vessel in Alaska.

In October the DIANE, with Captain Ed Lee, sailed for Anchorage, little suspecting the tug would not return to Puget Sound for over three years! During her long sojourn in Anchorage, she worked at a variety of jobs—servicing drill rigs, ship-assists at Anchorage, hauling petroleum products from Dutch Harbor to Bristol Bay, towing barges of general cargo between Anchorage and Kodiak, and running anchors for sea-floor pipeline construction. By December

1969 the DIANE needed a thorough refitting and drydocking. And, as Foss-Seattle was the proper place to do the work, she came down in late December and remained in the shipyard all winter.

In April, again all shipshape, she towed an oil barge to Dutch Harbor, discharged the load and reloaded black oil for distribution to the Bristol bay canneries. She then returned to Cook Inlet to take over the FOSS-251 and haul containerized cargo for Sea-Land during the fishing season in southwestern Alaska. The DIANE picked up canned salmon at three canneries and barged the loaded containers to Kodiak and Anchorage for trans-shipment to Seattle on Sea-Land's ocean carriers. At the end of the fishing season, the need for the added barge service was over, so the DIANE returned to Seattle as it was too late in the Alaska season for further towing, but she could very easily operate on Puget Sound. The new work must have agreed with her for once started, she stayed on the Sound for two and one-half years. Then for the fourth time she returned to Alaska because a harbor tug was needed during the construction of oil terminal facilities in Valdez. The DIANE assisted with the handling of large cargo barges arriving from California and Washington ports with construction materials. The job lasted from August 1974 through March 1975 and then, due to the need of engine repair, she was relieved by the DONNA FOSS. The DIANE returned to Seattle, cured the engine ills but went back to general towing on the Sound, keeping on the go month after month well into 1978.

During the summer of 1978 she had a special job towing rock barges between Neah Bay and LaPush, Washington for the rebuilding of the large LaPush breakwater. In seven weeks the DIANE hauled over 50,000 tons of rock. The perfect weather prevailing both in the Straits and on the Washington Coast for the entire time made the record tonnage possible.

After the breakwater job, the DIANE returned to Foss-Seattle and resumed the work she was doing two months previously. She apparently has become a permanent member of the Foss linehauler group, towing port to port.

LELA FOSS In Port Angeles Harbor, August 1966. (Courtesy of the author's collection)

LELA FOSS (2)

Built:	1966	Propulsion:	Caterpillar
	Pacific Shipyard		325-horsepower
	Anacortes, Washington	Primary Service:	Bellingham
Length:	37-feet	Status:	In Service
Beam:	14-feet		

The second LELA, a steel tug completed in June 1966 was the fifth in a series of nine new harbor tugs programmed for local use in the Puget Sound ports served by Foss. She started out in Tacoma, remained a few months and then went over to Port Angeles in September 1966 to help out the regulars, the FOSS-8 and NANCY FOSS, in juggling log rafts and boomsticks.

The LELA remained in Port Angeles harbor service until late 1968 when she was replaced by the more powerful harbor tug, GRACE FOSS. The LELA then returned to Tacoma to do the same type of work she did in Port Angeles.

In January 1972 Foss transferred her to Bellingham to replace the outdated wood tug, BIRCH BAY, as second harbor tug to the SAMISH BAY (later the JOE FOSS). The BIRCH BAY having seen her day, was relegated to the lay-up farm in Seattle.

The SAMISH BAY and LELA worked together until June 1973 when a lessening of harbor work in Bellingham made two tugs unnecessary and the SAMISH BAY transferred to Port Angeles, leaving the LELA as the remaining harbor tug. Her primary work has been with the Georgia Pacific Pulp Mill, shifting chip barges and logs, but she does take care of general harbor calls asking for tug assistance. The LELA, with Captain Dick Edwards, carries on with the all-purpose service, usually on just a five-day, forty-hour week, but they get the jobs done and on time even with the limited hours—a little fish in a big pond, but the only fish.

MARGARET FOSS (2)

Built:	1943	Propulsion:	General Motors (Twin)
	Levingston Shipyard		1,800-horsepower
	Orange, Texas	Primary Service:	Coastwise and Ocean
Length:	135-feet	Last Operating Day:	April 8, 1968
Beam:	33-feet	Status:	Sold - Foreign

The MARGARET FOSS, a large World War II ocean-class tug, numbered ATA 126, was built to do heavy towing and convoy assistance for the United States Navy. But shortly after completion, she was transferred to the British Royal Navy and renamed MINDFUL. She finished out the War years for the British before being returned to the United States. The navy then in 1945 reclassified her as the Ocean Rescue Tug ATR 48.

In 1947 she was purchased at a government surplus sale by the Moran Towing Company of New York and renamed GAY MORAN. She served the towing interests of Moran for only two years before being sold to Redstack Towing Company of San Francisco in 1949 and renamed SEA LION. In 1955 she was again sold—this time to East Coast owners and renamed HARRY J. MOSSER. Two years later ownership passed to Mobile Towing and Wrecking of Mobile, Alabama, and for the sixth change her name became MARGARET WALSH. She remained under Mobile Towing and Wrecking ownership for eight continuous years—a record time for the ATR 48. But, then having no further use for the MARGARET, she was offered for sale.

Foss, with expanding ocean operations on both the West Coast and Alaska, was in need of another big tug and the MARGARET could be the answer. An inspection was made of the tug and though some defects were in evidence, the asking price was in line, so Foss purchased her on February 7, 1966 and added Foss after her name—the MARGARET FOSS became the first and last diesel-electric tug owned by the Company. She had two 900-horsepower diesel engines driving two main generators, and the two generators in turn furnished power for the propeller-shaft motors. The electric drive allowed the main engines to run at a steady speed at all times.

Two weeks after the MARGARET became a Foss, Captain Jug Nolze and a twelve-man Foss crew left Mobile with the MARGARET for Charleston, South Carolina where they picked up three cargo barges for delivery to Panama. The PACIFIC RANGER was to take over the barges in Panama, but it so happened the RANGER was ahead of schedule and met the MARGARET off the south coast of Jamaica and there took charge of the barges. The MARGARET returned to Charleston on March 24, 1966 and picked up the FMS #6 (Floating Machine Shop) at the Navy yard for delivery to Tacoma. However, the MARGARET towed the barge only to Panama where the LESLIE FOSS was waiting to complete the tow. The MARGARET then was dispatched to Louisiana to the Atchafalaya River and took in tow the drill tender J. W. NICKLE for delivery to Cook Inlet, Alaska. The tug and tow arrived in Panama on April 16th and after transiting the Canal towed non-stop to Long Beach, California, averaging six knots for the 2,900-mile trip. After fueling at Long Beach, the MARGARET on May 9th left for Cook Inlet, intending to make a direct run.

Two days later the ADELINE, having completed a towing job in San Francisco, joined forces with the MARGARET to help on the long uphill pull to Alaska. But when they arrived off the Washington Coast, the

MARGARET FOSS *At Foss yard Ballard in lay-up status, after arriving from Vietnam July, 1967. (From the author's collection)*

MARGARET developed electrical troubles in the main power units. Fearing a complete breakdown, Foss sent the PATRICIA out from Seattle to relieve the MARGARET on the tow. On May 10th the two Miki tugs continued on to Cook Inlet and the MARGARET proceeded to the Foss-Seattle repair yard.

For the next four weeks extensive electrical and mechanical repairs were made to put the MARGARET in seaworthy condition and by mid-June the big tug was ready. In late June she was underway with the LST-barge FOSS-210 for Clatskanie, Oregon to pick up a load of drill pipe for Cook Inlet. However, the MARGARET left the FOSS-210 in Clatskanie and went down the coast to Oakland and hooked onto two barges for delivery to the Inlet. But she didn't get far as the ARTHUR FOSS took over the tow in Georgia Straits, B.C. and the MARGARET brought the ARTHUR's empty Alaska barges back to Seattle, tying up on July 9th.

In August and early September, the MARGARET completed a round trip with a lumber barge between West Coast Lumber ports and Honolulu. Arriving back in Seattle on September 15th she went immediately to the repair yard to be outfitted for an extended voyage to Vietnam, as Foss had contracted with the Government to make two separate tows from the East Coast to Vietnam. The AGNES FOSS was already engaged in the first tow and the MARGARET was selected to make the second. She was about to enter a theatre of war for the second time in her life.

On September 25, 1966 the MARGARET left Seattle with a Foss barge for delivery at San Diego before going to Long Beach to pick up her Vietnam tow, consisting of one large Army tug and two barges that were being brought around from Charleston, South Carolina by the MARY FOSS. The two Foss tugs coming up from the South arrived in Long Beach about the same time. The MARY left immediately to tow a disabled ship back to Long Beach and the MARGARET's crew started right in to make up their tow for the long haul across the Pacific. With Captain Jay

Jacobson in charge for this trip and Chief Engineer Dick Goldsmith looking after the engines, the MARGARET pulled out of Long Beach the evening of October 3rd, towing the Army Tug LT 1952 and one barge—the second barge was lashed on the deck of the waterborne barge. The final destination: Vietnam, 8,000 miles away with stops at Honolulu and Guam for fuel.

On the leg to Honolulu, thirty to forty-knot winds and rough seas buffeted them all during the thirteen-day voyage. However, they arrived in Honolulu October 16th with no apparent damage to the LT or the barges. At 1900 hours, October 17th, the U. S. Coast Guard broadcasted a tidal wave alert and ordered all vessels out to sea. The MARGARET circled off Oahu all night until the alert was cancelled the next morning.

With weather clearance the MARGARET and her tow left Honolulu, but they didn't get far; while still inside the harbor, a fire in the engine control console necessitated a return to the pier. Necessary repairs were carried out quickly and she was underway again at 1700 hours on October 18th, bound for Guam.

The weather started out fine on the second leg of the voyage, but deteriorated two days later. During the twenty-two days to Guam they were constantly beset with twenty-five to forty-knot winds. For nine days the seas were moderate to rough and for five days very rough, with the tug rolling and pitching heavily, according to Captain Jacobson's daily Log.

With Guam still eight hundred miles away, the Chief informed Captain Jay that the starboard engine would be under repair for a day to fix a fused and burned motor control current regulator, but the port engine would keep the MARGARET pulling ahead. After the repair with both motors back on the line, they were able to complete the three-week trip to Guam on November 8th.

At Guam, the crew was notified that upon arrival in Vietnam, the tug would go on charter to Alaska Barge & Transport then operating a fleet of tugs, mostly Miki-class, in South Vietnam under contract to the United States Government. Several A.B. & T. tugs were in drydock in Hong Kong, so the Foss tugs were needed as temporary replacements. The AGNES FOSS, already in Vietnam, was included under the terms of the nine-month charter agreement between Foss and A.B. & T.

The MARGARET was delayed in Guam for forty-eight hours undergoing repairs to a troublesome radar and shore mechanics worked around the clock for the two days, making engine and main motor repairs. The MARGARET was able to leave Guam behind on November 11th for the third and final leg of the trip. After only one day at sea, the weather turned foul with lightning, torrential rain, strong winds, and steep seas. Captain Jacobson reported the MARGARET performed as before—yawing, rolling, and pitching heavily! For the next five days they were pounded by heavy, rough seas. Even passing through San Bernadino Straits in the Philippines and entering the South China Sea, the weather remained bad with winds over twenty-five knots the entire time.

At 1350 hours on November 23rd, the MARGARET passed into the Vietnam War Zone, then after three more days at sea, on November 26th, the long rugged fifty-three day voyage ended at Saigon. On November 27th tug and crew went on the agreed charter to A.B. & T. for service at their discretion in Vietnam waters.

The MARGARET's first local trips were barge shuttles on the Saigon river during daylight navigation hours. The trips halted on November 30th when a bearing on the starboard main engine blower burned out. The repair took place in the river mooring Bouy #6, Vung Tau. After 72 hours of day-and-night work, the blower was repaired, and at the same time the towing winch was overhauled and the engine controls worked over. She started out towing again on December 28, but not for long—the port main engine blower this time, so back to the buoy for two more days of repairs. Then with both blowers functioning, the MARGARET went back to work towing between Saigon, Vung Tau, Cam Ranh Bay and Qui Nhon. Whenever the MARGARET's engineers had the chance they worked on the saltwater cooling system, the injectors on both main engines, electrical short circuits, the refrigerating system, pulling and changing main engine pistons and heads and attempting repairs on the radar. The engineers were fighting their own private war with the MARGARET's machinery.

On the night of January 13, 1967 the MARGARET was called away from her regular work to do a rescue job—the freighter GOLDEN GATE had lost her propeller at the Saigon River entrance and was in danger of grounding. The MARGARET headed out immediately in a blacked-out condition, down the dark River without benefit of lights or radar, but with a patrol escort. They reached the ship in time and towed her up to Saigon, arriving in the morning.

In late January, the MARGARET worked out of Cam Ranh Bay, towing coastwise. On one of her runs in February, after arriving at Nha Trang, they were ordered to shift barges at a shallow water mooring. There were no small tugs available and the job had to be done. While shifting the barges the MARGARET grounded. Inspection revealed water entering the general storeroom and after-chain locker. Within a few hours both compartments were flooded, but the crew was able to seal off the area.

An underwater examination team found cracks in the shell plating below the storeroom compartment, so a shoreside repair crew welded the fractures in the hull and another crew cemented the hull from inside the pumped-out rooms. Four days and the job was complete, or so they thought. Water continued to enter the chain-locker and further investigation revealed additional cracks. To correct the defects overlay plates had to be welded on the hull. Three more days and the MARGARET was again ready to go to work.

During the remaining weeks of February, March and April she was assigned to more coastwise duties, towing barges between ports of Cam Ranh Bay, Phan Thiet, Vung Tau, Vung Ro, Nha Trang, and Phen Rang. Nearly fifty barge tows were safely made, delivering war material and supplies.

In early May she was assigned a new duty: assisting landing ships on and off the beaches at Duc Pho. She continued in this hazardous service for several days until A.B. & T. ordered her to Nha Trang where the weary crew were elated to hear that the MARGARET's tour of duty in Vietnam was over—three months early.

On May 14th, Captain Jacobson headed the MARGARET to Hong Kong for the repairs necessary in order for Foss to accept the tug after the A.B. & T. charter. On May 17th, she arrived at Tai-Koo shipyard for two weeks of extensive overhaul.

The AGNES FOSS, also released, was at Hong Kong for survey and repairs at the same time as the MARGARET. So the question was, who would tow the other home!

The AGNES was selected because she was in far superior condition for the long trip. On May 31st, the crew of the AGNES flew home and the MARGARET's crew moved over to the AGNES after the Foss Company had accepted both tugs in their repaired condition. The two boats left Hong Kong on June 7, the AGNES towing the unmanned MARGARET on the long 5,700-mile non-stop voyage to Seattle.

After a safe and comfortable crossing, the two tugs arrived at the Foss Yard in Seattle on July 2nd, and outside of rust streaks spoiling the paint jobs, both tugs looked in good shape, and so did Captain and crew, but they did look a little like South Pacific rovers.

The MARGARET, with her performance record not the best, remained idle all summer and fall of 1967 as the new ocean-class tugs handled all heavy duty assignments. But an opportunity came her way in December. At the time, Foss was heavily involved in the Amchitka-AEC cargo movement and with severe winter weather battering the Gulf of Alaska and Aleutian Islands, they decided a heavy-built steel tug would be the safest way to go, especially with the warning of the near-sinking of the storm-damaged JUSTINE FOSS while enroute to Amchitka two weeks earlier. The MARGARET's hard-pressed Vietnam skipper, Jay Jacobson, was on the JUSTINE at the time.

With all the new tugs otherwise committed, the MARGARET was broken out of lay-up to make the run to Amchitka. So on December 6, Captain Don Gordon left Seattle with the MARGARET, towing the loaded LST Barge, FOSS-200. Captain Don had good luck for the first thousand miles, then one of the typical Pacific winter storms drove down in sudden fury. The MARGARET had to heave-to in the Gulf off Icy Bay. The wind rose to hurricane force and the seas were high and steep. The strain on the winch was too great and the towline started to slip on the drum. At 1600 hours on December 14, the brake couldn't hold the load any longer and the towline flew off the drum right to the bitter end. Driven by the wind, the barge drifted away to the northward at two-and-a-half knots.

Fortunately, Puget Sound Tug & Barge's SEA WITCH was within a few miles of the MARGARET, so Don Gordon called on the radio and asked the Captain to try and hook the barge and tow it to shelter. With good maneuvering the SEA WITCH was able to get her wire aboard and tow the barge to Gull Cove in Icy Straits, and the MARGARET followed along to calmer waters.

In the quiet haven, the MARGARET was able to make a deadline hookup to the barge for the run to Seattle for repairs and relash the barge cargo. The MARGARET and the barge left Gull Cove December 17 and arrived Seattle on the 23rd, without complications—much to the joy of the crew and their families, in time for an unexpected Christmas at home.

On December 31, 1967 with winch repairs complete, the cargo relashed, and Captain Jay Jacobson now aboard, the tug left Seattle with the FOSS-200 in tow bound for Amchitka, Captain Jay hoping his luck with the MARGARET and the weather would change for the better, but it was not to be.

The first sign of trouble came less than two days out of Seattle when a warning light on the barge signified the motors on the reefer vans were not functioning properly. Then the next day the MARGARET's radar went dead. So they hauled for Ketchikan to effect repairs to the reefer units and the radar. This time the repairs were easy and in six hours they were underway.

Shortly after entering the Gulf of Alaska on January 13, 1968 the old radar gave up the ghost completely. A whole new unit was air-freighted to Kodiak and the MARGARET went to Kodiak, installed the new unit and then after waiting out a storm, got underway for Amchitka on January 14. For all of twenty-four hours everything was normal.

However, at 0600 hours January 15th, the MARGARET radioed that the wind was reaching gale force and reported that the deck cargo on the barge had shifted and sections of pipe were hanging over ths side, forcing them to seek refuge in Alitak Bay. Inspecting the barge, they found that the cargo had again shifted dangerously and some of the pipe washed overboard. The intensity of the storm held them in Alitak Bay for three days before they were able to head out for Kodiak and better facilities for restowing the cargo. They arrived in Kodiak on January 19th and longshoremen went to work on the restow. During the stay in port, the temperature held at sixteen degrees accompanied by heavy snow!

By 2000 hours January 21st, Captain Jay reported that the stanchion-welding on the barge was completed and the deck-cargo restowed. They left Kodiak on January 22nd, but by evening they were weatherbound in Kupreanof Straits with fifty-knot winds and rough seas. Two days later they were again weatherbound in Uganik Bay for 48 hours. They finally arrived in Dutch Harbor for fuel on January 29th. During the fuel stop an electronics expert tried to repair two of the tug's dead radios. Only one was repairable.

By the morning of February 3rd, 36 days out of Seattle, the MARGARET was within six miles of Amchitka. However, the weather took a sudden turn for the worse with the wind gusting at seventy knots and heavy seas battered Constantine Harbor on Amchitka Island. For the next four days they jogged back and forth between Amchitka and Kiska Island waiting for the weather to moderate. At last on the night of February 7th, they were able to dock in the Harbor.

By February 11, with half of the cargo discharged, a heavy surge started to build up in the harbor, causing the barge to pound against the pier, inflicting structural damage. The MARGARET pulled the barge away against a fifty-knot gale and driving snow. Working out to the middle of the harbor, they dropped the hook and ran the engines slow ahead to hold position, but by the fourteenth the wind was hurricane force and the MARGARET had to leave the harbor to get away from the battering. She stayed outside, holding up to the seas until February 16, when the weather eased enough to get back to the pier and discharge the remainder of the cargo. Two days of unloading and they were on their way back to Seattle.

The southbound voyage was made in continuous bad weather. The storms along the way caused extended periods at anchor in sheltered bays. The 2,500-mile return voyage required twenty-four days!

An anti-climax to a long and discouraging voyage occurred upon arrival at Shilshole Bay in Seattle on March 13. The engineroom auxiliary quit—causing loss of power to the tow winch and capstan, requiring a harbor tug to assist in breaking up the tow gear and hauling in the tow wire. They finally arrived at the Foss Pier at 1830 hours after a record-setting voyage length of seventy-four days to Amchitka and return. It was a happy crew that set foot on home ground, happy to be free of all the MARGARET's tough luck. Captain Jacobson probably felt the greatest relief, freed of the heavy day and night responsibility that was his for the last seventy-four days.

The voyage repair work to the MARGARET was not extensive and on March 21st, with Captain Don Barbeau aboard, they took in tow McDermott's heavy Derrick Barge #7 for Cook Inlet. The 1,500-mile trip was made in eleven days with no problems, an unusual feat for the beleaguered MARGARET. She returned light to Seattle, arriving April 8th.

The Chief Engineer had an extensive voyage repair list this time and repair work was started, but as time went on it appeared that all the programmed towing work for the season could be accomplished without the use of the MARGARET. Several factors, including heavy Coast Guard manning requirements governing inspected vessels over three hundred tons, and the MARGARET's poor general mechanical and structural condition made it impractical and uneconomical to keep the tug in service. But she did remain in ready-reserve in Seattle until the fall when she was towed to Tacoma for lay-up.

In early October, representatives from a Mexican cement company, having heard of the MARGARET's availability for purchase, arrived in Tacoma to inspect the boat for possible use in Mexico. The tug appeared to fit their needs, and so on October 8, an application was made to the U.S. Maritime Administration to sell the vessel foreign and convert her registry from U.S. to Mexico. Approval was granted on October 30 for the change in flag. With the way cleared, the tug was then sold on November 8th to Cementos California of Ensenada.

The MARGARET was reactivated and renamed C.C.#7 and some repairs were carried out at Foss-Tacoma. On December 4, 1968 the CC#7 left Tacoma for Ensenada to begin a new life hauling barges of limestone between the quarries of Punta China and Ensenada.

In early 1979 word was received from Cementos California that the CC#7 was in good working condition, making three trips per week to Ensenada and a few trips to LaPaz each year. The CC#7 has been hauling barges of limestone for the past ten years and she has moved a total of 3,553,184 metric tons. Quite a record for a tug that had a less than satisfactory past record. But the environment and the work demands were vastly different. Anyway, the Mexican climate must agree with the thirty-six year old tug.

MELIA FOSS

Built:	1966	Propulsion:	Caterpillar
	Martinolich Shipyard		765-horsepower
	Tacoma, Washington	Primary Service:	Puget Sound
Length:	65-feet	Status:	In Service
Beam:	21-feet		

The MELIA FOSS—named for a daughter of Christine Foss Udall, Arthur Foss' daughter—was completed in Tacoma in early May of 1966, second of her type built by Martinolich to replace the aging Puget Sound wood tugs. After completing test runs in Tacoma, she went to work for the Seattle office on the North Vancouver car-barge service. The MELIA continued as the primary vessel on the run until the newly repowered and rebuilt GARY FOSS replaced her in mid-July, 1966.

After the GARY took over, the MELIA assisted on the Puget Sound towing programs handled by Foss-Seattle. She has remained close to home base with the exception of one month in the summer of 1973 when she towed two barges from Seattle to Ketchikan for loading with canned salmon. She remained in Ketchikan, with Captain Walt Kardonsky in charge, for a short period on a stand-by basis to assist Foss Alaska Line tugs arriving with tandem tows of container-barges. Then in mid-August the MELIA went over to Chatham Straits, picked up a barge load of canned salmon and delivered it to the New England Fish Depot in Anacortes. The MELIA's load was one of many brought down by Foss tugs in moving out the 1973 salmon pack.

After her return from Alaska in August and for the next several years, the MELIA was assigned to tow sand and gravel barges from Steilacoom to Seattle, bulk cement barges between Bellingham and Seattle, chemical barges from Hooker in Tacoma, Monsanto in Seattle, and Georgia-Pacific in Bellingham, to various pulp mills on the Sound. She also did assist work in various ports docking ocean-going vessels and in the late seventies, she towed oil barges to ships in need of bunkering.

The MELIA and her crew made an unprecedented type of oil delivery in Seattle harbor in August 1979. Due to a strike in Vancouver, British Columbia, the Alaska cruise ship VERACRUZ was forced to come to Seattle for fuel oil before starting north. But there was a problem, the hurried run to Seattle came about over the weekend with no opportunity to establish the vessel's credit for fuel, so the Company furnishing the oil requested Foss, the delivering carrier, to obtain cash on the barrel head in U. S. funds before pumping any oil into the ship's tanks. Foss agreed and at 0500 on a Sunday morning, with the VERACRUZ anchored in the Bay, the MELIA brought the oil barge FOSS-97 alongside with 2,500-barrels of heavy fuel and 300-barrels of diesel—the load had an FAS value of approximately $70,000.

The Foss representative climbed aboard and was ushered into the Captain's cabin where a sealed bank bag with $55,000 was turned over to him. The ship needed more time to obtain the balance of the money, but pumping was started to deliver $55,000 worth of fuel. Two hours later the pumps stopped with 600 barrels yet to go. Then the Captain produced $7,000 from his own funds and along with the Purser, they agreed to raid the Casino for the balance. This understanding satisfied Foss, so pumping resumed. As promised the Casino cash was in hand to keep the oil flowing to the last barrel. By 1000 Sunday morning, the ship had fuel, Foss had the money, everybody was happy except the passengers—they had lost one day of their Alaska cruise. As for the MELIA, perhaps she should carry a cash register now that fuel is being sold on a cash basis!

She has continued in oil-barge service, cash notwithstanding, making the rounds of all the major ports, doing exactly what she was designed to do, intermediate towing, and she does it with very little down-time, so important to the tight scheduling necessary in the busy Foss ship-bunkering program.

The Foss "fuel by barge" service reached an all-time high in November-December 1979 when the four-barge fleet delivered one million barrels of bunker fuel to 175 ships. A tight schedule developed and in order to take care of the bunkering jobs on hand, the MELIA and her crew, headed by alternate captains, Jack Ogden and Jack Hagen, worked right through the Christmas holidays.

The MELIA, with barge FOSS-96, spent Christmas Day in Port Angeles bunkering the logship GEMINI. Then, less than twenty-four hours later, she had reloaded her barge in Seattle and was enroute for Olympia to bunker the log ship GREEN STAR. She then made a run of 140 miles to the Mobil Oil Refinery at Ferndale and loaded her barge with bunker fuel for the Seattle Steam Plant. No doubt with a heavy order file, the MELIA will continue to run day and night, from port to port and ship to ship, delivering an average of 6,000 barrels of fuel per vessel.

MYRTLE FOSS (2)

Built:	1966	Propulsion:	Caterpillar
	Martinolich Shipyard		765-horsepower
	Tacoma, Washington	Primary Service:	Puget Sound
Length:	65-feet	Status:	In Operation
Beam:	21-feet		

The second MYRTLE, named for a daughter of Hildur and Chris Foss (a nephew of Andrew), was the second of two additional "M"-class tugs built from tried and proven plans of the MATHILDA FOSS, former SEA QUEEN. The three "M"-class tugs, MATHILDA, MELIA, and MYRTLE were equipped with 765-horsepower engines in order to handle heavier tows than their immediate predecessors, the 600-horsepower "J" boats.

The MYRTLE started out towing in mid-1966 at Port Angeles, but she was listed as a Tacoma tug and her home port has never changed. The Port Angeles division put her to work towing logs out of Neah Bay for Crown Zeller-bach as the tug PACIFIC, based in Port Angeles for several years, was often called away for barge tows to Alaska, leaving only the THEODORE FOSS—over seventy-five years old—to provide continuous delivery of log rafts to Port Angeles for the Crown-Z mill.

Towing logs out of Neah Bay required accurate timing of tides and weather on the tug Captains' part as westerly winds and swells combined with a west-flowing tide could easily break up and scatter a raft. To the Skippers on this open water run, heavy westerly weather was the bane of their existence. Many times the tugs were weather-bound in port. It was frustrating and not unusual to wait at anchor in Neah Bay for two weeks at a time waiting for a break in the weather with the crew fighting off boredom with coffee, paperbacks, cribbage, and tug upkeep. However, nowadays, when the weather on the Straits becomes too violent for the tug and tow to start out, the rafts are tied up in the protected booming grounds at Neah Bay and the tug returns to Port Angeles to go on barge tows until conditions improve on the Straits for log towing.

In good weather and in season, fishing from tugs on the Neah Bay run has always been a pleasant diversion on an otherwise slow tow to Port Angeles. Many claims are made on the prowess and success of the tugboat fishermen, but they do catch fish as salmon entrees appear on the mess tables with convincing regularity.

The MYRTLE has worked in the Straits and upper Sound areas continuously for the past thirteen years except during diversions due to bad weather. Her only venture Coastwise was a round trip to Petersburg, Alaska in July 1973 towing an empty cargo barge north and two loaded barges of canned salmon south to Anacortes.

Similarly, like the proverbial women's work—a tug's work is never done—that aptly includes the MYRTLE. The Skippers that have kept her on the move have been Budd Turner, Ron Crabtree, Bill Acorn, Ed Branchflower, and Bob Wiley, the men mainly responsible for keeping the MYRTLE "Always Ready"!

OMER FOSS (2)

Built:	1966	Propulsion:	Caterpillar
	Pacific Shipyard		325-horsepower
	Anacortes, Washington	Primary Service:	Tacoma Harbor
Length:	45-feet	Status:	In Service
Beam:	13-feet		

The second OMER was sixth of the nine modern, steel harbor tugs built for Foss to replace the old low-power wood boats. The OMER joined the fleet in December 1966 and after a month of "break-in" service in Tacoma, Foss assigned her to Port Angeles, to join the LELA and FOSS-8 in shifting log rafts and assisting log carriers in and out of the Port dock.

The OMER remained in Port Angeles until August 1973 when she was replaced by the SAMISH BAY from Bellingham. The new tug was equipped with a Kort-nozzle for better maneuvering and more thrust, which gave her an advantage over the OMER in "juggling" big ships.

Foss returned the OMER to Tacoma Harbor, where she towed barges around the port area with an occasional sand and gravel barge tow between Steilacoom and Tacoma. During the next four years she followed the same routine with a two-man crew working twelve-hour days, except then a surge of business occurred requiring a second crew working a twelve-hour night shift.

In 1977 the OMER added a strange incident to her history and to the annals of the Foss Company. It wasn't a calamity, but it was mysterious and could have been tragic. On a Sunday in November the OMER was stolen from her berth at the Foss float!

Ocean freighters, while waiting for a berth, usually anchor in Tacoma Harbor and Foss tugs often provide ship-to-shore launch service for the crew. During this particular Sunday afternoon, the DONNA and OMER were providing transportation from and to a Greek freighter. Several of the ship's crew had been taken ashore during the day and by late evening all but four had returned to the ship. About midnight, the remaining four men staggered up to the Foss float, in need of transportation for one thing. The Mate on the DONNA FOSS informed them that the DONNA had to leave for Seattle immediately, but the CATHERINE would be available within an hour to run them out to their ship. (The OMER was also at the float, but without a crew.)

The first report that all was not well came from a call to the night dispatcher in Seattle from the CATHERINE FOSS at about 0100, stating that a tug looking like the OMER was running, without lights, on an erratic course toward the anchored Greek ship. The CATHERINE was tied up on another job and could not break free to check on the situation. The question was whether it was a regular pleasure boat or the OMER—turned into a pleasure boat.

The only vessel in Tacoma available to check on the OMER's whereabouts was the Crowley tug, BARBARA S. She made a quick run up the waterway to the Foss float and verified that indeed the OMER had disappeared. The BARBARA S. began a search in Tacoma Harbor for the missing tug. There was no sign of the OMER. Eventually, a report from an outbound freighter leaving Tacoma Harbor complained of narrowly missing a small tug running without lights at the outer boundary of the harbor.

The BARBARA S. headed out and found the OMER with no one aboard running at slow speed and turning in circles. The BARBARA's crew stopped the OMER, put the rudder amidships and towed her to the Foss dock. Upon inspection she was found to be no worse for the escapade. There was a whole case of empty beer bottles scattered around the wheelhouse so the OMER no doubt did some strange maneuvering. But sending the boat out to run around the area with no on aboard and without lights was the height of recklessness—a serious collision and possible loss of life could easily have occurred. Fortunately, the harbor traffic at the time was light.

After a general cleanup on Monday, the OMER was ready to assume her normal duties, with an American crew. Foss made a claim against the ship's local agents for the expense involved and in time the claim was paid, but the identity of the four sea-going hijackers was never divulged.

In early 1978 the OMER came to Seattle and worked for Manson Construction at Pier 42, tending the derrick barge, HAAKON, and other equipment used in the construction of the new, huge container-terminal. When completed, the terminal occupied the whole area from Pier 36 to Pier 46.

During her time in Seattle, the OMER and her two-man crew, Captain Jan Snyder and Deckhand Gary Lansdon, took part in subduing a tug fire. They received high praise and thanks from the men of Washington Tug & Barge for their timely action in preventing a serious loss to one of their vessels. While docking an empty gasoline barge at Pier 43, W.T.& B. Company's tug, SKOOKUM, caught fire. The fire, of an electrical origin, quickly spread through the pilothouse and crew's quarters. The OMER, near by and seeing the danger, raced over, took off the crew and shifted the gasoline barge away from the burning tug. Then the OMER returned and fought the fire until the Fire Department arrived and finished extinguishing the flames. The SKOOKUM was repaired and resumed towing several months later.

After several additional weeks in service for Manson Construction in Seattle, the OMER, in the spring of 1978 returned to her home port of Tacoma to take up where she left off. And from all indications, her address for some time will be Foss-Tacoma.

DAVID FOSS Shown departing Seattle for S.W. Alaska with container barge FOSS 251 on contract to Sealand Service in 1968. (Courtesy of Foss Tug Co)

DAVID FOSS (1)

Built:	1967	Propulsion:	Caterpillar (Twin)
	Albina Shipyard		1,200-horsepower
	Portland, Oregon	Primary Service:	Southwestern Alaska
Length:	66-feet	Final Operating Day:	January 11, 1975
Beam:	24-feet	Status:	Foundered

Some of the Foss tugs had short lives. One of them, the DAVID, had less than a decade of service before joining Davy Jones' collection of sunken ships. But, no doubt, the tug by steady, efficient work paid for her original cost in her alloted years.

The DAVID, named after a great grandson of Theodore, was fifth in the series of sister-tugs, commonly known as "D" boats. The versatile "D's" performed equally well towing logs on Puget Sound, petroleum barges in Southeastern Alaska, or assisting in offshore oil support work. The DAVID's active duty began on June 19th when she headed for Cook Inlet to work as a utility tug. She worked out of Anchorage until the freeze-up in October dictated her return to Seattle.

Apparently, the DAVID was destined to be permanently based in Alaska, for she returned to Anchorage in the Spring and remained up North, except for overhaul, for the rest of her useful life—operating in Southeastern and Southwestern—even going out to Dutch Harbor at the tip of the Alaska Peninsula and as far away as the mouth of the Yukon River.

Few tugs spend an entire winter in Southwestern Alaska, but the DAVID did—she wintered in Cook Inlet or Valdez during four different winter seasons, and the harsh weather may have contributed to her unexpected fate. However, for one winter, the DAVID left ice-prone Cook Inlet and dropped down to Ketchikan in October to replace the aging EDITH FOSS on the Southeastern Alaska run for Union Oil. Earlier in the year the DAVID's sister-tug, DELORES FOSS, had taken over the Southeastern oil run for Standard Oil. So, there were then two "D" boats delivering oil, both owned by Foss, yet operating for competitive companies.

In April 1969 after being relieved of the oil run by a third sister-tug, the DEAN FOSS, the DAVID was recalled to Cook Inlet and she stayed in Alaska for the next six years, serving Sea-Land, Standard Oil, Associated Divers, and Foss Alaska Lines. Only once, in April 1973 did the DAVID return to Seattle for drydocking and voyage repairs. She was out'a month later and Captain Karl Hansen with his five-man crew left right away for Anchorage, little knowing the DAVID would never again visit Seattle.

The beginning of the end came after eighteen months of towing, tending, and stand-by in the Inlet, when she went on charter to Standard Oil of California in December 1974 to tend the drill rig GEORGE FERRIS in lower Cook Inlet. Though ice pans were prevalent near the drill rig location at the time, only the upper Inlet experienced solid pack ice. By shifting farther south the rigs were able to continue work.

The DAVID's demise started on the morning of January 11, 1975 on a typical winter day in Cook Inlet with the wind blowing out of the northeast at forty knots and a six to eight foot sea running. The temperature was below freezing and new concentrations of ice threatened the tug. Due to the adverse conditions, the DAVID held off about four miles from the rig. About 0630, Captain Lyle Ackerlund and Mate Ken Anderson noticed the DAVID's stern was no longer rising to the sea and clearing water from the deck. The Chief Engineer, George Rancich, was called to transfer fuel forward in order to raise the stern. Conditions appeared normal when Rancich went below, but before long water suddenly began pouring into the engine room from an open conduit tube containing service lines leading to the lazarette—the after storage-hold.

Apparently sea water had been entering and building up in the lazarette for some time, possibly due to a fracture in the stern section. When the water rose to the level of the open tube the engine room began flooding. With the force of water jetting out of the tube, there was no way to plug the flow and the engine room began filling regardless of the bilge pumps. The rising water shorted out all the electrical systems, but the main engines were kept running full out in an attempt to get closer to shore.

Realizing the imminent danger, the crew inflated the rubber life raft on the now slanting submerged afterdeck and climbed in. As the last crewman and Captain Ackerlund jumped aboard, with the tug settling rapidly, the raft's holding line was cut and with the raft floating free, the crew paddled well clear. A minute later the crew heard the main engines stop and the next minute, with all her modern equipment to no avail and with all the crew's possessions, the DAVID plunged to the bottom in a welter of foam and heaving water.

As a "Mayday" call had been transmitted at the first sign of trouble, and with the dawn breaking about 0800, a large Evergreen Company pontoon helicopter landed alongside the raft and DAVID's crew, numb and stiff, crawled aboard. They were ferried ashore to Kenai for medical examination and after thawing out, were pronounced okay. With dry clothes of sorts they were flown back to Seattle to acquire a new set of gear and to crew another tug.

Attempts to locate the DAVID by sonar were unavailing, probably due to current action and silt, so after three weeks the search was stopped and the DAVID declared a total loss. Cook Inlet had claimed its second Foss tug in the past ten years and Davy Jones gained another prize.

JOE FOSS (2)

Built:	1967	Propulsion:	Caterpillar
	Pacific Shipyard		420-horsepower
	Anacortes, Washington	Primary Service:	Port Angeles Harbor
Length:	42-feet	Status:	In Service
Beam:	14-feet		

The JOE FOSS, built as the SAMISH BAY, was delivered complete in 1967 to Foss for use by Bellingham Tug & Barge. She was seventh in the series of the new harbor tugs ordered from Pacific Shipyard to provide better service for Puget Sound ports. The SAMISH BAY, assigned to Bellingham Bay, worked steadily in general harbor service and log towing for the next six years.

By 1973 shipping tonnage doubled in some ports, particularly Port Angeles, and the heavier and larger log ships calling at the port required more horsepower and quick response from assisting tugs in docking and undocking. In Bellingham the work load in 1973 diminished to the point where the smaller LELA FOSS could meet the demands, so the SAMISH BAY, with her innovative Kort-nozzle advantages, was transferred to Port Angeles to assist the hard-working PEGGY FOSS. With the SAMISH BAY on the job, the OMER FOSS, a smaller tug helping the PEGGY, was transferred from Port Angeles to Tacoma where her tasks would be lighter.

With the two strong built-alike tugs teamed up in Port Angeles, handling the big log carriers became a safer and more efficient operation. Except for annual drydocking in Seattle, the SAMISH BAY, renamed JOE FOSS in October 1974, has remained in Port Angeles. With her sister-tug she is always ready to tow anything that floats.

RICHARD FOSS

Built:	1967	Propulsion:	EMD (Twin)
	McDermott Shipyard Group		3,000-horsepower
	Amelia, Louisiana	Primary Service:	Puget Sound
Length:	110-feet	Status:	In Service
Beam:	30-feet		

The RICHARD FOSS, named for Peter and Margaret Campbell's son, a grandson of Sidney and Barbara Foss Campbell, was the first ocean-class tug built from the keel up for the Foss Company. Several other ocean-class Foss tugs were considered new, but they were rebuilt from ex-World War II vessels. At the time, this was the most expeditious method for increasing the fleet to serve Foss' expanding ocean and coastwise towing commitments.

In late May 1967 the RICHARD, complete in all respects and under Captain Don Gordon, left Galveston for Seattle with six new Foss barges. The RICHARD had two 240-foot flat deck barges on the towline and each barge carried two 150-foot barges riding "piggy back." With good weather and steady running, she averaged better than nine knots on the 5,550-mile trip, arriving Seattle in only four weeks, much to the satisfaction of the Operations Department, urgently needing a high power ocean tug.

During the summer and fall of 1967 the RICHARD was engaged in the Alaska oil program, towing drilling and pipeline equipment from West Coast ports to Cook Inlet. In November, winter weather drove her south, way south for 5,500 miles, but with a stopover in Seattle for fuel and to pick up the ex-Army Troopship GENERAL M M PATRICK for delivery to Panama. Arriving at the Canal she turned the vessel over to the ARTHUR FOSS for final delivery to an East Coast shipyard for conversion to a container ship.

The RICHARD then took over two barges from the ELLEN as she was having power difficulties near Panama on the way to Long Beach, California. The RICHARD finished the ELLEN's tow and then returned to home base to take on another long towing job.

In January 1968 the United Fruit vessel SAN JOSE caught fire and burned in the Western Pacific. As a result she was considered a total loss, but after being towed to Guam, the fire-ravaged ship, upon further inspection, was considered worth repairing. After bids for the work were received from West Coast shipyards and with the bids reasonable, the repair was approved. The work was awarded to Todd Shipyard of Seattle and the towing to Foss. The RICHARD was ready and available, so on February 7th, with Captain Guy Johnson in command, a skipper short in stature but long in ability, left Seattle for Guam and arrived on March 3rd, after a good weather trip. Captain Johnson and his crew wasted no time in hooking up to the SAN JOSE and getting underway—time was money on a lump-sum contract. They were able to depart the next day on the long route home, it was a slow tow averaging only five knots, the drag from the SAN JOSE's propeller being partly responsible. What could have been a serious mishap occurred on April 10th, when a tropical storm hit them a thousand miles northeast of Hawaii. By coincidence, the RICHARD's subsequent trouble occurred within one hour of the time that the HENRY FOSS, three thousand miles away battling Typhoon Jean, experienced similar towline failure while towing a drydock to Guam!

The RICHARD reported by radio on April 10th that despite being hove-to in storm-force winds, the surge-chain shackle parted allowing the 450-foot SAN JOSE to go adrift. Captain Johnson later reported to Foss-Seattle that the sea was too rough to attempt a recovery and he would wait out the storm. He also informed them the seas were as high as the tug's boat deck and the crew could not safely get out or move around on deck due to the cascading water. However, by the next day the weather had moderated sufficiently for the crew to stay on deck and re-rig the towing gear. After four hours of wet and heavy work in sloshing water, the SAN JOSE was again on the towline and headed for Cape Flattery. Thankfully, the weather on the last 1,500 miles turned out to be a sailor's delight—a soft breeze under a blue sky. Tug and tow arrived Seattle April 23rd, after a round trip of seventy-five days, covering 10,000 miles.

In June 1968 the RICHARD ran light to the Columbia River and picked up the lumber barge KOKO HEAD at a Portland shipyard. The barge, after undergoing a major rebuild from a severe grounding accident in January 1968, was ready to go back on the lumber haul to Honolulu. The RICHARD towed the barge to Longview, Everett, and Coos Bay, for a full load of lumber and from Coos Bay she headed for Honolulu on the first of two similar trips. When the HENRY FOSS, the usual tug on the lumber run, returned from Japan to take over the KOKO HEAD, the RICHARD headed for Seattle to commence Alaska towing.

Starting out in October 1968 the RICHARD towed two barges of oil exploration and construction equipment to the Pan American drilling site near Port Moller on the north side of the Alaska Peninsula. The ALASKA CONSTRUCTOR, ELLEN FOSS, and AGNES FOSS, brought in additional equipment for the drilling operation. The cargo was off-loaded over ramps to the beach with the tugs holding the barges in position. After completing discharge the RICHARD returned to Seattle with the empties and tied up for voyage repairs.

During early 1969 the RICHARD completed two round trips to Amchitka for Holmes & Narver with equipment for the Atomic Energy Commission project. The second voyage, with good weather, was completed in thirty-three days, seven under the Amchitka average. The Operations Department always hoped for smooth sailing as the type of weather encountered had a direct bearing on the profit or loss under a lump-sum contract.

On June 30, 1969 with Captain Ernie Guchee in command, the RICHARD started out on another run to Amchitka; the trip almost turned out to be fast and uneventful with the crew looking forward to arrival is Seattle and a few days off. However, it wasn't to be. On the July 22nd morning radio schedule with the Seattle office, they were directed to rendezvous with the MARY FOSS in sheltered waters about 400 miles north of Seattle and trade tows. The RICHARD would then have two barges bound for Bethel in the Bering Sea! The grumbling on board could be heard above the howl of the 30-knot wind. But go they must and go they would. The RICHARD's crew had learned to accept the vicissitudes of tugboating.

The crew's hope now was for a quick trip to Bethel and return home, but it didn't work out this time either. While still headed for Bethel they were informed that from Bethel, they were to proceed to the Adak Navy Base in the Aleutians and load Navy cargo, then go on to the end of the Aleutian Chain and discharge the barge at the military base on remote Shemya Island.

The crew, in a state of disbelief, nevertheless again took the news as all part of the job and headed westward—the diversion lengthened the voyage yet another two weeks. On the return trip they threatened to silence the radio! That is, the Seattle channel. The old adage, more days more dollars, had lost its appeal.

Another surprise awaited them upon arrival in Puget Sound on September 6. The closest they came to Seattle and home was the ammunition base at Bangor. They had received new orders to pick up the old C-1 freighter, CAPE CATOCHE, loaded with outdated ammunition and tow it to a disposal area off the Washington Coast. Arriving at the appointed position two days after leaving Bangor, they were met by a Navy demolition crew. The CAPE CATOCHE was scuttled and at a pre-set depth, the ammunition detonated. The RICHARD, standing by five miles off, felt but little concussion or sea disturbance, so deep was the explosion. With the final delivery in the Log Book, they left immediately for the Foss pier and, at last on September 10th, seventy-three days after leaving Seattle, the crew was home.

Another stretch of continuous operation started in early 1970 for the RICHARD when the tug, with Captain George Ducich in charge, towed the loaded oil barge, FOSS-98, from Anacortes to Amchitka. Upon discharge of the 38,000 barrels of oil, they returned to Seattle and immediately loaded the FOSS-98 for Hawaii with refined oil for Hilo, Kahului on Maui and Barbers Point on Oahu. The outbound voyage was without incident and after completion of discharge on Oahu, they were dispatched to the oil refinery at Oleum, California to take on a load of oil for Eureka and Crescent City, California. From Crescent City they returned home to Seattle after seventy days, arriving on April 27th.

The next seven months of 1970 were spent towing barges to ports in Southwestern and Southeastern Alaska. Then late in the year she was assigned to the Southeastern Alaska van run for Foss Alaska Line. Her 3,000-horsepower was needed to maintain the tight schedule that otherwise would be affected by adverse winter weather and the consequent slower speed of the smaller tugs.

With the return of spring, the RICHARD was put on the Seattle-Anchorage run for Permanente Cement Company in conjunction with Coastal Barge Line. In this service she made one trip per month towing the barge ANCHORAGE, loaded with bulk cement below and mobile homes on deck.

The RICHARD had an uneventful 1971 season on the Anchorage run until the unfortunate October trip. After the usual discharge in Anchorage, she departed with the empty cement barge for Seattle on October 8. Then, during the day of October 9th, the weather began deteriorating and by evening a full gale raged with heavy southeasterly seas and dense rain.

The RICHARD and her barge were six miles east of Outer Island bucking the gale when the towline parted casting the barge adrift. With rough seas and gusting wind no attempt could be made to rescue the barge even by picking up the short insurance line that was trailed from the stern of the barge for the tug to hook on in case of just such an emergency as had occurred. But the breaking, tumbling seas so increased the danger of being washed overboard that working on deck was impossible.

The RICHARD, in need of shelter, ran into Nuka Bay near Seward to await daylight and the possible chance of picking up the drifting barge in more favorable weather and smoother water. Early in the morning they headed for Outer Island to search for the ANCHORAGE and in two hours spotted it—stern-to on a rocky ledge jutting from the southeast corner of Rabbit Island. Running up as close as possible, the crew could see the barge had a 45-degree port list and had suffered hull damage. The bottom was holed from just aft of amidships to the stern and she was grinding and working against the rocks in the heavy southerly swell. The RICHARD having informed Foss of the stranding, stood by to await the arrival of surveyors. Later in the day a chartered plane with the appraisers examined the barge from the air and determined that she would pound to pieces and would be completely destroyed in short order. So she was declared a total constructive loss. The RICHARD, unable to assist in any way, headed back to Seattle, hoping for better luck on the next tow, a run to Amchitka.

In 1972 she towed between Seattle and ports in Southeastern Alaska, except for a diversion in mid-November. Shortly after leaving Anchorage with an empty LST barge for Seattle, the RICHARD, with Captain Jay Jacobson now in charge, received orders to drop the barge at Seldovia and proceed to Beaver Inlet, about six hundred miles southwest of Seldovia, where the disabled United States Coast Guard Cutter JARVIS was waiting for help. An ironic situation—a commercial vessel going to the aid of the Coast Guard! The RICHARD arrived at the Inlet on November 19th and towed the dead ship to Dutch Harbor, making the run in twelve hours.

The Coast Guard requested the RICHARD to stand by the JARVIS, to hold the cutter fast alongside the quay and safe from the adverse wind and weather. She tended the JARVIS until November 29th, when temporary repairs were completed and then escorted the JARVIS out of Dutch Harbor through Unalga Pass into open water where the cutter was able to take a safe departure for Honolulu, her home port, and there obtain needed permanent repair.

The RICHARD, with three farewell blasts of the whistle, headed for her waiting barge and home. Upon arrival, the crew received a well-done citation from the Coast Guard for assisting the JARVIS in her troubles.

In September 1973 the RICHARD, after several months of towing between Seattle and Anchorage with the cement barge SEWARD, began full-time van-barge towing for Foss Alaska Line. FAL's new barges were larger and carried more containers, adding to the in-port cargo time and spending hours that normally would be used in running. So to compensate, tugs of the RICHARD's type, with more horsepower were necessary to maintain the published weekly schedule.

The RICHARD continued in service for Foss Alaska Line through 1976 although not always on the Southeastern run. In July 1974 she made two trips to Anchorage delivering full barge loads of automobiles and in 1975 she made two seasonal trips to the Bering Sea. Captain Red Hendershot reported tough ice conditions on the first voyage in June as the ice was late in moving out of the Bering Sea. On the Bethel-to-Nome leg of the voyage, June 13th, the RICHARD was ice-bound off Nunivak Island and forced to wait for an opening. Then on June 14th they made an attempt to break out, but for seven days fought against heavy unrelenting ice before finally getting through. Voyage #2 was good sailing in open water all the way.

The RICHARD returned to the Southeastern Alaska van-run in the fall and continued for Foss Alaska until her high horsepower was needed on a new tug service established by Foss on Puget Sound. By late 1975 with oil tanker traffic up considerably on the Sound and with the State tanker-escort law in force, whereby every loaded tanker over 40,000-tons must have tug escort, ship-assist tugs having ample horsepower became a necessity.

The RICHARD's 3,000-horsepower was well-suited for escort and ship-assist work for tankers going to the Ferndale and Anacortes refineries. After annual repair in early January 1976 she was assigned to work out of the Bellingham office assisting tankers, replacing the 1,200-horsepower, 32-year-old LORNA FOSS. However, the LORNA, because of the increasing ship traffic, remained in Bellingham on stand-by, but without a regular crew.

The RICHARD is still in service on the northern Sound as one of the several tanker escort tugs, with George Hobson and Jerry Brown the alternating Captains, doing the piloting. On occasion when escort duty is slack (rather unusual), the RICHARD engages in towing barges between Seattle and the Northern Puget Sound ports served by Foss. The RICHARD makes a round trip between Seattle and Bellingham with a loaded barge in half the time required for the smaller "M" and "J" class tugs. She does wonders for the Seattle central dispatch department when they are running behind schedule on a long upper Sound barge tow. An assist by the RICHARD and the job is done on time as scheduled.

CLAUDIA FOSS

Built:	1968	Propulsion:	Caterpillar (Twin)
	Albina Shipyard		1,700-horsepower
	Portland, Oregon	Primary Service:	Puget Sound
Length:	84-feet	Status:	In Service
Beam:	25-feet		

The CLAUDIA, named for a daughter-in-law of Sidney and Barbara Foss Campbell, was the first "C"-class tug built by Albina for Foss. The CLAUDIA and later the CLARA, were built to the design and plans of the time-tested CATHERINE FOSS. The three boats were intended for medium coastwise towing and general towing in Puget Sound.

After a trial period, the CLAUDIA, under Captain Walt Davis, started towing in May 1968 for Foss Alaska Line on their Southeastern Alaska container-barge run. The CLAUDIA with van-barge FOSS-275, made the usual FAL ports of call—Ketchikan, Petersburg, Juneau, Sitka, and then returned to Seattle via Ketchikan. A round trip lasted twelve days and the trip length was closely adhered to during the four years on the run. The alternate skippers, Captains Walt Davis and Paul Peterson, with their knowledge of weather, tides and currents, were largely responsible for the CLAUDIA's steady performance record.

For two months in late 1969 the CLAUDIA, temporarily leaving the van-run, had a change of climate and a change of jobs. A highly maneuverable twin-screw tug was asked for by the J. Ray McDermott Company to assist in construction of an offshore oil platform near Santa Barbara. The CLAUDIA had the tools so the California coast became her new area of operation. She finished up her oil-rig tending in a little over the expected two months and then returned to Seattle and resumed her familiar run for Foss Alaska Line until McDermott again asked for her services, this time in Cook Inlet.

To free the CLAUDIA for work in the Inlet, the CLARA took over on the van run in May 1972. The CLAUDIA's experienced Southeastern crew remained on the Foss Alaska run by transferring to the CLARA and the CLAUDIA recieved a new Seattle crew. She left Seattle in late May for the Inlet, where once again under contract to McDermott, she assisted in offshore oil pipeline construction, staying with the job until the freezing weather hit in late October and forced her to return home.

Foss-Seattle then put her in a new class—linehaul tug. She started towing rail-car barges on the Seattle-Vancouver international run and except for the summers of 1973 and 1974 on Foss Alaska Line service, she remained with the car-barges until late 1977.

The CLAUDIA left the Vancouver run in October to barge construction material to the Trident Nuclear Submarine Base at Bangor, Washington. For seven months she pushed gravel barges between the pit at Maury Island and Bangor, making seventy-five round trips, using 500-ton barges. Captains Gary Kroll and Jack Hagan were the skippers responsible for moving a total of 100,000-tons of aggregate in just seven months.

From the gravel haul the CLAUDIA went back to "railroading," the crew now considering joining a second union—the Brotherhood of Railway Trainmen—and getting two pensions!

DEAN FOSS

Built:	1968	Propulsion:	Caterpillar (Twin)
	Albina Shipyard		1,200-horsepower
	Portland, Oregon	Primary Service:	Southeastern Alaska
Length:	66-feet	Status:	In Operation
Beam:	24-feet		

The DEAN, named for Andrew Dean Hager, grandson of Henry Foss, was sixth in the series of "D"-class tugs built by Albina and designed by Foss for intermediate towing, range and horsepower.

Upon arrival in Seattle from the Portland shipyard in early May 1968 and after quickly passing a second inspection, she started right out on the Seattle to North Vancouver rail-car barge run under the direction of alternate Captains, John Hulet and Dave Davis, old hands on the sixteen-hour run. The DEAN remained on the car-barge tow with the FOSS-118 for the next eleven months, not missing a trip and holding to schedule. Then having served her time in inland waters, she was ready to graduate to the rougher open water in Alaska.

With stores aboard for six months and full bunkers, she left Puget Sound on April 14, 1969 to rendezvous with the DAVID FOSS in Wrangell, Alaska to relieve the DAVID on the oil delivery route for Union Oil Company, becoming the ninth Foss tug to take part in the distribution of petroleum products around Southeastern Alaska. The service began out of Ketchikan when the Union Oil contract became effective in 1930 with the LORNA FOSS towing the FOSS-11. Between the LORNA's time and the present day, the JUSTINE FOSS, FOSS-19, MARGARET, ROLAND, ROGER, EDITH and DAVID all served on the oil run. The Ketchikan-based boats were solely involved in distribution to out-ports, logging camps, and canneries. Two larger tugs, the ANDREW and MARTHA, with 6000-barrel oil barges brought the oil from Union Oil Company's terminal at Edmonds, Washington to the Southeastern distribution centers of Ketchikan and Juneau. However, the ANDREW's and MARTHA's part in barging the oil North was taken over by tank ships in 1945 but customer delivery service remained with the Foss Tug & Barge system, now carried out by the DEAN.

The Ketchikan oil run was well-liked by the tug captains—the added attraction of good hunting and fishing no doubt had a strong appeal. Captains Harry Butcher, Walt Davis, and Al Anderson all stayed on the job for several years and the present skipper of the DEAN, Henry Lund, has been on the run since late 1972.

With the exception of an annual trip to Seattle for drydocking and major engine work, the DEAN remains in Southeastern Alaska for the entire year towing the 12,000-barrel refined oil barge SEA-76. The DEAN serves about thirty-six different locations ranging from the major ports of Sitka, Wrangell, Petersburg, Juneau and Haines to the small communities of Hydaburg, Tenakee, and Point Baker. Included along the route are many logging camps, all requiring petroleum products. Some of the places have interesting names; Labouchere Bay, St. John Harbor, Thorne Bay, and Murphy's Chance. Stops are also made at the fishing resorts of Yes Bay and Bell Island—no communities are overlooked.

The DEAN works an average of twenty-three days a month regardless of Alaska's often blustery weather. She's a well-handled and seaworthy boat. During her idle days she lays up at the Union Oil Float at Ketchikan and her crew then has time for R and R at home.

During the fifty years of work for the Union Oil Company, with a variety of boats and crews, the basic idea has always been the same: a Foss tug towing a Foss barge to satisfied customers.

GRACE FOSS (2)

Built:	1968	Propulsion:	Caterpillar
	Pacific Shipyards		365-horsepower
	Anacortes, Washington	Primary Service:	Puget Sound Ports
Length:	42-feet	Status:	In Service
Beam:	14-feet		

The GRACE, completed in 1968 at the Pacific Shipyard in Anacortes, was number eight in the series of modern steel harbor tugs built for Foss and their operating companies. Two sizes of tugs were planned in the modernization and replacement program—in the 37-foot class five were built and four in the 42-foot series, including the GRACE. She is a modern version of her sturdy wooden ancestors, the little "steam pots" with their inimitable whistles and the early "smokers" with their deep-throated rhythmic-sounding oil engines.

With the arrival of the new tugs at the ports of Bellingham, Everett, Tacoma, and Port Angeles the old, under-powered, outdated harbor tugs were either given light part-time work and put on the reserve-list or sold outright. Port Angeles had the veterans FOSS-8 and NANCY.

The new GRACE, assigned to Port Angeles, handled log rafts at ship's side, towed to-and-from log storages, and assisted log ships in docking and undocking. The GRACE remained on the job at Port Angeles until early June 1975, when she gave way to a stronger tug.

With the use of large ships in the log trade, more power became a necessity for ship-assists. The PEGGY FOSS, a sister-tug of the GRACE, took over as she had more horsepower and faster response due to the Kort-nozzle installation around the propeller.

GRACE FOSS With Port Angeles in the background towing a log raft across the harbor, August 1966. (From the author's collection)

The GRACE now became a general relief boat on the Sound, filling in at out-ports when local boats needed extra help. Since 1976 the GRACE has been on the move from port-to-port, doing three stints in Everett, two each in Port Angeles, Tacoma, and Seattle.

In the fall of 1977 the GRACE had a special job in Lake Washington tending the Foss derrick barge FOSS-300, on a clamshell-bucket dredging job at the Newport Beach Yacht Club. Since then she has resumed her role as relief boat for all the small Foss harbor tugs, becoming a true itinerant worker until mid-1979 when she was assigned on a steady basis to the Everett harbor fleet.

MARTHA FOSS (3)

Built:	1968	Propulsion:	Caterpillar
	Martinolich Shipyard		1,200-horsepower
	Tacoma, Washington	Primary Service:	Puget Sound
Length:	80-feet	Status:	In Service
Beam:	26-feet		

The launching ceremony of the third MARTHA FOSS on July 22, 1968 was attended by one hundred and fifty guests. However, not everyone came for the keel-wetting—some were present to view the MARTHA's new propulsion system, featuring a ninety-inch Kort nozzle housing the propeller, giving added thrust with increased maneuverability. A special deck feature interesting only to the sailors in the group was a hydraulic crane which could swing full circle and lift 2,000 pounds at full extension, a practical labor-saving device for handling the heavy log rafting gear used on Neah Bay rafts that the MARTHA was slated to tow.

After two months of outfitting, testing, and with stores aboard, the MARTHA was ready for work. So in September 1968 she was assigned to Port Angeles for log towing as expected. Her primary job, along with the MYRTLE FOSS, was to tow log rafts on the Straits from Neah Bay to Port Angeles for the Crown Zellerbach pulp mill.

Crown Zellerbach, a leader in the pulp and paper industry, and a prime customer of Foss since the late 1920's, employed Foss at that time to tow log cribs out of the Sail river on the Straits. Then between 1930 and 1950 Foss towed logs from Crown's operations on the Sekiu and Hoko Rivers. Since 1950 Crown Zellerbach Straits-area logs are rafted at the Neah Bay booming ground and Foss tugs tow the rafts from Neah Bay to Port Angeles where the pulp-type hemlock is sorted out for use in the mill and the fir, cedar, spruce, and grade hemlock, is sold to domestic sawmills and at times to the export log market.

Log towing has always been a major thrust of the Foss-Port Angeles Division and at one time in the early 1940's, eight tugs were in use. But in 1979 with the reduced log in-put volume due to the unavailability of timber, only three tugs were necessary to handle the workload: the JOE, PEGGY, and MYRTLE, with an assist from the MARTHA when an extra tug was needed.

A few years ago there were booming-grounds at Sekiu, Pysht, and Crescent Bay in addition to Neah Bay; and all requiring tugs to tow away logs, not only to Port Angeles, but to mills located in Puget Sound. But now the Crown logging operation at Neah Bay is the only one using the Straits on the American side. So with fewer tows, the MARTHA can be used for ship-assists and for towing between Port Angeles and the Puget Sound log ports with a barge tow worked in now and then, especially if the weather prevents log towing.

In towing out of Neah Bay and Port Angeles, weather, ocean swells and tides determine when and where the rafts may safely be towed. All conditions must be "go." Towing logs on the Straits and Admiralty Inlet is a challenge to out-maneuver the weather; and captains and crews of the MARTHA and MYRTLE towing in these waters are recognized for their judgment and skill. Spilling logs enroute creates a hazard for small boats and entails a recovery expense and in many cases a serious loss. Log towing is a tricky trade and only a few men and towing companies are capable of safely handling the slow-moving ponderous tows.

The MARTHA stayed on inside waters until the summer of 1974 when the Ocean Division, short of tugs, had to borrow her for a quick trip to Alaska. The short trip turned out to be nearly four months covering four different assignments. The MARTHA with Captain Dave Edwards left Seattle on July 16, 1974 towing a general cargo barge for Naknek in the Bristol Bay region of Western Alaska. After discharging, the tug on the southbound run to Seattle made stops for freight at Cold Bay, Kodiak, and Anchorage. While enroute she was diverted to Juneau, arriving there August 20th. Captain Dave dropped off his barge and picked up another loaded cargo-barge for discharge at Uganik on Kodiak Island and Dillingham in Western Alaska. When the barge was empty the MARTHA went to Seward, reloaded the barge and finally returned to Seattle.

With the tour of southwestern over, the MARTHA had a chance to look over Southeastern Alaska, as a week after arriving home she left Seattle on a round trip to Ketchikan with a cargo-barge for delivery to the tug DAPHNE. The larger tug was to make the final delivery to Anchorage, so the MARTHA headed south with DAPHNE's empty barge arriving Seattle October 26th. The MARTHA turned around and headed north again five days later. This time she towed two empty pulp-chip scows from Bellingham to the sawmill at Klawock in southeastern Alaska. The chips went into the barges like a waterfall and the loading was accomplished in less than one day and the same day the MARTHA pulled out for the Georgia Pacific Pulp Mill at Bellingham, arriving November 12th. Within a few days she was back towing logs out of Port Angeles, staying on log delivery to Sound ports until the spring of 1975.

Starting in May, the MARTHA was called upon again by the ocean division to make two barge tows to southwestern Alaska, as the scheduled tugs could not handle the heavy summer volume.

In 1976 the MARTHA made a voyage down the coast, again for the Ocean Division. The trip was a "first-ever" delivery to the particular area for the Foss Company. On April 1st, with Captain Arne Nielsen in charge, she towed the flat-deck barge FOSS-185 from Seattle to Sacramento, California. The cargo consisted of four pre-fab bases on which factory modules were to be built for use in the North Slope oil operation. The MARTHA had the distinction of being the first Foss tug to navigate the Sacramento River to the capitol of California. By April 12th, she was back to the trade she knows best, log towing.

In January 1977 Foss was awarded a contract by the Weyerhaeuser company for towing log rafts from the South Bay log dump near Olympia to the Weyerhaeuser mills in Everett. Since the contract called for towing large rafts, up to fifty-four sections, on a regular basis with a tow about every ten days, the MARTHA with her ability and success in towing the heavy Straits rafts, was the logical boat for the Weyerhaeuser job. The CHRISTINE FOSS relieved the MARTHA at Port Angeles and she shifted bases to Seattle, a more central location. With the MARTHA now operating close by the major ports of Seattle, Tacoma, and Everett, she was frequently called on for ship-assists and barge work between the sixty-hour South Bay trips.

In early 1979 the MARTHA was temporarily loaned to Port Angeles, because a major backlog of rafts at Neah Bay had accumulated due to long periods of unsuitable towing weather. Extra tugs were needed to move the many rafts quickly to market as the weather had turned favorable. The MARTHA, MYRTLE, and MATHILDA took on the job and the three "M's" made short work of the backlog.

With the raft inventory at Neah Bay again normal, the MARTHA returned to log towing on the Sound. But no doubt, for a change of pace the MARTHA, with Captains Budd Turner and Ron Crabtree, will go North again towing an easy-moving barge instead of a dead-drag log raft.

DONNA FOSS (2)

Built:	1969	Propulsion:	Caterpillar (Twin)
	Albina Shipyard		1,500-horsepower
	Portland, Oregon	Primary Service:	Puget Sound
Length:	66-feet	Status:	In Service
Beam:	24-feet		

The second DONNA arrived at Foss-Seattle from the Portland builder's yard in late September 1969, seventh in the series of "D" class boats. The tug carries the name of Drew Foss' wife.

Within two days of arrival, under command of alternate Captains John Hulet and Dave Davis, she took over the North Vancouver rail-car run with Foss Barge-118. The DONNA remained on the car-barge run four years except for three months' service in Santa Barbara Channel, California in late '69 and '70, tending an oil drilling rig. Then in late 1973 the DONNA lost her Vancouver run when tandem car-barge tows became necessary due to the increased traffic volume and a larger more powerful tug was required to maintain the schedule.

As a result, the DONNA left the car-barge run and became one of the principal line-haul tugs on Puget Sound until the fall of 1974 when the demand for tugs to move material and equipment for the Alaska pipeline construction exceeded the capacity of the regular coastwise tugs. To ease the problem, tandem tows were started and a caretaker-tug was needed to tend barges at a stop-over point up north, so the DONNA was sent to Idaho Inlet, Alaska, the last major shelter for tugs and tows before entering the Gulf of Alaska and the rough winter crossing to Valdez. The DONNA tended "in transit" loaded cargo barges waiting to cross the Gulf. During the good weather months, Foss tugs had been hauling tandem barge tows of mobile homes and camp units from Southern California direct to Valdez, but with winter weather in the Gulf of Alaska the risk was too great to take two loaded 328-foot barges across at the same time. So for safety and insurance considerations, the linehaul tug dropped off one of the loaded barges in Idaho Inlet for safekeeping with the DONNA and then continued across with the single barge. After discharge at Valdez, the heavy linehaul tug would return to Idaho Inlet, trade barges with the DONNA and take the second loaded barge on to Valdez, discharge the cargo, return to Idaho Inlet, pick up the light first barge and head South with both barges for another round. The unexciting barge-tending went on all the long winter for Captain Jack Hagen and his crew—until March arrived and the line-tugs could again tow tandem non-stop across the Gulf.

When the DONNA left Idaho Inlet she went to Valdez and for the next eighteen months took over the position of harbor-assist tug, docking and undocking barges and ships or shifting supply and equipment barges. By August 1976 most of the material for the Valdez oil terminal had been unloaded and in position, so the DONNA had to go south to look for work.

The balance of 1976, all of 1977 and the first half of 1978 she towed on Puget Sound for long-standing Foss accounts—cement, chemical, pulp, sawmill and railroad companies. Whatever a Foss tug was expected to do, the DONNA did for her customers.

Then in July 1978 she was once again called North—this time to Cook Inlet to handle routine towing work out of Anchorage. By December, with winter setting in and the season's work complete, the DONNA returned to Puget Sound barging—taking up where she left off in July.

All of 1979 turned out to be a repeat of 1978 and if the regular Anchorage tug, the DUNCAN, needs help, no doubt the DONNA will be the one to respond.

PEGGY FOSS (3)

Built:	1969	Propulsion:	Caterpillar
	Pacific Shipyard		460-horsepower
	Anacortes, Washington	Primary Service:	Puget Sound - Port Angeles
Length:	42-feet	Status:	In Service
Beam:	14-feet		

The third PEGGY FOSS was completed in September 1969 the ninth and last of the new replacement tugs, updating the Foss day-boat harbor fleet. The PEGGY and also her sister-tug, SAMISH BAY, were fitted with a Kort-nozzle propulsion system which increased the rated horsepower from 360 to 460 and improved the rudder response, so essential for quick maneuvering.

Her first station was Olympia, but she was under jurisdiction of the Tacoma Division. The PEGGY by her superiority retired the veteran tug, CARL FOSS, and the CARL went into lay-up, eventually to be sold.

The PEGGY was active in most of the commercial towing activities in Olympia Harbor; towing and shifting chip scows, log rafts, boomsticks, and assisting ocean-going freighters in and out of berth. But as time went on, the daily need for the PEGGY in Olympia Harbor decreased, and the need in Tacoma Harbor increased, so in November 1972 she was reassigned to Tacoma. Foss then turned over the Olympia work to Olympia Towing Company but retained and maintained the ship-assist work by sending over Tacoma tugs whenever needed.

The PEGGY's active role in the Tacoma Harbor fleet lasted until June 1975 when the Port Angeles Division called for another tug to help with the increased volume of log-raft shifting and log-ship tending, brought on by the heavy Japanese export log demand. With the size and number of log ships arriving and departing every week, needing berthing assistance and log-raft service, another tug similar in design to the local SAMISH BAY was necessary. The PEGGY fitted the need so after annual overhaul in Seattle, she joined the SAMISH BAY. With the arrival of the PEGGY, the GRACE FOSS, the second tug in Port Angeles, but less qualified than the PEGGY, was transferred to Tacoma for small-tug harbor work.

With Port Angeles continuing to be a top log-exporting port, the PEGGY and the JOE (ex-SAMISH BAY) continue the established daily routine of tending log storages, shifting boomsticks and rafts, performing log-raft ship service, shifting barges and making up log tows for the line-haul tugs. However, docking and undocking ocean-going carriers is their priority job, for without the activity resulting from the many log ships most of the harbor work would be at an end and the PEGGY, now the second tug, would be out of a job.

PHILLIPS FOSS (2)

Built:	1969	Propulsion:	EMD (Two)
	McDermott Shipyard Group		3,000-horsepower
	Amelia, Louisiana	Primary Service:	Coastwise and Alaska
Length:	112-feet	Status:	In Service
Beam:	31-feet		

The PHILLIPS, built to replace Foss' aging World War II Miki's, was the first of three similar ocean-class tugs McDermott delivered to Foss in a twelve-month period. With outfitting complete in July 1969 the PHILLIPS, with Captain Arnold Reynolds, left Amelia light for Panama to relieve the ARTHUR FOSS of two barges and deliver them to New Orleans. The PHILLIPS' initial towing was unusual for a Seattle tug by making her break-in trips running back and forth in the Gulf. But where the work was offered—so went the tug. From New Orleans the PHILLIPS ran to Houston and picked up a drydock section for delivery to Panama. She then returned to Houston and towed the GENERAL HERSHEY to the Canal Zone for the ARTHUR FOSS to take on to San Pedro. The PHILLIPS, at last on the Pacific side, reclaimed the waiting drydock section and pulled the heavy drag up the coast to Alameda, California. She then shifted over to Richmond, picked up a ship hull and towed it to Portland, Oregon. The PHILLIPS' seven rapid traverses were finished and she headed for Seattle, arriving in her home port for the first time on October 4, 1969. The PHILLIPS had completed four ocean tows, spanning eighty-six days since leaving Amelia.

With just nine days in port, she headed back to the Gulf Coast, towing the drill rig, PENROD 46, from Astoria to Port Arthur, Texas. It was a slow, long haul and an awkward tow, taking forty days. Completing delivery of the oil rig, she went to Galveston, hooked on to the S.S. ROANOKE, and towed the ship to Astoria, Oregon. The ROANOKE slipped along easily so the PHILLIPS only needed twenty-three days to make the Columbia River, arriving in early December 1969.

The year 1970 was a busy one for the PHILLIPS. She operated continuously from January through December. Early in the year, with Captain Ernie Guchee, she made several round trips between Puget Sound and the Columbia River, transferring deactivated government ships from the Olympia lay-up fleet to Portland yards. At the end of the job she took a tandem barge tow of construction equipment from the Columbia River to Honokahau, Hawaii. This time she traveled west and east instead of her usual south and north.

After returning the two empty barges to Seattle and with only twelve hours in port to take on fuel and supplies, the PHILLIPS, again with Captain Guchee in charge, left for Oakland on February 25, 1970 to pick up the Matson

PHILLIPS FOSS With barge ISLANDER at Kobe, Japan while on run between Japan and Korea in 1970. (Courtesy of Foss Tug Co)

Steamship Company container-barge ISLANDER. The final destination was Inchon, Korea, 5,000 miles across the Pacific. The PHILLIPS was to initiate a container-barge run from Inchon to Kobe, Japan. Upon arrival in Korea after the long ocean haul, she started right out on the 800-mile shuttle run through the Yellow Sea, Korea Strait, and the Inland Sea of Japan to Kobe. The PHILLIPS continued the service until October when Matson discontinued the program. Then, taking along the barge, she headed down the East China Sea to Hong Kong and from there to Manila, Guam, and Honolulu, loading containers at each port for California discharge. The PHILLIPS arrived home on December 14 after nearly a year at sea including the 300-day assignment for Matson. The crew enjoyed the Far East interlude and they have cameras and gadgets to remind them of the vacation—with pay.

The PHILLIPS' next job started a long association with Foss Alaska Line, beginning with a new run to southwestern Alaska. In early 1971 Foss Alaska Line announced an extension of service to western Alaska. The plan called for cargo delivery to:

1. Kuskokwim Area: Freight to be forwarded up the Kuskokwim River to the port of Bethel.
2. Bering Sea: Service to Nome and St. Michael.
3. Peninsula and Bristol Bay: Service to cannery communities as required. Foss Alaska Line announced three sailings during the ice-free season from mid-May into October—the barges to carry container cargo, including refrigerated units for perishables, as well as break-bulk cargo, cars, construction equipment, storage tanks, and miscellaneous supplies.
      4. On the return trips, Foss Alaska Line would carry fish and general southbound cargo.

The PHILLIPS, again with Captain Guchee, inaugurated the westward service and so with a tandem tow, she left Seattle June 1, 1971 on the pioneer voyage. The ports of call included Bethel, Nome, and St. Michael. St. Michael, headquarters for Yukon River traffic, was on the schedule, but with reservations. The description of St. Michael found in Volume Nine of the U.S. Coast Pilot for Pacific and Arctic Coasts is a decided contrast to the town's once booming activity in the gold rush days. "St. Michael's present population 205, now shows little evidence of the days when the town was of major importance in the Yukon River traffic. Gone are most of the buildings of the Army post, the warehouses of the trading companies, and the tall hulks of the once great Yukon river fleet. The village has a church and a school, but no hospital and no physician. A traveling nurse from the Bureau of Indian Affairs calls at the school." Not a very promising description for estimating freight tonnage, but considerable volume did develop in spite of the austere conditions.

The PHILLIPS successfully completed the first delivery to the westward and arrived back in Seattle on July 6 to load for the second voyage. She made voyage number two, but upon returning, Foss assigned her to the Anchorage run for the next three months and called up the LESLIE to replace the PHILLIPS on the final voyage of the season to the Bering Sea.

On November 2, 1971 the PHILLIPS, this time with Captain Jay Jacobson in command, left Seattle with the last scheduled cargo barge to Amchitka Island on the Holmes and Narver Atomic Energy Contract. This was the last of seventy-three sailings spanning a period of nearly five years. After a forty-five day round trip, the PHILLIPS and BARGE-202 arrived in Seattle December 17—the last Foss vessel to visit remote Amchitka Island for many years.

The year 1972 found the PHILLIPS on a variety of routine assignments except that once again, she towed for Foss Alaska on the three seasonal voyages to the "westward."

For an interesting change, in May of 1973 the PHILLIPS, with Captain Chuck Crawford, spent two weeks' leisure time visiting in the South American seaport of Callao, Peru. They left Beaver, Oregon in early April with a bargeload of West Coast forest products for delivery to Callao. With the "manana" type of unloading, the cargo discharge required two weeks, so there was ample time for shore leave. The PHILLIPS returned the empty barge to San Francisco and then headed up the coast to Seattle, arriving in early June.

During the next few years, the PHILLIPS was primarily engaged in the Permanente Cement Company barge-run to Anchorage, and between runs she towed the Foss chemical barge from Georgia Pacific's plant in Bellingham to the G.P. plant in Samoa, California.

Then, beginning in February 1976 the PHILLIPS was assigned to the Foss Alaska Line container-run to southeastern Alaska. This she did for the next two and one-half years, running alternate weeks with the LESLIE FOSS to provide weekly service.

In late 1978 and early 1979 the PHILLIPS engaged in coastwise towing, but in the spring of 1979 she returned to the southeastern Alaska van run for an indefinite period. From the way she gets around, her slogan should be "HAVE TOWLINE—WILL TRAVEL."

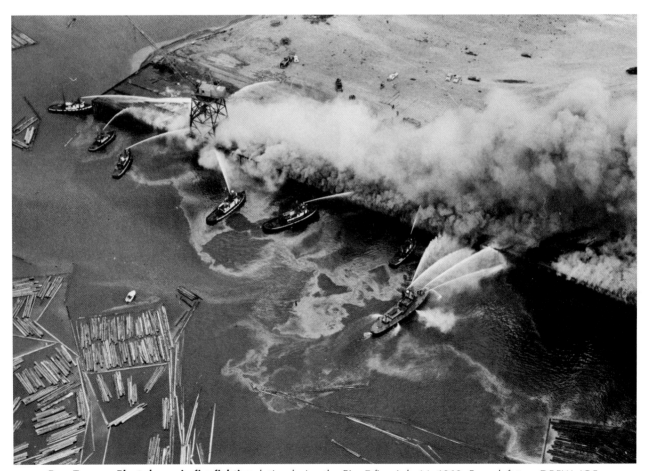

Foss Tacoma Fleet shown in fire fighting duties during the Pier 7 fire, July 14, 1963. From left tugs DREW, JOE, *PETER, CHRIS, BRYNN, FOSS #17. (Photo courtesy of Winfield Brown)*

James A. Cole

SECTION VII – FOSS REACHES TUGBOAT PRE-EMINENCE

Tugs Acquired 1970 – 1979

DUNCAN (2), JEFFREY, LESLIE (2), SHELLEY

CLARA, ANNA (3), WENDY, MARGARET (3)

AGNES (2), BARBARA (3), JUSTINE (3)

STACEY, SANDRA (2), SIDNEY, DREW (2)

IVER (3), PETER (2), PETER (3), MARY (2)

The 1970's open up more new routes: Foss Alaska Line—Seattle to Bering Sea ports. Chemical barge run—Tacoma to Eureka and Pittsburg, California. Kaiser Cement run on West Coast and Canada. Navy contract for delivering cargo barges to Adak, Aleutian Islands. Gulf and East Coast contract-towing with two assigned tugs. Adding 26,000 horsepower, the speed and efficiency of the Ocean fleet are increased.

Special tows and work accomplished: To West Africa, delivering an oil drilling support barge. Sealifts to Prudhoe Bay. To Chile and Ecuador tending pipelaying barges. Dredge delivery to Saginaw, Michigan.

Foss purchases first pusher-type towboat with elevated pilot house for handling high-side barges. The Company institutes oil tanker escort-service on Puget Sound, using high-power tugs. Cook Inlet tug requirements taper off for assisting oil drilling.

Then, in the later 70's business subsides below the normal level and Foss raises it back up by aggressive marketing.

Through the years, thirty regular runs and fixed assignments have been established, employing twenty-nine tugs—a compliment to management.

DUNCAN FOSS (2)

Built:	1970	Propulsion:	Caterpillar (Twin)
	Albina Shipyard		1,500-horsepower
	Portland, Oregon	Primary Service:	Southwestern Alaska & Puget Sound
Length:	66-feet	Status:	In Service
Beam:	24-feet		

Foss named their eighth "D"-class tug DUNCAN after a son of Sidney and Barbara Foss Campbell. The DUNCAN was the last of the "D" boats built by Albina for Foss. She came up from Portland in May 1970 and in less than a week after arrival at the Foss pier, the DUNCAN began her Alaska service by towing a container-barge to Cook Inlet. From there she went on shuttle runs between Southwestern Alaska ports during the fishing and canning season—hauling container cargo for Sea-Land Services, Inc.

The winter was spent in the warmer waters of Puget Sound doing general towing out of Seattle. Then in the spring of 1971 she headed back to Cook Inlet to do ship-assists and general towing around Anchorage, staying for the entire season. In December she returned home to escape the Cook Inlet ice, but she didn't escape more hard work. For the next several months the DUNCAN towed rail-barges on a steady run between Seattle and Vancouver, British Columbia. But she again abandoned Puget Sound in the spring and returned to Anchorage to assist in a cable-laying job in Turnagain Arm.

Finishing up the cable job in the fall of 1972 the DUNCAN was then free to go south, but she didn't get far. In September Foss had stationed the DAVID FOSS at Kodiak as a ship-assist tug for Sea-Land, but after a month on the job, the DAVID was transferred and the DUNCAN called on to take over. The job lasted for nearly three years—assisting Sea-Land ships and occasionally taking part in rescue missions in the open water off Kodiak Island.

A citation was presented to the DUNCAN for a rescue that occurred in February 1973. Two crewmen of the fishing vessel DORIS KAY were in the process of shifting their vessel from the Kodiak transient dock to the inner boat harbor when a sudden and typical Alaska storm, with 100-knot winds, struck the thirty-six-foot vessel. Huge seas broke over the boat, knocking out the windows, flooding the engine room, stopping the motor, and washing the men overboard. The boat was driven aground along the shore of Near Island and started to break up.

The Kodiak police, informed of the tragedy and knowing the seaworthiness of the DUNCAN, rushed to Captain Bob Washburn, hurriedly explained the perilous situation of the two fishermen. With no hesitation the crew got underway and headed the DUNCAN out and across the Channel, making for the vicinity of the disintegrating fish boat. They found one man still alive clinging to floating wreckage and pulled him aboard. They searched the waters for the second man, but unable to locate him, returned to Kodiak for volunteers to check the beaches of Near Island, hoping the man had reached the shore safely. The DUNCAN landed a search party on the island, found the man alive, but suffering from exposure.

Mayor Blake McKinley of Kodiak and the City Council passed a resolution citing and commending Captain Washburn and the DUNCAN's crew for their bravery and unselfish devotion in saving life in hazardous circumstances. It was indeed fortunate for the two men that the DUNCAN was kept up to the Foss motto—Always Ready.

In August 1975 the DUNCAN turned her job over to the KODIAK KING and returned to Seattle via Cook Inlet for a major engine overhaul. But the DUNCAN again showed up in Cook Inlet in the spring for the season's work and she had returned each April to serve Foss customers that each year require more and more service to keep up with the rapid growth of the area.

James A. Cole

JEFFREY FOSS Leaving on a routine assignment to Alaska in 1976. (Courtesy of Foss Tug Co)

JEFFREY FOSS

Built:	1970	Propulsion:	EMD (Twin)
	McDermott Shipyard Group		3,000-horsepower
	Amelia, Louisiana	Primary Service:	Seattle - Alaska
Length:	112-feet	Status:	In Service
Beam:	31-feet		

The JEFFREY, named for a son of Duncan and Claudia Campbell and a grandson of Barbara Foss and Sidney Campbell, completed trial runs and outfitting in June 1970 third in a class of 112-foot replacement tugs for the Foss Ocean and Coastwise Division.

Upon acceptance of the JEFFREY by Foss at the McDermott Shipyard, Captain Joe Uskevich and his Seattle crew left Amelia on June 19, bound for Seattle. Considering the trip was a break-in voyage, everything went well, even the weather was cooperative and after a calm run up from Panama in thirteen days, the JEFFREY pulled into the Foss-Seattle dock, ready for action.

Four days after arrival, she left on her first major towing job—a tandem tow to Anchorage and return. As the JEFFREY had no aches or pains to report when she returned, the crew and the tug had only a few days lay-over, then it was off to the Bering Sea and the Aleutian Islands for a second voyage, towing barge loads of supplies for delivery to Bethel and Adak. The JEFFREY became a familiar sight in southeastern and southwestern Alaska, in fact, for the next two and one-half years her runs were primarily to Alaska, but she did make an occasional trip to California and to Hawaii. During the JEFFREY's long Alaska service she made four trips to Amchitka Island, all made in the final year of the Atomic Energy Commission's project. Then after three years of coastwise towing, she was selected for a long distance ocean tow.

In July 1973 the JEFFREY completed the longest tow in Foss history from point of origin to point of delivery. She towed the oil drill-tending barge, NAVIFOR II, a distance of 10,000 miles from Seattle to Port Gentil, a port in the small West African country of Gabon. Captain Uskevich made the trip with the JEFFREY, and he reported an average speed of ten knots for the fifty-day outbound voyage, encountering pleasantly warm weather with the ocean flat—a good combination for a cruise and for ship's work.

The NAVIFOR II, and ex-Navy LST, was converted to the oil-drill support vessel at the Seattle yard of Marine Power & Equipment Company. The barge was completely equipped with machine shops, generators, cranes, repair equipment, and accommodations for up to ninety men when in service off the coast of Gabon.

Returning from the African tow in mid-August, the middle of the Alaska towing season, and with the boat in top condition, the JEFFREY, with only a two-day layover, but with a new crew, left for Alaska on the Foss barge-run to Anchorage. She stayed with Alaska towing for the balance of 1973.

In 1974 the JEFFREY was selected to make the Foss Alaska Line's two annual trips to western Alaska and Bering Sea ports. On the last voyage, made during the ice-free season in late August and under Captain Al Anderson, she called at the ports of Bethel, Nome, St. Michael, and Unalakleet. As the discharge of the two barges wasn't completed until late September, she headed right out for home since the Bering Sea usually starts to freeze over in early October and remains frozen until late spring.

Foss Alaska Line is a major freight carrier to southwestern Alaska and Bering Sea ports and their barges regularly carry container loads of food, clothing, and hardware. but on the JEFFREY's last trip of 1974 the barges carried a more varied cargo—thirty-five small fishboats, fifteen mobile homes, four heavy-duty modules to serve as courtrooms and jails, a 300,000-gallon water tank weighing fifty-four tons, a snowplow and a school bus, and also kitchen sinks (twenty-three of them) and all consigned to Bethel.

During the winter of 1974-1975 the JEFFREY was on the run between Long Beach California and Valdez, Alaska hauling tandem tows of house modules, used as camp units for the construction crews working on the Valdez-Prudhoe Bay pipeline.

After six months as a house mover, the JEFFREY left on a voyage that pitted man and tug against the freezing forces of nature at their icy worst—the trip furnished material to re-write the annals of tugboating in the frozen Arctic. The JEFFREY, along with twenty-two other tugs including the ARTHUR and HENRY FOSS, took part in a tremendous and exciting tug and barge operation. Cargo barging of such magnitude had never before been attempted by tugboats.

Each year since 1968 thousands of tons of supplies and equipment were marshalled in several Puget Sound ports to await loading on ocean-going barges for delivery to the oilfields of Alaska's North Slope. In early July the Sealift of tugs and barges left Puget Sound to meet at Port Clarence several hundred miles south of Point Barrow. The boats arrived at rendezvous about three weeks later to await the brief period when the polar ice recedes far enough from the Arctic coastline to permit the tugs and barges to round into Purdhoe Bay, unload the cargo and escape back around the northernmost tip of North America at Point Barrow before the ice moves in for another eleven months. Under usual conditions the ice-free time is only about four weeks duration, in the month of August.

Crowley Maritime, Inc. managed the yearly Sealift under the name of Arctic Marine Freighters. In addition to Crowley's own tugs and barges, the use of other towing companies' equipment was sometimes necessary due to the volume of cargo that had to be delivered by barge in a matter of days. Foss assisted in the regular Sealifts in the first years with the ARTHUR FOSS. However, the Sealift of 1975 required a total of twenty-three tugs towing forty-seven barges, and Foss was asked to supply three tugs and six barges. The cargo tonnage to be moved totaled 160,000 and was worth $500-million! Aboard the barge were a number of the most spectacular items ever to travel any sea. Some of the modular units housing processing machinery were as high as a ten-story building! These modules loaded on ten of the forty-seven barges were top-priority cargo as the oil companies had to have the equipment to complete the flow stations for separating crude oil and natural gas.

The first tugs and barges of the 1975 Sealift left Seattle in early June, but the JEFFREY FOSS departed later on July 5th with two barges in tow, again under command of Captain Uskevich, her regular skipper. The ARTHUR and HENRY had left a week earlier, each with two barges. The JEFFREY dropped anchor on July 25th at the 1975 rendezvous point near Wainwright, Alaska to await the Arctic ice pack to recede, expected to happen in a week or two.

The comments on the JEFFREY's log sheet ten days later read, 'Same as before, day in and day out. Heavy drift ice in all directions. Rain and fog, temperature 42°.'' Then on August 6th, the flotilla had to make a "strategic withdrawal" south to Icy Cape to prevent ice damage and an ice lock-in. Heavy ice surrounded the fleet with thick fog and a temperature of 32°, according to the JEFFREY's radio report. August 14th was a big day for all the tugs' crews—mail arrived from home. August 20th was another big day—the Crowley supply boat dropped off a pallet board of fresh fruit, vegetables and meat for each crew! The food was airlifted from Seattle.

August 22 came and went, with no change in almost a month from the arrival date. August 22 was the latest in the year, except in 1931, that the annual ice break-up had ever occurred at Point Barrow, so now it would be a battle with the ice to get to Prudhoe.

By August 26th, the days of waiting had turned into weeks for the 184 crew members on the tugs with each day filled with frustration and boredom as the polar ice refused to recede. The next day storm force winds played havoc with the fleet. Three barges broke loose from their tugs and grounded on sandy beaches. (They were later pulled off and repaired.)

On August 28 the decision was made to single up the tows (one barge per tug) with the ten barges of priority modulars to make a try if even the narrowest of an open lead in the ice should form. Failure to deliver the modules would delay completion of the pipeline by many months, so no chance could be passed up. The ten particular tugs picked, including the JEFFREY, to tow the priority barges, were chosen because they had the least draft and could stay close to the beach in shallow water where the ice was thinner.

On September 2 the ten tugs and barges were put on standby "Sealift command." Then early on September 3 a small lead opened up and with ice patrol planes scouting ahead for further leads, the first four tugs started through the opening to round Point Barrow. In the JEFFREY's log, Captain Uskevich wrote, "Going around Barrow with air reconnaissance scouting ahead for leads. Encountering heavy pack ice and crunching into ice. Temperature 26° and fog."

It took two days to force through the 165 miles from Barrow to Prudhoe Bay, encountering heavy ice all the way. The tugs reported, "ice everywhere—as far as the eye can see, and the huge modules fill the horizon like the skyline of a city—Arctic Skyscrapers." At 2100 on September 4 the JEFFREY arrived in Prudhoe Bay with her priority barge, the first tug of the 1975 Sealift to arrive in Prudhoe. Later in the evening the tugs SIOUX, SPARTAN and SEA MONARCH arrived with one barge each. The temperature on arrival was 20°, with new surface ice forming and snow falling.

After taking on fuel, the four tugs headed west toward Point Barrow to assist the next group and their barges. With two tugs working each barge, the second group successfully arrived in Prudhoe on September 7. A total of 22,000 tons had now been delivered. The JEFFREY and her running mates left Prudhoe on September 9 to rejoin the remaining fourteen tugs and thirty-seven barges still dodging ice flows off Wainwright.

On September 10 the JEFFREY's log reads: "Can't get around Barrow. Heavy mean ice and thick fog. Some bergs are moving; all sizes, 20 to 30 feet high and acres of thick ice." By September 11 the tugs were forced into Elson Lagoon, a shallow body of water comparatively free of ice, in order to escape the heavy pressure from ice building up in the open area. For five days the tugs remained trapped in the Lagoon until a wind change fortunately gave them a chance to escape and work safely around Point Barrow. They were able to rejoin the remaining fleet on September 16.

Back on September 11, the oil companies had decided that the less vital and smaller size cargo could be shipped overland from the ice-free port of Seward, and so three tugs and five barges (including ARTHUR FOSS) left the icefields for Seward. However, at Wainwright no one was giving in to the Arctic ice. There were still thirty barges that somehow had to get to Prudhoe Bay, and Arctic Marine Freighters were going to make every effort to get through if the wind and weather would just turn southeasterly.

Then, on September 24, Captain Uskevich reported to Seattle that fifteen tugs and the next fifteen barges on the priority list were heading in single file toward Point Barrow. But a few hours later, the report came that heavy pack ice blocked the route with new ice forming hourly. The temperature was 25° and dropping. The entire fleet turned around and retreated to Point Franklin. By nightfall the temperature had fallen to 15°. A decision had to be made. Should the fleet remain, waiting for an opening that might never come and risk the chance of getting frozen into the Arctic ice for the next ten months, with potential damage and delay running in the millions of dollars. The oil companies, standing the cost of all delays, decided to take the big gamble and hold on. The cost of the delay due to the ice conditions was running $200,000 per day! Up to September 16, the unrelenting ice barrier had cost the oil companies almost $10 million!

Finally, on September 28 with the aid of the coast guard ice breaker BURTON ISLAND and the cutters STORIS and CITRUS breaking out a lane ahead, the tugs and barges in single-file procession stretching over the horizon, rounded Point Barrow. The temperature held at 5° above zero and a six-inch layer of new ice had formed in addition to the year-old pack ice. On September 30 the first lead tug, after breaking and crunching through the ice for 160 miles, arrived battered but safe in Prudhoe Bay. Back in the procession with many miles to go, the JEFFREY and other tugs were having problems. At 1315 on September 30th, the JEFFREY radioed that they were stuck solid in pressure ice with heavy buildup on the tug's port side, and air temperature standing at 12°. The cutter, STORIS, arrived on the scene to assist, but upon stopping she froze fast. However, they were able to break free the same night and, fortunately, with no serious damage. At 1930 October 1, the JEFFREY arrived in Prudhoe Bay with her second barge and by the afternoon of October 2 the last of the priority convoy had safely arrived in Prudhoe Bay. The Captains reported ramming their tugs through ice fourteen to sixteen inches thick during the last 100 miles!

With Prudhoe Bay now nearly frozen solid and the temperature dropping to near zero and new ice forming by the hour, it was obvious the twenty-five barges would have to remain and be frozen in at the "Bay" for the next ten months. In addition to the barges, two tugs, the HERCULES and SPARTAN, were to winter-in and tend the barges until the entire area froze solid, stopping all movement.

At 2240 hours on October 2 the JEFFREY joined the single-file column for the escape through the narrow lane close to shore. After two days forcing and ramming through the ice, a beating which the tugs were never designed for, the fleet, with the help of air reconnaissance and the coast guard, rounded Point Barrow to safety. The most stupendous and the most costly civilian Sealift in peacetime history was declared a success, but it had nearly turned into a $500-million disaster. Of the forty-seven barges that originally went north, twenty-five were safely delivered to Prudhoe Bay, and twenty were towed to Seward for discharge and their cargo delivered overland to Prudhoe. Two loaded barges were returned to Seattle to await more favorable conditions in the Sealift of 1976. The Sealift of 1975 had been carried out in the most difficult summer ice conditions *ever* recorded in Arctic history.

The JEFFREY, along with several other tugs on their way south, stopped at Port Clarence and picked up the remaining loaded barges left behind in the race for Prudhoe. The barges were delivered to Anchorage and Seward with the JEFFREY taking her barge to Anchorage. After discharging the cargo, the tug and her weary crew finally headed for home, and on November 4, 1975 they arrived in the much longed-for calm and friendly surroundings of the ice-free Foss dock. The 124-day odyssey was over!

On November 22, 1975 the Foss Company held a Prudhoe Bay recognition dinner in honor of the crews of the three Foss tugs taking part in the Sealift. The placecards read, "In appreciation to the men at sea and their ladies at home, for making the Foss Launch & Tug Company's participation successful in the 1975 Prudhoe Bay Sealift. Well Done."

As a result of ice damage, the JEFFREY spent considerable time in drydock repairing the wear and tear inflicted by three months of battering by the Arctic ice. But by mid-December, she was back at sea assisting in the Alaska pipeline construction, this time hauling barges between Seattle and the ice-free port of Valdez.

In the spring of 1976 the JEFFREY was assigned to Foss Alaska Line and continued in their service during the summer and fall months. Under Captain Red Hendershot, she made the three annual Southwestern Alaska and Bering Sea supply runs for Foss Alaska. On the southbound trips they picked up cargoes of canned salmon at the ports of Egegik, Port O'Brien, and Larsen Bay; cargoes valued in the millions of dollars! Then in the winter and spring months the JEFFREY, along with the LESLIE, maintained a weekly schedule of sailings to southeastern Alaska.

After adhering to a fixed schedule for several years, the JEFFREY in April 1979, was assigned to a new job, but not in a new operating area. Having more horsepower, she replaced the SANDRA on the Chevron oil-delivery run in Bristol Bay and the Bering Sea, spending the usual six months on the run, with the veteran skipper of the route, Captain Bob Burns, in command. She returned to Seattle with oil barge FOSS-256 on November 4, a successful season in her log book.

After a short checkup, the JEFFREY joined the PHILLIPS on the Foss Alaska Line container-barge run to Southeastern, replacing the LESLIE.

As her assignment is long-term, the JEFFREY will, no doubt, become an Alaska "Sourdough" boat, having already passed the cheechako stage, and with no errors or omissions.

LESLIE FOSS (2)

Built:	1970	Propulsion:	EMD (Twin)
	McDermott Shipyard Group		3,000-horsepower
	Amelia, Louisiana	Primary Service:	Ocean and Coastwise
Length:	112-feet	Status:	In Service
Beam:	31-feet		

The LESLIE, second of four similar tugs built by McDermott for Foss, was completed and accepted in early May, 1970. Then, after stores were aboard and the crew signed on the Articles, the LESLIE, with Captain Jay Jacobson in charge, ran light to Houston and picked up a new ocean-class barge loaded with oil drilling equipment for delivery to Port Angeles. The new tug performed well on the 5,500 mile trip, arriving at Port Angeles in twenty-nine days and on time for her meeting with the ARTHUR FOSS, waiting to take the barge to Prudhoe Bay.

During the LESLIE's first year of operation with Captain Jacobson, she made several trips to Southeastern and Southwestern Alaska, interspersed with trips to California and Honolulu. During the winter she completed a succession of round trips to Amchitka, towing a thirty-thousand-barrel oil barge.

The LESLIE operated away from the Seattle base during the summer of 1971, shuttling barges brought North by other tugs from meeting points in Southeastern Alaska and delivering them to Adak, Anchorage, Kotzebue, Platinum and Naknek. Then in the fall of 1971, the LESLIE returned home to tow direct from Seattle to Southwestern Alaska and the Bering Sea.

In 1972, the LESLIE, with Captain George Ducich, towed the Permenente cement barge from Seattle and Bamberton, British Columbia, to Anchorage, Alaska, making one trip every thirty days. The favorable weather and the steady performance of the LESLIE combined to make a trouble-free towing year.

During the winter and summer months of 1973, she operated for Foss Alaska Line towing van-barges on a schedule between Seattle and the Southeastern Alaska ports served by Foss. In May, with the ice breaking up in the Bering Sea, the LESLIE, with Captain Bob Hegerberg in command, sailed on the first of three voyages for Foss Alaska Line to the Bering Sea ports of Bethel, Nome, St. Michael, and Unalakleet.

When the winter weather arrived in December, closing off the Bering Sea, the LESLIE, now with senior Skipper Tauno Salo in charge, turned south to warmer climates, towing the derrick barge ELIZABETH from San Francisco to Talara, Peru for Belco Petroleum Company of Callao. After completing the 4,000-mile tow to Talara under favorable conditions, the LESLIE, in mid-January, returned to Seattle via Panama. In Balboa she stopped to pick up a new Foss rail-car barge to be used on the Vancouver car-barge run; the barge was towed down from Houston for transfer to the LESLIE—this gave her a payload northbound.

In July, 1974, the LESLIE, with Captain Chuck Crawford in command this time, left Long Beach, California, on the first of seven round-trip voyages between Long Beach, Seattle and Valdez. Captain Crawford and the LESLIE remained on the run until April, 1975, when she was replaced for the duration of the towing contract by the Pacific Tow & Salvage tug, PACIFIC RANGER. During the LESLIE's time she towed two LST-class barges each carrying forty modular camp units to be used as living quarters for construction crews on the Alaska Pipeline.

During the nine months of LESLIE's run to Valdez, the heaviest weather encountered was not in the stormy waters of the Gulf of Alaska as would be expected, but off the Oregon coast. On one trip southbound and during the day of November 18th, the LESLIE, with two empty barges, ran into a deep low-pressure area off the Columbia River. Her speed dropped to less than five knots, and by daylight next morning the southwesterly wind had strengthened to fifty knots and was increasing. To protect the tug and barges, it was necessary to heave-to and wait out the storm, so Captain Crawford held the tug into the seas and maintained only a light strain on the two-inch wire towline. By morning of the following day, November 20th, the wind was a screaming seventy knots, building up thirty-five foot seas, and the barges being empty were acting like sails, dragging the tug backwards. It was a case of helpless waiting—the LESLIE drifted, the storm in charge. At 1300 hours, with no let-up in sight, Captain Crawford called the Foss office and advised that if conditions continued to deteriorate, he might be forced to drop the towline on one or both barges for the safety of the LESLIE and her crew. However, knowing the near-impossibility of retrieving drifting barges in such severe weather conditions, the Captain agreed to hold on for a few more hours. The decision turned out to be right as by nightfall the wind and seas started to ease up. By next morning the waves were not breaking and the wind was less violent, so they were able to start towing, and in the right direction. The LESLIE, her Captain and crew, came through the storm with only a roughing up and a loss of sleep, and ready to take on another onslaught from Aeolus.

A year later, in about the same location but in average weather, the LESLIE, with Captain Chuck May, witnessed an implausible situation that destroyed the value of their barge and cargo. The costly mishap occurred on December 31, 1975 with the unmanned, loaded, bulk-cement carrying barge SEWARD under tow from Redwood City, California to Seattle. This time, the LESLIE's weather was moderate and conditions on the barge normal. But late in the day the crew noticed the SEWARD suddenly take a list. The heel rapidly increased and before the tug could get near, the barge capsized. The SEWARD turned over, but strangely did not dump her load. The on-deck bulkheads were completely under water and the bottom totally exposed. The barge continued to float in its overturned position and after determining by inspection that it would remain so, the LESLIE continued up the coast with the SEWARD, but at a much reduced speed.

The LESLIE, with the barge still upside down, pulled into Port Angeles for inspection and survey. The surveyors found that the 4,000 tons of cement had hardened throughout the barge and they decided that any attempt to remove the cargo and recondition the SEWARD would be impractical and too costly. So the barge was turned over to the underwriters and declared a total loss. Eventually, the SEWARD was towed to Tacoma where it still remains after several years, still in the same condition. Apparently no one is willing to chance a scrapping job. The loss of the SEWARD left Permanente Cement Company with only one barge, the P-272, as the SEWARD's sister barge was lost in 1971.

In early 1976 the LESLIE was assigned to the Foss Alaska Line barge service to southeastern Alaska, leaving from Seattle every other Wednesday, making twenty-six trips each year. Darrel Wilson, her regular Captain on the van run, only had to point the LESLIE north and let her go on her own—she knew the way. But since December 3rd, 1979 the LESLIE has had to learn two new routes, still in Alaska.

She headed right out for Cook Inlet with the 36,000-barrel oil barge, FOSS-256, to spend several months barging oil between the Inlet, Valdez, Cordova, Kodiak, and other area ports on a demand basis. Then in the spring of 1980 when the open season again comes to the Bering Sea, Captain Bob Burns and his crew will go up to Anchorage, relieve the LESLIE's regular crew, take over the tug and barge, and head for Dutch Harbor to go on the long-established Chevron run delivering oil in the Bristol Bay-Bering Sea region for the usual six month period.

The schedule will keep the LESLIE occupied until November 1980 and then she will, no doubt, put her 3,000-horsepower to work on other Alaska runs—the spell of the North is strong in the LESLIE.

SHELLEY FOSS

Built:	1970	Propulsion:	Caterpillar (Twin)
	Albina Shipyard		2,850-horsepower
	Portland, Oregon	Primary Service:	Seattle Harbor
Length:	90-feet	Status:	In Service
Beam:	30-feet		

The SHELLEY FOSS, launched in Portland June 17, 1970 was designed and planned to take over ship-assists in Seattle Harbor. The work had been ably carried out for the past twelve years by the CAROL and SHANNON FOSS, but ship tonnage and the number of the ships arriving and departing had increased to a point where a larger and more powerful tug was needed, hence the SHELLEY. The tug was named for the daughter of Sandra Campbell Wright, granddaughter of Sidney and Barbara Foss Campbell.

A distinctive characteristic of the tug is the design of the pilothouse with the window glass slanted inward to minimize glare. She is also fitted with viewing ports in the pilothouse "eyebrow" to better see tie-up lines and movements of ships being maneuvered in and out of docks. Most important mechanically, the SHELLEY is equipped with twin Kort steering nozzles, each housing an eighty-eight-inch propeller, boosting her actual power by forty percent over a conventional twin-screw installation, and increasing her maneuvering ability. Her bow and stern-line winches were especially designed for more efficient line handling, as both winches are controlled from the main console in the pilothouse and are located alongside the main engine controls.

SHELLEY FOSS *Running lite across Seattle Harbor to assist a ship into berth – May, 1979. (From the author's collection)*

The SHELLEY arrived in Seattle from Portland on September 4th and spent the next week gearing-up at the Foss pier. On September 11th she went around to her new base at Pier 37, ready to start "juggling" ships. The SHELLEY, an immediate success in the Harbor, was soon called Queen of the Harbor tugs by shipowners, agents and pilots. The usual wording of a request by ships' agents for assist-tugs was, "We need two tugs to help our ship into dock; unless the SHELLEY is assigned, then one tug will do." She is available twenty-four hours a day, seven days a week, but even so, she loses out when arrivals or departures double up. In her eight years of service, the SHELLEY has docked and undocked nearly 12,000 ships!, with a total tonnage of nearly 168-million tons, and this doesn't include the big Navy ships at Bremerton.

The Navy asks for the SHELLEY's assistance on all major vessel shifts including the large aircraft carriers moving in and out of the Navy Yard. Usually, the SHELLEY is accompanied by five Navy tugs when assisting the mammoth ships.

Her two Captains, Ray Halstead and Dan Meagher, experts of long standing in handling ships, and their steady crews maintain the SHELLEY in top condition; her operating report shows few repair requests and all maintenance items checked off as completed. Other than the annual two weeks for drydocking and engine overhaul, she holds to her "Always Ready" status—even for community projects.

The SHELLEY and her two alternate crews, in addition to tugboating, are adept and most accommodating in public relations. The SHELLEY is always the tug called on to take special guests on waterfront tours. Also students, some as young as grade school, have toured Seattle Harbor aboard the SHELLEY as part of their on-site education.

In a display of public interest and patriotism, the SHELLEY's traditional Foss color scheme was changed, temporarily, during the 1976 Bi-Centennial. In short order she was transformed from her usual Foss green-and-white combination to America's red, white and blue. The six-man crew of the SHELLEY, headed by Captain Dan Meagher, with additional help from other Foss enthusiasts, applied the patriotic colors in two days of intensive painting—the job was done while berthed at Foss' former Seattle harbor moorage, Pier 28. For two colorful days the SHELLEY was relieved of her normal harbor duties to accomplish the striking transformation, and she looked like a Fourth of July parade float when the artists finished. The pilothouse ended up white with blue stars and the encircling visor bright red, with the top hand rails and trim painted flag blue. The lower deckhouse was accented with red, white and blue vertical stripes; the bulwarks were white and the deck machinery blue. The hull was solid red. A big Centennial logo was carried on the pilothouse. The SHELLEY was literally a waving flag in Seattle harbor, drawing many salutes from passing craft and visitors alike during the Nation's 200th-year celebrations.

Being stationed in Seattle, the SHELLEY took part in many unusual events in the harbor. On a stormy day in October 1977 a fire broke out under Pier 91, caused by a short circuit in an electrical cable. Shortly before the fire a wave-tossed log had damaged the Pier sprinkler system rendering it useless, so a fireboat was hurriedly called. The ALKI responded, but due to the high tide and heavy swells, the fireboat was unable to direct the powerful streams of their monitors and hoses under the dock. The Fire Department requested assistance from Foss tugs to act as a breakwater. The SHELLEY and the AGNES rushed over and stood off the Pier to break the westerly swells surging along the piling. Because of the reduced wave action, the ALKI was able to direct the water on the fire. A third tug, the DOROTHY FOSS, helped out by tying up to the pier so she could be used as a platform for the firemen to work closer to the fire. As the tide lowered, more and more water could be directed right at the flames, and finally, after five hours, the fire was under control and the tugs were released. It wasn't tugboating, but it was Harbor Service.

Another happening the SHELLEY played a part in was a fund-raising scheme for the KCTS Television Station to raise money for the Station's educational program. A day on the SHELLEY, watching her operate, was auctioned off, and the successful bidder paid $250.00 for the privilege. All the money, of course, went to KCTS, and the SHELLEY hosted the winner for a day's tugboating.

With all the SHELLEY's activities to look after, she is almost a permanent fixture in Seattle Harbor, but not quite—with her high horsepower, she does leave to go on tanker escort work when an extra tug is required on the northern Sound. If ship work is slow on a particular day, she makes a barge run from Seattle to Port Townsend, or she helps out in Tacoma on ship-assists. Occasionally, a special job comes up requiring a tug on short notice and the SHELLEY responds. Just such a situation arose when the Hood Canal Bridge was blown apart by hurricane-force winds.

On February 13, 1979 an unusual and violent wind storm, for the Puget Sound region, hit the Hood Canal area particularly hard. Hundred-knot winds and twelve-foot seas buffeted the pontoons that formed the floating part of the bridge. The slabsided pontoons were acting like a breakwater and the pressure was too much for the anchor cables and at 0800 they parted, allowing the west-end sections to fill and sink.

Prior to 0800, the SHELLEY, with Captain Dan Meagher aboard, was ordered by Foss to the bridge site, upon urgent request of the State Highway Department. They reasoned that if a section of the bridge should break loose and float down the Canal, the SHELLEY would be able to recover it and work the parts into sheltered waters. But unfortunately, by the time the SHELLEY arrived at 1030, the west-end pontoons were already in sheltered water—three hundred feet below the surface. The SHELLEY, unable to help the severed bridge in any way, did take the Highway engineers on a waterside survey of the damage before returning to her Seattle station.

The disaster was keenly felt by Captain Dan Meagher, as he was skipper of the CAROL FOSS when she played an important part during the bridge's construction, twenty years previously. The CAROL had towed the very same pontoons from the builder's yard in Seattle to Port Gamble, the assembly point, and then later on to the bridge site. Captain Meagher had charge of the tugboat work in assembling, positioning, and anchoring the pontoons, so he had more than a passing interest in the Hood Canal Bridge. Most likely he will be called on to do the job all over again when the new bridge is built. However, with Seattle becoming one of the top container-ports in the world, bringing in more and larger ships, the SHELLEY, before long, won't have time to go beyond Four Mile Rock and Alki Point.

CLARA FOSS

Built:	1971	Propulsion:	Caterpillar (Twin)
	Albina Shipyard		1,700-horsepower
	Portland, Oregon	Primary Service:	Puget Sound
Length:	80-feet	Status:	In Service
Beam:	25-feet		

The CLARA FOSS, named for Clara Berg Wright, niece of Thea Foss, was an updated version of the CLAUDIA and CATHERINE, the first two "C"-class tugs. She was built to handle container-barges for the Foss Alaska Line run to Southeastern Alaska, but eventually, as the barges increased in size, she lost out to the big ocean class tugs. After her initial run up from Portland, the CLARA made her first nine-day container trip under Captain Paul Peterson in early May, 1971—the first of many runs for Foss Alaska Line. Then in July, the CLARA took a ten-month leave of absence from the van run.

In June the Foss Ocean Division secured a contract with the Santa Fe Pomeroy Construction Company for support work in an offshore oil pipeline construction job in South America. The requirement was for a medium class, highly maneuverable tug to assist in the laying of an underwater pipeline. With the special type service in mind, the CLARA was chosen. The disadvantage in the contract, compared to other pipeline work Foss had assisted in, was the location at Quintero Bay, Chile, 6,000 miles from home base, possibly causing communication and supply problems.

Nevertheless, on July 2nd, the CLARA, with Captain Chuck Crawford in the pilothouse and towing the pipe-barge SEMINOLE, left Portland, Oregon bound for the pipeline site near Valparaiso. The trip south was uneventful except for a minor "tragedy." The day before arriving in Acapulco to take on fuel, the engineer started transferring diesel from tank to tank to simplify fueling. The fuel in one tank was higher than expected and the oil started coming out the vent pipe, which happened to be located right by an escape hatch over the Mate's below-decks room. Because of the tropical heat, the hatch was open and the Mate sleeping in his bunk was just under the hatch and the overflow. He suddenly had a rude awakening. In seconds, overflowing diesel oil had poured down in a solid stream soaking the Mate, the mattress, furnishings, deck and bulkheads. By the time the pumping and the descriptive language stopped, many gallons had accumulated in the cabin. After much cleaning, laced with more appropriate words, and a new mattress, the room was again livable except for the oily smell. The drops of oil found here and there weeks later, and the smell, were a constant reminder to the Mate never to leave port without a good supply of spray cologne!

For seventy-five days the CLARA and her crew worked from seven to seven every day tending the pipeline project. The twelve-hour days went on until the last of September.

By the time the CLARA had completed her assignment in Chile, Foss had secured a similar contract with Houston Construction Company for pipeline construction at Esmeraldas, Ecuador. To get the job started, the BARBARA FOSS left Seattle October 19, 1971 with the derrick-barge VIKING bound for a point of exchange with the CLARA on her way north with the SEMINOLE. On November 6, the tugs traded barges at the tip of Baja, California, and the CLARA went on to Esmeraldas with the VIKING, arriving November 19. For the next four-and-a-half months she worked again as pipeline tender. In late March 1972 with the work completed, the CLARA and the VIKING headed for Seattle, exchanging Tug Boat Spanish for Shore Side English. On May 2nd, after ten months away, Captain Crawford and the crew were back home. They had earned a long rest, but the CLARA started right out again.

After minor voyage repairs, she returned to the Southeastern Alaska van-barge run for Foss Alaska Line, and for the next three-and-a-half years remained on the route towing van-barge 275, serving the ports of Ketchikan, Wrangell, Petersburg, Juneau, and Sitka. Paul Peterson, Bob Myette, Walt Kardonsky and Darrel Wilson were the skilled Captains piloting the CLARA during her long continuous service.

Then as cargo volume increased and time in port working cargo lengthened, the CLARA was unable to maintain the schedule. As a result, in December 1975 she was taken off the run and replaced by one of the high-powered ocean tugs. The CLARA, then with alternate Captains Spencer Workman and Jim Martin in charge, became the number one tug on the North Vancouver to Seattle rail-car barge haul, remaining on the route until April 1978.

Most every tug in the Foss fleet with 750-horsepower or more, has served at some time or other on the car-barge run between Seattle and North Vancouver. The CHRISTINE FOSS in January of 1957 initiated the service and at that time only one barge was used carrying fifteen 40-foot rail cars, but through the years, the size of the barges and the rail cars increased, necessitating more and more tug horsepower. In 1974 tandem tows were started which required tugs like the CLARA, tugs larger than the "D"-class boats which had been on the run for five years.

For the first seven years of operation, the northern terminal was at Squamish, B.C., in Howe Sound, but in 1964 the terminal was shifted to a closer, more modern facility at North Vancouver.

By 1975, with a tremendous increase in the export of Canadian forest products, a third barge was added and a "D"-boat used to tow the single barge. At times, to take care of the volume of cars, three tugs and four barges were used on the run. Then in 1978 with the availability of still larger tugs (2,400-horsepower), the rail division began using two tandem tows (four barges) which provided daily service between Seattle and Vancouver. However, before the end of 1978 shipments were curtailed due to strikes in British Columbia; nevertheless, Foss continued the daily service and the tandem tows.

The rail-barge program has moved a tremendous volume since its inception and the volume indicates the success of the service. Between 1960 and 1978, 3,415 trips were completed, transporting 75,000 loaded rail cars to Seattle for on-going distribution to the forty-eight states.

Late spring, 1978 found the CLARA off the Vancouver run and back in Alaska, somewhat farther north than her last time in southeastern Alaska. An intermediate-class tug was needed in Cook Inlet during the 1978 season in addition to the regular "D" boat assigned to the area, so the CLARA, again with Captain Chuck Crawford in charge, ran light to the Inlet and worked for Chugach Electric Company on cable laying, also barging materials for the Beluga River Power Station, and in between times tending diving rigs.

In September the CLARA took over the DONNA's run with the FOSS-110, a small, refined-oil barge used between the refinery at Nikiski, Alaska and Kodiak Island. The CLARA remained on oil delivery until relieved by the WENDY in November, as a larger tug and oil barge were necessary during the adverse winter weather. Regardless, the CLARA had operated continuously in Southwestern Alaska for the past seven months and it was time she returned home for voyage repairs.

The CLARA's engines were given a major overhaul during the 1978-79 winter, preparatory to returning to Cook Inlet in April. As expected, the CLARA returned to Alaska for another season's work. One more season North and she will automatically become a member, along with the CHRISTINE, ALASKA HUSKY, and others, of the SOURDOUGH FLEET and entitled to fly the Big Dipper blue-and-silver-starred flag—earned after seven Alaska seasons.

ANNA FOSS (3)

Built:	1970	Propulsion:	General Motors
	Hudson Marine Services		950-horsepower
	Seward, Alaska	Primary Service:	Puget Sound
Length:	67-feet	Status:	In Service
Beam:	23-feet		

Of all the used tugs purchased by Foss, the ANNA came with the most unusual name—MR. CHUCK. The tug was built in 1970 by the Hudson Marine Services for shallow river work in Alaska. As a river boat she was of light draft, wide beam, high power, and a square bow for pushing barges on the winding rivers flowing into various Alaskan waters. By pushing instead of towing, towboat and barge become one tightly connected unit to insure positive control and handling, so essential in swift-flowing, bar-strewn rivers.

Hudson Marine apparently ran into financial difficulties as the official documents show that in late 1970 a lien was filed against the tug by the Internal Revenue Service. This lien was satisfied in March 1971 but on June 16, 1971 another lien was filed, this time by the Department of Labor, State of Alaska. The fate of MR. CHUCK ended up in Admiralty Court in June 1971 largely brought on by a suit of the General Electric Credit Company against the vessel and owners, Hudson Marine. On August 17th, the Court ruled the boat, her engine, all machinery, tackle, and furniture would be sold free and clear at Public Sale. General Electric Credit Company bid her in, then in turn, sold her six days later to the George Engine Company.

George Engine Company held ownership until January 1972 when they sold her to Foss. Shortly after, the WEDELL FOSS towed MR. CHUCK from Juneau to Seattle in company with a Foss Alaska Line barge.

During the early months of 1972 MR. CHUCK, at the Foss shipyard, received a thorough going-over, but no modifications were necessary to adapt her for Foss' planned use. Before final outfitting and painting with the identifying green and white, she was given the name of ANNA FOSS to keep the name alive, as the last ANNA, a MIKI, had been sold eighteen months previously to Luzon Stevedoring Company.

282

The ANNA had a rather difficult first assignment; she had orders to tow a 185-foot cargo barge from Seattle to the Yukon River for Foss Alaska Line. With Captain Lyle Akerlund in charge, she left Seattle on May 19th, towing the FOSS-185. For this type of run and with rough sea conditions to be met on the way North, the ANNA towed the barge rather than attempt to push it, although she was still equipped as a pusher boat. The weather was not favorable, but even so, she averaged 5½ knots when under way. Considering she was a river-class tug, not designed for crossing the Gulf of Alaska and bucking Western Alaska weather, her 2,400-mile voyage was remarkable—of course, she had to hole-up at times for protection. Tug and barge arrived at the first port on the Yukon River, Alukanuk, on June 16th, twenty-nine days after leaving Seattle.

For the next six weeks the ANNA shuttled cargo to and from the Yukon River ports of Alukanuk, Mountain Village, St. Mary's, Pilot Station, Fortuna Ledge, Emmonik, and Kotlik. She lightered cargo up-river from the Foss Alaska Line tug and barge anchored at the mouth of the river and she also brought return cargo down-river to load on the FAL barge for delivery to Seattle.

In mid-August, the ANNA and her small barge tied up at Sunshine Slough on the Yukon, and the crew went home by air to wait until the next FAL linehaul tug and barge arrived off the river with more cargo. The ANNA's crew returned in mid-September to lighter the cargo for the last FAL trip of the open-water season. When the job was finished, the crew again flew home for other work and the PHILLIPS FOSS towed the ANNA to Kodiak for winter tie-up.

The ANNA remained at Kodiak until May 25 1973 when a crew, headed by Captain John Klapp, was flown up from Seattle to return the tug to the Yukon River and repeat the lightering service of last year. Right on schedule on June 13th, the ANNA and her barge met the LESLIE FOSS off the river mouth and loaded cargo from one of LESLIE's barges and headed upstream on a cargo-delivery run to the river ports. The ANNA remained on the Yukon until mid-September when the last of the year's cargo was discharged up-river and a back-load of salmon had been loaded aboard the ANNA's small lighter barge. Then on September 18 1973 tug and barge headed for Seattle under her own power. After a slow and safe voyage of twenty-three days, on October 11th, she arrived home, barge and cargo intact.

The ANNA was idle in Seattle for several weeks until Foss-Tacoma finalized new plans for her. She was ideally rigged to push "LASH" barges (Lighter Aboard Ship) from the "LASH" ships anchored in Tacoma harbor to loading docks and moorings in Tacoma. Foss placed her in this service. However, it kept her busy for only six operating days a month, so other jobs were provided, but before starting to work, alterations were made to the ANNA.

In early 1974 the Foss yard began construction of a second, raised pilothouse, forty feet above the water. This would give the ANNA's crew good all around visibility when pushing chip and other high-side barges. The ANNA's two Captains, Gerry O'Conner and Jerry Gooding, were known as Foss' high-altitude skippers.

In mid-April the ANNA, with her high-rise pilothouse ready for use, the only one in the fleet, started on linehaul service around the Sound. She was now doing what she was designed for, pushing her barges—Foss' only river towboat. The ANNA has juggled and pushed barges of forest products steadily since 1974 except for shifting the small cargo "LASH" barges in Tacoma whenever the big ocean "LASH" ships come in with their nested-aboard barges.

The ANNA had a respite from her barge routine when she had a part in a Seattle-based movie. She gained national recognition in November 1977 when Universal Studios filmed a television special of the show "Emergency" with action scenes in Seattle Harbor. The movie appeared on television in the spring of 1978. The film featured the Washington State Ferry KLICKITAT suffering a simulated engine room explosion while on a routine Sound crossing to Seattle with a load of cars and passengers aboard. The film stressed the efficiency and capability of the Seattle Fire Department and the Paramedic Unit in saving the ferry and its passengers from a disaster by fire. The ANNA and barge FOSS-2 were supposedly on a routine job when the "Mayday" from the KLICKITAT came over the radio. The ANNA altered course and rushed to the side of the burning ferry and all the "passengers" were safely evacuated to the barge. Fireboats then came alongside the FOSS-2, tied-up and used the barge deck to run hoses and equipment to the ferry and enact the aid and rescue part of the filming. At the conclusion of the Harbor scenes, Universal Studios expressed their satisfaction with four days of shooting and, of course, the passengers thanked the ANNA's crew for their timely "rescue." The ANNA was chosen for the part over all other Foss tugs because of the high-rise pilothouse for better sight in following the action.

The ANNA appears to be involved for life in wood-chip runs. She moves barges from the Seaboard Mill in Seattle to the Crown Zellerbach pulp mill in Port Townsend and from the Simpson mill in Shelton to Crown-Z, and to Crown-Z from Pope and Talbot in Port Gamble. Also chips to Scott Paper Company in Everett from Shelton.

If ever a tug is in the chips the ANNA is—even if they are not blue.

WENDY FOSS

Built:	1964	Propulsion:	EMD (Twin)
	San Diego Marine Construction		3,000-horsepower
	San Diego, California	Primary Service:	Ocean and Coastwise
Length:	110-feet	Status:	In Service
Beam:	27-feet		

WENDY FOSS, ex-PACIFIC MARINER, while under construction for the Olsen Lumber Company, was acquired direct from the shipyard by Pacific Tow & Salvage Company.

During her time with PT&S the MARINER engaged in a variety of towing assignments. On her first run in 1964 she towed loaded lumber barges between Oregon and northern California mills to southern California ports, and surprisingly, for Olsen Lumber Company.

Then in November 1964 the MARINER ran light to Oakland and relieved the DONNA FOSS of the Sea-Land container barge COLUMBIA. For the next four months, she continued on the container haul from Portland to Oakland. The termination of the run came about in an unfortunate manner on February 27, 1965 off the Columbia River bar. The weather on the 27th was typical for the winter months, with strong winds and rough seas, even so, to the MARINER's crew, everything on the tug and barge seemed under control. However, in just minutes, the barge developed a list, and the Captain, realizing something was seriously amiss, stopped the tug and had the Mate stand by the tow winch, but by the time they were ready to take in the tow wire, the barge started to sink rapidly. They had no alternative except to cut the barge loose. She sank at once and sixteen loaded containers and ten trailer-chassis floated off, but they too sank quickly.

The loss of the barge ended the MARINER's container towing. A replacement barge was provided in two weeks, but the HENRY FOSS was assigned to the run. The PACIFIC MARINER, however, spent the rest of 1965 on the West Coast doing general towing. Then, early in 1966 she started out on what turned out to be one of the longest tows of her career. She left Long Beach for a three month trip to South Vietnam, towing two barges with two more riding piggyback. Captain Tom Kelly of Long Beach had the MARINER in charge, and with good weather cooperating, the round trip went smoothly and they arrived back in Long Beach in the spring of 1966.

Then in May, with Arnold Reynolds as Captain, the PACIFIC MARINER was assigned to tow the drill rig, CUSS-I, from Long Beach to the Cook Inlet oil fields. The MARINER delivered the rig to the southern Cook Inlet port of Homer, where other Foss tugs relieved her for the final delivery farther up the Inlet.

The MARINER next went down the Coast to Portland, Oregon and picked up another drill rig, the JOHN C. MARTHENS and towed it non-stop to Cook Inlet at an average speed of 4.5 knots. According to Captain Reynolds, the JOHN C. MARTHENS was the largest drill rig ever to work in the Inlet.

With an important tow waiting for the MARINER she made a quick turn-around and returned light to Long Beach. After a few days shore leave, Arnold Reynolds and the MARINER went full-bore for Honolulu to pick up a 38,000-barrel oil barge for delivery to South Vietnam. On the way over, when nearing the Philippines after a routine crossing, they were diverted to Manila with orders to tie up the oil barge and take in tow four flat-deck barges for Vietnam. They delivered the quadruple tow safely and then returned to Manila, picked up the oil barge, and delivered it unchallenged through the War Zone to Saigon. The MARINER remained in Vietnam and went on charter to Alaska Barge & Transport who had a Government contract to supply tug service for the U.S. Army.

One of the PACIFIC MARINER's first major assignments was tending the dredge NEW JERSEY at Tiu Hau, north of Vung Ro. The project consisted of dredging out a harbor and channel for bringing in and unloading cargo from supply vessels. The channel was to be dredged to thirty-eight feet, but a major problem developed. The bottom was volcanic sand and the river where Tiu Hau was located had strong currents, so the volcanic sand was constantly shifting. As soon as the dredge completed a segment, the current filled up the channel or the current rerouted the channel away from the new course. After wasting considerable time bucking the stubborn river, the job was scrubbed and the plan for a deep-water port remained just a plan.

The MARINER returned to general coastwise towing out of Saigon and an occasional Mekong River run through the active firing zone. Captain Reynolds reported no accidents during his stay in Vietnam aboard the tug, although on a tow up the Mekong, he was following two minesweepers when suddenly both sweepers blew up. Enemy mines caused the devastating explosions. The MARINER made it through the rest of the way by hugging the shallow water on the edge of the channel. Just navigating the Mekong and the Delta was treacherous enough without dodging enemy action at the same time!

Captain Reynolds left Vietnam in late February 1967 but the PACIFIC MARINER remained in the War Zone for the Military Sea Transport Service and for Alaska Barge and Transport, to supplement their own fleet of tugs. With Captain Les Easom, she finished her charter in March 1968 and left for the States the same month, making the crossing via Manila. The last lap, the run from Manila to Long Beach, was made in twenty-nine days at an average speed of eleven knots.

After operating foreign for two years and practically non-stop, the MARINER was in need of an overhaul. She was in the yard until mid-May before pronounced in fit condition to re-enter service.

During the remainder of 1968 she completed several coastwise trips, a voyage to Cook Inlet, Alaska, a tow to the Hawaiian Islands, all for Pacific Tow & Salvage. She continued in their towing service during the next three years, primarily on the West Coast. Then in September 1971 Foss needed an additional tug, so the PACIFIC MARINER was assigned to tow the loaded oil barge FOSS-98 from Long Beach to three ports in the Hawaiian Islands. Upon return to Seattle with the empty oil barge, and as all the regular Foss ocean tugs were on jobs, the MARINER was retained for service out of Seattle.

During her assignment for the next three months she towed Foss Alaska Line barges between Seattle and Southeastern Alaska. Then with the slack winter season, the regular Foss tugs became available for the Foss Alaska Line run and the MARINER returned to Long Beach.

By early May 1972 the Foss fleet was again fully occupied, so the MARINER headed for Seattle to assist by towing on the same Southeastern van run, this time with Captain Walt Kardonsky in charge. She remained on the "common carrier" service through December 4, 1972 then entered tthe Foss shipyard for re-fit and interior remodeling. Prior to this, during the last week on the van run, the MARINER officially became a unit of the Foss fleet by being named WENDY in honor of Peter and Margaret Campbell's daughter, a granddaughter of Sidney and Barbara Foss Campbell.

Her overhaul complete in March, the WENDY returned to Foss Alaska service and carried on until mid-1973 when she was shifted to general towing, Coastwise and to Alaska, with her former Captain, Arnold Reynolds, in command, who had transferred serveral years earlier from PT&S to Foss-Seattle. Captain Reynolds' orders called for towing two loaded lumber barges from Port Angeles to Wilmington, California and after discharging the lumber, he was to proceed to Ventura and load heavy equipment for Honolulu. This he did and upon cargo discharge at Honolulu he returned the WENDY and her barges to Seattle, arriving at the Foss pier in late June. For the remainder of the summer and fall she towed on the established Foss runs to Alaska.

In November 1973 PT&S asked for the WENDY and two Foss ocean deck-barges on a temporary basis, for transporting industrial bulk salt between Cedros Island, Mexico and Long Beach. After a trial delivery of a tandem tow to Long Beach of fully loaded barges, the job was confirmed for the winter, so the tug went on bareboat charter to PT&S. The charter continued until early March, then the WENDY was sent to Seattle and turned back to Foss.

She was assigned to tow on the usual Alaska runs for the balance of 1974, including a trip to the mouth of the Yukon River. The following year, she made several barge tows to Valdez, Alaska with material for the Alaska Pipeline project as well as making routine runs to Anchorage with general cargo barges; 1975 turned out to be another Alaska year.

Then in 1976 a twenty-nine-year CHRISTINE FOSS tradition was broken when, on April 24th, the WENDY, with Captain Bob Burns in command, left Seattle with the oil barge FOSS-111, bound first for Cordova and then on to the Bristol Bay area for the usual and seasonal six-month oil delivery run under the terms of the long-standing Standard Oil Contract. 1976 was the first year the CHRISTINE FOSS was not assigned to the annual Bristol Bay service. But the WENDY, twenty-one years newer than the CHRISTINE and of steel construction, with more horsepower, was better able to meet the expanded and tight schedule then in effect.

She turned in a successful first season arriving back in Seattle seven months later, on November 28th, about three weeks later than normal due to the added deliveries on the route.

The WENDY and Captain Burns returned to the oil run for the 1977 season, but with a newly converted oil barge, the FOSS-256, which held a third more cargo, necessary to better meet the increasing demand for Standard Oil products in Western Alaska. The 1977 season gave the tug crew a variation in scenery as the regular run was adjusted to make deliveries to several canneries on the south side of the Alaska Peninsula, including plants at King Cove, False Pass, Sandpoint, and Chignik. These customers were normally served by a Standard Oil tanker, but the WENDY and BARGE-256 were handy to the area at the time and they were able to make two separate calls at the south-side ports. 1977 was the last year the WENDY drew the Bristol Bay assignment as the SANDRA, a new boat and much more comfortable for the long, routine season, took over the run for 1978.

After lying dormant all winter at the Foss pier, the WENDY became an active tug in March when Washington Tug & Barge Company of Seattle called on Foss for help to tow their rail barge between Seattle and Sitka. The regular tug on the run, a boat similar to the WENDY, was scheduled to enter a local shipyard for three months of major repair. The WENDY went on bareboat charter to WT&B through May 1978 then their own tug, the ALAPUL, returned to service and the WENDY switched to the Foss Anchorage run and coastwise towing for the next five months.

In late October 1978 she made the first voyage of a multi-year Foss contract towing the chemical barge PENN-SALT TYEE from Tacoma to Eureka and Pittsburg, California. The Foss ocean division, with the new contract in hand, returned to towing chemical barges after an absence of two years, since 1976 when the Georgia Pacific, Bellingham to Eureka towing contract expired.

The WENDY did not remain on the run for long as Foss shifted her to another new assignment, this time in Alaska. The job was one of the most hazardous winter jobs on the Coast, towing a 36,000-barrel oil barge between Nikiski, on Cook Inlet, and the ports of Valdez, Seward, and Kodiak. During the winter months towing in the stormy Gulf of Alaska and the ice-clogged waters of Cook Inlet would be a trial and risk for the best of boats, but the WENDY met the challenge bow-on and she came through each trip safely. Her first Alaska winter season was a success, effectively serving the interests of Standard Oil, Union Oil, and Tesoro Petroleum. The Captains responsible for bringing her through the tough winter season were Chuck Crawford and Fred Strang—she arrived back in Seattle in early April 1979 her mission safely accomplished.

After routine voyage repairs, she returned to general towing on the Coast and Alaska, and once again, as during many voyages in the past thirteen years, Captain Arnold Reynolds was in charge.

MARGARET FOSS (3)

Built:	1963	Propulsion:	Stork-Workspoer (Twin)
	Main Iron Works		2,200-horsepower
	Houma, Louisiana	Primary Service:	Puget Sound
Length:	100-feet	Status:	In Service
Beam:	25-feet		

Many times, used equipment comes on the market that fits into a company's operating plan and policy, and the Foss Company found after inspection of the DENNIS W. GUIDRY at New Orleans in August 1974 that the tug would fit the Foss concept. Even though Foss was engaged in building new equipment rather than buying used vessels, the DENNIS W. GUIDRY, so it appeared, would be able to go right to work on any of the established Foss runs—a case of a tug in hand being worth two on the stocks. So the tug, after nearly eleven years of work with the Guidry fleet operating in the Gulf of Mexico and the Caribbean, was purchased by Foss for heavy towing on Puget Sound and to Alaska.

The GUIDRY's only apparent disadvantage was the difficulty in securing engine parts, as no other tug in the Foss fleet had Stork-Workspoer engines, and all major parts had to be shipped from the factory in Holland. The Foss maintenance and repair personnel had little practical experience with the GUIDRY's engines, so the necessary engine work to get the tug ready for sea was done by a repair firm in New Orleans familiar with Workspoer engines. As the trip progressed, the MARGARET's engineer, with all the time he spent on the engines, had ample proof the "work" part of the engine's name meant just that.

The name GUIDRY was changed to MARGARET FOSS before leaving for Seattle, and her colors changed to green and white. Now that she was a member of the Foss fleet, the Foss dispatchers hoped that the misfortunes of the second MARGARET FOSS, purchased eight years earlier in Mobile, Alabama, would not carry over to the newest MARGARET. But Captain Joe Uskevich, assigned with a crew of eight to bring the new MARGARET home to Seattle, was not too sure that she would not inherit the jinx. Anyway, only time would tell.

On September 22nd, with a full load of fuel aboard, the MARGARET left New Orleans for Seattle, 5,500 miles away. Her estimated time of arrival was October 16, 1974—at least the year turned out to be correct.

During the evening of September 24, Captain Joe was advised by radio to return to Morgan City, Louisiana, as a new job came in, and pick up two dump scows for delivery to San Francisco. They had 500 miles to backtrack and arrived in Morgan City, on the Atchafalaya River, September 27th, and left with the scows on September 30th.

However, before they reached the open sea, a radio warning came of a tropical depression in the Gulf and they were ordered to seek shelter in the river. Like an old-time river towboater, Captain Joe returned upriver "a ways" and tied the scows to strong overhanging trees along the shore. The MARGARET tied-up alongside and they waited out the storm front. Next afternoon the all clear sign came and they dropped down the river again, headed for the Panama Canal.

The following four days, the MARGARET and her two scows proceeded at a lazy, five-and-a-half knots in moderate seas. Then, at 2100 on October 6, without any warning, the scows drifted away from the tug. A quick inspection revealed that the last two-and-a-half wraps of the towline had slipped around on the drum and the bitter end snapped out of the socket and over the side. The entire length of the MARGARET's towline was now hanging straight down from the lead scow. They hove-to and waited for daylight to recover the wire.

During the next day, tug and tow were hooked up again by a set of wire bridles to hold the scows in position. Then preparations were made for retrieving the towline and the heavy chain surge gear. For the next two days attempts were made to pull the towline aboard, but with lack of equipment and adverse weather and sea conditions, they were forced to turn back for help.

The MARGARET now headed for South Pass, at the mouth of the Mississippi River, at a four knot speed, towing the scows with 1,500 feet of 12-inch nylon line and a shot of chain added. The tug's winch wire was still plumbing the depths, hanging from the scow. On October 13th, off South Pass, with smooth seas and a helper tug, the tow gear was retrieved and they proceeded to the river port of Venice, Louisiana for winch repair. During the four days in Venice the towline was checked over and respooled, engine adjustments made, tow winch repaired and electronic repairs carried out. The MARGARET was able to get underway again for Panama at noon, October 17th.

This time their distance run was less than 160 miles when the Chief Engineer informed the Captain that the port engine was in need of immediate repair, and he did not have the proper parts. Captain Joe called in and he was informed by radio to await the daylight arrival of a helicopter on October 19th, with the engine parts. In the morning of the 19th, the MARGARET was requested to return to within one hundred miles of shore as the helicopter did not have sufficient range. The Captain brought the MARGARET within the one hundred mile distance by mid-day—but no helicopter.

The morning of the 20th came and passed and still no helicopter. Finally, word was received that a larger helicopter had to be used and would be enroute later in the day. But by the end of the day—no helicopter. Then, at 0800 October 21st, the helicopter finally showed up and delivered the parts to the jogging tug. The Chief Engineer went right to work on the engine, but in keeping with the nature of events, the parts were the wrong size! Informed of the error, the parts house promised another copter would meet them at 0800 on the 22nd with the correct parts. Finally, at 1430 on the 22nd, after two unsuccessful attempts, the helicopter made it to the MARGARET and delivered the parts. This time the parts were right and at 2200 they were underway for Panama. Thirty-one days had passed since the MARGARET left New Orleans and they were only one hundred miles south of the Mississippi River entrance, about two hundred thirty miles from New Orleans!

The run to Panama was made without trouble at a poor speed of five-and-a-half knots, arriving on November 2nd. They made the Canal transit on November 5th and at last were northbound for San Francisco. Tug and tow moved along at six knots until they were three hundred miles south of Long Beach, then the ex-GUIDRY threw them another curve. The #8 rod bearing burned out on the port engine and the engine was lost for the rest of the voyage as major repairs would be required. They limped into Long Beach with the starboard engine and gave up the tow to the PATRICIA FOSS.

The MARGARET headed light for Seattle on one engine—one down, one to go. They cruised along at eight knots until Cape Flattery, then the Chief found the filters on the starboard engine plugged and upon further inspection he discovered shavings from several bearings in the filters. The MARGARET ran out of engines, so Captain Joe called for help. The MARTHA FOSS responded, arriving late in the day, and she towed the hard luck victim to the Foss yard in Seattle. Captain Joe and his crew arrived at 1000 on December 3rd, after a seventy-three day trip which turned out to be nearly as bad as an LSD trip.

The MARAGRET shifted to the Foss shipyard and remained "hors de combat" for the next five months. Repair crews dismantled the main engines right down to the bases. New parts were air-shipped from Holland and both engines were entirely rebuilt. Other modifications were made in the engine room including automation. The galley and crew's quarters were improved and the tug generally brought up to Foss standards.

By early May 1975 the MARGARET was ready and for the next month towed on the Foss British Columbia car-barge runs and the chemical barge run.

Then with the engines proving out, the MARGARET started on the Foss Alaska Line container-barge run to southeastern Alaska in early June 1975 with Captain Dave Edwards in charge. The MARGARET remained in van service for the remainder of 1975.

In 1976 she towed on various Alaska runs, primarily to Anchorage and Valdez, until November, and then after a month in lay-up she began three years of towing on the Seattle-North Vancouver rail-car barge run—her Dutch engines running trouble-free.

In April 1979 she entered the Foss shipyard for a major overhaul on both main engines in comformity with the Foss planned maintenance program, which applies to every tug in the fleet. By fall 1979 she was back on the rail-car run, her troublesome first year failings now in the closed file—the MARGARET jinx finally laid to rest.

AGNES FOSS Shown on towing assignment in the Columbia River. (Courtesy of Foss Tug Co)

AGNES FOSS (2)

Built:	1970	Propulsion:	EMD (Twin)
	McDermott Shipyard Group		3,000-horsepower
	Amelia, Louisiana	Area of Operation:	Ocean, Coastwise, and Alaska
Length:	112-feet	Status:	In Service
Beam:	31-feet		

The Foss Company's second AGNES was built by McDermott for the Inland River Transportation Company of Clayton, Missouri. They named her OCEAN STAR and she towed between ports on the Gulf Coast and the Caribbean. Though her home port was St. Louis, she had none of the characteristics of a Mississippi river boat. The OCEAN STAR was a standard design McDermott ocean-class tug of 3,000-horsepower, a sister-tug to three others that McDermott built and delivered to Foss in 1969 and early 1970—the PHILLIPS, LESLIE and JEFFREY.

When the OCEAN STAR was offered for sale, Foss, knowing the merits of the PHILLIPS-class tugs, made an inspection and, satisfied, purchased the boat on an as-is-where-is basis.

With appropriate colors of green and white and carrying the name AGNES FOSS, she left Morgan City, Louisiana on July 16th under the command of Captain George Ducich and arrived in Seattle on August 11, 1975. Next day she moved over to the Foss Shipyard for minor modifications to fit her for Coastwise and Alaska service. Then she went to work for six months towing barges from Seattle to Valdez for Fluor Company, contractors building the Tank Farm and other facilities to handle North Slope oil.

The following year, between February and May, the AGNES made two round trips between Seattle and Houston, Texas. The first trip she ran light to Houston, picked up a new rail-car barge, the FOSS-274, and delivered it to Seattle for service on the Seattle-Vancouver, B.C. run. The next week she returned to Houston for a new ocean-class cargo barge, the FOSS-288, and delivered the 288 to Seattle for use in the Alaska and Coastwise trade.

The Texas trips completed, she spent the summer on the Alaska barge run to Anchorage and the following winter helped out in Seattle harbor on ship and barge assists. With both the CAROL FOSS and the SHANNON FOSS in Tacoma for repowering, the AGNES substituted for them in Tacoma and Seattle on harbor work. Her six months of port duty showed the versatility of a modern ocean-coastwise tug and this very quality was a deciding factor in a change of bases for the AGNES in late 1978.

When the harbor stint was over she went on the Southeastern container-barge run for Foss-Alaska Line and stayed with it until the fall of the year. Then in September 1978 Foss assigned her for an indefinite period to Pacific Tow & Salvage at Long Beach, for double duty—local shifts and ocean-coastwise work.

The AGNES, under the direction of Pete Campbell, in charge of operations at the time, was kept on the move, and she might have become a permanent resident, except for attractive long-haul offerings showing up on the East Coast. So, in February 1979 with Captain Paul Plate in the pilothouse, she left California towing a loaded oil barge for Wilmington, Delaware. Then from Wilmington she went to Houston for her next job and towed a barge to Panama. From the canal, in mid-summer of 1979, the AGNES returned to the West Coast, towing two barges of heavy offshore oil pipe for construction of an underwater pipeline connecting a new oil rig offshore from Santa Barbara, California to shoreside tanks. Then after making a barge tow from Long Beach to Portland, she headed back to the Gulf Coast towing an empty Foss barge for loading at Panama and delivery to Houston.

From all appearances the West Coast has lost the AGNES for an indefinite time—she has joined the DREW as Foss Company's representatives on the Gulf and East Coasts.

BARBARA FOSS (3)

Built:	1976	Propulsion:	EMD (Twin)
	McDermott Shipyard Group		4,300-horsepower
	New Iberia, Louisiana	Primary Service:	Alaska-Coastwise-Ocean
Length:	120-feet	Status:	In Service
Beam:	34-feet		

The third BARBARA FOSS, a new and completely engine-automated tug, was built for heavy-duty towing as part of the upgrading program to modernize the Foss ocean fleet. Upon acceptance by Foss, the BARBARA, under command of Captain Chuck Crawford, left Galveston, Texas for Seattle on July 5th, arriving three weeks later with no first-voyage miseries to report.

Then on August 4th, under Captain Crawford, the BARBARA left Seattle running light to the Arctic to do a job for Crowley Maritime, Inc.. She arrived at her destination, Prudhoe Bay, on August 15th, to pick up and return two empty barges that had been frozen in the Bay since the previous October. The route at this time of year was completely free of ice so the trip was accomplished with little difficulty, tug and tow arriving Seattle, September 2nd.

After minor voyage repairs the BARBARA, again with Captain Crawford, returned to her place of origin, the Gulf Coast, taking along a Foss barge to pick up components for the Alaska pipeline pumping system at Valdez. The thirteen-thousand-mile round trip from Seattle to Houston to Valdez and return to Seattle was accomplished in just over two months! That's moving—not even the seaweed and barnacles could hook on.

During 1977 and 1978 the BARBARA, based in Seattle, did a variety of barge towing along the Pacific Coast and to Alaska, some routine and some not so routine, such as towing a submarine from San Diego to Puget Sound. When not on Coastal work, the BARBARA, as a help to the regular tugs, escorted oil tankers to the Ferndale, Cherry Point, and Anacortes refineries.

In 1978 the BARBARA received the traditional "Smart Ship Award" presented to the best-dressed vessel on display during National Maritime Week. The way the tug is maintained, she no doubt will take the honor any Maritime Week she is in port. The BARBARA missed the festivities in 1979 being at sea returning from a tow to Anchorage.

The BARBARA in mid-1979 found a steady job where her 4,300 horsepower could be put to good use on heavy, dead-weight tows. She began a towing contract for a long-time Foss customer, Kaiser Cement Company. Kaiser had recently completed building a new barge for hauling bulk cement between plants and delivery ports on the West Coast and Alaska—from Tilbury Island, B.C., all the way to Long Beach, California. Stops were made at Bamberton, B.C., Seattle, Portland, Redwood City, California and Anchorage. Captain George Ducich, veteran Foss skipper, directs the BARBARA on the cement runs.

From all indications, the BARBARA will be in the cement business, with Kaiser's help, for some time to come. She has been an active tug, but her history is ahead of her—the BARBARA has a lot of water yet to plow.

JUSTINE FOSS (3)

Built:	1976	Propulsion:	EMD (Twin)
	McDermott Shipbuilding Group		4,300-horsepower
	New Iberia, Louisiana	Primary Service:	Ocean - Alaska
Length:	120-feet	Status:	In Service
Beam:	34-feet		

The latest JUSTINE, completed and outfitted at the McDermott yard in July 1976 was second of the four new automated tugs built for the Ocean Division of the Foss-Dillingham Maritime Group. The first two tugs of the series, BARBARA and JUSTINE, were powered with 4,300-horsepower engines for heavy towing jobs, but the last two of the class, SIDNEY and DREW, were equipped with 3,000-horsepower to handle average tows more economically, using less fuel.

On her first trip, the JUSTINE, under Captain Al Anderson, towed a cargo barge from New Orleans to Seattle via Long Beach, arriving in Seattle on September 16, 1976—a trouble-free run of almost 6,000 miles.

The JUSTINE spent the next several months in general Coastwise and Alaska towing, with time out in May of 1977 to be the Foss tugboat representative during National Maritime Week in Seattle. Many thousands of visitors toured the vessel during the time and the gangplank remarks generally showed pleased surprise and praise for the superior living quarters and the advanced stage of design and equipment on a modern, ocean-going tug. The Foss "show-off" crew made good tour guides; they had all the answers to the hundreds of questions asked during the seven-day open house.

In June 1977 the JUSTINE, with Captain Anderson, left on the first of three trips between the Lone Star gravel pit at Steilacoom and Bethel, Alaska on the Kuskokwim River in the Bering Sea area. The contract called for towing two barges, each carrying 4,000 tons of sand and gravel for construction of an airport by Associated Engineers and Constructors. The unusual and long haul of commonplace sand and gravel kept the JUSTINE and her eight-man crew on the go through September.

During the next twelve months the JUSTINE completed several towing jobs on the Coast and to Alaska, including a six-week assignment for Crowley Maritime, towing two 400-foot rail-car barges between Seattle and Whittier, Alaska.

The JUSTINE's towing jobs up North were different and interestng and the variety didn't stop with her next assignment. In October 1978 Foss Alaska Line was awarded a two-year contract by the Military Sealift Command to haul general cargo and equipment between Seattle and the Navy Installation at Adak in Alaska'a Aleutian Islands. The contract called for delivery of one barge-load to Adak every three weeks, year around.

In order to maintain the schedule, it was necessary to have the point of origin for the Adak voyages in Southeastern Alaska and Sitka was selected. Each week the regular Foss Alaska Line tug with its container-barge, transported the Military Sealift Command containerized cargo from Foss Alaska Line headquarters in Seattle to the Foss Alaska Line terminal at Sitka. After arrival in Sitka the containers were stored in a marshalling area to await the arrival of the JUSTINE and her barge to pick up the assembled cargo.

To inaugurate the start of service on November 3, 1978 the JUSTINE, with a special, knowledgeable crew, handpicked by Captain Anderson and the Foss office, made up the tug Bristol fashion at the Foss Alaska Line Terminal in Seattle for an "open house" inspection for officers of the Military Sealift Command. They were duly impressed with the apparent capabilities of the JUSTINE and the Foss hospitality. Later in the evening after the amenities, a novel event took place, that is for a tugboat—the Chief Engineer, Don Nicklas, chose to be married in the pilothouse of the JUSTINE! The logbook related that all ship work came to a halt until Chief Nicklas and his lady were spliced—they asked the minister for a long-splice, so it took a little longer to make the tucks. Even so, a reception followed, short but toasty, and within the hour the crew were back in their work clothes and unfortunately for Chief Nicklas, the engines and not the bride needed his attention. Mrs. Nicklas quickly became a "sailor's widow" as the JUSTINE left in short order on Voyage #1 to Adak.

By Christmas, 1978 the JUSTINE had departed Sitka on Voyage #3 with typical Alaska winter weather facing the tug and her special crew. An excerpt from her Log of December 2nd shows what the JUSTINE faced:

"Veritable hurricane all day long—winds southwesterly and westerly at sixty, with gusts to ninety knots—thirty to fifty-foot seas—barometer 959 millibars—the "low" moved into Prince William Sound just ahead of us—barge out of sight most of the time—some seas breaking over top of wheelhouse—everything riding as good as possible though. Signed—Allan Anderson."

The JUSTINE delivered her tow intact and continued to do the job day-after-day—weather or no.

STACEY FOSS & SANDRA FOSS At their base in Bellingham. (Courtesy of Foss Tug Co)

STACEY FOSS

Built:	1976	Propulsion:	EMD (Twin)
	Fairhaven Shipyard		2,900-horsepower
	Bellingham, Washington	Primary Service:	Puget Sound
Length:	112-feet	Status:	In Service
Beam:	34-feet		

Fairhaven completed the STACEY in all parts, a contrast to her sister-tug the SANDRA, only partially finished at the Fairhaven yard. The STACEY was to be based in Bellingham as an escort and assist-tug for tankers delivering oil to northern Puget Sound refineries and in charge of the senior skipper of the Foss Bellingham Division, Captain Dick Blake, a veteran of forty years.

After earning a blue ribbon at her sea trials, she then towed the incomplete SANDRA to Foss-Seattle for three months' "finishing-up" work. The Fairhaven Shipyard, in financial difficulties and unable to complete the SANDRA, made a deal with Foss to accept the tug on an "as is" basis.

Both Bellingham-built vessels were designed by L. R. Glosten & Associates of Seattle, and they incorporated interesting features. A walk-around console in the pilothouse provided convenient access to the controls from any position, besides greatly improving the visibility. Fixed Kort nozzles surrounded the propellers to increase the thrust and rudder action. To simplify tandem towing, double-drum towing winches carrying 2,000-feet of two-inch wire on each drum were installed. The interiors were deluxe with carpeting in the crew's quarters, hardwood paneling throughout, and individual temperature control in each cabin. The accommodations are a far cry from the not too distant days of the multi-bunk forecastle—next to the forepeak and below the anchor windlass—no privacy and plenty of pitching.

The STACEY, as planned, started her scheduled service on Puget Sound on July 23, 1976, but after only one week's work, Foss Alaska Line requested her to tow their container barge for two trips to Southeastern Alaska. With veteran Foss Alaska Line Skipper, Captain Darrell Wilson in command, the STACEY performed to everyone's satisfaction.

After completing the second trip, the STACEY was returned to Captain Blake and alternate Captain Bud Klemp for tanker-assistance service out of Bellingham. The two expert Captains have successfully docked about 6,000 heavy-tonnage oil tankers during their time with Foss, so the tug was in good hands.

The STACEY's escort work with tankers is vital as accompanying tugs must be on hand to control the big ships in case of an emergency, accident or loss of power. State government regulations require all loaded tankers of over 40,000 dead-weight tons to have an escort tug or tugs equivalent in horsepower to five-percent of the tanker's dead weight tonnage. However, all tankers over 125,000 tons are banned from traversing Puget Sound.

The major oil companies opposed the law on the grounds of economic hindrance to the industry and that regulation of waterways is under control of the Federal Government. The State and industry ended up in court, but in the meantime the law remained.

Most of the tankers discharging oil to the refineries are over 40,000 tons, and several are over 100,000. Atlantic-Richfield has two tankers of 120,000 tons and they require a combined escort tug horsepower of 6,000. If a second large tanker is moving simultaneously with one of the "biggies," then additional tugs are dispatched from Seattle or Tacoma to provide escort from Dungeness to port-of-discharge.

The tankers arrive from major oil producing areas of the world on a regular basis, with crude oil from South America, Indonesia, and the Middle East. In August of 1977 the first crude oil from Alaska's North Slope arrived at Arco's Cherry Point refinery.

On August 5, 1977 the tanker ARCO JUNEAU, 120,000 tons, and loaded with 824,000 barrels (34,608,000 gallons!) arrived with the first oil from the North Slope flowing through the Alyeska Pipeline to the southern terminal at Valdez. The JUNEAU, which is the length of three football fields, arrived at the escort location east of Port Angeles in the early morning and was met by the RICHARD and STACEY FOSS. The tug captains reported the escort run turned out to be clearly routine as the blanketing early morning fog lifted rapidly and they could proceed at normal speed. The two tugs docked the ship in good order and the historic ten-million-dollar cargo arrived safely as scheduled amid a good deal of pro and con reportorial comment. The STACEY and RICHARD have handled the all-important tanker escort and assist work on a steady basis since October 1976, so the tankers have the protection of experienced escorts.

Since the arrival of the ARCO JUNEAU from Valdez in 1977, many tankers have delivered North Slope crude to Cherry Point and the volume is on the increase. In January 1979 the SANDRA FOSS joined the STACEY and RICHARD in the Bellingham Division to meet the current need for tanker escort-work on the northern Sound. The three able tugs, always ready and waiting, are the active part of the over-all plan of the escort service pioneered and developed by Foss Launch & Tug Company.

SANDRA FOSS (2)

Built:	1976	Propulsion:	EMD (Twin)
	Fairhaven Shipyard		2,900-horsepower
	Bellingham, Washington	Primary Service:	Puget Sound
Length:	110-feet	Status:	In Service
Beam:	34-feet		

The SANDRA, released incomplete to Foss by the Fairhaven shipyard in Bellingham, became a finished tug at the Foss yard in Seattle. She and her sister-tug STACEY FOSS were the last two vessels built by the Fairhaven yard before quitting business. The STACEY left Bellingham for Foss-Seattle in late July under her own power and with the unfinished SANDRA in tow. The day after the two tugs pulled out, the Fairhaven Shipyard closed down.

During the following four months, Foss transformed the SANDRA inside and out from a bare bulkhead boat to a complete, sea-going tug with all the latest navigation equipment and fitted with deluxe crew accommodations and appointments. After successful trial runs, the SANDRA, shining in her newness and looking able to range far and wide, was allocated to the Foss Ocean Division for towing to Alaska, but she didn't go North as her first several months were spent working for the Puget Sound Division on tanker escort-work, assisting the RICHARD and STACEY.

Her initial voyage for the Ocean Division, with Captain Fred Strang in charge, was a barge tow to southeastern Alaska and return in late November.

Then for several months she again worked out of Bellingham on tanker escort-work, but in mid-June she returned to the Ocean Division. During the remainder of the 1977 season Foss sent her on both the southeastern Alaska van-run for Foss Alaska Line and the routine barge-run to Anchorage. Later during the winter of 1977-78, she again went on tanker assist work with general barge towing mixed in—she still hadn't found her proper slot.

Nor did she in 1978 when selected as the tug to make the annual six-month Chevron Oil delivery-run from Dutch Harbor in the Aleutians to ports in Bristol Bay. On May 1st, with Captain Bob Burns, long-time skipper on the run, she towed the loaded 38,000 barrel oil-barge FOSS-256 from Point Wells direct to Naknek for discharge. Then working out of Dutch Harbor, the oil supply base, the SANDRA delivered oil during the ice-free season to Naknek, Dillingham, Bethel, Port Moller, Sandpoint, King Cove, Kodiak, and Cold Bay. After carrying out the six-months schedule, tug and barge returned to Seattle, and by arriving on October 26th, she made the earliest return from the Bristol Bay oil-run in many years—SANDRA's extra speed and power made the difference.

Less than two days after arrival, she was able to go right out on escort work. The ready response shows the excellent upkeep that the SANDRA had by Captain Bob Burns, Chief Engineer Joe Cannon, and the entire crew—even though away from home port facilities.

The increased tanker traffic on Puget Sound, requiring additional tug escort, necessitated a third tug be assigned to Bellingham on a steady basis and the SANDRA, having the proper tools, joined her old partners, the RICHARD and STACEY. The SANDRA is on the vessel operations board to continue escort work until the tanker traffic on the Sound no longer requires a third tug, which could happen if the Arabs turn off the tap.

SIDNEY FOSS

Built:	1975	Propulsion:	EMD (2)
	McDermott Shipyard Group		3,000-horsepower
	New Iberia, Louisiana	Primary Service:	Ocean and Coastwise
Length:	120-feet	Status:	In Service
Beam:	34-feet		

The SIDNEY FOSS, named for S. D. Campbell, Board Chairman of Foss Launch & Tug Company, was completed and accepted for service from McDermott in November 1976. The SIDNEY, assigned to the Foss Ocean Division, was the third of the four new tugs built by McDermott for the Dillingham Maritime group. All tugs in the series were given full engine-room monitoring and automation. They were complete and modern in all respects. The SIDNEY is considered the ideal type tug, economical yet able to handle general ocean and coastwise towing.

After a two-day run with the tug from New Iberia to Houston, Texas, the Seattle crew flew home for a short wait as a new Foss barge being built at Galveston was not completed and ready for the SIDNEY to tow. The barge was to be loaded at Houston with technical flow-metering components for the Valdez major oil-pumping station at the southern terminal of the Alaska Pipeline.

Foss received word on December 20th that the new barge was about loaded, so the SIDNEY's crew returned to Houston. Under command of Captain Joe Uskevich, they left Houston on December 21st towing the barge with its valuable pipeline cargo. After an uneventful voyage, stopping only at Port Angeles to take on fuel, the SIDNEY arrived in Valdez on January 26, 1977. Completing the cargo discharge, she returned to Seattle for the first call at her home port and the usual first voyage check-up.

SIDNEY FOSS *While on seatrials in the Gulf of Mexico. (Courtesy of Foss Tug Co)*

During the remainder of 1977 the SIDNEY, with Captain Uskevich, completed five barge tows to Anchorage, one barge trip to the Aleutians, one run to California, and a November trip to Kodiak with two barge loads of mobile homes. The year turned out to be one of fast turn-arounds for the SIDNEY—24,000 miles of water passed by her keel in just twelve months.

The SIDNEY produced another successful year in 1978, running steadily coastwise and to Alaska and in 1979 she continued to make time and reputation on the same runs including the Bering Sea deliveries for Foss Alaska Line. She just about finished out the year in FAL service, but the day after Christmas, with Captain John Klapp in charge, she left Seattle to pick up two Foss barges loaded with Weyerhaeuser lumber at Longview, Washington and Coos Bay, Oregon. She pulled out with the barges on December 29th, bound for Port Arthur, Texas. For steady work the SIDNEY is scheduled to return to Foss Alaska Line. With her fast action record the SIDNEY is aptly named.

DREW FOSS (2)

Built:	1977	Propulsion:	EMD (Twin)
	McDermott Shipyard Group		3,000-horsepower
	New Iberia, Louisiana	Primary Service:	Ocean and Coastwise
Length:	120-feet	Status:	In Service
Beam:	34-feet		

The second DREW, fourth and last in her class of new Foss ocean tugs, was completed and ready for service at New Iberia in March 1977. She carries the name of Henry and Agnes' son Drew and compliments Drew Campbell, Margaret and Peter Campbell's son, a grandson of Sidney and Barbara Foss Campbell.

For the DREW's first assignment she towed a loaded Foss Ocean Division barge from Galveston, Texas to Portland, Oregon in just twenty days—a good beginning. With the cargo discharged tug and barge headed home to Seattle, arriving on May 8th.

During the next five months the DREW, with Captain Fred Strang, a Foss skipper for many years, completed several trips to Alaska including a tandem tow of construction equipment to the Bering Sea port of Bethel.

Then on November 3rd, again with Captain Strang setting the courses, she left Tacoma with one of the Foss 286-foot ocean deck-barges in tow for Charleston, South Carolina. The barge carried a rather unusual deck cargo—three smaller barges! The three riders were 106-foot oil-waste barges and they rode piggyback on the carrier barge. The waste barges, three of eighteen built by Tacoma Boatbuilding Company for the United States Navy, weighed in at 110 short-tons each, and they were loaded by Manson Construction Company's super-derrick barge HAAKON.

The sailing orders given Captain Strang stated that after delivery of the tow to Charleston, estimated to be December 1st, the DREW and the deck barge would probably return to Seattle. But business dictated otherwise. The DREW, due to work offered, remained on the East Coast, towing steadily and with no particular home base—job to job, port to port, a tramp tug.

In November 1977 however, the Foss Ocean Marketing Division initiated a program to establish a competitive towing position in the East Coast, Gulf, Central and South American markets. The IVER FOSS, already on hand, started off the operation, making tows in the Gulf and Caribbean area and by the time the DREW arrived in Charleston, more offerings were coming in. The DREW's arrival on December 1st coincided with the award to Foss of a contract to tow an entire cement-making plant from ports on the East and Gulf Coasts to Venezuela (detailed in the history of the IVER FOSS (3). The DREW was immediately assigned to the job and headed for Baltimore to load cargo. She passed out of Chesapeake Bay, Christmas Day, on the first of several voyages to Venezuela.

In early June 1978 while enroute to Venezuela on her fourth voyage, the DREW was diverted into Port Everglades, Florida, where the IVER FOSS relieved her of the tow and the DREW proceeded to New Orleans, Louisiana, to take in tow one of the heaviest drags the tug would ever encounter. She was about to add a chapter of unusual and enterprising towing to Foss Company history.

On June 10th the DREW, again with Captain Fred Strang, who had just returned from time off, left New Orleans towing the 6,000-horsepower suction-dredge NEW YORK and a small service barge. Destination: Bay City, Michigan. This marked the first time in the Company's ninety-year history that a Foss tug navigated the Great Lakes. The dredge, owned by Great Lakes Dredge & Dock Company of Chicago, was the largest cutter-suction dredge in the world. It was to be used for three months in channel maintenance at Saginaw Bay, Michigan, for the Army Corps of Engineers.

This was the first instance that an ocean tug actually towed a large piece of floating equipment the entire distance of the St. Lawrence Seaway. On rare occasions when an ocean tug and tow required passage, special seaway tugs were used and the ocean tug ran independently. After lengthy discussions and some persuasion, the DREW was given a chance to prove that the ocean tow hook-up was safe and maneuverable. The Seaway authorities were cautiously impressed with the results as tug and tow successfully navigated the canals and complex lock system on the 182-mile run from Montreal.

Captain Strang provided a seaman's description of the DREW's historic 3,000-mile voyage, starting in New Orleans and ending with delivery of the dredge at Bay City!

Leaving the Mississippi River entrance on June 11th, the DREW ran southeast across the Gulf of Mexico to a postition off Key West, Florida. Then she headed north along the Atlantic seaboard and passed off Nova Scotia on June 26th. Then northwest through Cabot Strait into the Gulf of St. Lawrence. Passing close by the north side of the Gaspé Peninsula on June 29th, they entered the St. Lawrence River and the beginning of the Seaway. The 1000-mile distance from the Gulf of St. Lawrence to Montreal is free of locks and canals and Canada maintains the upstream section of the river to a minimum depth of thirty-five feet. Tidal conditions extend up the St. Lawrence to Trois Rivieres (eighty miles from Montreal). When the Seaway opened for navigation in 1959 the Great Lakes became accessible by sea and created nearly fifty deep-draft ports bringing the center of North America to the commerce of the world. The Seaway has been described as an engineering feat on the magnitude of building the pyramids.

The DREW arrived in Montreal on July 2nd and then began the tedious "uphill" voyage into the Great Lakes. Departing Montreal, they passed through the St. Lambert Locks and the Cote Ste. Catherine Locks. These two locks raised the vessel fifty feet to the level of Lake St. Louis and made it possible to bypass the Lachine Rapids. From Lake St. Louis they passed through Soulanges, a sixteen-mile segment which includes the two Beauharnois Locks. These locks gave an additional lift of eighty-five geet. Passing through the Beauharnois Canal on July 4th, the DREW entered Lake St. Francis and later on passed through a series of locks near Massena, New York and Iroquois, Ontario. The DREW was then in position to enter the first of the Great Lakes—Ontario.

The only access to Lake Erie, the second of the Lakes, was via the twenty-seven-mile Welland Canal which by-passes famed Niagara Falls. There were seven locks along the Canal, raising the tug and tow 326-feet into Lake Erie. Lake Erie covers 9,930 square miles with an average depth of fifty-nine feet—Captain Strang figured that was ample for a safe passage with the DREW!

On July 7th, the DREW crossed the entire length of Lake Erie, then entered the Detroit River on July 8th and passed into Lake St. Clair, the St. Clair River and St. Mary's River, before entering Lake Huron. From the south end of Lake Huron it was an easy run north to Saginaw Bay and on to Bay City, Michigan, arriving on July 10th, concluding the epic "first" for an ocean tug.

There was little time for sightseeing or celebrating the arrival of a Foss tug in Michigan for Captain Strang and his crew. After taking on fuel and supplies, the DREW was off to Cleveland, Ohio, to pick up the dredge MOGUL. From the southern shores of Lake Erie they retraced their route, this time going east, to enter the Atlantic Ocean. Their destination was Staten Island, New York. Fortunately, the Atlantic weather was mild—the big dredge would have been ornery in heavy weather—and they arrived safely with their charge on July 24th.

The DREW was given her annual drydocking and voyage repairs in New York while waiting for the Seattle office to put together another historic adventure. During the interval, the crew was sent home for much-needed time off; the tug had been going steadily for over nine months.

In early September, the DREW, now in charge of Captain Paul Plate, a twenty-year Foss veteran, was ordered to run light from New York to Houston, Texas to pick up what turned out to be a very valuable cargo for a barge. They arrived on September 17th and on the 21st were under way with a Foss barge loaded with ten-million-dollars worth of oil-rig equipment for Natal, Brazil; a small port on the east coast of South America, some three hundred miles south of the equator. The oil-rig outfit had pieces up to fifty-nine feet in height making the barge a bit tender. But the high-priced cargo was delivered safely to Petrobras, the Brazilian National Oil Company. Another "well done" for the DREW. The 4,200 mile voyage was completed in twenty-one days, averaging 8.3 knots; speed was essential to cut down the chance of running into foul weather.

Right after cargo discharge, the DREW and her barge returned to Houston for orders as Foss intended to keep the DREW, and possibly a second tug, on the Gulf Coast to be on hand for further offerings in the Gulf area and along the Atlantic Seaboard—if the tugs were not there, the jobs would go elsewhere.

But the DREW was there and at the right time, for in April 1979 McAllister Bros. Towing Company required a tug to deliver oil by barge to two ports on the East Coast. The DREW got the job, so in mid-April, with Captain John Klapp, she left Philadelphia with a McAllister oil barge for Wilmington, North Carolina to take on a full load of bunker fuel for delivery at the Delaware River port of Paulsboro, New Jersey.

Within a week of the trip to Paulsboro, Captain Klapp received orders from McAllister that effective April 25th, the DREW was to go on a regular run between an oil loading terminal on Long Island, New York, and the New England Power & Light Company's plant at Brayton Point, Massachusetts—an eighty-five-mile tow. The new run was a pleasant surprise for Foss as the job lasted for three-and-a-half months. The DREW, towing a 70,000-barrel oil barge, made a round trip every forty-eight hours, completing fifty round trips and delivering three-and-a-half million barrels of fuel during the assignment. The DREW's charter ended on August 5th, when McAllister had a tug of their own available to put on the job.

The DREW made use of off-time and went to Jersey City for drydocking and maintenance. After a week in the shipyard she headed for Jacksonville, Florida to pick up and deliver a barge to Great Lakes Dredging Company at Puerto Cabello, Venezuela. Two days after arrival on August 28th, the DREW was under way, this time to New Orleans, towing a dredge and two auxiliary barges. She maintained a speed of 5.8 knots with the heavy drag, until within a day of her destination, then weather complications set in.

Abstracts from the DREW's log indicated that three days after departure from Puerto Cabello the notorious hurricane *David* passed within two-hundred-seventy-five miles of the tug and tow, but with appropriate course changes by the DREW and veering away by *David*, the weather was tolerable. After *David* passed by without leaving its destructive trademark, a new hurricane, *Frederick*, formed and was now heading west some 1,400 miles east of the tug.

By September 6th, the DREW was about six-hundred-and-sixty miles from New Orleans and *Frederick*, according to the radio, had been down-graded to a tropical storm with maximum winds of forty knots with a center seven hundred miles east of the DREW. So far so good, then early September 10th, *Frederick* regenerated into a severe hurricane, about three hundred miles southeast of the DREW and heading for the tug at about five knots. *Frederick* had its watery "eye" on the DREW because on the morning of September 12th, the two collided in the Southwest Pass of the Mississippi River. Even though the eye of the hurricane passed one hundred miles to the east of the DREW, the side winds nearly blew the paint off. Captain Klapp made the following comments on his log sheet for September 12th:

"Entered S.W. Pass at 1000. Winds N.E. 60 and rain. Weather poor; right in the face of approaching Hurricane *Frederick*. No pilot available. Mississippi River closed to traffic. Received permission from Coast Guard to run up to Pilot Town for a port of safe refuge."

Tug help had been requested in order to hold a safe position in the Mississippi, so at 1140 the ELIZABETH SMITH hooked on to the DREW for added power, necessary to forge up the River. The extra tug was providential as by 1535 the wind had peaked at a steady one-hundred knots from the northeast and the speed of advance during the day, even with 4,800-horsepower, was only one knot. But by 1815, running all out, the tugs and their tow were safely anchored at Pilot Town. The winds remained steady at 80-100 knots until 2100 when the brunt of the storm passed and the winds eased to a quiet 40-60 knots.

The DREW remained at anchor for the next two days, waiting for a pilot as they were all engaged in moving up the backlog of priority deep-sea ships. Then on September 15, 1979 with a pilot aboard, Captain Klapp and his charges arrived in New Orleans. The weather on arrival—sunny and clear with light winds!

The DREW tied up at Todd's Shipyard to wait for the next assignment from the Foss marketing division. The Captain and Chief Engineer stayed aboard on standby and the crew returned to Seattle for "R and R" at home. From all indications it will be a long time before the DREW will be running courses in the Foss home waters—her whistle has even taken on a southern accent.

IVER FOSS (3)

Built:	1977 Main Iron Works Houma, Louisiana	Propulsion: Primary Service:	Caterpillar (Twin) 2,400-horsepower Puget Sound
Length:	98-feet	Status:	In Service
Beam:	32-feet		

The IVER FOSS, built and outfitted by Main Iron Works for Foss, was the fourth in the series of five MAMO II-class tugs ordered by Dillingham Tug and Barge of Honolulu.

When IVER was ready to join the fleet in July 1977 the Foss Ocean Division had entered the East and Gulf Coast towing market, so they put the IVER on call in New Orleans for charter work originating in the Gulf Coast region. However, only the Captain and Engineer remained aboard to maintain the boat in a ready condition, and the rest of the crew would return from Seattle when the first charter was secured.

Within a month the IVER went to work and for her first job towing out of the Gulf, she engaged in double-barge tows to Miami, St. Croix in the Virgin Islands and Puerto Cabello, Venezuela. Next she completed a triple tow, including a dredge, from Miami to St. Lucia Island in the southern Caribbean for Great Lakes Dredge and Dock Company. Then she towed a barge load of drilling supplies to a site on the east coast of Mexico.

In June 1978 the IVER, starting on a new Foss contract and needing a cargo barge, took over the ocean-class barge the DREW FOSS was towing north. Six months earlier Foss secured a contract for shipping an entire cement-making plant from various ports along the Gulf and Atlantic Coasts to Cementos Caribe in Puerto Cumarebo, Venezuela. Components of the plant were to be loaded at Baltimore, Fort Lauderdale, Tampa, and New Orleans. The cargoes consisted of an assortment of material from sophisticated computer systems to nuts and bolts to ten-ton pieces of equipment—a total of forty-million pounds.

The IVER made four of the seven trips required to deliver the plant during a period from December 1977 to December 1978. She made the final voyage of the contract, ending up in Mobile, Alabama on December 5th.

During the long contract the IVER had two alternate skippers, Captains Vagn Kjeldtoft and Arnold Reynolds, both of the Seattle area, each having charge for three months at a time. The names do not sound a bit Spanish for Captains commanding a tug running to South America.

In late 1978 with the demand for tugs increasing rapidly on the West Coast and Alaska, the IVER was called home to assist the Puget Sound-based fleet. She left New Orleans for Seattle in late December with two barges in tow, arriving a month later—ending her seventeen month tour of duty on the East and Gulf Coasts. Ever since, the IVER has divided her time between the Seattle-North Vancouver rail-car barge run and doing ship-assist work in Seattle Harbor. From all indications the IVER's adventuring days are over; she is now a member of the home fleet.

PETER FOSS (2)

Built:	1977	Propulsion:	Caterpillar (Twin)
	Main Iron Works		2,400-horsepower
	Houma, Louisiana	Primary Service:	Puget Sound
Length:	98-feet	Final Operating Day:	October 6, 1977 (For Foss)
Beam:	32-feet	Status:	Transferred to Dillingham Tug & Barge

The second PETER FOSS, completed in late May 1977 by Main Iron Works, was the third of five new MAMO II-class tugs ordered by Foss and Dillingham for intermediate ocean, coastwise, and inter-island towing. The first two tugs, MAMO II and MIKIALA, were allocated and delivered to Dillingham Tug & Barge of Honolulu. However, PETER FOSS, the third tug in the series, became a part of Foss.

In late June, the PETER, right from the builder's yard, ran light to Galveston, Texas, and picked up for delivery to Seattle two new ocean-class barges recently completed for the Foss Ocean Division. After a stop in Long Beach for engine adjustments, the PETER arrived with the barges on August 18th, at the Foss-Seattle yard. The PETER spent the next six weeks in the shipyard undergoing gear-box modifications and installation of additional equipment.

Foss planned to use her on the Seattle-North Vancouver car-barge run on a steady basis. However, during the six-week layup, Dillingham Tug & Barge suddenly needed a third new tug and could not wait for their next scheduled tug to be delivered in early 1978 by the Main Iron Works. So by a delayed exchange, the PETER FOSS was transferred to Dillingham and in return Foss would receive Dillingham's alloted vessel due in early 1978.

The PETER operated for Foss only between September 29th and October 6th. Then on October 8, 1977 the crew from the Honolulu tug MIKIALA, with orders to take over the PETER, flew up from Portland where their tug was waiting for a tow to be made up. The following day the PETER with her Hawaiian crew left for Portland. Before the tug headed for Honolulu the documents transferring ownership of the PETER were completed and she became the MOANA HELE. The MIKIALA, in late October, departed for home towing the MOANA HELE and a cargo-barge. Shortly after arrival in Honolulu, the MOANA HELE started out in the inter-island cargo barge service.

In February 1978 the final part of the exchange of tugs was completed when Foss accepted delivery of the fifth boat, the one originally planned for Dillingham. The new Foss tug bears the name PETER, so PETER FOSS was without a boat named after him for only four months.

PETER FOSS (3)

Built:	1978	Propulsion:	Caterpillar (Twin)
	Main Iron Works		2,400-horsepower
	Houma, Louisiana	Primary Service:	Long Beach, California
Length:	98-feet	Status:	In Service
Beam:	32-feet		

The third tug to bear the name PETER left the Main shipyard in late January 1978, complete and ready for acceptance trials on the Mississippi River. After satisfactory test runs, she became part of the Foss fleet in early February 1978. PETER (3) was the fifth and last in her class of island and coastwise tugs built for Foss-Dillingham.

Originally planned for Dillingham Tug & Barge as the MOANA HELE, the tug went to Foss instead to replace the third tug in the series intended for Foss but taken by Dillingham.

In mid-February, under charge of Karre Ogaard, the PETER left New Orleans supposedly for Seattle, but after a year she still hadn't arrived at her intended destination—but she didn't disappear. While transiting the Panama Canal, Foss was advised that a large tanker, the THEOMANA, needed a tug escort from Balboa to Long Beach, California due to steering gear problems. The PETER, right on hand, was assigned the job, so on February 25th she left Balboa and accompanied the tanker to Long Beach. The PETER ran close by to take over in case the steering system on the THEOMANA should fail. But as no problems developed, the tanker and tug were able to average twelve-and-a-half knots on the 2,900 mile run, arriving in Long Beach March 7th.

Prior to PETER's arrival, Pacific Tow & Salvage, a part of the Dillingham Maritime Group, obtained a contract from the Navy to provide ship-assistance and other support activity for naval vessels in the Long Beach area. Two high-quality ship-assist tugs were required to satisfy the Navy contract, and the PETER again at hand, and well-suited, was the obvious choice to work along with the PACIFIC SATURN—Pacific Tow & Salvage's own tug.

The PETER was immediately outfitted for harbor assist work and joined the Navy, but she didn't get to see much of the world—only the confines of Los Angeles Harbor! For local work she operates with two "live at home" crews, working twelve hours on and twelve hours off. The shoreside crews have little use for the PETER's modern accommodations and complete galley except for the coffee pot, though no doubt there will come a time when the PETER will put out to sea and all her modern equipment and comfortable cabins will be a joy to an outside crew. But for the time being she is only a pulley-haulley tug, but according to the Navy her work is "well done."

MARY FOSS (2)

Built:	1962 McDermott Shipyard Group Amelia, Louisiana	Propulsion:	Caterpillar (Twin) 800-horsepower
		Primary Service:	Puget Sound
Length:	63-feet	Status:	In Service
Beam:	20-feet		

The MARY FOSS, another product of the McDermott shipyards, was built in 1962 for the American Towing Company of Morgan City, Louisiana. They named her E.K. ROCKWELL and for many years she worked out of Morgan City and the Atchafalaya River in the Bayou country of Louisiana. After 1970 her name was changed to AMERICAN CHIEF, a better identifying name for the Company.

In May 1974 American Towing sold her to Inlet Marine of Anchorage, Alaska and they renamed her GEMINI. Inlet Marine brought the tug around to their home base and put her to work towing between Seattle and Anchorage during the eight-month, ice-free season. Frequently, the GEMINI wintered in Seattle to take advantage of the milder weather and the complete repair facilities available.

In early 1979 Inlet Marine was forced to sell their fleet of three tugs, including the GEMINI. A tragic plane crash in Alaska killed several executives of Inlet Marine and the loss brought on the liquidation of the Company.

Inlet Marine's three tugs were delivered to Seattle and put up for sale. One tug was purchased by Dunlap Towing Company of La Conner, Washington, one by Puget Sound Freight Lines, and the third tug, GEMINI, was purchased by Foss on March 14, 1979.

The new acquisition became the MARY FOSS. The Company now had two tugs named MARY; however, the first MARY, the MIKI tug, has been in surplus status since August 1976 and tied up at Foss-Seattle.

The newer MARY, after several weeks of repair, modifications, and upgrading, began general towing on Puget Sound. In her first nine months of operation she proved efficient at both log and barge towing. Her Captains were well satisfied with her performance, even though her 800-horsepower was light for current demands. But her port-to-port time shown in her log sheets indicates she is what her skippers call "a going concern."

The MARY will have to maintain an impressive record to stay on the preferred list as the new super "D" boats are scheduled for service in 1980 and with 1,700-horsepower engines, they will be tough competition. However, with the big difference in book value in favor of the MARY, she will still make a creditable showing on the bottom line.

AFTER-WORD

In comparison with past years, 1980 and 1981 were somewhat uneventful and routine, the tugs were largely employed on regular runs providing service to Alaska, coastwise, Puget Sound and British Columbia. The bunkering of ocean ships reached new highs in 1980 as well as other local services including ship assists and tanker escort work.

In 1980, a new Dillingham Company, Ocean Transportation Services was formed in Houston, Texas utilizing Foss equipment operating on the Gulf Coast. O.T.S., as the new company is known, is marketing services for tug and barge operations on the Gulf Coast of the U.S., Mexico and Central and South America.

In changes of assignment, the AGNES returned to her home port of Seattle in early 1980, from operating areas on the Gulf and East Coast, for runs to Alaska. The DELORES after eleven years on the Chevron Southeastern Alaska oil run was replaced by the DONNA near year's end, 1979 and the DELORES was re-assigned to Puget Sound towing. The MARGARET was assigned to service in Southwest Alaska during the 1980 and 1981 seasons. The WENDY after delivering a tow from the West Coast to Florida in the spring of 1981 was transferred to the newly formed Ocean Transportation Services joining the DREW as a full time Dillingham representative on the Gulf Coast.

The MARY purchased by Foss in 1979, and utilized by Foss Puget Sound operation was assigned to a new service for Foss Alaska Line, operating out of Ketchikan serving several of the smaller Southeast ports that are not served on the regular weekly van run, provided by Foss Alaska.

During 1980 and 1981 there were changes in tug ownership and status. As mentioned briefly in the individual stories, the WEDELL, LORNA 3 and PATRICIA 2 were sold during 1980. In September 1981 the MARY 1 was sold to Griffen Marine of Sausilito, California. After a few days of reactivation the MARY, now aptly named GRIFFEN, left the confines of Ballard for a new future towing barges in Mexico.

The twin ocean class tugs ARTHUR and HENRY were listed for sale but by the Fall of 1981 there had been no takers.

During 1980 three special medium-size tugs were built by Main Iron Works of Houma, Lousiana for primary use on Puget Sound. The new tugs are classed as "Super-D" boats. They are 76 feet long and powered by two Caterpillar 900 horsepower engines. The cabins are spacious, the galley is on deck, and with improved soundproofing and insulation, living aboard has been made more pleasant.

First of the Super-D's, the BENJAMIN, named for a grandson of Sidney and Barbara Foss Campbell was delivered in July of 1980 and operated on the Gulf Coast until the Spring of 1981. At that time it was reassigned to Puget Sound operations arriving in Seattle in early April.

Second of the series, the DAVID, was completed in August of 1980, arriving in Seattle in late October, about the same time the third tug, the EDITH was ready to go in Houma. Using the name EDITH (wife of Wedell) again, marks the only instance in the company annals that the same name was given to four different tugs. The EDITH arrived in Puget Sound in late November 1980 and was immediately assigned to Tacoma where she is operating as one of the three ship assist tugs in that port.

In mid-summer of 1981 a contract agreement between Foss and Tacoma Boatbuilding Company was signed for construction of four of the most modern and revolutionary tugs in the maritime industry. The new tractor tugs, as they are called, with their unique cycloidal propulsion system will be able to produce thrust in any direction and will be able to proceed forward or backward without having to reverse engines. The tugs will be able to move sideways or be brought to a complete stop while going full ahead within a distance of their own length. The twin engine tractor tugs will be rated at 3,000 and 4,000 horsepower with a length of 100 and 106 feet.

The conceptual design of the new Foss tractor tugs was developed by Don Hogue, manager of Administration-Ocean Division, and Jim Cole assistant manager—Foss shipyard. The new tugs should begin entering service in mid-1982.

The new automated, high-power tugs successors to Andrew and Thea's two-horsepower launch, HOPE, represent the sophistication required to compete in today's highly developed tugboating industry, and Foss has a history of being progressive and innovative. The motivating Foss policy of constantly updating equipment that started in the early 1900's has been to always improve in order to insure safe, prompt service, and the prevalent saying of years ago still applies to the ever-active fleet: "Tugs of Foss gather no moss." Their long and proven record shows it to be true. However, much credit is due to the shoreside staff for their effective daily planning and farsighted administration throughout the years, making possible the excellent performance. Nevertheless, the crews worked hard, long and often in danger from the seas—their log book pages filled with pertinent entries showing struggle, adventure, monotony, routine, and hazards that are the common lot of tugs and drews alike.

Typically, most of the tugs in "Ninety Years of Towboating" will experience many more interesting events deserving of recognition, but they must be left to future recording with the exception of two of the tugs which had major events that altered their history. One a happy ending, the other a heartbreaking ending, and both occurring just prior to publication time.

The ARTHUR FOSS #1, owned by Northwest Seaport as a Museum ship was never expected to leave her permanent mooring in Kirkland again. However, after two years of effort made possible by many volunteers, mostly amateurs, all machinery was once again in running order, by early 1980 after twelve years of inactivity. After another year of repairs, clean up, outfitting, and drydocking the ARTHUR was able to represent Northwest Seaport in the 1981 Maritime Day Parade and then her proudest moment in many, many years—competing in the 1981 Antique Tugboat races in Olympia in September and averaging 11.6 knots. The ARTHUR serves as an example of what can be accomplished by a few willing people with limited funds dedicated to the preservation of old ships and our maritime heritage.

On a much sadder side of maritime history the tug PROSPER (page 186-187) was repossessed by a local bank when the owner failed to make payments. The PROSPER was towed to Everett's 14th Street dock where it remained for several weeks until it sank on September 26, 1981. There was no one to take care of the tug or pump out the water from leaks that developed in a vessel of her age. There had been interested parties in buying the vessel, but she sank before any sale could be made. She remained in her sunken state for two weeks. When the vessel was raised inspectors stated that repairs would be more than her worth. The PROSPER was towed up the Snohomish River where she was dismantled by Shaffer Crane & Rigging Service. On October 25, the forty-seven year old Atlas diesel was lifted out of the water logged hull, and shortly afterward the hull was towed to a Marysville disposal yard. The PROSPER made her final departure but will remain in the memory of those who served aboard her as well as many in our maritime industry.

In point of time, eight bells rang for this account of Foss tugs and tows at the end of 1979. The watch is over, the smooth log written up, the lines coiled down. The pilothouse telegraph reads: "FINISHED WITH ENGINES."

FOSS . . . . Serving The Puget Sound Maritime Industry since 1889.

Newest additions to the Foss fleet, in late 1980, the sister tugs DAVID, EDITH and BENJAMIN bring an extra dimension and towing power and tug maneuverability to Puget Sound. (Courtesy of Foss Tug Co)

The SHANNON shown shifting the partially loaded oil barge FOSS 97 in Seattle during the summer of 1962. *(Photo courtesy of Foss Tug Co)*

CRAIG alongside the loaded lumber barge, KOKO HEAD in Everett, prior to departing for Honolulu in August *1967. (Photo courtesy of the author's collection)*

The CAROL and DEBORAH FOSS assisting the partially loaded tanker, Point Loma, through the Lake Washington Ship Canal to the Republic Creosote Dock at Kennydale, Washington in 1966. The ship was unloading 15,000 tons of coal tar. It was the largest ship to enter Lake Washington in many years. (Courtesy of Foss Tug Co.)

The ANNA with help from the WALLACE *towing the new Great Northern Railroad bridge thru Deception Pass enroute to location across the Swinohmish Slough near Anacortes in 1952. (Photo courtesy of Foss Tug Co)*

The DREW with dredge New York *and support barge, near Bay City, Michigan in June, 1978 concluding a 3,750 mile tow from New Orleans, LA. (Courtesy of Foss Tug Co)*

The entire ocean-going fleet of Foss tugs as of November, 1953 on Lake Union. From left, the AGNES, LESLIE, BARBARA, JUSTINE, DONNA, CHRISTINE, MARTHA, and WEDELL. (Courtesy of Roger Dudley)

INDEX

COMPANIES

PEOPLE

PICTURES

*The **OSWELL FOSS** towing a log raft in the Lake Washington Ship Canal in 1965. (Courtesy of The Seattle Times)*